MASTERPLOTS II

JUVENILE
AND
YOUNG ADULT
LITERATURE
SERIES
SUPPLEMENT

MASTERPLOTS II

JUVENILE AND YOUNG ADULT LITERATURE SERIES SUPPLEMENT

2

Gir–Pla

Edited by
FRANK N. MAGILL

Project Editor
TRACY IRONS-GEORGES

SALEM PRESS

Pasadena, California   Englewood Cliffs, New Jersey

TMC
011.62
Mast
1991 Suppl.
V.2

Editor in Chief: Dawn P. Dawson
Project Editor: Tracy Irons-Georges
Research Supervisor: Jeffry Jensen
Production Editor: Janet Long
Proofreading Supervisor: Yasmine A. Cordoba
Layout: William Zimmerman

Library of Congress Cataloging-in-Publication Data
Masterplots II. Juvenile and young adult literature series: supplement / edited by Frank N. Magill; project editor, Tracy Irons-Georges.
p. cm.
Supplements the Juvenile and young adult fiction series (1991) and the Juvenile and young adult biography series (1993); includes for the first time poetry collections, plays, short-story collections, and books on art, history, sociology, and science for young readers; the cumulative indexes cover the contents of the earlier series as well as those covered in the Supplement.
Includes bibliographical references and indexes.
1. Children's literature—Stories, plots, etc. I. Magill, Frank Northen, 1907- . II. Irons-Georges, Tracy. III. Masterplots II. Juvenile and young adult fiction series. IV. Masterplots II. Juvenile and young adult biography series.
Z1037.A1M377 1991 Supplement
011.62—dc21   96-39759
ISBN 0-89356-916-X (set)   CIP
ISBN 0-89356-918-6 (volume 2)

First Printing

LIST OF TITLES IN VOLUME 2

MASTERPLOTS II

Juvenile
and
Young Adult
Literature
Series
Supplement

A GIRL CALLED AL

Author: Constance C. Greene (1924-　　)
First published: 1969; illustrated
Type of work: Novel
Type of plot: Domestic realism
Time of work: The late 1960's
Locale: An American city
Subjects: Coming-of-age, death, and friendship
Recommended ages: 10-13

Two seventh-grade friends learn about separation, death, and friendship while living as neighbors in an urban apartment building.

> *Principal characters:*
> THE NARRATOR, a down-to-earth, conventional seventh-grader
> ALEXANDRA ("AL"), her best friend, a self-proclaimed nonconformist
> AL'S MOTHER, a sophisticated single parent
> MR. RICHARDS, the assistant superintendent in the narrator's building
> MR. KEOGH, the girls' homeroom teacher
> HERBERT SMITH, a frequent date of Al's mother
> THE NARRATOR'S MOTHER, a pragmatic woman
> THE NARRATOR'S FATHER, a gently sarcastic man
> TEDDY, the narrator's irritating nine-year-old brother

Form and Content

Constance C. Greene's *A Girl Called Al* is the story of two seventh-graders who become neighbors in a city apartment building. The authoritative and worldly Al, pigtailed and plump, is a sophisticated nonconformist who fascinates the more conventional narrator, and their growing friendship is the basis for the book's action.

At Al's request, Mr. Keogh, the girls' homeroom teacher, approaches the school principal in an attempt to obtain permission for Al to take a shop class in the place of cooking and sewing courses, but this appeal is denied. As a result, the narrator introduces Al to her special friend, Mr. Richards, the building's assistant superintendent; Mr. Richards, a retired bartender, constantly chews a toothpick and skates on his kitchen linoleum with rags affixed to his shoes as a cleaning technique. When Mr. Richards is made aware of the fact that Al's parents are divorced and Al's father is largely absent, he offers to help Al and the narrator construct bookshelves similar to those that the boys are making in shop class. The reader learns later in the novel that Mr. Richards' empathy for the lonely Al may be the result of a long-standing separation from his own family; Mr. Richards' wife left him early in their marriage, and the old man has contact with neither his daughter nor his grandchildren.

One evening, Al's sophisticated single mother goes out for one of her frequent dinner dates. Al is invited for supper at the narrator's apartment. Also present are the narrator's practical mother, her comedian father, and her typically irritating nine-year-old brother, Teddy. Al makes a favorable impression on the family, and the narrator, walking her friend home to an empty apartment at the end of the evening, is struck by Al's independence. The differences between the two families also become apparent when the narrator prevails upon her mother to invite Al's mother for tea; the narrator's mother complies and, obviously as intimidated by her sophisticated neighbor as her daughter is, begins a frenetic cleaning campaign in preparation. The tea, the epitome of social correctness, pleases the narrator, who feels proud of her mother.

As the girls' friendship develops, the narrator learns that Al waits daily, and in vain, for the arrival of a letter from her father announcing his plans to visit. Al's mother has a number of male companions, all of whom Al lumps into a single category and compares unfavorably to the idealized version of her own father that she has created. One day, the narrator remarks to Al that she has difficulty understanding Mr. Richards' lack of a relationship with his daughter. Al reacts strongly to the observation, and the narrator realizes that she has hurt Al's feelings by pointing out the reality of Al's nonexistent relationship with her father. The narrator apologizes to her friend, and Al begins to think more realistically about her absentee parent. At last, Al agrees to have dinner with one of her mother's boyfriends, and the dinner turns out well, to Al's surprise. Another milestone occurs when Al makes her first clothing purchase without her mother's approval; she buys a pink sweater with money that her father has sent her. The outing causes Al to realize that her father, despite his good intentions, is probably not going to be a part of her life as she has always hoped.

Meanwhile, the girls' bookshelves are nearing completion. Stopping at Mr. Richards' apartment one morning, however, the girls find their friend in bed and unresponsive. Surprisingly, it is Al's usually distant mother who calls for help and comforts her daughter. Mr. Richards has had a heart attack, and Al and the narrator visit him in the hospital, where they find their friend weak but pleased to see them. As they leave the room, the girls overhear Mr. Richards claim them as his own grandchildren. That night, Mr. Richards dies, and both girls attend the funeral; none of Mr. Richards' family members is present. The novel closes with the narrator's revelation that both girls are maturing; the narrator has a date, and Al has lost weight and changed her hairstyle. Memories of Mr. Richards bring the narrator happiness.

Analysis

A Girl Called Al is easily accessible to younger readers. The novel is presented in short sentences, and the narrator's voice is refreshingly age-appropriate; the narrator is relatively uncomplicated, trusting, and given to frequent misunderstandings of the adult world. Greene's decision neither to name the narrator nor to provide first names for adults except for Al's father-substitutes adds an extra dimension to the work. On one hand, the narrator becomes an "Everyman," allowing the individual reader to relate more easily to the narrator's role. The focus of the story remains completely on Al herself, and the reader is shown how an unconventional new friend can take precedence over everything else. The fact that the important male figures—Al's homeroom teacher, Mr. Richards, the well-meaning beau of her lonely mother—are named illustrates the difference between these real-life men and the nonexistent father whom Al romanticizes. Young readers can identify with the narrator's reaction to forming a friendship with someone who seems foreign and exciting, and the narrator's ability to maintain her down-to-earth attitude in the face of such exotic behavior can be viewed as encouraging and grounding. Greene hints that the narrator is aware that Al's tough exterior is largely a façade; that the narrator accepts her friend despite this knowledge is an important lesson.

Greene's novel is also noteworthy for the way it deals with loss. Al's mother is a struggling parent who works, dates, and rears her daughter alone. Al herself feels an emotional distance from her glamorous mother and a very real, physical distance from her absentee father. Mr. Richards is estranged from his wife, daughter, and grandchildren. The reader even gets a sense of the abandonment felt by Mr. Richards' child, as Mr. Richards tells of his efforts to contact his daughter and offer her money and inadequate gifts. The variety of situations involving separation in this deceptively short and simplistic book is prodigious, and the author deals with each circumstance fearlessly and with honest emotion, resisting the temptation to produce the requisite happy ending in each situation. Mr. Richards dies alone, without the hoped-for reunion with his daughter and grandchildren. Al's father fails to put in the anticipated appearance. In both situations, however, the characters accept their realities: Mr. Richards discovers surrogate granddaughters in Al and the narrator, and Al grows more receptive to the idea of her mother's male companions.

Greene also tackles the more common thematic elements of peer pressure and being "different." Al is overweight, and the narrator tries to help her friend deal with the taunting remarks of classmates while encouraging her to consume carrot sticks instead of high-fat snacks. Greene presents difficult problems, but she suggests constructive solutions. She also offers an impressive array of adolescent crises. Most readers in the appropriate age group will be able to identify with something in Greene's novel, even if it is simply the idea of being too "normal" in the presence of an exotic friend.

Critical Context

Constance C. Greene's major and best-known works are coming-of-age stories that feature a variety of the crises of early adolescence. *A Girl Called Al* is the first novel about the title character in Greene's popular series, which also includes *I Know You, Al* (1975), *Al(exandra) the Great* (1982), *Just Plain Al* (1986), and *Al's Blind Date* (1989). Greene's work also features other popular protagonists, such as the title characters of *Isabelle the Itch* (1973) and *The Love Letters of J. Timothy Owen* (1986); the latter novel marked Greene's foray into novels for older adolescents.

Greene has stated that her own children, as well as personal childhood memories, have inspired and informed her books. Her writing has earned her critical acclaim; *A Girl Called Al*, for example, is an American Library Association Notable Book.

Ellen Puccinelli

THE GIRL WHO CRIED FLOWERS
AND OTHER TALES

Author: Jane Yolen (1939-   )
First published: 1974; illustrated
Type of work: Short fiction
Subjects: Coming-of-age, death, love and romance, nature, and the supernatural
Recommended ages: 10-18

In Yolen's first collection of fantasies, she adapts magical and timeless symbols from myth and folklore to depict strong characters struggling to balance their relationships with nature and human society.

Form and Content
The Girl Who Cried Flowers and Other Tales contains five short fantasies in which human and mythical characters are linked closely with elemental forces of nature. Each tale is accompanied by full-page and double-page illustrations by David Palladini. Some are black-and-white drawings of the tales' symbolic characters, objects, and landscapes in bold outlines. In the color illustrations, the predominance of dark earth tones matches the stories' natural settings and haunting atmosphere, while highlights of brighter color draw attention to significant images—sunlight and sunsets, signal fires, snow and ice, flowers, the faces and figures of characters.

In creating the main character for the title story "The Girl Who Cried Flowers," Jane Yolen was inspired by Sandro Botticelli's *Primavera* (c. 1478), a famous Italian Renaissance painting based on classical myths, and by ancient lore about trees inhabited by the spirits of beautiful women. Olivia, found in an olive tree as a baby, becomes a generous woman who cries whenever someone asks for the beautiful flowers that drop from her eyes, until she promises her husband that she will stay happy and never cry. Eventually, her conflicting desires to please both her husband and the townspeople lead to her transformation into an olive tree, which produces olives for her husband to harvest and a magical array of flowers that bloom until his death.

"Dawn-Strider" portrays a giant who retreats into the night and imprisons the beloved sun child, Dawn-Strider, in his cave because his rough reflection in the lake by day confirms his belief that everyone fears him. Dawn-Strider and a human child transform the giant from Night-Walker to Sun-Walker, teaching him to find happiness by following the sun and enjoying their friendship. In "The Weaver of Tomorrow," a curious girl stubbornly seeking the truth about the future is sent to live with the old woman who weaves the golden threads of human life. Eventually, Vera learns that her curiosity has brought her sorrow, since all threads lead to death, but it has also led her to a beloved mentor and her inescapable destiny as the weaver for the next hundred years. "The Lad Who Stared Everyone Down" depicts a boy punished for arrogantly insisting that nothing is greater than he is. After accepting the challenge to stare down the sun, the lad is doomed to a lifetime of staring at the image burned permanently into his eyes.

In the fifth tale, "Silent Bianca," a young woman with white face and hair speaks in slivers of ice "that cut through lies." By using her magic voice to trick the guards into returning home, she wins entry to the palace, thus proving to the king's councilors that she is as wise as the king. He marries her and benefits from her loving advice whenever he patiently warms her words at his hearth.

Analysis

Like Yolen's many other original fantasies and fairy tales, these stories strike the reader as being both familiar and strange, both old and new. With their simplicity of plot and characterization, their wondrous images from the realms of nature and magic, they are as accessible and appealing to children as traditional fairy tales. Yolen's evocative poetic style and subtle but not simplistic morals attract older readers as well. Typical of many modern stories by feminists and children's writers is the focus on young women and children who strive to find their place in the world and form meaningful relationships; they are often braver and wiser than their more powerful adversaries and relatives.

Beginning with settings remote in time and place, Yolen has interwoven familiar patterns from myth and folklore. Only "The Girl Who Cried Flowers" has a somewhat specific setting in ancient Greece, when people believed in tree spirits. "Dawn-Strider," like a traditional pourquoi tale explaining the nature of the universe, tells how the sun established its daily course across the sky. "The Weaver of Tomorrow" dramatizes the old metaphor of time's tapestries woven on a loom until death breaks the thread of each individual life. "The Lad Who Stared Everyone Down" is a cautionary tale about the dangers of pride; the growth and repetition of the boy's boastful list of people whom he has stared down creates a cumulative pattern found in many folktales and children's stories. As Yolen explained in "The Brothers Grimm and Sister Jane," a 1993 essay about her lifelong reading of fairy tales, she was profoundly influenced by the Grimms' story "The Three Little Men in the Woods" and "used the idea of something unnatural coming from a girl's mouth in the story 'Silent Bianca.'"

The three middle tales are united by the theme of time and their focus on children bold enough to confront stronger and older characters. After the children in "Dawn-Strider" teach the giant that love is stronger than fear, he stops impeding the sun and enjoys human companionship by day. Time becomes meaningless to the boy in "The Lad Who Stared Everyone Down" after the sun burns his eyes. He is the only main character in these tales whose life is destroyed by his folly. "The Weaver of Tomorrow" contains a more complex message about realizing that the passage of time brings both fulfillment and pain; after rushing to learn about the future, Vera feels trapped by responsibility and the grief of observing that death is inevitable both for the old woman whom she loves and for herself.

These tales contain elements that Yolen has identified as "magic, sacrifice, and reward, all the wonderful accoutrements of a fairy tale." The first and last tales are linked by their focus on women with strange and magical gifts and the bittersweet ironies in their moral themes. In "The Girl Who Cried Flowers," marriage brings happiness, but love makes the husband selfish and short-sighted, like the giant in "Dawn-Strider." Olivia needs to experience both happiness and sadness, to serve her neighbors as well as her husband. As a magical tree, she can give fruit and flowers to everyone, yet her humanity is sacrificed. Silent Bianca's happy ending closes the book on a more hopeful note. She is rewarded for using her magic cleverly, finding an appreciative husband who brings her snowy beauty and icy words to warm gradually at his fire.

The characters in these tales experience isolation and strangeness, but they need to love and learn from others. This dilemma symbolizes the situation of the storyteller and the tales themselves. Olivia's husband attracts her with his skillfully told, happy stories, but he should share her with others and allow her to cry at tragic stories. Like the art of weaving the tapestry of life and the gift of crying flowers or speaking in slivers of ice that few people bother to thaw and hear, the storyteller's craft blends the natural and the spiritual, bringing both joy and sadness to the artist and to thoughtful people who appreciate her gifts. In a later collection, *Dream Weaver* (1979), Yolen calls the old blind weaver's stories "the heart and soul made visible" and refers to the tales as "resonances of the teller's life: my life."

Critical Context

Jane Yolen first became a leader in the revival of storytelling and fantasy writing in the 1960's. These traditions had lost favor in the United States by the mid-twentieth century because of the spread of mass media, the growing popularity of psychological and social realism in children's fiction, and adult concerns about the unrealistic content and damaging influences of many older tales. Yolen, a songwriter as well as a writer and editor of poetry, fiction, and nonfiction, saw the storytelling revival as an outgrowth of the folk movement in the 1960's. *The Girl Who Cried Flowers and Other Tales* appeared in 1974, the same year that the annual storytelling festival began in Jonesboro, Tennessee. The following year, Bruno Bettelheim's extremely influential book *The Uses of Enchantment*, affirmed the literary and psychological importance of fairy tales for children. In her own defense of folklore and fantasy, *Touch Magic* (1981), Yolen compares magical stories to mirrors and many-faceted dreams; for young and old, they reflect both dark and light facets of the human condition, offering morals that are not easily seen.

After the success of this first collection and early picture books such as *The Girl Who Loved the Wind* (1972), Yolen wrote scores of other tales based on myths, legends, history, and folklore. They have appeared in picture books illustrated by many important artists and in collections by Yolen and others for children and adults. "The Weaver of Tomorrow" reappeared in Yolen's *Tales of Wonder* (1983), a volume of short fantasies for adults. She has been compared to earlier writers such as Hans Christian Andersen and Oscar Wilde for her ability to weave traditional folk motifs into eloquent, evocative original tales that reflect symbolically the concerns of the author's milieu. Yolen's stories are important for both children and adults because they retain the utopian outlook of traditional fairy tales without ignoring the conflicts and complexities of human experience. Silent Bianca is like the heroine in many fairy tales by Yolen and other modern writers: Although misunderstood by others in her society, she is wise and brave and wins the heart of a man who is her equal.

Tina L. Hanlon

THE GLASS MENAGERIE

Author: Tennessee Williams (Thomas Lanier Williams, 1911-1983)
First presented: 1944
First published: 1945
Type of work: Drama
Type of plot: Psychological realism
Time of work: 1939-1945
Locale: St. Louis
Subjects: Coming-of-age, emotions, family, jobs and work, and love and romance
Recommended ages: 15-18

Tom Wingfield, in search of his true identity, learns about the detrimental effect of the conflict between illusion and truth, between tradition and reality, and between what life has dealt out to him and what he can do to reshape it.

Principal characters:
> TOM WINGFIELD, a poet who is stuck with a job in a warehouse
> AMANDA WINGFIELD, Tom's mother, whose emotional entanglement with the past calls into question her relationship with the present
> LAURA WINGFIELD, Tom's sister, whose physical disability corresponds to and mirrors her mental disturbance
> JIM O'CONNOR, an egotistic, self-centered gentleman caller, the alleged emissary from the world of reality

Form and Content

According to Tennessee Williams, *The Glass Menagerie* is a "memory play." It is narrated from the perspective of the character Tom Wingfield. What Williams calls "personal lyricism" is employed in the play not so much to challenge the account-ability of Tom's narrative as to display, from a character's point of view, the impact that illusion has on individuals. The play, for example, portrays a large group of characters whose obsession with the past complicates their connection to the present. Illusory worlds are created by these characters, either to cherish the not-so-accurate memory of an idealized past or to protect an already-tattered emotional integrity. It is typical of Williams, a self-proclaimed romantic dramatist, to create characters who prefer dwelling in a fantasy world. Yet, the playwright, aware of the inevitability of the conflict between illusion and reality, also leaves the audience with no doubt about his cynical and bitter attitude in dramatizing the sometimes self-deceptive but always debilitating nature of his characters' illusory world. Flashbacks are used effectively to underscore the struggle that characters must undergo when they do not know how to disentangle themselves from the past.

The main plot of *The Glass Menagerie* centers on what happens to the Wingfield family on one unforgettable evening. A childhood illness has left Laura Wingfield crippled; one of her legs is slightly shorter than the other and is held in a brace. Self-consciousness and a lack of self-confidence have turned Laura into an extremely shy person. She prefers living in a dream world created through her fantasies and her collection of glass animals. Laura's mother, Amanda Wingfield, believes strongly in tradition. Her faith in the traditional Southern practice of having a "gentleman caller" has led her to make an arrangement for Laura to meet with one of Tom's coworkers at the warehouse.

Jim O'Connor shows up one evening at the Wingfields' apartment as the "gentleman caller." He behaves like a gentleman, charming Amanda and strengthening her belief in this tradition. During the meeting, Jim's outward glamour and glibness temporarily rekindle hopes in Laura's closed heart. She tells him how much she admired him in high school and entrusts him with her favorite glass animal, the unicorn. When Jim clumsily breaks the unicorn's horn and tells her that they are not compatible with each other, Laura loses even more of her ever-dwindling confidence in herself and furthers her alienation from reality.

At the end of the play, Laura is apparently thrown off her emotional balance and ready to retreat permanently into her fantasy world. Amanda, holding Tom responsible for the fiasco of Jim and Laura's meeting, blames him as the manufacturer of dreams and illusions. Tom, now fully aware of the detrimental effects of the conflicts between the past and the present and between illusion and reality, decides to leave the family and take on the challenge of shaping his own life.

Analysis

The Glass Menagerie is a play about coming-of-age. Tom's maturity is demonstrated by his final decision to leave the family, a decision that is made with the awareness of the inevitable clash between illusion and reality, between reaction and action, and between what life has given him and what he can control. In the opening of the play, Tom announces that unlike a stage magician who "gives you illusion that has the appearance of truth," he gives the audience "truth in the pleasant disguise of illusion." Amanda is just such a stage magician, manufacturing illusion in the appearance of truth. Her problem is neither that she is insensitive nor that she is an overprotective mother attempting to keep her children under her wings. Her dilemma is that she is an anachronistic figure who clings "frantically to another time and place." Tradition, the main cause of Amanda's obliviousness to changes in society, is as important to her as her relationship with reality. Her faith in the "gentleman caller" tradition not only results in a failed marriage but also leads to the disastrous meeting between Jim and Laura.

Amanda's husband does not appear in the play, but his character plays an important role in demonstrating and accentuating Amanda's blindness. Mr. Wingfield, a bona fide gentleman caller, was hand-picked by Amanda to marry. He was also an irresponsible pleasure-seeker who later deserted the family for his own enjoyment of life. His abandonment of the family, in addition to announcing the death of the marriage, challenges the credibility of the "gentleman caller" tradition. Amanda is too nostalgically myopic, however, to see the portentous implication and too hopelessly dazzled by its glamour to admit its destructive potential. Thus, the circular movement of the play is not only underlined by the fact that Laura ends where she starts but also displayed in the emotional toll that two generations have to pay for living in an world of illusion.

Laura's tie to her make-believe world is as strong as Amanda's is to the past. Because of her apparent physical deformity, she has become sensitive to what people think of her. Her physical condition thus represents her mental distress; she is crippled both physically and mentally. In search of companionship, she builds her own fantasy world with her glass-animal friends and with a Victrola and many old records. Laura, however, is more than a prisoner of her own deformed consciousness. She is also a victim of moribund traditions, such as that of the "gentleman caller." The tragic nature of her life is made even more painful when the audience realizes that she is cognizant of the delicate nature of her fantasy world but that she does not see any alternative that can substitute for the security and companionship that her fantasy world provides her.

Jim is another magician who manufactures illusion in the appearance of truth. During his visit to the Wingfields' apartment, he tries to act like a gentleman, but his selfishness and egotistic nature are reminiscent of those of Amanda's former husband. Jim's interest in Laura arises only when he discovers that she still remembers all his "glorious" achievements in high school. He then practices public speaking skills on Laura, insensitively invites her to dance although he is aware of her physical condition, and continues to talk about the power of love after he bluntly breaks Laura's heart by refusing to see her again.

The Glass Menagerie ends with Amanda blaming Tom as the one who lives by dreams and illusions. Tom is not content with his work and dreams of becoming a poet. He represents the awakening generation of young people who are in a desperate search of their true identity. Tom is acutely aware of his responsibility, not in the traditional terms of being loyal to a family but in the sense of human choice. By deciding to break away from dying traditions, he has taken over control of his own destiny and turned himself into the speaker of "truth in the pleasant disguise of illusion."

Critical Context

Tennessee Williams' first major play, *Battle of Angels*, was produced by the Theatre Guild in Boston in 1940 and brought him recognition. *The Glass Menagerie*, his second play, helped to solidify his position in the American theater, establishing him as a leading playwright. The play was completed in 1945, around the time that World War II was coming to an end. Many literary works produced at the time were related either directly or indirectly to the war. *The Glass Menagerie* was one of the first works in that era to depict young people's restlessness and struggles in trying to identify their relationship with the past, with tradition, and with society. The play has been used in both high school and college classrooms to display the detrimental effect of the struggle between illusion and truth and between the past and the present. It encourages young people to establish self-esteem, develop confidence, and think for themselves about the dreams for which they are willing to live and die. While Williams' later plays deal mostly with the adult world, *The Glass Menagerie* perfectly captures the fantasy world of young adults.

Qun Wang

GLOOSKAP'S COUNTRY AND OTHER INDIAN TALES

Author: Cyrus Macmillan (1880-1953)
First published: 1922; illustrated
Type of work: Short fiction
Subjects: Animals, love and romance, nature, race and ethnicity, and the supernatural
Recommended ages: 10-13

The acts of the eastern woodland cultural hero Glooskap, as well as many other myths and legends, are recounted in this volume.

Form and Content

Cyrus Macmillan first published these thirty-eight tales as elements of two separate collections, *Canadian Wonder Tales* (1918) and *Canadian Fairy Tales* (1922). He takes the myths and legends of the Micmac and Blackfoot peoples of Canada and rewrites them as stories for young readers. Overall, Macmillan preserves the plots and characters, although he provides imaginative details that do not come from his sources. For example, in "How Summer Came to Canada," he mentions items such as the Southern Cross and orange blossoms, the existence of which the indigenous peoples of Canada did not know until fairly recent times.

Many ontological tales appear in this collection. Readers discover why rabbits and bears have short tails, why seasons alternate, why birds migrate, and why leaves change color. Although only seven tales actually relate the deeds of Glooskap, Macmillan links those seven with eleven others concerning figures associated with Glooskap into a series of eighteen tales, from "Glooskap's Country" to "The Passing of Glooskap." The first of these recounts the mysterious background accorded Glooskap by legend. For example, he dwells with old Dame Bear, who may or may not be his mother, and a seemingly eternal child, who may or may not be his younger brother. "The Passing of Glooskap" relates his departure from North America to an unknown land across the sea, which, again in the ambiguity of legend, appears to be both an otherworldly afterlife and a physical resting place. Between these tales are others in which Glooskap punishes evildoers and regulates the universe. Six tales of the series deal with Rabbit, one of Glooskap's followers and one of the tricksters familiar in North American traditions.

The remaining twenty tales are gathered without concern for plot connections, although "The Indian Cinderella," the first story after "The Passing of Glooskap," mentions that an aged man had lived at the time of Glooskap. The first eighteen tales, plus the twelve that follow them immediately, are Micmac legends from the eastern woodlands, while the final eight are Blackfoot legends from the prairies. The Blackfoot stories present a universe distinct from that of the Micmac legends; the first Blackfoot narrative, "Star-Boy and the Sun Dance," describes the Sun in very different terms than does "The Moon and His Frog-Wife," showing the Sioux solar concept to be much different from that of the Algonquin peoples.

Analysis

Some readers of recent times may find Macmillan reckless in his approach to legendary and mythological material. For example, he originally offered many of the narratives as "wonder tales" or "fairy tales," phrases that may appear condescending, considering that these stories were taken from religious tradition and are, in some sense, considered true by the original tellers and audiences. By contrast, although similar Greek and Roman narratives are often rewritten for young audiences, they are usually termed "myths," implying their original role. At best, Macmillan's original terms prove misleading. The choice of "Indian tales" is somewhat more neutral, but still not as precise as it might be. Also, the text's treatment sometimes suggests a fairy tale more than a legend or myth. For example, when Macmillan calls the trickster "Bunny the Rabbit," rather than simply "Rabbit," he imposes a cuteness not in the original tale.

Macmillan generally succeeded, however, at a hard task. He not only had to adapt his material from one medium to another (oral recitation to printed book) but also had to interpret it for another culture. Although the supernatural agencies tend to become more picturesque than awe-inspiring, as in the original myths, this result is as much a function of moving the stories into another civilization (for which Glooskap and Wolf Wind have no inherent significance) as it is a matter of Macmillan's treatment of the stories.

A related issue involves Macmillan's choice of language; words denoting the supernatural depend on particular perceptions that may not be fully understood in another context. For example, Macmillan renders *manitou*—which could mean "spirit," "god," or sometimes even "magician"—as "fairy." The origin of "fairy" in European and British folklore suggests that this is a decent approximation for many uses of *manitou*, but North American readers often think of a mischievous sprite, rather than a powerful demigod. In a similar fashion, the small entities who haunt remote places (akin to Henry Schoolcraft's "turtle people," or *pukwujinini*), become the "little people." The type of man-eating, usually large, humanoid, known as *wendigo* becomes a "giant" in Macmillan's text. On the other hand, he treats the supernatural characters and events in the legends as a traditional storyteller would, as if they were a normal part of life, as much to be expected as the animals and plants.

Occasionally, the ancestral atmosphere of the tales is weakened by a whimsical treatment; for example, in "Rabbit and the Grain Buyers," Rabbit lives in a house with a European-style bed and prepares a typical twentieth century advertisement for his business. In another, "Rabbit and the Indian Chief," characters wear spectacles, and in another, "Ermine and the Hunter," the pre-Columbian natives are aware of merchant ships crossing the ocean.

Of Macmillan's narrative choices, perhaps the most potentially disturbing to modern readers is the repeated suggestion that the native people, whose ancestors once were ruled by Glooskap, are largely creatures of a bygone world. Although stories of cultural heroes such as Glooskap often take place in a nostalgic world that has somehow diminished, the racial overtones, as Macmillan recorded them, are usually lacking. In "The Passing of Glooskap," he actually states that the native people are destined to perish, as have many of the indigenous animal species; confusingly, later in the same tale, he comes close to the beliefs of some native people, suggesting that the remnant who are faithful to their old ways will survive to see a return of the happy and pure world of their ancestors.

Nevertheless, Macmillan's tales are fair representations of American Indian legends. The tales, if tamer and more saccharine than the original myths and legends, still preserve the essential plots and tone. Nowhere did Macmillan slight American Indian culture; he treated the passing of the golden age of Glooskap and the coming of the Europeans as tragic. Often, Macmillan's text communicates the joy, irony, sadness, or moral concern of the original legends. In the Rabbit tales, for example, in which Rabbit fights with the moon, overcomes giants, and outwits opponents, the raucous and sometimes brutal humor common in trickster narratives dominates. Macmillan wrote as an individual who wished to share some tales that he enjoyed; the liberties that he took and the fidelities that he maintained are aspects of his attempts to make the stories live in a different medium and for a different audience than their originals.

Critical Context

Cyrus Macmillan, in general, belonged to a tradition of white writers who recorded and interpreted American Indian myth, legend, and folktale throughout the nineteenth and early twentieth centuries in both the United States and Canada. One of the earliest and most famous of these was the U.S. writer Henry Schoolcraft, who recorded Algonquin (primarily Ojibwa) and Iroquoian traditions in *Algic Recherches* (1839). Unlike Schoolcraft, who either misunderstood or purposely rewrote some narratives, Macmillan proved generally accurate. Like many such writers, Macmillan believed that American Indian culture was close to extinction and desired to preserve a portion of this narrative tradition. He collected the tales, intending them primarily, but not solely, for young readers.

Macmillan was not a prolific writer. *Glooskap's Country and Other Indian Tales* represents much of his output for young audiences. Nor was he a pioneer like Schoolcraft. He wrote fluidly, however, and largely resisted the temptation to rewrite the tales. Despite his occasional departures from his sources, Macmillan skillfully adapted most of what he found, preserving even the seeming contradictions in the stories. While Rabbit is described as kind in "How Rabbit Lost His Tail," in "Rabbit and the Grain Buyers," he mercilessly (if amusingly) feeds various creditors to one another. Macmillan's American Indian tales makes accessible for young audiences some lively and interesting stories that, if not truly in danger of extinction, often remain unfamiliar to most readers of any age.

Young readers may find the tales a sympathetic and entertaining introduction to woodland and prairie legends. Reading the stories collected by Macmillan could spark an interest in many other collections of tales, including those focusing on different Glooskap traditions. Also, students may decide to explore other mythical traditions and compare their heroes and ontologies with those recorded by Macmillan. More sophisticated students might wish to compare "fairy tales" and "myths" in order to discover their similarities and differences. Those who enjoy nature lore might appreciate some of the stories about animals and the changing seasons, such as "How Rabbit Lost His Tail" and "How Glooskap Made the Birds."

Paul James Buczkowski

GOBLIN MARKET AND OTHER POEMS

Author: Christina Rossetti (1830-1894)
First published: 1862
Type of work: Poetry
Subjects: Family, sexual issues, and the supernatural
Recommended ages: 10-15

Laura, pining away after being tempted into eating forbidden goblin fruit, is saved from death by her sister, Lizzie.

Form and Content

Goblin Market and Other Poems opens with the long narrative of the title piece, includes forty-four much shorter poems of varying subjects, and ends with sixteen devotional poems on aspects of the Christian experience. Composed over a period of fourteen years, the works in the volume are understandably disparate in theme, with only the title poem specifically aimed at young readers. It is "Goblin Market," a fascinating and elusive fairy tale originally illustrated by her older brother, Dante Rossetti, for which Christina Rossetti is most famous.

Told by an omniscient narrator, the story begins with the goblin cry of "Come buy," a lure heard by two fair-haired sisters, Laura and Lizzie, as they walk in the twilight. What the goblins are selling is some of the most temptingly described fruit in all of literature. Lizzie recognizes the danger of the call and tries to hurry her sister away, but Laura stays in the glen after dark, dreamingly speculating about the flavor of the exotic fruits. As the goblins approach Laura, the girl laments that she has no gold with which to purchase their wares. "You have much gold upon your head," they tell her, and Laura exchanges a part of her body, a blonde curl, for the fruit. In a frenzied gluttony, the girl consumes the supernatural fruit and then wanders home with "one kernel-stone" in her hand.

When Laura arrives, Lizzie wisely upbraids her for staying late in goblin haunts and reminds her of Jeanie, a girl who tasted goblin fruits and then pined away and died for want of them. After the initial taste of the fruit, it seems, one is unable to either hear or see the goblins again and must then suffer from an unsatisfied craving. Laura finds herself in this condition, telling Lizzie that her "mouth waters still" as she resolves to buy more fruit the next night. Laura now functions only in "an absent dream," declining both psychologically and physically. When the two go to the glen that evening, Laura is horrified to find that she can no longer hear the goblin cry, although it rings hauntingly in the ears of her sister.

Laura continues to ache for the fruit and even plants the kernel stone, watering it with her tears. When it fails to grow, she dwindles further and lies near death. At this point, Lizzie decides to visit the goblins herself, and she heads for the glen with a silver penny to buy fruit for Laura. It is not the money, however, that they want—they want Lizzie to eat the fruit too. When she refuses, the goblins suddenly maul her and, in what is nearly a rape scene, squeeze the fruit against her mouth to make her eat. Yet, Lizzie remains pure and resists the goblins until they retreat disgustedly into the woods.

Lizzie runs home full of "inward laughter," somehow aware that she holds Laura's cure in the fruit on her body, and she tells her sister to "Hug me, kiss me, suck my juices." As Laura licks the fruit off Lizzie, it burns her and makes her writhe "as one possessed." Laura is purified and cured, opening like a spring flower the next morning. As the poem ends, the setting has advanced several years and the girls are now mothers who warn their own daughters of the dangers of goblin men. As Laura has learned, "there is no friend like a sister."

Analysis

Although "Goblin Market" is told in a simple narrative form appealing to young readers, its main themes are interwoven in a complex manner through both overt and subtle references and imagery. The most apparent subject of the poem is that of temptation and the consequences of indulgence, on the one hand, and resistance, on the other. Laura, willful and romantic in nature, is juxtaposed to the sensible Lizzie, who is, in effect, her other half. The two together represent the conflicting impulses that push one toward either experience or innocence, excess or prudence. Such temptation is repeatedly expressed in terms of oral craving and heightened sensory detail. "Sweet-tooth Laura" ignores the warnings of her sister in favor of the "sugar-baited words" of the goblins, indulging in a gluttonous feast until she can eat no more, but Lizzie, contrastingly, will "not open lip from lip" as the goblins force food against her mouth. While the poem's message is clear, the ultimate ramifications of this theme require close consideration from the reader.

The question arises, for example, of what specifically the fruit represents. The majority of evidence suggests that the goblin wares, referred to as "fruit forbidden," are Edenic in quality and indicate Rossetti's tendency to include traditional Christian morality in her works, a fact corroborated by the devotional pieces included in *Goblin Market and Other Poems*. The fruit then denotes sexual sin, and the goblin men, with their "evil gifts," serve in the role of Satanic tempters. Laura, in feasting on the fruit, is in danger of losing her virginity like Jeanie, "Who should have been a bride;/ But who for joys brides hope to have/ Fell sick and died." A premature loss of innocence is further suggested by the descriptions of Laura both before and after she consumes the fruit: Previously compared to a lily and chaste moonlight, after the encounter she is "like a leaping flame" and sits in bed "in a passionate yearning" for "baulked desire." Also suggestive of sexual experience is the fact that Laura pays for the goblin fruit with a part of her own body, the clipped lock of golden hair.

The outgrowths of this theme of temptation are the related subjects of redemption and self-sacrifice. It falls to Lizzie to redeem Laura from her fallen state. Laura, similar to Eve in that she has eaten of the "fruit forbidden," suffers as "Her tree of life drooped from the root." Lizzie, interestingly portrayed as a female Christ figure, offers her own body up for sacrifice through some preternatural knowledge that doing so will save her sister. Covered in fruit juice in a decidedly Eucharistic parallel, she tells her sister to "Eat me, drink me, love me." What follows is essentially a purification by fire for Laura: After drinking the burning juice from her sister's body, she is washed clean of her symbolic sin and is able to laugh again "in the innocent old way." Lizzie's ability to give of herself is held up as the highest moral good of the poem, almost divine in its implications.

As with any great work, however, certain questions raised by "Goblin Market" remain unanswered. Why, many readers ask, is there no clear-cut assignation of guilt in the poem? Although the reader is to believe that Laura has committed a deadly sin, she is never truly held culpable, and Rossetti instead reserves her negative judgment for the wholly evil goblin men. Also curiously absent are any positive male figures, even after the sisters have children of their own, making the work a favorite among feminist critics. The shorter poems of the collection, although intriguing, do not have the same narrative mystery or curious power of "Goblin Market."

Critical Context

Goblin Market and Other Poems is considered a Victorian classic, and the seeds of its creation clearly lie within the nineteenth century. Among the works that form a basis for the title poem's story line is Thomas Keightly's *Fairy Mythology,* well known to the young Christina Rossetti, which recounts a folktale about a boy who pines away after yielding to the temptation of fairy food. Also discernible within Rossetti's work is a Keatsian influence on imagery and mood: the highly sensual descriptions of food in "Goblin Market" most likely owe their genesis to those in "The Eve of St. Agnes."

It is perhaps because of this strong grounding in the nineteenth century that the book has suffered some decline in readership. As Rossetti's most famous book of verse, *Goblin Market and Other Poems* enjoyed considerable popularity in the Victorian and Edwardian nursery, but, by the twentieth century, it was less widely read in households and classrooms. Critics of a post-Freudian mind-set are less likely than the Victorians to accept the work as a simple morality tale and will instead question the compatibility of the poem's Christian message with the latent violence and eroticism of its imagery. Rossetti's later writings for children—*The Prince's Progress* (1866), *Sing Song* (1872), and *A Pageant* (1881)—are usually considered more straightforward than "Goblin Market," but they have never achieved its fame. Despite shifting critical standards, the poem remains an elusive work that evades concrete judgment.

Joni Thornburg

GODS, GRAVES, AND SCHOLARS
The Story of Archaeology

Author: C. W. Ceram (Kurt Willi Marek, 1915-1972)
First published: Götter, Gräber, unde Gelehrte: Roman der Archäologie, 1949;
 illustrated (English translation, 1951)
Type of work: History
Time of work: 4000 B.C. to 1949
Locale: Italy, Greece, Egypt, Iraq, and Mezoamerica
Subjects: Science and travel
Recommended ages: 13-18

Through an examination of the lives of important archaeologists from the eighteenth to the twentieth century, Ceram reveals both the romance of archaeology and the history of the civilizations that he discusses.

Principal personages:
   HEINRICH SCHLIEMANN, an archaeologist who discovered Homer's
      Troy
   ARTHUR EVANS, a professor of prehistoric archaeology at Oxford
      University, the excavator of Crete
   JEAN-FRANÇOIS CHAMPOLLION, the decoder of the Rosetta Stone
   HOWARD CARTER, an archaeologist who discovered the tomb of
      Tutankhamen
   PAUL EMILE BOTTA, the discoverer of the eighth century B.C. palace of
      the Assyrian King Sargon
   AUSTEN HENRY LAYARD, the excavator of Nimrud
   ROBERT KOLDEWEY, an archaeologist who discovered and restored
      Babylon
   LEONARD WOOLLEY, an explorer of Ur
   JOHN LLOYD STEPHENS, an archaeologist who recovered the Mayan
      civilization
   EDWARD HERBERT THOMPSON, an archaeologist who explored the
      Yucatan

Form and Content

   C. W. Ceram relates the story of archaeology by focusing on the people who made major contributions to the field. He divides his volume into five books: "The Book of the Statues" deals with classical Italy and Greece; "The Book of the Pyramids" treats Egypt; "The Book of the Towers" considers Assyria, Babylon, and Sumeria; "The Book of the Temples" recounts the exploration of Mezoamerica; and the brief "Books That Cannot Yet Be Written" touches on discoveries that were then recent (such as the

Dead Sea scrolls, found in 1947) and mysteries still unsolved (such as the Easter Island script).

Johann Wincklemann, whose writings did much to popularize the excavations of Pompeii and Herculaneum, begins Ceram's procession of contributors to the study of archaeology. The hero of the first part of this study, however, is Heinrich Schliemann. When Schliemann's father gave him a book with a picture of Aeneas carrying Anchises out of the burning city of Troy, Schliemann remarked that someday he himself would find that lost city. Thirty-nine years later, he did. Schliemann learned languages easily; he taught himself all the major languages of Europe and then, in 1856, Homeric Greek. In 1869, Schliemann retired from the grocery business a rich man and began his excavations.

Homer's epics were regarded as myths that were not based on historical fact, but Schliemann believed otherwise. In 1870, accompanied by his twenty-year-old wife, he began digging at Hissarlik, Asia Minor, with a hundred workers, and there he found the ruins of nine cities stacked one on top of another. While his choice for Homer's Troy—the third city from the bottom—proved wrong, archaeologists have identified the third from the top (labeled VIIa) as the most likely candidate. Schliemann had proved Homer right and the experts wrong.

In 1876, Schliemann turned his attention to Mycenae on the Greek mainland. No one questioned the existence of Agamemnon's city, but authorities maintained that the king's grave was located outside the walls of the citadel. Relying on another classical text, by Pausanius (second century A.D.), Schliemann excavated within the citadel and found five graves with fifteen bodies, which he claimed were those of Agamemnon, Cassandra, Eurymedon, and the others killed by Clytemnestra and Aegisthus upon the king's return from Troy. Again Schliemann erred—the royal tombs that he found predate the Trojan War by about four hundred years—but he was right to claim, "It is an entirely new and unsuspected world that I am discovering for archaeology."

Ceram tells equally fascinating stories about other great explorers of the ancient world. Like Schliemann, Jean-François Champollion learned languages easily, studying Latin, Greek, Syriac, Chaldean, Coptic, Hebrew, Sanskrit, and Persian. At the age of nineteen, he was named professor of history at the university of Grenoble. In 1822, he published *Lettre à M. Dacier relative à l'alphabet des hiéroglyphes phonétiques*, indicating how hieroglyphics were to be decoded. Champollion rejected the idea that hieroglyphics were pictographs; he understood that they were phonetic without being strictly alphabetic.

As he tells the stories of the great archaeological discoverers and discoveries of past centuries, Ceram offers capsule histories of the cultures that he discusses. One learns, for example, that the pharaohs built pyramids to protect their bodies after death, so that the protective spirit (*ka*) and soul (*ba*) would have a bodily home. The grandiose tombs in fact had precisely the opposite effect. By the beginning of the eighteenth Egyptian dynasty in antiquity, most of the pyramids had already been robbed. Even the tomb of Tutankhamen had been entered in antiquity but had been resealed to be discovered by Howard Carter in 1922.

Analysis

C. W. Ceram (the pen name of Kurt Willi Marek) was not a professional archaeologist. A journalist who became interested in the subject while a prisoner of war in Italy in 1945, he delighted in celebrating the contributions of amateurs to the field. Schliemann represents his ideal, the grocer who proved the experts wrong. Other figures include Georg Friedrich Grotefend, a twenty-seven-year-old schoolteacher when he began deciphering cuneiform, and Henry C. Rawlinson, who added to the knowledge of the subject after serving in the Persian War Ministry.

Because he was not a trained archaeologist, Ceram offers no firsthand discoveries. Even his descriptions of the excavations were based on his imagination of what explorers would have seen, heard, and felt. He also minimizes the conflicts between the amateurs whom he praised and their professional colleagues, who often rejected the discoveries of less well trained explorers. Naturally enough, Ceram focuses on successes, but in so doing he ignores the many failures and frustrations that beset archaeologists. A careful student of the literature, Ceram made few mistakes, although he does erroneously claim that the monotheistic pharaoh Ikhnaton called his new city Tell-el-Amarna, the modern name for Akhetaten.

Ceram uses his journalistic skills to enliven his subject. He succeeds in making what might appear to be a dusty field "bubble forth again" and bringing the dead civilizations of the past to life. What he discusses he treats well, but his work ignores certain important areas. The Far East is a world in itself, so he may be pardoned for not including that region in an already lengthy text. His decision not to discuss Hiram Bingham's discovery of Machu Pichu in Peru is more curious. Bingham was an amateur archaeologist, although trained in history, and so should fit into Ceram's panoply of nonprofessionals who contributed to the field. Moreover, Ceram discusses in some detail the Aztec and Mayan cultures; the world of the Incas merits a place in his "Book of the Temples." Ceram did not revise his work substantially in later printings and editions. He made slight additions—noting, for example, Michael Ventris' 1953 success in deciphering Linear B, an ancient Greek language—but gave few details of this and other important developments in the field in the 1950's and 1960's.

Critical Context

With *Gods, Graves, and Scholars*, Ceram hoped to do for archaeology what Paul de Kruif's *The Microbe Hunters* (1926) had done for microbiology. In this attempt, Ceram was immensely successful: His book was a best-seller. By the time of Ceram's death in 1972, the work had been translated into twenty-five languages, had become a standard textbook for young adults, and had sold more than four million copies. Ceram also inspired others to offer popular accounts of archaeology, such as Karl E. Meyer's *The Pleasures of Archaeology* and Henri-Paul Eydoux's *In Search of Lost Worlds*, both published in 1971.

Ceram himself also continued to write about the subject, following up the critical and popular success of *Gods, Graves, and Scholars* with seven other volumes. Among the most important of these was his second book, *The Secret of the Hittites* (1956). Ceram had touched briefly on the Hittites in *Gods, Graves, and Scholars*, placing them in "Books That Cannot Yet Be Written." As his volume on the subject indicates, by 1947 much already had been discovered about this ancient empire, the rival of Egypt and Syria. As early as 1834, remains of the Hittite culture had been discovered, although not until 1879 did the English Orientalist Archibald Henry Sayce identify the discoveries as Hittite. As in *Gods, Graves, and Scholars*, Ceram focused on the personalities of the major contributors, telling his story through biography. Ceram did, however, actually visit an excavation, and he writes feelingly of the discomforts that archaeologists endure.

Ceram's *Hands on the Past* (1966; published in England under the title *The World of Archaeology*) allowed archaeologists to tell their own stories. Ceram excerpted seventy-five works, again beginning with Wincklemann, but including Bingham and others who had not been represented in his first book. Because some of the writing is dense, this book has less appeal for young adults, but it is nevertheless an important resource.

The First American (1971) turned to an area that Ceram had previously ignored—the archaeology of his adopted United States. His main concern was with the American Indians of the Southwest, but he also treated the mound builders of the Midwest. As in his earlier accounts, Ceram neatly synthesized the work of others and presented his material in an exciting and accessible form. What C. A. Robinson observed in the *Saturday Review of Literature* for January 28, 1956, in discussing *The Secret of the Hittites*, is true for all of Ceram's writing: Ceram "is an almost ideal popularizer, for he is able to make every page interesting by intimate knowledge of the subject and skill of presentation."

Joseph Rosenblum

GOD'S TROMBONES
Seven Negro Sermons in Verse

Author: James Weldon Johnson (1871-1938)
First published: 1927
Type of work: Poetry
Subject: Race and ethnicity and religion
Recommended ages: 13-18

Using African rhythms, echoes of actual spirituals, and bold imagery, the "old-time preacher" makes believable, through word pictures, familiar scenes and stories from Holy Writ.

Form and Content

As an expression of Harlem Renaissance inventiveness and as a part of the continuum of cultural creativity during the 1920's, *God's Trombones: Seven Negro Sermons in Verse* is James Weldon Johnson's adaptation of African American folk sermons into an artistic form. The book contains eight poetic sermons—"Listen Lord," "The Creation," "The Prodigal Son," "Go Down, Death," "Noah Built the Ark," "The Crucifixion," "Let My People Go," and "The Judgment Day"—written as monologues in the familiar call-and-response mode associated with the plantation preacher. Unlike Paul Laurence Dunbar, the author's distinguished forerunner who became famous for writing dialect poetry, Johnson elects not to use dialect in his poems. Nevertheless, *God's Trombones* does offer African rhythms and African American folk expressions, although Johnson maintains that the sermons are also saturated with Old Testament phraseology and King James English.

Genesis provides the basic material for "The Creation" and "Noah Built the Ark"; the Exodus account of Moses and the burning bush unfolds into distinct contemporaneous overtones in "Let My People Go"; details taken from the Gospels of Matthew, Mark, Luke, and John are recognizable in "The Crucifixion"; from Luke, Jesus' parable on intemperance is made picturesque in "The Prodigal Son"; and Revelation provides a heavenward vision in "Go Down, Death" and "The Judgment Day." Of particular note, the sermons are studded with echoes of actual spirituals and delivered in the tradition of the nineteenth century orator, where message and art (gestures and phonology) are intertwined.

Analysis

The trombone is Johnson's metaphor for "the wonderful voice" of the "old-time Negro preacher." In the book's preface, Johnson asserts that the "trombone possesses above all others the power to express the wide and varied range of emotions encompassed by the human voice—and with greater amplitude." The rhythmic, free-verse lines of the sermons make clear that the Southern preacher intones, moans, pleads, blares, crashes, and thunders. Furthermore, the preacher loves "the sonorous, mouth-filling, ear-filling phrase because it gratifies a highly developed sense of sound and rhythm in himself and his hearers." Creating a picture in words out of his own imagination becomes the most personal aspect of the preacher's mission.

Portrayed in the sentimental plantation tradition and the comic minstrel tradition as a buffoon, the stereotypical "old-time Negro preacher" was characterized as an ignorant lazybones, contented with guffawing and strumming the guitar or banjo, or as "a semi-comic figure." In contrast, Johnson's preacher not only laughs and is witty but also weeps, struggles, and suffers. Crushed all too often beneath the heaviness of injustice, as is made plain in "Let My People Go," the poet's preacher is described as a human being, confronting crises both personal and cultural.

Preaching a personal God, the preacher reproduces in his oratory themes, imagery, and idioms familiar to his congregation. When Eve succumbs to the serpent's wiles, the preacher is a witness. When the prodigal son journeys to a far-off country and yields himself to debauchery and dissipation, the preacher is an onlooker. Together with his listeners, the preacher relives the betrayal by Judas: "Oh, look at black-hearted Judas—/ Sneaking through the dark of the Garden/ Leading his crucifying mob/ Oh, God!/ Strike him down!" Sweeping his listeners (and oftentimes himself) to "a sure-enough heaven," he makes concrete a blissful abode for "those who've come through great tribulations."

Frequently appearing in the prayers and sermons are the thoughts and feelings of the Eternal Father. With the aim of inspiring his listeners, the preacher addresses God with an anthropomorphism that brings Him down to the human level: "O Lord—open up a window of heaven,/ And lean out far over the battlements of glory,/ And listen this morning."

In "The Creation," the preacher posits a God who ponders His reasons for being alone while He self-assuredly plans His masterwork, the world. Stepping forth to design, sitting to think, and kneeling "to make man," the "Great God" bats his eyes, peers around, smiles, expectorates, raises his arms, waves his hand and then drops it, claps his hands, and permits a rainbow to embrace him. Then, "stepping out on space" and later "stepping over the edge of the world," he is lonely but fearless. In addition to the anthropomorphism, rhythmic progressions that suggest both literal and figurative meanings are evident in the poet's use of intricate word groups. Rhythm is achieved through the linkage of the alliterative ("Great God," "green grass," "fishes and fowls," "beast and bird," "seven seas") with vibrant metaphors and similes ("Blacker than a hundred midnights" or "Like a mammy bending over her baby") combined with onomatopoeia ("spangling," "hurled," "hollowed," "bulged," "blossomed," "cuddled," and "scooped") to produce a musical effect.

Echoes of actual spirituals give the poet's sermons their poignancy, power, and wide appeal. Put together by unnamed bards under language limitations but "almost always in dead earnest," as Johnson states in *The Book of American Negro Spirituals* (1925) and *The Second Book of Negro Spirituals* (1926), the spirituals possess dignity. As concise and condensed paraphrases of Hebraic stories and scenes, they serve as subject matter for the preacher. Words and expressions in the sermons—such as "lonesome," "ride by this morning," "Mary's Baby," "golden street," and "pearly gates"—evoke familiar spirituals. The final line in "Listen Lord" reminds the listeners of the song "In Dat Great Gittin' Up Mornin'." The preacher borrows details from "When I Fall on My Knees" to warn the prodigal son to flee Babylon's debauchery and seek penance from a beneficent Father. "Noah Built the Ark" relies on the song "My Lord Says He's Gwineter Rain Down Fire" for its closing. Constructed from beginning to end upon spirituals, the last three sermons are the least original. "The Crucifixion" relies on "Were You There" and "Look—How Dey Done My Lord" for its structure and themes; "Let My People Go" echoes "Go Down, Moses"; and "The Judgment Day" suggests four spirituals: "In Dat Great Gittin' Up Mornin'," "My Lord Says He's Gwineter Rain Down Fire," "My Lord What a Mornin'," and "Too Late, Sinnah."

The sermons contain a range of human feelings. The preacher raises the congregation's hopes ("For the Lord God of Israel/ Will not forsake his people"), fills them with terror ("God is going to rain down fire"), and then arouses their pity ("Oh-o-oh, sinner,/ Where will you stand"), all in an effort to induce a change ("Sinners, repent while yet there's time"). Avouching theological and ethical views in a manner designed to move rather than convince, he sounds a reproof ("Young man—/ Young man—/ Your arm's too short to box with God") that becomes an exhortation ("Don't ever get friendly with Satan") and then a red-hot warning ("God's a-going to sit in the middle of the air/ To judge the quick and the dead"). In order to make himself understood by all, the preacher gives wide play to his imagination. Relying on his own creativity as he describes real experiences, he makes the illusive concrete, and his listeners "see" through his perceptive eyes: "And I feel Old Earth a-shuddering—/ And I see the grave-bursting—/ And I hear a sound,/ A blood-chilling sound."

The language of *God's Trombones* is standard American English except for a sprinkling of African American speech derivatives. Johnson does utilize the double negative, such as in "They didn't make no sound," "But she didn't feel no chill," and "Not a cloud nowhere to be seen." He also frequently uses "done," as in "When I've done drunk my last cup of sorrow" and "But Noah's done barred the door," and employs some colloquialisms, such as "lit the sun and fixed it in the sky," "most far," "down between," "streets all crowded," "only just gone," "pretty soon," "Eve got to walking," "got drownded," "Back there," "worked for about," "Look here," "dashed on in behind them," and "right then."

Critical Context

With *God's Trombones*, James Weldon Johnson ensured the survival of a rich oral tradition. Young adult readers will note that each verse is a scene engagingly employing rhetorical word clusters, winsome sensory images, charming figures of speech, and measured rhythmical beats made for enjoyable reading and dramatizations. Being a mediator between the divine and mortals, Johnson's preacher is not a trickster figure bent on power, vanity, or lechery. It is not by happenstance that the character of Reverend Shegog in William Faulkner's novel *The Sound and the Fury* (1929), published two years after *God's Trombones*, suggests Johnson's preacher, rather than such earlier characters as Dunbar's Reverend Parker. The enduring appeal of Johnson's book resides in its moral suasion.

Bettye J. Williams

GOING BACKWARDS

Author: Norma Klein (1938-1989)
First published: 1986
Type of work: Novel
Type of plot: Domestic realism
Time of work: The 1980's
Locale: New York City
Subjects: Coming-of-age, death, and family
Recommended ages: 13-18

As he finishes high school and copes with the uncertainties of his emerging manhood, Charles must also come to terms with the mental deterioration of his grandmother, who suffers from Alzheimer's disease, and the drastic but loving decision that his father makes on behalf of family harmony.

   Principal characters:
      CHARLES GOLDBERG, a sixteen-year-old student who suffers from an
         adolescent inferiority complex and wonders if he will ever be a
         success
      KAYLO GOLDBERG, his musically talented ten-year-old brother
      DR. SAMUEL GOLDBERG, his genial father, a pathologist
      MEGAN GOLDBERG, his boisterous mother, who owns a catering service
      GUSTEL GOLDBERG, his grandmother, once a dynamic and talented
         woman, now suffering from Alzheimer's disease
      JOSIE, the family's African American housekeeper, a surrogate mother
         to Charles
      KIM, a Korean American teenager who is Charles's best friend
      WENDY, a dancer and classmate, who occasionally dates Charles

Form and Content
   In his first-person narrative, Charles Goldberg describes his family as loving yet fraught with tensions. His own perplexities are heightened by sibling rivalry with his gifted younger brother, Kaylo, and the constant needling that he must endure from his well-meaning father. His mother seems preoccupied, out of touch, and oblivious to his needs. Only Josie, their African American housekeeper, provides genuine maternal guidance, with empathy and humor. In his mirror, Charles sees a physically unattractive youth, gauche with the opposite sex and not really up to the challenge of the special high school for which he has barely managed to qualify. Although lacking in glamour, his parents, by contrast, seem moderately successful, with his father's medical practice and his mother's partnership in a catering business.
   Conflicts in the family become centered on Gustel, Charles's grandmother, whose mental and physical decline as a result of Alzheimer's disease is particularly poignant because of the dynamic person that she has been. Her hard work as a masseuse enabled

her son to complete medical school; her drive brought an immigrant Jewish family into the American middle class. Now, her active and pleasurable life, with its many friends and hobbies, is gone. No longer able to live alone in her Florida home, she plays havoc with the Goldbergs' New York apartment. Her nightly prowls frighten Kaylo, whose closet walls are decorated with the "memoirs" that she scrawls in Yiddish. Although her son is still the acknowledged deity of her universe, Gustel no longer remembers his name. Forgetting even to dress herself, she cannot control her bodily functions. As the active lives of all the Goldbergs are increasingly disrupted, even Josie is reduced from housekeeper and gourmet cook to nursemaid, abused by Gustel as "the Shvartza" and accused of stealing pearls and perfume.

Charles, nevertheless, attempts to get on with his life. On a zoo visit with his friend Kim, he observes how another ethnic culture is dealing with the "going backwards" that is old age; Kim's elderly grandfather, although still mentally alert, is blind and tiresomely reminisces about the Korea of his youth. Goaded by his father, Charles gains sufficient courage to approach Wendy, an almost anorexic dancer in his school. Wendy dates Charles, but her own insecurities prevent their relationship from developing much beyond an awkward bantering. Yet, Charles begins to discover that the world at large does not necessarily find him as unsatisfactory as he regards himself.

Faced with mounting complaints from every member of his family, Dr. Goldberg realizes that he can no longer care for his mother at home. Accompanied by Charles for moral support, he makes a grim inspection of nearby nursing homes. Even the best ones appear to reduce their once-vibrant residents to a status resembling unruly children. The prospect of warehousing the woman who has made every sacrifice for him seems intolerable to Dr. Goldberg, but he sees no alternative.

On the night before she is to leave for the least objectionable nursing home that can be found, Gustel dies suddenly and peacefully in her sleep. Her funeral is spare and dignified, although Dr. Goldberg does, uncharacteristically, throw an angry tantrum when he later comes upon the survivors dividing up his mother's possessions.

Family life gradually returns to normal. Charles finishes high school and goes away to college, where he survives academically and even meets his first serious girlfriend. Not surprisingly, in this book of Oedipal undercurrents, she is African American—an educated, sophisticated version of Josie. Later, when the reassuring rhythms of campus life are interrupted by the sudden death of his father, Charles does not lose his newly gained composure. He is able to provide emotional support for his mother, who finally shares his father's secret with him. Gustel's "happy death" on the eve of her departure for a nursing home had been no coincidence. Rather than commit her to the cold hands of strangers, her son had quietly administered the proper dose of sleeping pills to ensure her passage with peace and dignity.

Charles and his mother realize that daring acts of mercy are not performed with impunity when they involve life and death. Under his burden of conscience, Dr. Goldberg suffered and possibly even succumbed to an early death. His sympathetic family is left to contemplate their strange legacy, their own genetically conditioned future, and the hazards of "playing God."

Analysis

Going Backwards belongs to the genre of the adolescent family novel; problems abound, yet the home environment is ultimately reassuring and affirming. Although some of the deepest dilemmas of the human condition are faced, the family members still have time for fun and can laugh through their tears at their own foibles. There are several skillfully crafted family scenes, usually centered on the consumption of food, in which Norma Klein's comic gift is evident. The dialogue sparkles with the rhythms and wit of this clever group of New Yorkers.

The book is also a *Bildungsroman*, a coming-of-age story in which a young person apprehensively makes the transition from dependent childhood to the responsibilities of maturity. It is the child who weeps when his once powerful grandmother regresses through Alzheimer's disease to become only a helpless burden on the family. It is the emerging adult who must cope with sexual insecurities and the social and ethical issues raised by interracial romance and euthanasia.

Klein wrote most convincingly about the people she knew best, urban professional people of Jewish heritage. Yet, her openness to diversity was evident in the majority of her books. In *Going Backwards*, Charles observes the familial and social values of his Korean American best friend. His first serious romance is with an African American woman. Although this romance seems a bit contrived, Klein did prepare her readers by demonstrating Charles's filial attachment to Josie, the housekeeper.

Compassion for the elderly and dying is an important concept that is too often served up with heavy-handed didacticism in young adult fiction. Klein's more subtle touch in *Going Backwards* is welcome. Rarely have both the grotesquely comic and the poignant aspects of Alzheimer's disease been better detailed in fiction, for whatever age group. The ethical dilemma of euthanasia is also sensitively dramatized. The final conversations between Charles and his mother suggest that they understand Dr. Goldberg's decision and even admire his courage. Nevertheless, Charles admits that he would find the same action next to impossible for himself. Ultimately, judgment is reserved in this most painful of ethical dilemmas.

Critical Context

Going Backwards is one of Norma Klein's most powerful novels; it is a personal statement as well. She acknowledged that Dr. Goldberg was a fictional counterpart to her own father, a psychiatrist, while Gustel was a rendering of her grandmother. Dr. Goldberg's decision had been Dr. Klein's as well, and his daughter had learned of it much as Charles did in the novel. With her narrative, Norma Klein was obviously working through her feelings about her own family secret.

From the beginning of her career, Klein demonstrated her willingness, even eagerness, to violate taboos. Her bold exploration of the varieties of adolescent sexuality attracted attention, and criticism, but she further startled her readers by introducing even more delicate subject matter. *Family Secrets* (1985) explored the fragility of contemporary family structures in the era of repeated marriages and no-fault divorce. *Older Men* (1987) examined obsessive, quasi-incestuous family relationships. At the time of her death in 1989, she was working on several innovative projects. A first-person narrative of gay sexual awakening was in the works. The problems of young people with physical and mental disabilities were to be explored realistically. Klein sometimes gave way to her propensity to sermonize on behalf of liberal causes, even to the artistic detriment of her fiction, and she could be wrathful toward those she considered reactionary. She must certainly be remembered as a pioneer in the realistic and sympathetic treatment of the issues facing urban youth in the last half of the twentieth century: sexual exploration, racism, suicide, mental and physical disability, regional and ethnic conflicts, teenage pregnancy, and child pornography. Compassion was the dominant note in her writing; it is almost impossible to find a truly despicable character in any of her books. Her genuine love for the fictional personalities that she created, much more than the alleged shock value of her books, strongly defines her work.

Allene Phy-Olsen

THE GOLEM

Author: Isaac Bashevis Singer (1904-1991)
First published: 1982; illustrated
Type of work: Novel
Type of plot: Fantasy and folktale
Time of work: The sixteenth century
Locale: Prague, Bohemia
Subjects: Love and romance, religion, the supernatural, and war
Recommended ages: 10-15

The legendary clay giant is miraculously brought to life to save a community of Jews, only to threaten their safety after an attempted misuse of his powers.

Principal characters:
RABBI JUDAH LEIB, a scholar of mysticism and magic
GENENDEL, his charitable wife
JOSEPH, the golem, a clay giant
MIRIAM, a servant girl who grows to love Joseph
COUNT JAN BRATISLAWSKI, a duplicitous nobleman

Form and Content

The Golem retells a story from Jewish folklore. Initially intended for an adult readership, *The Golem* first appeared in a 1969 edition of the Yiddish language periodical *The Jewish Daily Forward.* Author Isaac Bashevis Singer wrote all his fiction in Yiddish, only afterward publishing an English translation.

In the 1982 publication of *The Golem* as a children's book, Uri Shulevitz's chiaroscuro drawings capture the interplay of light and dark that conveys the story's tone. They also illuminate the story's medieval setting.

A classic tale of misdirected ambition, *The Golem* draws on legends dating back to the sixteenth century. These legends center on a clay giant, or golem, created by the historical figure Judah Loew ben Bezalel, a noted Kabbalist, or practitioner of Jewish mysticism. The golem is intended to champion the Jewish community in time of need.

Singer blends several of the legends surrounding the golem into a single narrative. He begins by introducing the reader to Rabbi Leib, humble as well as learned, and therefore suited to his sacred task. The rabbi is instructed about how to bring the golem to life and for what specific purpose: to exonerate a Jewish banker—and with him the entire Jewish community—from a charge of killing a Christian child for ritual purposes.

This first part of the narrative reaches its climax when the golem disrupts the banker's trial by bringing the supposed victim, very much alive, into the courtroom. It is revealed that the child was locked away by her own father, Count Jan Bratislawski. The count, an inveterate gambler, vengefully accused the banker of murdering the girl after the banker refused to finance his fall deeper into debt.

The ethics of the situation become complicated in the second part of the story. Now that the golem, named "Joseph" in Singer's version, has fulfilled his mission, Rabbi Leib decides to extinguish his life. The rabbi is dissuaded, however, by his wife, Genendel, who proposes that Joseph lift an enormous rock in their backyard, under which is believed to be buried a great treasure; the rabbi is persuaded by her argument that many could be aided by the recovered gold. This plan, although motivated by compassion, confuses the golem's purpose, and chaos ensues.

Rabbi Leib loses control over the golem, who becomes more human and, at the same time, more dangerous, if innocently so. Finally, orders come from the emperor that Joseph is to be drafted into the army. Concerned about the unmanageable golem running amuck and the Jews being blamed, the rabbi enlists the help of Miriam, an orphan who serves his family—including Joseph, who dotes on her. Miriam agrees, reluctantly, for she herself has grown fond of Joseph. Succumbing to an all-too-human weakness, Joseph becomes drunk on the wine that Miriam supplies to him, and, in the narrative's second climax, the rabbi is able to erase the Holy Name on his forehead, rendering him lifeless. The sense of relief that ends *The Golem* is disturbed, however, by the discovery one morning of Miriam's empty bed, generating rumors ranging from suicide to a reunion with her beloved Joseph.

Analysis

Singer dedicated *The Golem* to "the persecuted and oppressed everywhere, old and young, Jew and Gentile, in the hope against hope that the time of false accusations and malicious decrees will cease one day." Dramatized in the story is how bigotry and prejudice mar the lives not only of individuals but also of entire communities. The distress of the falsely accused banker sends shock waves through his community, the Jews as a people being implicated in his purported crime. The blood libel charge, alleging the use of the blood of a Christian child in baking the matzo (unleavened bread) for the Jewish festival of Passover, has resulted in violence against Jews from the Middle Ages through the twentieth century, when it was revived by Nazi propaganda.

The story demonstrates the ignorance that nurtures bigotry through the accused banker's protestations of his innocence: First, Jewish dietary laws forbid the use of blood, and, second, rabbinic instructions explicitly restrict the ingredients of the Passover matzo to flour and water. The illogic of prejudice is exposed when a gambling, dissolute person's word is accepted in court over that of an upstanding one simply because they belong to different religious groups. The extreme fear generated by bigotry and persecution is demonstrated in the panicked reaction of the Jewish community to the charge against one of their own, as well as by the supernatural measures that are employed in the community's defense. Embodying this monstrous fear, ignorance, and irrationality is the golem himself, dangerous in his mindlessness.

Identifying the golem as a monster leads to comparisons with the creature in Mary Wollstonecraft Shelley's novel *Frankenstein* (1818). Both are brought to life to ward off death. Both exhibit human desires for love and companionship, and both agonize over being denied such blessings because they are somehow not fully human. Nevertheless, as critic Alida Allison contends, the golem is not ostracized in the same cruel manner as is the Frankenstein creature. Given a name—unlike Victor Frankenstein's creation—the golem becomes a member of Rabbi Leib's household and is tolerated in the classroom, where he goes to learn the alphabet. He also engenders loving feelings in a young woman, to the extent that she herself disappears once he is gone.

Allison traces the difference in the fates of these beings to their origin: unchecked personal ambition, or hubris, on the part of the Frankenstein creature; fulfillment of a sacred charge on the part of the golem. It is significant that Shelley's monster becomes a murderer but that the golem never does.

Yet, it is this possibility that, according to critic Eric A. Kimmel, finally makes ending the golem's life a necessity for Rabbi Leib. As Kimmel points out, the rabbi finally turns to Miriam after Joseph is to be drafted into the emperor's army because a golem "accoutered with weapons of war and taught to fight in the service of an earthly monarch is an image of overwhelming horror." Although he admits that Singer does not elaborate on this theme, to Kimmel the modern implications are obvious: When Singer wrote his story in the mid-to-late twentieth century, the world's golem was nuclear energy. Kimmel draws this parallel: Like Joseph, nuclear power was originally intended to protect lives, but instead it destabilized them, raising concerns among people and societies over their ultimate survival.

Questions about safety and belonging would not be unfamiliar to Singer's young readers. The young can identify not only with Joseph's playfulness but also with his confusion over society's rules and mores and with his longing for acceptance. Increasingly, as their needs for family, guidance, and education go unmet, they can also identify with Miriam's loneliness in her orphaned state. It could be argued that, like Joseph, young people risk embodying the failings of the adult world around them—a world of prejudice and war, a world that makes orphans of its children.

Critical Context

The ancient legend of the golem began appearing in novels, plays, and films beginning in the late nineteenth century. The golem was even featured in a Marvel comic book in the 1970's. Most treatments of the legend were written for adults, until Beverly Brodsky McDermott's picture book *The Golem: A Jewish Legend* appeared in 1976. *The Golem: The Story of a Legend*, written for children by Nobel Prize winner Elie Weisel, followed in 1982, the same year that Singer—also a Nobel Prize recipient—published his version.

All three authors generally tell the same story, with variations. The versions diverge most significantly regarding Genendel's role in the narrative's downturn of events. McDermott omits her participation entirely, while Weisel includes hers among other similar schemes—well-intentioned or otherwise—to misdirect the golem's purpose. Critics seem at a loss to explain Singer's choice here. Is Singer reflecting the traditional view of women in much Western literature since the Bible as temptress, or is he simply streamlining the narrative?

In any case, appearing twenty-some years after Singer's first fictional work for children, *The Golem* continues to demonstrate Singer's conviction that "No matter how young they are, children are concerned with so-called eternal questions." *The Golem* also resembles Singer's other writings for children in its basis in folklore. According to Singer, being rooted in folklore "alone makes children's literature so important," adding that without it, "literature must decline and wither away."

Amy Allison

GONE-AWAY LAKE

Author: Elizabeth Enright (1909-1968)
First published: 1957; illustrated
Type of work: Novel
Type of plot: Domestic realism
Time of work: The 1950's
Locale: A hidden lake in Upstate New York
Subjects: Family and friendship
Recommended ages: 10-13

Two cousins discover a hidden lake and make friends with the elderly brother and sister who live there; by summer's end, the hidden lake colony is rejuvenated.

> *Principal characters:*
> PORTIA BLAKE, a girl "beginning to be eleven"
> FOSTER BLAKE, her six-and-a-half-year-old younger brother
> JULIAN JARMAN, their cousin
> UNCLE JAKE and AUNT HILDA, Julian's parents
> MINNEHAHA CHEEVER (MRS. LIONEL ALEXIS CHEEVER), an elderly
> widow
> PINDAR PAYTON, her brother

Form and Content

Gone-Away Lake recounts the happenings of a single summer. In Elizabeth Enright's usual episodic fashion, each chapter centers on a single event, usually one taking less than a day. The action begins with Portia and Foster Blake on their annual train journey to visit their aunt and uncle in the country; for the first time, they travel alone. Other things, too, mark the upcoming summer as different: Uncle Jake and Aunt Hilda have bought a new house, and their Boxer dog, Katy, has just had puppies. Exploring the woods behind the new house, Portia and her cousin Julian discover a stone with the inscription "LAPIS PHILOSOPHORUM / TARQUIN ET PINDAR / 15 JULY 1891," cross a swamp leading to a colony of derelict summer houses, and then, surprisingly, encounter two elderly people living there.

After meeting Mrs. Cheever and her brother, Pindar Payton, the children learn of the summer colony's deterioration after its central lake vanished. The old people, having returned to Gone-Away for financial reasons, are completely self-sufficient: They clothe themselves out of steamer trunks of old garments; supply themselves with food from their gardens, milk from their goats, and honey from their bees; and repel the swamp's many insects with A. P. Decoction, an antipest remedy developed after many trials. "I wonder how many human beings have voluntarily rubbed their skins with a solution of boiled skunk cabbage and wild garlic," recalls Mr. Payton, observing that that particular version attracted the mosquitoes "in conventions" instead of repelling them.

In successive visits, Julian and Portia hear the story of the Philosopher's Stone and other reminiscences of the old people's friendships at the lake. They grow fond of their new friends, now known to them as Aunt Minnehaha and Uncle Pin, who give them an old house to refurbish as a clubhouse. Their determination to keep Gone-Away a secret, however, results in a near-tragedy when Foster, following their tracks, sinks into the "Gulper," a treacherous area in the swamp. His rescue by Uncle Pin and return home in an ancient Franklin ("an equipage that looked more like a giant insect than a car") bring about the main turn in the book's action as the Gone-Away elders meet the Jarmans.

The story accelerates as a club is formed with a group of young people, the Gulper is safely bridged, Foster and his friend Davey take over a clubhouse of their own, and Aunt Minnehaha and Uncle Pin begin to enjoy more company than they have seen, or wanted, for years. Treasures shared among the generations include turn-of-the-century dresses for the girls and one of Katy's puppies for Uncle Pin. When September comes, one exploration remains: the isolated Villa Caprice, once the home of the pretentious Mrs. Brace-Gideon. Portia and Foster's parents, present for this event, fall in love with the decrepit house and, as the book gently concludes, are evidently planning to buy and reclaim Villa Caprice.

Each chapter has at least one lively picture; those showing the old houses and their crowded interiors are particularly appealing. Although Enright herself began as an artist and drew the illustrations for her previous books, the line drawings for *Gone-Away Lake* and its sequel, *Return to Gone-Away* (1961), are by Beth and Joe Krush.

Analysis

Gone-Away Lake, like nearly all of Enright's books for children, is unabashedly a family story. As such, it divides its attention among a number of characters rather than focusing on a single protagonist. Unlike many family stories of its time, however, *Gone-Away Lake* continually reinterprets the idea of family. At first, Portia mothers Foster; on the train, to celebrate their first unaccompanied trip, she allows him to have three different kinds of pie for lunch. On their arrival, she remembers how much she likes her immense Uncle Jake, a newspaper editor, and his kindly wife, Hilda, "a talented creator of breakfasts." Her appreciation of adventurous cousin Julian, an avid collector of butterflies, snakes, turtles, and many other interesting specimens, is echoed by Mrs. Cheever: "If cousins are the right kind, they're best of all: kinder than sisters and brothers, and closer than friends." Portia, astonished, "had supposed that this was her own personal discovery." The old people form a parallel family, combining deep affection with a strong need for privacy; they live in separate houses at opposite ends of the settlement. Other parallels are seen in the animal world: Katy, with her puppies, and a mourning dove hatching eggs just outside Portia's window. Fittingly, the end of this family story is marked by the reunion of the Blake family as the parents arrive to collect Portia and Foster and all the families combine to explore Villa Caprice.

Intertwined with the family theme is the idea of friendship, both within and across generations. Julian and Portia have an egalitarian and satisfying relationship, paralleled by Foster and his friend Davey, who are both equally obsessed with space travel. The affection and respect shown by Mrs. Cheever and Mr. Payton toward each other are mirrored in their treatment of their new young friends. The theme is reinforced by memories from other times, in stories about Mrs. Cheever's childhood friend Baby-Belle Tuckertown and her brother Tarquin, who coincidentally was Mr. Pindar's best friend. One such retold story, "The Knife and the Buttonhook," examines the meaning of friendship as Tarquin temporarily snubs Pindar in favor of a pretentious young guest, only to regain his senses when Pindar's father masterminds an elaborate practical joke.

As one would expect of a writer who published many short stories for adults in *The New Yorker*, Enright crafts each chapter with an attention to structure and language not always found in children's books. "The Summer Cats," for example, tells of the rescue of Mrs. Brace-Gideon's cats during her annual musicale. Every year, the cats, acquired as kittens at the beginning of summer, were taken to be chloroformed in mid-September; learning of this, Minnehaha and Baby-Belle were determined to rescue them. The story's appeal, with tomboy Baby-Belle ruining an elegant new dress and then stuffing it up the chimney, is strengthened by its frame of memory; its hearers are now the same age that Minnehaha and Baby-Belle were at the time. Throughout the book, Enright's language is a delight. "The mother mourning dove was on the nest looking as neat and soft as a pair of folded gloves." The country setting allows Enright to use her keen powers of observation. Mrs. Cheever's bog-grown arethusas "were lovely flowers, each one solitary, leafless, its pink blossom eared like a little fox."

Critical Context

Although well received by reviewers at its publication, *Gone-Away Lake* has never attracted as much critical attention as Elizabeth Enright's first major book for children, *Thimble Summer* (1938), which won the Newbery Medal and which also focuses on a single summer in the country. That novel combines the family themes with two external forces: drought and the Great Depression. In her later family stories, Enright concentrated more on family and less on outside problems, with the result that many young readers prefer her Melendy family books to *Thimble Summer*. Like Portia and Foster, the Melendy children begin as an urban family, in *The Saturdays* (1941), then move to the country for *Four-Story Mistake* (1942) and *Then There Were Five* (1945). Enright's final Melendy book, *Spiderweb for Two* (1951), shows the older Melendy children launching into adolescence and inventing a mystery for the younger two—a departure from her usual plotting that she never repeated.

Gone-Away Lake received a New York Herald Tribune Festival Award; the book's success with readers encouraged Enright to write a sequel, *Return to Gone-Away*, about the events following the Blake family's move to Villa Caprice. Some critics have suggested that Enright's predominantly white, middle-class characters do not represent a cross-section of American society. Others laud the books' sensitive language, family relationships, and descriptions of nature. *Gone-Away Lake*, like the Melendy books and *Thimble Summer*, was reissued in paperback in the 1980's. The intergenerational theme of the Gone-Away books continues to have appeal, as this theme became a significant one in juvenile books of the later twentieth century.

Caroline C. Hunt

THE GOOD EARTH

Author: Pearl S. Buck (1892-1973)
First published: 1931
Type of work: Novel
Type of plot: Domestic realism
Time of work: The late nineteenth century through 1912
Locale: Anhwei, China
Subjects: Family, gender roles, poverty, and race and ethnicity
Recommended ages: 15-18

Wang Lung rears his family and, with faith in himself and devotion to the land, moves from poverty and almost utter destitution to extensive land-ownership and wealth.

> *Principal characters:*
> WANG LUNG, a farmer who is so attached to land and familial tradition that these receive the love that his family needs
> O-LAN, a slave whom Wang Lung purchases to be his wife and whose selfless dedication to her husband and children persists through extreme adversity
> WANG LUNG'S UNCLE, a freeloader whose hold upon Wang Lung's support is disclosed to be more than familial
> CHING, a neighbor whose kindness and loyalty make him a lifelong servant and friend to Wang Lung
> LOTUS, Wang Lung's concubine
> NUNG EN, Wang Lung's eldest son
> NUNG WEN, Wang Lung's second son
> THE "POOR FOOL," Wang Lung's mentally retarded first daughter
> PEAR BLOSSOM, Wang Lung's second concubine

Form and Content

The Good Earth is an epic depiction of agricultural life during the last half-century of the Manchu or Ch'ing dynasty (1644-1911) in China. The Chinese man of the soil is embodied in the character of Wang Lung. Wang Lung brings the slave O-lan to his earthen house where he cares for his aged father and from which he farms his land. After O-lan bears him two sons and a mentally retarded daughter, the region is devastated by drought and famine, and Wang Lung takes his father, children, and wife many miles south to a city, where they become street beggars while Wang Lung earns what he can as a rickshaw runner. O-lan will give birth later to a second girl and, after leaving the city, to twins, a boy and a girl.

In this first part of the novel, the customs of prerevolutionary China are detailed as part of the story. Filial respect, not only for the father but also for the father's brothers, is absolute. Wang Lung must obey his father's wishes, even though the old man is immobile and losing his memory and good sense. In addition, Wang Lung must take his shiftless uncle, along with the uncle's wife and son, into his household as dependents. The uncle imposes upon his nephew's charity with impunity: Wang Lung learns that his home is spared the ravages of bandit gangs only because his uncle is a member of a particularly vicious gang.

While there is something of merit in the tradition of filial piety, little can be found in favor of the concurrent status of women. In all but very wealthy families, "girl" is synonymous with "slave." Girls and women are bought and sold as wives, concubines, and servants. A woman achieves status only by bearing one or more sons. Infant girls may be put to death for the sake of convenience. O-lan herself strangles at birth her second girl during the height of the famine when there is no possibility of adequate nursing or care. Another measure of status of women is the size of their feet. The feet of girls in wealthy or solvent families are bound from birth to maturity in order to create small, delicate feet. O-lan, a slave who is physically unattractive in other respects, becomes repulsive to Wang Lung at one point because of her large feet. He had not been bothered by their size during the famine and after the family returns to the land and makes a success of the farm. With the worst of these hardships behind them, however, Wang Lung sees things differently and purchases Lotus, a delicately featured concubine with tiny feet.

The acquisition of Lotus marks Wang Lung's achievement of wealth and prestige. It is in this second part of the novel that Wang Lung's sons begin to assert themselves as individuals and to part from the tradition of patriarchy that had been sacred to Wang Lung. Meanwhile, O-lan, having given her entire life to her husband and having been responsible in no small degree for his success, dies in the agony of cancer and without the love of her husband.

The conclusion of the novel passes stylistically from simple narrative to an approximation of biblical lyric, cadenced and polysyndetonic—for example, "Then Wang Lung was humbled and anxious and he was submissive and he was sorry and he said . . . " The formalism of the language is in accord with Wang Lung's function as a representative of prerevolutionary China. The world passes away from him as none of his sons commits himself to farming: His youngest son leaves to become a soldier, and his first and second sons are determined to sell his land.

Analysis

The emphasis in the first twelve chapters of *The Good Earth* is on the earth itself and on Wang Lung's identification of himself with it. The next twelve chapters focus on Wang Lung's three sons and their disaffections with one another and with their father, whose attachment to the land they do not share. The last ten chapters include the deaths of O-lan; Wang Lung's father; his true friend, Ching, who had given from his own meager store a lifesaving handful of beans to Wang Lung during the famine; and Wang Lung's uncle. These chapters elaborate on the corruption of character wrought by luxury and on the consequent divisions in the house of Wang. These themes correspond to the books of the Wang family trilogy that Pearl S. Buck fashioned, consisting of *The Good Earth, Sons* (1932), and *A House Divided* (1935), published together in 1935 as *The House of Earth*. The sequels continue the narrative of Wang Lung's three sons and concentrate on the militaristic brigandage of the youngest, who comes to be known as Wang the Tiger.

The emphases of both *The Good Earth* and the completed trilogy constitute a view of the cycles of life, both terrestrial (fertility, fruition, and decay) and human (struggle, achievement, and decline). In its mythic quality, *The Good Earth* is richer than its sequels, which have more to do with enterprise and brigandage. Land in *The Good Earth* is, while not explicitly identified as female, the maternal sustenance of Wang Lung, who may be viewed as umbilically dependent on the earth. This relationship is reflected in the four women who nurture Wang Lung and satisfy his needs: O-lan, fully attuned to the earth and the mainstay of her husband, whose acquisition and retention of abundant land is made possible by her surrendering to him a horde of jewels of which she comes into fortuitous possession; Lotus, the concubine, who satisfies his lechery as he becomes wealthy from his land holdings; his "poor fool," the daughter who makes it possible for him to experience human love; and Pear Blossom, the very young slave and his second concubine, who eases his passage from active life into senescence. When Wang Lung leaves his palatial house and returns by preference to the earthen house where he began, thereby completing his life cycle, his only companions are Pear Blossom and the "poor fool," themselves analogous to the fruitfulness and barrenness of the good earth.

O-lan, the "poor fool," and Pear Blossom are consonant with the true earth in both its positive and its negative phases. Lotus is identifiable with the sickness induced by luxury and by exploitation of the earth. Wang Lung's sensual obsession with Lotus makes him selfish and inconsiderate. His mental cruelty to O-lan during this period parallels his loss of immediate contact with the land. The cure for his sexual lust is the earth: "and when he was weary he lay down upon his land and he slept and the health of the earth spread into his flesh and he was healed of his sickness."

Paradoxically, his love of the land precludes his full love of any human, whatever the measure of his devotion to father, wife, children, or his friend Ching. Only with his "poor fool," whom he had held and comforted during the famine as starvation brought her close to death, does he experience the selfless love that is the very nature of O-lan. It is this paradox that contributes to the novel a greatness not often found in best-sellers.

Critical Context

The Good Earth was a phenomenal best-seller, eagerly celebrated by a Western world in which knowledge about daily life and social turmoil in China had been quite limited. It was the second of Pearl S. Buck's thirty-five novels, including her screen-play *Satan Never Sleeps* (1962), and must be acknowledged as her masterpiece. Her life's literary mission, opening the world of China to the world of the West, is entirely realized in this novel, the aesthetic greatness of which was obscured by critics either favorably disposed to her exposition of Chinese life or, as in the case of Asian intellectuals and elitists, captious about her inaccuracies and misconceptions. The author answered the latter convincingly and well, reinforcing her argument with personal experience and irrefutably accurate observation. The true companion piece to *The Good Earth* is *The Mother* (1934), a universalization of motherhood as the cycle of life, which, in its interdependence of positiveness and negativeness, is the mythic personification of the earth.

Roy Arthur Swanson

GOOD-BYE AND KEEP COLD

Author: Jenny Davis (1953-   )
First published: 1987
Type of work: Novel
Type of plot: Domestic realism and psychological realism
Time of work: The late 1970's and early 1980's
Locale: Cauley's Creek, Fincastle County, Eastern Kentucky
Subjects: Coming-of-age, death, emotions, family, and sexual issues
Recommended ages: 13-15

When her father dies in a strip-mining accident, Edda must be surrogate mother for her baby brother and confidante to her mother while creating a space for her own identity to take root.

Principal characters:
  EDDA COMBS, a young girl who struggles to keep her family together and to make sense of the adult world
  ED COMBS, her father, who dies in a mining accident
  FRANCES COMBS, her mother, who is in constant emotional crisis
  JIMMY, Edda's active and much younger brother
  BANKER, Ed's seventy-five-year-old great-uncle, who lives with the family
  HENRY JOHN FITZPATRICK, Ed's coworker, who later courts Frances
  ANNIE ADAMS, Frances' best friend
  CHARLIE HENSON, one of Edda's few school friends
  AMY EVERSOLE, another of Edda's friends
  ALEXANDRA, Henry John's daughter

Form and Content

"I am resting from my childhood," Edda Combs says near the end of *Good-bye and Keep Cold*. She knows that when she breaks her winter reverie, she will have to be an adult. Again. She is waiting to be free of a childhood she lost when she was eight, when Henry John Fitzpatrick blew a dynamite charge too early and accidentally killed Ed Combs, her father. That was the day Edda that took charge of sixteen-month-old Jimmy and realized that Uncle Banker would not be much help. It was also the day that her mother, Frances, turned inward and shut down.

Jenny Davis' novel depicts the lingering psychological damage done when a child must become an adult too soon, without trivializing the love that keeps this family intact. It traces Edda's search for identity and self-worth, yet it is also her mother's search. "I'm tired, Edda. I'm going to bed," Frances says, and Edda is frightened more by the physical shell of her mother than by the physical loss of her father. Frances, struggling through her bereavement, remains profoundly depressed for most of the next ten years, leaning heavily on Edda for support. It is twenty months before Frances even considers getting a job; actually, Henry John finds her one. Jimmy must go to stay with a sitter; he develops night terrors and spends his days digging by the fence. Edda, however, enjoys some normalcy: She learns to ride a bike, stays overnight at Amy Eversole's house, and develops a school friendship with Charlie Henson. She also watches Henry John's courtship of her mother.

Frances' friend Annie hints to Edda that the neighbors are gossiping, and Edda is thrust back into her role of family protector. Eventually, Henry John is driven away by Edda's jealousy, Annie's vindictiveness, and Frances' thoughtlessness when she uses the shelves that he built to create a photographic shrine to Ed and his family. Shortly after a family vacation at the ocean, Edda has a fistfight with a boy who accuses her father of contracting venereal disease from Annie. In a moment of rage, Edda confronts Annie, and her mother's friendship with this woman is ruined. Having loosed this terribleness, Edda is "no longer able to stand guard" and wants no more adult knowledge. After a period of internalized rage, Frances frees herself by formally divorcing her dead husband and moving the family to Lexington.

This action should be the turning point, but Edda discovers that she does not fit in at high school any more than at Cauley Creek. Frances continues to confide in her as a sister, and Edda becomes the family bookkeeper. Finally, Henry John returns to give his new wife's handicapped, unwanted baby, Alexandra, to Frances. The past romance is rekindled; Henry John eventually divorces his wife and marries Frances, but it is too late for Edda to regain her childhood. After high school and college, she is back at the oceanside, waiting and listening, just as her mother did before her.

Analysis

Good-bye and Keep Cold provides an unflinching and distressing look at one family's life in the early 1970's in the back country of Eastern Kentucky. Davis, an environmental activist, shows the personal side of the destructiveness of strip mining. She argues that there is real ambivalence in people's attitudes toward the mines and the mountains that they destroy. The love of the mountaintops and "hollers" keeps the people there; the necessities of survival cause them to ignore the scarred landscapes of "mountain-top removal," even after the Strip Mining Act of 1975. This dichotomy is reflected in a heated argument between Henry John and Annie when he accuses the indigenous population of sloth and laziness; she says that the lack of craftsmanship is a mark of despair. This ambivalence is also at work in the Combs family: The mining operation claims Ed's life and later gives Frances a much-needed job. Davis also uses Eastern Kentuckian canon about the paramount importance of belonging to an established family in order to highlight the merits and the destructiveness of such interdependency and to show the parallel development of both daughter and mother toward emotional and social maturity.

"We're a little colony of outsiders," Frances says, feeling alienated from life in Cauley Creek. She will not discuss her childhood as an orphan, and she satisfies her desperate need for belonging with Ed, Annie, and her children. Devastated when Ed dies, Frances becomes disorganized and detached. Banker is the only stable adult in this family, and he only listens. Henry John, a second-generation Irish immigrant and an outsider himself, cannot break through that isolation, and even Edda and Jimmy think that their mother often looks through them. Edda stops visiting "Heaven," her father's favorite glade, long before her mother stops talking to his ghost. Frances' dependency places Edda in conflict with herself and with her mother; she cannot achieve a separate social identity in this closed society until her mother does so and thus remains a loner throughout the story.

Davis provides no easy answers for adolescent survival in such a high-risk environment. At the novel's end, however, Jimmy has weathered childhood dangers and some adolescent delinquency, and Edda is almost emotionally independent of her family. "Nobody's perfect," Annie says, and there is hope that this family will transcend life's circumstances.

Another theme is the unifying force of family love. Edda, Jimmy, and Banker, whose room is a safe haven, are wrapped tightly in that love. Henry John is excluded because, although Frances feels "cherished" by him, she cannot see the possibilities that he represents. She is eventually driven to create a visual representation of family on the living room shelves. This purposeful activity is healing for her, but it shatters Henry John's courtship.

It seems that nothing Frances can do allows her to avoid unpleasantness, which only adds to her fatalism. Surprisingly, the discovery of Ed's adultery with Annie, who has surreptitiously been the cause of much trouble in this family, actually breaks her self-absorption. "Perhaps we aren't meant to avoid anything, " she philosophizes. "We're in for it all." Allowing her anger to become conscious means that Frances is able to act on it and leave it behind.

Edda's self-discovery parallels that of her mother. At one point, she realizes that she hates both her parents—and so her anger at them also becomes conscious. Eventually, Edda puts them in her "private book of fools" and moves forward. Her mother continues inappropriate confidences, but now Edda knows that she should not hear, does not want to hear, and even when she must listen, she blocks out understanding. "Good-bye," she says, "good-bye and keep cold." This reference to a Robert Frost poem is significant. Perhaps Edda herself is the young orchard "cut off by a hill from the house" and out of sight; she too must be left in the cold for awhile before she can mature. "No orchard's the worse for the wintriest storm," Frost writes, and that is the hope for Edda.

Critical Context

Good-bye and Keep Cold was Jenny Davis' first novel, and it is a hallmark treatment of a dysfunctional family. Many psychologically realistic young adult stories allow the problem to supersede the plot or provide an unrealistic happy ending. In this novel, real problems are faced head on, and the ambiguous ending offers both hope and despair.

Davis has published other books for young adults. In *Sex Education* (1988), a class project about caring for someone has disastrous consequences for two students when they take on a young pregnant girl as their assignment. In *Checking on the Moon* (1991), the protagonist helps her grandmother run a coffee shop in a dangerous section of Pittsburgh. When her brother's girlfriend is raped, the community works together to reclaim its neighborhood. Davis, who also writes short stories and poems, says that "a good deal of what I write is hope on paper."

This is Davis' gift to the young reader. Her protagonists must overcome terrible odds, but those who persevere and have valor will emerge victorious and whole. She is not afraid to treat tough subjects and to let her readers work through the challenges facing their generation, yet she is sensitive enough always to offer them hope for the future.

Jane Laurenson Neuburger

GOOD-BYE, MR. CHIPS

Author: James Hilton (1900-1954)
First published: 1934
Type of work: Novel
Type of plot: Domestic realism
Time of work: 1848 to World War I (1914-1918)
Locale: Brookfield School, a fictitious preparatory school in England
Subjects: Education and friendship
Recommended ages: 13-18

A series of episodes describing a beloved teacher, this novel reminds readers of their own favorite teachers while providing a nostalgic look at turn-of-the-century England.

> *Principal characters:*
> MR. CHIPPING, a teacher of Latin and Greek at Brookfield School who
> is affectionately known as "Mr. Chips" or simply "Chips"
> KATHERINE BRIDGES CHIPPING, Mr. Chips's wife
> MRS. WICKETT, Mr. Chips's landlady, who had once been in charge of
> the school's linen room
> MR. RALSTON, a young headmaster whose progressive ideas cause
> conflict with Chips
> MAX STAEFEL, the school's German master, who is killed in World
> War I while fighting on the Western Front

Form and Content

Good-bye, Mr. Chips is an episodic novel about the most beloved teacher at a British preparatory school. Although many of its vignettes appear in chronological order, the novel has no single narrative. It achieves its unity, not through a single story line but through the figure of Chips himself. Each episode provides another detail about the novel's central character and the crucial role that he played in the lives of his students.

Mr. Chips is a composite of the "ideal teacher," a representation of the dedication and love found in all who excel at this profession. Nevertheless, James Hilton takes great pains to make Mr. Chips seem ordinary. He is not the greatest scholar on the faculty of Brookfield School. He does not win the admiration of his pupils through skill at games or athletics. He was not even a particularly good teacher or administrator when he was young. Rather, like many other teachers, he improved year by year, eventually coming to symbolize Brookfield School.

Mr. Chips was born in 1848 and visited the Great Exhibition (also known as the Crystal Palace Exhibition) in London when he was three years old. In 1870, he was hired by Brookfield School's old master, Wetherby, who died the following summer. In later years, he would be the only teacher left who recalled the school's early days.

Mr. Chips is recognizable everywhere because of his tattered academic gown, a habit of interjecting the words "umph" and "um," and the jokes that he uses when teaching his lessons. He has a old-fashioned view of education and the value of classics. Chips sees Latin and Greek not as real languages, but as the source of a few phrases that gentlemen use to adorn their speech. He resists new techniques of pedagogy and was all the more successful for being a member of "the old school."

After more than a quarter century of teaching, Mr. Chips is appointed housemaster in 1896. That same year, he vacations in the Lake District of northwestern England. On a hike there, he meets Katherine Bridges, twenty-five years old to his forty-eight. With her blue eyes, straw-colored hair, freckled cheeks, and relaxed nature, Chips falls in love with Katherine at once, and they are married that same summer. Ideologically, Katherine is as different from Chips as she could be. She is a "new woman" who admires the ideas of such social reformers as Henrik Ibsen (1828-1906) and George Bernard Shaw (1856-1950), authors whom Chips detests. Under her influence, however, his thinking becomes sharper. He is also exposed to a tenderness and sense of beauty lacking in his life. With Katherine by his side, Chips for the first time becomes truly loved, not merely respected, at Brookfield School. This brief interlude of happiness comes to an end, however, when both Katherine and their baby die in childbirth on April 1, 1898. Chips then falls back into the role of a bachelor so completely that most people forget that he had ever been married.

Mr. Chips retires in 1913 at the age of sixty-five but returns to the school as acting headmaster during World War I. He dies soon after, a dedicated teacher to the end.

Analysis

The title *Good-bye, Mr. Chips* is taken from an expression that appears twice in the novel. On the night before their wedding, Katherine whispers "Good-bye, Mr. Chips" in the belief that, once they are married, they will never be the same again. Near the end of the novel, Linford, a new boy at school, departs from tea with the aged teacher with the words "Good-bye, Mr. Chips," unaware that Chips will die the next day. These two episodes illustrate the factors that give Chips's life its meaning: Katherine and the students of Brookfield School. From Katherine, Chips learns to temper justice with mercy and to balance learning with love, gentleness, and an appreciation of beauty. From his students, Chips derives his whole reason for living. The students of Brookfield School become Chips's children, and he remembers their names and faces all the rest of his life. As he lies on his deathbed, Mr. Chips overhears one of the masters saying what a pity it was Chips never had children. At this, the old man opens his eyes and says "But I have, you know . . . I have . . . thousands of 'em . . . and all boys."

Good-bye, Mr. Chips provides a nostalgic portrait of a teacher whose life is dedicated to his students. Although the schooling familiar to today's juvenile and young adult readers differs sharply from that described in the novel, they will see many parallels between Mr. Chips and their own favorite teachers. In fact, shortly after the novel was published, Hilton was inundated with letters from people who wrote to tell him about their own "Mr. Chips" in diverse corners of the world. The book became an overnight sensation and was Hilton's first successful novel. His character of Mr. Chips continues to remind readers of a teacher who was stern but caring, idiosyncratic and a bit "odd," unforgettable despite all of his or her foibles, and widely loved by generations of youngsters.

Hilton's novel teaches a number of lessons that make it particularly well suited to younger readers. *Good-bye, Mr. Chips* demonstrates, for example, that people must continue to develop throughout their lives. When Mr. Chips nervously took his first prep (a type of study hall) at the age of twenty-two, no one would have guessed that this was the man who would one day become synonymous with Brookfield School. Chips's success is gradual, proving that one need not be instantly popular in order to succeed in the end. Mr. Chips also demonstrates that it is the extent to which one cares for other people that earns their admiration, not the extent of one's knowledge or wealth. Hilton mentions several times that Chips is not regarded as a superb scholar or as having a keen intelligence. His students learn from him not because he knows so much but because he cares so much about them. Mr. Chips represents a sort of gentility that was becoming rare even in his own day. When the German master, Mr. Staefel, is killed on the Western Front, Mr. Chips ignores the fact that he was fighting against England. He announces Mr. Staefel's name among the honored dead at Chapel, inspired by what this teacher meant to Brookfield School, not the side on which he was fighting during the war. Even those who are appalled by this breach of propriety admire Chips's motives. He soon gains a reputation for being "pre-war," a product of the values of an earlier (and perhaps more noble) time.

Critical Context

Good-bye, Mr. Chips was influenced by two distinct literary traditions. On one level, it may be described as a "most memorable person" novel along the lines of F. Scott Fitzgerald's *The Great Gatsby* (1925), Nikos Kazantzakis' *Vios kai politela tou Alexe Zormpa* (1946; *Zorba the Greek*, 1952), or Truman Capote's *Breakfast at Tiffany's* (1958). Novels in this tradition usually contain elements of both comedy and sentimentality, describing an individual whose unique personality had an impact upon numerous people. *Good-bye, Mr. Chips* differs slightly from the other novels in this tradition, however, by not being told in the first person by someone who "knew" the central character and was inspired by them. Instead, Hilton adopts a third-person omniscient voice in the novel.

At the same time, *Good-bye, Mr. Chips* may also be described as a "life at school" novel bearing some similarities to Colette's *Claudine à l'école* (1900; *Claudine at School*, 1956), E. R. Braithwaite's *To Sir, with Love* (1959), John Knowles's *A Separate Peace* (1959), Bel Kaufman's *Up the Down Staircase* (1963), Robert Cormier's *The Chocolate War* (1974), and central sections of Charles Dickens' *David Copperfield* (1849-1850). "Life at school" novels range widely in tone—from starkly tragic to broadly comic—and often contain a strong element of nostalgia.

By combining these two literary traditions, *Good-bye, Mr. Chips* exhibits a style and tone that is utterly unique. Young people relate to it because, despite the passage of time, its central figure is similar to individuals whom they encounter in their own education. Older readers enjoy it because of the nostalgic look that in provides of a bygone day. Originally written as an extended short story for the *British Weekly* and *Atlantic Monthly*, *Good-bye, Mr. Chips* is light, sentimental reading with a gentle moral that can be enjoyed by readers of all ages.

Jeffrey L. Buller

GORILLAS IN THE MIST

Author: Dian Fossey (1932-1985)
First published: 1983
Type of work: Science
Subjects: Animals, nature, and science
Recommended ages: 15-18

Fossey's chronicle of her thirteen years of field research with mountain gorillas awakens interest in the great apes and in issues related to wildlife conservation, the impact of humans on nature, and the rigors of scientific research.

Form and Content

Gorillas in the Mist is a popular account of Dian Fossey's research and her other experiences while studying mountain gorillas in Africa. The book, consisting of a first-person narrative and descriptive passages, is divided into twelve chapters. In some cases, a chapter follows the history of a particular gorilla group or an extended patriarchal family. This approach results in some overlapping between chapters, since some described events involve more than one group of gorillas.

Fossey went to Africa in December, 1966, as a protégé of the famous anthropologist Louis Leakey and under the sponsorship of the Wilkie Foundation and the National Geographic Society. The first chapter describes her attempts to study the gorillas from a base camp in Zaire, in the Virunga Mountains. The work was interrupted when Fossey was evacuated by soldiers during a rebellion. She reestablished contact with some of the same gorillas from a new base camp in Rwanda, in the Parc des Volcans.

Two chapters give general impressions of the terrain, ecology, wildlife, native people, and gorilla populations around the Karisoke camp in Rwanda. Six chapters follow several gorilla groups, giving descriptions of intergroup and intragroup social relationships, individual characteristics, migrations, nest making, feeding behavior, play, sexual activities, contents of feces, births and deaths, development and care of infants, vocalizations, aggression, curiosity, illnesses and injuries, changes in group composition, and the gorillas gradual acceptance of Fossey.

Fossey observed the animals for nearly three years before one of them touched her. That silverback male, named Peanuts, and another male, Digit, were among Fossey's favorites. The gorillas eventually became so accustomed to her presence that adults would allow playful youngsters to sit on Fossey's lap. The book dispels old stereotypes of gorillas as fierce "King Kong"-type monsters. Much of gorilla family life is described as involving tranquil periods of feeding, resting, and play. Yet, Fossey also relates how the adult males fought with one another for females and defended their groups against attacks by poachers. When a male captured a new female for its harem, it sometimes killed the female's infants that had been sired by other males.

Two chapters describe animal and human visitors to the Karisoke Research Centre. Fossey was more accepting of the animals: Chickens, dogs, a monkey, duikers (antelope), bushbuck, buffalo, rats, and other creatures roamed freely in and around the camp. She resented visits by tourists and had difficulties with most of the students who came to work with her. Fossey did have a long relationship with *National Geographic* photographer Bob Campbell, and she was grateful for the help of African trackers and porters, some of whom were with her for many years.

Two chapters involve poaching and trapping and the devastation that these activities cause among gorillas and other wildlife. Fossey organized antipoaching patrols and paid African assistants to dismantle poachers' traps and snares. Whenever possible, she rescued animals from the traps. Two sick, frightened infant gorillas were brought to Karisoke after they were captured for a zoo. In attempting to defend their babies, most members of the infants' families (not groups in the study) had been killed. Fossey nursed them back to health but could not save the two young gorillas from their fate as short-lived zoo specimens. A third baby gorilla was released back into the wild. Several gorillas in Fossey's study groups, including her special friend, Digit, were killed or seriously injured by poachers. Digit and a male called Uncle Bert were decapitated, and Digit's hands were hacked off.

The main text is followed by an epilogue, which is a plea for the preservation of wildlife areas and endangered species in various parts of the world. Two years after the book was published, Fossey was murdered at Karisoke.

Analysis

Although many scientific terms are used throughout the book, *Gorillas in the Mist* tells such an engaging story that it can interest readers without scientific training. Readers come to know gorillas as complex, intelligent, curious, charming creatures, with family lives and conflicts not unlike those of humans. Although primarily intended for adults, this book can be of interest to older teenagers; sophisticated terminology and mature topics make it inappropriate for younger readers. Appendices and an extensive bibliography at the end are designed for those with more scientific background. The book is a mixture of scientific reporting and less-documented, often-impassioned opinions. From a scientific standpoint, as the first multiyear field study of mountain gorillas (*Gorilla gorilla beringei*, a different subspecies from lowland gorillas), Fossey's work cannot be ignored.

The patience that is necessary in field research and the difficulties of living in the bush, without modern conveniences, are clearly described. For young people interested in science, the book can serve both to inspire and to point out the potential drawbacks of such work. As a popular narrative, however, the book does not give a realistic picture of the meticulous, unglamorous, highly controlled, and statistical nature of most scientific research. In contrast to reports in academic journals, which are often inaccessible to high school or undergraduate readers, Fossey's work paints vivid images of her subject. Fossey wrote a doctoral dissertation at Cambridge University in 1976 entitled *The Behavior of the Mountain Gorilla*, which was her attempt to comply with academic standards. She has been widely criticized by other scientists and conservationists, partly for the subjective nature of her work, but more vehemently for the bizarre behaviors in which she indulged in order to combat poaching. According to several accounts, and by her own admission, Fossey attempted to frighten poachers away from the wildlife refuge of the Parc des Volcans. She reportedly humiliated and injured or tortured some of them, and she may have burned some of their homes.

The death of Digit and other gorillas had a tremendous impact on Fossey. She valued and loved these animals so much that she could not understand conflicting human needs. Perhaps one of the greatest values of Fossey's book, beyond being merely informative, is that it can stimulate the consideration of many complicated issues. How detached should scientists be from their research subjects? What influence does the presence of an observer exert on behavior? What methods are appropriate or inappropriate for research on animals or humans? What do humans have in common with the great apes? Should the welfare of wildlife be valued above the welfare of people? How can people and wildlife coexist? Should tourism be used to provide funds for conservation? Is the killing of intelligent animals the same as murdering humans? Does the end justify the means when trying to protect innocent creatures? Is it a good idea to try to preserve gorillas and other animals in captivity?

To deal with these issues adequately, and to view Fossey's life and work from a clear perspective, it is necessary to examine other works. Despite controversies that have arisen about the author, in the final analysis *Gorillas in the Mist* is one of a growing body of works that have aroused public awareness and sentiment in favor of the protection of primates and other animals.

Critical Context

Public interest in the behavior of chimpanzees and great apes was first stimulated in the 1960's by many articles in *National Geographic* and reports in other popular media. Along with Fossey, Jane Goodall, who worked with chimpanzees, and Biruté Galdikas, who studied orangutans, were pioneers in discovering and communicating to the world the endearing character of these animals. Fossey's book was widely popular when it was first published, and interest surged again when a film loosely based on it was released in 1988. Young readers may be somewhat misled if Fossey's book is their only source on the subject, and even more so if they only see the film version of *Gorillas in the Mist*.

More details of Fossey's life are included in *Woman in the Mists* (1987), by Farley Mowat. *The Dark Romance of Dian Fossey* (1990), by Harold T. Hayes, is highly critical of Fossey, as is Sy Montgomery's book *Walking with the Great Apes* (1991). Montgomery also chronicles the work of Goodall and Galdikas, who are subject to similar but much milder criticism. He and other writers go so far as to charge that Fossey was mentally ill.

Gorillas in the Mist, along with such easy-to-read books as Goodall's *Through a Window: My Thirty Years with the Chimpanzees of Gombe* (1990); *The Education of Koko* (1981), by Francine Patterson and Eugene Linden; and *Almost Human: A Journey into the World of Baboons* (1987), by Shirley C. Strum, can be worthy starting points for more serious study of primates. The work that Fossey started was continued in Rwanda until it was disrupted by civil war in the early 1990's.

Laura L. Klure

A GRASS ROPE

Author: William Mayne (1928-   )
First published: 1957; illustrated
Type of work: Novel
Type of plot: Domestic realism and mystery
Time of work: The mid-twentieth century
Locale: The Yorkshire Dales, in northern England
Subjects: Animals, family, nature, and the supernatural
Recommended ages: 10-13

> *Two families in the remote Yorkshire Dales share an ancient mystery concerning a unicorn and hunting dogs that is solved both by the use of common sense and by a belief in the supernatural.*

> *Principal characters:*
> MARY OWLAND, a small girl who believes implicitly in the truth of fairy stories
> NAN OWLAND, her older sister, who is in her first year of high school
> PETER DYSON, a boy of Mary's age, the owner of a dog named Hewlin
> ADAM FORREST, the head boy of the local high school
> MR. and MRS. OWLAND, the owners of Lew Farm
> MRS. DYSON, the landlady of The Unicorn, an inn
> CHARLEY, an old farmhand of Mr. Owland

Form and Content

This charming story of the solving of an ancient mystery by four schoolchildren is set in one of the more remote areas of England. The continuity of life in the two valleys, Vendale and Thoradale, is shown by the fact that forebears of the two families depicted in the novel are part of a legend from medieval times. The families live in exactly the same places in the present as in the legend and bear the same names, even down to the dog, Hewlin.

Into this quiet, hill-farming community rides Adam Forrest on his bicycle, ostensibly to earn some money by repainting The Unicorn Inn, which is run by the Dysons, one of the families of the legend. He has another mission, however, set him by the headmaster of the local high school, where he is head boy: to "solve" or explain the ancient legend that involves a Dyson ancestor eloping with an Owland heiress. He was drowned and the Owland treasure was lost, along with a pack of hunting dogs and a mythical unicorn.

In the course of eighteen short chapters, the mystery unfolds gradually to its conclusion. Mary Owland believes the legend quite literally and is prepared to discover for herself the fairyland where the unicorn supposedly dwells. Her sister, Nan, both wants to protect her and is embarrassed by her naïveté in front of Adam. In fact, although Adam is considerably older than the other children, including Peter

Dyson, he treats them with great ease as equals.

The ancient sign on the inn offers them the most clues, including an ancient hunting horn that they clean and blow. While Mary believes that it will summon the dogs from fairyland, the others work out the echo effects of the sound and fit this into the solution to the mystery. It is Mary, however, in search of the gates of fairyland with her grass rope—believed in the legend to be the only way to capture the unicorn—who brings the story to a climax. She sneaks out of her farm one night and discovers a tunnel beneath a waterfall called Dysons Dig. Her parents discover that she is missing and, fearing that she may have fallen down an old mineshaft, go searching for her. Her discovery provides the remaining clues to the mystery of the legend. The hunting dog that she believes she has captured turns out to be a fox cub, which she is allowed to keep as her reward. Honor is maintained by all parties in the solution.

A Grass Rope is illustrated with line drawings by Lynton Lamb and a much-needed map. Lamb's buildings and landscapes capture their stony texture, but his figure drawing is woefully disproportioned.

Analysis

One of William Mayne's many qualities as an author for which critics have often commended him is the almost poetic quality of his prose. This is nowhere more clearly seen than in his depictions of the Yorkshire Dales, both in their Brontë-esque remoteness and grandeur and in the details of a working sheep farm. Although farming is a struggle in the stony and barren soil and with the predations of foxes in the henhouse, what comes across in the novel is the settled and contented nature of the inhabitants, their natural intelligence and sympathies, and the depths of their roots. The novel is set in the summer, and Mayne's description of the sunlight, moonlight, and starlight, the cloud formations and visibility, inform the whole atmosphere. Readers can sense how Mary believes so easily in fairyland; the setting itself, as described by Mayne, is magical.

In addition to geographical remoteness, strangeness is also provided by the use of local dialect, especially by Peter and Charley, the farmhand. Mayne, who is from Yorkshire himself, has an unerring ear for this dialect. His narrative descriptions contrast with the dialogue in their complex and detailed visual imagery, which gives the style its particular poetic quality. The dialogue, of which there is a generous amount, also has a fantastical quality at times, as the motifs from the legend color the subject matter and the thought patterns of the children.

Although the setting is depicted as a self-enclosed world, the details of everyday farm life, from digging holes and mending walls to collecting eggs, give it a concreteness, a way to identify with the characters' lives. The schoolwork that the children bring home is universal, although, in this remote setting, it is the academic material that seems remote. Mayne portrays the simple lifestyles of the children and the natural closeness of the families beautifully. Adam, the outsider, is drawn into their homes, and the process by which he is accepted by both younger children and parents is sensitively handled. The emphasis is on cooperation; on a farm, everyone must do allotted chores in order to survive, and visitors must help. In some ways, the depiction evokes the frontier family life in the books of Laura Ingalls Wilder.

The pace of the story is leisurely, avoiding the frantic excitement of many adventure stories for children. Mayne's desire to tell a story is balanced by his equal desire to paint a picture in words. The two goals come together as the continuity of country life and traditions unfolds in the explication of the legend. The final explanations do not "explain away" the legend. It is quite the contrary: They authenticate the reliability of country tradition. The accretions may be magical, but the basic facts have proved to be true.

This approach leads to Mayne's underlying thematic proposition: that both poetry and science, both imagination and logical thinking, are valid ways of searching for truth. Although children in their psychological development may move from magical thinking to logical operations, reflected in the contrast between Mary and Nan, neither way is better. Mary's magical thinking leads to discoveries that the others would not have made. Mayne's own style seems to mirror this exactly: The concreteness of his details and his clarity in weaving the plot are balanced against the symbolism and imaginative leaps of his descriptions and dialogue.

Critical Context

The publication of *A Grass Rope* firmly sealed William Mayne's reputation as a gifted and sensitive children's writer, especially with the awarding of the Carnegie Medal for the book in 1957. Like many of Mayne's novels, it derives its strength from a detailed portraiture and the love of a specific Yorkshire locale. Such atmosphere and careful scenic painting are not always seen as virtues in children's literature; neither is the elliptical, often tangential style or the unspecific sense of audience. His prolific output—forty books in twenty years—and his typically careful and intelligent writing helped raise the status of children's literature in the 1950's and 1960's and established him firmly in the canon of British children's literature.

A Grass Rope is perhaps, in its near fantasy elements, more akin to *Earthfasts* (1966) rather than Mayne's better-known school stories, such as *A Swarm in May* (1955). Both *Earthfasts* and *A Grass Rope* are set in the Yorkshire Dales, show a fascination with a fairy world underground and the characters' attempts to enter a magic gate to attain it, and share a sense of the solidity of history and the living past. More important, both conduct a debate on the limits of scientific methodology as a way of knowing truth. Mayne handles the personal and family relationships far more successfully here, however, than in the later book.

Among other writers, perhaps the closest to Mayne in style is a Yorkshire compatriot, Jane Gardam. Her book *The Hollow Land* (1981) has a similar feel to *A Grass Rope*: The younger children are seen exploring a similar northern landscape full of the living past, dialect language and local customs are used to create a keenly experienced setting, and, out of this setting, plots naturally develop in a relatively leisurely way.

David Barratt

GREAT EXPECTATIONS

Author: Charles Dickens (1812-1870)
First published: 1860-1861
Type of work: Novel
Type of plot: Moral tale and social realism
Time of work: The 1820's and 1830's
Locale: The marsh country, Satis House, and London
Subjects: Coming-of-age, crime, emotions, friendship, and love and romance
Recommended ages: 15-18

Pip—an orphan reared by a simple yet kind-hearted blacksmith—pursues the wealth, social status, and manners of a refined gentleman and becomes a snob until he learns the difference between Christian behavior and worldly behavior.

> *Principal characters:*
> PIP, a seven-year-old orphan who is manipulated by a convict and a spinster over a period of thirty years
> JOE GARGERY, Pip's brother-in-law and loyal friend, the most sympathetically portrayed character in the novel
> ABEL MAGWITCH, the convict whom Pip befriends on the marshes and his secret benefactor
> MISS HAVISHAM, the deranged heiress who was betrayed on her wedding day and now brings up her ward Estella to hate all men
> ESTELLA HAVISHAM, the beautiful and stately adopted daughter of Miss Havisham with whom Pip falls in love
> MR. JAGGERS, a well-known and highly respected London lawyer who serves as Pip's guardian and dispenses money to him from Magwitch
> JOHN WEMMICK, a clerk in Mr. Jaggers' office who becomes Pip's good friend and who shows him hospitality
> HERBERT POCKET, a man who nicknames Pip "Handel" at their London lodgings and tells him Miss Havisham's story
> ORLICK, a mean employee of Joe Gargery and later of Miss Havisham who attacks Pip's sister and subsequently Pip
> BENTLEY DRUMMLE, Pip's fellow boarder in London who vies with him for Estella's love and later marries her

Form and Content

Great Expectations is an account of a young boy's moral education. A study in human weakness, it depicts the rise in social status of the seven-year-old orphan Pip, the novel's narrator and chief character and a kind of Everyman. On Christmas Eve in a cemetery, Pip meets Abel Magwitch, an escaped convict who makes him steal some food and a file from the forge where he lives with his sister and her husband,

Joe Gargery, a blacksmith. Shortly thereafter, Pip is hired by a wealthy old woman named Miss Havisham to be a playmate for her beautiful adopted daughter, Estella.

Jilted years ago on her wedding day, Miss Havisham is a recluse. She lives in a world of the past at desolate Satis House, a home whose name means "enough"; the ancestor who built it believed that whoever lived there could never want more. During his frequent visits to Miss Havisham's home, Pip begins to believe erroneously that her fortune will make him a gentleman, will bring him the love of Estella, and will provide him with prosperity. These are his great expectations.

Miss Havisham, however, has no hopes for happiness and no intention of leaving a legacy of happiness to anyone. Rather, she is a schemer who enjoys making nearly everyone around her miserable. She teaches Estella to hate men, exploits Pip, and vexes her ever-hopeful relatives. Although Pip eventually receives money from another source, Estella continues to scorn him and to be as coldly distant as a star. What Miss Havisham does is turn Estella and Pip into snobs.

In London, Pip matures while dealing with many strange situations. From Mr. Jaggers, a criminal lawyer who becomes his guardian, Pip discovers that he does indeed have a benefactor and great expectations. Jaggers gives Pip some money, and his clerk John Wemmick helps him. Pip takes up lodgings with Herbert Pocket, a relative of Miss Havisham from whom he learns her story and the manners of a gentleman. Soon, Pip feels superior to others, neglects his friends back home, and falls into debt. Proud and selfish, he feels ashamed to have the patient and polite but unpolished Joe Gargery visit him. When Magwitch drops by unexpectedly, Pip finds out that he is his benefactor. The felon tells him that the money he has been sending to Jaggers is part of a fortune he has made as a sheep farmer in Australia. Although aghast, Pip resolves to protect the escaped convict.

As Pip learns more about Magwitch, he begins to redeem himself. He finds out that Molly, Jaggers' housekeeper, was Magwitch's lover. Wemmick tells him that Molly strangled a rival in a fit of jealousy over Magwitch. Jaggers gained her release, and she has been working for him since then. Estella, ironically, is the daughter of Molly and Magwitch—not the genteel maiden of Pip's fantasies. During one of Pip's visits to Satis House, Miss Havisham promises to procure nine hundred pounds for Pip so that he can purchase a business partnership for Pocket at Clarriker's. Shortly thereafter, Miss Havisham dies in a fire at Satis House. With his act of generosity toward Herbert and an excursion to smuggle Magwitch out of England, Pip overcomes his selfishness. The latter, however, is unsuccessful. Wounded in a scuffle with the convict Compeyson, Miss Havisham's former lover and his former partner in crime, Magwitch is captured and taken to a prison infirmary. Pip visits the dying convict there and tells him that he has a beautiful daughter, a lady whom Pip loves. He is referring to Estella.

Although she does not care for him, Estella marries a sulky oaf named Bentley Drummle. When he returns from an eight-year sojourn in India, Pip hears that Drummle has died from an accident involving the ill-treatment of a horse and that Estella has remarried a Shropshire doctor with whom she is living prosperously on the fortune that she inherited from Miss Havisham. One day, Pip sees Estella in Piccadilly. Her carriage stops and the two talk briefly, shake hands, and part. The novel originally ends with Pip estranged from all who were associated with his great expectations.

When *Great Expectations* was published in book form, Dickens rewrote the ending, offering some hope for his main character. Pip visits Satis House and finds Estella still a widow; she is kinder to him, and Pip again envisions a future together.

Analysis

Great Expectations is the product of a time period when traditional values had been seriously declining and an extensive dehumanization of the multitudes had been ongoing. Mid-Victorian England was a land of extremely fixed social divisions. This is Charles Dickens' greatest novel. It was written with a sense of mastery, contains a superbly constructed plot, has a host of memorable characters, and is full of good scenes. It is more complicated than most of Dickens' novels, but not difficult to read. A commentary on the superficiality of middle-class attitudes during an era when an Englishman's achievements were esteemed enormously, *Great Expectations* depicts the self-seeking and self-destroying fantasies of the nineteenth century and contends that the decent but impoverished individual has greater worth than the idle yet affluent socialite.

Dickens redefines for his times the status of a true gentleman and emphasizes how money can change people and create class distinctions. Pip dreams of living on money that he has done nothing to earn. An attack of brain fever that sends him into a deathlike coma late in the novel leads to his rebirth. Joe Gargery helps him regain his health, and Magwitch helps him to learn the importance of humility.

The first half of *Great Expectations* contains one of the finest portraits of the frustrations of childhood in English literature. Dickens adapts several motifs from folklore. Miss Havisham, Estella, and Magwitch might be regarded as the fairy godmother, beautiful princess, and terrible ogre of this Dickensian fairy tale. Young Pip and Estella are victimized by an adult world that treats them as things rather than as persons. Both are manipulated by forces beyond their control. Pip's love for Estella is associated with the snobbery that makes him wretched; it is never reciprocated.

Snobbery is a facet of the theme of social injustice in the novel. What Dickens commends throughout are the simple, benevolent impulses of human nature—those possessed by Joe Gargery. What he condemns is the love of money—an obsession that motivates many of the other characters. The novel closes with an emphasis on forgiveness.

Great Expectations is a forerunner of the twentieth century development novel, a tale of lost illusions that describes the progress of a young man who travels from the country to the city, climbs the social ladder, and loses his innocence.

Critical Context

Great Expectations was published in weekly installments in *All the Year Round*, a British paper. The first installment appeared in December, 1860; the last came out in

August, 1861, the year that the novel was published in book form. It was at the urging of his friend Edward Bulwer-Lytton that Dickens revised his ending. *Great Expectations* is one of Dickens' last two completed novels, the other being *Our Mutual Friend* (1864). Critics regard the two books as bringing to fulfillment the social themes that Dickens had been developing for nearly three decades. Young adult readers of *Great Expectations* will identify readily with the problems of Dickens' characters.

James Norman O'Neill

THE GREAT GILLY HOPKINS

Author: Katherine Paterson (1932-   )
First published: 1978
Type of work: Novel
Type of plot: Domestic realism, psychological realism, and social realism
Time of work: The 1970's
Locale: A fictional community based on Takoma Park, Maryland
Subjects: Coming-of-age, family, religion, and social issues
Recommended ages: 10-15

Gilly Hopkins learns that life is tough but that it is this quality that makes it worthwhile, providing the chance to master something difficult.

> *Principal characters:*
> GILLY (GALADRIEL) HOPKINS, a twelve-year-old foster child who is starving for her mother's love
> MAIME TROTTER, a poor and uneducated woman who is filled with traditional values of love and self-responsibility
> WILLIAM ERNEST, a seven-year-old foster child who is considered intellectually slow
> MR. RANDOLPH, an old, blind black man, a neighbor of Trotter
> COURTNEY, Gilly's mother, a hippie

Form and Content

Some young adult literature, especially that written for younger audiences, presents an adolescent protagonist who has been given an unfair life, only to resolve all the problems at the end of the book in an unrealistic, unforeshadowed way. *The Great Gilly Hopkins* threatens to fall into this category but avoids doing so by maintaining an honest, realistic approach and thus offering a hard, but positive ethical perspective.

The story quickly establishes the main characters. Gilly is an intelligent girl who has developed a hard shell as the result of being rejected by her family and forced to grow up while being shifted from one foster home to another. Gilly arrives at her new foster home ready to set up her emotional barriers that she has developed from past experiences. Foster mother Maime Trotter welcomes Gilly and introduces her to William Ernest, a foster child considered to be mentally slow, and her neighbor Mr. Randolph, a poor, blind, black man who shares their evening meals. Author Katherine Paterson strips Maime Trotter of the less important qualities—an education, a clean house, money—so that her more important wisdom about human relationships and self-responsibility is both obvious and acceptable to the reader.

Gilly starts school and begins her standard routine: first demonstrating how intelligent she is, then purposely failing at her work. At the same time, she continues to write to her mother, believing that someday she will return, and complains about her new foster home, prompting a visit from the welfare department. Gilly also steals money from Mr. Randolph and heads for the bus station. In the final chapter, Gilly stands in the airport with her maternal grandmother, waiting for her much anticipated meeting with her idolized mother. Since self-responsibility is at the center of the novel, it is important to note that Gilly is responsible for initiating the change in her situation, for putting herself in this position. By this time, Gilly's qualities, both good and bad, have come out, and the reader has become sympathetic and anxious for the novel's resolution. It is a standard progressive plot, leading to this climax—a climax that must be not only happy but also satisfying, which it is.

Analysis

The Great Gilly Hopkins presents the core of Katherine Paterson's ethos in Maime Trotter's words that life is tough but it allows for the possibility of doing well at a tough job. The novel centers on self-responsibility. No matter how hard life is, no matter how unfair, it is up to the individual to make the best of the situation. In making the best of a difficult task, the task of life, the individual wins, even in defeat.

This central ethos is based on and surrounded by basic, traditional Presbyterian Christianity, not the born-again or charismatic movements, and in many ways, this context ties the story more closely to the writings for adolescents around the beginning of the twentieth century, such works as *Little Women* (1868-1869), by Louisa May Alcott; *Heidis Lehr und Wanderjahre* (1880; *Heidi*, 1884), by Johanna Spyri; *Anne of Green Gables* (1908), by L. M. Montgomery; and *The Secret Garden* (1911), by Frances Hodgson Burnett. Yet, whereas these books, although excellent, are often didactic, *The Great Gilly Hopkins* is not. The Christianity in Paterson's works is kept in the background, even mocked, and the shift from an emphasis on God to self-responsibility is an important one. This is most evident in the climatic conclusion, where the protagonist Gilly tells Maime Trotter to "Go to hell" and to not "try to make a stinking Christian out of me." Other social concerns surround the novel's center. The family and the neighborhood are not of the lily-white, upper-middle-class variety, and the story deals with such issues as racism, nonstandard families, and handicapped or intellectually challenged individuals.

Beyond these themes is a stylistic brilliance. Paterson mixes tragedy and humor well, and the juxtaposition both highlights and softens the unflinchingly honest views. Also, the characters, including the adults, who are often treated as caricatures in adolescent fiction, are both unique and believable. As with all good fiction, they linger, like friends, long after the book is finished. In addition, Paterson's obvious affection for both Gilly and Maime Trotter is mixed with an equally obvious concern for realistic honesty. All these qualities result in a work that young adults will readily understand.

Critical Context

Katherine Paterson has written several novels for young adults with similar heroines that offer various perspectives on the same ethical concerns about self-responsibility.

Perhaps her best-known work is the Newbery Medal-winning *Bridge to Terabethia* (1977), in which Leslie Burke, a young girl much like Gilly without the rough edges, teaches Jesse Aarons what life is all about. She tells him that the world is frightening, terrible, and fragile, that it is up to him to pay back to the world in beauty and caring what she has loaned him in vision and strength. In *Lyddie* (1991), an adolescent girl filled with determination and intelligence must discover, just as Gilly did, that there is "nothing to make you happy like doing good on a tough job." After Lyddie has faced many external, unfair, and difficult situations in life—such as class, race, and gender inequities—she comes to Paterson's central theme: "'I'm off . . . ,' she said, and knew as she spoke what it was she was off to. To stare down the bear! The bear that she had thought all these years was outside herself, but now, truly, knew was in her own narrow spirit." In the Newbery Medal-winning book *Jacob Have I Loved* (1980), the main character and narrator is yet another adolescent girl, Louise, who believes that she has received unfair treatment in comparison to her twin sister (much the same as in the biblical reference to Jacob and Esau on which the title is based). Once again, she learns that it is up to her to make what she will of her life. In the end, Louise becomes a nurse and delivers twins, discovering that it is necessary to leave the healthy twin aside while she helps the weak twin, an obvious reference to her own situation at birth.

This basic ethos fits into what is perhaps the greatest concern of human existence, that of free will verses fate. In contemporary literature, this theme is dealt with in another manner in the works of Robert Cormier, where the characters are deprived of their free will by an uncaring, brutal society. The ethos differs in that Cormier's characters either succumb or are forced to abuse power to gain even a small amount of self-responsibility. The perfect example of this struggle occurs in *The Chocolate War* (1974) and *Beyond the Chocolate War* (1985), in which Jerry Renault attempts to "disturb the universe" by standing up against the establishment. Readers are left to wonder whether he has won or lost. It is obvious in Katherine Paterson's novels that her characters have won, even if, such as in *The Great Gilly Hopkins*, it is a victory in defeat.

Harry Edwin Eiss

GRIMM'S FAIRY TALES

Authors: Jacob Grimm (1785-1863) and Wilhelm Grimm (1786-1859)
First published: Die Kinder- und Hausmärchen, 1812, 1815, revised 1819-1822 (English translation, 1823-1826)
Type of work: Short fiction
Subjects: Animals, coming-of-age, family, and the supernatural
Recommended ages: 10-18

The young protagonists in these exemplary tales encounter ill will, danger, and challenges and survive the vicissitudes of life by using their wits or by having their diligence and virtue rewarded.

Form and Content

Grimm's Fairy Tales as the collection is known today is the Grimms' seventh and final edition, published in 1857. It contains 210 tales, excluding 32 from previous editions. All 242 tales appear in numbered sequence in Jack Zipes's English translation, *The Complete Fairy Tales of the Brothers Grimm* (1987). The tales vary in length and complexity. Wilhelm Grimm improved them over the years by adding more dialogue, which brings the tales to life. Many of the characters and creatures also speak in catchy rhymes that are easily remembered.

Jacob and Wilhelm Grimm, known as the Brothers Grimm, collected the tales from acquaintances and from previous collections in German and other languages, most notably Charles Perrault's *Histoires: Ou, Contes du temps passé, avec des moralités* (1697; *Histories: Or, Tales of Past Times,* 1729), commonly known in French as *Contes des fées* or *Contes de ma mère l'oye* and in English as *Perrault's Fairy Tales* or *Tales of Mother Goose.* Therefore, it was inevitable that they would find different versions of the same tale. Where the variations are substantial, they appear as separate tales but are grouped together.

Some elements common to many of the tales are recognizable as standard fairy-tale formulae. Protagonists are apprenticed or locked in towers for seven years, and they must accomplish three tasks to break a spell. They are described through motifs rather than specific attributes: Princesses are beautiful, while witches are ugly.

Largely as a result of the popularity of certain of the Grimms' fairy tales, such as "Cinderella," "Little Red Riding Hood," "Sleeping Beauty," and "Hansel and Gretel," the opening formula "Once upon a time" and the closing formula "They lived happily ever after" have come to define fairy-tale style. Nevertheless, according to critic Maria Tatar in *The Hard Facts of the Grimms' Fairy Tales* (1987), the collection also includes "fables, tall tales, anecdotes, cautionary tales, and all manner of other narratives that struck the Grimms as folklore."

The content of the tales has been the subject of much critical debate. Their simplicity supports many diverse interpretations, and their widespread popularity makes them an attractive subject of research in education, psychology, folklore, German studies, theology, and comparative literature. *Grimm's Fairy Tales* is an organized body of work that points back vestigially to the pre-Christian myths of Northern Europe. Yet, Wilhelm Grimm's radical revisions from edition to edition have given many critics pause and suggest caution against attributing too much significance to any particular detail. In the final version of "Rumpelstiltskin," the miller's daughter is placed in a predicament by her father's assertion that she can spin straw into gold—a complete reversal from the first version, in which her problem was that everything she spun turned into gold. Images are not used consistently from tale to tale. They also have different value in different times and places. The core of *Grimm's Fairy Tales*, however, contains wishes and fears common to all peoples.

Analysis

The original German title of *Grimm's Fairy Tales* means "fairy tales for children and for the home." Both entertaining and didactic, the stories are meant for children and their parents. For children, whose lives lie ahead and hold infinite possibilities, the popular tales extend the promise that all will turn out well for the good and virtuous. That this end is often accomplished with the aid of magic appeals to children's sense of wonder at the world and reinforces what they need to believe. For parents, and adults in general, the tales serve as a reminder of children's vulnerability and their reliance on kind and good adults to care for them. Everyone's heart goes out to Hansel and Gretel, and no one wants to be seen as a wicked stepmother.

"Cinderella" is the quintessential fairy tale that not only contains all of its main figures and features but also embodies its standard themes. These themes were consciously emphasized by Wilhelm Grimm in his repeated rewriting of the fairy tales, and they reflect the biographies, beliefs, and ethics of the Brothers Grimm, who were orphaned at an early age and had to care for their younger siblings.

The main theme of "Cinderella" is of going from rags to riches. Following an early reversal of fortune that plunges Cinderella into degrading poverty, she persists through difficult times and triumphs in the end. This outcome reflects the Grimms' Protestant work ethic, the importance that they placed on self-reliance, and their belief that virtue will be rewarded.

Cinderella receives miraculous help from the tree that grows on her mother's grave and from a white bird. (The six Grimm children received help from their maternal aunt, without whom they might have starved.) Another theme of the fairy tales is that one never knows from whom, or indeed from what, one will receive assistance. Therefore, all people, animals, and plants should be treated with respect. In the fairy tales, animals often turn out to be people under a spell. Animals are personified, and cruel punishments are meted out to those who maltreat them.

Both Cinderella and the prince must work hard to find each other: Cinderella must get to the ball three evenings in a row in suitable clothes, and the prince must find out who she is. The theme that perseverance yields results runs through many of the tales.

As a postscript to Cinderella's happy marriage to the prince, the evil stepsisters' eyes are pecked out by pigeons. Rewards and punishments are justly deserved in *Grimm's Fairy Tales*, and the tales often end on a sobering note.

By way of contrast, tales that depict people defeated by their own stupidity and gullibility, with ironic titles such as "Clever Hans" and "Clever Else," are interspersed in the collection to provide comic relief. While the Grimms often use the theme of stupidity for amusement, they wisely achieve the greatest effect with a nonjudgmental tone. One of their truly ambivalent tales is "Lucky Hans." In return for seven years of service, Hans is given a large gold nugget. On the way home, he trades it for a horse, the horse for a cow, the cow for a pig, the pig for a goose, and the goose for a grindstone, which he accidentally knocks down a well, only to exclaim, "Nobody under the sun is as lucky as I am!" Is the tale an ironic portrayal of stupidity, or does it portray someone who has achieved enlightenment? Like many of the apparently simpler tales, "Lucky Hans" supports both simple and profound interpretations.

Critical Context

Grimm's Fairy Tales have been immensely popular ever since the first edition and are second only to the Bible in the number of copies sold. They are classics, read in homes and schools and studied in universities. Walt Disney produced three feature-length animated films based on the Grimms' fairy tales: *Snow White and the Seven Dwarfs* (1937), *Cinderella* (1950), and *Sleeping Beauty* (1959).

The fairy tales have become part of Western cultural heritage. Heard and read repeatedly in childhood, they are assumed to be part of everyone's frame of reference. British author Angela Carter developed the psychosexual aspects of "Blue Beard" (omitted from the Grimms' final edition) and "Little Red Riding Hood" in her collection *The Bloody Chamber and Other Stories* (1979). They depend for their effect on the reader's familiarity with *Grimm's Fairy Tales*. So do American author James Finn Garner's amusing collections *Politically Correct Bedtime Stories* (1994) and *Once Upon a More Enlightened Time* (1995), which use the same titles as the fairy tales that they parody.

Jacob and Wilhelm Grimm became interested in fairy tales as a means of entertaining their younger sister Charlotte and her friends. Soon, they took an academic approach to the subject. The Grimms intended to present the fairy tales as folktales, even writing some of them in dialect, and destroyed the manuscripts of the first edition. Scholars have subsequently succeeded in identifying almost every source, oral and literary, as listed in the notes to Zipes's translation. Whether the Grimms' tales are authentic folklore is a moot point in view of their enduring popularity. They fulfill a continuing need of the human psyche that transcends social class.

The landscapes evoked in the tales often seem idyllic and imaginary to North Americans, but they still exist in Europe. The Grimms lived in the city of Kassel in Germany. On the outskirts of the city, a beautiful rococo castle, Schloss Wilhelmsthal, stands surrounded by woods and fields. On the hill behind it is a tall tower much like Rapunzel's, and a row of magnificent fountains leads through the castle gardens to a glass summerhouse where musicians play on summer evenings.

Jean M. Snook

GUADALCANAL DIARY

Author: Richard Tregaskis (1916-1973)
First published: 1943; illustrated
Type of work: History
Time of work: July 26, 1942-September 26, 1942
Locale: Solomon Islands, South Pacific
Subjects: Death and war
Recommended ages: 13-18

Tregaskis describes the landing of American soldiers on Guadalcanal Island during World War II and their day-to-day struggle to capture the Japanese air base and defend it against enemy counterattack from the air, land, and sea.

Principal personage:
RICHARD TREGASKIS, a war correspondent

Form and Content

Adopting the format of the diary, Richard Tregaskis records what he hears and sees as he follows the men assigned to wrest from Japanese control the strategically important airfield on Guadalcanal Island. The narrative opens aboard a naval ship steaming toward the island, situated in the Solomon Islands east of New Guinea. As he passes among the officers and enlisted men bound for battle, Tregaskis records scenes of final preparation, troops sharpening their bayonets, cleaning their rifles, making jokes and small talk. With the officers, the correspondent discusses troop morale and military objectives in the coming offensive. Religious services counterpoint lectures on jungle warfare, booby traps, and Japanese snipers.

After almost two weeks of ship-board preparation, the day of the "big event" arrives. Tregaskis is assigned a place on the launch of the assault commander, Colonel LeRoy P. Hunt. The landing is uneventful: The enemy, caught by surprise, has fled into the jungle. At first, the Americans suspect a trap and expect an ambush, but none arrives. Instead, large stores of equipment and supplies are captured by the landing forces, including food, ammunition, gasoline, trucks and automobiles (a Ford V8 sedan), brand-new bicycles, an power plant, and even a fully stocked infirmary.

The Japanese military begins a counterattack immediately, although for several days it consists of only a few planes and small warships that do little damage. Skirmishes with the enemy are frequent, however, and sniper attacks are a constant threat. Tregaskis accompanies the troops into the jungle, describing the difficulties of fighting an enemy that is a master of cave warfare. The countryside is riddled with connecting caves that form a labyrinthine haven for the Japanese troops. Shoot at the enemy in one hole, one Marine complains, and he comes up in another.

The bloody cost of the war is shown in the number of losses on both sides, which Tregaskis reports after each battle, and in personal encounters with the wounded and dead. Occasionally, Tregaskis includes a vivid example of the bloodshed, describing in one case a Marine who had been torn apart by a bomb. What he does not see himself, he reports in more general detail, relying on what others have experienced. An assault on nearby Tulagi, for example, is reported in the words of the officer who commanded the operation. Tales of heroism are recorded as they are told to him by witnesses.

In addition to the mosquito-infested jungle, the Americans are described fighting along steep ridges, across open fields and rivers, and among coconut trees—ideal perches for Japanese snipers. Several weeks after the landing, the intensity of the battles in the jungle and in the air increases; a large Japanese invasion is rumored to be imminent, and soon the enemy attacks in force. The action culminates in the Battle of the Ridge, the fiercest of the battles that Tregaskis witnesses. When a sniper's bullet barely misses his head, he finds that the war has "suddenly become a personal matter."

Air battles are almost a daily routine, and the author describes many, watching them as though he were at a concert. After several weeks and several battles, reinforcements arrive and with them other news correspondents. Having exhausted his personal supplies and having seen enough of the war, Tregaskis leaves Guadalcanal Island, hitching a ride aboard a military bomber bound for a reconnaissance mission over Bougainville and a distant American base. A brief scare as enemy Zeros attack his airplane gives him a parting reminder of how closely he has lived with fear, danger, and death for two months in the jungles of Guadalcanal.

Analysis

The principal focus of this war diary is on the people and events that shape the battle for Guadalcanal. Although Tregaskis is present throughout the narrative as observer, his attention is almost always on what others do and say, on what happens, what he encounters, and what others report to him. By minimizing commentary and eschewing any discussion of the battle from the point of view of the historian or military theorist, the author imbues his narrative with the intimacy of personal experience and the immediacy of the eyewitness.

Although criticized by some reviewers for its unadorned style and lack of polish, which may have been mistaken for artlessness, *Guadalcanal Diary* is appealing because its narrative is plain, because the sequence of events is uncomplicated, and because the narrative is uncluttered by anything that was not part of what the correspondent saw and heard. Tregaskis does not dwell on the thoughts and emotions of the officers and enlisted men whose ordeal he records. Certainly, conversations are reported, and from them readers learn what the men feel and think, but Tregaskis himself does not probe the minds of the soldiers or attempt to plumb the depths of their feelings. He does not try to speak their fear, suffering, or anger at the enemy. He reports virtually without comment what they say, letting the reader surmise the rest.

This objectivity is seen in the way in which Tregaskis subordinates description to the reporter's duty to tell what happened. Only enough of the setting is described to let the reader understand how bullets behave when one is caught in a jungle skirmish.

The jungles and caves in which the enemy hides have no significance beyond their deadly threat and contribution to the difficulty of island warfare. When Tregaskis describes a dogfight, his eye is on nothing but the elements of battle: "This time the planes were set against an almost cloudless sky, and had a long course of blue to traverse before they reached dropping point over the airport." Only occasionally will he embellish his style with such literary devices as simile and metaphor: "The tiny speck of the fighter, looking like a bumblebee . . . was diving now. And we heard the rattlesnake sound of his guns."

This lean approach to battle scenes is consistent with the author's restraint in reporting the more graphic physical details of battle. Although he witnesses many scenes of death and dying, he does not report them in every detail; rather, he lets two or three occasional descriptions, strikingly vivid, speak for many. The effect is to convey the book's major theme subtly but with lasting impact: The American troops who fought in this humid, unglamorous little island far from any spotlight did so with selfless honor, unclamoring dignity, and unflagging spirit. Tregaskis does not exploit the old cliché that "war is hell." Instead, he tells of men confronting the hazards of hard conditions and defeating the enemy with basic decency. His prose befits that point of view—simple, spare, sharply focused, factual.

The restraint that marks the prose style and descriptions of battle scenes is also evident in the way in which Tregaskis treats the enemy. His approach is remarkably free of racist epithets and the rhetoric of outrage that one might expect to find in a book written and published when anti-Japanese sentiment was strongest. Although the enemy soldiers are referred to as "Japs," now and then as "Nips," the author's treatment is not tainted by the kind of bias that would rapidly date it and ultimately destroy its value. Tregaskis is not so detached from the people and events that he appears unfeeling, unmoved by scenes of human suffering and dying; yet, he does not allow himself to become so caught up in what he sees as to lose reportorial balance and the kind of objectivity that allows a work to survive.

Critical Context

Guadalcanal Diary was described as a classic from the moment of its publication. In 1955, it was printed in a special edition for the young adult reader. The qualities that recommend it to young readers, as well as older ones, are easy to see. Its style is simple, its story is clearly presented, and its subject is of universal interest and importance: war and the experiences of those who wage it.

Tregaskis was fortunate in the choice of his subject and in his timing. The book was published while the Pacific war was still on the front pages of American newspapers. Although he later reported on wars in Europe, Korea, and Vietnam—nine, all told—none of his efforts is as memorable as this book. It serves well as an introduction to all modern wars, for it describes the combatants, conditions, and events of war with a realism that is sufficient to his purpose, to explain events in sequence, highlighting what is significant without pausing too often or too long on the gore. The record that emerges stands alongside Stephen Crane's classic novel *The Red Badge of Courage*

(1895) as a view of battle from the soldier's perspective. Tregaskis' narrative, however, describes what its author actually sees and hears. It has the enduring quality of good, realistic narrative, and the enduring value of objective truth.

Bernard E. Morris

THE HANDMAID'S TALE

Author: Margaret Atwood (1939-   )
First published: 1985
Type of work: Novel
Type of plot: Fantasy
Time of work: An unspecified future
Locale: The Republic of Gilead (formerly the United States)
Subjects: Gender roles, sexual issues, and social issues
Recommended ages: 15-18

The story of Offred, told by herself, is set in a near future when the United States has become the Republic of Gilead, ruled by a male hierarchy that requires a strict subservience from women.

> *Principal characters:*
> OFFRED, the narrator, a Handmaid
> MOIRA, Offred's friend who rebels against her repressive society
> THE COMMANDER, Offred's master
> SERENA JOY, Offred's mistress

Form and Content

Offred, the narrator of *The Handmaid's Tale*, is one of a class of women who are trained to serve the master class—in this case, the Commander and his wife, Serena Joy. Offred remembers and indeed yearns for the husband and child that belonged to her in the time that the Republic of Gilead was the United States. All the democratic rights that were taken for granted in America have vanished in this future world—including a woman's right to marry, to hold a job, or to do ánything without the approval of her master and mistress.

Offred speaks as a character who has partially become accustomed to this new world. She is aware that it came about because of the social chaos of American democracy. There was too much violence; people were too free to do as they liked. At least this is how the United States is viewed from the perspective of Offred's authoritarian society. Yet, Offred has not been brainwashed. Like Winston Smith in George Orwell's *Nineteen Eighty-four* (1948), she has a mind of her own, but she has to conceal it. She is afraid of being punished for her independent thoughts. She has a friend, Moira, who represents everything that Offred would like to be. Moira is outspoken and rebellious. She does not accept the subjection of women for a moment or believe that any class of people has the right to rule others.

Offred is wistful about the past. It is hard to recall, however, when her present is so filled with her duties as a Handmaid. She is surprised when the Commander takes an interest in her—proposing they attend a costume party and then making sexual advances to her. In the Republic of Gilead, Handmaids such as Offred are only meant to be procreators—that is, they have sex with their masters only for the purposes of childbearing. The Commander, however, obviously chafes under the rigid, puritanical regime, and he looks to Offred to relieve his frustrations, even though he is breaking the very rules that he is pledged to uphold.

Offred uses the Commander's attentions to win a few freedoms for herself, realizing that to the Commander she is merely a plaything and that he cannot be trusted with her real inner feelings. She must also be cautious because Serena Joy, the Commander's wife, would surely have Offred punished if she were to discover that Offred and her husband had a sexual relationship outside of their officially sanctioned mating sessions. Offred finds her true lover in Nick, who is also employed by the Commander and his wife. Nick risks certain death if his liaison with Offred is discovered, yet the couple (again like Winston Smith and his beloved in *Nineteen Eighty-four*) are compelled to express their humanity by carrying on their secret affair. In each other they find an outlet for expressing all those emotional human needs that their society represses by restricting both males and females to prescribed roles.

Offred's fate is not entirely clear because the novel ends with an appendix that reveals that Offred's narrative has been discovered by a later society—one that apparently has restored something like the equality of the sexes and individual liberties that Offred desired. From the perspective of the appendix, then, Offred's narrative becomes a kind of Old Testament, a record of the human quest for self-expression and redemption.

Analysis

The Handmaid's Tale is Margaret Atwood's extrapolation from the debates about feminism and women's roles in the 1970's and 1980's. In fact, Offred remembers her mother's feminist activities in the days before the revolution that created the Republic of Gilead. Offred's mother was a fierce opponent of pornography, which is the target of feminists who deplore its tendency to demean women. Offred's mother participated in a book-burning of pornographic works—an event, the novel seems to imply, that displays the fanaticism that contributed to the reaction against feminism and the drive for women's rights. Atwood apparently believes that even a good cause can be harmed by extremism that contributes to an antidemocratic atmosphere. If it is acceptable to ban or burn certain books that offend women's sensibilities, then why is it not right to ban or burn feminists who offend other people's sensibilities?

That Atwood intends to convey this judgment against both feminist and antifeminist extremists seems to be confirmed by her novel's dedication to Perry Miller, the premier historian of American Puritanism, and to Mary Webster, one of Atwood's ancestors hanged as a witch in Connecticut. Like the Puritans, the rulers of the Republic of Gilead believe in the literal word of the Bible. They also believe that they are establishing God's kingdom on earth. Their religion governs their view of politics, of human sexuality, of the family—in short, of everything. Yet, like Reverend Dimmesdale in *The Scarlet Letter* (1850), Nathaniel Hawthorne's great novel about Puritanism, the Commander cannot live by such strict and dehumanizing rules. What he wants is for Offred to kiss him—an act strictly forbidden. What is more, he wants her to kiss him with passion. In other words, the Commander wants not simply to rule or to dominate or to believe that he is in the right, but to feel passion and to create passion in others. Unfortunately, his human feelings are driven underground, and he must consummate his affair with Offred in secret, just as Reverend Dimmesdale can make love to Hester Prynne only clandestinely. In both cases, it is the woman who must submit passively and who also must conceal the secret of her love even at the peril of death or of ostracism from her own community.

Offred is a young woman searching for her own sense of herself—apart both from the strictures of her masters and from her memories of the past. She knows that she cannot be free, yet she persists in trying to define her own feelings. This is why she is telling her own story and why she turns to Nick. He is almost the only person with whom she can express herself without censoring her words.

Much of the tension in the novel is built on Offred's dilemma. How much risk is she willing to take in order to exercise her will? How much can she trust Nick? Can she balance her desire to conform, so that she will not be punished (physically and mentally), with her need for an outlet for her emotions? Is the Commander's wife beginning to suspect her? Offred must practice incredible self-discipline and perceptiveness.

Offred is not heroic. She is no Moira, who risks everything in order to be herself. In a way, however, Offred is more compelling because she compromises. She is an apt symbol for every man or women caught in a totalitarian society that demands absolute obedience and crushes rebels. Offred's will and her imagination are not broken by this fundamentalist republic; on the contrary, her creativity and determination flourish as she insists on telling her own tale.

Critical Context

The Handmaid's Tale has become a classic. While it can certainly be called a feminist work of literature, it is not uncritical of contemporary feminism and of other social movements that, in their intensity, can turn intolerant and bring out the very antisocial and antihuman conditions that they protest.

Several critics have compared Atwood's novel to *Nineteen Eight-four* because both novels show the plight of individuals in a one-party state that puritanically controls people's lives. Like George Orwell, who picked 1984 as the year in which the totalitarian tendencies of the late 1940's might culminate, Atwood picks an unspecified but near future in order to suggest the place to which the social trends of her own time might be leading.

Although Offred is clearly past her teens but still of childbearing age—her age is not specified—*The Handmaid's Tale* can also be looked upon as a *Bildungsroman* or coming-of-age novel, which shows how the main character educates himself or herself. Often, the heroes or heroines of these works discover that society is corrupt and unjust. They learn this truth through personal relationships that also teach them to reject the adults who have control over them. Like Mark Twain's Huckleberry Finn,

Offred has an instinctive grasp of what is right and wrong, even if society tells her otherwise. She has a conscience and a sense of humanity that transcend the laws of political systems and the rules of society.

Carl Rollyson

HATCHET

Author: Gary Paulsen (1939-   )
First published: 1987
Type of work: Novel
Type of plot: Adventure tale
Time of work: The present
Locale: The northern wilderness of Canada
Subjects: Coming-of-age and nature
Recommended ages: 10-15

Brian Robeson finds himself hurled alone into the wilderness with only a hatchet and his wits to help him survive and find a way to reach his father.

Principal character:
BRIAN ROBESON, a thirteen-year-old who is overcome with the emotional distress caused by his parents' divorce and who is trying to make sense of the changes in his life

Form and Content

Hatchet is a story that describes a young boy's adventure in the wilderness, where he learns to be self-sufficient and emotionally secure and to cherish life and all that comes with it, both good and bad. When Brian Robeson finds himself alone in the wilderness, his physical challenges parallel the emotional challenges with which he has been dealing since his parents' divorce. A steel hatchet with a rubber handgrip worn on his belt becomes his only tool for survival; it symbolizes the strength and maturity that will grow within Brian.

The realistic, omniscient narration begins with Brian's mother giving him the hatchet and a leather sheath for his belt on the way to the airport. At first, he thinks of the hatchet as "hokey," but he places it on his belt in order to please his mother. Brian then boards a Cessna 406 bushplane to visit his father for the summer. His father has been working in the Canadian oil fields, and Brian is excited by the thought of being with him again. Once the plane is aloft, however, the pilot has a heart attack. Brian attempts to fly the plane but crashes it into a remote Canadian lake. Dragging himself from the cockpit and swimming to shore, Brian begins to comprehend his situation: He is alone, cold, and wet, without any supplies, without any adults to help him, and without the faintest idea of where he is or what he is supposed to do. All that he has is the hatchet. After the first miserable night near the lake, Brian realizes that he must do something if he wants to survive, and he tries to recall everything that he knows about survival. Through many trials and errors, he learns that his hatchet can be used to make shelter, design tools, hunt food, and protect him.

Through all these physical challenges, Brian dwells on "the secret" that he alone knows about his parents' divorce: He had seen his mother meeting with another man before his parents were divorced. His struggle to keep this secret gnaws at his emotional well-being until it becomes all-consuming. While facing nature's challenges, however, Brian becomes aware that life is indeed not fair, that one must make the best of any situation. He comes to realize that his father and mother are separate entities from himself and that they had their own challenges to face and resolve, issues that had nothing to do with Brian.

In the end, after facing his own mortality several times, Brian also learns that he can rely upon himself for his physical and emotional needs. He has become a mature, less emotionally dependent individual who can survive in the face of diversity and challenge.

Analysis

Hatchet delivers a wonderful vicarious adventure. The thoughtful, vivid descriptions and the clear development of character and plot allow readers of all ages to appreciate the wonders of life and the glory of nature. Addressing the fears of all adolescents, author Gary Paulsen uses the wilderness to parallel the emotional and physical pains of coming-of-age. His description of both the grandeur and the danger of the wilderness evokes awe and trepidation.

At the start of the novel, Brian is struggling with the changes in his life caused by his parents' divorce. Finding himself truly on his own leaves Brian with a primitive urge to survive at all costs. While learning step-by-step how to find food, water, and shelter, he grows physically and emotionally stronger. These changes in Brian's character develop rapidly as he carves out an existence using only his hatchet. In the beginning of the story, the hatchet symbolized the young Brian. His mother gives it to him with the words "Just like a scout. My little scout," which convey Brian's immaturity and frailness in his mother's eyes. He is embarrassed, worried that the pilot will sees the "hokey" hatchet on his belt when he arrives at the airport. When Brian is alone in the wilderness, however, the hatchet becomes his source of life, much like his mother had been, protecting Brian from nature's elements. Without it, he could never have survived.

Brian faces many setbacks because of unclear thinking and poor decision making. Charles Darwin's theory of the "survival of the fittest" applies to Brian's constant battle with nature. Brian adapts and learns to cope with all adversities—from insects to wild animals to storms. His emotional growth comes from the recognition of the magnificence of life. He learns that life's problems can be overcome and that struggles can be won with clear thinking and common sense.

Lessons about living from his mother, father, and teachers also guide Brian through his adventure. The awareness that he is strong enough to survive alone comes when he first calls his camp "home"—one of his own creation. He has truly grown into an independent individual who does not rely on anyone else to survive. When rescue workers finally arrive, Brian is not in a hurry to leave; he has almost enjoyed the independence that he has achieved.

Many adolescents can identify fully with the anger and confusion deep within

Brian. His adventure symbolizes the emotional highs and lows of young people. After each success, Brian faces a new problem. Life becomes unbearable, but then, all at once, life becomes wonderful. The changes that Brian undergoes involve maturity, self-sufficiency, and the belief that anything is survivable. This message is one of great importance to relay to young adults who are facing the trials associated with coming-of-age.

Critical Context

Gary Paulsen has truly captured the adventurous spirit of many teenagers. Young readers and their teachers have come to enjoy, share, and recommend Paulsen's books to peers who enjoy adventure stories. His tales of protagonists-versus-nature portray characters who battle the elements while gaining a sense of self. Guided and cajoled by the forces of nature, Paulsen's characters develop and change in a quick, clear, and efficient manner. The readability levels of his works lie between the fourth and eighth grades, which makes these easy-to-read novels quite adaptable for either independent or school-oriented reading.

Hatchet is a classic tale of a boy's struggle with the problems of coming-of-age. Its sequel, *The River* (1991), allows the reader to resume the adventure and watch as Brian Robeson continues to master his universe. The reader is allowed to struggle with and feel the pain of the protagonist, as well as to revel in his joy at surviving. Paulsen's many adventure stories include *The Island* (1988), in which a young boy discovers that isolation from the world will not help him solve his problems; *Woodsong* (1990), a personal work based on Paulsen's own experience in the Iditarod dogsled race; *Dogsong* (1985), a realistic and romantic quest of Russe, a young Eskimo, in the snow-covered wilderness; and *Canyons* (1990), a spiritual tale and quest adventure that weaves the life of a contemporary adolescent with the life of an adolescent Indian boy who was hunted and killed by soldiers in the nineteenth century. All these stories, and many more adventures from this prolific writer, speak to the primitive sense of survival and adventure in the human spirit.

In Paulsen's novels, the relationship between humankind and nature is revealed as both symbiotic and challenging. Humans need nature in order to survive, and the need to overcome and tame it has been a mystical quest that all people experience to some degree at some time in their lives, although they may not be able to recognize or name those experiences. Paulsen delightfully describes this quest to overcome and understand the nature of human existence. *Hatchet* and Paulsen's other vivid, captivating nature-oriented stories give readers an opportunity to commune with nature and revel in its splendor while appreciating its danger and reverence.

Denise Marchionda

THE HAUNTING

Author: Margaret Mahy (1936-   )
First published: 1982
Type of work: Novel
Type of plot: Fantasy
Time of work: The 1980's
Locale: New Zealand
Subjects: Family, gender roles, and the supernatural
Recommended ages: 10-13

*When Great-Uncle Barnaby Scholar dies and his namesake Barney Palmer be-
comes the object of mysterious hauntings, deeply hidden secrets surface that had
disturbed relationships in both the Palmer and the Scholar families.*

Principal characters:
    BARNEY PALMER, an ordinary eight-year-old boy who is suddenly
        subjected to supernatural hauntings by his supposedly long-dead
        magician uncle
    TABITHA PALMER, his chubby, overly talkative sister, who considers
        herself the family's novelist and who becomes Barney's confidante
        and helper
    TROY PALMER, his thin, taciturn, teenage sister
    DOVE PALMER, their deceased mother, a Scholar family member
    JOHN PALMER, their father
    CLAIRE PALMER, their beloved stepmother, who is pregnant
    GREAT-GRANDMOTHER SCHOLAR, the embittered, unyielding Scholar
        matriarch
    GREAT-UNCLE GUY SCHOLAR, a compassionate bachelor uncle and
        pediatrician
    GREAT-UNCLE COLE SCHOLAR, the missing, mysterious member of the
        Scholar family, who has been presumed dead

Form and Content
    From the onset of *The Haunting* to its satisfying conclusion, author Margaret Mahy
delves into the dynamics of how a family's secrets, even those deeply embedded in
the past, constrain the relationships and inhibit the emotional development of its
members. Although written with elements of fantasy, Mahy's story is firmly based in
everyday family life. She downplays setting and focuses on the importance of family
interaction, which, in *The Haunting*, is intergenerational. Mahy portions out family
secrets, maintaining a high level of suspense throughout the story. Problems in the
Scholar family insinuate themselves into the Palmer family via eight-year-old Barney,

who is being haunted. (The Scholars are the late Dove Palmer's family, the "extra" set of relatives now that John Palmer has remarried.)

The novel opens with Barney experiencing a haunting in which the apparition of a young boy in a blue velvet suit tells him, "Barnaby's dead! I'm going to be very lonely." Barney's hauntings are precipitated by the death of his Great-Uncle Barnaby Scholar. In *The Haunting*, the key secret, from which others spawn, is the existence of magicians in the Scholar family line. Great-Grandmother Scholar has perpetuated the belief that these magicians are always male. Therefore, when Barney experiences hauntings, family members believe him to be the next magician. In page-turning suspense, Mahy involves all members of the Palmer and Scholar families in helping Barney unravel the mystery of these hauntings. As deeply hidden secrets are disclosed, the mystery and suspense mount.

Experiencing the initial haunting leaves Barney shaken: He thinks he is being told that he is dead and faints with relief when he arrives home and finds out that it was his Great-Uncle Barnaby who died. Because his mother, Dove, died when he was born, Barney is plagued with the fear that, in some way, he caused her death. He dearly loves his new stepmother, Claire, who is pregnant. Believing that childbearing is a dangerous business, he refuses to upset her by telling her about his hauntings. He is afraid that she might lose the child she is carrying or, like his mother, die in childbirth.

Barney has no one in which to confide. Unexpectedly, his sister Tabitha becomes his confidante, helping him to piece together mysterious bits of Scholar family history through her meeting with Great-Uncle Guy. With the advent of visits from Scholar relatives, further information surfaces, including the news that Great-Uncle Cole, who was missing and presumed dead, is indeed alive and well—and on his way to visit Barney.

Great-Uncle Barnaby and his brother Cole, unbeknownst to their family, had remained lifelong friends. Now that his brother and only friend is dead, Cole mentally communicates with Barney under the mistaken notion that Barney will be the next magician in the family. He plans not only to befriend Barney but also to take him away from his family. When Cole arrives at the Palmer house, Tabitha inadvertently invites him in. Cole seems friendly, gentle, and benign, but Barney fears that he has come to take him away. At the peak of tension, Claire enters, reassuring Barney that he is her family and that no one is taking him away against his will.

The unexpected arrival of John Palmer and the Scholars brings the story to its startling climax. Barney's other sister, Troy, confronts Great-Grandmother Scholar and proves that she and Troy herself are magicians, dispelling the misconception that all the Scholar magicians are male. Troy names herself a Palmer magician in deference to her mother, who knew that Troy had a special "golden," "magical part" of her mind. In doing so, Troy honors the fact that she is a female magician. She refuses to condone Great-Grandmother Scholar's denial of her gift. Further, she refuses to condone the way in which her great-grandmother mistreated her children. The past, now revealed, clears the way for a better understanding of the future.

Analysis

Although her novels are set in New Zealand and her genre is fantasy, Mahy's characters search for identity, encounter jealousies, and suffer alienation, self-doubt, and the same general agonies that seem to be the universal phenomena that people experience during life's transitional phases. In *The Haunting*, she includes adults whose emotional and social development has been interfered with. She focuses on alienation, loss, misunderstandings, incomplete information, and the consequences of denying a special gift. Her resolutions depend on reaching into the past and inviting it into the present in various ways. In *The Haunting*, Mahy uses Barney as a vehicle to introduce magic, which becomes the catalyst that releases past secrets. As bits and pieces of the past come together, emotional and social development resume.

Two themes that Mahy addresses are loss and alienation. The Palmer family lost a wife and mother. John Palmer, left with his grief, his job, and three children to rear, turned inward and moved forward blindly, never addressing his grief and not knowing how to help his children through their difficult time. So, in a real sense, until John remarried and Claire became the new wife and mother, Barney, Tabitha, and Troy lost communication with their father. As Barney's hauntings continue, Claire becomes greatly concerned about him. At dinner one night, Troy assuages Claire's concern that she is not being a good mother. She explains Barney's fears about Claire's pregnancy and delivery. She reassures Barney, telling him that Dove had a weak heart "but that Claire's got a heart like an ox." She explains that after Dove died, Barney had the most difficult time because the woman who had taken care of the Palmer children disliked little boys and paid little attention to Barney. Later, Troy reveals that she created three imaginary playmates to ease Barney's loneliness. When asked why she had never said anything before, Troy pragmatically answers, "There's just no point in telling everything you know unless it's going to *change* something." Through her confrontation, Troy diminishes Barney's fear and facilitates better communication in the Palmer family.

If the Palmer family had lost a wife and mother (and, psychologically, a father), the Scholar brothers psychologically lost their mother, their childhoods, their sense of compassion, and their ability to share friendships—all because of their mother's unyielding discipline. Because Cole dared to defy her, she refused to acknowledge him, refused to send him to school, and refused to correct rumors that he was retarded. Cole's only ally among his brothers was Barnaby; the others were too frightened of their mother to stand up to her. When Cole left home and a drowning accident was reported, his mother let the family believe that it was Cole, not his companion, who drowned. For years, only Barnaby knew that Cole was alive.

Through these suppressions, secrets remained hidden and misconceptions abounded: Great-Grandmother Scholar perpetuated the belief that only Scholar males were magicians; Barney was believed to be the next magician because of his hauntings; Barney thought that, in some way, he had caused Dove's death and that Claire and her baby's safe delivery depended on his not upsetting her by telling her about the hauntings; both families believed that Cole was dead; and no one knew that Great-

Grandmother Scholar and Troy were magicians, except for Troy. Through cautious interfamily and intergenerational interaction, multiple secrets and misconceptions are unveiled. In an uplifting ending, truth becomes the force that sets the players free. Troy's secret is revealed, but she must figure out how to achieve balance in her life and still be able to experience the wonder of being a magician. Cole, whose childhood was denied him, becomes a frequent visitor to the Palmer home and begins to learn how children interact and what a normal childhood might have been like. John Palmer learns how to relax and communicate with his children, and Tabitha, Mahy hints, may be the one to melt Great-Grandmother Scholar's icy heart.

Critical Context

Margaret Mahy's novels for juveniles and young adults are filled with magic, wonder, unlikely encounters, and twists of plot and are enriched by her carefully crafted dialogue and descriptions—all of which bring a special wonder and sense of empowerment to her protagonists, leaving the reader both swept up in the magic of the story and feeling uplifted through her positive imagery. Examples of other novels in which she sets up situations that must be resolved by examining the past are *The Changeover: A Supernatural Romance* (1984), *Aliens in the Family* (1985), *The Catalogue of the Universe* (1985), *The Tricksters* (1986), and *Memory* (1987), to name a few. She develops plots with the adroitness of a mystery writer; there is usually a twist that the reader would not have anticipated. The breadth of her erudition and her unusual imagination make her a master storyteller and her books a delight to read. Because of her consummate skill as a writer of fantasy who grounds her works in reality, Mahy gives her readers a broader understanding of the complexities of the world that they inhabit.

Sandra Ray

THE HAUNTING OF HILL HOUSE

Author: Shirley Jackson (1919-1965)
First published: 1959
Type of work: Novel
Type of plot: Thriller
Time of work: The late 1950's
Locale: A haunted mansion in New England
Subjects: Death, family, friendship, suicide, and the supernatural
Recommended ages: 13-18

Eleanor Vance escapes her overbearing sister and attempts to find a life of her own as she spends a summer helping in the investigation of a haunted mansion.

> *Principal characters:*
> ELEANOR VANCE, a thirty-two-year-old who still suffers the guilt of her mother's death
> THEODORA (THEO), a young woman who showed amazing prowess in an extrasensory perception (ESP) experiment
> DR. JOHN MONTAGUE, an anthropologist interested in the analysis of the paranormal
> LUKE SANDERSON, the reckless nephew of the owner of Hill House
> THE DUDLEYS, the strange couple who work as servants at Hill House

Form and Content

The Haunting of Hill House is a subtly eerie gothic horror story of an introverted young woman's efforts to free herself from her personal prison and of the tragedy that results. It is brief, with only a few major incidents, although many details and symbols are woven together to create an emotionally complex story. Shirley Jackson uses the trappings of the genre to create a realistic psychological study of the troubled heroine and her sense of alienation.

The ghosts of Hill House remain offstage as the novel relies on suggestion for its shudders, with almost all of the story revealed through Eleanor's eyes. After an argument with her sister over the use of their jointly owned automobile, Eleanor makes a bid for freedom in a trip to Hill House. She has been summoned to participate in a study of hauntings there because her home was pelted with a rain of stones when she was young, an incident for which she may have been responsible through telekinesis. Dr. Montague has also summoned a young woman known only as Theodora, who has exhibited strong extrasensory powers. Joining them is Luke, the reckless nephew of Hill House's owner.

Upon their arrival, Theodora and Eleanor seem on the verge of becoming friends as they engage in humorous conversation following a meeting with the rigid house-keeper, Mrs. Dudley. It is a friendship the lonely Eleanor desperately needs, which is exhibited in her fabrication of a life for herself that incorporates elements that she saw on her trip, including stone lions and a cup decorated with stars.

As she and Theo explore the strangely designed Hill House, Eleanor develops a real feeling of happiness in spite of her eerie surroundings. "Journeys end in lovers meeting," she constantly repeats to herself, indicating that she has found a sense of belonging.

In a fireside talk, Dr. Montague explains Hill House's origins and tragedies. It was built by Hugh Crain as a country home, but his first wife died in a carriage wreck before ever seeing the house. His second wife died in an unexplained fall. The home was eventually left to his two daughters, who fought over it. After the older sister's death, the house was willed to her companion, who may have been delinquent in answering her cries the night of her death. The companion, overwhelmed by accusations from the surviving sister as well as from townspeople, eventually committed suicide. It is this portion of the story that is most important to Eleanor, since the companion's life resembles hers. Eleanor failed to hear her ailing mother's cries for assistance until it was too late.

Shortly after Montague's account, strange events begin. Sounds in the night terrify Theodora and Eleanor while Luke and Montague are distracted. Later, old writings with Eleanor's name appear as if the house were calling to her. Eleanor panics at this sight and is placed at odds with Theodora, who begins to chide her about recognized embellishments of the truth.

Eventually the message "HELP ELEANOR COME HOME ELEANOR" appears on Theodora's bedroom wall, and red stains mar her clothing. This forces Theodora to move into Eleanor's room and to borrow her clothing, but they are not drawn together closer as friends. As they share the room, Eleanor believes that she is clutching Theodora's hand in the darkness, but she soon discovers that it was not Theodora's hand but empty space. Later, following a quiet moment between Luke and Eleanor, Theodora chides Eleanor about Luke, telling her that she is making a fool of herself with him. When they go for a walk, they find their path has diverged from reality. Hearing ghostly laughter, they flee back to the house.

Eventually, Dr. Montague's wife arrives with an assistant, who helps in an attempt to use automatic writing in order to identify the spirits that haunt Hill House. The results are inconsistent with historical fact. The hauntings continue until Eleanor slips from her room while everyone is asleep. She climbs a rickety staircase, perhaps on her way to duplicating the companion's death. Luke rescues her, but Dr. Montague concludes that Hill House is having a negative impact on Eleanor and that she must leave. Just as she may have caused the rain of stones as a child, the poltergeist-type events at Hill House may be the result of her psychic abilities.

As she prepares to depart in the same car in which she made her bid for freedom from her sister, Eleanor feels that she cannot leave Hill House. Already, she has been contemplating a children's song that essentially likens the house to a lover. Gleefully, she speeds away in the car, feeling that she is at last acting on her own. In the moments before she steers the car into a tree, she wonders why these events are happening and why the others do not stop her. She is finally free, but she remains at Hill House as a spirit to walk alone. Her fate illustrates the difficulty of breaking free of life's parameters: While the escape of one bondage is possible, a new type of bondage and loneliness results.

Analysis

While *The Haunting of Hill House* uses supernatural ambiguity, its primary focus is a study of Eleanor and her quest for a place to belong. Above all, the novel is an examination of alienation and its shattering effects. All events revolve around Eleanor and her sense of isolation and imprisonment. Her existence has always been one of bondage to other people. Her mother is exchanged for an overbearing sister who refuses Eleanor use of the car that she helped purchase. En route to Hill House, Eleanor fantasizes about taking up residence in a large house guarded by the stone lions and dreams of a cup of stars. In spite of Hill House's loud noises and other fears, she feels at home there because she has found a sense of community.

Eleanor pays a high price to break free of the bonds in which life has placed her. The very car that was both instrument and symbol of her escape from her sister becomes the instrument of her death and the tool that makes her an irrevocable part of Hill House. She frees herself from her sister and the stifling existence that she has known only to become trapped in Hill House. She has fulfilled her belief that journeys end with lovers meeting. As the book concludes with a repeat of the opening paragraph, Jackson reveals the grim message that even in her place of belonging, Eleanor still walks alone, imprisoned again.

While supernatural considerations are secondary in the book, they are significant in the study of Eleanor. Questions arise of whether ghosts are at play or all the events are generated by Eleanor's psychic abilities. Just as the rain of stones from her past may have been created telepathically by Eleanor, such events as the eerie writing and the disappearing red stains on Theo's clothing may have been generated by Eleanor's needs, with Hill House serving only as a conduit.

Eventually, it becomes apparent that just as things are not right in Hill House, where the angles are odd and disturbing, things are not right inside Eleanor. She is burdened by guilt and often lost within herself, alienated much like the Crain sister's companion whose suicide she mimics. When Eleanor comes to Hill House, a dangerous combination develops that leads to tragedy.

Although Eleanor Vance is thirty-two, the novel is a pertinent work for young adults since her struggle reflects the quest on which all adolescents embark for a sense of belonging, identity, and independence. It illustrates the dire results when that need is not fulfilled and suggests that often true freedom is impossible.

Critical Context

The Haunting of Hill House can be viewed as a triumph of the quiet horror story. It features many of the conventions of genre fiction, including the oddly constructed Hill House, apparently a place of residual evil. Themes of personal bondage and alienation from earlier works by Shirley Jackson, such as *The Sundial* (1954), continue in *The Haunting of Hill House* and in her final book, *We Have Always Lived in the Castle* (1962). It also echoes themes from her controversial short story about human sacrifice, "The Lottery" (1948), which depicts a young woman who is stoned by her community. Elements from *The Haunting of Hill House* and Jackson's other works have obviously influenced many popular horror writers. Her work blends psychological realism with fantastic elements to produce enthralling and insightful fiction.

Sidney Glover Williams

HEN'S TEETH AND HORSE'S TOES
Further Reflections in Natural History

Author: Stephen Jay Gould (1941-   )
First published: 1983; illustrated
Type of work: Science
Subjects: Animals, nature, and science
Recommended ages: 15-18

In this third volume of collected essays reprinted from his column in Natural History
*magazine, Gould educates and delights his audience with his further defense of
Charles Darwin's theory of evolution and the anomalies of the natural world.*

Form and Content

In *Hen's Teeth and Horse's Toes*, Stephen Jay Gould, a well-known scientist and a
writer of rare skill, makes complex scientific theories understandable to a lay audience
by interspersing everyday prose with technical and scientific language. His interjec-
tion of humble, humorous asides draws the reader into his sphere of the complex
theories and odd creatures about which he writes.

This book is a celebratory volume to commemorate the one hundredth anniversary
of the death of Charles Darwin (1809-1882). Thirty essays are grouped into seven
sections, headed by titles such as "Sensible Oddities" and "A Zebra Trilogy." Each
section contains three or more essays. Several have subheadings and contain five or
six essays. A prologue gives an overview of the material covered in the book.

The catchy titles of the essays pique the reader's interest: "Big Fish, Little Fish,"
"Quick Lives and Quirky Changes," "Worm for a Century, and All Seasons" are but
a few. The comparison of physical size between male and female of different species
is included in an essay disclosing the reproductive process of the anglerfish. Also
included is a chapter on the decrease in the size of the Hershey chocolate bar over
a twenty-year period. Physical oddities of mammals (human and otherwise), myths
and realities of the animal world, and nineteenth century scientific findings are all
described. A constant in this smorgasbord of information on natural phenomena is the
defense of Darwin's theory of evolution against the theory of creationism.

Gould does not carry over ideas from one essay to the next, although occasionally
there is a reference to a previous essay. This form of writing allows the reader to
read a chapter as an autonomous unit and still make sense of it. The exceptions in
Hen's Teeth and Horse's Toes are the essays about the role played by the Jesuit priest-
paleontologist Pierre Teilhard de Chardin in the Piltdown conspiracy, a major twentieth century scientific fraud. What had been presumed to be a skull of an early
primitive man, found in 1908 by Charles Dawson, turned out to be part man and part
animal. The hoax was uncovered forty-five years later.

Science, politics, and extinction are all subjects of Gould's penetrating investiga-
tions. On scientific puzzles, he gives not only his own viewpoint but the revelations

of others in his field as well, even though these viewpoints may disagree with his own. Gould presents complicated scientific information, but his language should be comprehensible to educated laypeople. His style of writing will appeal to a wide audience.

Line drawings and occasional photographs help to clarify some of the complicated facts that might be difficult to understand with text alone. For example, in the chapter "Helpful Monsters" an electron microscope photograph of a fly illustrates a point. Only a few footnotes are provided in this book. For the more curious, a bibliography of eight pages and a comprehensive index follow the text.

Analysis

Darwin's theory of evolution is supported and defended throughout *Hen's Teeth and Horse's Toes*. Gould argues the roles that genetics and environment play in the drama of evolution, drawing on the work of William Bateson. Gould addresses debates occurring within evolutionary theory, the political and nonintellectual controversy beginning to stir anew in 1980. Behavior, both inherited and learned, is explored as an adaptation to local environments.

Gould's first essay, "Big Fish, Little Fish," introduces the female anglerfish and its dwarf male partner as a delivery system for sperm. A one-and-a-half-inch male anglerfish imbeds itself into a ten-inch female. The two fish become one unit, sharing tissue. The fused male depends on the female for nourishment and provides sperm to ensure a new generation and the continuity of the species. In the second essay, "Sensible Oddities," Gould writes of the carnivorous nature of parasitic wasps, quoting experts in the field. The female wasp often displays what humans deem cruel and immoral behavior in order to lay its eggs and feed its young.

In the last chapter of this trilogy, "The Guano Ring," Gould compares the inflexible intelligence of most animals, with decisions made as a result of certain signals, with that of humans, who decide using rational thinking. For example, birds know how to care for only the young that are inside their nests. On the Galápagos Islands, the blue-footed booby nests on a bed of guano (droppings). Squirting guano all around to produce a symmetrical white ring to mark its nest, it lays its eggs. One to three eggs are laid, which are hatched in the same order. Within the white area is an invisible ring, and should a hatchling be pushed outside that ring by an older sibling, it will not be fed and will die. Gould points out that by responding to simple signals as these birds do, the proper biological behavior required to advance the species is performed. The constraints of this kind of intelligence—responding to inflexible rules—permit boobies to reduce their broods in order to allow the strongest to survive.

Each of the six essays in the "Personalities" section portrays a different scientist and his research. In introducing these scientists and their theories, Gould highlights their contributions. Gould also shows how a theory in one age, found to be in error at a later time, may lead to important conclusions at a later time; scientists learn from errors as well. A chapter on Louis Agassiz, considered America's most influential nineteenth century naturalist, relates how, in spite of a visit to the Galápagos Islands, he retained his creationist view of a preordained, divine plan for species. Gould refutes creationism throughout this work, and the essay "Worm for a Century, and All Seasons" is a tribute to Charles Darwin.

Gould offers examples of adaptation, both biological and cultural, that all readers can understand. In "Kingdoms Without Wheels," he recounts how armies in biblical times used chariots and carts in the desert. By the sixth century A.D., the much more efficient camel was used as transportation.

In the title essay "Hen's Teeth and Horse's Toes," genetics is explained using the example of the modern horse, the possessor of one toe, reduced from the five that its forebears probably had. The third toe of the original five evolved into a hoof, while short splints of bone above the hoof indicate the former presence of a second and fourth toe.

Gould ends his volume of essays with a discussion of zebras. Under the title question, "What, If Anything, Is a Zebra?," he conjectures whether zebras are striped horses or a separate species. Gould answers the question that many have asked since childhood, "Are stripes on a zebra black on a white animal, or white on a black animal?"

Exciting ideas, complex theories, and biological oddities couched in understandable language make science fun to learn. *Hen's Teeth and Horse's Toes* imparts scientific information using a less-than-formal tone that appeals to young adult readers.

Critical Context

Hen's Teeth and Horse's Toes is the third volume in a series of essays originally published in Stephen Jay Gould's monthly column "This View of Life" appearing in *Natural History* magazine. The earlier books, *Ever Since Darwin* (1973) and *The Panda's Thumb* (1980), were also compilations of column essays. *Ever Since Darwin* more directly addressed Charles Darwin's theory of evolution, outlining the theory, its application, and related issues. Gould writes about the impact that social and political views have on science. In *The Panda's Thumb*, the essay "Women's Brains" stands out and contains several excerpts from studies concluding that women's intelligence is inferior to that of men. Gould accepts the data but takes issue with the conclusions. His defense of Darwin's theory against that of the creationists runs through both volumes.

Gould's books bring to mind those by anthropologist Loren Eiseley, who also wrote for a popular audience. In *Darwin's Century* (1958), Eiseley gives much credit to the scientists of the nineteenth century, as does Gould in *Hen's Teeth and Horse's Toes*.

Gould is a highly respected scientist who has taught geology, biology, and the history of science at Harvard University. *Hen's Teeth and Horse's Toes* is not a textbook, per se, but it may be assigned as additional reading in high school or college courses. Gould's humorous prose and reminiscences about his youth lighten the task of learning complex scientific concepts. His books will be read for generations to come.

Hen's Teeth and Horse's Toes sheds new light on subjects discussed in his earlier volumes. One may read the essays individually or the book as a whole. The writing is so thoroughly enjoyable and the information so interesting that any reader will be inspired to seek out more works by Stephen Jay Gould.

Anne Trotter

HIROSHIMA

Author: John Hersey (1914-1993)
First published: 1946
Type of work: History
Time of work: August 6, 1945, through August, 1946
Locale: Hiroshima, Japan, and surrounding areas
Subjects: Death, social issues, and war
Recommended ages: 15-18

These detailed stories of six survivors of the first atomic-bomb attack raise social and psychological issues and show human strength and kindness despite almost unthinkable horror.

> *Principal personages:*
> TOSHIKO SASAKI, a personnel clerk in a tin factory
> DR. MASAKUSA FUJII, a physician with a private clinic
> MRS. HATSUYO NAKAMURA, a tailor's widow
> FATHER WILHELM KLEINSORGE, a German Jesuit priest
> DR. TERFUMI SASAKI, a doctor on the surgical staff of the Red Cross
> Hospital
> THE REVEREND KIYOSHI TANIMOTO, the pastor of the Hiroshima
> Methodist Church

Form and Content

Hiroshima has the immediacy of fiction but is factual, taken from extensive interviews with six survivors of the atomic bombing of Hiroshima, as well as from some written documents. The third-person narrative is sympathetic but almost clinically objective. John Hersey's voice is apparent in his choice of events and details: of Japanese life, of the bomb's devastation, of the victims' personal reactions and feelings.

The work originally appeared with four sections, which cover increasingly longer periods of time. The first, "A Noiseless Flash," introduces the six people, none of whom know why they lived when others died. Flashbacks and the depiction of the moment before the bomb detonated establish the characters and situations of those involved, but the focus is on the instant of the explosion and its immediate effects. Most of the six survivors are trapped by rubble but can free themselves; Dr. Terfumi Sasaki only loses his slippers and eyeglasses, while Toshiko Sasaki (no relation) is seriously injured, imprisoned by falling bookcases. Hersey emphasizes both the capricious nature of the bomb's impact and the stunned ignorance of its victims regarding what exactly happened.

The second section, "The Fire," describes the first several hours after the atomic bomb, as a firestorm sweeps the flattened city. Mrs. Hatsuyo Nakamura rescues her children and flees, like many others, to Asano Park, a relatively intact private estate on the river. Toshiko Sasaki is finally dug out, but she receives no medical help, waiting under a lean-to with two others who are horribly wounded. The Reverend Kiyoshi Tanimoto finds his wife, who was elsewhere when the bomb fell, but primarily dedicates himself to helping others, as do Drs. Masakusa Fujii and Terfumi Sasaki and Father Wilhelm Kleinsorge. The available medical care and water rations are woefully insufficient.

The third section, "Details Are Being Investigated," continues the stories of survival, heroism, fear, injury, and death. The effects of radiation poisoning begin to show; there are rumors, but little is known about this peculiar bomb attack. Citizens return to the ruins, retrieving any personal belongings remaining. The surrender of Japan, which ends the chapter, seems almost an anticlimax for the sick, exhausted people of Hiroshima.

"Panic Grass and Feverfew," although comparable in length to the other sections, covers a full year, showing longer-term results of the atomic bomb. Its title ironically combines references to the plants that, spurred by radioactivity, cover the city in lush green and to the physical and mental problems lingering after the explosion, from anxiety to the deadly fevers and damage to the blood of radiation sickness. The six protagonists recover, but all face mental and physical scars. Hersey ends with the question of whether such warfare is ever justified.

On the fortieth anniversary of the bombing of Hiroshima, Hersey released a new edition with an added section, "The Aftermath." The six survivors are still tired and ill, although most have found some personal *modus vivendi*. Hersey discusses the world's failed attempts to restrict the testing of atomic weapons, symbolized by Kiyoshi Tanimoto's mostly unsuccessful career as a peace activist.

Analysis

Hiroshima is credited with inaugurating the "nonfiction novel" and anticipating the movement known as New Journalism. John Hersey—already a Pulitzer Prize-winning novelist and well-known war correspondent—uses many of the techniques of fiction to make this true story immediate and emotionally effective. He originally planned to present his own observations of the ruined city, but he was inspired by Thornton Wilder's *The Bridge of San Luis Rey* (1927) to structure an interwoven narrative featuring several principal personages.

The two women and four men are vivid, distinct individuals, but they also stand for the hundred thousand killed and even more injured or made homeless by the bomb, providing an emotional impact that numbers lack. They function as representative Everyman characters, with the same concerns, needs, and sentiments as Hersey's readers. The actions of the six people during and after the bomb blast follow naturally from their characters as Hersey views them, a natural mixture of fear and courage, cooperation and self-interest.

The book is also notable for its concrete observation, presented primarily in an objective, even clinical tone. By not interpreting the scenes, Hersey leaves the reader to form an impression, rather than be told—but that impression is subtly guided by what the author presents. For example, he further creates sympathy through homey, telling details, such as Mrs. Nakamura keeping her prized sewing machine safe by putting it into a water tank, only to retrieve it and find it rusted solid. When Hersey is directly didactic, especially in the final half of the book, he actually conveys the book's lessons less effectively.

Some have suggested that Hersey's understatement may be attributable to the fact that the grief was not his to speak about and that the survivors themselves, in addition to any cultural reticence and the barrier of speaking through a translator, were still too exhausted and psychologically troubled for histrionics when interviewed. For whatever reason, the result is quite strong, and the awesome and awful subject matter keeps the work from ever being pedestrian.

Hiroshima repeatedly examines four themes: the value but unpredictability of human survival, the importance of awareness and communication, the necessity of cooperation, and the peril that humanity faces from destructive technologies. All of these permeate Hersey's novels and journalism; they also shaped the author's life of writing and of activism in causes ranging from education to civil rights. He is often called an existentialist writer because of his emphasis on human freedom and responsibility, and *Hiroshima* shows his high regard for the common people, surviving and helping others without control over events, often without even knowing the real situation. The most extreme and grotesque suffering is shown not from the point of view of the victim, but from the perspective of the person helping those victims, whose compassion helps Hersey avoid sensationalism.

Some see *Hiroshima* as a tract for nuclear disarmament, while others see it as merely descriptive and hence too accepting of the bomb's reality. Actually, the question that Hersey quotes from a Jesuit report—"whether total war in its present form is justifiable, even when it serves a just purpose"—is exactly that: not an answer, but a question, which Hersey finds imperative for all people to confront for themselves.

Critical Context

Few works have had the immediate impact of *Hiroshima*. On August 31, 1946, for the first time in its history, *The New Yorker* magazine devoted an entire issue to one essay. When the book was published, also in 1946, the Book of the Month Club considered it so important that it distributed free copies; Albert Einstein personally bought one thousand copies. Editions quickly appeared in almost every country—except, ironically, for Japan. John Hersey donated his profits to the International Red Cross.

In 1948, a school edition appeared from Oxford Book Company. The first of Hersey's books to be used in college history, social science, and journalism classes, it is also taught in high schools and in college literature classes. Far from becoming dated, its approach and political concerns are even more appropriate to the nuclear age, with growing educational and cultural influence.

Like Anne Frank's *The Diary of a Young Girl* (1952), *Hiroshima* provides individual human stories through which young adults can come to grips with unimaginable, inhuman events. Younger readers may find the book a way to voice their own fears about nuclear weapons, while older teenagers will find much to consider and discuss, politically and philosophically. For any age group, the characters and events are emotionally effective and fascinating, although some details are unsettling and even disgusting. The treatment of Japanese culture and individuals may suggest this book for a multicultural curriculum, although the emotionally distanced presentation and its mainstream white American author may argue against it in favor of the work of actual survivors, such as Keiji Nakazawa's *Manga*, a Japanese comic book read by adults and published in book form as *Barefoot Gen* (1987) and *Barefoot Gen: The Day After* (1988).

General critical reactions to *Hiroshima* have been mixed. While many like Hersey's use of fictional devices in the service of nonfiction, others have been suspicious. Ironically, while some critics fault *Hiroshima* for its cold objectivity, others find it unacceptably didactic. Hersey's impassioned advocacy of ordinary social values was especially unfashionable in art of the 1950's, and his reputation suffered accordingly. Nevertheless, *Hiroshima* is undeniably a landmark work, effective on both emotional and literary levels. Although Hersey won a Pulitzer Prize for his novel *A Bell for Adano* (1944), it is *Hiroshima* for which he may be best remembered.

Bernadette Lynn Bosky

THE HITCHHIKER'S GUIDE TO THE GALAXY SERIES

Author: Douglas Adams (1952-   )
First published: The Hitchhiker's Guide to the Galaxy, 1979; *The Restaurant at the End of the Universe,* 1980; *Life, the Universe, and Everything,* 1982; *So Long, and Thanks for All the Fish,* 1984; *Mostly Harmless,* 1992
Type of work: Novels
Type of plot: Adventure tale, fantasy, and science fiction
Time of work: The early 1980's, the end of time, and prehistory
Locales: England, an alternative Earth, and various alien spaceships, habitats, and planets
Subjects: Friendship, nature, and travel
Recommended ages: 10-18

Arthur Dent learns about the universe around him, not only how much there is to learn but also how crazy, chaotic, and chancy life can be.

> *Principal characters:*
> ARTHUR DENT, a middle-aged Englishman taken on the journey of his life from the end of the universe to prehistoric Earth and various times and places in-between
> FORD PREFECT, an alien "from a small planet somewhere in the vicinity of Betelgeuse" who is a roving researcher for the guide and who helps Arthur acclimate to the craziness of the universe
> ZAPHOD BEEBLEBROX, the two-headed former President of the Galaxy and pilferer of the spaceship *Heart of Gold*
> TRILLIAN, the only other human survivor of the original planet Earth and pilot of the *Heart of Gold*
> MARVIN, THE PARANOID ANDROID, a robot with a personality who accompanies Arthur, Ford, Trillian, and Zaphod through most of their travels
> SLARTIBARTFAST, one of many designers of the original Earth and another friend and guide to Arthur
> DEEP THOUGHT, the computer that answered the question of life, the universe, and everything and then designed the computer to provide the question
> FENCHURCH, Arthur's girlfriend on the second Earth
> RANDOM DENT, the daughter Arthur never knew he had

Form and Content

Douglas Adams' Hitchhiker's Guide to the Galaxy series brings the absurdity of Franz Kafka and the comedy of the Three Stooges into the realm of science fiction. *The Hitchhiker's Guide to the Galaxy* sets the tone for the entire series: Arthur Dent is taken from his sedentary life in a small English town and, in the space of an hour, learns his best friend is actually an alien and researcher for the series' eponymous travel guide, witnesses the destruction of his home for a highway and then of the Earth for the construction of a hyperspace express route, is taught how to sneak onto the spaceship of his planet's destroyers, learns that Ford Prefect's fifteen years on the planet produced an entry about it in the guide of exactly two words ("Mostly harmless"), is forced to listen to the captain's dangerously bad poetry, and is promptly, along with Ford, kicked out an airlock and into open space. The novel goes on to detail the search by aliens from a higher dimension for the answer to life, the universe, and everything, the answer given by the supercomputer Deep Thought being "forty-two." The book ends with Arthur, Ford, and their friends Trillian and Zaphod Beeblebrox, who rescued them from certain death, meeting Slartibartfast, a planet designer. They learn that the Earth was in fact a computer designed to produce, after ten million years, the question to go with the answer and that it was destroyed five minutes before the question was finally to be calculated.

The Restaurant at the End of the Universe begins with the group on the *Heart of Gold* fleeing an attack and ending up at the restaurant of the title. There, they witness the destruction of the universe in the "Gnab Gib" ("Big Bang" backward) over dinner and a floor show. After the universe ends, they steal a ship that time warps them back to the rock concert of all rock concerts, where they learn that their ship is to produce the grand finale's light show by diving into a star. Escaping this mess divides the group: Arthur and Ford end up on a ship of colonists about to crash into the Earth several million years before their own time; Trillian and Zaphod Beeblebrox go to meet the man who runs the galaxy and learn that he knows nothing outside the four walls of his cabin.

Life, the Universe, and Everything commences with Arthur and Ford again meeting up with Slartibartfast, this time to help him stave off the return of the robots of Krikkit, an evil force out to rescue their masters from their time-envelope prison. All of Arthur's friends are eventually reunited, and the ending of the original trilogy is the saving of the universe and the destruction of the Krikkit robots.

In *So Long, and Thanks for All the Fish*, Arthur hitchhikes to a planet and learns that it is in fact the Earth (although without the dolphins), a disconcerting fact to a survivor of its destruction. He meets Fenchurch, a woman who also realizes that something is strange, and the two go in search of the answer. They learn that the Earth was destroyed, but that the dolphins found a replacement Earth and switched every-thing just as the first planet was destroyed, leaving behind the final message that is the novel's title. Arthur and Fenchurch find the planet holding God's last message to his creations: "We apologize for the inconvenience."

Mostly Harmless ends the series with Arthur meeting the daughter he has not yet had and Ford trying to track down why the newest edition of *The Hitchhiker's Guide to the Galaxy* is producing strange events. What ensues is an alien plot to control the galaxy and the ultimate, final destruction of the universe.

Analysis

On the face of it, the Hitchhiker's Guide to the Galaxy series appears to be all fun and games. Crazy things continually happen, particularly to Arthur, who can only muddle through, never sure of what will come next. A more complex reading reveals that what lies at the heart of the series is something not touched upon often in either young adult or mainstream fiction: the randomness of life and the ability to deal with whatever is put in one's path by it. Arthur Dent as representative human is thrust into a world not of his making—a world, in fact, actively hostile to his existence. That he survives as long as he does is testament both to chance and to his friends, who also must live with the uncertainty of existence. Central to this idea is the fact that even knowing the answer to life is not in itself an answer because both the question and answer can never be known.

The last two novels of the series teach the most important lessons for young adults, although their tone is less exuberant than the first three and the plots are more straightforward. The destruction of the Earth and the debate about humankind's supposed superiority in the web of life give much to ponder, as does the eventual destruction of all that is. While such issues are handled in an amusing way, astute young adults will find concepts that they will confront in one form or another for the rest of their lives.

The series was not originally intended specifically for young adults, and younger readers will most likely not see these ideas in the stories. For them, the sense of play upon which the novels are structured will keep them entertained and returning repeatedly to Arthur's universe. Older readers will see in Arthur a much-needed role model in a complex world—he never fully understands all that is around him, but he never gives up. Regardless of this lack of total comprehension, or perhaps precisely because of it, the series can provide an fascinating road map for what lies ahead in life for everyone. Its seriocomic handling of important concerns allows young adult readers to begin to confront the world around them and their own place in it.

Critical Context

The Hitchhiker's Guide to the Galaxy series is a seminal work precisely because of its irrepressible irreverence. Originally a British Broadcasting Corporation (BBC) radio show in the 1970's that was made into a BBC television production in the early 1980's, the series has also appeared as radio transcripts (in 1985) as well as in an illustrated version of the first novel (in 1994). While the series has received much acclaim, two other comic novels by Adams, *Dirk Gently's Holistic Detective Agency* (1987) and *The Long Dark Tea-Time of the Soul* (1988), have not received much fan support despite critical attention. In whole or part, this reaction can be attributed to the almost addictive pleasure of reading his other works. The latter books also contain interesting ideas to ponder, but in a more fantastic, supernatural setting. At their best, Adams' novels are insightful reading for children of all ages and levels of maturity.

Joshua Stein

THE HOUR OF THE WOLF

Author: Patricia Calvert (1931-   )
First published: 1983
Type of work: Novel
Type of plot: Adventure tale
Time of work: The 1980's
Locale: The Iditarod Trail from Anchorage to Nome, Alaska
Subjects: Coming-of-age, family, friendship, nature, and suicide
Recommended ages: 13-18

> *After a failed suicide attempt, Jake Matthiesen is sent to Alaska, where he enters the Iditarod Dog Sled Race in memory of Danny Yumiat, a friend who dies before he can compete in his own Big "I."*

Principal characters:
JACOB (JAKE) MATTHIESEN, a high school student with low self-esteem who is sent to Alaska to finish high school after a failed suicide attempt
DANNY YUMIAT, an Athabascan Indian classmate who befriends Jake and interests him in dogsled racing
KAMINA YUMIAT, Danny's older sister
DR. WIN SMALLEY, a veterinarian and owner of the Smalley Animal Clinic, who provides a home for Jake while he lives in Alaska
JAKE'S FATHER, the best defense lawyer in the Midwest and a living legend whom Jake believes he will never be able to please

Form and Content

Unlike many authors who deal with the subject of teen suicide, Patricia Calvert downplays the events leading up to the suicide attempt and focuses her attention on the healing process as Jake Matthiesen learns to accept himself and take responsibility for his life. Unable to talk to his father, a successful Minneapolis lawyer who Jake claims is a living legend, and convinced he cannot be the kind of son who would make his father proud, Jake attempts suicide with his great-grandfather's old pistol, which he finds in the attic. Jake's father decides that the suicide attempt resulted from a combination of the pressures of living in a large metropolitan area and association with the wrong companions. After Jake's recovery from his wound, his father sends him to live with Dr. Win Smalley in Anchorage, Alaska, where he hopes that Jake will learn self-sufficiency or, as Jake believes, become a son of which his father could be proud. Leaving his successful father, his high-society mother, and his preppy sister, Jake continues to be haunted by self-doubt when he first arrives in Alaska.

Jake's life takes on a positive quality when he is befriended by Danny Yumiat, a popular Athabascan student who seems to be everything Jake would like to be. Danny asks Jake to work as his dog handler while he prepares to run the Iditarod Dog Sled Race, a 1,049-mile race from Anchorage to Nome. Before he can run the race, however, Danny dies in an apparent accident when he and one of his dogs fall through a section of thin ice during a training session.

Jake vows to enter the Iditarod as a memorial to Danny, but when he attempts to borrow Danny's dog, he learns that Kamina, Danny's older sister, has a similar plan. Jake is reluctant to challenge Kamina's decision to enter the Iditarod because she is a strong-willed individual who, according to local rumors, earned the nickname "Crazy Kate" because she used a knife to intimidate a man who offended her while she was going to college in Seattle. Although Kamina has a low regard for Outsiders (people not born in Alaska) such as Jake, she relents because Danny thought so highly of Jake. She loans him enough dogs for Jake to enter the race, but she makes it clear that she will "beat his socks off," a statement Jake knows is no idle boast considering Kamina's greater knowledge of racing and her superior team of dogs. Kamina also tells Jake that Danny's death was no accident; he killed himself because the pressure of living up to his plans to be a lawyer and leader of his people became too great for him to handle.

Because of his inexperience and lack of quality dogs, Jake is never a serious contender in the race. As Kamina and many other racers far outdistance him, the primary question becomes whether Jake will quit or continue on, in spite of the severe weather conditions and his own physical exhaustion. Whenever Jake is tempted to give up the race, however, the fact that he is running it as a memorial to Danny provides the incentive that he needs to continue following the pack of other racers. Near the end of the race, Kamina has to drop out because of a severely sprained ankle that she suffers in a fall from a cliff during a blinding snowstorm. After Jake rescues her, she loans Danny's sled to Jake, and, although Jake finishes last, earning himself the "Red Lantern Award," he does finish the race, something that many others who started the race were unable to do.

Analysis

Although *The Hour of the Wolf* deals with two suicide attempts, the story is surprisingly upbeat. By the end of the novel, Jake has regained his self-esteem because he was able to finish the Iditarod. Prior to the start of the race, Jake was unable to tell his father that he had entered. At the conclusion of the race, however, Jake has gained self-assurance. Now he can admit that he does not plan to return to Minnesota, enter college, and take a position in his father's law firm. Instead, Jake plans to stay in Alaska, attend the University of Anchorage to earn a degree in veterinary medicine, and possibly to enter the Iditarod next year.

Meanwhile, his father has gained enough respect for Jake that he can accept Jake's decision. In addition, he says that losing a recent case to a top-notch prosecutor has convinced him to cut down on his own legal work so that he can spend more time with Jake in the future than he has in the past. Even Danny's suicide is given a positive aspect through the use of the "spirit wolf" that shadows Jake during the final leg of the Iditarod, which Jake comes to believe is the spirit of Danny.

The individual-versus-nature theme is particularly well handled in this novel. Calvert's vivid depiction of the severe weather and physical exertion of the Iditarod enables readers to understand why even finishing last in the race is noteworthy. In fact, one of the subthemes of the novel focuses on the fact that how one competes is more important than where one finishes in a contest such as the Iditarod. The sense of accomplishment that Jake gains from finishing the race provides a sense of self-sufficiency that enables him to face "the hour of the wolf," the times of fear that all individuals confront in life. Although the book is an exciting adventure story, the fact that Jake struggles as much with his own need to be free of his family's expectations for him as he does with the forces of nature adds depth to the novel.

Calvert's depiction of Jake is one of the major strengths of the book. His progression toward greater self-confidence and acceptance of himself is firmly grounded in his experiences running the Iditarod. Calvert also handles the relationship between Jake and Kamina effectively, as they progress from mere tolerance to a closer relationship. Unfortunately, Calvert does not devote enough space to Kamina, even though she has the potential to be a memorable character. The other characters, particularly Jake's father, lack sufficient development to make them much more than background for the story. In particular, readers learn so little about Jake's father that his plans for a dramatic reversal in his relationship with Jake lacks the impact it might otherwise have had.

Once readers have finished the book, they will know much about dogsledding in general and the history and customs of the Iditarod in particular. Calvert has unobtrusively inserted a large quantity of information about those subjects into the book, thus increasing her credibility while not detracting from the story line.

Critical Context

Patricia Calvert's first young adult novel, *The Snowbird* (1980), was selected by the American Library Association as a Best Book for 1980. Since that time, she has continued to earn praise from critics and has won most of the awards available to young adult authors. Calvert's protagonists, like Jake Matthiesen, are usually physically and/or socially isolated individuals who learn to take responsibility for their lives, accept themselves, and relate to other people.

Although there is no evidence that they have influenced each other directly, Calvert and author Gary Paulsen share a high regard for sled dogs and for the value of testing oneself under extreme conditions such as the Iditarod Dog Sled Race. Readers who like *The Hour of the Wolf* will probably also enjoy Paulsen's novel *Dogsong* (1985) and his nonfiction accounts of dogsledding, *Winterdance: The Fine Madness of Running the Iditarod* (1994) and *Woodsong* (1991).

Ronald Barron

A HOUSE LIKE A LOTUS

Author: Madeleine L'Engle (1918-   )
First published: 1984
Type of work: Novel
Type of plot: Psychological realism
Time of work: The late twentieth century
Locale: Benne Seed Island, South Carolina; Athens, Greece; and Osia Theola, Cyprus
Subjects: Coming-of-age, death, emotions, and friendship
Recommended ages: 15-18

> *While spending time in Athens before traveling to a conference to work as a gofer, Polly O'Keefe reflects on her friendship with Max, who has made her life richer in many ways yet who has also betrayed her trust.*

Principal characters:
POLLY O'KEEFE, an intelligent sixteen-year-old girl
MAXIMILIANA "MAX" HORNE, an older woman who befriends Polly
ZACHARY GRAY, a young man who spends several days with Polly in Athens
MR. and MRS. O'KEEFE, Polly's parents
URSULA HESCHEL, Max's lover
XAN and KATE, Polly's younger brother and cousin
QUERON "RENNY" RENIER, an intern at the local hospital, whom Polly dates
OMIO HENO, VIRGINIA PORCHER, NORINE FONG MAR, KRHIS GHOSE, FRANK ROWAN, MILCAH ADAH XENDA, and BASHEMATH ODEGA, teachers or students at the conference in Cyprus
SANDY and RHEA MURRY, Polly's uncle and aunt

Form and Content

Like many of Madeleine L'Engle's novels for young people, *A House Like a Lotus* is written in the first person, as though it were a series of journal entries or an account told to a friend. There are no chapters as such, but the story alternates between the past and the present. *A House Like a Lotus* begins with Polly O'Keefe writing in her journal as she sits in Constitution Square in Athens, Greece. Within the first few pages, L'Engle draws the reader into the story, hinting that Polly is hurting emotionally, but not specifying the problem. The narration jumps backward to Polly's journey to Athens, backward again to the day that Max asked her if she would like to spend three weeks as a gofer at a conference in Cyprus, and finally backward once more to the day that Polly was introduced to Max. From this beginning, the narration alternates between Polly's activities in Greece and, later, in Osia Theola, Cyprus, and focuses on the story of her friendship with Max.

Polly meets Maximiliana "Max" Horne at Christmas, when her Uncle Sandy introduces her to his old friend, who has come to live for the winter in her family mansion, Beau Allaire, fifteen miles from Polly's home on Benne Seed Island. Polly and Max quickly become friends; the older woman needs the companionship that Polly provides, and Polly needs the intellectual stimulus that Max is able to give. Polly quickly becomes the child that Max could not have, and, in return, Polly begins to idolize Max. At first, no one questions why Max and her lover, Ursula, a neurosurgeon, would choose to spend their winter on an isolated island in South Carolina, but Polly eventually realizes that it is because Max is dying.

This knowledge is very difficult for Polly to cope with, as she has come to depend on Max. She feels isolated at school, where her younger brother and her cousin, Kate, are popular, and Max provides the friendship and attention that she craves. One night, however, when Polly is staying at Beau Allaire because Ursula is away, Max, drunk and crazy with pain and fear, tries to seduce Polly. Soon after this incident, Polly flies to Greece on her way to Osia Theola, Cyprus, where Max has arranged for her to work as a gofer at a conference.

In Athens, Polly meets Zachary Gray, a "spectacular-looking" young man who takes an interest in Polly and spends several days with her before she flies to Cyprus. Zachary, although handsome, intelligent, and rich, is pessimistic and negative about humanity, whereas Polly is optimistic and positive. Polly's conversations with Zachary allow her to review her friendship with Max as she tries to come to terms with events. Polly knows that she must try to forgive Max, who has acted completely out of character, but she feels as though "a splinter of ice had lodged deep in my heart."

It is not until Polly has met the teachers at the conference in Osia Theola, who have all had terrible personal experiences yet have come through them with love and compassion, that she is able to begin the process of forgiveness. Zachary follows her to Osia Theola, and, when she has a few hours off, takes her kayaking in the sea and nearly ends up drowning her. When Polly realizes that she is able to accept and forgive this selfish young man, she also realizes that she can accept and forgive Max and even move back into a love for her.

Analysis

Madeleine L'Engle is not afraid to tackle the tough themes—death, sex, love, responsibility, forgiveness, trust. *A House Like a Lotus* touches on all these, both in its story line and in the discussions between characters. At one point, Polly muses that she is "far more comfortable with ideas than with ordinary social conversation," and *A House Like a Lotus* is full of conversations about ideas. It is also a coming-of-age novel, in which Polly leaves the self-centeredness of childhood to learn to understand and have compassion for other people.

Max begins this growing-up process for Polly, helping her to see how a teacher whom Polly dislikes may actually be lonely and unfulfilled and, simple as it may seem, that her parents are separate individuals, with strengths and weaknesses of their own. Polly needs to learn that "all human beings betray each other and that we are going to be let down even by those we most trust." The trick that the mature person has is to be able to forgive the betrayal and view the betrayer with compassion. Polly ends up learning this lesson the hard way: Max's attempt to seduce her betrays their friendship in the most taboo way possible, since Max is a lesbian and regards Polly as the child she did not have. Polly must learn to look beyond this incident to the person Max really is and to have compassion for the pain and fear that drove Max to her uncharacteristic actions.

A House Like a Lotus also tackles the question of what love is: the love between parent and child, between husband and wife, between two friends. L'Engle's firm conviction is that love is inextricably combined with trust, and it has to be given; it cannot be taken. The relationship between Max and Ursula highlights the idea that love involves nourishing the loved person both emotionally and intellectually. Polly's relationship with Zachary helps her realize that love is more than simply sex and is, in actuality, unrelated to sex; Polly is attracted to Zachary, but "chemistry's not enough." When Polly is at the conference on Cyprus, her friend Omio points out to her that "to deny friendship is unlove." In her inability to forgive Max, Polly has been guilty of "unlove"; she has been selfish, only wanting to take the good things that Max has taught her but unable to give forgiveness back. When Polly is finally able to understand this concept, she can phone Max and honestly tell her that she loves her and that she, Polly, also needs to be forgiven.

All of L'Engle's books are informed in some way by her Christian faith, and *A House Like a Lotus* is no exception. The fact that Max is dying allows L'Engle to introduce discussions on the soul, on God, and on life's meaning. For example, the lotus of the book's title is a way of imagining the soul. Max has found this image in the Upanishads, part of the Veda, holy writings in Sanskrit: "In this body, in this town of Spirit, there is a little house shaped like a lotus, and in that house there is a little space. There is as much in that little space within the heart as there is in the whole world outside." The "little space" is the soul, and the soul is "the reality of your *you* and my *me*." Those who close the doors to their house in "self-protection or lust or greed" constrict their souls. When Polly is finally able to forgive Max by moving beyond self-pity and self-protection, she feels that the ice has melted within her and that her heart is "like a lotus," with room enough again for Max.

Critical Context

Readers of Madeleine L'Engle's other works, both for children and adults, will recognize many of the characters in *A House Like a Lotus*. Polly features in three other novels: *The Arm of the Starfish* (1965), *Dragons in the Waters* (1976), and *An Acceptable Time* (1989). Polly's parents, Calvin and Meg O'Keefe, were the main characters in L'Engle's Newbery Medal-winning novel *A Wrinkle in Time* (1962). Zachary Gray also appears in *An Acceptable Time* and in two of L'Engle's novels about another teenage protagonist, Vicky Austin. Several of the more minor characters also feature in previous novels. This recurrence is evidence of L'Engle's belief that people and events are interconnected and interdependent; what one person does, or does not do, affects others in ways that perhaps can neither be explained nor even imagined, but that are nevertheless crucially important.

Readers will also recognize many of the themes that recur in L'Engle's work. One of her first books for children, *And Both Were Young* (republished 1983), attempted to deal with the death of a parent and had to be rewritten at the publisher's request because it was believed that the subject was too difficult or upsetting for young people. Her novel *A Ring of Endless Light* (1980), a Newbery Honor Book, also deals with death in a sensitive way. What L'Engle is really concerned with, however, is life and how to live it most fully. Max, despite her illness and impending death, is vibrant, and she tells Polly that "no one is too insignificant to make a difference. Whenever you get the chance, choose life." L'Engle is convinced of the importance of each individual in the scheme of things, and her novels are concerned with the idea of interdependence—what one person chooses to do makes a difference and can affect the entire universe.

Karen Cleveland Marwick

THE HOUSE ON MANGO STREET

Author: Sandra Cisneros (1954-   )
First published: 1984
Type of work: Novel
Type of plot: Psychological realism and social realism
Time of work: The late 1960's and early 1970's
Locale: An inner-city neighborhood
Subjects: Emotions, family, friendship, gender roles, and social issues
Recommended ages: 13-18

> *A preadolescent girl recounts her experiences and dreams of overcoming economic and social entrapments by becoming a self-reliant woman.*

> *Principal characters:*
> ESPERANZA, the narrator
> NENNY, Esperanza's younger sister
> LUCY and RACHEL, sisters who are friends with Esperanza
> UNCLE NACHO, a supportive member of the extended family
> AUNT LUPE, an invalid relative who supports Esperanza's creativity
> CATHY, a friend whose family moves to a more Anglo-American neighborhood
> MARIN, a young Puerto Rican girl who lives with members of the extended family
> ALICIA, an young woman who is trying to overcome poverty and oppression through education
> MINERVA, an abused young wife who writes poetry

Form and Content

The House on Mango Street is presented in forty-four vignettes that run from a fragment of a page to two or three pages. The young narrator, Esperanza, provides coherence to the book: Her voice, in a scarcely interrupted monologue, is present throughout. The predominant point of view of the narrative is the first-person singular, but the narrator makes extensive use of the third-person singular while describing the other characters in the work.

One can view *The House on Mango Street* either as a nontraditional novel made up of sketches or as a series of thematically related short stories. In addition to the constant presence of the narrator, which brings together the vignettes as chapters of the same book, the work presents other structural features that define it as a novel—for example, the recurring image of a comfortable house, which becomes a metaphor for the independence that Esperanza desires. As in short stories, however, there is limited character development within the vignettes.

Esperanza was born in the bosom of a loving Mexican American family of modest resources. She recalls having moved frequently and having lived in rundown apartment buildings. Although her family owns their current house located on Mango Street, Esperanza does not feel satisfied in it.

The narrator provides descriptions of both the house in which she lives at the present and the house that her parents have promised their children. The house on Mango Street has no front yard and is small and constructed of red brick. It has small steps leading to the front door, and the windows are so small that the family does not seem to have space to breathe. The lack of enough room prevents the family members from having the privacy that they need; every time someone takes a bath, he or she must make an announcement first so that no one will accidentally walk in. The size of this house, however, is not the only problem. The reader perceives that it is an old building in which some of the bricks are crumbling, a detail that perhaps points to the material decadence of the neighborhood.

Esperanza's parents talk about having a home like those on television. It will be a comfortable white house, with a large open front yard planted with trees. It will have an interior staircase, three bathrooms, and abundant running water. Esperanza realizes that a home like this is only a dream for her family and decides that it will be up to her to get the house she wants in the future.

Esperanza's dream home becomes synonymous with individual economic and social independence, which one can obtain through education and the cultivation of one's native talents.

In addition to developing gradually the metaphor of a house as symbolic of a self-reliant existence, the narrative relates Esperanza's childhood games, alludes to the loving relationship that she maintains with her family, and describes the activities of the neighbors.

Analysis

The House on Mango Street offers a feminist view of society. Significantly, the book is dedicated "*A las mujeres*," to women, which seems to indicate that the experiences portrayed pertain especially to women. From the beginning, the reader perceives Esperanza as a member of a marginal minority group, one that traditionally has upheld the most conservative tenets of patriarchy. The narrator, although she is only in early adolescence at most, is aware that she does not wish to follow the steps of any of her female predecessors. Her observations and conclusions reveal that she is preparing to challenge traditional ideologies concerning the status of women. In the section entitled "My Name," among the earlier vignettes in the book, she comments on the origin of her Spanish name, Esperanza. She states that this was the name of her great-grandmother who, like her, was born in the Chinese Year of the Horse. She adds that according to the Chinese zodiac, it is bad luck to be born in that year if one is female, but she does not believe in this superstition. She thinks that the Chinese make such claims because they, like the Mexicans, do not like their women to be strong.

Esperanza opposes some of the traditional tenets of patriarchy. As a direct consequence of this opposition, she rebels against the concept of marriage as the only future available to a woman. Her rejection of oppressive marriages is apparent in several vignettes, such as the one in which she relates an unfortunate event in her great-grand-mother's life: She did not want to marry, but a man who wanted her for his wife captured her by placing a sack over her head and carrying her off. Her great-grand-mother was then an unhappy woman who "looked out the window all her life, the way so many women sit their sadness on an elbow," states the narrator.

Esperanza also opposes traditional gender roles. She does not welcome the idea of having women be exclusively responsible for domestic tasks and having to spend their lives waiting on men. She confesses that she is fighting a war in this regard, which she makes evident by leaving the table "like a man, without putting back the chair or picking up the plate."

A woman's freedom to select her own destiny and her right to receive earned respect are prominent ideas in *The House on Mango Street*. Although there is an abundance of images of women in the book, these women's lives are not successful. On the contrary, the narrator enumerates the multiple failures of these characters. All the women in the novel can be placed into one of two categories: either those who depend economically on husbands and fathers or those who have been abandoned by men. Esperanza's mother falls in the first group. She has many regrets, such as having to abandon her studies at an early age and neglect the growth of her artistic talent because of the family's poverty.

Among the female characters is Minerva, a poet who is only somewhat older than the narrator and who already has more responsibilities that she can handle. She has two small children and an irresponsible, abusive husband. The most appropriate feminine role model for Esperanza appears in "Alicia Who Sees Mice." The central character of this vignette is a young woman who is determined to overcome poverty and oppression through education. After rising early to prepare her father's lunch box of tortillas, Alicia takes two trains and a bus to go to college. Alicia is a good girl, says the narrator.

Since the narrator cannot see herself in the other characters, she engages in self-analysis and meditates on the house that will make her free. *The House on Mango Street*, however, offers more than revelations about the inner world of one teenage girl; it is also a striking disclosure of the inner workings of the Hispanic family and the strong support system its relatives create. Significant expressions of encouragement for the narrator come from her home and from the members of her extended family. Hence, the reader surmises that Esperanza will be successful in her quest for self-sufficiency, which will become tangible when she has a special house of her own.

Critical Content

The House on Mango Street was the first narrative work by Sandra Cisneros. It has become a valuable work of fiction in contemporary Chicano literature, forming part of the core readings in diverse ethnic studies curricula. Cisneros' volume of poetry *My Wicked Wicked Ways* (1987) contains pieces whose motifs the reader can relate to themes appearing in *The House on Mango Street*. Two other volumes of poetry, *Bad*

Boys (1980) and *Loose Woman* (1994), include some social commentary motifs as well as lyrical compositions. In Cisneros' other works, such as the short-story collection *Woman Hollering Creek and other Stories* (1991), feminist themes are more evident, emerging from a variety of narrative voices that represent female children, adolescents, and adults.

The House on Mango Street is inspiring reading material for young people. Cisneros encourages changes in the traditional roles and social conditions of women and members of minority groups while she emphasizes the universal human values of love and respect.

Cida S. Chase

HOUSEKEEPING

Author: Marilynne Robinson (1944-   )
First published: 1980
Type of work: Novel
Type of plot: Psychological realism
Time of work: The 1960's to the 1970's
Locale: Fingerbone, a fictional town in the Pacific Northwest
Subjects: Coming-of-age, family, nature, and suicide
Recommended ages: 15-18

After her mother's death, Ruth, with the help of her eccentric aunt, begins to understand the nature of impermanence and claims independence from a society that excludes her.

> *Principal characters:*
> RUTH STONE, an adolescent girl in junior high school
> LUCILLE STONE, her younger sister
> SYLVIE FOSTER FISHER, their maternal aunt

Form and Content

Fingerbone, the cold, damp setting of *Housekeeping*, was the site of a spectacular train derailment years ago, when Ruth and Lucille's grandfather, Edmund Foster, and his Fireball train plunged off the bridge and sank into the lake. An awareness of the lake and the train's presence beneath its surface permeates the entire novel. After the accident, other widows left Fingerbone, but the girls' grandmother remained. As an adult reminiscing about her childhood and the women in her family, Ruth narrates the story in an unusual meditative style; the plot is driven less by character action than by Ruth's active imagination and emotions. Although it deals with serious subject matter, *Housekeeping* is a comic novel, and Aunt Sylvie is one of the most memorable characters in contemporary literature.

The action of the story begins when Ruth and Lucille's mother, Helen, uproots her daughters from their apartment in Seattle, abandons them on their grandmother's porch, and drives her borrowed car over a cliff into the deepest part of the lake. The girls remain under their grandmother's care for five years. When she dies, her persnickety sisters-in-law, Lily and Nona, move into the old house to watch over the girls. Missing their familiar surroundings in Spokane's Hartwick Hotel, the old women conspire to persuade Helen's sister, Sylvie, to take over rearing the girls. Sylvie, a transient, has been away from Fingerbone for sixteen years and has acquired strange habits, such as sleeping on park benches, eating her supper in the dark, and listening for the freight trains that she once rode. Upon Sylvie's arrival, Lily and Nona flee Fingerbone.

Lucille becomes lonely when the spring thaw and heavy rains flood the town. After the waters recede, she tests her new guardian by skipping school and hiding at the lake with Ruth. The girls are stunned to see Sylvie walking out over the lake on the train trestle. Beginning to doubt their aunt's mental stability, the girls imagine that they will be taken from her care. When they return to school, Lucille feels pressure from the community members, who cannot abide Sylvie's eccentricities. Caught between her aunt and Fingerbone residents who disapprove of her behavior, Lucille chastises Sylvie for offending her sense of propriety.

One night, the girls go fishing to escape the gaze of the townsfolk. They stay out all night and argue about their mother. Ruth notices a resemblance between Helen and Sylvie, but Lucille insists that Helen was orderly, responsible, and a proper role model, nothing at all like Sylvie, whose accumulating clutter of tin cans and newspapers floods the house. Lucille, who accuses Ruth of preferring Sylvie over their mother, works to improve herself by attending school, associating only with "proper" girls, and dreaming of moving to Boston. Finally, Lucille leaves the house and moves in with Miss Royce, her home economics teacher. That day, Ruth remarks, she lost her sister.

The next morning, Sylvie steals a rowboat and takes Ruth across the lake to a wooded valley. Sylvie, named after mythic wood sprites, disappears in the woods, forcing Ruth to be self-reliant. She rejoins Ruth, and that night they row under the trestle and wait for the trains to pass. Ruth thinks about the train derailment and her drowned mother under the lake's smooth surface. They stay on the lake overnight and catch a freight train back into Fingerbone the next morning.

Unable to tolerate Ruth's acceptance of Sylvie, the pious citizens of Fingerbone believe that they must rescue the girl and bring her back into their ordinary society. The sheriff announces plans for a custody hearing. Frightened, Sylvie begins traditional housekeeping—cleaning up the parlor, burning old magazines—but her last-ditch effort is too late. To avoid being separated, Ruth and Sylvie put "an end to housekeeping" by setting fire to the house and leaving Fingerbone. They escape across the railroad trestle over the lake and drift on freight trains for many years. When Ruth tells her story, she recalls the headline of the local newspaper when they left Fingerbone—"LAKE CLAIMS TWO." The citizens of Fingerbone, including Lucille, presumed that they had drowned.

Analysis

The most remarkable feature of Marilynne Robinson's novel is its lingering, rhythmic language and distinctive style. In *Housekeeping*, Robinson's language refreshes her readers' understanding of reality by making them see the world anew. She transforms the simple metaphors of house, lake, and train into a beautiful meditation on the nature of security, loss, and transiency.

Ruth is a survivor. The first line of *Housekeeping*—"My name is Ruth."—echoes the beginning of another survivor's tale, Ishmael in Herman Melville's *Moby-Dick* (1851). Both novels can be read as *Bildungsromans*, novels chronicling a young person's journey from adolescence to maturity. Throughout the novel, Ruth, whose name means sorrow, mourns her mother. The omnipresent lake dredges up the unwelcome changes and dislocations that Helen's suicide brought upon Ruth and Lucille. Nature itself represents the change and impermanence that Ruth fears. On her outing with Sylvie, Ruth imagines her mother coming back from the lake. She longs for the wholeness that her mother represents. Yet, Ruth acknowledges the futility of her dream and concludes, "It is better to have nothing."

At a critical moment in their relationship, Ruth and Lucille disagree over memories about their mother. Ruth remembers her as indifferent, while Lucille thinks that she was orderly and sensible—the perfect mother that she wishes Helen had been. Despite Ruth's vehement objections, Lucille maintains that their mother lost control of the car. These conflicting memories reflect Ruth and Lucille's strategies for coping with their mother's suicide and the uncertainties that it creates. Ultimately, Lucille retreats into an established social order, while Ruth drifts with Sylvie between Spokane and Billings. Ruth strains to catch a glimpse of the old house whenever their freight train rattles through Fingerbone.

The novel's title ironically opposes Sylvie's transient habits with traditional housekeeping. Good housekeeping means policing boundaries: keeping dirt and trash outside and maintaining order indoors. Sylvie's transient housekeeping, itself an oxymoron, implies a loss of boundaries between inside and outside. *Housekeeping* illustrates how a rigidly conformist world often excludes some individuals. Many forgotten transients died when the train derailed. Like Sylvie and other marginalized people, Ruth believes that she is outside ordinary society. While Lucille stays in Fingerbone "stalemating the forces of ruin," Ruth learns her family's history from Sylvie and discovers that living takes place in the world outside the confines of houses and Fingerbone. For Ruth, transiency is a means of taking her house with her. Her rite of passage occurs when she crosses the bridge with Sylvie and becomes a transient. Rather than shutting out the world, Ruth embraces it and learns that nature, like a train, can embody both movement and stasis; it changes, yet remains the same.

Housekeeping is also a novel about the West, but it rejects the simplistic cowboy images associated with John Wayne films. Ruth's story opens with the matriarchal lineage of her family. She blames her grandfather for uprooting her female ancestors and settling in Fingerbone. Yet, it is Edmund's plunge into the mysterious depths of the lake that allows Ruth's imagination to wander outside the house. Ruth discovers the natural processes of life, which she later comes to appreciate. Ruth and Sylvie set out for a new territory of female experience.

Critical Context

As a *Bildungsroman*, *Housekeeping* revises the male tradition of Mark Twain's *The Adventures of Huckleberry Finn* (1884) and J. D. Salinger's *The Catcher in the Rye* (1951). With its strong female protagonist who rejects traditional domestic roles, the novel is comparable to Zora Neale Hurston's *Their Eyes Were Watching God* (1937). Despite the absence of male characters and the story's emphasis on female experience, male readers are not excluded from the novel.

Reminiscent of Sarah Orne Jewett's *The Country of the Pointed Firs* (1896), *Housekeeping*'s local color flavor indelibly evokes its Pacific Northwest setting and emphasizes a deep sense of place. Readers might also notice the influence of Henry David Thoreau's *Walden* (1854), in which Thoreau relates his solitary experience of keeping house in the woods near Walden Pond. *Housekeeping* was Robinson's first novel, and she also wrote a nonfiction book, *Mother Country* (1989), which exposes the British government's irresponsible operation of the environmentally hazardous Sellafield nuclear power processing plant.

Trey Strecker

THE HUNCHBACK OF NOTRE DAME

Author: Victor Hugo (1802-1885)
First published: Notre-Dame de Paris, 1831 (English translation, 1833)
Type of work: Novel
Type of plot: Allegory, historical fiction, and social realism
Time of work: January-July, 1482
Locale: The neighborhood around the Paris cathedral of Notre Dame
Subjects: Death, love and romance, politics and law, and social issues
Recommended ages: 13-18

Despite his horrible face and a misshapen body, Quasimodo ultimately shows that ugliness can coexist with a beautiful soul.

Principal characters:
QUASIMODO, the hunchbacked bell-ringer of Notre Dame Cathedral
CLAUDE FROLLO, the archdeacon of the cathedral and the epitome of the intellectual
ESMERALDA, a beautiful sixteen-year-old gypsy dancer and nanny goat trainer
PIERRE GRINGOIRE, a poet and playwright
PHOEBUS DE CHÂTEAUPERS, the handsome captain of the Royal Archers
LOUIS XI, the king of France

Form and Content

Set in France during the reign of Louis XI, *The Hunchback of Notre Dame* is a historical novel of epic proportions that appeals to a broad readership. Victor Hugo vividly re-creates the teeming Paris of the late Middle Ages, with its sharp roofs and narrow, muddy streets, as well as the people, customs, and pageantry of fifteenth century France. He also presents conflicts and themes that resonate with adults both young and old because they are at the core of the human condition.

The novel's action is divided among a number of crucial days spread over six months (January to July), enhanced by fascinating short essays on various subjects ranging from alchemy to the future of architecture. If at first the narrative concentrates on Pierre Gringoire walking around Paris, it soon shifts to the other characters as Hugo describes in omniscient fashion or through authorial intrusions their thoughts and movements, which he often explains and compares in the light of modern events and ways of thinking, such as the Revolution of 1830 or the need to abolish the death penalty.

Claude Frollo, the archdeacon of Notre Dame, had adopted some twenty years before an ugly and deformed infant found on Quasimodo Sunday (hence his name), whom he had reared within the confines of the cathedral. Now, in 1482, Frollo is involved in transforming base metals into gold through alchemy, and the hunchback has become the official bell-ringer. When the priest sees the gypsy girl Esmeralda dance on the public square, he is so struck by her beauty, gracefulness, and innocent sensuality that he has Quasimodo kidnap her. After she is rescued by the handsome Captain Phoebus, she falls in love with him, while Quasimodo is publicly punished, much to the crowd's enjoyment. Only Esmeralda takes pity on the young wretch and gives him water to drink, awakening eternal feelings of gratitude and adoration in Quasimodo.

Unable to overcome his obsession with Esmeralda, Frollo follows her to a tryst with Phoebus and wounds him—a crime for which Esmeralda is accused and sentenced to death. Frollo promises to save her, however, if she agrees to love him, but she refuses. Rescued at the last minute by Quasimodo, she is whisked inside the cathedral (a medieval sanctuary) and devotedly watched over by him. During the night, in an exciting chapter, her friends—the seething, frightening underclass of thieves and cutthroats—attack the cathedral in a vain attempt to free her, in a scene reminiscent of the storming of the Bastille in 1789. After Frollo tricks Esmeralda into leaving her refuge, he again offers her the choice between himself and death, and again she chooses death. She is therefore turned over to the authorities and hanged. Quasimodo, realizing at last his protector's involvement, hurls Frollo off a tower of the cathedral and then, observing the bodies of both Esmeralda and his master, cries, "Oh, all that I ever loved!"

In a few paragraphs, Hugo mentions King Louis' death the following year, Gringoire's literary success, and Phoebus' marriage.

Analysis

Hugo wrote in his accompanying note to *The Hunchback of Notre Dame* that he had seen the Greek word *ananké* (fatality) scratched on a wall inside the cathedral and that "it is around this word that this book has been written." Fatality is an important theme in the novel, as is love in its various forms. In addition, the antithesis between the grotesque and the sublime—a concept dear to the author—shows that ugliness, far from reflecting vice and sin, signifies instead virtue and greatness of soul. Similarly, neither is knowledge for knowledge's sake synonymous with wisdom. Such worldviews have repercussions for young adult readers since they, like the protagonists, often consider the personal forces driving them and the moral choices confronting them in trying to live well.

From the beginning of the novel, the characters' lives are ruled by an absurd fatality that is at once physical, historical, hereditary, and social. The monstrous Quasimodo is turned into a subhuman animal creature (one chapter is entitled "The Dog and His Master"), destined to suffer misfortune. On the other hand, Phoebus, whose name associates him with the Greek sun-god, is the epitome of superficial beauty, which assures a professional success further guaranteed by his aristocratic origins. Frollo, the scratcher of the word *ananké*, is destroyed metaphysically and literally both by his heretical quest for gold and by his evil pursuit of Esmeralda. For her part, because she is a gypsy and therefore an outcast, she is fated to be rejected—like the foundling

Quasimodo, but for different reasons—by an intolerant and xenophobic populace. The "vast symphony in stone" that is Notre Dame is not immune from decline and metaphorical death either. As Hugo predicts in no uncertain terms, the cathedral—mysterious, immense, filled with symbols—is itself doomed to extinction by the advent of the printing press. Books will replace the stories told in stained glass windows or in sculpted scenes around the portals.

Love is one fatality common to all. Frollo's passion for Esmeralda is based on an intense sexual and psychological need to possess her, just as he wants to possess ultimate knowledge. The jealousy that he feels is motivated as much by unrequited desire as by his realization that the hold his position should give him over Esmeralda is completely useless since she never gives in to his threats. Driven by powers outside his control and frustrated by her refusals, he can only cause her unjust destruction. Phoebus is more careless than wanton in his response to Esmeralda's love: An empty-headed braggart, he is obviously flattered, but, like her, he also has a "tragic end": He gets married. Thanks to Esmeralda's act of kindness, Quasimodo reveals that behind his repulsive exterior shines a luminous soul. Self-sacrifice and devotion are better proofs of love than Frollo's egotism or Phoebus' opportunism.

While Quasimodo is transformed through love, Esmeralda remains throughout the book an angelic vision. Among all the horror and pain, she is the only figure of absolute purity and light, and as such she is often compared to the Virgin Mary. Indeed, she incarnates beauty in the face of ugliness, pity in the face of cruelty, true love in the face of fickleness. That she was misled by Phoebus' good looks points out her human fragility and her own kind of fatality. Quasimodo should have been her companion: His heart of gold is more real than the alchemical gold sought by Frollo, and his inner beauty more lasting than Phoebus' surface one. In the final chapter, aptly called "Quasimodo's Marriage," the ill-fated hunchback dies of love embracing the body of Esmeralda.

Critical Context

Although *The Hunchback of Notre Dame* was preceded by other French historical novels, such as Madame de La Fayette's *La Princesse de Clèves* (1678; *The Princess of Clèves*, 1679) or Alfred de Vigny's *Cinq-Mars* (1826), the work that had the most immediate influence on Victor Hugo's conception was Sir Walter Scott's *Quentin Durward* (1823). Not only did Hugo want to surpass Scott in his portrayal of the world of Louis XI, but, as he wrote in his review-essay on the English novel, he too intended "to express a useful truth in an interesting story." Hugo also helped usher in a renewed interest in and admiration for everything medieval, especially gothic architecture. Furthermore, he was the first to present large crowds in motion, a group-character later used by Leo Tolstoy in Russia and Émile Zola in France, among others.

Through his visionary imagination, Hugo knew how to weave a dramatic narrative, how to evoke an authentic historical era, and how to depict a setting vividly and picturesquely. All this explains why *The Hunchback of Notre Dame* was and remains such a great success. Excelling in poetry, drama, and fiction, Hugo continued to explore the struggles of the individual against nature in *Les Travailleurs de la mer* (1866; *Toilers of the Sea*, 1866), against society in *L'Homme qui rit* (1869; *The Man Who Laughs*, 1869), or against history in *Quatre-vingt-treize* (1874; *Ninety-three*, 1874). In *The Hunchback of Notre Dame*, he rationalized the presence of evil in the world by attributing it to human powerlessness before fatality. *Les Misérables* (1862; English translation, 1862), especially, went even further by advancing the proposition that there is no evil in good and that there is good in evil.

Pierre L. Horn

THE HUNDRED DRESSES

Author: Eleanor Estes (1906-1988)
First published: 1944; illustrated
Type of work: Novel
Type of plot: Psychological realism
Time of work: The present
Locale: A school in a small town
Subjects: Education, friendship, poverty, and social issues
Recommended ages: 10-13

Afraid of becoming the object of ridicule, Madeline stands by as Wanda Petronski, a girl from the wrong side of tracks, is tormented by her classmates; the results teach Madeline that complicity in wrongdoing is itself wrongdoing.

> *Principal characters:*
> WANDA PETRONSKI, a motherless girl who is overlooked by her teacher
> and ridiculed by her classmates for claiming to have one hundred
> different dresses in her closet at home
> PEGGY, the most popular girl in the class, who delights in tormenting
> Wanda about her hundred dresses and pointing out that Wanda wears
> the same dress to school each day
> MADELINE, Peggy's best friend, who is almost as poor as Wanda and
> who fears that standing up for the other girl will make her the object
> of Peggy's derision

Form and Content

A Newbery Honor Book, Eleanor Estes' *The Hundred Dresses* is a straightforward yet psychologically complex story about friendship and the ethical implications involved in standing by and saying nothing while another person is being harmed. Louis Slobodkin's illustrations reinforce the message of this story, which is written in seven short chapters and narrated in the third person. Even very young children will be able to understand the premise of the story, while the adult who reads *The Hundred Dresses* to children will find the narrative both moving and substantial enough to compel his or her interest.

Wanda Petronski, whose Polish name sets her apart from her classmates as much as her address on Boggins Heights, the poor part of town, comes to school every day in the same faded, yet clean, blue dress. She sits in the last seat in the last row of her classroom, among the troublemakers, and is generally ignored by her teacher and by her fellow students.

The children pay attention to Wanda, however, after the day she claims to have one hundred dresses at home. Peggy, a privileged and popular girl, decides that it will be amusing to make fun of Wanda for this apparent lie, and Peggy's friend Madeline, while uncomfortable with Peggy's behavior, does nothing to stop it. Madeline is poor, although not as poor as Wanda, and fears that Peggy will turn her attention on her if she stands up for Wanda. After all, Madeline's own dresses are castoffs from Peggy's closet, and it would be painful and embarrassing to have Peggy point this out to everyone. Thus, while Madeline does not participate in mocking the other girl, she protects her own place in the classroom community and in Peggy's good graces by doing nothing to prevent Peggy from having fun at Wanda's expense.

Peggy, Madeline, and the other students soon learn that their teasing has had serious implications on the Petronski family's life and happiness. They also learn that Wanda had not really been lying about the hundred dresses; she had actually drawn one hundred beautiful and original dresses for the class art contest. By the time that the students realize their error, Wanda's father has withdrawn her from school and moved to the city where, he writes, "No more holler Polack. No more ask why funny name. Plenty of funny names in big city." Wanda's classmates' games, it appears, had not been amusing to Wanda or to her family.

Madeline and Peggy go to Boggins Heights to look for Wanda, but the family has already moved. They then write to Wanda, who, in a letter to the class, replies that things are going well for her and that she would like Madeline and Peggy to have two of her drawings.

After a long period of honest and painful reflection about her own passivity in the face of Peggy's cruelty, Madeline decides that she will never "stand by and say nothing again." To observe an unfairness and not act to stop it, Madeline realizes, is at least as bad as committing such an act. In fact, Madeline realizes, she was more in the wrong than Peggy, since she realized that Peggy's actions were wrong and Peggy had not. Neither Madeline nor Peggy will ever be able to make things right for Wanda and her brother and father, but Madeline will never again remain inactive before an injustice or an act of cruelty.

Madeline also learns a lesson about grace when she realizes that the pictures Wanda designated for her and for Peggy were, in fact, drawn especially for them: The girls wearing Wanda's creations are Madeline and Peggy. Despite being alternately teased and ignored by Peggy and Madeline, Wanda had chosen to remain caring, generous, and sympathetic toward them. Her art was not an escape from her tormentors but rather a gift to them. The story ends with Peggy's conclusion that Wanda liked them despite their behavior and with Madeline blinking away "the tears that came every time she thought of Wanda standing alone in that sunny spot in the school yard close to the wall."

Analysis

The meaning of *The Hundred Dresses* is simple and timeless: All people have human obligations to one another, and sidestepping these obligations is both unethical and immoral. Such inaction may have serious consequences. In the psychologically sophisticated narrative of *The Hundred Dresses*, Estes also acknowledges the difficulty inherent in making oneself conspicuous by acting to stop an injustice. No person wants to risk becoming the object of ridicule by standing up for another person. Like Madeline, one can find excuses for why a victimized person deserves that ill-treatment and is hence unworthy of rescue. Yet, as Madeline realizes, those excuses are just that—excuses. They are not reasons; indeed, there can be no reasons for complacency when others are being harmed. Excuses do not absolve one of complicity in the misery of another person or group. While it can be difficult or painful to stand up for the outcast, it is necessary to do so.

Estes' message of human obligation and interconnectedness should be clear to most readers. By making the consequences of Peggy's and Madeline's behavior evident early in the novel and then showing the evolution of Wanda's estrangement through flashbacks, Estes avoids the charge of preaching. Readers will, like Peggy and Madeline, wonder why Wanda has stopped attending school. The narrative takes the reader through Madeline's reconstruction of past events to speculate about why Wanda is missing and to wonder why, despite the fact that Wanda is a quiet and compliant student, her teacher has consigned her to the back of the room with the "bad" kids.

Indeed, one of the subthemes of Estes' exploration is the consequence of "writing off" certain children. Wanda sits at the margins of her classroom, and her teacher makes no effort to bring those at the margins into the world of the class. The rest of the children, for their part, accept that it must be right and proper that Wanda exist on the fringes of their lives. Wanda lives in Boggins Heights and thus sits in the back of the classroom. No one attempts to help the girl, with her broken English and her reading problems, to become a part of her town or school community. No one asks her to explain what she means when she says that she has a hundred dresses; they simply assume that she is lying. Wanda does not matter to anyone until she has stopped attending class; the children have taken their cues from their teacher, who has accepted the premise that well-scrubbed, protected, and outgoing children are her primary concern as a teacher. Because Wanda seems to show little academic promise, seems generally confused, and speaks haltingly, and because she has no protector, she is given no nurturance within the classroom or school community. Sensitive and perceptive readers may begin to look around their own classrooms to see if any Wanda Petronskis are there.

Critical Context

More somber in tone and subject than *The Moffats* (1941), *Ginger Pye* (1951), or *Rufus M* (1943), books for which Eleanor Estes became celebrated, *The Hundred Dresses* is less a celebration of childhood than an argument against the injustices that even children can perpetuate on one another. This plea against racism and discrimination toward those who are ethnically or financially different was published before the current concern with these issues. A psychologically complex examination of why people do not speak out against injustice, *The Hundred Dresses* is also a forceful argument for why people must do so. Estes' narrative places readers in the mind of Madeline, who is not the victim of injustice, nor someone who has simply come across it. Rather, Estes has made the reader explore with her protagonist what it feels like to have done wrong to another person and how a person can atone for having caused harm.

Angela M. Salas

I AM! SAYS THE LAMB

Author: Theodore Roethke (1908-1963)
First published: 1961; illustrated
Type of work: Poetry
Subject: Animals and nature
Recommended ages: 10-18

At first, playful names, strange sounds, and zany subjects mock the adult world from the child's perspective, then the mood turns somber as Roethke explores a world of snakes and marshes, mildew and rot, the seeds of life, the smells of death.

Form and Content

The twenty-two poems in the first section of *I Am! Says the Lamb*, entitled "The Nonsense Poems," address younger children in ways that appeal to minds free of conventional restrictions, filled with wonder, and charmed by the play of sounds, rhythms, and meanings. They are accompanied by drawings as playful as the verses in their depiction of the poet's subjects, such as a Kitty-Cat Bird and Myrtle the Turtle. Through these characters, the adult world is explored, transformed by nonsense and the magic of language into objects of delight for children.

Theodore Roethke applies the principle that in foolishness, there is an element of divinity, in topsy-turvy an element of truth—or, as Emily Dickinson put it, "Much madness is divinest sense/ To a discerning eye." The poems assume that the young reader (or, better, listener) possesses the discernment necessary to see that the adult world makes sense often, perhaps only, when it is viewed madly. The adult, unless a poet, forgets that a simple chair is animated by a power that enables it to disappear. Its existence is proven (or discovered) empirically: "To know a Chair is really it,/ You sometimes have to go and sit." Adults impose order and meaning on the world, see it as "out there," whereas the poems in this first part of the book posit the notion that children see in a continuum, assuming that other creatures and things are mere extensions of themselves, their feelings and their view of the world. The poems capture the obverse of this view as well, see the world "out there" filled with mysterious forms that cannot be understood. "The Gnu," for example, sums up this dilemma deftly in a couplet: "There's *this* to Remember about the Gnu:/ He *closely* Resembles—but I *can't* tell *you!*" To the child, the world sometimes both denies and threatens.

In the section "The Greenhouse Poems," twenty poems address a more mature audience with more mature themes and subjects. The greenhouse of the title symbolizes the artificial version of nature as creative force. It houses and harnesses this creative force and is not only fed by the sun but also illuminated by it. The mood of these later poems is more somber, and the shift toward sobriety is reflected in the use of language and stanzaic patterns. The poems in the first section are on the whole short and heavily rhymed. The stanzaic patterns and line lengths in the poems of the second part are irregular, and rhyme disappears after the first five poems. The free verse of these poems suggests a throwing off of restraints and growth. Both the language and the illustrations reflect a shift toward serious subjects: dying, alienation, and suffering—the old florist stands "all night watering roses, his feet blue in rubber boots." In these final poems, behavior is viewed in the moral terms of the adult. The youth in "Moss-Gathering," for example, having gathered moss from the marsh, feels guilty. "I always felt mean," he says: "As if I had broken the natural order of things in that swampland;/ Disturbed some rhythm, old and of vast importance,/ By pulling off flesh from the living planet;/ As if I had committed, against the whole scheme of life, a desecration." In the illustration that accompanies this poem, the youth is shown trudging along a path that winds out of sight, followed by a bird. It is not clear whether the bird is the youth's companion or pursuer, or whether the youth is disappearing into the woods or simply going home. Roethke offers two worlds—that of the child, illuminated by merry nonsense and innocence, and that of the older child, filled with beauty, mystery, and fecundity. At the dark edges of this adult world, however, some part of the reader, like the youth, suffers and disappears into mystery.

Analysis

The poems in the first section address the beginners, who, like Roethke himself, are charmed by the experience of worldly things, yet aroused, often intimidated by them. Roethke empathizes with the child's fears and confusions while feeling the child's awe that accompanies the confrontations. The child's view also offers a metaphor of the grownup's compulsion to explore the mysteries of the world, especially of nature. The child never leaves the adult, and the more astute, more adventurous adult returns from time to time to the viewpoint of the child for fresh discoveries.

The varied subjects of the second half of *I Am! Says the Lamb*—flowers, fungus, the poet's father, the greenhouse and its crew of three ladies, and the swampy soil—challenge the poet to explore nature's myriad manifestations and celebrate them. Many of the images in the later poems are of digging down to the roots of nature, into the soil, scraping off fungus, unearthing the tendrils that flower into orchids; the imagery reflects the poet's urge to dig into the heart of nature itself, dig through objects into their unseen and unseeable spirit. The poet's aim is to discover the source of beauty, the source of life. Mingling is an important part of that process, mingling with the soil as if the poet, in being close to the earth, could somehow take on some of its creative power. As a whole, the poems stand as evidence of the creative urge, perhaps of its success.

Critics have said that Roethke's poetry probes the unconscious level of experience in search of archetypal patterns. If this interpretation is correct, these poems may be viewed as expressions of the poet's desire to discover manifestations of nature and the natural processes, a pattern of birth and death, of nurture and dependence, of emerging and receding. For the poet, foraging for sustenance by digging up the earth is but a physical corollary to the intellectual and spiritual probing of physical experience. It may also reflect the poet's intellectual probing of the spiritual world that encloses the mystery of life, giving it existence and sustenance.

For Roethke, nature holds the magical power of generation, the creation of being. Flowers, plants, fungus—these are the objective forms of the metaphysical process of birth and death, of life manifest. The child's wonder is the adult's faith that nature is the beginning and end of everything and is ultimately circular: Birth gives way to death, and from death comes life. The individual—be it orchid, bat, or poet—is but a transitory manifestation of the ongoing, life-giving spirit of nature, one that exists, like the "Weed Puller," "Alive, in a slippery grave."

Throughout the poetry, the personal element is strong. Although the poet provides a fond portrait of his father, the greenhouse ladies, and the old florist who squirts tobacco juice on a bug, mainly the poems view their subjects from a solitary perspective, the individual confronting manifest nature, often alone. Some critics have seen in Roethke's poetry a withdrawal from social subjects, situations, and problems. The poems in the second section may reflect a similar urge to withdraw, but one can hardly explore the world of the spirit without being solitary, and if the natural forces and their manifestations are most clearly seen and experienced in isolation, solitude is essential. Roethke seems to have accepted the privacy of reflection as a condition of poetic exploration.

Critical Context

In the tradition of Edward Lear and Lewis Carroll, Theodore Roethke offers, in the nonsense of the rhymes, names, and subjects in the first set of poems, a world in which children can laugh and frolic. It is a world in which the imagination is given free reign to create helter-skelter levity by distorting the ordinary way in which children are taught by adults to view the world. Freed from the restraints of sober sense, bears talk and serpents sing. The rhythms are as bouncy as the nonsense that plays on the predicaments of children—their fears, feelings, and outlooks and their fascination with magic.

The poems for older children and adults have the air of magic about them, too, and the imagination plays among the dark places that adult children would find if they would go exploring in nature. An occasional moral marks the early poems and is mocked; in the later ones, more ominous strains are heard in the lines, and images reveal a side of nature that frightens the child and warns the adult. The forces of nature are exposed in images of the wind's violent thrashing and the "ghostly mouths" of the "Orchids." The weed puller, it is suggested, digs his own grave, "Hacking at black hairy roots" and finding "fern-shapes,/ Coiled green and thick." Roethke's adult world is not far from the demonic forces and grotesque forms of the fairy tale. Here, it is disguised as poems for adults.

Bernard E. Morris

I KNOW WHAT YOU DID LAST SUMMER

Author: Lois Duncan (1934-   )
First published: 1973
Type of work: Novel
Type of plot: Moral tale and mystery
Time of work: The early 1970's
Locale: Albuquerque, New Mexico
Subjects: Crime, emotions, friendship, social issues, and war
Recommended ages: 13-18

Four teenagers responsible for a hit-and-run accident realize that they have been unsuccessful in keeping the act a secret when threats to each of them reveal that someone else both knows about and seeks revenge for the crime.

Principal characters:
    JULIE JAMES, a high school senior and the backseat passenger in a car
        involved in the hit-and-run accident
    BARRY COX, the driver of the hit-and-run vehicle, who swears his three
        passengers to secrecy
    HELEN RIVERS, Barry's girlfriend, a self-centered television weather
        girl who is in the front seat of the car
    RAY BRONSON, Julie's former boyfriend and the other backseat
        passenger in the car
    BUD, a Vietnam War veteran who currently dates Julie
    COLLIE, a young man whom Helen meets at her apartment complex

Form and Content

I Know What You Did Last Summer is a somber examination of responsibility and the effects of the Vietnam War on the youth who served in it. Narrative and dialogue are sober in style as each of the four teenagers involved in a hit-and-run accident searches his or her own conscience, examines the effects of the incident on other factors in their lives, and painfully learns the results of group actions. Tension and suspense build to a plot twist and the revelation of the avenger's identity. Red herrings and suspicious characters keep readers guessing, although clues to the avenger's motive and identity are planted throughout the skillfully crafted plot.

Lois Duncan hooks her readers on the first page with a suspenseful opening paragraph that hints of events to follow: "The note was there, lying beside her plate when she came down to breakfast. Later, when she thought back, she would remember it. Small. Plain. Her name and address hand-lettered in stark black print across the front of the envelope." The seriousness of the matter and the setting are established at the outset. The author sets a troubled mood, provides basic information about characters and place in the story, and reveals something about Julie in particular and other characters in general. The plot contains two levels: the personal problem that the main characters must handle and the mystery that must also be solved.

This blend of morality and mystery features believable characters with whom the reader can identify. The teenagers involved may not always be admirable, but they are realistic. The story is told primarily from Julie's perspective. A year has elapsed since the four teenagers driving much too fast hit a young boy on a bicycle and left the scene. Barry convinced his passengers that it would do no good to report the crime. In his words, "Taking the blame won't bring him back. No one will ever know who did it." Although Ray had second thoughts and later reported the accident, it was too late; the boy was dead.

The four have gone their separate ways over the year since the accident, and, as the story opens, Julie finds two envelopes waiting at the breakfast table. The first is a much-anticipated college letter of acceptance, and the second is an anonymous note containing the message "I know what you did last summer." Julie's letter is soon followed by a series of threatening notes and telephone calls to the other three. A few nights later, Barry is lured to the college football field by a mysterious telephone call. He is shot and ends up paralyzed. Helen is also attacked, and she, Julie, and Ray begin to fear that the attacker is bent on killing them all.

In an effort to defend themselves, Julie and Ray join forces to discover the identity of the avenger. They go to the home of the boy who was killed and find only a girl not much older than Julie. She informs the pair that she is the boy's half sister and that her mother is in another town because of a breakdown suffered after the accident.

The story reaches its climax on an evening when Julie and Helen are both attacked by a young man whom Julie has dated as "Bud" and whom Helen has met as "Collie" in her apartment complex. Both are saved, and Julie and Ray realize that they can never erase or undo the accident but that they can face it. The ending of the novel is far from optimistic.

Analysis

This multilayered novel deals with a number of issues. *I Know What You Did Last Summer* can be read purely as an exciting and suspenseful mystery story, but the issues of peer pressure, going along with others instead of acting on one's own, taking responsibility for one's actions, and the long-range effects of the Vietnam War on those who were involved are central to the work as a whole. Loyalty and inaction also play a part. Which is more important, loyalty to friends or to oneself? What are the consequences of inaction?

All four teenagers involved find that a price must be paid for keeping silent about the crime, as do others whose lives are also altered by the accident. The four acted irresponsibly by leaving the scene of the accident, and each has dealt with it in his or her own way. Ray, consumed with guilt, leaves town for a year. Julie, also consumed with guilt, has chosen to erase the incident from her mind. Barry has tried to rationalize his behavior, and Helen agrees to anything in order to keep her dream of marrying Barry alive. None of them is willing to break the self-imposed code of silence. Although the accident was unintentional, the selfishness of Barry and Helen has led all four into lives of guilt and deceit. In addition, the sense of responsibility felt by the boy's mother for the accident affects her sanity and alters the structure of her family.

The novel is set against the backdrop of American family and social life of the early 1970's. Self-centered Helen has the seemingly American dream job of a television "weather girl." Rich, spoiled Barry is a football hero who dates Helen for only two reasons: She is a television personality, and his parents don't like her. Ray is able simply to take off for California. Julie lives with her widowed mother and dreams of going to college at her mother's alma mater. The victim's blended family is no longer a functioning unit. Into this mix steps Bud/Collie, the psychologically disturbed war veteran. His presence forces the four teenagers to look again at the boy's death and the effects that the event has had on their own interpersonal relations. When she meets the boy's family, Julie says that she is sorry she came to the house. It was easier for her when the family was only a name in a newspaper article; now they are real, and she is directly involved with them. Julie and Ray realize the ramifications of the cover-up and confront the logic that enabled them to justify their code of silence.

Duncan propels readers to the conclusion that one's actions are important and one is responsible for them. People must also learn to recognize others for what they are instead of listening to or following undesirable companions. Peer pressure is inevitable, but it is important to stand up for one's own beliefs. The world may not always be kind or fair, but there are many positives to offset the negatives.

Critical Context

Lois Duncan's place in young adult literature is assured. Her books are popular with teenagers and valued increasingly by teachers and librarians. Books dealing with the theme of personal integrity are useful vehicles for classroom discussion. *I Know What You Did Last Summer* is a realistic novel laced with tragedy and one that provides no happy ending for all of its protagonists, which is a departure from traditional upbeat endings for young adult mysteries. Duncan's work following this novel confirms her mastery of the suspense/mystery novel and her continuing interest in responsibility and group loyalty. In *Killing Mr. Griffin* (1978), another blend of morality and mystery, a group of teenagers are involved in a situation that turns unintentionally deadly. The selfishness of two of the group's members leads them all into lives of guilt and lies. Susan is easily swayed when Mark decides to kidnap their English teacher. The teenagers are in the process of performing this act when the teacher has a heart attack and dies.

In 1992, Duncan became the fourth recipient of the Margaret Edwards Award. Sponsored by the American Library Association, the award recognizes writers whose books have given young adults a window that will help them understand themselves and their role in society. The books singled out by the award committee include both *I Know What You Did Last Summer* and *Killing Mr. Griffin*. The award committee cited Duncan's diverse world of individuals: the fortunate, the underprivileged, the weak, the strong, the good, the evil, the impatient, and the submissive.

Duncan's work has been praised by her readers, reviewers, and peers. A number of her novels have been honored by the Mystery Writers of America, *The New York Times*, and the American Library Association. All feature characters who struggle with truth and courage to reach maturity.

Lynn Sager

I REMEMBER MAMA

Author: John van Druten (1901-1957)
First presented: 1944
First published: 1945
Type of work: Drama
Type of plot: Domestic realism, historical fiction, and moral tale
Time of work: 1910
Locale: San Francisco
Subjects: Coming-of-age, emotions, family, and health and illness
Recommended ages: 13-18

Katrin, a young woman in her early twenties, remembers her teenage years in San Francisco and the things that happened in her family that helped her grow up.

> *Principal characters:*
> KATRIN, a young woman in her early twenties
> MARTA (MAMA), her mother
> LARS (PAPA), her father
> DAGMAR, her little sister
> CHRISTINE, her other sister
> NELS, her older brother
> AUNT TRINA, her aunt
> AUNT SIGRID, her aunt
> AUNT JENNY, her aunt
> UNCLE CHRIS, her uncle, Marta's brother

Form and Content

Katrin, who wants to be a writer, remembers growing up in San Francisco in her Norwegian American family. In addition to her father, mother, brother, and sisters, there are a boarder, Mr. Hyde, who reads to the family each night from the classics; Katrin's three aunts, who visit often; and Uncle Chris, who travels and has a reputation for drinking, for his temper, and for living with a woman to whom he is not married.

Katrin's first memory is how the family would sit at the kitchen table every Saturday night and count the money in the "Little Bank," always hoping that they would not have to go to "Big Bank" to get more. Mr. Hyde returns home and reads to the family. The next day, Uncle Chris arrives; he has recently taken Aunt Jenny's boy, Arne, to the hospital for a knee operation, and when he finds that Katrin's sister Dagmar is sick, he takes her to the hospital too. After Dagmar's operation, the hospital will not let Katrin's mother, Marta, in to see her for twenty-four hours, so she pretends that she is cleaning the floors in order to visit Dagmar. Mr. Hyde comes home to say that he must depart immediately, and he gives them a check for his past rent. Aunt Jenny comes in and says that Mr. Hyde has been cashing checks all over the neighborhood and that he does not even have an account. Because Mr. Hyde also left all of his books for the family, Marta insists that he owed them nothing.

As graduation and the school play approach, Katrin tells her friends that she is hoping for a dresser set as a gift. Her sister Christine tells her that instead she is getting her mother's brooch, and Katrin is not happy. Later, as Katrin leaves for the performance, Christine tells her that her mother traded the brooch for the dresser set. Upset, Katrin performs badly in the play and afterward gets the brooch back, gives it to her mother, and apologizes. Her mother gives her the brooch and serves Katrin her first coffee to let her know that she is grown-up.

When Uncle Chris is dying, Marta goes with her sisters to see him. He explains that there is no will and no money. He had always wanted to make Nels a doctor, because he himself was always lame and his one desire was to help others to walk. When he is gone, Marta shares the notebook that shows that all the money went to helping children such as Arne to walk.

In the last scene, when Katrin gets another rejection in the mail, Marta decides to take Katrin's stories to a famous writer visiting San Francisco, because the newspaper says that she is a food lover and Marta has recipes. They trade recipes, and the writer reads five of Katrin's stories. The woman says that Katrin must write about what she knows, so Katrin writes the story of Mama and the hospital and sells it for five hundred dollars. It is revealed that there is no account at the bank, and Katrin reads her story.

Analysis

The primary theme of *I Remember Mama*, since it is seen through Katrin's eyes, is Katrin's process of growing up through these years. She learns the importance of family, not to take money for granted, what selfishness is, dedication to the family, and what it is to be a writer. There is pain for Katrin as she grows up, and the audience feels her pain with her. Although Katrin is not in all the scenes, they are all from her memory and it is her play, and so one can assume that they are all part of her growth and learning experience.

John van Druten's characters are somewhat symbolic of different qualities and values, as family members must always seem to a teenager, at least in memories. Aunt Jenny and Aunt Sigrid are mostly selfish and petty, Aunt Trina is mostly sweet, Mama is always perfect, Papa is always loving and mostly the provider, Christine is brutally honest, Dagmar is mostly young, Nels is always wise, and Uncle Chris is always gruff, at least until Katrin gets to know him better.

One of the themes of this play is the nature of selfishness and unselfishness. In the opening scene, one sees how unselfish the family members are with one another as they all try to figure out a way that Nels can afford to go to high school: Marta offers to forgo her warm coat for a while longer, Nels offers to work in Dillon's grocery after school, Papa offers to give up tobacco, and Christine offers to mind the Maxwell children on Friday nights. With all these sacrifices, the plan works. It seems a selfish thing for Mr. Hyde to give Marta a bad check for his back rent, which it is, but he does leave all of his books, which the audience knows are dear to him and which Marta knows will be important for the children. She responds unselfishly when she burns his check and insists to Aunt Jenny that Mr. Hyde owed them nothing. Nels takes over the nightly reading after Mr. Hyde is gone. Katrin acts selfishly when she makes it clear that she must have the pink celluloid dresser set as a graduation present. It is because Christine cannot stand the selfish way in which Katrin is acting that she tells her that Mama traded her family heirloom brooch that she was going to give Katrin so that she could give her the dresser set. When Katrin realizes how selfish she has been, she performs badly in her senior play, arranges to trade back the dresser set for the brooch, and returns the brooch to her mother. Uncle Chris has a reputation of thinking only of himself. Aunt Jenny says that boxes of oranges are the only things that he ever gives away and that he spends all his money on drink and on the woman with whom he lives. The family later finds out that Uncle Chris is completely unselfish, however, when they discover that he has given all of his money over the years to pay for operations to help children walk. His kindness and unselfishness is reflected in Dagmar's great care for animals. She cares greatly for Uncle Elizabeth, her male cat that she thought was a female, and over the course of the play acquires a dog and rabbits, asks if she can have a horse, and decides that if Nels is going to be a doctor, she will be a veterinarian.

Katrin learns about the importance of writing what one knows. In the past, she has written stories about things that she has read about, such as the painter who becomes blind and tragically cannot paint anymore, but then regains his sight and paints better than before. She assumes that her own life and family are not interesting enough to use as material. After the visiting writer reiterates what Katrin's own teacher has always said, that she needs to write about what she knows, she realizes that her own family is interesting and wonderful. She writes about her mother finding a way to see Dagmar in the hospital and is successful.

Critical Context

I Remember Mama is based on a collection of stories by Kathryn Forbes called *Mama's Bank Account* (1943). John van Druten's play opened on Broadway at the Music Box Theatre on October 19, 1944. It was staged realistically, by the author, with three turntables allowing for changing of scenes. It received unanimous praise from critics and was so well attended that it ran until June 29, 1946, for a total of 713 performances. Several critics mentioned that the adaptation from stories made it episodic and unconventional as a play, that the focus was on the characters, and that there was no actual plot in the usual sense, but that the play nevertheless worked wonderfully and made an excellent and heartwarming evening of theater. They also mentioned that its popularity made it a financial success, which was especially exciting for van Druten because another of his plays, *The Voice of the Turtle*, was a success at the theater next door.

Although it was not written for young audiences, the play may be popular with them because of its focus on Katrin and her brother and sisters, and because the challenges that she faces as she grows up are so familiar to young people.

Luther Hanson

I WILL CALL IT GEORGIE'S BLUES

Author: Suzanne Newton (1936-   )
First published: 1983
Type of work: Novel
Type of plot: Social realism
Time of work: The early 1980's
Locale: Gideon, North Carolina
Subjects: Coming-of-age, family, and friendship
Recommended ages: 13-18

Neal relies on his secret love of jazz piano as a way of coping with the oppressive life within his dysfunctional family, but he learns that his younger brother, Georgie, has no way of dealing with their overbearing father.

> *Principal characters:*
> NEAL SLOANE, a fifteen-year-old minister's son who conceals his developing piano talent from his father and others
> GEORGIE SLOANE, Neal's younger brother, who is developing psychological problems
> MRS. TALBOT, Neal's piano teacher and confidante
> RICHARD E. SLOANE, Neal's overbearing father, a minister who worries more about his public image than about his family
> MRS. SLOANE, Neal's mother, who is torn between caring for her children and fulfilling her role as a minister's wife
> AILEEN SLOANE, Neal's rebellious sister
> PETE CAUTHIN, Aileen's nineteen-year-old boyfriend and Neal's nemesis

Form and Content

I Will Call It Georgie's Blues is an insightful study of adolescent life within a family in denial of reality. Reverend Sloane is concerned with maintaining the façade of a perfect family, and his efforts toward this perfection have damaging effects on his children.

Aileen dates Pete Cauthin, a nineteen-year-old still trying to graduate, and she is in danger of failing English even though that would mean more time at home when college could provide an escape. The younger, frightened Georgie is in danger of losing his grip on reality altogether. Neal is usually calmer in dealing with his father, although, at fifteen, he is growing less tolerant of his father's overbearing methods. It is ironic that Neal is as tenacious at concealment as his father. As the novel opens, Neal's two-year source of solace with "Mrs. T," his piano teacher, is threatened. He has kept his music lessons a secret from his family and the townspeople, but his visits to his teacher's home are beginning to raise questions.

While seeking access to Mrs. T and to the jazz that is his deliverance, Neal is swept into a swirling turmoil that is beyond his control. The earliest hints of this situation develop when he learns that Georgie has made a secret, on-credit purchase from grocer Mr. Bailey, a fact that Neal helps him conceal. He soon forgets about the incident as his mother tries to limit his visits to Mrs. T., and Mrs. T suggests that he reevaluate the secrecy and nature of his time with her.

Tension builds within the family as Reverend Sloane wrangles with Aileen. Neal inwardly applauds her defiance and begins to take stands against his father as well, such as refusing to mow the churchyard for free.

It is while he is on a secret approach to Mrs. T's that Neal encounters Pete, who offers him a boat ride. As they ride, Pete makes lascivious remarks about Mrs. T, prompting a fight with Georgie. This incident wrecks the boat and heightens animosity between the boys, while also damaging notes for a musical composition on which Neal has been working.

When Mrs. T discovers the soaked Neal at her door, she takes him in but warns him that the secrecy of his music lessons is creating a bad appearance for her. She reminds him that he cannot keep his love of music secret forever if he wants to be a jazz performer, and she contends that it is much easier to live an honest life. Honesty, Neal says, is something he knows nothing about because he has never had an example. As he contemplates this conversation, Neal decides that his mother must have spoken to Mrs. T. He confronts her but discovers that he is wrong, and his mother concedes that she may have been wrong in her decision about his visits.

Neal becomes more aware of Georgie's problems one Sunday after they visit Georgie's friend Captain, an elderly man who lives on a boat. Georgie tells how safe he feels with Captain and how frightened he feels at home. Georgie fears that the Sloanes have been replaced by "false" people who only look like his family members.

Neal discusses this discovery with his mother, with whom he is actually beginning to communicate again. She explains her concerns about Georgie's mental health, but she does not know how to broach the topic with her husband. Reverend Sloane interrupts the conversation to berate Neal about the mowing issue, but eventually Neal is heartened by the fact that the "mutiny" against his father seems to be spreading to his mother.

That satisfaction is short-lived. Neal is discovered playing jazz in the church by Mr. Mac, but tensions in the Sloane family soon worsen as a result of a different matter. Reverend Sloane learns that someone has been spreading rumors that he has family problems and that he is about to lose his job. When he is called to the principal's office because Neal and Pete have had a fight, he reveals his worsening paranoia.

That paranoia peaks when he learns from Mr. Bailey that Georgie is the source of the rumors. Neal defends Georgie against Reverend Sloane's verbal abuse, and at last his father admits a need for counseling. Before they can seek that help, however, Georgie disappears. His purchases at the grocery were canned goods in anticipation of an escape. After a frantic search, he is found and taken to a nearby clinic for help.

The events bring about a catharsis for Neal, who goes into the church and begins to play the composition on which he has been working, a piece that he has decided to title "Georgie's Blues." He continues to play even as Mr. Mac and other townspeople discover him. Neal is at last ready to reveal his secrets, just as the family secrets have at last been exposed.

Analysis

While *I Will Call It Georgie's Blues* deals with a severely dysfunctional family, it is a significant book for all young people in its examination of the communication problems between youths and adults. The battle of secrecy versus honesty is at the book's core, and the dangers and difficulties of creating a façade are illustrated by the action of the plot.

The themes of secrecy and honesty are defined by three characters: Reverend Sloane, Neal, and Georgie. Reverend Sloane is so concerned with the unrealistic façade of perfection that truth has become something alien to him. When rumors of family troubles arise, he never stops to realize that the rumors are partially true.

Oppressed by his father but also his own fear of how his love of music will be received, Neal maintains his secret as his public image slowly crumbles. He has reached a point at which he can no longer act as the perfect preacher's son who never gets into trouble. Despite his own secrecy, however, he despises his father's façade and realizes its damaging effects.

While he is the character most removed from reality, Georgie is also the one who sees things clearly. While his interpretation of it seems delusional, Georgie is aware of his family's falsity. It is his exposure of the truth as much as his inability to cope with his father's harshness that brings the Sloane family much needed change and that frees Neal of his self-imposed restrictions. When Neal plays "Georgie's Blues," he is unleashing at last a song of truth.

Neal Sloane is a hero with whom many young readers will identify. He suffers the awkwardness of feeling out of place and is preparing to embark on a course that he fears will be misunderstood, despite reassurances from his mentor, Mrs. T.

While it deals with grim subjects, the novel is ultimately an illustration of spiritual triumph in the face of dark conditions.

Critical Context

I Will Call It Georgie's Blues, Suzanne Newton's sixth book, has been praised for its blend of teenage reality and humor. It has also drawn acclaim for its depiction of the strong central character, who, like the central figures in *M. W. Sexton Speaking* (1983) and *Care of Arnold's Corners* (1974), must wrangle with adult authority figures. *I Will Call It Georgie's Blues* received numerous awards in its year of publication. Newton's subsequent books have included *An End to Perfect* (1984) and *A Place Between* (1986).

Sidney Glover Williams

IF BEALE STREET COULD TALK

Author: James Baldwin (1924-1987)
First published: 1974
Type of work: Novel
Type of plot: Social realism
Time of work: The mid-1960's
Locale: New York City
Subjects: Family, love and romance, politics and law, race and ethnicity, and social issues
Recommended ages: 15-18

A black sculptor is unjustly imprisoned on a rape charge, and his pregnant girlfriend and her family struggle against the criminal justice system to free him.

Principal characters:
ALONZO (FONNY) HUNT, a twenty-two-year-old black sculptor jailed on the charge that he raped a Puerto Rican woman
CLEMENTINE (TISH) RIVERS, the nineteen-year-old woman, pregnant with Fonny's child, who loyally works to overcome the obstacles to Fonny's freedom
JOE RIVERS, Tish's father, who supports the plans of Fonny and Tish to marry, looks forward to the birth of the child, and works to raise cash to free Fonny
SHARON RIVERS, Tish's mother, who encourages the marriage, loves the baby that is to be born, and tries to persuade the rape victim that she has identified the wrong person
FRANK HUNT, Fonny's father, who loves his son and struggles to raise cash to free him
MRS. HUNT, Fonny's mother, a devout Christian who scorns Fonny and takes no action to help him or the family that forms around him
VICTORIA ROGERS, the Puerto Rican rape victim who identifies Fonny as the perpetrator
OFFICER BELL, the racist police officer who bears a grudge against Fonny and corroborates the charge against him
HAYWARD, the lawyer representing Fonny
ERNESTINE RIVERS, Tish's sister, whose persistence and resourcefulness help to win Fonny's freedom

Form and Content

If Beale Street Could Talk reveals the struggle between the forces of love and senselessness. The personal love between Fonny and Tish, as well as the family love that forms around the couple and the child that is on the way, is in conflict with the senseless scorn of Fonny's mother and the senseless malice of the criminal justice system. Set in New York, the novel is an exploration of a childhood relationship that grows into mature love, but James Baldwin's work is also a fierce indictment of hypocrisy in religion and racism in law enforcement. Love triumphs in *If Beale Street Could Talk*, but the price of that triumph is high, and the determination of the characters to pay the price demonstrates their heroism.

The narrative of this compact novel is framed by the final six months of Tish's pregnancy, a period that coincides with the struggle to get Fonny out of jail. Baldwin's work is divided into two books, the first much longer than the second. The first part begins with Fonny already in jail and Tish already in her third month of pregnancy, but Baldwin's use of flashbacks enables him to provide extensive background and end the first book with the arrest of Fonny. The second book begins with Fonny's dream of freedom and ends with the fulfillment of that dream.

The story is told by Tish, whose moving and disturbing flashbacks recount the development of the relationship between her and Fonny, as well as the stories behind the marriages of their parents and the circumstances leading to Fonny's arrest. Her connection to Fonny goes back to her childhood and reveals the depth of her intimacy with him. Tish recalls from their childhood her scratching of Fonny's forehead and Fonny's retaliatory spitting in her face. Tish remembers her first date with Fonny—a trip to church supervised by Fonny's mother—and she vividly remembers her loss of virginity with him.

From Tish, the reader learns of the sexuality of Fonny's parents, whose relationship is a collision between Christianity and crude desire. From Tish, the reader also learns about the marriage of her own parents: the sudden wedding of Joe, a porter in a bus station, with Sharon, an abandoned singer. From Tish, the reader learns that Fonny's arrest, which follows an incident involving a stranger's gross sexual advances on Tish in a fruit market and Fonny's violent reaction, stems from the hard feelings of the police officer who intervenes. Officer Bell wants to take Fonny to the police station, perhaps to beat him up, but the owner of the store, who is a witness to the sexual attack against Tish, supports Fonny and Tish, leaving Bell shamefaced and bitter. Later, when Bell has the opportunity, he pins a rape charge on Fonny.

Tish's announcement of her pregnancy occasions the gathering of the Rivers and Hunt families, but instead of producing cooperation, the meeting degenerates into a bitter, vulgar argument. While Fonny's father remains loyal to his son and joins Joe, Sharon, and Ernestine Rivers in their support of Tish and Fonny, Mrs. Hunt and her two daughters reject and dismiss Fonny.

Suspense runs high through the first one hundred pages of the novel because the reader does not know the charge against Fonny; when the accusation of rape is clarified, the suspense intensifies further as the challenge of disproving the charge must be met. Joe Rivers and Frank Hunt dedicate themselves to raising funds for Fonny's legal expenses, working extra hours and stealing materials from their jobs. Tish considers prostituting herself to raise funds. Sharon travels to Puerto Rico to seek out the victim, Victoria Rogers, and persuade her to reconsider her identification of

Fonny; after the two women meet, however, anguish overcomes Mrs. Rogers, and she disappears into the mountains. With the district attorney's case weakened by the loss of this key witness, Hayward, Fonny's lawyer, succeeds in arranging bail, and Ernestine acquires sufficient money from an actress whom she knows in order to supplement the family's holdings and make the necessary payment. Unfortunately, before Fonny is released, Frank's despair about the difficulty in getting Fonny out of jail and the discovery of his thefts at work overcomes him, and he commits suicide. Fonny emerges from jail in time for the birth of his child, but he is a transformed person, forever affected by the horror of his experience in jail.

Analysis

If Beale Street Could Talk appeals to young adult readers because the two figures at the center of the novel's conflict are themselves young adults. The struggle of Fonny and Tish is opposed by Fonny's mother on the one hand, yet supported by Fonny's father and Tish's family on the other. These vexing circumstances involving family ties engage young readers. In addition, the love story, particularly the innocence of Tish and the tenderness of Fonny, capture the emotions of readers who are learning about love and sexuality.

Baldwin's story explores social issues, including problems related to poverty, racism, housing, criminal justice, and religion, but a central question for the narrator is whether things in the world make sense. Does it make sense for a woman who emphasizes Christianity in her life to scorn her son in his time of greatest need? Does it make sense that a boy awakened to Christianity in a church should end up dead of a drug overdose? Does it make sense that schools are run to make sure that students do not become smart? Does it make sense that the most beautiful person in a young woman's life is a scruffy young man in old clothes? Does it make sense that a proud, perceptive, and dedicated artist must bear up against a society intensely pressing against him, demanding that he break? At the start of the novel, Tish admits, "I'm beginning to think that maybe everything that happens makes sense. Like, if it didn't make sense, how could it happen? But that's really a terrible thought. It can only come out of trouble—trouble that doesn't make sense." In the end, Tish and the reader are forced to consider the conclusion that life in America does not make sense but that love, achieved despite a series of agonizing sacrifices, can counterbalance senselessness.

Critical Context

When *If Beale Street Could Talk* was published, it held a place on the best-seller list for seven weeks. Reviews of the novel were mixed, with some readers finding the work to be powerfully realistic and dramatically convincing, but with others finding it to be either sentimental or bitter.

If Beale Street Could Talk brings to mind other works by James Baldwin: the treatment of family life and church affiliation raised in *Go Tell It on the Mountain* (1953); the accessible, fast-paced style of *Giovanni's Room* (1956); and the quest for sexual and artistic satisfaction in *Another Country* (1962). In addition, the rich references of these works to hymns and the blues recur in *If Beale Street Could Talk*, but there are also references to contemporary music by Aretha Franklin, Marvin Gaye, and others. Baldwin, perhaps in response to criticism that he is not sufficiently aggressive on racial issues, has *If Beale Street Could Talk* feature some of the rage embodied in the play *Blues for Mister Charlie* (1964); in particular, the rage of Frank Hunt is expressed in powerful black idiom, which contrasts sharply with the measured eloquence of the essay *The Fire Next Time* (1963).

Baldwin's prolific output of outstanding works may lead some educators to overlook *If Beale Street Could Talk*, but those who select the work for classroom use will discover that the novel is a lively, accessible, and stimulating one for young adult readers.

William T. Lawlor

IF I ASKED YOU, WOULD YOU STAY?

Author: Eve Bunting (1928-   )
First published: 1984
Type of work: Novel
Type of plot: Social realism
Time of work: The 1980's
Locale: California
Subjects: Coming-of-age, emotions, family, friendship, and social issues
Recommended ages: 13-15

When Crow, an adolescent loner living on his own, rescues a young girl from her attempted suicide, their chance meeting expands and alters both of their lives.

Principal characters:
 CROW, an adolescent who leaves his amicable foster home to live a
  relatively uncomplicated life until he rescues Valentine from the
  raging ocean
 VALENTINE, a young girl who sees her life as having no options

Form and Content

If I Asked You, Would You Stay? is a simple book dealing with complicated issues. It gently confronts the issue of adolescents who are forced, by the circumstances in their lives, to live without the security of a strong, supportive family as they grapple with emotional growth and evolving relationships. This story, although set in California with characters who have left their homes, deals with issues that all adolescents confront as they forge their own lives and identities. The desire to break free of the constraints imposed by adults and declare independence carries heavy burdens, which Eve Bunting expertly and covertly depicts.

The story in this direct and captivating novel is elegantly simple in its presentation while dealing with intricate issues. Charles Robert O'Neill—known as Crow—is a gentle seventeen-year-old who has spent all of his life shunted from one foster home to another. Crow leaves the home of kindly Mrs. Simon and his foster brother Danny. He wants to live unencumbered, without attachments to anyone. He chooses to live a private existence, letting no one know where he lives. He works, fends for himself, lets his foster mother know that he is well, and survives relatively well in a secret room above an old carousel on a pier. This secret place belongs to Sasha, a character whom the reader knows of only through Crow and his thoughts. He wants to save money so that he, like his namesake, will always be free. Crow's life is indeed uncomplicated. He goes to work and lives a peaceful, secretive existence.

Crow's tranquillity is shaken when he looks out his window and sees someone struggling in the ocean. He races out into the cold ocean, drags the swimmer onto a dinghy, and carries the swimmer to his room. Once there, Crow learns that the person he rescued is a young, desperate girl named Valentine, who wants to end her life. Valentine is neither pretty nor nice. Her entrance into his solitary, secretive world turns both of their lives upside down.

Crow, valuing his privacy, looks forward to Valentine's departure, but she is determined to stay for two or three days. Although he is annoyed that she is there, her promise to leave in a few days pleases Crow, who values his solitude and freedom from entanglements with others. He goes off to work and realizes that his life savings, his independence money, which he kept hidden in his room, could easily be found by Valentine. He rushes home and finds his money still there, but the loss of his private space still troubles him. Crow continually thinks of Sasha, whose room he is sharing. Although Sasha is not physically there, her presence is felt; Crow is careful about protecting her property and her rights. In his thoughts, he thanks Sasha for allowing him to share her space, while silently confirming that Valentine will be gone soon.

During the course of the novel, the layers of their troubled existences are unfolded as Crow and Valentine slowly learn each other's secrets. Crow's relationship to Sasha, as well as to his foster brother, unfolds. Crow often thinks of Sasha, a beautiful, serene, and secure woman, and also of Danny, his young and confused foster brother. Valentine's fears revolve around both her family and a person named Marty. In the few short days that they are together, Crow slowly learns of the reasons for Valentine's desperation.

Analysis

If I Asked You, Would You Stay? is a fine example of contemporary realistic fiction. In this brief novel, the principal characters, singly and together, confront a wide range of emotional issues as they each forge their own roads toward peace, serenity, and maturity. The subthemes of the novel—loss, alienation, fear, dreams, and the desire for independence—are themes that are prevalent among the young adolescents who are the readers of this book. This novel of emotional growth and trust is about people, not problems. The content and the characters are presented honestly and simply. The reader learns about the characters as they learn about each other. Details unfold gradually, leaving readers room to ponder details and draw inferences and conclusions. Bunting sensitively portrays the plight of these two adolescents as they deal with some of the problems and issues that unfortunately confront many adolescents.

This novel explores the characters' attempts to overcome problems that arise from external forces and physical or emotional desertion. It allows readers to explore closely the impact of these forces on the lives of characters and in turn on the lives of the readers themselves. Adolescents often fantasize about leaving their home and forging their own lives, independent of the scrutiny of adults. Bunting provides readers a window through which to view that fantasy.

The main characters of Crow and Valentine are, on the surface, like people whom the readers already know. They both seek escape and refuge—he from ties, she from fear and unhappiness. He creates a life for himself, while she considers death. Through a singular event, these two young people, confronting different conflicts, meet and expand each other's worldview. Readers learn about them through their actions and thoughts. The characters are well-developed, credible, and authentic, and they show gradual development as the story progresses. As these complex characters grapple with their adolescent hopes and fears, readers see Crow and Valentine undergo dynamic changes. Bunting's adept writing style enables readers to understand how and why these protagonists change.

The plot revolves around the characters, their problems, and the resolution to these problems. The plot structure is straightforward and readily understandable, and the plot is enhanced through the author's effective literary style. Descriptions of the multidimensional characters and the setting are vivid and believable. On the surface, Crow and Valentine could be anyone whom the reader knows. Adolescents often keep their inner thoughts and feelings to themselves, and it often is only through extraordinary circumstances that these emotions are revealed. As the story progresses, each character's complex situation is unfolded in a sensitive manner. Crow has made a life for himself, devoid of ties; Valentine seeks to sever ties. Like the adolescent reader, Crow and Valentine are on a quest for definition in their lives. Readers can envision multiple solutions to the problems of the characters. Although it is well grounded in the story, the final resolution may surprise readers who have come to expect more typical endings.

This is an important novel for adolescents. The feelings and conflicts within Crow and Valentine as they struggle toward independence ring true. They attempt to take charge of their own lives as they struggle with conflicting internal and external loyalties. The themes of loss, alienation, and fear are expertly depicted. Bunting offers readers the safe harbor of a fictional world in which they can try on various roles and identities as they live vicariously through and grapple with these issues.

Contemporary realistic fiction such as *If I Asked You, Would You Stay?* provides readers with windows through which to view life. Good realistic fiction treats characters and their problems candidly and respectfully, and the problems of adolescents in modern times provide clear justification for this genre. Adolescents enjoy reading about people with whom they can identify. Bunting, in this novel as well as in her many other fine works, evidences a clear understanding of her characters and of society.

Critical Context

Through realistic fiction, readers can identify with characters, try on different roles and identities, and live in a vicarious world. This world may include adventures and experiences that readers ponder but never actually experience. This important genre allows readers to see that their lives and problems are not unique. Through books, young people can become responsible decision makers. Through her rich characterizations and a smooth writing style, Eve Bunting has the power to transport readers into another person's thought and feelings.

Through her young adult novels and picture books, Bunting relentlessly confronts social issues. Keen understanding and compassion permeate her more than 150 books.

Whether dealing with deep subjects such as the death of a friend in *The Empty Window* (1980), urban violence in *Smoky Night* (1994), and the Holocaust in *Terrible Things* (1980), or with lighter adventures, such as quests and ghost stories, Eve Bunting is the consummate storyteller. Her books will endure and leave a profound mark on society and the literary world.

Carole S. Rhodes

IN COUNTRY

Author: Bobbie Ann Mason (1940-   )
First published: 1985
Type of work: Novel
Type of plot: Domestic realism
Time of work: 1984
Locale: Hopewell, Kentucky, and Washington, D.C.
Subjects: Coming-of-age and war
Recommended ages: 15-18

During the summer after her graduation from high school, Sam Hughes attempts to learn about her father, who died in the Vietnam War before she was born, and tries to help her uncle, who returned from the war with psychological scars.

> *Principal characters:*
> SAMANTHA (SAM) HUGHES, a young woman who is trying to understand her relationship to a father she never knew in an effort to understand herself and her future
> EMMETT, Sam's uncle, who returned from Vietnam scarred psychologically and perhaps damaged by Agent Orange
> IRENE, Sam's mother, who has remarried and begun a new life in Lexington, Kentucky
> MAMAW HUGHES, Sam's paternal grandmother, who seems to hold a key to her father's identity
> DAWN, Sam's friend, who is pregnant and planning marriage

Form and Content

Bobbie Ann Mason's *In Country* examines a few significant weeks in the life of Sam Hughes during the summer after her high school graduation. Irene, her mother was widowed when Sam's father died in Vietnam only a few months after their marriage, but now she has remarried and moved to Lexington. Sam has elected to spend her last year of high school in her old home, living with her mother's brother, Emmett. The two seem more like brother and· sister than uncle and niece, partly because his role in the Vietnam War has left Emmett in a sort of extended adolescence, unable to decide what to do with his life. In fact, Sam seems the more mature of the two, even though at the time of the novel she too is uncertain where her life will take her. She thinks she might want to go to college, but she is not certain. She wonders about her future with her boyfriend Lonnie. She also longs to help Emmett cope with his problems, both physical and mental. Most of all, Sam wonders about the father she never knew and the war that took him from her; she senses that, in knowing him, she will somehow come to know herself. The novel becomes the story of Sam's quest during these few weeks in the summer of 1984.

The novel opens with Sam, Emmett, and Mamaw (Sam's grandmother) on the road to Washington, D.C., in Sam's decrepit Volkswagen. She bought it used a few weeks before, but now they have had to stop in Maryland to have its failing clutch repaired. The center section of the novel describes the events that brought Sam to this point.

One of those events is the announcement by Sam's friend Dawn that she may be pregnant and expects to marry her boyfriend, a future that Sam realizes she does not want for herself. Another more ambiguous event is a dance held by the local group of Vietnam veterans, which Sam attends with Tom, a friend of Emmett. Later that night, Tom tells Sam that his inability to make love is the psychological result of his experiences during the war. During the same dance, Emmett disappears and remains missing for several days, frightening Sam, who knows how vulnerable he is. In another event, Sam finds and reads her father's letters from Vietnam and learns that he chose her name, Samantha. Her grandmother also gives Sam her father's diary. Reading it, Sam confronts the wartime bloodshed in which her father (and presumably Emmett) participated. The pain of that realization makes her go "in country" by hiding out at Cawood's Pond, a place rumored to be full of snakes. After her first night there, Emmett finds Sam, and they quarrel bitterly about whether she can ever understand the effects of the war on the men who fought in it.

After this confrontation, Sam and Emmett collect Mamaw and set out for the Vietnam Veterans Memorial, where each seems to experience a healing moment of epiphany.

Analysis

A critical part of coming-of-age lies in the problem of self-knowledge, a problem that is particularly difficult for Sam Hughes because she is so detached from the elements of family that give most people their sense of identity. Sam never knew her father, and although she and her mother maintain a friendly relationship, her mother's remarriage and new baby effectively remove her from Sam's resources. Irene is vague about Sam's father when asked questions about him; she is even uncertain about where his old letters may be. Irene's parents, who also live in Hopewell, are not much more help. They live in a sterile world of small-town consumerism, a world that Sam has already come to mistrust.

In fact, most of the people who inhabit Sam's world are similarly rootless. Emmett floats aimlessly from the television to minor household jobs to alcoholic binges. He and Sam share a deep affection, and as a veteran he has experienced the most potent link to Sam's father that she can imagine. Crippled psychologically and perhaps physically by the war, however, Emmett is more in need of help from Sam than he is able to offer help to her. He has trouble connecting even with his girlfriend Anita, who shares Sam's concern for him. The other minor characters in the novel are equally unhelpful. Sam's friend Dawn is unable to share Sam's urgent sense that she has important things to learn about herself and life; Dawn has been happy working at the Burger Boy, just as she expects to be happy to marry her high school boyfriend and have his baby. Sam's boyfriend Lonnie is similarly limited. Even Sam's grandparents seem unable to tell her anything more than random snippets about her father; she suspects that they have never even read the diary they hand over to her. Still, she knows that they represent her closest contact to the dead man whom she longs to understand.

Two other elements of Sam's world deserve mention. One is the constant presence of Hopewell's community of Vietnam veterans. Their various troubles flicker through everyone's conversation across the novel—their illnesses (many of which seem related to chemicals of war), their marital crises, their job difficulties. At the same time that Sam is trying to understand what happened to her father and what has happened to Emmett, she is surrounded by men who seem to exemplify the varieties of damage that war can inflict. Another war also dominates Sam's imagination: the television series *M*A*S*H*, set in Korea but obviously developed as a network response to the growing distaste of Americans for the war in Vietnam. Sam and Emmett watch the series in syndication every night after dinner, and Sam frequently compares events in her real world to episodes from the series.

Sam seeks a picture of her father from his letters and diaries and in reports about the war from people such as Emmett. Yet, what she finds seems disappointing and as elusive as the white egret that is Emmett's symbol of the unattainable. Her father's letters are the shallow writings of a young man; his diaries suggest his inability to think very deeply about the people whom he is fighting to defend. What drives Sam to retreat to Cawood's pond, then, is her sense of helplessness to know her father in any way that she can find acceptable. What Emmett makes her understand when he comes to rescue her is the impossibility of her search. She can never know the dead past. She can never know what it meant to fight in that far-off country and time. What she discovers in seeing her father's name on the wall of the Vietnam Veterans Memorial is the only way left for her to touch him: As she looks around, she identifies with all the others who have made the same journey and for the same reason that she has.

Critical Context

Most war novels attempt to describe the experiences of war, and, perhaps significantly, few novels have attempted description of the Vietnam conflict. Most successful works, such as Tim O'Brien's *Going After Cacciato* (1978), have been aimed at adult audiences. The achievement of *In Country* lies in its intention to make that conflict accessible to young people, not primarily by describing warfare itself but by addressing themes of self-discovery that are particularly relevant to youth. Surprisingly, the novel's protagonist is a young woman. Bobbie Ann Mason is skilled at representing the everyday world all people recognize; here, as in the short fiction of *Shiloh and Other Stories* (1982), she interweaves details of television shows, popular music, and advertising with Sam's efforts to understand herself and her relationship to the man who died fighting in a war that seems more remote than the Korean War she has watched so often on *M*A*S*H*.

This interweaving of the themes of the Vietnam War and of coming-of-age allows the reader entrance into a painful period in history, a period that Mason does nothing to prettify and a period that, like Sam's father, holds a key to the United States' understanding of itself as a nation.

Ann Davison Garbett

IN THE BEGINNING
Creation Stories from Around the World

Author: Virginia Hamilton (1936-   )
First published: 1988; illustrated
Type of work: Short fiction
Subjects: Nature and religion
Recommended ages: 13-18

This anthology of twenty-five Creation stories from oral traditions, retold by the author, presents a variety of cultural interpretations about the origins of the earth and its people, the relationships between humans and gods, and the nature of good and evil.

Form and Content

In this Newbery Honor Book, Virginia Hamilton retells Creation stories from the oral traditions of cultures around the globe. Each story is about three-to-five pages long, with watercolor illustrations by Barry Moser on each facing page and usually within the text as well. At the end of each story, Hamilton includes a commentary explaining the source of the story, special thematic or narrative qualities, and its cultural context. She also includes a brief introductory "Note from the Author" explaining what Creation stories are and an afterword entitled "More About These Myths" in which she elaborates on the common features of the stories. *In the Beginning* concludes with a list of "Useful Sources," a bibliography of some fifty items. Because of the simple layout and vivid, bright illustrations, the book is intellectually accessible and visually inviting to readers from adolescence onward.

Despite their variety in plot and origin, these Creation stories illustrate the common effort of early societies to explain the great questions of existence. All address universal human concerns about how life began, the relationship between humans and the gods, and the causes of suffering, evil, and death. The stories also address other fundamental questions, such as the relationship and sometimes the conflict between men and women, between humans and animals, and between the gods. The book includes familiar stories from the Western tradition, such as the Greek stories of Pandora, who opened a forbidden box and released despair and misery into the world; Prometheus, who gave fire to humans; and the Hebrew stories of Adam and Eve ("First Man, First Woman") and the Creation story from the Book of Genesis ("Let There Be Light"). *In the Beginning* also includes many lesser-known myths as well, such as "Phan Ku," a Chinese story of a giant born from the nothing that was and whose body eventually became the world; the Nigerian story of "Olorun the Creator," who had the earth made so that he could send people there from heaven; and, from northeastern India, the story of "Sedi and Melo the Creators," woman (the earth) and man (the sky) whose marriage threatened all those who lived between them.

Analysis

Collectively, these stories include points of amazing similarity, underscoring the universality of human interpretation, imagination, and concern. Many stories, for example, claim that in the beginning there was only light, or darkness, or an ocean; others begin with a god who becomes the world or begets the world and its creatures. In her afterward, Hamilton offers some loose categories. For example, she identifies earth diver stories, in which a creature swims down through the water to find dirt from which to make the earth; cosmic egg stories, in which a god emerges and begins the Creation; world-parent stories, in which all creation comes from a mother-seed, or stone; and stories that tell of a time before earth and sky were separate or before the earth was solid. Many depict forces of life opposing those of death or depict a world in constant tension between conflicting gods. These similarities will not be lost on younger readers and probably would help them begin to grasp and synthesize ideas, as they note comparisons and points of contrasts. Some stories reflect a pessimistic view of the elements and gods, perhaps suggesting the challenge of survival; others are more lighthearted.

Individually, these stories offer glimpses into the minds of earlier peoples in specific places around the globe as they tried to make sense of abstract concerns with only the physical world and their own imaginations, experience, and knowledge of human nature to provide answers. The stories illustrate the limits and resources of that experience, and many describe the landscape from which they came. In the Icelandic saga, the source of the gods and Earth is Imir, an evil frost giant. In a story from the Marshall Islands in the Pacific Ocean, in the beginning there was only the ocean, and a god took the islands out of his basket and placed them in the sea; when he let one island slip out if his hand, it landed out of line with the others, and so remains.

Although grand in scope, the stories of *In the Beginning* describe very human characteristics and thus make compelling and engaging reading simply at the level of narrative. Gods often reflect the jealousy, cruelty, and pride of human beings, and so the world suffers from their weaknesses. In the story from the Kono people of Guinea, Sa, or Death, angered that the God Alatangana took one of Sa's daughters as his wife without Sa's consent, punished them by determining that their children would be of different races and speak different languages so that they would not understand one another. Ti-i, the first man in a Tahitian myth, was evil and "liked to see others suffer," so he cast a spell over the world through a white heron; peace changed to unhappiness, unease, and war. Ti-i's wife, Hina, "full of good," helped save the world from destruction. Prometheus' compassion led him to give wisdom and fire to humans, making them greater than animals, but in doing so defied Zeus, who took revenge by creating Pandora.

Equally human qualities of humor and cleverness are illustrated as well. In "Wulbari the Creator," from the Krachi people of Togo, Wulbari was heaven and hovered only five feet above the earth; the people below him kept bumping into him, so Wulbari had to move higher in the sky to give them room. Ananse the spider later tricks Wulbari and in doing so creates darkness, the moon, stars, and the sun. While describing fundamental understandings of the nature of life, these stories, through Hamilton's careful retelling, remain intimate, clear, and intensely familiar; myth and religion become matters of storytelling, of people relating the experience of being human.

Critical Context

Virginia Hamilton is a prolific and widely read author of children's books, with works ranging from realistic and historical fiction to mystery, fantasy, and folktales. *In the Beginning* is one of her books of retold tales for which she has won numerous awards, including *The People Could Fly: American Black Folktales* (1985) and *The Dark Way: Stories of the Spirit World* (1990). The tug of tradition and the importance of recognizing one's relationship with a cultural past are noted as frequent themes in many of her books. In *The Time-Ago Tales of Jahdu* (1969), *Time-Ago Lost: More Tales of Jahdu* (1973), and *The All Jahdu Storybook* (1991), Hamilton uses realism, fantasy, allegory, and folktale to illustrate the link between a contemporary boy and the past. Her novel *The House of Dies Drear* (1968), one of her most successful works, combines realism and mystery with the history of the Underground Railroad. Although highly readable and engaging, Hamilton's books challenge readers to think about their identity and their role in their families and encourage them to see themselves as part as a larger cultural community. *In the Beginning* extends that invitation to understand, accept, and embrace the great human effort to create stories that will make sense of the world.

Retelling and presenting twenty-five Creation myths and packaging them to suggest some kind of unity is a daunting task, yet the author succeeds by relying on simplicity and by letting each story, or perhaps culture, speak for itself. Hamilton does not simplify or censor the stories to make them more familiar, or even arrange them in any order that might suggest familiarity and a hierarchy or line of development. Each story stands alone, neither sentimental nor ominous, but instead dignified, vital, and, most important, human. Hamilton handles the language carefully and intimately, giving each story a tone and color of its own. The book's illustrations contribute to this sense of each story having its own identity, and Moser's paintings share and underscore the quiet vibrancy of Hamilton's language. His portraits of Raven, man, and woman in the Eskimo story "Raven the Creator" suggest humor, elegance, and strength of character. His depiction of gods playing in the water-marsh in "Olorun the Creator" is a fanciful yet ghostly image of dancers, legs bent and arms outstretched— an almost touching depiction of gods in human forms.

Through good storytelling, commentary, illustration, and bibliography, *In the Beginning* provides entertaining and thought-provoking tales that encourage and invite greater inquiry about myths and the people and places that produced them; each tale leaves the reader wondering what happened next. This is a fine, scholarly, yet readable addition to the large number of publications for both younger and older readers that seek to make the connection between folktales and religion.

Patricia Gately

INDIAN TALES AND LEGENDS

Author: J. E. B. Gray
First published: 1961
Type of work: Short fiction
Subjects: Animals, friendship, love and romance, religion, and social issues
Recommended ages: 15-18

This collection focuses on selections from the two great epics of India, The Mahabharata *and* The Ramayana, *and includes a variety of shorter tales from Buddhist and Hindu traditions.*

Form and Content

Indian Tales and Legends offers insights into traditions from India using tales that originated in the East before the Christian era. According to J. E. B. Gray, the compiler of the collection, the sources for these stories were written Sanskrit and Pali, the classical languages of Brahmans and Buddhists, respectively. Consequently, these tales highlight the history, beliefs, and values of Hinduism and Buddhism. The collection includes twenty-nine short tales (two to nine pages each) and three short tales from "The Vetala's Stories." Forming the centerpiece of the book are longer selections from the great epic *The Mahabharata* (in an episode entitled "Nala and Damayanti") and six tales from *The Ramayana*. Transmigration (rebirth on Earth according to one's deeds in a former existence) and the caste system (rigid barriers for marriage and social interaction set by Hindu society) are fundamental concepts reflected in the tales. Although the collection does not focus on a single theme, all the tales use relatively simple stories to direct readers' thoughts to higher values. To highlight the collection's style and content, summaries of three of the tales are offered here.

The Ramayana, one of the major epics of India, written in Sanskrit by the poet Valmiki in 300 B.C., is a long and intense love story focusing on the hero Rama and his unfailingly devoted wife, Sita. An understanding of Hindu ideals can be gained through the events of the epic. In *Indian Tales and Legends, The Ramayana* is presented in prose, with a series of only six episodes from the epic. In the first, Rama is given the task of conquering the demon Ravana and is married to Sita, who will be his lifelong companion. In later episodes, Rama is banished and tested with the disappearance of Sita. His task is difficult, even with the assistance of monkeys, who are the earthly forms of gods. Rama's self-sacrifices allow him to meet the demands made of him and to overcome Ravana. He is installed as king, and Sita returns to a land "free of evil." The epic ends with the words "He who reads or listens to this tale of Rama, composed in olden times by Valmiki, will be freed from sin. To him, prosperity and all good will come."

"King Great Virtue" is one of five Buddhist birth stories selected from the Pali *Jatakas*, which tell of former existences of the Buddha. Even as an infant, the young prince of Benares brought much happiness and was righteous; at the age of sixteen, he became ruler with the name King Great Virtue. He ruled wisely and well, but in time a banished former minister persuaded the king of Kosala to seize the kingdom of Benares. King Great Virtue and his ministers were captured, buried to their necks, and left for the jackals. The king, however, was not only virtuous but also brave and resourceful; he tricked the jackals, released himself and his ministers from the earth, and, with the help of demons whom he had counseled wisely, was transported to the rooms of the usurpers of his kingdom. The demonstration of his merits led King Great Virtue to regain his lands and save his people. "It was by fortitude alone," the king mused at the end of the tale, "that I regained the splendour which I lost, and bestowed the gift of life upon my thousand ministers; truly, without ever losing hope, one should persevere, for the rewards of noble deeds bring true prosperity."

"The Indian Jackal" is a short tale of a jackal who fell into a tub of indigo. With his newfound regal color, he sought to advance his position in life by spreading lies about his anointment by a forest goddess. He was revered for a time but treated his fellow jackals with contempt. Arranging a trick themselves, the other jackals waited until he was alone at night and enticed him to howl. The indigo jackal thus gave himself away as a mere jackal rather than royalty, and he was promptly killed by hungry tigers. The tale ends with a moral: "Such is the fate of a fool who deserts his own side and joins the enemy."

Analysis

Indian Tales and Legends is a collection of classic tales that draw in readers with fast-paced action and exciting plots. The descriptions of settings and physical details are simple or assumed to be known unless these are essential to the plot. Similarly, readers learn only selected things about characters. The stories focus on the events that demonstrate the characters' virtues, usually with unexpected twists that make the tales memorable. In this way, these Indian tales are similar to collections of tales from other cultures. In other ways, these stories are particular to the culture and history of India. Readers' comprehension of a story in the collection is dependent not only upon its words but also upon their own knowledge and experience. A possible problem for those who are not natives of India or familiar with Hindu and Buddhist traditions is that these readers do not bring to the tales the background experience that the original storytellers may have assumed. From whichever culture they come, however, folktales can appeal to and inform readers on many levels. Children have always loved folktales; adults may also be enthralled by the story, but they understand its deeper meanings as well.

This collection of Indian tales includes many with animals as main characters, as well as stories of earthly forms of gods and of kings, villains, witches, and demons. Both animal and human characters demonstrate the power of good and evil and highlight virtues to which all aspire. Frequently occurring themes in the tales are the value of friendship and love, the destructiveness of greed, and the power of honesty. Patience and consistency over time are praised, especially in tales that make up epics, and knowledge and bravery are also valued.

The stories in this collection are masterfully didactic tales intended to transmit Hindu and Buddhist religious and social values. These values are sometimes only implied, but they may be specifically noted at the end of the tale. Indeed, characters may state as a soliloquy what their adventures mean or what they have taught them. In other tales, titles or the names given to characters reflect the values being taught. It is clear that many of these tales originated as teaching tools to inspire young people to reach their goals. The tales still can serve this function for adolescent readers, but they can also introduce readers from other cultures to a world outside their own. Readers can take a child's perspective and delight at the antics of hawks, cats, mice, owls, goats, vultures, hares, and tortoises. They can also delve deeper and gain understanding of the symbols and values presented through the tales.

Critical Context

J. E. B. Gray's *Indian Tales and Legends* does not regularly appear on lists of books for adolescent readers. It is suitable for them, however, if they are interested in Indian traditions and tales. Additionally, the collection could serve as an introduction for individuals or in classes as a way of expanding their understanding of literature beyond the American and Northern European tales that are typical high school fare in the United States. Each of the tales can stand alone; readers can choose to sample only parts of the collection. As a whole, the collection illustrates well the style and content of Indian tales, which can be especially useful since the origin of many Western tales can be traced to India. Adolescent readers and their teachers should be aware, however, that the book includes only a single page of introduction to the collection. No comments or footnotes are offered for individual tales. Consequently, deeper understanding of the symbolism that underlies the surface of the stories requires that readers already have background knowledge or seek this knowledge from other sources.

As a translator, Gray was obviously careful in his work. The writing is clear, and sentences are usually simple, reflecting the voice of the storytellers who once shared these tales aloud. Occasionally, explanations of terms that might be unfamiliar to modern Western readers are woven into the stories themselves. Also, the names in the tales often include diacritical marks, such as Rāmāyana or Mahāli. More important, the collection includes a pronunciation guide, with example words. Much care was taken in selecting tales for this collection, allowing young adults to sample the variety and contrasts that pervade Indian tales—whether they are neophite explorers of the literature of a land previously unknown to them or more seasoned lovers of literature armed with the knowledge to understand Indian literature at a deeper level.

Lynda R. Ludy

THE INNER CITY MOTHER GOOSE

Author: Eve Merriam (1916-1992)
First published: 1969; illustrated
Type of work: Poetry
Subjects: Crime, poverty, race and ethnicity, and social issues
Recommended ages: 13-18

Merriam offers powerful rhymes with strong rhythms that shock the reader with the stark contrasts of America's inner cities.

Form and Content

Eve Merriam's sixty-five poems in *The Inner City Mother Goose* are moving portrayals of the evils lurking in the guts of cities across the United States. The illustrations by Lawrence Ratzkin are black-and-white photographs and drawings that visually balance the white-on-black and black-on-white print of the poetry pages. In only ninety-five pages, this book explodes two-line verses to full-page parodies of the original Mother Goose rhymes. The reading of this piece is neither contextually nor prosaically difficult. The book seems to stimulate readers to look deeper, to examine further.

The poems themselves as listed in the table of contents may have original titles such as "Now I Lay Me Down to Sleep" and "Pussy Cat, Pussy Cat, Where Have You Been?" Others have easily recognizable similarities to familiar titles, such as "Poverty Program Hot, Poverty Program Cold" and "What Are Winter Nights Made Of?" Blunt criticisms of politicians, law enforcement officers, drug dealers, and absentee land-lords fill the pages, which cry to be crimson and gold instead of ebony and crystal.

Not only are public servants condemned but also the shopkeeper who cheats customers, the landlord who does not repair apartments, the school board members who merely rename schools after African American leaders but do no more. The role of the media is mildly knifed in verses about television shows, newspaper local advertising, and commercials.

Washington, D.C., and New York City are specifically named in photographs or in words, but cities such as Chicago or Los Angeles could as easily fit the images and poems. Any melting pot of humanity might have the same contrast of good and bad, hope and despair. As drugs and crime invade most sections of the United States, even small cities of the Midwest such as Lima, Ohio; Worth, Illinois; and Portage, Michigan, have educational programs for youths to make them aware of modern problems.

The dust jacket of the original work shows a photograph of a large mousetrap on the front and back. A drawing of a simple mouse near the baitless trap and the title, author, and illustrator names appear in red crayon, graffiti-style printing. The back cover quotes critic Ramsey Clark, who compares the book to the works about ghetto children by Lewis Carroll and Jonathan Swift.

Analysis

The songs and poems of the original Mother Goose—such as "Humpty Dumpty," "There Was an Old Woman Who Lived in a Shoe," and "London Bridges"—appeal to children of toddler and preschool ages even though they were written to address adult social issues. In much the same way, the new forms of *The Inner City Mother Goose* appeal to adolescents because of the staccato earthy rhythms of the poetry and the nonlyrical jabs of the thoughts. Through Merriam's poems, young people discover that poetry is not always pretty word pictures about nature. Teenagers often like to experiment with writing verse, and this book may introduce them to a way in which to begin penning their own poetry.

A mature audience is needed for these poems and images, one that can separate, for example, the acts of the stereotypical "pig" police officer from the positive accomplishments of law enforcement agencies. The book calls for readers who can categorize and excise the glaring sins of one segment of the population from humankind as a whole.

The black-and-white photographs and other visual images provoke the reader into thinking about the injustices within a system dedicated to the concept of equality for all. Students of the graphic arts, especially photography, can see the power of the use of light, shadow, geometric designs, enlargement, size reduction, double exposure, and full-page and double-page spreads. Some of the pages have as many as seven photographs, while others are half of a double-page spread. Graphically, the imbalance of words per page reflects the message about inconsistency in society. For example, one page containing twelve words faces a page with one hundred fifty words; both poems rant against the welfare system.

In units studying multicultural diversity, the history of America's disadvantaged learners, *The Inner City Mother Goose* would certainly have a place in the curriculum. This work could be a launching point for discussion, historical study, psychological interpretation, and literary comparison.

A study of semantics could also follow or introduce the book. What is meant by "numbers games," "Mister Big," "pusher," "junk," "the Man," and "this little pig"? Students can trace the meanings of these words from their beginnings through their meanings in the literature of the 1960's and 1970's to current terminology. A comparison of words used in slang by white and black youths might stimulate lively discussions.

Critical Context

In the 1970's, *The Inner City Mother Goose* was used in classes for teacher education preparation in children's literature. By the 1990's, it was mentioned in children's literature textbooks as a work for adult readers presented in the form of a children's picture book. The work has sometimes been omitted from school reading lists or taken off library shelves because of the use of a few words that are considered unacceptable. Within the body of the verses, strong language reflects street talk rather than the vocabulary of the intelligentsia. Yet, it seems that young adults are drawn to books of this type precisely for these reasons. Moreover, authors such as Eve Merriam are viewed by this audience as having something important to say and not being afraid to disturb the people in power—traits that are admired by many young adults.

The issues analyzed in *The Inner City Mother Goose*—the freedom of speech, the freedom of expression at the college level, and the Civil Rights movement—have made the book attractive to general audiences, professors, college students, and critics. The slow and painful process of change in a society is shown as a challenge in this collection of poems and graphic images.

This poetry collection appeared in the middle of Merriam's career. Her works, both those for adults and those for younger readers, often touch on controversial social issues. She explores sexism in *Boys and Girls, Girls and Boys* (1972), a picture book for children, and celebrates feminism in *Mommies at Work* (1961) and *Growing Up Female in America* (1971). Merriam also writes lighter works: *It Doesn't Always Have to Rhyme* (1964) makes the study of poetry forms fun, *The Birthday Cow* (1978) contains fifteen poems celebrating the humorous aspects of contemporary life, and *Halloween ABC* (1987) is a simple children's book. *The Inner City Mother Goose* appears to be the most impassioned of her literary products.

Margot Ann Keller

THE INVISIBLE MAN

Author: H. G. Wells (1866-1946)
First published: 1897
Type of work: Novel
Type of plot: Science fiction
Time of work: The late 1890's
Locale: England
Subjects: Science and social issues
Recommended ages: 13-18

A reckless young scientist, using himself as the subject of his experiments, becomes invisible, wreaking havoc on himself and on civilization, which must mobilize to defeat him.

> *Principal characters:*
> GRIFFIN, the invisible man
> MARVEL, the poor tramp whom Griffin persecutes and turns into his
>   fellow conspirator
> DOCTOR KEMP, Griffin's former colleague and now his adversary

Form and Content

H. G. Wells's *The Invisible Man* begins with several mysterious scenes involving a stranger who keeps bundled up and will not leave his lodgings. He is irascible and contemptuous of other people's curiosity about him. He tells his landlady that he wishes to be left alone to conduct certain experiments. His behavior is somewhat understandable because people do try to pry into his affairs, and they are far less intelligent than he is. He believes that he has no one in which to confide because everyone treats him as a curiosity.

Only gradually does the stranger's plight make itself known. He has somehow made himself invisible, and he is desperately trying to reverse the process that has erased his living substance. However haughty he may seem, his unique dilemma is exciting and troubling. How will he cope with this unprecedented situation? Indeed, he is so self-absorbed that nothing else matters. He cannot be troubled to consider anyone else's feelings or how his behavior and the implications of his actions are a threat to society. Rather, his position seems to reinforce his feelings of superiority. Who could possibly be his match, or realize the implications of his invention?

The invisible man's identity is not revealed until he takes refuge with an old friend, Doctor Kemp, whom the invisible man (now identified as Griffin) hopes to include as a collaborator in his experiment and as a buffer between himself and a hostile and frightened populace. Griffin dismisses the terror that he has caused, and Kemp quickly sees that his colleague has lost all sense of proportion. Griffin has become a kind of monster, dedicated only to his scientific cause.

A horrified Kemp feigns an interest in Griffin's plans, realizing that to oppose him openly would only result in more violence: Griffin does not hesitate to injure people who stand in his way. To him, they are stupid obstacles, and he has no qualms about obliterating them or twisting them to his purposes. It is painful to witness his torturing of Marvel, a poor tramp. Like the other characters in *The Invisible Man*, Marvel is a vivid, colorful creation. He is given a distinct voice. He may seem pathetic—an easy target for Griffin's jeers—but his individuality and his right to his own life are precious things that Griffin would deny him.

Because Griffin's explanation of his experiments and of his scornful view of humanity are withheld almost until the end of the novel, Wells is able to maintain extraordinary tension and suspense. How has Griffin made himself invisible? Why has he done so? How has his invisibility affected him? The answers to these questions are held until the denouement of the novel, until the narrative has worked through several exciting scenes of pursuit and destruction. Not until the unbearable nature of Griffin's isolation is complete is he given an opportunity, in the scenes with Kemp, to explain himself.

These final scenes constitute Griffin's confession, defense, and defiance of society's conventions. At this point, he sounds demented—a man overtaken by his intellectual passions, in the grip of ideas that have shriven him of his humanity. Although Griffin's cruelty would seem to deprive him of any sympathy, the novel ends with a touching image of him, "naked and pitiful on the ground, the bruised and broken body of a young man about thirty." The scene suggests that Griffin is also a victim, hardly yet mature and deluded, fragile, and misled—a representative of erring humanity, vulnerable and tragic.

Analysis

Griffin is so absorbed in his own views that he does not detect the revulsion that Kemp feels for his colleague's murderous plans. Griffin means to use science as an instrument of coercion; the scientist will become a dictator, deciding who shall live and who shall die. He sees no irony in the fact that his great discovery has made him invisible to humanity. His breakthrough literally separates him from the rest of the human race, which treats him as a frightening alien. He, in turn, no longer feels any bond with his fellow human beings.

That Kemp should triumph over Griffin suggests natural limitations to the damage that a scientist like Griffin can inflict on society. Intelligence without moral vision runs amok. To be smart without also being sensitive to others virtually guarantees that Griffin will not be able to find a partner for his studies. Kemp triumphs because he recognizes that ideas in isolation from society can prove lethal.

Wells's work is prophetic not only about the dangers of the single-minded pursuit of science but also about the need for cooperation and the sharing of knowledge. Griffin's instinct is to hide what he knows, and only when he is desperate does he seek a confederate. Even then, he shuts out the possibility that Kemp might have a different view. Such authoritarianism, in itself, constitutions the defeat of the very scientific quest that Griffin initiates.

Griffin fails to gain Kemp's allegiance precisely because he does not recognize Kemp's humanity. Griffin has turned against human values, and thus he guarantees his own doom. Society will have to crush him just as he has planned to crush it.

There is something heroic in Griffin's dedication to science, but his quest has become perverted. Science offers the possibility of specialized knowledge, of improving the human condition, and of learning more about nature. Scientists must realize, however, that they are part of what they study and that they cannot divorce themselves from it. Wells shows that Griffin becomes a criminal as soon as he becomes invisible. Invisibility increases his sense of isolation from society and intensifies his sense of uniqueness; invisibility does not contribute to Griffin's understanding of nature.

Wells also emphasizes Griffin's youth. That he is only thirty suggests that no matter how brilliant a scientist he may be, he must mature as a human being. Without considering the context of society, of history, of ethical considerations, the young scientist is lost. In this sense, he knows far less than the simple people whom he arrogantly dismisses. In Griffin's hands, science becomes a tool of tyranny—a way of denying all individuality, a way of blending all of humanity into the mad scientist's vision of carefully controlled experiments. People become test subjects. He sees society as merely material that he can manipulate.

The Invisible Man is a novel of grim realism, with a unique sense of the apocalyptic framed by a profoundly authentic, panoramic view of English society. Wells presents vivid, rounded characters, with colorful accents and personalities. Equally impressive is his depiction of middle-class English society, which sturdily organizes itself to capture Griffith and to reinstate order. In addition, he rightly forecasts a future of frightening inventions that society must learn to control.

Critical Context

The Invisible Man has an honored place as one of the first works of modern science fiction. H. G. Wells, a science student and teacher, was keenly interested in how the twentieth century would develop its technical knowledge. Yet, he was equally concerned with the scruples of the scientific experimenter.

In a sense, with *The Invisible Man* Wells has rewritten Mary Shelley's science-fiction classic *Frankenstein* (1818). In that novel, Victor Frankenstein tries to improve humanity by using parts of human bodies to create a perfect being. Frankenstein also isolates himself from his community, allows his enthusiasm for scientific discovery to outweigh moral considerations, and consequently produces a monster. He reacts to his terrible invention with horror and contrition, realizing that he has cut himself off from humanity. Griffin, on the other hand, is the model of the disinterested scientist. He is solely concerned with his experiments. He will destroy anything that impedes his scientific progress. He is the modern professional—cool and self-contained. He has no emotional involvement with anything but his experiments.

The Invisible Man is also about the struggle of Wells's characters to cope with new scientific attitudes. For this reason, his novel generated enormous excitement when it first appeared. Unlike previous science fiction, Wells's work combined a vigorous narrative and action-packed scenes with sharp dialogues about ideas and the direction in which civilization was headed. His economical and sure grasp of dramatic structure ensured that his work was read by a broad audience with varying degrees of education.

The Invisible Man remains a classic. Reprinted countless times, it is often taught and analyzed. It has lost little of its fresh, documentary-like form, as if Wells were writing as much like a journalist as a novelist. A keen observer and a seer, he allows the story its own momentum, never holding scenes or characters hostage to his vision. His manner and his message fuse, and this union of thought and feeling, structure and point of view, account for the novel's longevity.

Carl Rollyson

THE INVISIBLE THREAD

Author: Yoshiko Uchida (1921-1992)
First published: 1991; illustrated
Type of work: Autobiography
Time of work: 1928-1952
Locale: Japan, California, and Utah
Subjects: Adolescents and race and ethnicity
Recommended ages: 13-18

Children's writer Uchida describes her life as a Japanese American growing up in Depression-era California, her family's internment in a relocation camp during World War II, and how these factors shaped her sense of identity.

Principal personages:
YOSHIKO UCHIDA, a shy young Japanese American girl struggling to find her identity, who faces the problems of prejudice and internment during World War II
DWIGHT UCHIDA, Yoshiko's energetic father, a businessman
IKU UCHIDA, Yoshiko's caring, open-hearted mother
KEIKO UCHIDA, Yoshiko's older sister

Form and Content

Yoshiko Uchida's *The Invisible Thread* describes her life as the daughter of Japa-nese parents growing up in Depression-era California. While Uchida's story is autobiographical and told in the first person, she does not use a strict, chronological format. Rather, she relates events from her life as a series of reminiscences. Each of Uchida's stories illustrates aspects of her life that contributed to the development of her identity as a Japanese American. Photographs of Uchida, her family and friends, and the places they lived illustrate the work.

Uchida begins her story by describing her average, American childhood in Berke-ley, California, during the Great Depression. Her portraits of her older sister, neigh-borhood friends, and life in the suburbs could apply to any child, but, as she also tells about her dissatisfaction with the endless stream of Japanese guests whom her parents entertain, it becomes clear that she must also reconcile two distinct cultures in her life. While Uchida found the visitors boring, for her parents these friends formed an "invisible thread" connecting Uchida's parents to the country and customs that they had left behind. Anecdotes from the early part of Uchida's life show that she absorbed much of her parents' Japanese culture: food preferences such as sukiyaki, her mother's Japanese poetry and stories, and customs such as bowing to acquaintances. When Uchida went to Japan on a trip, however, she felt like a stranger, missing American food and American ways.

Uchida devotes half of her book to the seminal event in her life: her family's internment in a relocation camp during World War II. After Japan bombed Pearl Harbor, the government arrested her father, sending him to jail in Montana, and later forced Uchida (now a college senior), her sister, mother, and other Japanese families into a relocation camp. Uchida, her family, and many of her friends found themselves prisoners of their own country simply because they looked like the enemy. Their first relocation home was at Tanforan Racetrack Assembly Center, an abandoned racetrack in California, where Uchida's father eventually joined them. They were later moved to Topaz Japanese Relocation Center, a permanent camp in the middle of the Utah desert. Here, the Japanese American citizens created a community under difficult living conditions. Uchida and her sister were able to leave the center before their parents did, and both found homes and jobs on the outside. After the war, the family reunited and continued their lives. When Uchida returned on a visit to Japan after the war, she had a new appreciation for her Japanese heritage, finding beauty and worth in the customs and stories of her parents' homeland. Uchida used much of this background in the children's stories that she went on to write.

Analysis

The title of the story, *The Invisible Thread*, refers to the bond between the Japanese and American aspects of Uchida's world. As a child, she developed an awareness of the dichotomy between the American and Japanese parts of her life, and this dichotomy figured strongly in Uchida's search for self-identity. In choosing events to include in her autobiography, Uchida concentrates specifically on stories that illustrate this duality. She felt divided: Although she considered herself American, she still had to worry about whether neighbors would object to a Japanese family moving in next door, and she asked "Do you cut Japanese hair?" when she went for her first professional haircut. While many young adults do not have such obvious differences with the society in which they live, they are confronting their own sense of alienation and search for self-identity and will find much in common with Uchida's struggles.

Structurally, the book has two sections, although it is formally divided only into chapters. The first part of the book relates events typical of Uchida's background and how these events influenced the person she became. Each chapter is a collection of memories around a theme or event—what Sundays were like in the Japanese community, her parents' history, family vacations, a visit to Japan. Uchida adopts a nostalgic tone in these stories, one anecdote leading to another and all illustrating experiences that Uchida believes shaped her life. While her stories progress through time, they do not form a strictly chronological narrative. Such events as visits from Japanese guests and Sunday activities remained constant throughout Uchida's early life. She tells these things much as a storyteller tells about the past, moving from topic to topic and choosing stories to illustrate specific points. When she discusses the events surrounding her family's internment, her story becomes much more of a narrative with a beginning, middle, and end. While the period of her family's internment covers only a few years, Uchida's story of this time accounts for half the book, indicating the significance of these events in her life.

The story of the forced relocation of thousands of Japanese American citizens into camps during World War II is an often-overlooked story. For years, few history books made mention of it. Uchida's personal account of her experience provides young people with an intimate look at the feelings of confusion, depression, and determination that so many Japanese Americans experienced. A gifted storyteller, Uchida gives her account a sense of immediacy, making it difficult to remember that she is describing events happening more than fifty years earlier. She relates with forceful clarity the starkness of the camp in the Utah desert, the dust everywhere, and the primitive conditions of half-finished living quarters.

In spite of the injustice of her forced internment, Uchida's account lacks any deep bitterness or resentment about the things that occurred. When she describes the general approval of the government's actions, her tone reflects the bewildered acceptance by the Japanese Americans of what was happening to them. Her expressions of anger or disappointment are simple statements, not tirades. Uchida's understated tone in such statements as, "We were angry that our country had so cruelly deprived us of our civil rights. But we had been raised to respect and trust those in authority," conveys the essence of Uchida's Japanese American personality. While she does describe hard times and difficult conditions, Uchida does not dwell on the negatives. Instead, she emphasizes the efforts that everyone made to go on with their lives, to create a community with schools and organized social events.

Uchida does not make an overt comment about how her internment shaped her identity, but she does tell the reader about a postwar visit to Japan, when she felt for the first time the true importance of Japanese culture in her life. The implication is that her experiences with prejudice and persecution as a result of her Japanese heritage helped her to reexamine who she was and to come away with a new sense of herself as a person who is both Japanese and American.

Critical Context

Yoshiko Uchida was a noted children's author who published collections of Japanese stories for children and many stories with Japanese American protagonists. She also wrote other autobiographical works that focus specifically on her experiences in a relocation camp during World War II: *Journey to Topaz* (1971), *Journey Home* (1978), and *Desert Exile* (1982). Because relatively few works focusing on the Asian American experience exist for young adult readers, Uchida's book is valuable for the insight that it gives. Another work that does focus on the Asian American experience is Laurence Yep's autobiography *The Lost Garden* (1991), and Uchida and Yep share the common theme of searching for an identity between two cultures.

Uchida's autobiography makes an important contribution to the literature available on World War II. While *The Invisible Thread* is factual, Bette Greene's *Summer of My German Soldier* (1973) presents a fictional account of how the war touched a young American girl in the United States. Anne Frank's *The Diary of a Young Girl* (1947) makes less remote the tragedy of German concentration camps by allowing readers to develop a personal relationship with one of the victims of German injustice, while

Uchida achieves much the same effect by providing an account by one of the victims of American injustice. The contrast between the situations provides young readers with the opportunity to examine war and its effects on people and governments.

JaNae Jenkins Mundy

IRISH SAGAS AND FOLK-TALES

Author: Eileen O'Faolain (1902-1988)
First published: 1954
Type of work: Short fiction
Subjects: Coming-of-age, friendship, love and romance, the supernatural, and war
Recommended ages: 13-18

This collection of popular Irish myths not only is entertaining and exciting but also introduces readers to heroes who are from Irish culture, history, and literature.

Form and Content

Eileen O'Faolain did not write the stories in *Irish Sagas and Folk-Tales*; rather, she retells them. The book is not one story, or simply a collection of stories; it is organized into four parts that correspond to accepted thematic divisions of Irish mythology and tales. The stories in each section are arranged in a loose chronological narrative when possible and, most important, are written for general readers. O'Faolain, while maintaining idioms, uses standard English dialect instead of a stylized dialect, a practice in some collections that can be confusing.

In the first section, O'Faolain relates tales from the Mythological Cycle whose protagonists are the Tuatha De Danaan, or the people of the Goddess Danu. In later stories, these people become known as the Sidhe, or Faeries who live in the other-world (usually underground) after their defeat by the Milesians. The Sidhe, a race of gods and their children, interact freely with mortals. In "The Quest of the Children of Turenn," three mortal brothers must complete what seems to be impossible tasks in order to atone for killing the father of a De Danaan, Lugh of the Longbow. They travel through many countries to battle and kill many kings before they complete their quest, only to perish in their last task. Ultimately, they regain honor in death.

The next tales, "Midir and Etain" and "The Children of Lir," are also about the De Danaan. In the former story, a Faery prince, Midir the Proud, falls in love with a mortal woman, Etain. They wed, but Midir's jealous Faery wife, Fuamnach, has Etain turned into a butterfly who is blown away by the wind. Etain is whisked around Ireland until one day Angus of the Birds, the Irish God of love, sees her. He realizes that the butterfly is a beautiful woman and marries her. Through a series of events, Etain is reborn and marries a king, but Midir finds her and changes Etain and himself into swans so that they may fly away and be together forever. "The Children of Lir" also features a jealous wife. Eva's niece and nephews become her children when she marries her brother-in-law, Lir, following her older sister's death. Eva turns them into swans. After many years, the children, now old men and an old woman, are freed from the spell and thankfully die in one another's arms.

In the next section, O'Faolain recounts tales of the Ulster Cycle that detail the exploits of the Ulstermen and their primary hero Cuchulain (Hound of Culann). The main portion of this section, "The Cattle Raid of Cooley," relates the epic battle of

Cuchulain and the Ulstermen against Queen Maeve of Connacht. The war begins when Maeve and her husband, King Ailell, boast about who has the most riches and treasures. They are equal in almost everything, but Ailell owns a famous white-horned bull. Maeve cannot be outdone; she and her warriors go to battle to capture the Brown Bull of Cooley from the Ulstermen, so that she will possess equal wealth.

At the time of the attack, the Ulstermen are asleep under a spell, so it is up to Cuchulain to defend the province. The tale tells of Cuchulain's feats of courage during battles against the army of Connacht. Cuchulain wins them all, and, although the Ulstermen finally awake and defeat Maeve and her army, she does escape with the Brown Bull. The tale ends with the Brown Bull and the white-horned bull in epic battle; Irish place-names resulting from this battle are explained.

Also included in this section is the epic love story of Deirdre and Naisi. When Deirdre is born, druids predict that the kings and heroes of Ulster will fight and die for her love and that she will ultimately bring great ruin and evil to Ulster. Many want her killed, but King Conor vows to marry her and sends her off with three women—a nurse, a teacher, and a poet—to be reared in the woods. When she is old enough, he will send for her and they will be married. Before Conor arrives, Deirdre and one of Conor's great warriors, Naisi, fall in love. For many years, Deirdre, Naisi, and his two brothers flee from Conor, until he says that he forgives them and asks them to return. They do and the prophecy comes true—the kingdom is tarnished by Conor's treachery and actions.

In the third section, "In the Time of Finn and the Fianna," O'Faolain narrates tales of the Finn Cycle about the legendary Finn Mac Cool. These southern Irish stories are in many ways similar to the Ulstermen tales, although they occur much later. The warriors, the Fianna of Erin, are great heroes who perform remarkable feats and deeds, such as defending themselves from spears with only sticks and shields, running as fast as deer, and killing giants. O'Faolain tells of Finn's rise to lead the Fianna and of his great deeds. Also, she recounts his pursuit of Dermot and Grania in a tale similar to Conor's pursuit of Naisi and Deirdre. "Oisin in the Land of the Ever Young" relates the feats of Finn's grandson, Oisin, the great warrior-poet in the land of the Sidhe. Oisin is one of the few Irish heroes who makes the journey to the otherworld. He returns to Ireland three hundred years later, only to see that the Fianna and his world have been replaced with a tarnished and weak Ireland.

In the last section of the book, O'Faolain turns to a few Irish folktales from the same time period as the sagas. There is a short tale about how Finn Mac Cool defeats giants with the help of small men and a tale about the Sidhe called "The Palace in the Rath." There also are folktales about the Black Thief and his near escapes from death and the journeys of three princes in "The Three Sons of the King of Antua." These folktales are short and usually have a moral, such as "The Haughty Princess," in which a princess must learn humbleness and modesty before she can marry a prince.

Analysis

O'Faolain makes an important choice in the tales that she retells in *Irish Sagas and*

Folk-Tales. For Irish people, these stories are an invaluable part of their culture. The images and ideas behind Irish heroes such as Cuchulain and Oisin continually surface in Irish history and literature. The leaders of the Easter 1916 rebellion against the British, for example, are compared to the heroic Cuchulain. A statue erected in their memory even includes this legendary figure. This mixture of myth and history makes understanding these tales important for readers wanting to know more about Ireland.

Some aspects of this book should be kept in mind. First and foremost, these tales started as part of an oral tradition and were handed down for many centuries. Only much later were they recorded by scribes, and scholars are unsure of the content of the original tales. Nevertheless, reading these tales relates values that the Irish have held for many years. The importance of family, honor, and the love of the land itself, all predominant themes in the tales, are as important in contemporary Ireland as they were in Celtic Ireland.

An understanding of these tales is also important for readers who want to study such Irish writers and poets as William Butler Yeats, Lady Augusta Gregory, and John Millington Synge. Many of Yeats's poems and plays, for example, are based on these very tales. His narrative poem "The Wanderings of Oisin" is about Oisin's journey to the land of the Sidhe; his play *Deirdre* (1906) is based on the tale "The Fate of the Sons of Usnach." Yeats also wrote a set of four plays on Cuchulain. Lady Gregory was interested in the Irish sagas, as was Synge, who based some of his plays on them and on Irish folklore. These are but a few examples.

Ultimately, O'Faolain's collection of sagas and folklore is valuable because she retells them in a language that is readily understood. She does not try to capture the Irish dialect and thereby leave readers struggling with pronunciations or guessing the meanings of words. Nevertheless, she is able to relate the tales in a manner that maintains the integrity of their ideas.

Critical Context

Eileen O'Faolain's *Irish Sagas and Folk-Tales* is one of her many books that relate Irish myths and folktales to young readers. She also wrote *Miss Pennyfeather and the Pooka: An Irish Fairy Story* (1944), *Children of the Salmon and Other Irish Folktales* (1965), and *The Little Black Hen* (1989), to name a few. These works demonstrate the author's commitment to keeping the storytelling tradition alive for another generation of Irish children and young adults. While most books about Irish mythology are written for scholars and are either direct translations of manuscripts or scientific studies of myths and their relation to culture, O'Faolain presents these tales for the enjoyment of all readers.

Alan I Rea, Jr.

THE ISLAND KEEPER

Author: Harry Mazer (1925-   )
First published: 1981
Type of work: Novel
Type of plot: Adventure tale, domestic realism, and moral tale
Time of work: The early 1980's
Locale: Duck Island, Canada
Subjects: Coming-of-age, death, emotions, family, and nature
Recommended ages: 13-18

> *Sixteen-year-old Cleo—overweight, unhappy at home, and heartbroken over the death of her beloved younger sister—runs away to an uninhabited island, where her peaceful retreat becomes a harsh struggle for survival after winter storms make return to the mainland impossible.*

Principal characters:
CLEO MURPHY, a teenager lacking in self-confidence who becomes a
     runaway
MR. MURPHY, Cleo's father
MRS. MURPHY, Cleo's grandmother
JAM, Cleo's sister, recently killed in an accident
GLEN, a clerk in an outdoor store in Canada
FRANK GARRITY, the mainland caretaker responsible for island
     surveillance

Form and Content

The Island Keeper is a study in physical and personal survival. Cleo learns through her experiences as a runaway that her problems, both perceived and real, can be understood and solved only by her; the behavior of others cannot be controlled. The adventure is experienced entirely from Cleo's point of view, with past events emerging through imaginary scenes and dialogue with family members. Reader interest is captured on the first page: As she boards an airplane, Cleo is reminded that "time heals all wounds," even those of "recent tragic events." Readers also learn that Cleo is unhappy with herself; she has poured perfume all over her body and hates the way that she smells. In addition, "She tried to pretend she wasn't fat and even if she was it didn't matter."

Sixteen-year-old Cleo Murphy comes from a wealthy family, but it is also a family confronted with tragedy and distanced by a failure to communicate effectively. The present family consists of Cleo, her seemingly uncaring father, and her highly critical grandmother. Her mother was killed in a car crash, and her beloved younger sister, Jam, has recently died in a boating accident.

Unable to relate to her family and unwilling to spend the summer at camp, Cleo runs away to a Canadian island, owned by her father, where she and her sister spent happy times. Armed only with some cash and without a plan, Cleo buys camping equipment and food supplies, steals a canoe from the island caretaker, and heads for the island and its furnished cabin. Upon her arrival at the cabin site, however, Cleo finds only its charred remains. She takes shelter in a cave and becomes the "island keeper" of the title. *Webster's Dictionary* defines "island" as "something isolated or having no communication" and "keeper" as "a person who guards and watches." After animals steal her food supply, Cleo survives in the wilderness by eating berries, greens, and fish. She plans to stay for the summer, and then through the fall. When she realizes that she can fend for herself and when her physical condition and self-confidence have improved, she is ready to return to the mainland and home. Early winter storms smash her canoe, however, and she is marooned without adequate food or clothing. An attempt to build a raft from logs ends in failure. Her existence now becomes not only a struggle for survival—for food, shelter, and clothing but also a battle against the forces of nature—bitter cold and snow.

Cleo learns to kill, clean, and cook animals in order to have food and warm clothing. Her destiny is her own, and she becomes a person of action instead of reaction. As the icy winter sets in and Cleo faces death, she fashions simple tools and creates a shelter. Through coping with her environment, she emerges a different person. Cleo comes to the realization that she has caused her own problems and predicament and that the solutions are within herself. Her only hope for escape is to wait for the lake to freeze over and walk back to the mainland over the frozen water.

Analysis

This novel addresses a number of issues of interest to teenagers. Although *The Island Keeper* can be read simply as a story of physical survival, the issues of emotional maturity, physical appearance, the death of family members, rebellion, the experience of running away from home, the need to attract attention in the hope of making family members appreciate one more, and the acceptance of others as they constitute key elements of the work. Loneliness and being alone are also factors—there is a difference between the two that must be realized. Harry Mazer's dedication at the beginning of the book highlights the theme of seeking and taking action: "to the young who stand at the threshold of an uncertain world. Courage."

Cleo is caught in a real crisis, and it is one that she has created. As she works to survive the island winter, she learns that self-discovery is the pathway through which she can free herself from this situation.

Cleo spends a total of seven months on the island. She arrives overweight, without preparations, unable to handle problems, and lonely. During her stay, she masters survival skills and learns to cope with the deaths of her mother and sister. She leaves thinner, confident, able to handle her problems, and ready to get on with her life. She realizes that no easy answers exist to life's complexities. Cleo's father and grandmother had searched for her and presumed her dead. They are still remote upon her return, and Cleo knows that they will not change their basic personalities. She accepts her family as it is, faults and all. She decides to return to boarding school. Instead of merely existing there, she now plans to assume an active role, buoyed by the thought of returning to the island during the summer.

Mazer leads readers to the conclusion that life is what one makes of it. Planning ahead is essential, and carelessness is unacceptable. Solutions to problems must come from within, not through attempts to change the actions of others. People create their own situations, and they must work their way through them. The problems that motivated Cleo to run away are still evident when she returns, but she is ready to confront these problems instead of trying to escape them. Another lesson learned is that money cannot buy happiness. Although the Murphys are quite wealthy, the family members are unable to relate to one another on a personal level.

Minor characters and those revealed through flashback are pivotal to plot development. The only loving relationship in Cleo's life, the one between her and her sister Jam, is re-created so that Cleo's loss when Jam is killed seems greater. Glenn, the clerk who outfits Cleo for the island visit, becomes a romantic fantasy for Cleo during her island stay. The caretaker, Frank Garrity, appears as the one human threat to Cleo's existence on the island.

Despite its life-and-death situation, *The Island Keeper* is not without humor. When Cleo must eat raw fish to survive, she hears her grandmother's voice saying "pure savagery." Cleo grins and replies, "That's me, your savage granddaughter!"

Critical Context

Harry Mazer is a major contributor to young adult literature and the creator of realistic and memorable characters. Although his books were sometimes considered controversial at the time of their publication because of subject matter and language, they are popular with teenagers and are valued and used by both teachers and librarians. Books dealing with such issues as survival, belonging, self-esteem, maturity, and death serve as useful vehicles for classroom discussion. In addition, the endings to his novels are often open and answers are not always provided, offering more avenues for discussion.

The Island Keeper is a realistic novel that features one of the few female protagonists in Mazer's fiction. The story has much in common with Daniel Defoe's *Robinson Crusoe* (1719), the story of a man alone on a desert island; Mazer has cited it as one of his favorite books. His beliefs that one cannot run away from problems and that survival must rely on self-sufficiency are also evident in *Snowbound* (1973), a novel that deals with wealthy and unprepared runaway teenagers who survive a snowstorm and return home with fresh insight. Mazer continued his examination of death and its effect on grieving teenagers in *When the Phone Rang* (1985). Often, there is no happy ending in Mazer's novels, a departure from the upbeat endings prevalent in young adult novels published during the 1970's and 1980's.

Mazer is the recipient of numerous awards and honors from associations of both teachers and librarians. His work has been appreciated and enjoyed by teenage readers, literary critics, and peers. In 1985, *The Island Keeper* was an Arizona Young

Reader's Award nominee. A majority of Mazer's books, including *Snowbound* and *When the Phone Rang*, have been listed as the American Library Association's Best Books of the Year for Young Adults. All feature characters who must solve problems on their own as they walk the path to maturity.

Lynn Sager

THE ISLAND ON BIRD STREET

Author: Uri Orlev (1931-   )
First published: Ha-I bi-Rehov ha-tsiporim, 1981 (English translation, 1984)
Type of work: Novel
Type of plot: Adventure tale and historical fiction
Time of work: 1943-1944
Locale: Warsaw, Poland
Subjects: Coming-of-age and war
Recommended ages: 10-13

   During World War II, a young Jewish boy survives alone in a ruined house in the Warsaw Ghetto.

   Principal characters:
      ALEX, an eleven-year-old who must learn to survive on his own when
         he is separated from his father
      FATHER, Alex's surviving parent, who desperately seeks to save him
      BORUCH, an old Jewish worker who saves Alex's life
      STASHYA, a young Jewish girl with whom Alex falls in love
      BOLEK, a Polish resistance worker who helps the Jews

Form and Content
   Uri Orlev's *The Island on Bird Street* is the inspiring story of an eleven-year-old boy's fight to survive alone in the devastated Warsaw Ghetto while he waits to be rescued by his father. Through the eyes of the narrator-protagonist, young readers experience the best and the worst of human behavior in this realistic work of historical fiction. The novel's authenticity is genuine since it is partially based on the author's own experiences during World War II. Orlev spent the years from 1939 to 1941 hiding in the Warsaw Ghetto with his mother and younger brother. The Nazis killed his mother and imprisoned him and his brother at the Bergen-Belsen concentration camp.
   In a moving introduction, Orlev asks readers to pretend that they live in a place where they are persecuted because they are different in some way from others. He reminds his readers, "It doesn't have to be the Warsaw Ghetto, because there are other ghettos, too." A map of the ghetto provides a visual aid in identifying the major points of action. Chapter headings, each with the imprint of a bird, effectively summarize each chapter. A table of contents is included.
   Hillel Halkin has provided a smooth, seamless English translation of the original novel in Hebrew. The novel is easy to read, literate, and full of believable dialogue. Orlev's tone is neutral, almost dispassionate at times.
   Alex, the protagonist, learns his father's secret: Father has a gun to use against the Germans. His mother has been missing for a week, and Father is determined to save his son's life. Life is hard for those few who remain in the ghetto. Alex's only friends

are his books and his pet white mouse. Unexpectedly, the Nazis begin rounding up the remaining workers at the rope factory for shipment to a concentration camp. Boruch, an old man, manages to slip Alex a gun and hurriedly instructs him to hide in the ruins at 78 Bird Street until his father finds him—whether it takes a week, a month, or a whole year.

With only his mouse for company, Alex learns survival skills. Through a combination of luck and ingenuity, he avoids Nazis and Polish looters while searching out food, water, and other survival needs. He makes his home, which he calls his "island," in the remains of a second-floor apartment that is accessible only by ladder. From this vantage point, the lonely boy watches the day-to-day routines of Poles who live outside the walls. Despite his fears, he instinctively helps Jewish resistance fighters who are fleeing from the soldiers and is forced to kill in their defense. He leaves the ghetto for the first time to find a doctor to help a wounded man.

As he becomes more confident, Alex increasingly leaves the ghetto to shop and play with other young people outside the walls. He is befriended by Bolek, a member of the Polish resistance, but refuses to leave 78 Bird Street. He meets Stashya, his first love. Alex is heartbroken when her family moves away. His existence becomes precarious, however, as Polish families move into the now-deserted ghetto. He is caught outside and hides from intruders, only to recognize his father's voice. He has waited five months.

Analysis

Set in Warsaw, Poland, during World War II, *The Island on Bird Street* is thematically a coming-of-age story as a young boy matures under barbaric conditions. When his father is taken away by German soldiers, Alex must survive on his own. The love of his father, who promises to return, gives him the will to survive. The novel describes hope, bravery, and courage against a backdrop of hate and violence. Readers will strongly empathize with Alex as he stares wistfully at life beyond the ghetto walls and reaches out to others for love and companionship. The novel is a personal odyssey through a childhood disrupted by the savagery of war as good battles evil in a world gone mad.

The action-filled plot unfolds in chronological order. One young boy must evade the combined forces of the German soldiers and those Poles who support the extermination of the Jews. At the same time, he is battling nature for survival. From the moment that he escapes the German soldiers until his climactic reunion with his father, Alex survives one crisis after another. The young reader is constantly bombarded with strong emotions and compelling action. Even older readers will enjoy the fast-paced action and adventure.

Young people will identify with the hero of the novel, eleven-year-old Alex. Although he is a Polish Jew, he is a universal character. He laughs and cries; he loves and hates. Isolated from others, he fills his time reading and playing with his pet. The reader feels a shared bond of humanity. Surrounded by ugliness and hate, Alex must distrust others in order to survive yet heroically aids a wounded resistance fighter. To save another's life, he kills a German soldier. A lonely boy, he is an observer of life beyond the walls of the ghetto. A parade of humanity, the good and the bad, passes before his eyes: the bully; the greedy doorman; Henryk, the Jewish resistance fighter; Dr. Polawski, the compassionate doctor; the brutal soldiers; Bolek, who is brave and kind; and Stashya, Alex's sweet first love. These flat secondary characters are vehicles for demonstrating the historical fact that among both Poles and Jews, some people were forces for good while others were evil.

Orlev uses metaphor in his introduction in describing the ghetto as the island in Daniel Defoe's *Robinson Crusoe* (1719) and draws parallels between Alex's desperate battle for survival with that of Robinson Crusoe. The metaphor is extended when Alex finds safety on his "island" on Bird Street. Like Crusoe, Alex is alone and fighting for survival.

Although the realistic setting is drawn from the author's experiences in the Warsaw Ghetto, the novel transcends time and place. The historical facts of the Holocaust are realistically interwoven with ghetto life, slave labor factories, and the death trains. The final, brave rising up of the Warsaw Jews against the Germans is integrated into the plot. Originally published in Israel, the novel personalizes a part of Jewish history for young people. For Jews, it will help them remember their roots; for others, it will serve as a reminder that no group should be denied its roots or basic liberties.

The Island on Bird Street is an eloquent testimonial to the courage, selflessness, and determination of many people of different faiths during World War II. A study in contrasts, it also exposes the apathy, hate, greed and desperation that allowed the Nazis to come to power and engage in their policies of extermination. As Boruch says, "All this must be remembered so that other peoples will know what can happen when a madman is elected to be leader."

Critical Context

For Uri Orlev, survivor of the Belsen-Bergen death camp, the Holocaust was his childhood. Through his writings for young people, he re-creates the past as a warning to future generations. *The Island on Bird Street* is an excellent addition to Holocaust literature for young people. When originally published in Israel, the novel received the 1981 Mordechai Bernstein Award, the highest award for children's literature given by the University of Haifa. It was also cited as a 1982 International Board on Books for Young People (IBBY) Honor List Book for Israel. The novel has been widely used in the Holocaust curricula in middle and secondary schools.

Another work written by Orlev and translated by Hillel Halkin is *Lydia, Queen of Palestine* (1995), a novel based on the life of the Israeli poet Arianna Haran. Ten-year-old Lydia describes her childhood misadventures, her distress over her parents' divorce during World War II, and her life after the war in Palestine. In Orlev's *The Lady with the Hat* (1995), seventeen-year-old Yulek, the only member of his immediate family to survive the German concentration camps, joins a group of Jews going to live on a kibbutz in Israel; unbeknownst to Yulek, his aunt living in London is looking for him. In *The Man from the Other Side* (1991), fourteen-year-old Mark Marek and his grandparents, who live on the outskirts of the Warsaw Ghetto in World War II, shelter a Jewish man just before the Jewish uprising.

Inez Ramsey

IT DOESN'T *ALWAYS* HAVE TO RHYME

Author: Eve Merriam (1916-1992)
First published: 1964; illustrated
Type of work: Poetry
Subjects: Education
Recommended ages: 10-15

This volume of Merriam's spirited poetry contains several lovely, serious poems of considerable stature, but most are lighter poems reflecting a profound love of language.

Form and Content

Eve Merriam wrote both fiction and nonfiction for young people over a thirty-year period, from 1962 to 1992. Merriam, who was wordstruck and versatile, created poems that are not only lyrical but rich in other ways as well, including wordplay and humor. *It Doesn't* Always *Have to Rhyme* is representative of Merriam's body of poetry for young people. Indeed, the only way in which this volume is not characteristic of Merriam's body of work is that no political satire or social concerns are explicitly treated.

It Doesn't Always *Have to Rhyme* was Merriam's second volume of poetry for young people and also the second volume in a trilogy including *There Is No Rhyme for Silver* (1962) and *Catch a Little Rhyme* (1966). It contains fifty-nine poems spread over eighty pages. Because the poems are not arranged by any apparent classification scheme, the book invites browsing, and thus new interests or appreciations may be discovered. The majority of the verses focus on the nature of poetry, various poetry forms, basic elements of poetry, word meaning, and wordplay. One concrete poem is included among the free verse and rhyme. As a result, this volume is particularly useful in English language arts classes.

With the title, some readers may be in for a surprise: There is considerable rhyme in the volume. It is often presented, however, in places and ways that are unexpected, although artful. Because Merriam had a lifelong love of literature and theater, it is not surprising that her poems are also rich in rhythm and in sound (including rhyme). Many of the verses beg to be read aloud. Humor, another characteristic of Merriam's writing, is liberally sprinkled throughout *It Doesn't* Always *Have to Rhyme.* Young people may smile, chuckle, or even laugh out loud as they read her light verse. Also presented, however, are poems of what some critics might call a more substantial stature. These are the poems that involve one or more of the reader's senses and allow them to experience the exquisite beauty of language in unique forms. In all her poems, Merriam speaks to the experience of her readers and often evokes an emotional response. In this way, she is an authentic poet.

Small, rather whimsical line drawings by Malcolm Spooner accompany fifteen of the poems. While nicely rendered, they neither clarify nor extend the poems and merely act as decoration.

Analysis

Merriam often revealed what she thought of poetry and its use: in speeches, essays, and workshops or sharing sessions and in her poems, even those for the young. "Inside a Poem," the opening of *It Doesn't* Always *Have to Rhyme*, reveals that Merriam considered poetry as rhythm, rhyme, and perfectly chosen words arranged to provide a unique experience or moment in time available nowhere else.

This volume is rather eclectic in that it presents several themes and poetry forms under the umbrella of language appreciation. It reveals her broad range in the poet's use of rhythm and rhyme and in her love of language in general. Further demonstration of Merriam's versatility may be observed in the provocative imagery of such poems as "Simile: Willow and Ginkgo," "Leavetaking," and "Solitude."

The importance that Merriam placed on rhythm and rhyme in poetry is addressed directly and indirectly (through example) in "Inside a Poem." It begins

> It doesn't always have to rhyme,
> but there's the repeat of a beat, somewhere
> an inner chime that makes you want to
> tap your feet or swerve in a curve;
> a lilt, a leap, a lightning-split:—

One may observe that while there are four regular beats in each line, there is a fascinating pulsating rhythm caused by variance in the number of unstressed syllables in different lines (thereby increasing or decreasing speed), punctuation, internal (and unexpected) rhyme, and insightful use of consonants and long and short vowel sounds. All of this strongly enhances the meaning of the poem. This sort of manipulation of elements is characteristic of Merriam's work. She uses rhythm and rhyme often and well, but always to enhance meaning.

Since Merriam was also a creative writing teacher, it seems likely that she often had the clear intent not to teach lessons but to encourage learning and to offer food for both thought and entertainment. Her poems that offer lessons do so in the most inviting ways, giving clever, cheerful, even witty explanations or examples of their subject matter. Some of the lessons are on poetry writing. "Leaning on a Limerick" offers four examples of limericks, with the first two inventively giving instructions for their writing. Similarly, "Quatrain" offers two instructive examples of that form, while "Couplet Countdown" presents six examples in countdown fashion, beginning with a couplet having six beats per line and concluding with "Terse./ Verse." Language lessons that may be more broadly helpful in poetry composition or other writing are evidenced in "Metaphor," "A Cliche," "Nym and Graph" (as in "homonym" and "homograph"), and "Why I Did Not Reign," a humorous lesson on spelling words with the vowels "ei" and "ie." "Mnemonic for Spelunking" may well help audiences finally master whether it is stalactites or stalagmites that hang from cave ceilings, and "Be My Non-Valentine" may cause a giggling rush for a thesaurus—to find that perfect word for one's own "non-valentine."

Merriam's enthusiasm for sounds, words, and wordplay pervade the volume. "A

Jamboree for J" is a jolly jaunt into alliteration. Through clever examples, "Serendipity," "Ululation," and (in "Having Words") the concept of taking umbrage are illuminated. Wordplay fans and punsters appreciate such inclusions as "Gazinta" (as in "Two gazinta four two times"); "One, Two, Three—Gough!"; "Beware of the Doggerel"; and "Unfinished Knews Item."

Demonstrating her versatility, Merriam includes one concrete poem, "Onomatopoeia II," amid the free verse and rhyme that make up this volume. Preceding "Onomatopoeia II," on the facing page, is the same poem—this time entitled only "Onomatopoeia"—in a more traditional form. Presenting the work in two forms and on facing pages is a stroke of genius. About the working of a rusty spigot, the first poem is initially easier for most readers to comprehend, but artful placement of the same letters, syllables, and words in the second poem adds meaning through visual impact. Thus, these poems offer by example a lesson about how the visual presentation of a poem may enhance its meaning.

Merriam viewed poetry as a vital, joyful discovery of meaning—offering something to everyone. She insisted that people be involved with poetry in her workshops and in her writing. "How to Eat a Poem" begins with the poet's urging, "Don't be polite./ Bite in." " 'I,' Says the Poem," the final entry of this volume, concludes, "*I cannot speak until you come./ Reader, come, come with me*." Merriam instructed people to forget poetic terms, to do the beats naturally, think of the meaning to them, read aloud, and derive pleasure from it. Another of Merriam's hallmarks is the healthy respect that she had for readers of all ages. Her poetry never talks down to audiences; on the contrary, it challenges them.

Critical Context

It Doesn't Always *Have to Rhyme* has been cited consistently in major children's literature textbooks and literature reference sources. It has always garnered favorable reviews—most being very favorable. Only the rare reviewer has praised the volume as a whole but noted that a few of its poems fall a little flat. Such criticism has been the extent of the negative reaction to this work.

In 1981, Eve Merriam won the highly respected National Council of Teachers of English Award for Excellence in Poetry, which was created in 1977 to honor living poets for the body of their work. As the fifth recipient of that award, Merriam had published only eleven of the twenty-three volumes of poetry for young people that she ultimately wrote. That honor speaks to the enormous strength of her work, as does the statement by some literature experts that Merriam was probably one of the most anthologized poets for children during the time that she wrote for them. Other critics have referred to Merriam as one of America's most beloved poets.

It Doesn't Always *Have to Rhyme*, along with the trilogy bookends *There Is No Rhyme for Silver* and *Catch a Little Rhyme*, established Merriam as a major poet for young people; *Catch a Little Rhyme* was adapted into a sound recording at Caedmon. One rarely hears or reads about only one volume in this trilogy, further affirming the strength of the work—both its parts and its sum. Some have contended that the trilogy was part of Merriam's efforts to help young people enjoy, know about, and, if so inclined, write poetry. That contention is difficult to refute.

Sandra F. Bone

ITALIAN FOLKTALES

Author: Italo Calvino (1923-1985)
First published: Fiabe italiane, 1956 (as *Italian Fables,* 1959; as *Italian Folktales,* 1980)
Type of work: Short fiction
Subjects: Animals, coming-of-age, love and romance, social issues, and the supernatural
Recommended ages: 15-18

In this collection of two hundred popular folktales from all Italian dialects, retold or recast by the author, the central theme is coming-of-age into a world of both tribulation and imagination.

Form and Content

Folktales are traditional stories told repeatedly by successive generations of storytellers. Italo Calvino's *Italian Folktales* is not a collection of folktales per se, because he both embellishes the stories and combines elements of various versions to form polished literary renditions. Nevertheless, Calvino neither patronizes nor slavishly imitates his sources; instead, he skillfully reconstructs the folktales in a style worthy of the original narrations. He presents two hundred short tales, from all Italian dialects. The collection includes animal and fairy tales, religious allegories and legends, and adventure and anecdotal stories. In addition, Calvino provides an informative introduction and notes on the original sources, the Italian locales of the versions selected, and, when available, the names or descriptions of the original storytellers.

Calvino primarily presents tales from the oral tradition, collected in the nineteenth and early twentieth centuries, but there are notable exceptions; for example, "The Count's Beard" was collected as late as 1956. Ultimately, however, many of these folktales have roots in much earlier—if not ancient—literary sources. Elements from the myth of Cupid and Psyche are quite popular (in "King Crin"), as are those concerning the cyclops Polyphemus (in "One-Eye" and "The Florentine") and Danaë, the mother of the Greek hero Perseus (in "The Daughter of the Sun"). "The Palace Mouse and the Garden Mouse" is an adaptation of Aesop's famous fable of the city mouse and the country mouse, testifying to the longevity of such stories in folk tradition. Still other European literature influences the folktales: A Morgan le Fay figure appears in "The Sleeping Queen," and tales resembling medieval ballads and stories from the fifteenth century *The Arabian Nights' Entertainments* are also featured.

A logically structured plot is often absent in these folktales, but their fantastical nature and unpredictable appearance of magic make for extraordinarily rewarding entertainment. The quintessential Italian folktale, "The Love of the Three Pomegranates," for example, centers on a paradox: a desire to find a girl "both milk-white and blood-red." It continues with a series of marvelous situations that themselves transcend the limits of reality, so that death itself appears as a temporary condition, a mere pause between transformations and enchantments.

Furthermore, the tales often represent a dichotomy between the royal and the rustic. Enchanted palaces and aristocratic courts abound, but so do everyday toil in the fields and peasant labor. Consequently, the tales engage kings and queens, merchants and peasants, maidens and witches, friars and saints, devils and fairies, animals, and a cadre of fantastical creatures including giants, ogres, and dragons.

Many of the folktales have recognizable and popular story lines, with colorful Italian versions of the protagonists. For example, the diabolical Silver Nose (the Devil in disguise) plays the role of Bluebeard, who disposes of disobedient wives until he is bested by the wise peasant girl Lucia. Giovannuzza the Fox encapsulates all the daring of Puss-in-Boots. Giricoccola overcomes her sisters' scheming as proficiently as does Cinderella. Three geese or three orphaned daughters replace the three little pigs, who build their houses and vie with a hungry fox or wolf. A girl who travels to Borgoforte to care for her sick mother discovers troubles not unlike those of Little Red Riding Hood.

Analysis

The folktales that Calvino has selected do not generally offer advice to the audience; instead, their fantastical nature and witty presentation are intended to provide entertainment. Nevertheless, folktales often help establish proper social behavior and reveal the trials of mature life; that is, many contain a certain practical wisdom, and their preoccupation with important events and rituals of life (and indeed death) nourish a wide range of emotions.

As such, folktales often concern oppositions: wealth versus poverty, beauty versus ugliness, stupidity versus cleverness. They do not necessarily favor one attitude over the other; specific tales may reveal the benefits and dangers of either side and thereby offer partial praise and partial condemnation for certain actions. In some cases, an overly clever life may be as troublesome as one of bumbling stupidity; in others, a life of ignorance may be blessed with complementary fortune. Perhaps the best example of the latter is the irascible fool Giufà, whose misfortunes almost always turn a lucky profit and whose own mother dupes him for her personal gain. Giufà is an interesting character—he appears in six folktales form Sicily—and represents a fascination for life's inconsistences inherent in many Italian folktales.

Consequently, satire contributes significantly to these folktales. "The Science of Laziness" encapsulates this idea. Therein, an unproductive child is send to a "professor" of the art of laziness. This child quickly outdoes his mentor and graduates with highest honors. While the folktale does not advocate sloth, the humorous heroism of the protagonist undermines the opposite, expected code of behavior, which the reader easily appreciates.

On the other hand, some folktales address the disastrous results that regularly afflict the transgressor of social mores. The little girl in "Uncle Wolf" is eaten as a consequence of her own greed. Her counterpart in "Buffalo Head" bears a curse for her impolite and insensitive actions. A parent's foolishness or rashness can bring suffering to a child, as "The Cloven Youth" and "Nick Fish" readily testify. Thus, folktales regularly suggest acceptable conduct.

Coming-of-age is a pivotal theme, and a typical pattern of this journey emerges easily. A young girl or boy, who often competes with siblings, must overcome hardships in forests or other rustic places, where potential dangers and guides such as wildwood kings and old crones hide, or in magical otherworlds, usually underground. The impetus for the journey is often a parent's transgression, and the child, if successful, both wins the advantages of maturity (such as a spouse and mastery of one's own home, if not an entire kingdom) and mitigates the circumstantial difficulties that adulthood brings (death is often conquered, symbolically if not literally). These folktales preserve an alchemical mystery; they reinforce the notion that rejected things often are keys to great treasures. "Animal Speech" is a poignant commentary on this situation: Dismissed by his father for learning "worthless" communication with animals, a boy struggles to employ his talents to reach the highest possible earthly status, that of pope. In sum, most stories in Calvino's collection eventually address the youth's journey into adulthood; they stylize, symbolize, and romanticize the rites of passage into the trying world of adults, while concurrently recognizing both the pleasures and the limitations of childhood.

Since life is a process of limitless change, so metamorphosis plays a central role in folktales. This is especially apparent in those tales that concern marriage: Men may find their brides in doves, chickens, or frogs, and women may discover their grooms in pigs, parrots, or any other conceivable animal who takes on a human form when an enchantment is broken. Sometimes, certain characters assume animal form to assist the hero, as Sandrina becomes a filly for the sake of her beloved Fioravante in "Fioravante and Beautiful Isolina." Love both enlivens and haunts these folktales, and Calvino skillfully allows its transformative power to unfold.

Folktales mediate between social classes. Consequently, characters on society's fringe play roles as central as those in absolute authority. Although they often appear as minor characters of minute intellectual acumen, thieves also may face heroic extremes, as "Crack and Cook" exemplifies. In this story (the two characters also appear elsewhere), Crack cleverly exonerates himself, but does so by using Crook's horrific death advantageously. Thus, a good trick and luck's blessing are as worthwhile as all the advantages of superior social status. Similarly, princes often win their brides (who represent a different social class) or save relatives through skillful guile, and thereby further explore life's irrational nature.

Finally, many folktales stress, either implicitly or explicitly, the importance of religion in Italian life. Stories of or interventions by certain Catholic saints occupy several tales. St. Joseph, the Virgin Mary, St. Anthony (who plays the ancient role of fire-bringer in "St. Anthony's Gift"), and the Apostles are all present. Yet, no religious figure—besides Jesus himself—is more popular than the trickster St. Peter, who in Calvino's collection appears in nine tales from Friuli and Sicily. This St. Peter is a notorious character, akin to Giufà: deceptive, slothful, gluttonous, and proud. In short, he represents all those things that his master and fellow pilgrim Jesus is not. Nevertheless, St. Peter is an endearing character, truly human in his weaknesses, and his absolute mistakes in judgment reinforce for the Italian people the need for a salvatory relationship with Jesus. Still other folktales address the significance of Catholicism on the Italian consciousness more seriously; for example, "The Three Orphans," a religious allegorical tale from Calabria, recognizes the pervasive allure of the paths to Hell.

Critical Context

Although Italo Calvino notes that Italian folktales do not linger on life's more grim aspects, nevertheless many may be inappropriate for younger children. The dark humor, suggestive language, sexual innuendo, and frank eruptions of bodily functions all contribute to masterfully retold folktales, but they also confirm that these stories were not composed solely for children. Amputations and other grisly fates await many characters, witches are burned at the stake, parents often abandon their children, and, unlike the boy in "Animal Speech," not all children forgive their parents' misgivings. In fact, family relationships are often compromised, if not antagonistic: In "The Widow and the Brigand," the son of a treacherous mother subsequently puts her to death. While these melancholic aspects almost always yield to a successful ending for the young protagonist, their portrayal of humanity's darker aspects may be unsettling to the unsuspecting reader.

The seeming lack of logical plot may be confusing at first, but once embraced it provides a rewarding experience into the imagination and creative wisdom of Italian folk traditions. Calvino is not overly concerned with the anthropological significance of these folktales, nor does he force interpretations from them; rather, he successfully aims to entertain with wondrous Italian fantasies. In this way, his work is an important literary rendering of traditional stories in their Italian versions, and he introduces a compelling cast of characters. Giufà, Bella Venezia, Nick Fish, and Giricoccola survive because they and their misadventures address human emotions, aspirations, and troubles; ultimately, they celebrate the ways in which the human spirit triumphs over the trials of human existence.

Stephen C. Olbrys

IVANHOE

Author: Sir Walter Scott (1771-1832)
First published: 1819
Type of work: Novel
Type of plot: Adventure tale and historical fiction
Time of work: The twelfth century
Locale: England
Subjects: Love and romance, race and ethnicity, and war
Recommended ages: 15-18

The chivalric endeavors of Ivanhoe, Richard the Lion-Hearted, and other characters provide a vehicle for Scott to portray the political intrigue, racism, and other bigotries of medieval England.

Principal characters:
IVANHOE, the disinherited son of Cedric the Saxon, the lover of Rowena and a friend of King Richard the Lion-Hearted
KING RICHARD, the Norman king of England, long absent at the Crusades
REBECCA, a Jewish woman of great healing skill, intelligence, and beauty, the daughter of Isaac of York
CEDRIC THE SAXON, a Saxon noble dedicated to the end of Norman rule in England
ROWENA, Cedric's ward, the last of the line of Saxon royalty
PRINCE JOHN, Richard's brother and a pretender to the throne
ISAAC OF YORK, a wealthy Jewish moneylender
BRIAN DE BOIS-GUILBERT, a Knight Templar

Form and Content
   Ivanhoe is a rather sharp-edged story of intolerance, both personal and social, in the Middle Ages. Although it is one of the earliest historical novels, written by Sir Walter Scott, the originator of the genre, history is but vaguely represented in the work, except in the personages of such authentic characters as Richard the Lion-Hearted and his brother, Prince John.
   At the time portrayed in the novel, Crusaders are trickling back to England from Jerusalem. The England of the story is racked with dissension. The ruling nobility, including the crusading King Richard, are Norman conquerors. A small number of the defeated Saxon nobility remains to foment the overthrow of the Normans. Ivanhoe's father, Cedric, is the leader of this faction. Cedric has disinherited Ivanhoe for being in love with Rowena, the last of the line of Saxon royalty and Cedric's ward. In addition to the tension between the ruling and subservient classes and the familial strife between Cedric and Ivanhoe, the novel contains political intrigue between

Richard and Prince John, who wants to usurp the throne, and racial and religious tension in the personages of Isaac of York and his daughter, Rebecca, who are Jewish and therefore despised by Saxon and Norman alike.

The several story lines of the novel play themselves out by only occasionally intersecting. The dominant tale is the account of racial prejudice against Rebecca. After Ivanhoe is kind to her father, she returns the favor by healing him of wounds received at a tournament and consequently falls in love with him. Although Ivanhoe is properly grateful, he is cold to her because she is Jewish. When Rebecca is abducted by a Knight Templar, Brian de Bois-Guilbert, who has become infatuated with her, her father finds little help in obtaining her release, again because they are Jewish. Finally, she is tried as a witch because of her skill in healing and her religion.

Another major story is that of Richard the Lion-Hearted. He has just returned from the Crusades but is still thought to be imprisoned. His brother, Prince John, is plotting to take over the throne with the help of a following of greedy nobles. John is petty, childish, unthinking, and uncaring, and the nobles are ultimately disloyal. Richard is a happy knight more bent on doing random good deeds than on governing a country; he falls into company with the likes of Robin Hood (here called Locksley) and has adventures.

Finally, one finds the story of the lovers Ivanhoe and Rowena. The dissension between Norman and Saxon has kept them apart because of Cedric's ambition to marry Rowena to the Saxon noble Athelstane, who could have some pretensions to a Saxon throne if the Normans were ever overthrown. His nostalgia for a pure Saxon country keeps him from realizing that the Norman and Saxon cultures have already merged too far to be ever separated again.

Analysis

Scott dealt with many themes in *Ivanhoe*, including racism, intolerance, the chivalric code, and class relations. At the same time, he was attempting to define the historical novel as a new form. The dedicatory epistle that prefaces the book is a clear explanation of his attempts to create believable characters set on a stage of historical occurrences, but without overwhelming the reader with archaic language or mountains of bookish details. The novel both succeeds and fails on most levels.

The portrait of Rebecca as a sympathetic character, a paragon of wisdom and kindness, brings to a personal level the cruel and blind prejudices of all the non-Jewish characters against her. The portrayal of her father, however, serves only to validate the prejudices expressed by the societal racism. Although he is admittedly in a difficult position in the society, he personifies the stereotype of the avaricious, lying, fawning Jewish moneylender. This is, unfortunately, to be expected when the publication date of the novel is taken into account but might be confusing for a reader who does not have a sense of how pronounced anti-Semitism was in the early nineteenth century.

Racial intolerance against the Jews is accompanied by the intolerance of the class struggle between the Saxons and the Normans. As members of the ruling class, the Normans have imposed upon the society their own language (Norman French) and code of behavior (the chivalric code). They despise the Saxons as primitive, uneducated boors who should gladly be subservient. As one of the last of the former ruling Saxons, Cedric rejects both the language and the code. Other Saxons, however, especially those of the new generation, such as his son Ivanhoe, have come to terms with the new society. They have joined the Crusades and become enamored with the concept of chivalric endeavors. King Richard is determined to integrate the Saxons as part of the new society. Even the languages have merged into a commonly spoken tongue known as English. The struggle to separate the Norman and Saxon cultures and hold one supreme is doomed to failure but is still carefully nurtured by both Cedric and Prince John, who cannot see the union of cultures that has already begun.

One of the most interesting themes in the book is the depiction of the chivalric code as wasteful, cruel, and senseless. A major event in the book is a jousting tournament. While describing the bright crowds at the event, both the brave knights and the manners of those present, Scott quietly points out the blood-lust of the spectators, who are more avid to see a death than a display of skill and are preoccupied with the numbers of horses destroyed and men wounded and killed. The wise Rebecca, in a later scene in which a castle is under siege, points out to Ivanhoe the darker side of chivalry. The adherents forsake home and family to go off to kill those who have done them no real harm, in order to tally up points of "honor." King Richard embodies the most subtle condemnation of chivalry. In his lighthearted eagerness to be the perfect knight errant, having adventures and saving the oppressed, he has abdicated his kingly responsibility to govern the country and ensure justice for all. He has left this task to his brother, Prince John, who is only concerned with reaping from the country what he wants. Thus, chivalry on an individual scale has wreaked havoc on the country that Richard is supposed to preserve.

As a historical novel, *Ivanhoe* may perhaps succeed as a prototype, but it fails as an example. Scott allowed romanticism to gain ascendance over history as the setting for the tale. The tournament is much too merry, the armor too flexible and maneuverable, the woods too full of Shakespearean jesters, Arthurian knights, and Robin Hood and his band to be considered accurate. While this romanticism is no doubt one reason for the popularity of the novel when it was written, and to later generations looking for an adventure tale, it lends an atmosphere of fable to the work that is inconsistent with history as a vehicle for the story.

Critical Context

Ivanhoe is not widely read today, either by young people or by scholars. As a romance, the social attitudes are dated, and, as an historical novel, it is too full of romance. While it is interesting as Sir Walter Scott's earliest attempt to place a novel in ancient history, other works are more successful. For example, his novels set in Scotland, such as *Redgauntlet* (1824), the story of a failed Jacobite rebellion which is rather reminiscent of Cedric's dream to overthrow the Normans, or even later works based in England, such as *Kenilworth* (1821), which is set in the Elizabethan era, have greater critical and reader appeal. Nevertheless, his effort to establish guidelines for the genre of the historical novel and his skill at the imaginative re-creation of a sense of place as opposed to the mere recitation of historical fact have influenced writers to the present day. Unfortunately, the overt racism of *Ivanhoe*, as well as its disjointed, loosely connected style, make the book a suspect choice for many schoolrooms and young readers.

Konny Thompson

JAMES AND THE GIANT PEACH

Author: Roald Dahl (1916-1990)
First published: 1961; illustrated
Type of work: Novel
Type of plot: Fantasy
Time of work: The early 1960's
Locale: Southern England, the sky over the Atlantic Ocean, and New York City
Subjects: Friendship, the supernatural, and travel
Recommended ages: 10-13

Magic crystals turn an ordinary peach into an extraordinary transatlantic adventure for James Henry Trotter and a variety of unlikely insects.

Principal characters:
>JAMES HENRY TROTTER, a boy who is forced to live in slavelike servitude with his aunts after the death of his parents
>SPONGE and SPIKER, James's cruel and greedy aunts, who live on an isolated hilltop in southern England
>LADYBUG, one of the travelers, who is afraid that every incident will precipitate total destruction
>OLD-GREEN-GRASSHOPPER, the wise elder of the group
>MISS SPIDER, a polite traveler who defers to James's opinion whenever a decision is needed
>EARTHWORM, a crybaby who is constantly fearful because he is blind
>CENTIPEDE, a bully and loudmouth who causes dissension during the flight
>GLOW-WORM and SILKWORM, minor characters

Form and Content

James Henry Trotter is a four-year-old who lives by the sea with his gentle and loving parents and is free to play in the sand with his many companions. One tragic day, his parents are gobbled up by a rhinoceros that escaped from the London Zoo. James's home is sold, and he is sent to live with his aunts, Sponge and Spiker, on a remote hilltop, geographically as well as emotionally distant from his idyllic past.

The main story of *James and the Giant Peach* actually begins three years later with a much-altered James. Instead of a happy-go-lucky toddler, he is now a slave to his selfish and self-centered aunts. James is beaten regularly, deprived of food, isolated from other children, and forced to do all of his aunts' work.

One beastly hot summer day, James chops wood for the kitchen stove and his aunts lounge in the shade drinking lemonade. The child recalls the days when his parents were alive and his life was full of love and friendship. James is startled by the appearance of a tiny man who hands him a bag of what appear to be sparkling green crystals. Upon closer inspection, James discovers that the minuscule particles are in motion. The elf tells James that they are magic that will transport him away from his dreadful life if he will only follow directions. In his haste to do as the elf has instructed, James trips and spills the crystals at the base of an old peach tree. He tries to recover the lost magic, but the wormlike particles burrow into the earth as quickly as James reaches for them.

Within twenty-four hours, the tree has produced an enormous peach that draws crowds from nearby towns. Reporters document the miraculous occurrence, and the aunts begin charging admission to see the peach. Amid all the hubbub and melee, Spiker and Sponge forget about James, locking him out of the house when they retire for the night. He is drawn to the peach and finds a tunnel in the fruit that leads to a door opening into the peach stone. When he pushes on it, James finds himself in a beautifully furnished room occupied by talking insects that are the size of large dogs: Ladybug, Old-Green-Grasshopper, Miss Spider, Earthworm, Centipede, Glow-worm, and Silkworm.

After each of the magically transformed inhabitants greets James, Centipede completes his job of gnawing through the stem of the peach, and the adventure begins. A series of near disasters follows from the moment that Centipede detaches the peach from its tree. The travelers experience two bumps when the enormous peach flattens Sponge and Spiker, but it gains momentum and continues rolling down to the sea. The cliffs of Dover cannot harm the peach, but a school of sharks poses a significant threat. James devises a scheme to attach threads, spun by Miss Spider and Silkworm, to seagulls, which will then hoist the peach and its occupants out of harm's way. Transported by 502 birds, this fantastic inverted hot-air balloon begins its voyage across the Atlantic Ocean.

Soon, other dangers confront the crew. Centipede hurls insults at a colony of Cloud-Men, who pitch hailstones back at him. Another group of Cloud-Men, in charge of painting rainbows, attacks the Peach when it crashes into one of their masterpieces, spilling a bucket of purple paint onto Centipede. A torrential storm nearly drowns the group, but all survive and Centipede is thrilled because he is cleansed of the purple paint. The ultimate tragedy occurs when a four-engine airplane soars through the mass of silk threads and detaches the peach from the flock of seagulls. Luckily, James and his friends are over New York City, where the Peach impales itself on the spire of the Empire State Building.

The adventure ends with a ticker-tape parade through the streets of Manhattan. Each of the wanderers finds happiness in New York—especially James, who is free to play with his multitude of new friends.

Analysis

Roald Dahl wrote much of *James and the Giant Peach* in verse, which is one source of the book's humor. At one point, Centipede breaks into song about the glories of the foods he has tasted, including scrambled dregs, noodles made of poodles, and mice with rice. It is inevitable that his final stanza compares all these rare epicurean delights with the most marvelous food in the world—their home—the giant peach.

Dahl's sharp wit and caricatures evoke laughter on a variety of levels, providing enjoyment for both adults and children. As Spiker and Sponge argue the merits of their respective beauty, younger children are reminded of the wicked stepmother's "Mirror, mirror on the wall" rhyme in "Snow White." For more sophisticated readers, the references to Hollywood and to film stars provide a totally different perspective based on the prior knowledge that Dahl was married to Patricia Neal, an Oscar-winning actress.

As in many of Dahl's other books, such as *Charlie and the Chocolate Factory* (1964), the protagonist is a gentle child who has done nothing to deserve his difficult life. This idea gives rise to the book's dominant theme—that effort eventually transcends hardship, that good overcomes evil. When the peach returns to land, James is surrounded by love and friendship, which is all he ever wanted. He is free to play and enjoy childhood, having been transformed from the saddest and loneliest child in the world to one of the most popular.

Some of Dahl's other works have been criticized for including vulgarity and witchcraft, but *James and the Giant Peach* avoids controversial issues. Instead, Dahl employs one of his prevalent themes: revenge. The wicked aunts, who have tortured James and changed his world into a prison, receive their just punishment when they are flattened by the peach. As the story progresses, it becomes clear that the aunts' fate was precipitated by more than their treatment of James. Miss Spider relates how Spiker and Sponge caught and gleefully dispensed with several of her relatives. All the insects, as well as James, rejoice that justice has been served with the elimination of Sponge and Spiker.

Cruelty and violence, other objectionable attributes in Dahl's works, are downplayed in the aunts' deaths, as well as in the incidents with the Cloud-Men. Just as the cruel sisters deserve their fate, so too does Centipede merit punishment for taunting the giant hail-makers. The other incidents of death and destruction—James' parents being eaten by an angry rhinoceros and the plunge of the rainbow-painter—are related quickly and forgotten. By ensuring that no one else is killed by the peach as it whirls to the sea, Dahl avoids gratuitous violence. The juggernaut precipitates a stampede, causes a flood of chocolate, and even skins a woman's nose, but not one animal or person is injured.

Critical Context

James and the Giant Peach is a modern classic that has established a permanent position in children's libraries. Roald Dahl frequently commented that he owed his writing success to the bedtime stories that he created for his own children, and this book reads as if the author were telling a remarkable story to a group of children sitting at his feet. The book maintains this chatty feeling throughout, which makes it a perfect read-aloud choice. Chapters are short and frequently end with cliffhangers that leave the reader, or listener, begging for more.

These attributes, and the delightful illustrations by Nancy Ekholm Burkert, afford a sense of accomplishment for reluctant readers. For the same reasons, the book accommodates younger readers whose attention spans allow them to attempt chapter books. As a combination of fantasy and fairy tale, *James and the Giant Peach* provides a gratifying introduction into more difficult fantasies such as C. S. Lewis' *The Chronicles of Narnia* (1950-1956), Robert C. O'Brien's *Mrs. Frisby and the Rats of NIMH* (1971), or Lynn Reid Banks's *The Indian in the Cupboard* (1981).

Linda M. Pavonetti

JENNIFER, HECATE, MACBETH, WILLIAM MCKINLEY, AND ME, ELIZABETH

Author: E. L. Konigsburg (1930-   )
First published: 1967; illustrated
Type of work: Novel
Type of plot: Psychological realism and social realism
Time of work: The 1960's
Locale: An elementary school
Subjects: Coming-of-age, emotions, family, and friendship
Recommended ages: 10-13

Two fifth-grade girls, Jennifer and Elizabeth, become friends as they play at being witches.

> *Principal characters:*
> ELIZABETH, the narrator, a shy adolescent who has no friends until she meets Jennifer
> JENNIFER, a self-declared witch, who allows Elizabeth to become her apprentice
> CYNTHIA, a classmate who is neat, pretty, smart, and almost perfect around adults but mean to her classmates

Form and Content

Jennifer, Hecate, Macbeth, William McKinley, and Me, Elizabeth is written in the first person, with Elizabeth serving as the narrator. Two children, Jennifer and Elizabeth, participate in ongoing imaginative play about being witches. The story does not focus on witchcraft or any of the darker elements that are sometimes associated with stories about witches. Instead, the focus is on the growing friendship between two girls.

Elizabeth first meets Jennifer as she is walking alone to school one day. Jennifer hops out of a tree and asks about the cookies in Elizabeth's lunch bag. After discussing how she knows that there are cookies in the bag (witches know everything), Jennifer, who is a self-declared witch, permits Elizabeth to become her apprentice. From then on, each trip to and from school becomes an adventure for Elizabeth because she may have contact with Jennifer. At least once or twice a week, Jennifer leaves notes for Elizabeth tacked to the tree where they first met. These notes arrange Saturday meeting times, mostly at the library, for the two of them to learn more about becoming witches. Jennifer, however, has some of her own rules for her apprentice witch, such as eating nothing but hot dogs one week and then the next week eating at least one onion a day. As the relationship between the two girls grows and changes, Elizabeth becomes more self-confident, and eventually the two are able to have an equal friendship as partners.

The book consists of ten short chapters, each written in a humorous and easy-to-read manner. The viewpoint of the narrator, Elizabeth, is that of a participant rather than an observer. Therefore, the reader is intimately involved in the story instead of being an spectator. Author E. L. Konigsburg provides a credible story in which the reader is able to understand why Elizabeth and Jennifer act and react as they do. Although the illustrations are limited to a small number of black-and-white sketches, the written descriptions provide detailed images for the reader, mostly through the dialogue of the characters and the personal thoughts of the narrator. The resolution to the story is not contrived; it comes about because of a series of carefully developed, realistic, and logical situations.

The book has a whimsical feel to it that invites constant speculation about what will happen next. Jennifer is unusual and carefree enough to leave one wondering if she does have some sort of magical powers: Perhaps she really is a witch. Yet, in examining her closely, the reader will be able to determine logically how Jennifer knows what she knows and why she acts as she does. *Jennifer, Hecate, Macbeth, William McKinley, and Me, Elizabeth* is an entertaining book that will remain in the mind of the reader for a long time.

Analysis

A number of issues of concern to adolescents are presented in Konigsburg's work: finding peer acceptance, making friends, growing in maturity, finding oneself, coping with family relationships, and living in a diverse world. Primarily, the book addresses peer relationships and acceptance. The story portrays two children who are forming a friendship and who are in some ways alike but in other ways quite different. The meaning of real friendship is demonstrated, and the author's underlying message is that friends should support and help one another rather than be hurtful.

Self-conflict provides the primary plot for the story. Elizabeth is presented as a shy girl needing a friend. She is a new student who walks to school alone each day and who is afraid that she will cry when walking into class late with everyone looking at her. Adolescence is often a time of uncertainty, one filled with self-doubts and fears about other people's perceptions. Therefore, these are believable scenarios with which many adolescents will be able to associate. Elizabeth's shyness is reemphasized through her actions and responses when she meets Jennifer, an imaginative and apparently self-assured individual. Elizabeth agrees to all of Jennifer's recommendations and suggestions related to becoming an apprentice witch. Because Jennifer is confident and is supportive of Elizabeth in subtle ways at school, Elizabeth complies with Jennifer's demands even when she does not want to do so. She gradually becomes aware of how Jennifer manipulates situations in order to force her to make decisions so that Jennifer will not have to take responsibility. Once Elizabeth discovers this, she takes control of a situation important to her, tells Jennifer exactly how she feels, and risks ending their friendship. Eventually, Elizabeth's growing confidence in herself allows her to become more assertive, and she no longer needs the game of becoming a witch. At this point, the two girls are able to become good friends and to begin acting as equals.

Konigsburg's story does not address conflicts that may be caused by racial bias. The fact that one of the girls is African American and the other is white is only referred to directly in one situation. The reader is mainly aware of the cultural diversity of the two girls because of the illustrations in which both appear. Because children in this age group are likely to begin developing personal perspectives about people of other cultures, *Jennifer, Hecate, Macbeth, William McKinley, and Me* offers a positive example by focusing on sharing and similarities rather than on tensions and differences.

Family relationships are also an integral part of this story. While readers, and Elizabeth, do not learn much about Jennifer's family, they do become involved in Elizabeth's family. She is an only child from a two-parent family; this lack of siblings contributes to Elizabeth's sense of shyness and isolation. Her parents interact with her on a regular basis as authority figures, not as friends. Other family members who comes to visit treat her as they might a small child, not taking into account her growing maturity. Although Elizabeth does not complain about these circumstances, ultimately she does begin to compare them with other families with whom she comes in contact. Nevertheless, her family accepts her as she is. As she gains more confidence with Jennifer, she also begins acting in a more mature manner at home.

The reader cannot be entirely certain whether Elizabeth will reach a point where she is accepted by her peers in the school setting. She has become more self-sufficient and self-confident, however, and is able to fit into more situations without the initial anxiety that she felt as a new person in the community. She becomes more involved in her world, attending Cynthia's birthday party and taking part in the class play, but the reader is left with the feeling that Elizabeth does not really need her classmates as she did when the story began.

Critical Context

E. L. Konigsburg is known for writing stories with dialogue that seems completely natural and realistic. In 1968, *Jennifer, Hecate, Macbeth, William McKinley, and Me, Elizabeth* was named a Newbery Honor Book, the same year that Konigsburg received the Newbery Medal for *From the Mixed-Up Files of Mrs. Basil E. Frankweiler* (1967), another story with a female protagonist. To have one book recognized by the Newbery committee is an honor, but to have two receive acclaim in the same year is truly exceptional. Even more impressive is the fact that these novels were her first two books. Konigsburg is identified in the field of children's literature as a notable author and one of those credited with introducing contemporary issues. She continued to write stories of realistic fiction for younger adolescents, including *About the B'nai Bagels* (1969), a story about a boy whose mother coaches his softball team; *Journey to an 800 Number* (1982), the story of a boy learning to appreciate his father during a summer visit; and *Throwing Shadows* (1988), a collection of short stories about people making discoveries about themselves. Her stories tell amusing tales that explore substantial, realistic themes throughout.

Leslie Marlow

JONATHAN LIVINGSTON SEAGULL

Author: Richard Bach (1936-   )
First published: 1970; illustrated
Type of work: Novel
Type of plot: Allegory
Time of work: Unspecified
Locale: A shoreline
Subjects: Animals, death, and religion
Recommended ages: 15-18

Jonathan breaks from the Flock in order to perfect himself as a seagull and then returns years later to enlighten other young gulls, teaching them that there is more to being a gull than catching fish.

> *Principal characters:*
> JONATHAN LIVINGSTON SEAGULL, a gull who grows to understand and achieve his full potential in flight and in life
> THE ELDER, the head of the Flock, who believes that Jonathan is irresponsible and banishes him from the Flock
> SULLIVAN, Jonathan's flight instructor and his best friend
> CHIANG, the spiritual and philosophical Elder of "heaven's" flock, who teaches Jonathan to perfect himself
> FLETCHER LYND SEAGULL, Jonathan's student and his successor

Form and Content

As an allegory of self-enlightenment, *Jonathan Livingston Seagull* is meant to have universal implications. The story resists being located in any particular time or place—it could be happening on any coastline in the world at any moment in history. Because seagulls are the only characters, the moral of the story applies not simply to one race or nationality of people but rather to every creature capable of thought. The allegory is deceptively simple. It is told through a combination of uncomplicated language (reminiscent of folktales) and black-and-white photographs that capture the elegant flight of the gulls. Author Richard Bach also invests the story with an amalgam of Eastern and Western philosophy—ideas broad in scope but simplified for the lay philosopher and common reader. The use of allegory, in which the particulars of the setting are vague, suggests that the themes addressed are both universal and timeless.

As the story opens, while his Flock feeds on a fishing boat, Jonathan is elsewhere over the ocean testing his speed and control in flight. Unlike the other gulls, who use their powers of flight only to obtain the day's meal, Jonathan views flight as an art form to be studied, tested, and perfected. He spends his time discovering how to access the full potential of his wing movements so that he can do barrel-rolls in mid-flight, so that he can control his turns at higher speeds, and, most important to him, so that he can go faster than any gull ever has before. Despite the admonitions of his parents that he should be more like the other gulls in the Flock, he continues his experiments. One morning, however, Jonathan's desire for speed sends him thundering through the Breakfast Flock at 214 miles per hour and endangering the other gulls. The Elder, instead of praising Jonathan for breaking the world speed record for seagulls, banishes him from the Flock for what he sees as "reckless irresponsibility." As an Outcast, Jonathan leaves the Flock and travels the world friendless.

At the end of many years alone, Jonathan is suddenly encountered by two golden gulls who lead him to a place beyond Earth not unlike heaven. In this heaven, the gulls are similar to Jonathan in their desire to craft and perfect the art form of flight. He develops a relationship with the wise Elder Gull, Chiang, who tells him that he will be able to fly fastest only when he has spiritually perfected himself as a seagull. When he finally achieves this enlightenment, however, Jonathan is not satisfied with simply teaching the students of this "heaven" Flock to do the same. Instead, he bids farewell to his friend and former flight instructor, Sullivan, and returns to Earth to teach the gulls of his old Flock what he has learned.

Jonathan is at first reviled by his old Flock, but he soon attracts a few interested students, the first of whom is Fletcher Lynd Seagull. He teaches his new students that freedom can be found only in discovering one's true nature and that an idea of the Great Gull exists in every gull. When at the end of the story he believes that he has taught all he can, Jonathan returns to his "heaven" Flock, and Fletcher is left to carry on his teachings.

Analysis

Although *Jonathan Livingston Seagull* is meant for readers of all ages, young adult readers in particular will find many of its themes thought-provoking and applicable to their own lives. The process of Jonathan's gradual enlightenment calls into question issues such as child/parent relations, individual/group relations, the value of the self, and the importance of being educated and of educating others. Overlapping these ideas are issues of fealty, whether to family, friends, society, instructors, or the self. The story suggests that faith in oneself is the most complete and fulfilling type of faith.

The primary focus of the story is the process through which Jonathan achieves perfection, or the perfect state of consciousness as a seagull. This process is informed by a combination of Eastern philosophy and Western religion. The reader is reminded that the "heaven" Flock where Jonathan achieves his self-actualization is not actually Heaven, but rather an alternative plane of consciousness. He is under the tutelage of Chiang who, complete with an Eastern name, is strongly reminiscent of a guru of Eastern thought—a kind of Buddha. It is suggested that the purpose of life is to find freedom through the perfection of the self and that individuals are reincarnated through many lifetimes before they can actually achieve this perfection. As in much of Eastern philosophy, the individual is here seen as merely another manifestation of matter in the universe; that is, an individual's "true nature" exists "everywhere at once across space and time." Jonathan asserts that the only thing he teaches—and that the only thing that is important to teach—is a realization of this universal oneness.

When Jonathan returns to Earth from the "heaven" Flock, however, the story becomes characterized by ideas from Western religion, particularly Christianity. Ideals of kindness and love become central to Jonathan's teaching. His student, Fletcher, is told to forgive the other gulls for casting him out, to see the good in every gull and teach them all to understand. Jonathan himself is considered wise by some gulls but crazy by others. Some of the Flock even go so far as to describe Jonathan as the "Son of the Great Gull Himself." All these ideas suggest that Jonathan is paralleled to Jesus Christ. Yet, despite these parallels, Jonathan insists that he is not the Son of the Great Gull, that his teachings are not religious. He argues that freedom through self-perfection is not necessarily a religious ideal. In this respect, it would seem that Bach is mounting a small and subtle attack upon Christianity; he suggests that some people may find it too easy to adapt these Eastern ideas to their own Western culture—and that it could corrupt the ideas to do so.

Despite these various complicated philosophical and religious considerations, the story suggests more general themes that young readers will find valuable to the development of their own personal ideals. The lessons to be learned from the story concern self-discovery: People should discover what is important to them as individuals and should then perfect themselves by pursuing these particular ideals, even at the cost of society's approval, and part of the process of perfecting oneself is the act of teaching others what one has learned. At every point, patient education is prized above all—the suggestion being that it is just as important to teach as it is to learn.

Critical Context

When it was published, *Jonathan Livingston Seagull* enjoyed more popular success than critical success. Although it was a best-seller and continues to be an emblem of the period in which it was written, academic interest in the book was negligible and remains so.

Regard for the book has waned since its initial success, partially because its themes belong to a particular era of late twentieth century American culture, the height of which was in the early 1970's. During this period, pop culture attempted to unite Eastern philosophical thinking with Western religion in order to develop a more inclusive or universal sense of the spiritual self. Another important novel of this period of American culture is Robert M. Pirsig's *Zen and the Art of Motorcycle Maintenance* (1974), in which a man attempts to reconcile two warring sides of his own consciousness. More recently, Benjamin Hoff's *The Tao of Pooh* (1982) and *The Te of Piglet* (1992) have continued ideas engendered during this period, despite the fact that much of this brand of spiritual thought lost popularity in the 1980's.

Richard Bach wrote other books on similar topics after *Jonathan Livingston Seagull*, including *Illusions: The Adventures of a Reluctant Messiah* (1977) and *Running from Safety* (1994), which also dealt with issues of obtaining personal wisdom and educating others about it.

Joshua Alden Gaylord

JOURNEY FROM PEPPERMINT STREET

Author: Meindert De Jong (1906-1991)
First published: 1968
Type of work: Novel
Type of plot: Adventure tale and psychological realism
Time of work: The early twentieth century
Locale: A Frisian village in The Netherlands
Subjects: Animals, emotions, family, and health and illness
Recommended ages: 10-13

A short journey becomes a grand adventure in growth toward confidence and understanding as Siebren accompanies his grandfather on a visit to a tiny aunt and a giant uncle who is both deaf and dumb.

Principal characters:
> SIEBREN, a nine-year-old who feels restricted by his duties as caretaker of his baby brother and who is eager to venture beyond his own village
> KNILLIS, his baby brother, for whose sickly condition Siebren feels partly responsible
> FATHER, a carpenter, who is often absent from home
> GRANDPA, whose dying sister occasions the journey on which Siebren accompanies him
> AUNT HINKA, Siebren's great-aunt, who nurtures his need for confidence and acceptance
> UNCLE SIEBREN, the giant deaf-mute with whom Siebren develops a relationship of genuine affection
> WAYFARER, the three-legged stray dog that melts Siebren's fear of dogs into strong attachment and insistence of adoption

Form and Content

Journey from Peppermint Street is a warm, inspiring tale of a young boy's journey toward wholeness. From the very first pages, the reader notes at once Siebren's restiveness. He feels like he is on a leash as his busy, pregnant mother makes him take care of his brother Knillis, hour after hour. He chafes, evidenced by his disobedience to his mother when he takes Knillis for a walk to the town's pond. Siebren is hungry for more freedom, more independence, more experience. He has never been beyond the borders of Weirom, their small village by the sea; his spirit craves discovery.

Author Meindert De Jong sets the situation up well. Siebren is in need of a change of scenery, and Grandpa obliges. He gets word that his older sister Anna is sick and may not live long, and he sets out to see his sister one more time. Grandpa agrees to take Siebren along; he will stay with Hinka, his great-aunt, in an abandoned monastery on the edge of the marsh. Siebren is ecstatic and, since he is the narrator, the reader experiences intimately the boy's deeply felt emotions—giddy anticipation at the outset, soon giving way to fear and anxiety. At heart, this is the story of a journey through childhood fears to a final destination of quiet, happy confidence.

The journey begins slowly. Walking gives one a lot of time to think, especially when not much happens along the way. In the first village through which they pass, Grandpa cleverly wards off an attack by a dog, much to Siebren's relief. What intrigues Siebren even more, however, is his discovery that Grandpa and the Miller of Nes have had a long-term dispute over seventeen cents that has turned them into enemies. Against the backdrop of that adult conflict, Siebren is won over by a dog, a helpless, crippled, hungry little runt that follows him and successfully begs for his compassion. The boy names him Wayfarer.

After some scary encounters and misadventures that speed up the action, Grandpa and Siebren finally reach the ancient monastery in which Aunt Hinka and Uncle Siebren make their home. That night, Siebren tries to sleep in a room with a cistern in the middle of it that contains Vrosk, the noisy frog. It is a wondrous new world for young Siebren, a world that both frightens and awes him. In the days that follow, he encounters a dead rat, a newborn calf, the biggest pike ever caught, and a subterranean tunnel that keeps them safe when a tornado blows the roof off the monastery, in addition to huge Uncle Siebren, who can neither hear nor talk, and little Aunt Hinka, who speaks to his heart and nurtures his confidence.

Because Aunt Anna has died, Grandpa must stay longer. It is his deaf-mute but lovable uncle who takes Siebren back home to Weirom and his anxious parents, who have been hearing dire reports about the tornado's destruction. Yet, all is well that ends well: Siebren returns to a loving family, where little Knillis for the first time says his big brother's name and where even Wayfarer is waiting eagerly for a reunion with his young master.

Analysis

Meindert De Jong demonstrates the impressive capacity not only for remembering a child's mental and emotional geography but also for reexperiencing that internal state. This talent allows him to render Siebren's physical and psychological journey with absolute authenticity.

Fear and confusion constitute a significant part of a child's growing up. This is particularly true for Siebren, who has lived a restricted, sheltered life. Once he leaves the confines of Weirom behind, he enters into an unfamiliar world that constantly reinforces his feelings of limitations and vulnerability. The fierce dogs of Nes make him feel as if he is about to enter the gates of hell. The dispute over seventeen cents confuses him about the maturity and wisdom of adults. A woman with a shotgun, the eerie dangers of the marsh in the dark, the Gothic creepiness of the monastery, the strange giant uncle he has never met, the roaring tornado that swallows everything in its path—all these encounters disturb his mind and shake his spirit. Although Siebren is young for an archetypal journey of initiation, this journey from the too-familiar world of Peppermint Street in fact initiates him into a level of experience and understanding that yields maturity.

The journey changes Siebren. He overcomes his fear of dogs through love for the stray, which he aptly names Wayfarer. He notes that silly disputes that bring alienation need not be permanent when his Grandpa sees the error of his ways and makes peace with the Miller of Nes. He discovers that the woman with the shotgun deserves credit for their safe arrival in the night. He learns that his fear of Uncle Siebren was ill-founded, that in fact his uncle is a jovial giant, full of hearty humor and fun, and that communication is possible with someone who can neither hear nor speak. He confronts the death of Grandpa's sister, but also the beauty of a newborn calf. The terror of the tornado is real, but it leads to Siebren's discovery of a secret passageway and a magic balm for what ails little Knillis. More than anything else, in Aunt Hinka he discovers an adult who takes all his fears and insecurities seriously, who understands and accepts him at the deepest level, who makes him feel loved and important. When he returns to Peppermint Street, Siebren is ready to celebrate the miracles of life that signify more than its fears and threats: the validation of trust, the power of goodness, the affection of a throw-away dog, and the spiritual nourishment of a caring and loving family.

In Siebren, De Jong masterfully creates a child with a rich interior life. The boy perceives life dramatically, in tension between the forces of light and darkness. Yet, as children often do, he also perceives life poetically, as when their journey reaches the edge of the marsh in the dark: "'Ten thousand thousand frogs, a million fireflies,' Siebren said in a soft, slow delight." When he has begun to feel at ease in the strange but awesome monastery, "Siebren closed his eyes. Everything was safe, and everything was new, and everything was holy—this early miracle morning." Siebren's journey has led him to a sense of wholeness.

Critical Context

Journey from Peppermint Street earned for Meindert De Jong the National Book Award for Children's Literature and is the last story that featured the Frisian setting of his childhood. At a time when books for younger readers increasingly reflected the harsher realities of a troubled world, this novel exuded the enduring virtues of a stable community full of trustworthy adults and traditional values, and it found a receptive and appreciative audience. Many readers had loved other De Jong books, including those that also had the author's birthplace of Weirom (Wierum) as their setting, such as *The Wheel on the School* (1954). That Newbery Medal-winning book begins with a child whose quest for bringing back the storks to town eventually energizes the whole community. *Far out the Long Canal* (1964), like *Journey from Peppermint Street*, deals tenderly with a young boy's yearnings for experience and connectedness. All these stories and De Jong's others impress with their strong sense of place, rooted as they are in the author's vivid childhood memories of dikes, floods, ice, and people. The particularity of a place and a culture, however, invariably accrues the universal, as it does in the books of De Jong and of Katherine Paterson, through the moving, insightful depiction of children who need the healing wholeness of confidence, courage, and love. Many of Meindert De Jong's books are still in print and continue to be read by young readers and their parents. Ironically, *Journey from Peppermint Street* is not.

Henry J. Baron

A JOURNEY TO THE CENTRE OF THE EARTH

Author: Jules Verne (1828-1905)
First published: Voyage au centre de la terre, 1863 (English translation, 1872)
Type of work: Novel
Type of plot: Adventure tale
Time of work: 1863
Locale: Germany, Iceland, and a cavernous underworld beneath the earth's surface
Subjects: Science and travel
Recommended ages: 15-18

A scientist and his nephew descend into the crater of an extinct volcano in search of a hidden world discovered by a sixteenth century alchemist.

> *Principal characters:*
> OTTO LIDENBROCK, a professor of philosophy, chemistry, geology and
>   mineralogy
> AXEL, his nephew
> HANS BJELKE, an Icelander

Form and Content

A Journey to the Centre of the Earth is a first-person account of an extraordinary voyage. Axel, the narrator, is a youth sent to study science with his multitalented uncle, Otto Lidenbrock; he is present when the professor finds a manuscript hidden in an old copy of the Icelandic epic *Heimskringla*. The manuscript contains an encrypted message signed by the celebrated alchemist Arne Saknussemm, which purports to give directions for reaching the center of the earth. Having solved the cryptogram, the professor immediately resolves to follow the directions and the narrator goes with him to Iceland; their party is eventually completed by an Icelander hired as a guide.

The narrator describes in great detail the equipment assembled by the professor. Their discussions regarding the usefulness of various items provide a running commentary on all that was then known about the structure of the earth's crust. Axel also describes the professor's eccentric but methodical attempt to offer him some relevant training by making him climb a tall tower, in order that he might overcome his tendency to vertigo. The descent into the extinct volcano is described with equal scrupulousness, with a full report of the scientific observations made by the professor. At first, the temperature increases the further down they go (as contemporary theory had predicted), but, as the story moves into purely hypothetical realms, it reverts to a more comfortable level.

Deep beneath the surface, the three explorers enter a vast, illuminated cave system that seemingly extends beneath the whole of Europe, and perhaps the whole of the world. It harbors many strange life-forms, including some that once existed on the surface but that have long been extinct. They find a subterranean ocean and set about building a raft on which they might cross it, heading south-eastward toward the region beneath continental Europe. They are menaced by a plesiosaur and are hastened on their way by turbulent weather, eventually reaching a further shore. Amid a veritable treasure-trove of fossils, they discover a human skull—and then, in a primeval forest, they catch a brief glimpse of a giant humanoid patiently watching over a herd of mastodons.

After discovering more signs of Saknussemm's passage, the three explorers begin to make plans for their homeward journey, but their progress is interrupted by a huge lump of rock. Their attempt to clear a path with explosives causes more disruption than they intended, and their raft is swept away, eventually being forced up a narrow shaft that the professor recognizes as the core of another volcano. The volcano's eruption hurls them out onto the surface of the earth, delivering them to safety on a tide of lava. They discover that they have been ejected from the mouth of Stromboli in southern Italy.

Analysis

A Journey to the Centre of the Earth was the second of the long series of "extraordinary voyages" that formed the backbone of Jules Verne's literary output and made him famous. It was one of the boldest of these novels, taking him into a hypothetical realm where he was forced to allow his imagination a freer rein than usual. Verne was careful, however, to take his inspiration from actual scientific discoveries and to populate his imaginary underworld with things that were known to have existed on the surface. Even the twelve-foot-tall humanoid, who now seems rather fanciful, is supported in the text with a mass of evidence intended to license the biblical claim that there once were "giants in the earth."

Verne was sufficiently carried away by the current of his speculations to land himself with an awkward problem when it came to getting his heroes safely home again. That necessity drove him—not for the last time—to the only kind of rank implausibility that he was ever prepared to entertain, but he was always prepared to make compromises for the sake of a final narrative flourish. He always liked to end his stories with a melodramatic climax.

Although Verne was careful to relate every aspect of his own tale to scientific discoveries, he was aware of the great literary tradition of fantastic voyages, and he took care to acknowledge that fact. The professor discovers the manuscript in a copy of the part-historical, part-mythical *Heimskringla*, and he does not reject its testimony out of hand when he finds that it is the work of an alchemist. The solving of the cryptogram pays homage to Verne's favorite writer, Edgar Allan Poe, whose works were still being translated into French by Charles Baudelaire while Verne was writing *A Journey to the Centre of the Earth*. The determination to stick as closely as possible to the revelations of modern science was, for Verne, an extension rather than a denial of the visionary dimension that he had found in the Icelandic sagas, the exploits of alchemists, and the fantasies of Poe.

Some critics have complained that Verne's books were not intended to be read solely by children and that it is something of an insult that they were marketed as "boys' books" in Britain and the United States. It is certainly a pity that most English translations of *A Journey to the Centre of the Earth* are severely cut, and that some of them insist on translating the leading characters' names as "Harry" and "Professor Hardwigg," but it is nevertheless the case that Verne's use of a young narrator reveals a determined attempt to awaken a sense of wonder in young readers. The text is straightforwardly and unashamedly didactic, but what it attempts to teach is not so much the facts of nineteenth century science as their wondrous implications. The story is a celebration of the sensation of being on the threshold of great discoveries—a sensation that all young adults ought to have, whether or not they are fortunate enough to grow to maturity in an era of expanding horizons.

The text of *A Journey to the Centre of the Earth* is an account of observations rather than actions. The characters are given ample opportunity to apply their ingenuity—and all three of them have a part to play—but what they do is always secondary to what they see. Few writers would have allowed them to glimpse the giant "shepherd" and then steal quietly away; most would have insisted on a more intimate, and probably more violent, encounter. That was not Verne's way; he was an imaginative tourist rather than an imaginative colonialist, and he set out to marvel rather than to interfere. There is a kind of reverence for the natural state of affairs in his work, which is conspicuously absent from almost all the fiction that followed where he led. Looking back with the wisdom of hindsight upon the natural and cultural devastation that followed in the wake of actual nineteenth century explorations, young readers may be better able to appreciate and respect that reverence than any previous generation.

Critical Context

The influence of *A Journey to the Centre of the Earth* is by no means restricted to later novels about interior worlds within the earth, although many were written. It provided a prototype for all novels of planned exploration, in which adventurers make the best calculations they can as to what they might encounter and make the best provision they can for meeting those challenges. It paved the way for Verne's own *De la terre à la lune* (1865; *From the Earth to the Moon*, 1873) and *Vingt milles lieues sous les mers* (1869-1870; *Twenty Thousand Leagues Under the Sea*, 1873) and hence for all their successors. The combination of imaginative ambition and semiscrupulous restraint displayed by *A Journey to the Centre of the Earth* won Verne later recognition as the first important writer of science fiction and in doing so helped to define the nature and ambitions of that genre.

In maintaining its exploratory fervor, twentieth century science fiction had perforce to rush further and further onward where Verne had feared to tread, with the result that Verne's efforts now seem a little tame. It must be remembered, however, that in 1863 *A Journey to the Centre of the Earth* did go where no one had been before, and it went boldly. When no such expedition had ever been dreamed of, it really was the case that planning the trip was half the fun and that it was as exciting to travel hopefully as it was to arrive. In that context, the tale's constant insistence on matters of detail is not merely excusable but vital. If this is borne in mind, the story remains eminently readable today, and there is still much to be learned from it.

Brian Stableford

THE JOY LUCK CLUB

Author: Amy Tan (1952-   )
First published: 1989
Type of work: Novel
Type of plot: Domestic realism
Time of work: The early twentieth century to the 1980's
Locale: San Francisco and China
Subjects: Coming-of-age, family, gender roles, and race and ethnicity
Recommended ages: 15-18

By juxtaposing the stories of four sets of Chinese mothers and their American-born daughters, Tan creates a multifaceted picture of what it means to grow up female and bicultural.

> *Principal characters:*
> JING-MEI "JUNE" WOO, the central character of the novel, a writer who is responsible for giving shape to her mother's life and to the lives of the other characters
> SUYUAN WOO, June's late mother, who was forced to abandon twin girls in China before coming to the United States and giving birth to June
> ROSE HSU JORDAN, a young woman, initially paralyzed by her husband's desire for a divorce, who gains self-worth and learns to be assertive with her mother's coaching
> AN-MEI HSU, Rose's mother, who refused to resign herself to her fate as did her own mother, a concubine who committed suicide
> WAVERLY JONG, a young woman who uses her mother's gift of invisible strength to become first a chess prodigy and then, against her mother's wishes, the wife of a non-Chinese man
> LINDO JONG, Waverly's mother, who used her wit and strength to escape a disastrous arranged marriage in China and flee to the United States
> LENA ST. CLAIR, an architect whom her mother accuses of living in a marriage as empty as her own first marriage in China
> YING-YING ST. CLAIR, Lena's mother, whose failed first marriage turned her into a "ghost"

Form and Content

The Joy Luck Club is a story cycle told by seven voices. It consists of four sections, each divided into four separate stories. The first and last sections present four mothers' stories, and the middle sections are devoted to the stories of their daughters. In each section, however, one story is narrated by June Woo, who, now that her mother is dead, must sit at her mother's place at the mah-jongg table—"on the East, where things begin"—and relate not only her own stories but also those of her mother.

Suyuan Woo, June's mother, started the San Francisco version of the Joy Luck Club, a regular social affair organized around a game of chance, in 1949, after she and the other Chinese "aunties"—the mothers of the book—had immigrated to the United States. The club originated, as they did, in China, as a means of raising the spirits of four women (Suyuan and three other nonrecurring characters) during the Japanese assault on Kweilin. Decades later and in another country, the aunties continue their social gatherings as a means of hanging onto their identities under the assault of yet another foreign culture.

It is through their American-born daughters that these women most experience this sense of loss—either because the daughters are too much like them, too "Chinese," or because the daughters have become so assimilated as to forget their origins. For all the young women but June, who remains single, the primary source of conflict with their mothers seems to arise from their marriages. Waverly Jong, whose first marriage to her childhood sweetheart was ruined in part by her mother's criticisms of her Chinese American husband, is fearful now of what Lindo will say about her daughter's engagement to the all-American Rich Shields. Lena St. Clair finds herself at odds with her mother because of the alienation wrought by her marriage, now breaking apart, to a selfish American. When Rose Hsu Jordan informs her mother that her marriage to yet another selfish American man has already broken down, An-Mei muses:

> . . . I was raised the Chinese way: I was taught to desire nothing, to swallow other people's misery, to eat my own bitterness.
>
> And even though I thought my daughter the opposite, still she come out the same way! Maybe it is because she was born to me and she was born a girl. And I was born to my mother and I was born a girl. All of us are like stairs, one step after another, going up and down, but all going the same way.

In *The Joy Luck Club*, continuity between generations is at once a blessing and a burden.

Analysis

The passage cited above is key to the novel. The sense that the daughters are reincarnations of their mothers is reinforced not only by June taking her dead mother's place at the gaming table but also by the mirror imagery that recurs throughout the book. Each of the sections opens with a kind of parable that unites the four stories that follow, such as the one that precedes the section entitled "American Translation." In this allegory, an anonymous mother, judging the mirrored armoire at the end of her married daughter's bed a bad omen, cures the defect by placing an opposing mirror at the head of the bed. Glancing in the mirror now, the daughter sees not her own reflection, but a reflection of her reflection. This phenomenon her mother calls "peach blossom luck," the happiness of seeing a seemingly endless parade of generations, each image a smaller version of the one that it reflects.

June, whose narrative voice dominates and unifies *The Joy Luck Club*, has lost her mother before the novel opens. Before her mother died, however, she revealed that June was not her only daughter. Indeed, June has two sisters, twins born of Suyuan's first marriage in China. The sorrow of Suyuan's life was that she was forced to abandon the infant girls along the roadside when, fleeing Kweilin as the Japanese invaded, she could no longer carry them. Suyuan never gave up hope of finding the twins, and shortly before her death, they were discovered to be alive and in China. She died, however, before receiving this news. Now, the aunties tell June, it is her job to travel to China to fulfill Suyuan's dearest wish of being reunited with the twins and—because the aunties have perpetuated the twins' belief that Suyuan still lives as a means of keeping her wish alive—to tell them of their mother's death.

When June, whose Chinese name "Jing-mei" signifies that she is the essence of her older sisters, arrives in China and meets the twins for the first time, she sees in them a double reflection of Suyuan. The twins, for their part, recognize June by her own resemblance to Suyuan, as well as from a recent photograph that she has sent them. The three sisters embrace, all murmuring "Mama, Mama." They celebrate the occasion by taking a joint Polaroid photograph, which instantly reveals a collective portrait of their mother: "Her same eyes, her same mouth, open in surprise to see, at last, her long-cherished dream." Their shared blood, June discovers, is their common language. Thus is the novel brought full circle.

The failure of communication between the cultures and the generations is another important theme of *The Joy Luck Club*, which opens with a parable about a long-cherished swan's feather that the Chinese mother harbors over the years, awaiting the day that she can relate its meaning to her American-born daughter in perfect English. June, who has fulfilled her mother's wish by her reunion in China with the twins, is thereby empowered to tell her mother's tale—in effect, to take her place not only at the mah-jongg table but in the narrative sweep of Amy Tan's book as well.

Critical Context

The Joy Luck Club, Amy Tan's first book, is avowedly autobiographical. Like the Chinese American daughters in the book, Tan shunned her own heritage while growing up in San Francisco in the 1950's and 1960's. When Tan took her first trip to China in 1987, like her character June Woo, she embraced a cultural identity against which she had long struggled; *The Joy Luck Club* followed in 1989. Since then, Tan has published other major works of fiction. In *The Kitchen God's Wife* (1991), a Chinese mother tells her daughter how her life has been distorted by male domination and class disparities. *The Hundred Secret Senses* (1995) concerns the relationship between a Chinese American woman and her Chinese half sister.

Tan is part of the generation of Asian American writers that first emerged in the 1970's to give voice to stories that previously were little known in the United States. Maxine Hong Kingston's autobiographical *The Woman Warrior: Memoirs of a Girlhood Among Ghosts* (1976), which began this new wave, was both a critical and a popular success, and it provided at least a partial model for Tan's tales about growing up Chinese American. By emphasizing mother-daughter conflict within the context of competing cultures, both *The Woman Warrior* and *The Joy Luck Club* provide fresh variations on classic themes of family relations and inheritance. For better or worse, in these books it is the female offspring who carry with them the aspirations of the previous generation.

Lisa Paddock

THE JOY OF MUSIC

Author: Leonard Bernstein (1918-1990)
First published: 1959; illustrated
Type of work: Art
Subjects: Arts and education
Recommended ages: 10-18

One of the world's most gifted musicians converses about the nature of music and captures the essence of different forms by focusing on famous examples.

Form and Content

The Joy of Music is in two parts, a felicitous combination of conversations that Leonard Bernstein was contracted to write for publishing company Simon and Schuster but never finished and the scripts of his subsequent television shows about music for the CBS series *Omnibus*.

Bernstein states in the introduction that he will deal with "purely musical meanings," which are the only ones worthy of musical analysis. Any questions that the reader may have about Bernstein's rejection of extramusical associations are dispelled in the two opening dialogues of part 1, "Imaginary Conversations." Two major art forms are represented, music and literature. Bernstein, the musician, counters the observation of a fictitious Lyric Poet that the "hills are pure Beethoven." Bernstein wins the debate, explaining at length that music is without any meaning except its own, "a meaning in musical terms, not in terms of words, which inhabit an altogether different mental climate." The musician, he suggests, hears so much in the music that it is "unnecessary to bring associations into the picture at all."

Having laid the philosophical foundation for his book, Bernstein devotes the next three sections of part 1 to problems that he encounters as a composer. Since these sections do not show him as a success, they provide a welcome contrast to his self-portrayal as an overbearing conversationalist and, ironically, win him the reader's understanding.

The first section on composing, written in the form of telegrams and letters between Bernstein and a fictitious Broadway Producer, shows Bernstein wanting to write a symphony but yielding to demands to write music for the theater. The choice is not only between abstract and program music but also between solitary work and collaboration. Bernstein was versatile. According to *Baker's Biographical Dictionary of Musicians* (1992), he was "equally successful in writing symphonic music of profound content and strikingly effective Broadway shows."

The second section on composing, written in the form of a luncheon conversation between Bernstein and his Professional Manager, shows Bernstein's difficulty in living up to his predecessor in American popular music: composer George Gershwin (1899-1937). Bernstein's early frustration at not writing a "hit" is humorously expressed in the understatement of his title: "Why Don't You Run Upstairs and Write a Nice Gershwin Tune?"

The third section on composing was written before the first two, which would have placed it, as indicated by its title, as an expository "Interlude" in the middle of the "Imaginary Conversations." Appearing as it does out of chronological order, it brings part 1 of the book to a close with a description of the composer's secondary function in setting film music. This order has its logic as well, for part 2 does not feature Bernstein as a composer but as an articulate commentator who is secondary to the works that he is presenting.

Preceding this part of the book is a brief photograph section with images from four of the following seven *Omnibus* television scripts that constitute part 2: "Beethoven's Fifth Symphony," "The World of Jazz," "The Art of Conducting," "American Musical Comedy," "Introduction to Modern Music," "The Music of Johann Sebastian Bach" and "What Makes Opera Grand?"

Whereas part 1 conforms to the concept of a book of conversations and is easily read, part 2, the television scripts, presupposes the ability to read music and the availability of a keyboard. Excerpts that the television audience heard played appear in the book in piano reduction scores. Those who cannot hear the notes that they see will have to play the excerpts or seek them out in recordings. The length of time that it takes to digest part 2 is inversely proportional to the extent of the reader's musical training and prior familiarity with the pieces Bernstein chooses as his examples.

Nevertheless, it is worthwhile even for the beginning student to read *The Joy of Music* because Bernstein offers something for everyone. CBS was staggered by the public response to the telecasts. According to Bernstein, they received "letters from plumbers and professors, little children and old men."

Analysis

Bernstein's shows for *Omnibus* were originally intended for adults, but many young adults are accomplished musicians, able to understand all of his examples. Bernstein has a flair for pedagogy. He presents new concepts such as recitative, counterpoint, and tone rows in a way that makes them understandable and recognizable. He provides examples of what does and does not work musically, and he encourages people to try things on their own.

Educated in music at Harvard University, the Curtis Institute of Music, and the Berkshire Music Center at Tanglewood, Bernstein was an eloquent graduate, and as a conductor he began the practice of talking briefly to the audience, introducing pieces with a few succinct remarks. The format of the *Omnibus* telecasts enabled him to talk at greater length and to have parts of pieces performed as examples.

Bernstein immediately realized the possibilities of a multimedia presentation and introduced a strong visual component in the television shows. His opening show on November 14, 1954, illustrates how he could demonstrate in detail on television what he could only assert in his first two "Imaginary Conversations," written in 1948. Both the conversations and the television show deal with Beethoven. In fact, the text of the telecast ends with a quotation from the first conversation. Bernstein's point about Beethoven is that he, more than any other composer, "had the ability to find exactly the right notes that had to follow his themes." That is easily said, but Bernstein proves it in the telecast by going inside the composer's mind, examining and playing alternate versions of themes from Beethoven's notebooks, showing changes in the first movement of the Fifth Symphony in facsimiles of the actual score and then letting his listeners hear the inherent "rightness" of the composer's final version. Bernstein made spectacular use of the television medium (as shown in the photograph section) by having the orchestral score of the first measures of Beethoven's Fifth Symphony blown up to huge dimensions on the studio floor. Twelve musicians with their different instruments stood on their respective parts of the score. When one sees what Bernstein was able to accomplish with television, it is obvious why video became his preferred medium and why he substituted the exciting *Omnibus* scripts for further "conversations."

All the *Omnibus* scripts are instructive and entertaining, yet one senses that Bernstein's supreme effort went into "The Music of Johann Sebastian Bach." (It is also disproportionately well represented in the photograph section.) As the sixth of seven telecasts, it was created at a time when Bernstein was sure of his audience and could count on their interest in the most demanding material. Consequently, he prepared a powerful and cohesive show on the musician's musician, Bach (1685-1750), claiming that "once you get to know Bach well enough to love him, you will love him more than any other composer." This is the earliest music that Bernstein explores, and his main example, the *Saint Matthew Passion*, is a challenge to the conductor, since it combines chorus and orchestra. Bernstein uses the words not in the original German but in English, for a more immediate effect on the American audience. The work is "pure drama, on the highest level."

Critical Context

The Joy of Music, in particular the *Omnibus* scripts, was an immense success. Many people who later became professional musicians made their career decisions as a result of watching Leonard Bernstein on television in the 1950's. He did not talk down to his audience, and he analyzed music with contagious enthusiasm. Moreover, he did not exhaust his topics. Each show served as an introduction, a glimpse of infinite possibilities for further exploration. Bernstein's next television series, his *Young People's Concerts*, was translated in 1962 into the more easily studied book-and-record form. More than a decade later, in 1973, Bernstein again reached a tremendously large international audience with his six Charles Eliot Norton Lectures at Harvard. Entitled "The Unanswered Question," after a composition by American composer Charles Ives (1894-1954), the series is a vindication of tonal as opposed to atonal music.

Bernstein was a pianist, composer, conductor, and brilliant music analyst. Most of his prodigious output was in composition. Many people know him for the memorable tunes in the Broadway show *West Side Story* (1957) and for the more serious *Chichester Psalms* (1965), commissioned for Chichester Cathedral in England. Bernstein did much for music in America. His *Fanfare I* (1961) was written specially for

John F. Kennedy's inauguration. Bernstein also conducted the New York Philharmonic to capacity audiences from 1958 to 1969.

The Joy of Music was the first manifestation of his rare ability to convey extraordinary analytical insights to large audiences from the general public. In a tribute written for the occasion of Bernstein's seventieth birthday in 1988, Humphrey Burton, former head of Music and Arts for the BBC, said *The Joy of Music* "should be on every music lover's bookshelf."

Jean M. Snook

JUBILEE

Author: Margaret Walker (1915-   )
First published: 1966
Type of work: Novel
Type of plot: Historical fiction and social realism
Time of work: The mid-nineteenth century
Locale: Georgia and Alabama
Subjects: Gender roles, poverty, race and ethnicity, social issues, and war
Recommended ages: 13-18

> *Born a slave, Vyry survives mistreatment and hardship but, because of her compassion for others and her faith in God, eventually sees her dreams come true.*

Principal characters:
VYRY, a slave, the daughter of the slave Hetta
JOHN MORRIS "MARSE JOHN" DUTTON, her white father
SALINA "BIG MISSY" DUTTON, his spiteful wife
JOHNNY DUTTON, their son
LILLIAN DUTTON MACDOUGALL, their daughter
RANDALL WARE, a free black man, who is forbidden to marry Vyry
JAMES "JIM" WARE, the son of Vyry and Randall
MINNA WARE, the daughter of Vyry and Randall
INNIS BROWN, a black field hand, Vyry's legal husband

Form and Content
    Jubilee is based on the life of Margaret Walker's maternal great-grandmother, Margaret Duggans Ware Brown, called "Vyry" in the novel, as her story was related to the author by her grandmother, Elvira Ware Dozier, or "Minna." As Walker explains in her book *How I Wrote "Jubilee"* (1972), however, the novel is not based solely on the oral tradition. It is also the product of ten years of research into historical documents. Therefore, although *Jubilee* is classified as a historical novel, rather than as a biography, it is very close to the truth.
    The novel is divided into three sections, each representing a distinct period in Vyry's life. "Sis Hetta's Child—The Ante-Bellum Years" describes her childhood as a slave on the Dutton plantation near Dawson, Georgia. After her mother's death, Vyry is reared by an elderly slave. At seven, she is taken to the Big House to be the maid of Lillian Dutton, who is actually her half sister, since both are daughters of the white plantation owner, John Morris Dutton, or "Marse John." His wife, Salina Dutton, or "Big Missy," hates and abuses Vyry, and, although Marse John seems kind, he never forgets that Vyry is his property. He will not permit her to marry Randall Ware, the father of her unborn child. When Vyry tries to run away, she is caught and whipped.
    The middle section is entitled "'Mine eyes have seen the Glory'—The Civil War Years." During this period, the Duttons become increasingly dependent on the good

nature of their slaves. Vyry helps to care for Marse John after he is injured in a carriage accident, but he dies still refusing to free her. The slaves also tend young Johnny and Lillian's husband, Kevin MacDougall, who come home to die after being wounded in battle. After her stroke, Big Missy too requires care. Fortunately, she does not live to see Yankee soldiers pillage the plantation, leaving Lillian injured and mentally unbalanced. Vyry thinks to contact her mistress's relatives in Alabama, and they take Lillian and her children to live with them. Now Vyry can leave the desolate plantation. Despairing of ever seeing Randall again, she marries a freedman, Innis Brown, who has been kind to her and to her two children, Jim and Minna. The Browns start off for Alabama, where they plan to claim land for their own.

In "'Forty Years in the Wilderness'—Reconstruction and Reaction," Walker describes the wanderings of the Browns and their increasing family. They are driven from one place by floods and fever, from another by the tyranny of a landlord, from still another by the Ku Klux Klan. Finally, in Greenville, Alabama, Vyry helps a young white woman in childbirth, and the grateful family arranges for Vyry to stay there as a midwife, assuring her of their protection and even building her a home. The one remaining problem, Jim's unhappiness, is solved when Randall Ware turns up alive and prosperous. Although he cannot have Vyry, Randall is happy to take Jim with him and place him in a school. Now the last of Vyry's dreams is to be fulfilled: Her children will be educated.

Analysis

Jubilee appeals to young readers not merely as an exciting book with a happy ending but also, more profoundly, because it shows how one can transcend the most miserable circumstances by trusting to God and preserving a spirit of generosity and compassion, even toward those by whom one has been injured. Vyry is a heroic figure. Moreover, her story is true.

As a child born into slavery, Vyry is even more helpless than other children. She loses her mother because, unlike Big Missy, Hetta cannot refuse the master's attentions. Worn out by constant childbearing, she dies young. Where another child would turn to her father for comfort, Vyry cannot do so, for Marse John will not acknowledge her as his daughter. Tortured and abused by Big Missy, Vyry has no one to whom she can turn. The other slaves cannot help, and her father will not.

In fact, although he is not sadistic like Big Missy and his overseer, Ed Grimes, John Dutton must be held largely responsible for the reign of evil on his plantation. His self-indulgence with the slave women is humiliating for Big Missy, who, unable to vent her anger on her husband, turns it on his black children. John Dutton's self-importance takes him into politics and away from his duties at home, leaving the plantation in the hands of Big Missy and Grimes; he then chooses not to notice how many slaves are disappearing or being murdered. Vyry has firsthand experience of her father's habit of lying; however often he promises to free her, she knows that he has no intention of doing so.

Vyry refuses to hate her father, however, in part because she is a devout Christian and in part because she is a practical person who knows that hatred harms only the one who hates. Ironically, she shows herself to be more responsible than her former master and mistress and more compassionate when they are as helpless as she once was. Even after she is free, she takes care of the family that did not care about her. Vyry does not leave the plantation until she has made sure that her half sister has a place to go and people to care for her. She is so scrupulous that, although she would seem to have a right to them, she will not take any of the treasured Dutton possessions, which she helped to hide from Yankee looters.

One of the themes of *Jubilee*, then, is that the practice of Christianity brings its own reward. Vyry's capacity for forgiveness keeps her from being bitter; her sense of responsibility gives her a clear conscience; her honesty brings her a sense of self-worth and earns the respect of Lillian's relatives; and her trust in God enables her to hope for a better future. Yet, the author also believes that God does indeed work in mysterious ways, often when life seems darkest. Her own great-grandmother found sanctuary in Greenville in the same way that her fictional heroine does. When the Browns reach Greenville, Vyry has almost given up on ever finding a home. Indeed, she will not let Innis begin to build one. Then, through a turn of events so unlikely that it can only be explained as providential, Vyry is once again presented with an opportunity for compassion, and this time she is rewarded with her heart's desire.

Critical Context

Before the publication of *Jubilee*, there had been many novels about the antebellum South and the Civil War written by white authors and expressing the point of view of white people. Augusta Evans Wilson's *Macaria: Or, Altars of Sacrifice* (1864) argued the justice of the Southern cause so skillfully that Union soldiers were forbidden to read it. In the twentieth century, works about this period included Stark Young's *So Red the Rose* (1934), Margaret Mitchell's *Gone with the Wind* (1936), and William Faulkner's *The Unvanquished* (1938). However sympathetically these novelists viewed the plight of slaves in the South, they were writing as outsiders. *Jubilee* is of immense historical importance, then, as the first realistic novel about slavery, the Civil War, and Reconstruction written by an African American, who, like most of the white Southern writers, could draw on family history for her fictional details.

During the 1960's, *Jubilee* fell out of favor because, unlike her militant poetry, Margaret Walker's novel was considered too moderate in tone. More recently, however, *Jubilee* has again become popular. The fact that Walker depicts her slaveowners and even the overseer Ed Grimes as human beings, rather than as monsters, is seen as one of the book's virtues, supporting its reputation for honesty and realism. Moreover, in times of increased racial tension, Vyry can serve as a role model for white and black people alike. In this portrait of her heroic ancestor, Walker is clearly paying tribute to all the strong black women who, throughout the centuries, have endured hardships, preserved the traditions of their people, and enabled their children and their culture to survive.

Rosemary M. Canfield Reisman

JULY'S PEOPLE

Author: Nadine Gordimer (1923-   )
First published: 1981
Type of work: Novel
Type of plot: Psychological realism
Time of work: The early 1980's
Locale: A small settlement in rural South Africa
Subjects: Family, politics and law, race and ethnicity, social issues, and war
Recommended ages: 15-18

Maureen and Bamford Smales learn more about themselves and their relationship with their servant July when a revolution in South Africa forces them from their suburban Johannesburg home to seek refuge in July's rural settlement.

> *Principal characters:*
> MAUREEN SMALES, a thirty-nine-year-old wife and mother of three who does not support South African apartheid
> BAMFORD SMALES, Maureen's husband, an architect in his forties who also sympathizes with the cause of the revolutionaries
> JULY (MWAWATE), a servant to the Smales family for fifteen years

Form and Content

The novel opens with July bringing tea to Maureen and Bamford Smales in bed as they wake one morning. It soon becomes clear, however, that this is far from a normal day: The Smales family and their servant July have driven for three days and nights through fields, staying off roads, to escape the violence in Johannesburg. A revolution to wrest control of South Africa from the white minority has begun. Instead of awakening in their seven-room suburban home, the Smales find themselves in a one-room circular hut that belongs to July's mother.

In twenty short chapters—unnumbered and untitled—*July's People* follows the lives of the Smales family in the rural settlement for about a month. Stripped of their routine and away from their home, the family begins to disintegrate. The three children meld into the community, relying less on their parents. The children adjust rather quickly, finding friends and adopting their habits and bits of their language with little difficulty. Maureen and Bamford, however, have a much more trying time psychologically. They discover how tenuous their control of their lives has been, how dependent they have been on convention, routine, and apartheid society. Although both Maureen and Bamford disapprove of minority rule in South Africa, they clearly have benefitted from being part of the privileged class. Now living in July's rural settlement with only extended members of his family, they learn what it is like to be dependent on someone else for the basic necessities of life and what it is like to have no place in society. Author Nadine Gordimer has reversed the roles of servant and employers; now July is in charge, and Maureen and Bamford must adjust to living in a new environment where they do not know the language or the customs and where their presence can be dangerous to themselves as well as to others.

A successful architect, Bamford aids the village by setting up a tank so that the community can use rainwater instead of dangerous river water. Having the only gun in the settlement, he also supplies meat by hunting warthogs. Psychologically, however, he suffers seriously after his two symbols of power brought from Johannesburg—his truck and his gun—are taken from his control. The reader learns more about Maureen's reaction to their new life, as the external narrator focuses more on her than on Bamford. Her past and present relationship with her husband and with July characterize Maureen's conflict. In this new world, her husband is a stranger to her, someone in whom she has little interest and for whom she has less respect. In this new world, she also confronts the truth about her fifteen-year relationship with July. She thought that she treated him well until she understands what it is like to be dependent. By the end of the novel, Maureen's life is deconstructed. She runs alone toward the sound of a helicopter, leaving behind the voices of her children and husband.

Analysis

Although it was not expressly intended for a young adult audience, *July's People* may attract young readers through its themes. A major theme is racial discrimination. South Africa's policy of apartheid, government-approved and -enforced discrimination, is not dealt with directly. Instead, Gordimer portrays how the policy affects various types of people: liberal, privileged white people; rural black people; and black people forced to split their lives between two worlds, the urban areas where they work and the rural areas where their families are forced to live. This approach opens the novel to themes beyond discrimination to those of initiation, mistaken views of oneself and one's world, role-playing, and role reversal—all themes relevant to young lives.

The novel is a narrative of initiation, but ironically the character coming-of-age is thirty-nine years old. Maureen Smales comes to evaluate her life—her naïve political views, her relationships with her husband and with July, and her responsibility to herself—only when she is removed from her society and forced to adapt to life in July's village. For example, she wants to share the workload in the community but is rebuffed because she does not belong. Through her own experience of isolation and worthlessness, she begins to understand more about July's life in Johannesburg, how her treatment of him was acceptable from her perspective but often insulting from his. A political liberal who opposes apartheid, Maureen learns how she participated in the system.

July's People centers on the effect of the revolution on July, Bamford, and Maureen. The irony is that Maureen and Bamford do not recognize the extent to which they participate in denying July some basic human rights until they are forced out of their protected environment. July has worked for the Smales family for fifteen years, living in their yard and never once sitting in their living room. Maureen believes that her relationship with July in running the household in Johannesburg leads her to understand him much better than her husband does, but she is mistaken in her belief that she understands July or his situation. In signing July's passbook every month, Maureen assures July his job at her house and a place to live on her property, but she does not seem to consider how such a system also contributes to enforced separation from his family. Working in Johannesburg, July has leave to return to his community, his wife and children, only once every other year. The climax of the novel comes when July, now assertive, speaks to Maureen in his own language, one she cannot understand. When July feels freer to speak and act as he desires, Maureen discovers that their relationship has been defined by apartheid: that he spoke with her always as servant to mistress under conditions where she had the option of not signing his passbook or not giving him work the next month.

The Smales family's movement from comfortable suburban life to isolation in a rural village and, more important, Maureen and Bamford's movement from figures of authority to characters who feel impotent and worthless suggest all sorts of questions about modern life. Who holds power and why? How can political and personal independence be achieved? How does wealth affect character? Can rationalization settle one's conscience in a world filled with injustice?

The ending of the novel is ambiguous, but not opaque. Maureen flees, leaving behind her husband and children. This act may seem selfish and despicable but may in fact be appropriate. During her stay in July's community, Maureen learns enough about herself to realize that her children have little need for her and that her marriage only functions as part of an oppressive societal structure. Her past life, as well as her present, is now unacceptable to her, and her flight may be her first step toward personal responsibility and independence.

Critical Context

Nadine Gordimer often uses the years immediately preceding her writing as the setting for her novels, but she departs from this pattern in *July's People*. In imagining a possible scenario for the revolution for majority rule in South Africa, Gordimer places the action in the near future. Like George Orwell's political novel *Nineteen Eighty-four* (1949), *July's People* is set in the early 1980's and addresses the issue of government oppression. Published in 1981, ten years before the last apartheid law was repealed, the novel contains historical references to demonstrations against apartheid such as the Soweto riots of 1976. Unlike Orwell's work, however, Gordimer's novel concentrates more on character than on a system of government. Her focus is on how characters are shaped by politics rather than on politics itself.

By blending history with an imagined narrative, *July's People* provides a good opportunity for interdisciplinary study. The novel is best read within the context of South African history, but in no way does it attempt to present an actual revolution. Rather, it offers a vision of how people living through such a period might be affected. Compact and focused, *July's People*, Gordimer's eighth novel, was one of three works singled out for praise when she received the Nobel Prize for Literature in 1991.

Marion Boyle Petrillo

JUST SO STORIES

Author: Rudyard Kipling (1865-1936)
First published: 1902; illustrated
Type of work: Short fiction
Subjects: Animals and nature
Recommended ages: 10-13

Kipling's anthropomorphic fables offer delightful explanations for natural phenomena.

Form and Content

Just So Stories is a collection of whimsical tales accompanied by the author's excellent pen-and-ink drawings and humorous verse. The stories are written in the first person and addressed to "O Best Beloved." (The "beloved" is Rudyard Kipling's eldest child, Josephine, who died at age six in 1899.) The narrative tone is the intimate voice of a doting father talking to a favorite child.

Like Aesop's fables, some of the tales in *Just So Stories* anthropomorphize animals to illustrate human virtues and failings. Like traditional folklore and myths, other stories in the collection explain the origins of natural phenomena.

"The Elephant's Child," one of the book's most popular tales, combines elements of folklore and allegory. Kipling tells how an elephant child's curiosity led elephants to acquire long noses. Since no one will answer the elephant child's question, "What does the Crocodile have for dinner?," the elephant child decides to ask the crocodile himself. The crocodile answers that he will "begin with Elephant's Child" and grabs the end of the elephant child's heretofore short nose. After a vicious tug-of-war match, the crocodile finally lets go, leaving the elephant child with a stretched-out nose. Yet, instead of being an indictment of curiosity, the ending of the tale validates this childlike quality: The elephant child finds several good uses for his long nose. "How the Rhinoceros Got His Skin" relates how the rhinoceros' bad manners and greed led to his loose-fitting skin. After stealing a Parsee's cake, the rhino takes off his skin and goes for a swim. In retaliation, the Parsee fills the rhino's skin with cake crumbs and burnt currants. The crumbs and currants cause such great itching when the rhino puts his skin back on that he rubs himself against a tree trunk until his skin hangs in folds. In other stories, the camel's arrogant exclamations of "Humph!" explain "How the Camel Got His Hump," and a cat's pride is deemed responsible for felines' limited involvement with humankind in "The Cat That Walked by Himself."

Other tales are more etiological myth (a story to explain the origin of something) than allegory. "How the Leopard Got His Spots" describes the development of camouflaging fur patterns in certain animals. Giraffes and zebras acquire spots and stripes to hide from a leopard, who decides to sport spots in order to beat his prey at their game. In "How the Whale Got His Throat," a resourceful mariner swallowed by a whale uses his raft to create a grate that blocks the whale's throat. "By means of a grating, I have stopped your ating," the mariner declares triumphantly.

Although the animals' worlds are peopled with humans in many guises—an African hunter, an Indian Parsee, a powerful magician, and a wise king named Suleiman-bin-Daoud and his 999 wives, among others—two stories stand out for their lack of animals. "How the First Letter Was Written" and "How the Alphabet Was Made" are etiological myths that relate how a Neolithic father and daughter playfully create language.

Analysis

Kipling once said that his "original notion" as a writer was "to tell the English something of the world outside England." An Englishman reared in India, Kipling grew up to be fascinated with other cultures. As an adult, he traveled extensively, visiting or living in such places as South Africa, Japan, the United States, and Bermuda. He sought to introduce his readers to distant lands through the exotic settings of *Just So Stories*: South America, the Middle East, India, and Africa, among other places.

In addition to enlightening readers about other cultures, Kipling's stories reveal his connection with and understanding of the world of children. He wrote *Just So Stories* when his three children were small, completing the book after the death of his eldest, favorite child, Josephine. The intimate narrative tone of the book suggests that the stories were written, on one level, to allow Kipling to reexperience his close relationship with his daughter.

This personal tone is expressed through Kipling's innovative use of language. His language is colloquial and informal, with rhythms closely matching those of speech. He uses words incorrectly and misspells them, as a child might. For example, it is the elephant child's "'satiable curtiosities" that get him into trouble. Kipling's style is also lushly descriptive in a way that delights children. He uses poetic devices such as onomatopoeia, forming a word by imitation of a sound made or associated with its referent ("greeny-crackly melons," "twirly-whirly eel," "ooshy-skooshy" sea); alliteration, starting two or more words of a word group with the same letter ("great grey-green, greasy, Limpopo River"); and repetition of phrases to evoke time, place, and mood.

Although verses follow each story, sometimes Kipling uses rhythm and rhyme within a story for whimsical effect, such as this passage from "How the Whale Got His Throat":

> . . . he stumped and he jumped and he thumped and he bumped, and he pranced and he danced, and he banged and he clanged, and he hit and he bit, and he leaped and he creeped, and he prowled and he howled, and he hopped and he dropped, and he cried and he sighed, and he crawled and he bawled, and he stepped and he lepped . . .

While using language in a way that appeals to children, Kipling also demonstrates his profound respect for the innocent vulnerability of the young by drawing a parallel between animals and children. The *Just So Stories* are anthropomorphic; that is, the animal characters speak and act like humans. In particular, they act like human children.

Kipling felt a strong empathy with children because of his own childhood experiences. At age six, Kipling and his sister were sent from India to England to live with grossly abusive relatives for six years. When asked as an adult why he and his sister never let anyone know the horror of their lives in what they called "The House of Desolation," he replied: "Children tell little more than animals, for what comes to them they accept as eternally established."

Through giving mute animals a voice in the *Just So Stories*, Kipling was actually giving children a voice. The animal-children in the stories are uninhibited and independent in a way that Kipling could never be as a child. They sulk, steal cake, run away from home, and even take revenge on their tormentors, as when the elephant child uses his newly stretched trunk to severely whip all the relatives who had unjustly spanked him for his "'satiable curtiosities." *Just So Stories* is an affectionate, exotic gift to Kipling's own adored children, and the book offers its audience an ideal vision of childhood as a time of innocence, independence, whimsy, and wonder.

Critical Context

Before the creation of Rudyard Kipling's naughty but lovable animal-children in *Just So Stories*, children's literature tended to offer children two models of behavior: the good child and the bad child. Kipling's stories declare that it is natural and right for children to exhibit all types of behavior as they form their identities.

Just So Stories celebrates the innocent spontaneity of very young children. Some of Kipling's other children's works go a little further by examining the moral development of children as they grow older. *The Jungle Books* (1894-1895), *Kim* (1901), and *Stalky & Co* (1899) relate how children's characters are formed as they learn to distinguish between good and bad, to be assertive, and to express unique identities.

Mowgli, from *The Jungle Books*, is the ultimate uninhibited child. An Indian orphan reared in the jungle by wolves, Mowgli is Kipling's child version of the "noble savage" described by Jean-Jacques Rousseau (1712-1778). Like Rousseau, Kipling believed that human nature would basically turn to good unless corrupted by the evils of civilization. Mowgli's challenge is to retain his good "animal identity" as he confronts the world of humans. Similar in theme to *The Jungle Books*, *Kim* relates the identity crisis of an Irish boy orphaned in India. Kim feels like a Hindu but, through sometimes painful experience, learns that he is a Sahib. *Stalky & Co.* tells how three boys survive the often brutal bullying by adults and older children at a boys' boarding school. Like Mowgli and Kim, the boys must struggle to keep their natural goodness intact so that they do not themselves grow up to be oppressors.

In all his works for children, Kipling shows his admiration for the innate nobility of humans and animals and his distaste for the brutality and corrupting influence of "civilized" adults.

Samantha Bonar

JUSTICE AND HER BROTHERS

Author: Virginia Hamilton (1936-   )
First published: 1978
Type of work: Novel
Type of plot: Science fiction
Time of work: A summer in the 1970's and the future
Locale: A rural midwestern town, probably in Ohio
Subjects: Coming-of-age, family, and the supernatural
Recommended ages: 10-15

> *Eleven-year-old Justice Douglass, struggling with changes in her family's life, learns that she and her two older brothers have psychic powers and the ability to travel into the future.*

Principal characters:
>   JUSTICE DOUGLASS, an eleven-year-old girl coping with her mother's absence during the day
>   THOMAS DOUGLASS, Justice's thirteen-year-old brother, a drummer
>   LEVI DOUGLASS, Thomas' identical twin
>   MRS. DOUGLASS, their mother, a college student
>   MR. DOUGLASS, their father, a stonecutter
>   DORIAN JEFFERSON, a boy in the neighborhood who also has psychic powers
>   MRS. LEONA JEFFERSON, Dorian's mother, the Sensitive who teaches Justice about her psychic abilities

Form and Content

Justice and Her Brothers, which takes place during a hot summer week, is told primarily from the point of view of Justice Douglass, the protagonist. Virginia Hamilton does, however, occasionally reveal the point of view of other characters, a move that sometimes seems abrupt or startling but that adds more depth and complexity to the novel than Justice's limited perceptions could provide. While the action of the plot can be sketched fairly simply, the novel focuses on Justice's changing relationship to her brothers, on both the supernatural and the domestic level.

Mrs. Douglass has begun taking college classes during the day, and Justice and her brothers are left alone for the first time. It is a lonely and difficult time for Justice, and much of the emotion of the novel comes from her turmoil. Levi helps take care of Justice—he cooks for all three children and intercedes with his brother for her occasionally—but Thomas is antagonistic and angry, frequently calling her names or shouting at her. In the opening scene of the novel, Justice sees one of Thomas' drumsticks move on its own and is frightened; this incident establishes both the supernatural aspects of the novel and the tension between Thomas and Justice.

The events of the novel move on two parallel tracks, one toward the Great Snake

Race, which Thomas has organized for all the boys in the neighborhood, and one toward Justice's realization of her psychic powers and potential. Justice practices stunts on her bicycle and looks for snakes near the strange and somewhat sinister Quinella Trace. She is determined to find the largest snake that can race the farthest and fastest. At the same time, she notices that Thomas seems able to control Levi mentally, and her growing fear of Thomas drives her to the home of Dorian Jefferson and his mother, Leona. There Mrs. Jefferson teaches Justice to use her own psychic powers to protect herself from Thomas and to move objects with her mind. At first, Justice does not remember the visits—Mrs. Jefferson is shielding her—but as her power grows, so does her knowledge of it.

After she has caught her snake, Justice learns that the object of the Great Snake Race is to collect the most snakes, rather than to race them. She is sure that she will lose, but when the snakes are counted the next day, she and the boys discover that her large snake was pregnant and has had offspring; she wins instead of Thomas. When they take the snakes back to the Quinella, Thomas probes Justice's mind and attempts to control her. She and Dorian battle psychically against Thomas, with Levi caught in the middle. When Thomas has been defeated, the four children link minds, and Justice transports them briefly into the future. Her power as the Watcher fully awakened, Justice realizes that the four of them are the "first unit," a new kind of human. The novel ends with the tension between Justice and Thomas not entirely resolved, but Justice has accepted her difference because she no longer is lonely.

Analysis

While psychic powers dominate the plot and events of *Justice and Her Brothers*, the novel is also about family relationships, identity, and growing up. Justice's entrance into adulthood begins with the acquisition of psychic powers rather than the more usual responsibilities teenagers must accept, but Hamilton is also clearly interested in depicting the emotional life of children and the effects of adolescence on the family structure as a whole.

Justice is lonely, deprived of her mother's presence for the first time and without any real friends; she is tolerated by the neighborhood boys only because Levi feels obligated to include her. Her desire to impress the boys by performing a dangerous bicycle trick and to win the Great Snake Race comes out of her need for companionship. Both of her parents see the loneliness in Justice, and her mother wonders whether she is doing the right thing by going to college now instead of waiting until Justice is older. Hamilton uses Mrs. Douglass' perspective to contrast the difficult choices of adulthood with the relative freedom that Justice still enjoys; while childhood is not represented as entirely idyllic, adulthood is complex and full of responsibility. When Justice becomes part of the unit and is no longer lonely, she also gives up much of her childhood. Although the novel ends with the four children riding bicycles as children do, there is a sense that such freedom and play will not last much longer.

The other key character struggling with growing up is Thomas. After the visit to the future, he declares that he will not give up who he is to be part of a unit, and much of his anger and hostility throughout the book seem to be a method of determining his identity. He psychically dominates his brother, at one point using images of Levi locked in a cell to keep him from saying things to their mother, and in the battle at the end he covers himself with leeches but makes Levi feel the pain. Because Thomas and Levi are mirror identical twins who have always been able to read each other's minds, their identities could easily merge. Thomas' control of his brother is a way to separate himself from Levi. He also has a stutter that disappears when he drums, and much of his pounding and banging serves as a way for him to control his speech. While he is certainly the antagonist in the book, he is simultaneously depicted as a character whose hostility and aggression come out of insecurity. Much of the tension between Thomas and the other family members is related not to his psychic ability but rather to his need to establish a separate identity.

Nevertheless, the psychic powers serve several purposes. First, they intensify the children's emotions and increase the dramatic tension. Thomas is a more frightening character because he can take out his hostility on his brother through controlling Levi's mind. Second, they provide the children with an increased range of possible actions and so make moral and ethical dilemmas weightier. Justice defeats Thomas in the psychic battle by making him feel his own pain; he has avoided personal responsibility in the use of his powers, and it is necessary that he stop doing so. Justice herself must be careful in what she does with them. Finally, as is the case in much science fiction, the psychic powers not only propel the reader into a fantasy world but also suggest that one take a closer look at the real world; Justice and her brothers' evolution into a new kind of human being raises the question of what kind of human being exists now.

Critical Context

Virginia Hamilton's career began in 1967, and since then she has written numerous books and won the Newbery Medal for *M. C. Higgins, the Great* (1974). Her work draws on a variety of African American experiences and spans a range of genres; in addition to novels and fiction for children, she has written biographies of W. E. B. Du Bois, Paul Robeson, and the fugitive slave Anthony Burns, and she has also published several volumes retelling folktales and myths. *Justice and Her Brothers* has two sequels, *Dustland* (1980) and *The Gathering* (1981), both of which have a more extensive future setting, a world of dust caused by the depletion of rain forests and nuclear catastrophe. *The Gathering* concludes with the children's power gone for the moment but all of them more mature and Thomas free of both his aggression and his stutter. The three novels together (known as the Justice Cycle) belong both to the tradition of children's literature in which supernatural powers lead to maturity and responsibility and to the science-fiction literature of dystopia (oppressive future societies). The Justice Cycle has significance outside the genre of children's literature because Hamilton is one of the few African Americans writing science fiction.

Elisabeth Anne Leonard

JUSTIN MORGAN HAD A HORSE

Author: Marguerite Henry (1902-   )
First published: 1945; illustrated
Type of work: Novel
Type of plot: Historical fiction
Time of work: 1795-1813
Locale: The Green Mountain country around Randolph, Vermont
Subjects: Animals, coming-of-age, and friendship
Recommended ages: 10-13

Young Joel Goss matures physically and psychologically as he loves, gentles, loses, and regains Little Bub, the founding stallion of the Morgan breed.

Principal characters:
JUSTIN MORGAN, an elderly singing master and schoolteacher who accepts the mongrel colt Little Bub as payment of a debt
JOEL GOSS, an apprentice sawyer and innkeeper and the young student of Morgan, who gentles Little Bub
LITTLE BUB, a colt of unknown ancestry who founds the sturdy Morgan breed
THOMAS CHASE, a miller and innkeeper who is master and surrogate father to Joel
EZRA FISK, a settler who leases Little Bub from Morgan
ROBERT EVANS, Fisk's hired hand, who enters Little Bub in pulling contests and races

Form and Content

From its dedication to Marguerite Henry's own Morgan horse, Friday, and to her friend Fred Tejan, who gentled him, *Justin Morgan Had Horse* proceeds through eighteen chapters of straightforward chronology, beginning with Joel Goss's apprenticeship in 1795 and ending with his recovery of Little Bub during the winter following the War of 1812. In her foreword, Henry establishes both the legendary qualities of the original Morgan horse and the authenticity of the breed's contribution to the settling of the United States. The novel concludes with a page of acknowledgements (including descendants of Justin Morgan and of Joel Goss) and a list of more than sixty works that Henry consulted to provide an authentic historical and geographical setting.

Henry's third-person narration, flavored with occasional letters and frequent conversations, allows the reader access to Joel's thoughts and emotions as well as glimpses into the minds of his friends. Little Bub displays his personality by his actions and by his distinctive snorting nicker; in addition, the reader sees the Morgan horse through Joel's loving eyes and through the comments of the Vermonters who admire the little stallion. Wesley Dennis' vivid illustrations, occurring every two or three pages, enhance Henry's depictions of her characters and especially of Little Bub.

Justin Morgan, the local singing master and schoolteacher, takes Joel as his helper on a summer-long trek to collect on a debt. Morgan accepts a pair of colts as payment. The muscular Ebenezer outshines Little Bub, who is thrown in for free, but Joel recognizes Little Bub's potential and identifies strongly with the runt, being slight and awkward himself.

Upon their return to Vermont, Joel's miserly father refuses to board Morgan any longer and insists that Joel immediately begin a seven-year apprenticeship with local sawyer and innkeeper Thomas Chase. Morgan finds lodging for himself and the colts nearby, and he arranges for Joel to gentle Little Bub after night school. Joel does so, supported by Morgan's friendship and Chase's fatherly understanding; he and the colt grow together until Morgan must sell Ebenezer and lease Little Bub to Ezra Fisk, an enterprising settler, to pay debts incurred during a lengthy illness.

Joel grieves deeply the loss of Little Bub's companionship until fate, in the person of Fisk's hired hand, Robert Evans, intervenes. Evans realizes that Morgan's young stallion excels in hauling, running, and overall endurance. With Fisk's permission, Evans enters Little Bub in a series of contests, all of which the Morgan horse wins. As Little Bub's reputation spreads, Joel renews their friendship, until Morgan's death parts boy and horse once more. For several years, Little Bub passes through a series of owners and out of Joel's life, until the two are reunited by chance after the War of 1812. A grown man, Joel can at last buy the Morgan horse; the story ends triumphantly with President James Monroe riding Little Bub in a victory parade as Joel proudly recounts the horse's deeds and declares his stallion "an American."

Analysis

Because *Justin Morgan Had a Horse* is based in fact, the novel contains a healthy dollop of fictionalized biography. Singing master Justin Morgan, apprentice Joel Goss (and his harsh, penny-pinching father), sawyer and innkeeper Thomas Chase, President James Monroe, and the mongrel stallion Little Bub (later known as "the Morgan horse") are rooted in history. Yankee stubbornness, Vermont pride, American pluck, frontier self-reliance, big-city foppishness, and British high-handedness add spice to Henry's approach to American history. Against the background of post-revolutionary war America, Joel Goss comes of age and finds his own set of values.

Although life in the United States has changed markedly in the centuries since Joel and Little Bub lived, the novel's treatment of the challenges faced by young people remains timeless. One such challenge involves the need for respect and approval. In search of unconditional love and acceptance, both young people and adults often seek the companionship of animals; gentling and mastering a horse gives Joel a much-needed dose of self-esteem, especially in the face of his father's continuing harshness and disapproval. Because Little Bub sets the standard for a new breed, and because Joel sensed the colt's potential when others scoffed at the runt, Joel experiences further affirmation from adults when his judgment proves superior to that of many experienced farmers and horse breeders.

In addition to the public praise that Joel gains as a result of his work with Little Bub, he seeks and receives a different sort of private acceptance: Before Joel recognizes Little Bub's physical potential, Justin Morgan recognizes Joel's mental and emotional potential. The gentle, elderly schoolmaster chooses Joel to accompany him on a summer-long errand not only because he trusts the boy and needs someone reliable to help him on the road but also because he knows that the sensitive, scholarly Joel needs time away from the demands of a harsh, intolerant, anti-intellectual father. Morgan nurtured Joel's mind and spirit; Thomas Chase nurtured his self-esteem and his yearning for practical knowledge. Henry portrays Chase as longing for a son of his own and as delighted with the hidden qualities that he can sense in the lanky, "runty" Joel; the combined influence of Morgan and Chase counteracts the acidic, materialistic negativity of Joel's father and further supports the theme of the search for acceptance.

Another theme of the novel, the individual in conflict with some facet of his environment, comes across clearly in Joel's daily life. Vermont in the late 1790's surrounds Joel with purely physical challenges: sawing logs by hand, using lamps and candles for light, facing winter without proper clothing, traveling on foot or by horseback, using muscle power instead of gas or electrical power for everyday living. Such challenges appeal to young people whose lives are circumscribed—and often stifled—by the continual presence, even encroachment, of technology. Although adults might wonder how Joel could find the energy for training Little Bub after a grueling day's work and several hours of night school, younger readers can identify with the need to fit something pleasurable into even the busiest day. Henry stresses the sheer physical toll of living by manual labor alone; yet the novel shows clearly that great joy can accompany or result from great labor.

Henry's novel suggests to young people that work brings its own rewards, that patience pays off, that gentleness can accompany courage, that simple dreams can come true, that animals can be excellent companions, and that society will eventually recognize and respect quality and integrity. Through its depiction of Joel's participation as a veterinarian in the War of 1812, the novel also emphasizes patriotism and the superiority of the American forces—their quality and integrity—while displaying the futility of war; it shows that animals as well as humans suffer when nations resort to armed conflict to settle their differences.

Critical Context

Within three years of its publication, *Justin Morgan Had a Horse* won the Junior Scholastic Gold Seal Award and the Award of the Friends of Literature and was named a Newbery Honor Book. Because of her meticulous research, her careful attention to character development (both human and animal), and her ear for the details of regional language, Marguerite Henry earned numerous other awards during her prolific writing career, including the Newbery Medal. Her more than fifty books of biography, geography, history, and animal stories have made her a perennial favorite not only of young adult readers but also of their teachers, who find the books a nearly painless method of enriching classroom education and of encouraging outside reading. Young readers respond positively to Henry's realistic scenes, believable protagonists, and satisfyingly hopeful outcomes—outcomes that occasionally earn her work the criticism of being sentimental. So famous are such novels as *Misty of Chincoteague* (1947), *King of the Wind* (1948), *Born to Trot* (1950), and *Stormy, Misty's Foal* (1963), that Henry has been called "the poet laureate of horses." The enduring appeal of *Justin Morgan Had a Horse* prompted Walt Disney Studios to adapt it for film in 1972.

Sonya H. Cashdan

KAFFIR BOY
The True Story of a Black Youth's Coming of Age in Apartheid South Africa

Author: Mark Mathabane (Johannes Mathabane, 1960-   )
First published: 1986; illustrated
Type of work: Autobiography
Time of work: March 21, 1960, to September 16, 1978
Locale: The shantytown of Alexandra, near Johannesburg, South Africa
Subjects: Adolescents, athletes, and race and ethnicity
Recommended ages: 15-18

Mathabane lives in conditions of hopeless poverty and oppression in apartheid South Africa until he is able to use his talents as a tennis player and as a student to win a scholarship to a U.S. college.

> *Principal personages:*
> JOHANNES (later MARK) MATHABANE, the oldest son of a poor black family in urban South Africa
> MAGDELENE MATHABANE, his mother
> JACKSON MATHABANE, his father
> GRANNY, his maternal grandmother, a gardener for wealthy white people
> FLORAH, his younger sister
> GEORGE, his younger brother
> ARTHUR ASHE, a black American tennis champion
> STAN SMITH, a white American tennis champion

Form and Content

Mark Mathabane's *Kaffir Boy: The True Story of a Black Youth's Coming of Age in Apartheid South Africa* delivers on all the promises made by its subtitle. It traces Mathabane's own story growing up in a very poor black family in the segregated Bantu township of Alexandra, near Johannesburg, following him from his birth in 1960 until 1978, when he boards a plane for the United States and college. The story is told in straightforward chronological order, in the first person, in fifty-four short chapters. Dialogue and description bring characters and settings to life—so well, in fact, that the sixteen black-and-white photographs do not add much to the prose.

In the first of three parts, "Passport to Alexandra," a clear sense of life in South Africa's black townships evolves. As the action begins, Johannes is awakened by shouting and banging. The police are making early-morning rounds, ostensibly to look for people who do not have the proper passbooks, which every black South African must carry, but also randomly to beat, loot, and vandalize. Johannes, just five years old, must look after Florah and George, his younger siblings, and face down the police. The scene is typical of the brutal ugliness of the boy's life. His family lives in a rough shack with no heat, water, or electricity. Johannes' father, Jackson, is imprisoned several times without a trial; when he is out of prison and working, he earns little money and spends most it on drinking and gambling. Often, Johannes and the children have only insects and grain to eat, and their mother, Magdelene, has less. Both parents are desperate for a way out of their misery. Jackson believes that clinging to traditional Tsonga customs and beliefs will bring some stability, if not comfort, while Magdelene finds her escape in an evangelical Christian church. Johannes rejects both belief systems.

In part 2, "Passport to Knowledge," Johannes begins to find his own way. After a long struggle with unsympathetic bureaucrats, his mother has obtained a birth certificate for Johannes, so that he may enroll in school. It is only through the determined assistance of a white woman that the certificate is granted. (Throughout the next decade, Johannes will learn to trust those white people who earn that trust—a position that will put him at odds with others in his community.) At first a reluctant student, preferring to hang out with other boys instead of attending school, Johannes soon sees that an education could help him escape violence and early death. He is bright and becomes an excellent scholar. One of his grandmother's white employers gives him cast-off books, and his mother takes in laundry in order to pay school fees. Johannes' father disapproves and will not help him in any way; once, he even burns the books that he thinks are driving his son away from him.

"Passport to Freedom" opens just after Granny's white employer has given Johannes an old wooden tennis racket. He soon discovers an aptitude for the game and eventually finds a job playing at a tennis club with liberal white people. Tournament play in South Africa, like everything else, is strictly segregated, but Johannes, who now calls himself Mark, is able to watch a match between American players Arthur Ashe (the first free black man Mark has ever seen) and Stan Smith. Smith befriends Mark, offers financial support, and arranges for him to receive a college tennis scholarship in the United States.

Analysis

Mark Mathabane did not write *Kaffir Boy* with a young audience in mind. As he explains in his preface, he found after he had been in the United States for some time, and as the political situation in South Africa came to the attention of more Americans, that he was asked more and more frequently what it had been like to grow up as a black South African under apartheid. Because few South African black people could become educated enough to write professionally in English, and because the apartheid government would not permit the publication of criticism of itself from within, the voices and stories of black South Africans went unheard. By re-creating his experiences, Mathabane hoped to educate adults in the United States about his native country and inspire them to work for change. Young people are naturally drawn to stories of other young people, however, especially those with emotions and goals similar to their own but in wildly different situations. The story of a young man who pulls himself up through determination and hard work, whose education enables him to find a better life, is an important one for young people.

An important theme in *Kaffir Boy* is Mathabane's refusal to reject all white people. Because he is willing from an early age to give individuals a chance to prove themselves—even though so many disappoint him—he is able to find friendship and support beyond his own community. In the dedication to *Kaffir Boy*, he mentions the white South Africans who helped him and Stan Smith and his wife, Margery, his first white American friends. So separate were the lives of white and black people under apartheid that Mathabane met few white people in the first fifteen years of his life. To open his first chapter, the author quotes a sign posted on the roads entering Alexandra township, warning those without permits (that is, white people) not to enter the area. Black and white South Africans were forced to remain ignorant of one another's lives, and fear was often the result. In fact, many of the white people Mathabane actually encounters help him in some way, including the woman who demands that his birth certificate be issued, Granny's wealthy employer who gives the boy old books and a tennis racket, young tennis players who break the law by playing tennis with him and driving him home, and Stan Smith. Within the black community, Mathabane is criticized for mingling with white people and is accused of trying to be white himself. Eventually, he is banned from black South African tennis, and he receives death threats. Mathabane stands firm in his belief that a person of any race might be good or evil, might help him or hold him back.

Yet, Mathabane is no apologist for apartheid or for his white oppressors, as the title of his book makes clear. The word "kaffir" is derived from the Arabic word for "infidel" and is a term used by white South Africans to insult black people. Although it carries the same force as the word "nigger" in the United States, Mathabane uses the term unflinchingly in his title. Some white people became his friends, but he has no illusions about his place in South African society. His descriptions of the pass rules, of separate buses and drinking fountains and residential areas for black and white South Africans, and of the rage he felt during the Soweto uprisings in 1976 constitute a ringing condemnation of apartheid and of those who upheld it. Although apartheid ended four years after this book was published, Mathabane's story remains important for those who wish to understand the conflicting emotions facing South Africans as they try to forge a new society.

Critical Context

The book to which *Kaffir Boy* is most frequently compared is Claude Brown's *Manchild in the Promised Land* (1965), a chilling story of Brown's own youth in Harlem. The two books share a grim tone overlaid with faint hope, strong language, and horrible but clearly authentic details of poverty existing side by side with plenty. For both young men, it is finally a college education that makes escape to a better world possible. The fascinating irony lies in examining the changes brought about in the United States and South Africa since the appearance of these books.

Mark Mathabane was surprised to learn, after settling in the United States, that black and white people did not mingle freely even in a free country and that his acceptance of white people was still controversial. His sequel to *Kaffir Boy*, entitled *Kaffir Boy in America: An Encounter with Apartheid* (1989), explores these issues further, as does a book that he cowrote with wife Gail, who is white: *Love in Black and White: The Triumph of Love over Prejudice and Taboo* (1992).

Cynthia A. Bily

KIM/KIMI

Author: Hadley Irwin (Lee Hadley, 1934-   ; and Annabelle Bowen Irwin, 1915-1995)
First published: 1987
Type of work: Novel
Type of plot: Social realism
Time of work: The early 1980's
Locale: A small Iowa town and Sacramento, California
Subjects: Coming-of-age, family, and race and ethnicity
Recommended ages: 13-15

Sixteen-year-old Kim Andrews loves her mother, stepfather and half brother but leaves home to find the family of her Japanese American father and her own identity.

> *Principal characters:*
> KIM ANDREWS, a biracial sixteen-year-old who is trying to find her deceased father's family, the Yogushis
> DAVEY ANDREWS, her twelve-year-old half brother, who helps Kim plan her trip
> MRS. MUELLER, the Andrews' babysitter and friend, who arranges for Kim to stay with the Okamura family in Sacramento
> BARBARA OKAMURA, Mrs. Mueller's friend, who begins Kim's introduction to her Japanese American heritage
> ERNIE OKAMURA, Barbara's son, who befriends Kim
> MRS. ENOMOTO, a teacher who introduces Kim to the experiences of Japanese Americans in the internment camps during World War II

Form and Content

Kim/Kimi is an account of a sixteen-year-old girl's struggle to develop her own identity. The opening line, "I don't understand you," reflects Kim Andrews' own confusion over who she is and what she is supposed to be. The novel, organized in chapters, is a chronological narrative of her journey to locate her Japanese American relatives and to understand her biracial heritage. *Kim/Kimi* is a notable title in multicultural literature since it is one of the first to explore the Japanese American culture for young adults. Within this short, easy-to-read novel, authors Lee Hadley and Annabelle Bowen Irwin, writing under the name "Hadley Irwin," explore the themes of racial intolerance and ethnic awareness.

Born Kimi Yogushi, Kim Andrews never knew her Japanese American father, who died before her birth. Adopted by her stepfather, she has grown up as an all-American girl in a small Iowa town. Although she has a loving family and good friends, Kim feels different because she looks Japanese. Confused and sometimes angered by racial slurs and stereotypes, she is determined to find her father's family, who disowned him when he married a non-Japanese woman. Since her mother is unable to help her, she plots with the help of her half brother, Davey, to fly to California while her parents are out of town.

Mrs. Mueller, Davey's mentor in the game Dungeons and Dragons, plans the quest. Kim is surprised when Ernie Okamura, a Japanese American college student, meets her at the airport. Mrs. Mueller did not tell Kim that she had arranged for her to stay with the Okamura family. Although she looks Japanese, Kim knows nothing about her "Japaneseness." Mrs. Okamura, understanding a need that Kim does not recognize, begins her acculturation.

Although Kim is appreciative of Mrs. Okamura's kindness, she is impatient to start her search for her father's family. She traces the family's address in the early 1940's and is shocked to learn that they were imprisoned at an internment camp, Tule Lake, during World War II. The search seems to have reached a dead end. Mrs. Enomoto, a Japanese American teacher who has access to Tule Lake records, volunteers to help. Herself an inmate at the camp, Mrs. Enomoto shares with Kim her childhood recollections of life at Tule Lake during the war.

Following new leads, Kim locates an address for the Yogushi family after their imprisonment. Although the house has been sold, the elderly occupant furnishes Kim with her aunt's address. Excited and scared, she prevails upon Mrs. Enomoto to contact the Yogushis. Her visit to her aunt and grandmother is a failure. When she cannot bring herself to tell them who she is, she instead leaves a picture of her father with them. Sick at heart, she returns to the Okamuras, where she finds her brother and friends from home waiting for her. When she again visits her aunt's home, her grandmother refuses to see her. The novel ends on a positive note when she receives a note from her aunt asking for time to think about the future while conveying her grandmother's acceptance of her.

Analysis

Kim/Kimi, with its themes of racial intolerance and ethnic awareness as they affect a young person's search for identity, is an excellent multicultural novel. The child of an interracial marriage, Kim Andrews must find her past to create a foundation for her future.

The authors present Kim's story as an archetypal quest. Mrs. Mueller guides the protagonist in her quest with the words, "Learning, remembering, forgetting. That is how we find out who we are." The heroine must overcome obstacles, including her own doubts and fears. Simple but satisfying, the plot follows her journey to California in search of her paternal grandparents. The story moves rapidly and reaches a climax with Kim's first, disastrous reunion with her grandmother. The authors avoid the usual pat, predictable ending. Indeed, an unhappy ending seems almost certain when Kim's grandmother refuses to see her on her second visit. The reader is left with a sense of hope at the conclusion of the novel, however, as the protagonist realizes that her grandmother has accepted her into the family.

In *Kim/Kimi*, one finds a unity of plot and characterization. The personality of the protagonist, Kim Andrews, is developed in a nonstereotypical manner. She is an all-American girl who knows little about non-Caucasians. Aware of her physical differences, she is angry and confused about her Japanese heritage. Although she is bright, she is frequently in trouble at school and earns poor grades. Ultimately, Kim must achieve a balance between her American lifestyle and her biracial heritage. Her desire to locate her father's family is tempered by her fears that they will reject her, as they rejected her father for his interracial marriage. Ultimately, Kim grows from an immature, impatient teenager, enamored with romance novels, into a mature young woman. Her quest leads not only to acceptance by her father's family but also to pride in her heritage.

Less developed, secondary characters provide balance within the themes of racial intolerance and ethnic awareness. While the protagonist has been the target of racial slurs at school, Davey, Mrs. Mueller, and Kim's friends, all Caucasians, support Kim's efforts to go to California. Kim's Japanese grandfather rejected her father's marriage on racist grounds, but several Japanese Americans, including the Okamuras and Mrs. Enomoto, help Kim in her quest.

Like the protagonist, readers may have little knowledge of the facts surrounding the imprisonment of Japanese Americans during World War II. Mrs. Enomoto, a teacher, serves as the vehicle for a first-person account of the experiences of Japanese Americans during the war. Although didactic in tone, her bitter account of life in the camps is necessary to the protagonist's understanding of her family's experiences and provides a powerful voice raised in protest against the fear and prejudice that led to such injustice and persecution.

While Kim's goal is locating her father's family, her Japanese American hosts help her see that she must also learn about her own "Japaneseness" if she is to develop a true sense of who she is. At first, she is unhappy and unappreciative of their efforts. As she learns more and struggles to overcome setbacks, Kim seeks their help in answering questions of her own, a testament to her coming-of-age.

The setting of the novel is integral to its themes. Kim's hometown in Iowa could be most small towns in the United States. Sacramento, California, with its large Asian American population is an ideal backdrop for the protagonist's introduction to a Japanese American community.

The writing style used by the authors is excellent. Sentence structures vary from simple to complex, while the dialogue is extensive and believable. Tone and mood vary, from Mrs. Enomoto's bitter recollection of Tule Lake to the protagonist's despair after her visits to her grandmother's home.

In *Kim/Kimi*, the authors have developed a poignant, gripping novel, gently crafted to explore the inner turmoil of a young adult of mixed ancestry. Balancing their protagonist's quest for her roots with broader issues of racism and social conscience, Hadley and Irwin have created a work with which young adults can identify.

Critical Context

Historically, there have been few young adult novels by or about Asian Americans. *Kim/Kimi* is a seminal work in that body of multicultural literature whose purpose is to break down racial and ethnic stereotypes. The novel dispels clichés while briefly opening a page in U.S. history. In a similar way, Yoshiko Uchida's novel *Journey to Topaz* (1971) mirrored harsh realities at the Topaz relocation camp while reminding readers that not all Americans hated the Japanese immigrants and their children.

For more than fifteen years, joint authors Lee Hadley and Ann Irwin pooled their individual writing talents to create novels of truth and beauty for young people. They often explored universal truths and social issues through the eyes of young adult protagonists.

Their novel *I Be Somebody* (1984) also explores racial themes, as a young black boy in the early twentieth century faces leaving his home when his community considers emigrating to Canada in order to escape prejudice in the United States. In addition, they wrote *Abby, My Love* (1985), a sensitive coming-of-age novel that deals with incest; it was named an American Library Association Notable Book and was chosen as one of the Child Study Association of America's Children's Books of the Year. In *Can't Hear You Listening* (1990), a teenage girl struggles for independence from an overprotective mother while trying to help a friend who is experimenting with drugs.

Inez Ramsey

THE KING WHO SAVED HIMSELF
FROM BEING SAVED

Author: John Ciardi (1916-1986)
First published: 1965; illustrated
Type of work: Poetry
Subjects: Social issues and war
Recommended ages: 10-18

Disturbed by the sudden appearance of a knight on a mission to slay a giant and save a kingdom, the king wants none of the hero's heroics.

Form and Content

On the surface, this little poem of 168 lines is an amusing fairy tale with a twist: A knight in armor suddenly appears, disturbs the peace of the kingdom, and becomes the one who must be conquered. The lighthearted tone adds a sharp edge to the underlying satire, which mocks the concept of the hero, the heroic ideal, and the whole fairyland tradition. Here, the kingdom is in a languid state of peace, and the direst threat is only a virus, which has afflicted the queen with a cold. The princess whiles away her time in the tower listening to a lark, and the giant lolls in the park smelling the flowers.

Into this tranquil world of sylvan repose and prosperity—the king thinks of exerting himself only to count his gold—the would-be savior noisily appears. Fiercely he insists on slaying the giant and saving the kingdom. Claiming the princess as his bride, as well as half the kingdom, is also among his plans. The queen is aroused from her bed; the giant runs away and hides. The knight's bellicose manner frightens the larks, and the princess, far from being enthralled, bursts into tears. The king, shocked but unintimidated by the clamorous intruder, orders him to leave or be shot. The king's only ambition is to allow his kingdom to fade peacefully into fairy myth and become "Long Ago and Far Away." Finally, he commands his cannoneer to fire at the knight and thus saves the kingdom from being saved.

This playful make-believe is cast in a form familiar to readers of old ballads: four-line stanzas with alternate rhymes. The pace is smooth and quick, running from a longer line of four stresses to a shorter one of three stresses through each of the forty-two quatrains. This pattern is used for a variety of narrative effects, such as a quick, summary conclusion of the previous line, or an amusing, unexpected turn: "The King was thinking of counting his gold/ But went to sleep instead." The language is as simple as the story itself, and the plot is hurried along by dialogue. Poet John Ciardi plays with the syntax in a way that adds to the self-mockery: "—So there *was* a Lark. In, as I say,/ The tree I put there to be . . . ." Adding to the amusement is commentary about what constitutes a proper fairy tale. There must be a giant, a castle to be saved, a princess to be won, and a hero, and so the storyteller includes them, along with larks aplenty—because, as he says in the beginning, "all the poems I ever see/ Put all their larks in the air." So that readers will not take this pleasantry too seriously, the poet continually reminds them that he is fabricating his tale as one should: "A (naturally) Princess in (yes) a Tower/ Was listening to (what else?) the Lark."

The drawings by Edward Gorey lend flawless accompaniment to the mythical atmosphere. A scaled creature with wings and a pointed tale looks dangerous, but he turns out to be as tame and frolicsome as a canine pet. The realistic details of the drawings contrast with their playful use. Large piggy banks lie scattered about the throne, the princess swoons in the tower with her head cushioned by passing clouds, and the approaching knight dominates the crest of a mountain far away. The pictorial sharpness of the artist's work makes the unreality of the fairy world clearer.

Analysis

The effect of the poet's tongue-in-cheek approach in *The King Who Saved Himself from Being Saved* is to keep readers distant from the fiction and to suggest that one not take the tale seriously. In addition, the characters are, except for the king, scarcely more than names. The knight, who is given the obvious, generic name of Hero, is never seen without his helmet. He remains a faceless force with one outstanding trait: an unwavering zeal that blinds the believer. Yet, the simplicity of the plot, its charming commentary, and, above all, its compelling logic—it is silly to start a fight in this peaceful world—engage one's attention and sympathy. Readers may be disarmed by the tone and manner of the poem's narrator, a congenial voice that continually assures that all this playfulness is mere artless fabrication. This staged innocence befits the characters in the story itself. The giant wants only to smell the flowers in the park, the princess passes her time in the tower watching the larks, and the queen lies in bed with a cold while the king snoozes on the throne. Once aroused by the intrusive knight, however, the king proves to be a practical sort who thinks the clamorous Hero is not only a nuisance but a fool so determined to do the heroic deed that he cannot see that the kingdom is in no need of saving. He is so caught up in his enthusiasm that he ignores the cannon's fuse as it rapidly burns toward the powder. Children will delight in the silliness; adults will see in it a commentary on the world outside the child's fiction.

By making fun of itself, by adding larks and castles by the sea because such "of course" poems as this fairy tale always have them, the poem forestalls any criticism that would see the piece as a mere child's poem. On one level, the poet is having a lark, but the stock characters and phrases are transparent enough to show a serious undertone. The more childlike and harmless this simple world appears, the more awful and frightening is the knight who comes with a fierce determination to save it.

The main focus of the narrative is on the problem presented by the errant knight. Implicit in the portrait is the knight's blindness, his inability to accept "reality," so dedicated is he to the chivalric code. The main message is unstated but nevertheless clear: Something is wrong with a belief that blinds one to reality. By making this kingdom not only peaceful but childlike in its innocence, the poem goes further and makes the chivalric code, represented by the knight, a force that threatens to destroy the kingdom. The traditional view of the Camelot ideal is turned topsy-turvy. Here, the knight is not a righter of wrong, a slayer of evil dragons and giants, for none exists. The knight himself is the monster, monstrous in his dedication to an ideal that, if it is not entirely outmoded, is out of place in this kingdom. There are places, the poem is saying, that do not need heroes. A more serious implication, however, hovers over the whole halcyon scene: Sometimes heroes do more harm than good. Sometimes they cause problems where none exists, as the king declares: "once they start saving you . . . / They don't know when to stop."

Critical Context

The text of the poem was first published in *The Saturday Review* of November 14, 1964; the book edition has a twelve-line rhymed dedication to James Cubeta. This work showcases John Ciardi's talent for appealing to both adults and children and is a testament to his popularity. He wrote several children's books, including *I Met a Man* (1961) and *The Wish-Tree* (1962). His adult readers would know him not only as a poet of considerable reputation but as a teacher, editor, and critic as well. His work is never far from either the serious or the witty and playful, as *The King Who Saved Himself from Being Saved* demonstrates.

The poet's intent in composing this tale may not have been to awaken children to the danger of believing too much in romantic ideals, but this message is inescapable, certainly to the adult reader. Appearing at a time when the concept of Camelot was perhaps at its crest, a year after the assassination of its chief inspiration, President John F. Kennedy, this poem offers a sobering comment on the tendency toward idolatry to which human nature is often is heir. Ciardi denied that his poem carries such a message, but the poem itself belies the author. Its point of reference is both historical and conventional, and since it mocks the world and ideals that it depicts, the implication is obvious: One should not take heroes or myths too seriously. The setting of the poem, as unadorned as a cartoon; its witty wordplay; and its few characters, who scarcely act, highlight in their simplicity the poem's central point—that ideals can carry one too far into make-believe. The adult reader who is familiar with Ciardi's poetry would recognize his penchant for satire and for calling attention to the fact that in the real world all things pass, including a society's most cherished ideals. Children will delight in the poem's amusing wit, as will adults, who will also feel its sharp point pressed against their tendency to follow heroes into oblivion.

Bernard E. Morris

THE KINGDOM UNDER THE SEA
AND OTHER STORIES

Author: Joan Aiken (1924-   )
First published: 1971; illustrated
Type of work: Short fiction
Subjects: Animals, family, poverty, religion, and the supernatural
Recommended ages: 10-13

This collection of stories is derived from Eastern European folktales.

Form and Content

Joan Aiken's *The Kingdom Under the Sea and Other Stories* includes eleven stories based on folktales from Eastern Europe, three of which the author found in the collection *Croatian Tales of Long Ago* (1924), written by Ivana Berlic-Mazuranic and translated by F. S. Copeland. Two stories are adapted from Christian legend, and the remainder refer to local mythologies. The stories are accompanied by striking illustrations by Jan Pienkowski that employ silhouette figures; they are sometimes used as borders for the text, set against the white background of the pages, but they are given beautiful colorful backgrounds in the full-page plates.

Some of the stories carry conventional morals and were evidently designed for that purpose. These tales include, as one would expect, the two items of Christian legend. In "The Goose Girl," Saint Peter asks to trade places with God for a day, so that he might savor the experience of absolute power, but discovers instead the burden of absolute responsibility. In "The Pear Tree," the angel Gabriel, disguised as a poor man, receives charity from three brothers whose sole possession is a pear tree and offers all three a wish in return. The two who use their wishes to become wealthy are not so generous next time that the disguised angel calls, and they are restored to their former penury. The youngest, who only asked for a dutiful wife, has retained his simple virtues and is given further rewards.

The other conventional moral tale in the collection is "The King Who Declared War on the Animals," in which an impoverished nobleman who looks after his animals well accumulates a whole set of humble liege-men, including such apparently useless servants as a mouse and a mole. When the nobleman incurs the wrath of a powerful king by marrying his daughter, however, the mouse and the mole call on their kinsmen to make the advance of the king's army impossible.

Formal morals are also attached to "The Venetian Princess" and "The Golden-Fleeced Ram and the Hundred Elephants," but they are less conventional. In the former story, a Serbian Tsar sets off to claim the hand of the daughter of the king of the Venetians, but he must nominate a champion to undertake various improbable tasks before he can do so. The tsar thinks that he has left all his nephews behind, but the least of them has tagged along unnoticed and completes the allotted tasks. "Woe to him who overlooks his own relations!" the conclusion of the tale proclaims. The latter story also involves an seemingly impossible task set by a king who is looking for an excuse to execute a subject whose golden-fleeced ram he covets. The young man in question finds a way to attract the hundred elephants whose tusks he requires to build an ivory tower, but he rebels against the necessity of slaughtering them and instead applies their strength to the destruction of the tyrant.

"Baba Yaga's Daughter" combines the themes of the familiar stories of Cinderella and of Hansel and Gretel. Vasilissa, made miserable by the hatred of her stepmother and two stepsisters, befriends the daughter of the cannibal witch Baba Yaga. When the witch eventually finds the girl in her strange house—after several near misses—she tries to put her in the oven but is tricked and ends up there herself.

The remaining tales are less like those most carefully preserved in Western Europe and America. In "The Kingdom Under the Sea," a fisherman asks Zora-djevojka the Dawn Maiden to show him the way to the sea-king's palace, where he thinks he might be happy, but he finds that his reckless desire to reach it has spoiled the life he had. In "The Imprisoned Queen," three brothers try to build a city but are frustrated by a *vila*, a wicked fairy. In order to complete their task, they must wall up the wife of the youngest son as a sacrifice. When her son grows up, he sets her free and the *vila* destroys the city. In "The Reed Girl," a prince with a magic horse is helped by Zora-djevojka to obtain the reeds in which three beautiful girls are confined, but his carelessness kills two of them before he returns safely home with the third. In "The Sun's Cousin," the witch Mokosh—who is foster mother to the sun during the midwinter—befriends a generous miller's daughter and tries to establish her as lady-in-waiting to the princess, but the girl prefers a different reward and marries the knight Oleg Ban. When the jealous princess sends an army to punish them, Mokosh refuses to help them. The sun, however, proves more generous than his mean foster mother.

Analysis

The tales in *The Kingdom Under the Sea and Other Stories* are plainly and economically told, without the kind of calculated prettification and authorial commentary that are often employed to make retold folktales more "suitable" for a modern audience. Aiken is content to present such unfamiliar mythical figures as Zora-djevojka the Dawn Maiden without elaborate introduction or explanation, save for the observation that she is "the Sun's beloved daughter." The language employed in the telling of the tales is easily comprehensible, but Aiken is not afraid to introduce exotic elements where they are appropriate.

Aiken does not emphasize the moral element in the tales, nor does she attempt to import morals into the tales that have none; if anything, she tends to collaborate in the covert undermining of morals that are a little too facile. Even in a conscientiously pious story such as "The Pear Tree," there is a note of subtle cynicism. Gabriel has no difficulty making the acquisitive brothers rich, but, when he is asked to find the youngest a "good Christian girl" to wed, he observes that the available supply is so desperately limited as to make the task almost impossible.

Many folktales have the paradoxical quality of using fantastic apparatus to defend the virtues of dull reality. "The Kingdom Under the Sea" is typical of this tendency, arguing that the fisherman ought to be content with his dutiful wife and healthy child instead of lusting after the wealth and comfort of the sea-king's palace. "The Pear Tree," "The King Who Declared War on the Animals," "Baba Yaga's Daughter" and "The Sun's Cousin" all sing the praises of the virtues of humility, self-restraint, and kindness, all of which require people to be content with their lot rather than entertaining unrealistic ambitions. It is interesting, however, that several of the stories distribute their rewards and punishments according to a different scheme.

"The Reed Girl" fails to punish the carelessness that causes the death of two of the imprisoned girls. Although the first death might be excused as a mere lack of foresight, the prince's repetition of the error is criminally stupid, and yet he is allowed to attain unrestrained happiness with the third reed girl. In "The Imprisoned Queen," on the other hand, the son's virtuous act in releasing his mother causes the destruction of the city—the *vila* who established the unjust situation remains unchallenged. Although virtue does triumph in "The Golden-Fleeced Ram and the Hundred Elephants," its victory involves a calculated abandonment of its own symbols: The ram that is the object of desire for the unjust and unwise king is simply discarded. The presentation of such exceptional tales alongside the others preserves an intriguing moral complexity that is—arguably, at least—more valuable than the kind of insistent preaching which refuses to notice that in the real world, the humble virtues are not often rewarded and even the most blatant injustice is rarely punished.

The exoticism of the collection is a considerable advantage because it offers children motifs and ideas that are likely to be new to them. The book does retain a base within the familiar, but it is careful to extend its range into the wilder frontiers of the imagination. It does so gracefully and colorfully, in terms of both its text and the supportive illustrations. *The Kingdom Under the Sea and Other Stories* is a handsome book that is a pleasure to behold and is therefore precious.

Critical Context

The Kingdom Under the Sea and Other Stories was the second collection of Joan Aiken's stories to be illustrated by Jan Piénkowski, following *A Necklace of Raindrops* (1968), the contents of which were much more various. This collection benefits from the refinement of the artist's technique as well as the utilization of stories from a common source; words and pictures are blended into a more coherent and more aesthetically satisfying whole. Many excellent collaborations between artists and storytellers of the first rank were produced during the 1970's, taking advantage of cheap and efficient technologies of reproduction; *The Kingdom Under the Sea and Other Stories* is one of the landmark works displaying the potential that such works had.

Brian Stableford

THE KING'S DRUM AND OTHER AFRICAN STORIES

Author: Harold Courlander (1908-   )
First published: 1962; illustrated
Type of work: Short fiction
Subjects: Death, family, gender roles, and social issues
Recommended ages: 10-15

> *These tales of fools, wise men, heroes, tricksters, and ordinary people entertain and teach simple, universal lessons against a background of traditional African life.*

Form and Content

The King's Drum and Other African Stories is one of many collections of traditional folk material from around the world by Harold Courlander. The stories in this volume are widely varied, as the author himself notes; he presents tales about human and animal tricksters, heroes and pseudo-heroes, conflicts and dilemmas that deal either humorously or seriously with human foibles and proverbial wisdom. None of the twenty-nine tales is more than a few pages long, in a small-page format. They are simply written and they are not sequential, so they can be read singly or in any combination. Seven of the tales feature animal characters rather than human ones. Seventeen pen-and-ink illustrations by Enrico Arno provide whimsy and an exotic flavor.

Seen in terms of their effect, the stories may be divided into three broad categories: explanations of nature, social or moral lessons, and purely humorous narratives. In the first category are tales that explain natural phenomena and the physical makeup or natural actions of animals. "The Message from the Moon," for example, explains the origin of death among human beings and also explains the hare's split lip. In "Why the Chameleon Shakes His Head," the chameleon hears the dog explain his partnership in hunting with the man and then witnesses how the man actually treats the dog after they have hunted together. The chameleon is shocked and since then has avoided all human beings. Now, whenever people see him in the forest, the chameleon is still shaking his head in amazement at the unkindness of the man.

One of the more serious, socially didactic tales tells of a father-in-law and his son-in-law who have a disagreement and of how the elders of the tribe bring them to reconciliation. In a more satirical vein, "A Song for the New Chief" shows that praise of public officials is a ritual activity and has nothing to do with the actual personality or popularity of the official.

Whether explaining nature, commenting on social customs, or simply entertaining, most of the tales contain at least some element of humor. The title story of the collection shows how Anansi, the spider trickster, outsmarts himself and loses the hand of the chief's daughter. "Nawasi Goes to War" is a hilarious, extended description of a merchant whose harmless attempt to look like a warrior is complicated by the boasting songs of his servant, forcing the merchant into a situation for which he is wholly unprepared and from which he emerges, through no virtue of his own, as a hero. "Ruda, the Quick Thinker" offers a classic example of a man whose silly actions belie his reputation for decisiveness and intelligence.

These tales will appeal to any young person who appreciates *Aesop's Fables* (fourth century B.C.), Rudyard Kipling's *Just So Stories* (1902), and similar works, and some of them will also appeal to younger children when read aloud.

Analysis

Courlander's anthology is a balanced selection from a wide variety of geographic locations in Africa south of the Sahara. The tales represent East Africa, Central Africa, Southern Africa, and West Africa, as well as many ethnic and cultural groups in this vast area. Young readers may gain a casual and comfortable introduction to the folkways of a major complex of cultures in Africa—cultures that are the source of tales and traditions still to be found not only in Africa but also in the United States, Brazil, and the Caribbean.

The division of tales given above considerably simplifies the collection's range of folk narrative genres, which include fool tales, trickster tales, tall tales, riddles, and origin tales. "Three Fast Men," for example, is an example of the tall tale. The two Ashanti tales of Anansi represent the trickster genre through a figure who is well known in West Africa and has survived as well in African American tradition as Aunt Nancy; the figure of Anansi even appears on at least one occasion as an opponent of the transcendent African American trickster, Brer Rabbit. "The Search: Who Gets the King's Daughter" exemplifies the riddle or unresolved enigma, best known in English through William Blake's poem "The Lady or the Tiger." "The Message from the Moon" is a typical origin tale, and "Ruda, the Quick Thinker" is a fool tale in the manner of the English folk cycle "The People of Gotham."

Thus, while the tales may be read and enjoyed at the level of *Aesop's Fables*, Jacob and Wilhelm Grimm's *Die Kinder- und Hausmärchen* (1812, 1815; *Grimm's Fairy Tales*, 1823), the adventures of Paul Bunyan, and the like, they are also rich in information about the types of folk narrative, everyday customs, and generally accepted opinions in Africa. For the young reader who is ready (and the adult who is interested), the "Notes on the Stories" at the end of the volume offer a wealth of information in simple language, devoid of scholarly bombast and nit-picking. Reflecting Courlander's experiences with the United States Information Agency (USIA), United Nations, and Voice of America, as well as years of independent collecting, his introduction to the notes sketches the diversity of topography and peoples in sub-Saharan Africa. The notes themselves provide differing background information, depending on the tale.

In "The Fisherman," a seagull asks land-locked birds about the time of low tide, and the note informs the reader that this demonstrates the truth of a Jabo proverb, which is also the last line of the tale: "Every man should be the master of his own profession." Another tale with a moral, perhaps related to a common proverb, is "The Song of Gimmile," which shows that an action once taken cannot be undone.

Courlander's note provides this explanation and goes beyond it by observing that the instrument accomplishing the public shaming of the king is a song and by pointing out that song is a common means of both communication and comment. Confirmation of the importance of both the song and the singer in African societies is found in the note to "The King of Sedo," from which readers learn that the Wolof, like most African ethnic groups, have their own word for the bard and for his instrument.

The notes function as anthropological background to the sampling of stories from different peoples, informing the reader, among other things, that the pun or play on words is an acceptable form of humor and satire, that the actual purpose of an insoluble enigma tale is to provoke discussion and argument among the listeners, and that public ridicule is a powerful civic weapon against unacceptable behavior. Although the morals of tales such as "The Lion's Share" are easily recognizable as universal folk wisdom, some of the customs illustrated in tales such as "A Father-in-Law and His Son-in-Law" are particular to the local culture. In this tale, readers learn that personal and family as well as legal matters are often adjudicated promptly by the community because "If trouble lasts, it will involve many people."

The stories alone are entertaining, and their world is no more alien—perhaps less—than that of the Arthurian legends and the fairy tales of the Brothers Grimm. With the notes, they are the beginning of an education in a real, rather than an imaginary, culture.

Critical Context

In 1936, Harold Courlander began a career of collecting African, African American, and African Caribbean songs, myths, legends and tales, as well as writing scholarly articles and fiction based on his knowledge of this material. *The African*, a novel that he published in 1967, tells the tale of a boy captured by slavers in Africa and brought to America, where he learns to adapt and survive. Although not Courlander's best-known work, it became famous for a time when he successfully sued Alex Haley for infringement of copyright in portions of *Roots* (1976). *The King's Drum and Other African Stories* was published approximately midway through Courlander's most active period in his career, which stretched to 1982.

Like *A Treasury of African Folklore* (1974, 1995), his mammoth volume of tales, myths, and legends from sub-Saharan Africa, *The King's Drum and Other African Stories* is a sampling of many localities and moods in this continent. The major difference is that the smaller collection concentrates on shorter and more accessible tales and is therefore both easy to read and suitable for beginning an exploration of the genre. What separates Courlander's book from many others of the kind is its eclectic geographic selection, his wide knowledge, and his avoidance of cumbersome scholarly apparatus.

James L. Hodge

KITTY IN THE MIDDLE

Author: Judy Delton (1931-   )
First published: 1979; illustrated
Type of work: Novel
Type of plot: Domestic realism
Time of work: September, 1942, to June, 1943
Locale: St. Paul, Minnesota
Subject: Friendship
Recommended ages: 10-13

Kitty and her best friends Margaret Mary and Eileen attend the fourth grade together at a parochial school in St. Paul, Minnesota, during World War II.

>   *Principal characters:*
>   KITTY, a fourth-grade girl who finds herself "in the middle" between two very different best friends
>   MARY MARGARET, one of Kitty's two best friends, a devout, studious, neat, and unspoiled girl
>   EILEEN, Kitty's other best friend, a self-assured, adventurous only child who knows how to get what she wants
>   SISTER URSULINE, the fourth-grade teacher at St. Anthony's School
>   DOLORES HENLEY, the least-liked girl in the fourth grade
>   EUGENE LEGGET, the handsome new boy at school
>   CHARLOTTE NEILSON, the occupant of the mysterious "haunted house"

Form and Content

Judy Delton's *Kitty in the Middle*, a short, easy-to-read book, is divided into eight titled chapters, each of which is illustrated with a black-and-white sketch by Charles Robinson. The novel features third-person narration, with omniscience limited to the title character, and an episodic structure that recounts the adventures of Kitty and her best friends, Eileen and Mary Margaret, at St. Anthony's School in St. Paul, Minnesota, during 1942 and 1943. The novel, which centers on the childhood domains of classroom and neighborhood, highlights the fears, frustrations, and joys of fourth-grade life, while adult concerns occupy only a vague and distant reality.

Kitty, the only child of caring parents, inhabits a well-regulated home in which her father returns from work promptly at 5:30 P.M. to a dinner of breaded veal on Monday, pork chops on Wednesday, and tuna on Friday. Kitty's chameleon-like personality is somewhere "in the middle" between Mary Margaret and Eileen, and she tends to take on the personality of whichever girl she is with. Mary Margaret, Kitty's "safe" friend, is a member of a large, devout Catholic family of modest means. Studious, religious, honest, and well-liked, she always looks immaculate in her spotless homemade school uniform and perfectly arranged "sausage" curls. Eileen, on the other hand, is Kitty's "dangerous" friend, a rather pampered only child, who longs to grow up, change her name to Dorothy, and travel the world. She knows her own mind and how to get what she wants, and she possesses the enviable ability to lie and smile simultaneously.

The novel opens, appropriately, with the first day of school, as Kitty's apprehension about her new teacher, the formidable Sister Ursuline, is only somewhat offset by the excitement of wearing her fashionable new shoes. Kitty comes to realize, however, that Sister Ursuline is a mere mortal after all when a mischievous boy places the nun in an embarrassing predicament by stepping on her veil and refusing to lift his foot. Pride also takes a fall when the least-admired girl in class shows up wearing shoes identical to those that only a day before Kitty had judged so superior.

The traumas of the first day of school behind her, Kitty faces a series of crises only too familiar to most readers in grammar school. Valentine's Day, always fraught with the potential for melodrama, marks the end of her first crush, when she discovers that the romantic valentine she receives from the object of her affection was given to every girl in class and that her "admirer" does not even know her name. Kitty faces another typical childhood fear by hiding in the bathroom to avoid the possibility of being called on in music class when she does not know the answer. Only after Mary Margaret advises her that giving one very wrong answer will prevent her from ever being called on again does she return to class.

After school, the girls occupy themselves making life-sized paper dolls from cardboard boxes, crashing a wedding at the local church (and even catching the bouquet), and pondering the identity of the occupant of the neighborhood's "haunted house." This continuous motif leads to the story's climax, when the girls finally summon up the courage to approach the house (by devising a scheme to sell pencils for "charity") and meet the occupant, Charlotte Neilson, a woman with a fascinating history and an attic full of wonderful old clothes. A former actress, she serves jasmine tea, encourages the girls to try on her old costumes, spins tales of her past, and offers the friends an enticing glimpse at life's possibilities.

Analysis

Like much successful juvenile fiction, *Kitty in the Middle* examines life from a child's perspective, allowing young readers to identify easily with its characters and situations. Although the novel's action takes place during World War II, Kitty's world does not seem unfamiliar to young contemporary readers, because the vision of childhood portrayed has universal currency. The novel's scope extends no further than schoolyard, neighborhood, and church, so that the historical setting supplies ambience and educational value, without detracting from the universality of childhood experiences. The young reader gains a sense of being a part of a community of children that transcends both geography and time.

The novel encompasses one school year, the unit by which most children measure their lives. Delton recognizes that small matters loom large in childhood and that school is the main stage in every child's life drama. The small but significant routines of the school day so familiar to all young people are effectively dramatized in *Kitty in the Middle*. The fear of being called on by the teacher, the thrill of Valentine's Day, and the first crush on a schoolmate will all resonate with schoolchildren, particularly girls. The anticipation of a new school year—accompanied by such overwhelmingly urgent questions as "Who is my teacher?" "Who is my class?" and "What will I wear?"—is dramatized both by Kitty's trepidation regarding Sister Ursuline and by the intense pleasure that she takes in her new shoes. Like most childhood fears and expectations, these prove to be exaggerated, as Kitty discovers that Sister Ursuline is subject to embarrassment like everyone else and that a pair of shoes alone is not a measure of one's worth as a human being.

Although the novel's depiction of grammar school rings true for most readers, *Kitty in the Middle* may resonate even more strongly for parochial school students. Delton's inclusion of such details as the pupils' beliefs that nuns have no hair and that attending Mass and Holy Communion the first Friday of the month nine times in a row guarantees entrance into Heaven, will strike a particular chord with Catholic school students (and their parents). The girls' continuous preoccupation with what is and is not a sin, and how to atone for a sin once one is determined, should offer comfort to young readers grappling with such significant issues themselves.

Kitty in the Middle reassures young readers who are in the process of puzzling out their own identities that an infinite variety of personality traits and behaviors exists and that discovering one's own particular characteristics is a lifelong process. Both Eileen and Mary Margaret have very strong, well-defined characters that illustrate that a wide diversity of human character is not only permissible but also desirable. Kitty, on the other hand, is still in the process of discovering her identity, taking on various aspects of her friends' personalities when she is with them in order to ascertain what fits and what does not.

Kitty in the Middle neither lectures to its readers nor preaches to them. Its value dwells in the subtle message imparted that children's concerns are not trivial and that their worries, fears, and joys are shared by young people everywhere. Delton nurtures in her readers the delights of friendship and the adventure of self-discovery, while whetting their appetites for exploring their world.

Critical Context

Kitty in the Middle, Judy Delton's first novel, is also the first book in the Kitty series, which includes a prequel, *Kitty from the Start* (1987), and the sequels *Kitty in the Summer* (1980) and *Kitty in High School* (1984). A prolific author, Delton also created the Angel series, including *Back Yard Angel* (1983), *Angel in Charge* (1985), *Angel's Mother's Boyfriend* (1986), and *Angel's Mother's Baby* (1989), and the popular Pee Wee Scouts books, a series of easy books for very young readers.

The Kitty books are directly descended from Maud Hart Lovelace's Betsy-Tacy and Tib series, published in the 1940's, including *Betsy-Tacy* (1940) and *Betsy-Tacy and Tib* (1941). The books share a Minnesota setting, a triumvirate of friends, a focus on the details of childhood, and corresponding characters. Tacy, like Mary Margaret, sports "sausage curls" and comes from a large, devout Catholic family, while Tib, like

Eileen, is a no-nonsense, pampered only child. Betsy, the series' central figure is, like Kitty, the "in-the-middle" character, a girl in the process of discovering her own identity and place in the world.

Judy Delton, like Beverly Cleary in such books as *Henry Huggins* (1950), *Ellen Tebbits* (1951), and *Beezus and Ramona* (1955), creates a warm, comforting, and familiar childhood world in which young readers can immerse themselves and believable characters with which they can identify. *Kitty in the Middle* fits snugly into this tradition of fiction that treats childhood in a realistic, insightful way, making its young readers feel at home and its older readers nostalgic for their own childhood days.

Mary Virginia Davis

KNEEKNOCK RISE

Author: Natalie Babbitt (1932-　　)
First published: 1970; illustrated
Type of work: Novel
Type of plot: Folktale and moral tale
Time of work: A preindustrial age
Locale: The imaginary country of Kneeknock
Subjects: Nature, religion, science, and social issues
Recommended ages: 10-15

Egan discovers the truth about the mysterious monster that has terrified the village of Instep for more than a thousand years, but in doing so he is forced to consider the possibility that if the monster did not exist, the villagers would invent him.

Principal characters:
　　EGAN, a boy of eleven or twelve who goes on his first visit to the annual fair at the base of the mysterious Kneeknock Rise
　　ADA, the female cousin with whom Egan is forced to stay during his visit
　　ANSON, Egan's uncle and Ada's father
　　GERTRUDE, Egan's aunt and Ada's mother
　　OTT, an uncle of Egan who generally lives with Anson and Gertrude but who has disappeared
　　THE CHANDLER, a friend of Egan's father who gives Egan a ride to the fair

Form and Content

In its fablelike account of a preadolescent boy's visit to his relatives, *Kneeknock Rise* raises important questions about the nature of faith and myth and about the pressure to conform. The imaginary geography of the setting and the unusual cultural practices of the inhabitants of Kneeknock make it clear that Natalie Babbitt's intention in writing this novel was not to create a realistic world but to invent a mythic place that was different enough from the contemporary world to make young readers think broadly about human behavior but similar enough to allow them to recognize themselves in the characters. The novel is set in the preindustrial past in a country that could be rural America but that, with its chandler, clockmaker, and fair, feels vaguely Western European, vaguely germanic.

The story in this brief, engaging novel is fairly straightforward. Egan, who appears to be about eleven or twelve in Babbitt's own illustrations, is invited by his Uncle Anson and Aunt Gertrude to visit during the annual fair. The fair is the most popular event of the country because of its proximity to the small mountain that lends its name to the town—Kneeknock Rise. People are both appalled and intrigued by the prospect of being close to the mysterious mountain that for more than a thousand years has terrified nearby inhabitants with the strange moaning noises that rise from it on stormy nights. Egan, too, is thrilled to visit the mountain that is said to be the home of the Megrimum, the monster that the townspeople believe to be the source of the moaning and of certain rumored attacks on sheep and dogs.

Egan's excitement about his first visit to Kneeknock and to the fair is tempered somewhat by his having to stay with his fussy aunt and his rather hostile female cousin, Ada. He is also bothered by the fact that another uncle, Ott, who normally boards with his Uncle Anson and Aunt Gertrude, has mysteriously disappeared.

Nevertheless, Egan rides to Kneeknock in the wagon of a chandler who is a friend of his father, and he enjoys the visit, despite the harangues of Ada and the nervous worrying of his aunt. During the visit, Egan comes across some poetry written by his missing uncle, and he is intrigued by the poems that speculate upon what adventurers will find on the other sides of the hills they climb and that ponder whether kings whose collected knowledge brings them worry and responsibility are truly wiser than fools who have no knowledge but are happy. Egan is attracted by the nonconformist themes of the poems, and he dreams about being an adventurer like his missing uncle. He even fantasizes about climbing Kneeknock Rise, battling and slaying the Megrimum, and returning to the village a hero, thus proving his merit and maturity to his obnoxious cousin and silly aunt.

Before long, Egan is given the opportunity to advance in the direction of his dreams. One afternoon when a storm is brewing, Ada pushes a bit too far in her teasing. All along, she has mocked him for not knowing the details of Kneeknock lore and ritual, and now she labels Egan a sissy and challenges him to climb Kneeknock Rise. He calls her bluff and does just that, much to her chagrin and to the dismay of the townspeople, who, although certain that he will be killed by the Megrimum, are too afraid of the monster themselves to make more than a half-hearted rescue attempt. Before they do so, however, Egan discovers not only that his missing uncle is resting safely on the supposedly dangerous Kneeknock Rise but also that Uncle Ott knows the secret of the Megrimum. He takes the would-be dragon slayer to the cave that the Megrimum is supposed to inhabit and shows Egan a steam vent on the cave floor. When it storms, his uncle explains, rainwater runs into the vent, is heated by underground volcanic forces, and is propelled as steam back through the vent, thus producing the famous moan of the Megrimum. The monster is nothing more than a geothermal teakettle. To test the theory, Egan throws a rock into the vent to block the opening and heads back toward the village, certain that he will be welcomed as a hero.

When the storm subsides and the villagers finally find Egan, they hurry him down from Kneeknock Rise and refuse to believe his account of the Megrimum, choosing instead to believe that he is feverish from his night out in the storm. A few begin to be convinced by Egan's claims, however, when it begins to rain and it seems that the moan has been silenced. Suddenly, there is a great explosion and the Megrimum's moan returns, to the great relief of the villagers.

At story's end, Egan returns home and discovers en route that his own climb up the hill has been enlarged and distorted by local gossips and that his attempt to slay the dragon has become part of the lore of the monster.

Analysis

As is often the case in folktales or fables, many of the characters of *Kneeknock Rise* are rather silly in their fears and beliefs, but the power of the novel is such that even as readers are led to chuckle about the silliness of the townspeople, they are forced to wonder if they, and all human beings, are not a little like them. Despite Egan's "scientific" debunking of the myth of the Megrimum, the people choose to believe in the monster, preferring to continue their apparently foolish rituals of lighting candles, hanging onions, and carrying wishbones for protection instead of being delivered from fear. The fable suggests that the need for belief in human beings is so powerful that people will sometimes deny reality and invent a system of belief.

Yet, if it makes such thought-provoking suggestions about the nature of human faith, the novel also suggests much about the power of peer pressure in shaping the collective beliefs of a community, an issue that is of extreme importance to young people. The novel hints at the fact that a number of individuals may indeed know the secret of the Megrimum but demonstrates that it is extremely difficult for anyone to disagree with public opinion and remain in the town. Uncle Ott, who knows the secret, must leave and wander the countryside in order to have a chance at happiness.

Critical Context

Many writers have retold folktales or have written fantasy novels for readers in this age group, and some authors, such as Robin McKinley in *Beauty: A Retelling of Beauty and the Beast* (1978) or Jane Yolen in *Briar Rose* (1992), have chosen to adapt a traditional tale to another plot and setting. Natalie Babbitt, however, is notable for her particular mode of fantasy in which she uses the narrative strategies of folklore and fable to craft fantasy novels that raise large moral questions, questions that seem even more mysterious and compelling to readers because they have the feel of legends and stories from an oral tradition. Although *Kneeknock Rise* was designated a Newbery Honor Book in 1971 and was received warmly by reviewers, it is probably less well known than Babbitt's *Tuck Everlasting* (1975), a fantasy novel that similarly explores moral issues as it presents the story of a family that has discovered a spring whose water produces eternal life. In both of these novels, it is clear that Babbitt's gift in fantasy is to invent compelling worlds that make readers think seriously about what individuals can give one another in community and about what it means to be human.

Donald R. Hettinga

THE LANDMARK HISTORY OF THE
AMERICAN PEOPLE

Author: Daniel J. Boorstin (1914-   )
First published: 1968; illustrated
Type of work: History
Time of work: From the seventeenth century to the 1960's
Locale: The North American continent
Subjects: Politics and law, religion, social issues, and war
Recommended ages: 13-18

Boorstin provides a survey of the history of the United States from its earliest times to the late twentieth century.

> *Principal personages:*
> THOMAS JEFFERSON, an American political thinker and the author of the Declaration of Independence
> GEORGE WASHINGTON, the first president of the United States
> FREDERICK DOUGLASS, a former slave and a leader of the abolitionist movement
> ABRAHAM LINCOLN, the sixteenth president of the United States
> ROBERT E. LEE, a Confederate general
> ULYSSES S. GRANT, a Union general
> SUSAN B. ANTHONY, a leader of the woman suffrage movement
> WOODROW WILSON, the president of the United States during World War I
> FRANKLIN DELANO ROOSEVELT, the president of the United States during the Great Depression and World War II
> DR. MARTIN LUTHER KING, JR., a leader of the Civil Rights movement

Form and Content

The Landmark History of the American People is a chronological study of the growth and development of the United States of America from its earliest fragile settlements through the latter part of the twentieth century. Profusely illustrated with contemporary drawings, paintings, and photographs, it follows the major development of the nation as it evolved from a scattering of primarily English colonies along the Atlantic coastline to the major world power that largely determined the shape and fate of modern world history. Daniel J. Boorstin's emphasis is on the political and social culture of a nation that believed, from even before its formal beginning, in the independence and freedom of the individual and the power of democracy.

Boorstin's controlling metaphor is that the United States is a collection of peoples who have learned, over the years and through a series of dramatic and traumatic events, to think as one people—in other words, to become a nation with a core basis of shared national beliefs and values that transcend a wide variety of backgrounds. The subdivisions in the first volume of this two-volume set illustrate this approach clearly: From "An Assortment of Plantations," the work moves to "Thirteen States Are Born," then changes to "American Ways of Growing," advances to "Thinking Like Americans," and ends with "The Rocky Road to Union." In this fashion, Boorstin traces the development of the American national consciousness from the Colonial period, when settlers considered themselves merely transplanted Englishmen and Englishwomen, to the strangely uniting tragedy of the Civil War, when the separate states were finally woven into a single nation.

Volume 2 of the history brings the newly reunited United States into the modern world and places its emphasis on how the national government used its newly acquired powers to enhance and advance the rights and responsibilities of all citizens, black people as well as white people, women as well as men. "The Go-Getters" outlines the role of economic freedom in the surprising yet perhaps inevitable development of American industry during the early years of the twentieth century. "People on the Move" develops the theme of immigration, both internal and external, in providing an impetus to the energy and dynamism of the United States. "Bringing People Together" and "Champions for the People" underscore the crucial importance of leaders such as presidents Woodrow Wilson and Franklin Delano Roosevelt in expanding the promise of American democracy to all citizens, especially the poor, minorities, and the working men and women who had for so long been disregarded and exploited by the industrialists and bankers. "To This Whole World—and Beyond" brings the story to a triumphant close—and the hint of a new beginning—with the account of the role of the United States in two world wars and its leadership of the "free world" in a period of international tension and potential mutual destruction by nuclear holocaust.

Boorstin's history is clear, concise, and honest. He does not absolve America for what might rightly be considered its short-comings and failures. He notes, for example, that the original draft of the Declaration of Independence contained an unsparing denunciation of slavery that was edited out for political reasons. The failure to address that fundamental flaw was to return generations later in the Civil War, the bloodiest conflict in U.S. history and one that continues to haunt the nation. The victory over Nazi Germany, Imperialist Japan, and Fascist Italy in World War II did not lead to the realization of the dream of a perfect world, as some had hoped, but to a protracted and nerve-wracking Cold War with a former ally, the Soviet Union. Boorstin chronicles this situation in his chapter "Winning a War, Losing a Peace." In short, Boorstin presents the American story without flinching, aware that it contains much that is both good and bad, but confident that an honest account is worth the effort.

Analysis

Daniel Boorstin is one of the most respected authorities on American history. His widely acclaimed writings, which span over half a century of work, set standards for accuracy, precision, and insight that are almost unparalleled in the discipline. At the same time, they have proven popular with general readers as well. In *The Landmark History of the American People*, he has given young adult readers in the United States a fair and balanced account of their nation's development that will allow them to make informed and critical judgments of how and why their country developed in the fashion that it did and permit them the opportunity to decide what they would—and could—do to influence its future course. In a very real sense, this work is a practical as well as an academic history of the United States; it is a civics lesson for the present as much as a history lesson about the past.

Boorstin's survey of U.S. history is scrupulously honest. While the content of the work naturally includes much that is favorable to the nation, such as its dramatic growth in prosperity following the Civil War, its emergence as an industrial power during the twentieth century, and its vital role in fighting the Axis Powers during World War II, Boorstin does not omit the less-than-perfect aspects of U.S. national life. These include the often indefensible treatment of American Indians, continuing economic inequality throughout much of the country's history, and racial injustice, which began with more than two centuries of slavery.

It is appropriate that both sides of history are covered in the work, for the major theme of Boorstin's study is how the uniquely American character has found ways to resolve conflicts, correct injustices, and widen participation in the nation's democratic form of government. The young reader who discovers how real and often difficult national problems have been solved learns a valuable lesson both in history and public life. This is the practical aspect of the work, and it is an important one.

Boorstin's style in *The Landmark History of the American People* is an impressive accomplishment. Well known for his numerous volumes of history for adult readers, the author here uses an approach that is direct and simple but never simplistic or condescending. While his chosen vocabulary is appropriate both for his subject matter and for the age range of his readers, this is still a history book that can be read, enjoyably and profitably, by adults as well.

Critical Context

Daniel J. Boorstin served for twelve years as Librarian of Congress, was director of the National Museum of American History of the Smithsonian Institution, and taught history for twenty-five years at the University of Chicago, where he held the chair of Morton Distinguished Service Professor. His historical trilogy *The Americans—The Colonial Experience* (1958), *The National Experience* (1965), and *The Democratic Experience* (1973)—won the Bancroft, Parkman, and Pulitzer prizes. Clearly, the author understands his subject and cares about it deeply and passionately.

That understanding and concern are clearly evident in *The Landmark History of the American People*. When the work was first published in 1968, readers and critics were attracted to the accessible style and unimpeachable authority of the history, which struck a balanced and objective, yet generally optimistic note. This deeply informed historical study transforms the facts of American history into living and contemporary aspects of the national experience. Its celebration of the United States as fundamentally a union of diverse peoples was especially noteworthy in the troubled era of the late 1960's and early 1970's and has remained a central reason for its continued popularity.

Michael Witkoski

THE LAST UNICORN

Author: Peter S. Beagle (1938-   )
First published: 1968
Type of work: Novel
Type of plot: Fantasy
Time of work: Unspecified
Locale: A nameless world of the imagination
Subjects: Coming-of-age, the supernatural, and travel
Recommended ages: 13-18

A unicorn's quest for her lost kin makes her a force for change and growth as she touches the people and places she meets along the way.

> *Principal characters:*
> THE UNICORN/LADY AMALTHEA, a unicorn who, unwilling to believe she is the last of her kind, goes in search of the other unicorns
> SCHMENDRICK, a wandering magician who, having freed the unicorn, decides to accompany and help her
> MOLLY GRUE, a disillusioned, middle-aged woman who decides to follow her dream
> THE WITCH, a woman who collects enchanted creatures in the quest to become immortal
> KING HAGGARD, a man who desperately seeks happiness
> PRINCE L'R, the young man who falls in love with Lady Amalthea, which turns him into a fairy-tale hero
> THE RED BULL, King Haggard's curse, weapon, and protector

Form and Content

The Last Unicorn most resembles a novel-length fairy tale. Even so, it is a fairy tale that knows itself to be one: Throughout the novel, author Peter S. Beagle offers a more realistic look on life that plays havoc with the conventions of the genre. The outlaws in the forest, for example, are not exactly merry—more poor and disillusioned. Moreover, the great deeds of heroism that the prince performs for his beloved do not exactly endear him to her—she does not like killing and bloodshed.

As is characteristic for fairy tales, the plot has a deceptively simple linear structure that is not interrupted by flashbacks, flashforwards, or parallel plots. Also characteristically, it is told in the third-person narrative voice. Heroes and villains can be found in this story, but, contrary to those in the polished Grimms' fairy tales, they are not painted in black and white. As in real life, there are many shades of gray, which makes even the villains at least understandable.

The story begins when a unicorn overhears two hunters mention that she is now the last of her kind in this world. Despite misgivings about leaving her beloved forest, she finally decides to find out whether this rumor is true. Indeed, she searches far and wide without finding any other of her kind. To make matters worse, it seems that human-kind has forgotten that unicorns are more than simply make-believe. When humans look at her, they see only a white horse.

Exhausted from her travels, one day the unicorn falls asleep beside a road. It is a dangerous mistake, for the owner of a passing carnival, an old witch, does recognize her. Seeing a chance to enlarge her collection of mythical creatures, the witch uses magic to capture the unicorn. Thus, the unicorn becomes part of an exhibit, along with a real harpy and many enchanted animals.

Aside from the witch, only one other person working at the carnival recognizes the unicorn: Schmendrick, a down-on-his-luck magician who seems unable to get his spells straightened out. He decides that it is wrong to keep her captive and, after some failed attempts with spells, unlocks the unicorn's cage with a stolen key. She in turn frees the harpy. In the ensuing chaos, the unicorn and magician escape.

Schmendrick has resolved to help the unicorn with her quest. An increasing number of clues point toward the Red Bull of King Haggard as the cause of the other unicorns' disappearance. On the way to his country, Schmendrick is captured by a gang of would-be Robin Hoods and distracts them by using his magic to conjure up an illusion of the real thing. Helped by the unicorn, he escapes. Molly Grue, a disillusioned version of Maid Marian, sees the unicorn and decides that she will come along.

Through a wasteland country and an enchanted city—the only rich place in the entire kingdom—the group finally reaches King Haggard's castle. Nearby, the Red Bull smells the unicorn. In order to save her, Schmendrick must turn the unicorn into a human girl. Thus, Lady Amalthea arrives at the castle.

While Schmendrick and Molly work for King Haggard and look for the unicorns, Lady Amalthea is being courted by Prince L'r. The poor prince has fallen head over heels in love, and he tries to prove himself by righting wrongs and slaying monsters. Gradually, the unicorn begins to lose herself in her forced human identity. Before she completely forgets her past, Molly and Schmendrick find the Red Bull and the other unicorns. Against her will, Lady Amalthea is turned into a unicorn again. A desperate fight wins her freedom and that of the other unicorns.

Analysis

One theme underlying many, if not most, fairy tales and stories about quests is that of growing up. A hero or heroine sets out into the world to accomplish a specific task and is changed in the doing. So too is the unicorn. She has never had to worry about anything, but now she must confront a harsh reality. Immortality does have its drawbacks: The mortal world has changed beyond her knowledge. Almost no one cares who or what she is anymore, and the world turns out to be much uglier and colder that her protected forest. Her kind has already been forgotten, and she, who may be the last unicorn, could die out among humankind.

Still, there is a truth to be found, and she leaves her forest to find it. Her serene state is rapidly eroded, however, and the process occurs all the faster when she is turned into a human and becomes suddenly mortal and vulnerable. Knowledge of mortality—repugnant to her as an immortal—and the accompanying emotions enable her to change, the one thing of which immortals are incapable. In the end, the ability to change is what enables her to grow beyond herself and save her kind.

The Last Unicorn is, in many respects, a novel of self-discovery. The positive characters—especially L'r, Amalthea, and Schmendrick—all have to find something hidden in themselves, something that they will need in order to survive and grow. That quest is easier for some than for others, but they all manage to follow their dreams, even when there is a cost. The negative characters—notably Haggard, the people in the enchanted city, and the witch—have given up and are content with keeping things as they are. They have stagnated into a kind of perpetual adolescence: They are no longer innocent, but they are not balanced adults either.

Nevertheless, every character in the novel is recognizable, not because they are generic—on the contrary, each of them is very much an individual—but because the way that they think, feel, and behave is familiar. They offer different ways to face reality and by their actions indicate the course that the author prefers: trying, never losing hope, and following one's dreams.

If there is a message to the novel, it is that dreams can come true, even if they do not always conform to one's expectations. This outcome should not discourage the dreamer. *The Last Unicorn* is a bittersweet reminder that things cannot stay the same forever. One mourns the loss of innocence and illusions, but celebrates the beauty of life that remains.

Critical Context

The Last Unicorn is probably Peter S. Beagle's best-known work. It is regularly reprinted and has been translated into several languages. The novel speaks of inner truths and of a process of growing up that even adults continue to confront, themes that are also present in other works by the author. The fact that this story is not bound to any recognizable time, place, or culture adds to its universal appeal.

In addition to *The Last Unicorn*, Beagle has written such works as *A Fine and Private Place* (1960), *I See by My Outfit* (1971), *The Fantasy World of Peter Beagle* (1978), *The Garden of Earthly Delights* (1982), *The Folk of the Air* (1986), and *The Innkeeper's Song* (1993). His screenplays include that for the animated film *Lord of the Rings* (1978). As with many popular novels, *The Last Unicorn* has also found its way to the film industry. In 1982, it was used as the basis for an excellent animated film (with an all-star voice cast), for which Beagle himself wrote the screenplay.

G. A. M. Vissers

A LIFE FOR ISRAEL
The Story of Golda Meir

Author: Arnold Dobrin (1928-   )
First published: 1974; illustrated
Type of work: Biography
Time of work: 1903-1974
Locale: Pinsk, Russia; Milwaukee, Wisconsin; and Palestine (later Israel)
Subjects: Activists, military leaders, and politicians
Recommended ages: 10-13

Meir commits herself as a young woman to the cause of Zionism and becomes an important leader in the struggle to build the new nation of Israel.

  Principal personages:
    GOLDA MABOWITZ (LATER GOLDA MEIR), an independent and strong
      girl and woman
    MRS. MABOWITZ, her mother
    MR. MABOWITZ, her father, who wants a better life for his family
    SHANA, Golda's older sister, a dedicated Zionist
    MORRIS MYERSON, Golda's husband, a Zionist with a great love for the
      arts
    DAVID BEN-GURION, the chief of the Jewish Agency in Palestine and
      later the first prime minister of Israel
    MENAHEM, the son of Golda and Morris, a cellist
    SARAH, the daughter of Golda and Morris, a *kibbutznik*
    MOSHE DAYAN, the Israeli minister of defense

Form and Content

A Life for Israel: The Story of Golda Meir was the first biography of Meir written for this age group. It covers the time from her birth until 1974, just after her retirement as prime minister of Israel. Each of the eleven chapters is brief; the longest is slightly more than seven pages long. The text is illustrated with nineteen black-and-white photographs that provide important information, especially for children who have no idea what an overloaded refugee ship looks like or how hard it is living in a tent camp. Two photographs of the Merhavia kibbutz, one showing barren ground in the 1940's and the other showing a lush oasis after years of hard work, are especially interesting. Also included is a chronology, a bibliography for further reading, and an index.

The story begins with the Mabowitz family living under religious persecution in Russia during the late nineteenth and early twentieth centuries. Golda's father sets out for a better life in America, and his family rejoins him in Milwaukee after he has started a business. Golda grows up listening to discussions by Zionists, who want to create a Jewish homeland, and runs away from home at fourteen to work with them. She marries Morris Myerson, and they move to Palestine to work on a kibbutz. Now known as Golda Meir, she becomes more politically active and effectively leaves her family behind as she rises in power. After decades of struggle, Israel becomes a nation, a Jewish homeland, and eventually Meir becomes its prime minister, leading the young nation through the Yom Kippur attacks of 1973.

Meir's life is illustrative of several important issues for young social studies students. It is the story of an immigrant family trying to find a better life in America, of a strong and independent woman in a man's world, and of an important series of events in Jewish history. Arnold Dobrin has a good sense of his audience and the special demands of young readers. Thus, he pauses to define terms such as "pogrom" and "kibbutz" and to identify historical figures such as Theodore Herzl, Chaim Weizmann, and Moshe Dayan. He also chooses not to use a distant, reportorial tone but instead to dramatize and fictionalize. He presents conversations around the dinner table, private discussions between Meir and her husband, and an appeal from a friend. The book opens, in its one departure from chronological order, with a breathless five-year-old Golda running to tell her mother that the Cossacks are coming. The reader knows from the first sentence that this biography will be told in something resembling a novel form.

Dobrin wrote with the full cooperation of Clara Stern, Meir's younger sister. Stern reviewed the manuscript, supplied her own memories and insights, contributed a celebratory preface, and provided family photographs, including rare glimpses of the Mabowitz family. Her cooperation lends authority to Dobrin's story and also adds to the feeling that this biography is an impassioned one—that does not simply report on a great woman but adulates her, that does not objectively describe a series of conflicts but pushes the reader toward an interpretation of them. While there is no such thing as truly objective writing, in this book the author's sentiments come through unusually strongly and clearly.

Analysis

For Dobrin, the central question about Golda Meir is not "What did this woman accomplish over the course of her illustrious life and career?" but "What in this woman's character made it possible for her to accomplish so much?" The emphasis is not on the events themselves, although they are related fully and in glowing terms, but on the internal and interpersonal conflicts that had to be resolved in order for her to fulfill her heroic destiny.

Many of these conflicts involved those people closest to her, and Dobrin highlights and individualizes these conflicts by presenting fictionalized representative scenes. In a conversation with her parents, young Golda explains her desire to continue her education beyond high school and to become a teacher. Her parents scold her and make it clear that they believe a woman's goal should be marriage, not education. By presenting the scene as a series of direct quotations instead of as reported and explained speech, Dobrin puts the emphasis on the conflict between these particular people, instead of presenting it as a clash of Old World versus New World values, or between parents and children.

This focus on Meir's own situation, avoiding any hint that her conflicts might be typical, is used throughout the book. For example, Dobrin presents a scene between Golda and Morris at the Merhavia kibbutz after a long day's work. Golda is exhausted, too tired to gather with the others for supper. Morris offers to bring food to her, but she summons the strength to eat dinner with the others: "Although every bone in her body ached, Golda joined the other young men and women in the dining room." By comparison with Morris, she seems the more noble because she refuses his offer for assistance and overcomes her own weakness. By presenting the dialogue between couple, Dobrin focuses the reader's attention on the two of them, so that comparisons between Golda's condition at the end of the day and the tiredness of the other *kibbutzniks* will not be drawn.

Because he was writing in the mid-1970's, in a United States engaged in an intense debate about women's roles, Dobrin struggles with Meir's conflicting responsibilities as wife and mother and as politician. He feels compelled to address the conflict head-on, to reassure his readers that Meir acted thoughtfully and purposefully. When Golda and Morris quarrel about her wish to work full-time after their two children are born, Dobrin explains, "Golda believed that it is important to be a good wife. She knew too that being a good mother is one of the most important jobs in the world. But she also realized that for some women, marriage is not enough." When the couple separate and Golda has custody of the children, her work keeps her away most of the time: "She didn't like being away from Sarah and Menahem all day but her sense of duty and her desire to help Jews everywhere forced her to find work that would lead to a better future for her people." The story of a heroic man who does great deeds but overlooks the people closest to him is a common one, and one suspects that were this biography about a male subject, his neglect of family would not be deemed worthy of comment. More to the point, biographies of Meir written ten or more years later than Dobrin's do not attempt to justify her ambition and focus more directly on her achievements.

Critical Context

A Life for Israel was important at the time of its publication, largely for being the first biography of Golda Meir for this age group. The book appeared shortly after Meir's retirement in 1974, when the world's attention was focused on her and when the United States was coming to respect the contributions women have made to national and international history. The book became immediately popular as a tool for helping explain to young people the incendiary politics of the Middle East and for celebrating the contributions of intelligent and strong women. More than two decades later, as schools acted on a new call for multicultural studies, a book such as this one that offers Jewish history and culture and a strong female central character found renewed demand.

Although *A Life for Israel* is no longer in print, it remains on the shelves of many public and school libraries. Its approach seems old-fashioned to some, but Arnold Dobrin's scholarship remains unquestionable. Although *A Life for Israel* may have been replaced in some classrooms by the more objectively toned (and somewhat easier to read) *Our Golda: The Story of Golda Meir* (1984), by David A. Adler, the passion of this work, the index and bibliography, and the irreplaceable photographs make it invaluable for students and teachers alike who seek a jumping-off place for further study.

Cynthia A. Bily

LIFE WITH FATHER

Author: Clarence Day (1874-1935)
First published: 1920
Type of work: Biography
Time of work: The late nineteenth century
Locale: New York City, the Day home, and a country home outside the city
Subject: Philosophers
Recommended ages: 13-18

Clarence Day, Sr., is depicted by his son in a series of affectionate and lightly satirical essays that show the several members of the well-to-do Day family.

> *Principal personages:*
> CLARENCE DAY, SR. (FATHER), a newspaper publisher and the head of the Day household
> LAVINIA (VINNIE) DAY (MOTHER), his wife, who supports and manages him
> CLARENCE DAY, JR., the oldest of the Day children and the narrator of the work
> GEORGE DAY, the next son
> JULIAN DAY, the third son
> THE BABY, the last of the Days' sons

Form and Content

Life with Father is a series of essays, many of them originally published in *The New Yorker*, *Harper's*, and *The New Republic*, in which Clarence Day describes, with affection and satire, what it was like to grow up in turn-of-the-century New York in a household dominated by Father, a larger-than-life-sized authority figure who loves his wife and children but is convinced that they need better management.

With Clarence, Jr., the oldest son and narrator, the reader is taken to Father's office, the Day summer home, and various other locales. Father's views of money management, religion, the employment of servants, illness and physicians, and the role of children in the household are described in individual, often hilarious essays.

During the course of the biography, the various Day children are introduced, as is Mother. Mother venerates Father but is astute enough to realize that his bluster hides a tender heart; she attends to his numerous lectures but in fact frequently acts as she wishes and holds her own views. Mother resists Father's efforts to teach her money management, invites guests to dinner over Father's protests, organizes her household as she pleases, and tries (with only partial success) to prevent Father from opening his son's mail.

Although *Life with Father* is a biography, it does not span the senior Day's life. The time frame of the work is partial, centering on the period of Father's life while his sons are growing up; occasionally, through flashbacks, the reader is able to deduce something of Father's younger years. Toward the end of the work, there is a time leap that describes Father facing serious illness. The final essay, dealing with Father's choice of a cemetery plot, reveals him confronting the possibility of death with the same gusto and spirit as he has faced the various events of his life. He threatens to buy a plot on a corner, "Where I can get out." Mother looks, "startled, but admiring," at her son, the narrator. The book ends with her comment that "I almost believe he could do it."

Analysis

Life with Father is both an affectionate account of a family and a lightly satirical study of a supremely self-satisfied man who sees himself as king in his castle, with his wife and children as servants. In return for catering to his every whim and endorsing all his views, they are lovingly treated, even cherished. Like Mother at the end of the book, the family members "almost believe" in Father's kingship.

In a wider sense, the work is a study of a view of family and the concept of the head-of-family that owes greatly to the Victorian age; Father is surely the last of the pure Victorians. His anxiety lest women might earn the right to vote, wear bloomers, hold political opinions, or participate in business is clear. In general, Mother agrees with him, saving her energies for smaller victories. Clarence Day, Jr., the narrator, maintains a careful tone that lets the reader know that Day simultaneously loves and venerates his father while disagreeing with many of his views.

The technique whereby Day, as an adult, relates his youthful perceptions of his father allows him to see his father through two pairs of eyes. Each perception is realistic. The young Clarence gradually grows in his sense of his father as exaggerated. The younger Day's ability to see Mother's management of Father, for example, lets the reader realize that the son is keenly aware that Father is the last of a species. Brief references in the text to the younger Clarence's later relationships with women suggest that he will see them as equals in a way that his father never does.

At the same time, the narrator shows the comedy inherent in a family with strong parents and lively children. Tiny incidents, such as Father's expectation of having ice water in the summer or his sewing of a button on his shirt, become crises of major proportions. Mother's practice of inviting guests to dinner throws off Father's schedule and causes him to wonder why people cannot be content to stay in their own homes. A female guest who asks gracious questions is pronounced an "incessant babbler" by Father, who is used to Mother's placid listening to his pronouncement on all topics. Through these and other incidents, Day comments both on the relative innocence of an earlier age and, more subtly, on the narrowness of vision that causes the incidents to be magnified out of proportion.

Despite the strong portrait of the title character, it is really the narrator who is memorable for his insight, warmth, and sense of realism. The younger Day is in fact more like his mother, deeply loving and admiring of his father but clear-sighted about not only his foibles but his biases and belligerence as well. The narrator knows that he is chronicling the end of an era; he is at once both thankful to have grown up in that era and now firmly outside of it. The later parts of the book, in which the narrator speaks more recognizably as an adult, make that transition.

Critical Context

The popularity of *Life with Father* can be demonstrated by the numerous reprintings of the work. First published a few years after the end of World War I, the book was viewed as an affectionate look at a past that would never be recovered but that had its own beauty: a stable family with devoted servants, a daily life with leisure for clubs and drives in the country, and family entertainment.

Contemporary readers of *Life with Father* will perceive the enormous imbalance of the roles of men and women. Mother has no official voice nor does she claim one, even though she manages Father coyly. Father sees himself as the center of his world and assumes with total serenity and self-assurance that everyone in it is there to attend him. What was initially read as affectionate satire is often a major obstacle for the contemporary reader.

Clarence Day, Jr., suffered for most of his life with acute arthritis. Unable to participate in an active social life, he nevertheless maintained a wide circle of friends with whom he corresponded. His writings for the major periodicals are characterized by the same wit, humor, and insight that mark *Life with Father, God and My Father* (1932), *Life with Mother* (1937), and his several other works. It is for this tone, as well as for his fine prose, that he will be remembered. Until fairly recently, in fact, sections from *Life with Father* or other works by Day were frequently anthologized in high school or college writing texts. The stereotyping found in this work, however, renders it difficult if not impossible for the contemporary reader to take seriously.

Katherine Hanley

A LIGHT IN THE ATTIC

Author: Shel Silverstein (1932-   )
First published: 1981; illustrated
Type of work: Poetry
Subjects: Coming-of-age, emotions, and friendship
Recommended ages: 10-15

Poems and line-drawings bear equal weight in these humorous, whimsical, and occasionally macabre musings about life from a young person's point of view.

Form and Content

Readers of *A Light in the Attic* quickly realize the value of complementary words and drawings, as Shel Silverstein uses both with incomparable facility to present his wry child's-eye view of all subjects that matter. Silverstein explores topics from feeling left out ("Play Ball") to bossiness ("Friendship") to clowns who are not entertaining ("Cloony the Clown") and bad attitudes ("Sour Face Ann") with keen wit and deep appreciation for the importance of not taking oneself too seriously. His sense of humor runs the gamut of possibilities—sometimes dry, occasionally sardonic, at times outrageously nonsensical.

Silverstein's illustrations complement his poems; rarely are they merely visual restatements of a poem's message. Some yield additional information necessary for understanding the poem; all are as integral a part of Silverstein's creation as the second voice in a duet. Readers of the poem "Surprise!" who wonder what Grandpa has sent back from India need only look at the elephant-shaped wooden box to guess. Occasionally, as in "Snake Problem," in which a twenty-four-foot python uses his body to spell "I love you," or "Quick Trip," a poem about being eaten by the "quick-digesting Gink," the meaning of the poem depends upon the drawing. One poem, "Union for Children's Rights," appears entirely in the signboards that a crowd of protesting children hold above their heads. "Buckin' Bronco" bucks the narrator almost off the edge of the paper. "Deaf Donald" uses sign language to tell the vital part of the poem, something conveyable only through illustrations. "Come Skating" shows a wool cap, a nose, and two astonished eyes peering through a jagged hole in the ice—the result of mistaking ice skating for roller skating.

Favorite children's subjects abound, but in unexpected contexts. Pirates are "blithery, blathery" or, like Captain Blackbeard, merely laughable because he recently got a shave. "The Dragon of Grindly Grun" weeps for fair damsels because he likes them medium rare and can only toast them well done. Silverstein's animals are eccentric, as can be imagined from the title "They've Put a Brassiere on the Camel."

Death appears as a subject several times in this volume, sometimes in jest, sometimes in fear, yet as natural in the continuum of topics in this book as it is natural to life itself. Likewise, Silverstein takes on pushy parents, bossy friends, pixilated baby-sitters who sit on the baby, and annoying nursery rhymes ("One Two").

Silverstein's whimsy takes off in countless directions, all worth pursuing. He never condescends and is never predictable. In its own outlandish way, *A Light in the Attic* is a collection of inspirational poems, beginning with the title poem, which suggests that "the lights are on and somebody *is* home," and ending with "The Bridge," which will only take the reader halfway, Silverstein notes. *The Light in the Attic* opens so many new possibilities for imaginative play that the remainder of the journey will seem easy.

Analysis

Silverstein never underestimates his readers. He knows that young people think as much as anyone about serious issues such as death, watching too much television, and growing old, and he addresses these topics and his readers forthrightly. Yet, given a choice, Silverstein prefers poking fun to pontificating. While he refuses to talk down to juvenile readers, he retains a childlike appreciation of the absurdity of life, whether that absurdity be exhilaratingly nonsensical or startlingly bleak.

He also knows how to have fun with words. His poem "Nobody" plays with the possible meanings when a negative term becomes a subject, while "Poemsicle" is a study in perseverance using "sicle" as a suffix. The universally beloved "The Meehoo with an Exactlywatt" is a takeoff on Abbott and Costello's "Who's on First?" comedy routine. "Ations" is an eighteen-line poem containing nine lines with final words ending in the suffix "-ation." "Anteater" puns to create an "aunt eater," and "Wild Strawberries" ponders the best way to tame an intractable berry.

Silverstein appreciates the satisfaction derived from a good comeuppance, as in "Ladies First," a poem about Pamela Purse who insisted on being first, right up to the moment that she met the cannibal Fry-'Em-Up Dan. "Fancy Dive" describes Melissa of Coconut Grove, who did "thirty-four jackknives, backflipped and spun,/ quadruple gainered, and reached for the sun,/ And then somersaulted nine times and a quarter—/ and looked down and saw that the pool had no water." If "Fancy Dive" touches the edge of grimness, "Who Ordered the Broiled Face" is downright and delightfully gruesome. "Overdues" describes an obsession with a library book that is forty-two years overdue. "Ticklish Tom" was tickled so much that he rolled out of school, through the town, into the country, and onto a railroad track; now "Tom ain't ticklish anymore." There is the "Strange Wind" that blew so strangely that hats stayed on and heads blew away.

Children's fantasies have their place in this volume. "Rock 'N Roll Band" fantasizes about every teenager's dream in singable four-line verses; also in verse are fantasies of breaking dishes in "How Not to Have to Dry the Dishes," catching the moon in "Moon-Catchin' Net," or polishing the stars in "Somebody Has To." A stingy imp in "Prayer of the Selfish Child" prays that if she dies before she wakes, her toys will break "So none of the other kids can use 'em." "How to Make a Swing with No Rope or Board or Nails" suggests growing a mustache and tying the ends to a tree limb. "Kidnapped" is a late-for-school fantastic solution most readers have considered at least once.

When Silverstein offers lessons, they are on the preposterous side of morality. You cannot make a milk shake by shaking a cow, he warns in "Shaking." What to do when a man with twenty-one heads and only one hat meets a man with twenty-one hats and only one head? Sell the hat to the man who loves them. The "Homework Machine" is a wondrous contraption, except for the fact that it cannot seem to get the right answer. Barnabus Browning in "Fear" was so scared of drowning that he just sat in his room and cried till it filled up with tears and he drowned. There are morals for parents, too, as in the poem "Little Abigail and the Beautiful Pony," in which Abigail's parents refuse to buy her a pony, insisting no one ever died from not getting a pony. Abigail does die, and Silverstein concludes "(This is a good story/ To read to your folks/ When they won't buy/ You something you want.)"

A few favorite Silverstein topics recur. He takes digs at hunting in "Arrows," hair-splitting in "The Toad and the Kangaroo," and perfectionists in "Almost Perfect." "Clarence" and "Channels" level sarcasm at television watching. "The Little Boy and the Old Man" compares two difficult, helpless stages of life: Both the little boy and the old man have trouble holding onto spoons and holding back their tears, and both think that no one pays attention to them.

Silverstein likes to vary traditional themes. "Rockabye" suggests that whoever put the cradle in the tree must have had it in for the baby. The prince "In Search of Cinderella" still loves his missing princess, but he is growing weary of feet. "Frozen Dream" is reminiscent of the song "When I Grow Too Old to Dream." To anyone who has read Dorothy Parker's poem "Suicide," the poem "Standing Is Stupid" will sound familiar.

At the heart of Silverstein's work is a keen appreciation for the value of silliness, as he suggests in the poem "Put Something In": "Draw a crazy picture,/ Write a nutty poem,/ Sing a mumble-gumble song,/ Whistle through your comb./ Do a loony-goony dance/ 'Cross the kitchen floor,/ Put something silly in the world/ That ain't been there before."

Critical Context

A Light in the Attic was the last in a series of best-selling, beloved, and occasionally controversial books that Silverstein produced before turning to writing plays for adults. The winner of a *School Library Journal* Best Books award (1981), Buckeye awards (1983 and 1985), George G. Stone award (1984), and William Allen White award (1984), the book remained on *The New York Times* best-seller list for months, as did his previous collection of poetry, *Where the Sidewalk Ends* (1974). Silverstein is best known for these two books but has published several other successful works for children, such as *Uncle Shelby's Story of Lafcadio, the Lion Who Shot Back* (1963), *The Giving Tree* (1964), and *The Missing Piece* (1976). He has also written songs (lyrics and music), motion-picture scores, and plays, and he has penned cartoons for national publications.

Silverstein mines several considerable talents to produce his children's books: His composer's ear, cartoonist's eye, and playwright's sense of dialogue all work together to produce work that is consistently engaging and respectful of the intelligence of readers of all ages.

Gena Dagel Caponi

A LITTLE LOVE

Author: Virginia Hamilton (1936-   )
First published: 1984
Type of work: Novel
Type of plot: Domestic realism
Time of work: 1982
Locale: Suburban Ohio and Dalton, Georgia
Subjects: Coming-of-age, emotions, family, race and ethnicity, and sexual issues
Recommended ages: 15-18

Sheema Hadley, an overweight seventeen-year-old African American girl who has used food and sex ("a little love") to medicate her shame and grief over the loss of her mother and abandonment by her father, reclaims her self-esteem with the genuine love and support of her grandparents and boyfriend.

> *Principal characters:*
> SHEEMA HADLEY, a sensitive but troubled teenager, who struggles to overcome the pain and shame of parental abandonment to find her identity as she moves from adolescence to adulthood
> GRANMOM and GRANPOP JACKSON, who have reared their granddaughter from birth and continue to provide her with wisdom, support, and caring
> FORREST JONES, Sheema's faithful boyfriend, whose love and belief in her assists Sheema in overcoming her paralyzing depression
> CRUEZY HADLEY, Sheema's natural father, whom his abandoned daughter seeks to find for security, identity, and "a little love"

Form and Content

A *Little Love* is the story of an adolescent girl who hides from the demons of shame and anger that have robbed her of her childhood, of a teenager's painful search for "a little love" to help her make the transition to adulthood. The book depicts a rite of passage, a journey in search of self, roots, personal voice, identity, and genuine love.

Virginia Hamilton begins her chronicle of a troubled teenager in a setting likely to cause distress to any self-conscious, overweight, depressed girl of seventeen tender years: a crowded school bus. School is over, and Sheema Hadley tries to hide from the insensitive taunts of fellow students who call her "She-mama" and make fun of the "lumps and rolls" that she cannot hide with her baggy clothing. The author uses a third-person narrator to tell Sheema's story, but she balances the voice of the omniscient narrator with frequent use of dialogue that makes her characters come alive in a most extraordinary way.

The novel's structure contains two main parts. The initial chapters that make up the first part of the book introduce readers to the main characters and to the conflicts in young Sheema Hadley's troubled childhood and adolescence. The locales of these initial chapters alternate between Sheema's school and her home, the world of the adolescent. It is a world of incomplete definitions of self, definitions attached to such labels as "student," "child," and "teenager." It is a world in which simple solutions, such as the search for "a little love," frequently plague young people, especially those who have known pain like Sheema's.

Sheema's pain comes from her acute sense of abandonment. Her mother died giving birth to her, and her father abandoned her to her grandparents and has never even called her on the telephone. The emotional turmoil that has plagued Sheema throughout her childhood and adolescence has resulted alternately in anger, shame, and guilt. To escape these demons and a plethora of other fears and anxieties, she has sought to medicate her pain with food that layers her body with lumps and rolls, trapping her "real, cute, little self on the inside." She has also sought to assuage her pain by seeking "a little love" in casual sexual encounters.

Three significant figures in her life offer Sheema more than a little love. Although she does not yet have the maturity to appreciate the genuine love provided to her by Granmom and Granpop Jackson and her faithful boyfriend, Forrest Jones, they do not abandon her. They encourage her to break away and make the journey in search of her identity. "Move on out and let in whatever," Granmom wisely encourages her. "Movin is livin. Changin is life." The first section ends with Sheema beginning to take control of her own life, beginning to make those painful preparations for her rite of passage into adulthood.

The second section of the book details Sheema's quest in search of herself. It is a frightening journey that takes her away from the comforts of the one home in which she has lived all her young life. It is a journey that deprives her of the security of her familiar suburban neighborhood in Ohio, takes her across Kentucky and Tennessee, and thrusts her into the Deep South in search of the father who abandoned her at birth. It is a fearful journey into the historic land of slavery that requires courage, determination, and more than a little love from the people in her life. Nevertheless, it is a journey that brings Sheema a surprise that will change her life. She thinks that she will find her father; she is surprised when she finds herself.

Analysis

Virginia Hamilton is a master storyteller whose novels reveal young people caught in the act of learning hard lessons about living and growing. Her stirring stories teach young readers without preaching or patronizing. In *A Little Love*, Hamilton presents a compelling character in Sheema Hadley, an African American teenager who will appeal to many young female readers regardless of their race or ethnicity. This book marks a change in Hamilton's approach to writing fiction for young people. Her previous works highlighted cultural themes important to young African American readers: the struggle for freedom, the proud heritage of people of African decent, and the quest for self-discovery. In this book, Hamilton begins to focus more on the theme of survival, a universal theme to which many young people can relate regardless of their background.

Survival of the deadly effects of parental abandonment is the major theme of *A Little Love*; it is a subject of significant importance to young people who live in broken and blended families where they have been physically and psychologically abused or abandoned by one or both parents. The emotional effects of the loss of a parent are similar for all young people. They feel anger that frequently borders on rage toward the parent who has abandoned them. They feel the pain of separation and lack the inner resources that they need to grieve the loss of the parent. They feel shame for being different from their peers who enjoy the support of parents in a "normal" home. They feel guilty and blame themselves for their parent's departure. They feel depression born of the guilt that they have assumed. Finally, they are racked by a multitude of irrational fears and personal demons that only loving, full-time parents can allay.

Without being overtly didactic, Hamilton paints a compelling portrait of an adolescent girl on the threshold of adulthood who learns to survive these devastating effects of abandonment. As many adolescents in similar situations do, Sheema at first looked outside of herself for "a little love" from casual sexual relationships in order to mask her pain and shame. These casual contacts simply heightened her shame and added additional guilt and depression that threatened her survival.

Sheema finally learns the lesson that ensures her ultimate triumph. She learns the importance of the genuine, caring relationships that she has taken for granted in her grandparents and in her faithful friend, Forrest. Ultimately, she learns that if she is going to survive the trauma of abandonment, she must stop making excuses and take full control of her own life.

Critical Context

Virginia Hamilton has written a number of acclaimed works—novels, short stories, and biographies—that enjoy places of eminence in the canon of juvenile and young adult literature. In 1974, she became the first author to win both the Newbery Medal and the National Book Award for the same book, *M. C. Higgins, the Great*. It is unfortunate that *A Little Love* has not been as well received as Hamilton's other works. It contains not only a model of survival from which young female readers will benefit but also a powerful example of an intergenerational relationship in Sheema and her supportive grandparents. For this reason alone, it deserves to be on supplemental reading lists for juvenile and young adult readers.

This book may also prove interesting to young adult and adolescent readers because of the dynamic dialogue of the book's diverse characters. There is no single black dialect, as some people mistakenly believe; there are many. Hamilton has deftly preserved a record of the dialect of African American youths living in the Midwest. In the authentic voices of Sheema's grandparents, the richness of the dialect of a previous generation is preserved. Finally, the vibrant differences between these two dialectical versions of black speech are further defined when contrasted to the language of African Americans in the Deep South.

Stanley J. Zehm

LIVES OF GIRLS AND WOMEN

Author: Alice Munro (1931-   )
First published: 1971
Type of work: Novel
Type of plot: Domestic realism, psychological realism, and social realism
Time of work: The 1960's
Locale: A small town in Ontario and the surrounding Canadian wilderness
Subjects: Coming-of-age, family, gender roles, and sexual issues
Recommended ages: 15-18

> *Del Jordon explores gender roles, the mysteries of sexuality, and small-town values as she struggles to maintain her perspective during her formative adolescent years.*

Principal characters:
  DEL JORDON, a down-to-earth observer of her small town who does not compromise with convention
  NAOMI, Del's friend and companion, who comes to see marriage as her principal goal
  ADDIE JORDON, Del's mother, a forceful but sometimes embarrassing example for Del
  DEL'S FATHER, a gentle and philosophical man who runs a failing fox farm
  FERN DOGHERTY, the boarder whom Del's mother takes in when she moves to town
  UNCLE BENNY, a half-senile laborer who lives near the Jordon fox farm
  GARNET FRENCH, a former criminal and fundamentalist laborer who becomes Del's lover
  JERRY STOREY, the intelligent but one-dimensional egghead with whom Del competes

Form and Content

Alice Munro's *Lives of Girls and Women* is a vivid and thorough depiction of a girl's coming-of-age in a remote Canadian town. Written first as a series of seven short stories and later revised around an autobiographical structure, this realistic and uncompromising novel reveals the complex choices faced by a young teenager. Through the eyes of the ever-observant Del, the novel focuses on the frailties of relationships, the mixed messages offered to girls, and the ravages of decay and death. Del refuses to blink as she observes those "who all their lives could stay still, with no need to do or say anything remarkable."

Each story illustrates Del's progression from child to woman. The early stories focus on the fringe characters living on a remote country road known for its poverty, harshness, and lack of class. Subsequent stories show Del's world expanding as she and her mother move to town. Watching the women and girls around her, Del notes the narrow gender roles that they have come to accept. In this intimate small town, where everyone knows everyone's business, she is privy to the dark side. As she freely admits, she is no "stranger to killing." She sees it on the fox farm and later in the suicides of townspeople. Fortunately, Del's mother is a powerful example, a woman driven by her passion for knowledge and her struggle to make ends meet. Like her mother, Del is a seeker of knowledge. Ignoring her mother's rejection of religion, she journeys through local churches, cataloging behaviors and beliefs. Although she comes to understand the demands of Christian faith, she is never quite sure that she wants to be saved. When her dog is shot, she wonders about a cosmos where God could remain indifferent. Her seeds of doubt serve as a prelude to the onset of puberty. In school, she and Naomi find themselves in not-so-subtle wars, where what boys "said stripped away freedom to be what you wanted, reduced you to what it was they saw."

As Del matures, she finds herself increasingly isolated as Naomi and other girl-friends make clothes, makeup, and plans for marriage their priorities. Although Del does not share these goals, she is persistent in her search for knowledge about the mysteries of sexuality. Soon, she gains firsthand experience. When Fern's boyfriend exposes himself to her, she sees the perversity of male sexuality. Later, with Jerry Storey, the school intellectual, she notes the absurdity of passionless experimentation. In the uneasy last days of high school, she discovers Garnet French, fresh out of jail and newly converted to religion. With Garnet, Del learns of the passion and power in lovemaking. In an earthy climax, she ends this relationship when he tries to force her to accept his faith and become his wife.

Del's rejection of Garnet marks the end of adolescence and the beginning of womanhood. Having rejected the "normal" paths chosen by Naomi and other young women, Del's goal will be to write the stories of her community. Although Del's proposed novel ends with the suicide of her young female protagonist, her own future is far from depressing. Somewhere, she knows, beneath the harshness and decay, is the stuff a meaningful life is made of.

Analysis

Lives of Girls and Women is a rich and detailed depiction of a girl's coming-of-age and her coming to terms with her community. Subthemes illustrate the limited gender roles for young women, the power of adolescent sensuality, and the difficulties of accepting death and inevitable decay. The power of this novel lies in Del's stubborn refusal to be cowed by these daunting unknowns. She is a protagonist who rejects stereotypical views of girls as fragile and easily damaged. This novel of initiation insists that all adolescents can pick and choose from life's lessons and face the future with confidence.

The major subject of the novel is the challenge for girls to create a healthy identity from the mixed messages of adult behavior. Fortunately, Del is a fearless, independent pioneer who plunges into unknown worlds with open eyes. As Del matures, she discovers that circumstances and intellectual and physical maturity will provide new challenges. Throughout this daunting period of blindly plunging into new experiences armed only with fragmented knowledge, her goal remains the same: to maintain a sense of self and continue to grow—even if this means she bangs heads with those around her.

Shrugging off the dreamy, ethereal haze of typical female coming-of-age novels, *Lives of Girls and Women* looks straight ahead at the realities of Del's environment. Del sees both the richness of the natural world of her father's fox farm and the killing of animals that sustains it. She sees both the inspiration of church hymns and the failure of theology to fill the voids in empty lives. She notes both the optimism of her mother and her teachers and the harsh reality of poverty and failed relationships. She documents both the dreams of her girlfriends and the reality of diminished expectations in marriages dominated by men. She remains sane in this gritty world because she accepts these complex realities, chooses what is valuable, and pushes on.

No novel tracing the path from childhood to adulthood can ignore the difficulties presented by sexuality, and Del is determined to understand its mysteries. She knows that sensuality is a boundary marking the lines between normal and the "magical, bestial act." She learns from the voyeuristic Mr. Chamberlain, from Jerry Storey's awkward naïveté, and from the electricity of passion with Garnet French. Although she comes to understand the power of sexuality, she is not destroyed by her experiences, and she does not pay a penalty for experimenting. Unlike her girlfriends, she refuses to connect sexuality with the inevitability of marriage. Rather, she sees sensuality as simply another source of knowledge.

From an early age, Del is aware of different expectations for men and women. She sees her aunt's subservient role to her Uncle Craig. She also hears her mother's warning about succumbing to the female "burden." Yet, she questions the warnings so often handed to women, "advice that assumed that being female made you damageable, . . . whereas men were supposed to be able to go out and take on all kinds of experiences and shuck off what they didn't want and come back proud." She watches Naomi groom herself for a future husband and notes the sordidness of placing marriage as the only worthwhile goal. When she rejects Garnet's attempt to force his religion upon her, she makes a stand for equality in relationships.

The lesson of Del's experiences is not simple and clear-cut. Although she has not mastered life's difficulties, she has also not been defeated. By choosing to be a writer who retells the stories she has observed, she will stay in her community, at least for the present, noting how the choices that women make can destroy their lives. The power of this novel is its depiction of balance in a woman's life, the interweaving of social, intellectual, and spiritual forces. *Lives of Girls and Women* is a history of one woman who accepts the absurdity, the humor, and the harshness of her environment. She is a young woman unafraid to confront the complex chaos of unknowns and determined to construct her own personalized vision for survival.

Critical Context

Lives of Girls and Women is a unique contribution to young adult fiction, both in its gritty portrayal of small-town life and in its depiction of female sexuality. Before its publication, few female coming-of-age novels existed, and none that documented the complex rites of passage so thoroughly. Although other novels discussed female sexuality, few traced its development from childhood to adulthood, and those that did so typically made the protagonist pay a price for her experimentation.

Lives of Girls and Women is significant also for its analysis of gender roles and its portrayal of the religious and social underpinnings in rural communities. Other works, including *Dance of the Happy Shades* (1968), *Something I've Been Meaning to Tell You* (1974), *Who Do You Think You Are?* (1978; also as *The Beggar's Maid*, 1979), *The Progress of Love* (1986), and *Friend of My Youth* (1990), explore similar themes in the farms and small towns of southern Ontario. Alice Munro, a self-described "anachronism," writes about characters who have roots, and "most people don't live that kind of life any more at all." Numerous critics have linked her works with the stories of Flannery O'Connor and Eudora Welty, two writers who also described in thorough detail characters enmeshed in their communities. Although Munro does not write solely for young adults, *Lives of Girls and Women* and many of her short stories describe the heartaches and triumphs of the female adolescent experience with a vividness that few writers can master. Without sensationalizing, Munro captures adolescents at crucial, often painful moments of discovery. The rich detail of her characters' lives helps to soften harsh realities and shed light on the interrelationships of family, community, sexuality, and the natural world.

Mark Vogel

THE LONELINESS OF THE LONG-DISTANCE RUNNER

Author: Alan Sillitoe (1928-   )
First published: 1959
Type of work: Short fiction
Subjects: Coming-of-age, family, jobs and work, poverty, and sports
Recommended ages: 13-18

Sillitoe's nine stories graphically present the economic, social, and psychological reality of working-class life in the industrial slums of mid-twentieth century England, particularly the dilemmas of young men coming-of-age in that environment.

Form and Content

Although the title of *The Loneliness of the Long-Distance Runner* is drawn from the first and longest story in the collection, the nine stories are essentially independent, related only in the most general terms: by contextual references such as to Borstal Reformatory, by similar inner-city slum environments, and by thematic concerns. A majority of the stories utilize first-person narration, and not coincidentally those stories are generally the most substantial and successful in the collection. The third-person stories lack the specificity, immediacy, and naturalness, and thus the power, of the first-person narratives.

Also significant to the success of the first-person stories is that, in all but one instance, the narrator is a teenage youth grappling with the kinds of situations doubtless experienced or directly observed by author Alan Sillitoe in his own inner-city slum upbringing. These events include burglary of a business and subsequent imprisonment ("The Loneliness of the Long-Distance Runner"); participation in the suicide attempt of a despondent, unemployed man whose wife has left him ("On Saturday Afternoon"); observation of another young man's attempt to survive a domineering mother and an even more demanding wife ("The Disgrace of Jim Scarfedale"); and enlistment in a ghetto gang and involvement in the gang's territorial skirmishes with rival groups ("The Decline and Fall of Frankie Buller"). Only "The Fishing-Boat Picture" is told by an older person, a postman near retirement and involved in the analysis of his failed marriage and subsequent visits by his spouse; the story is not intrinsically uninteresting, but its plot is too obviously imitative of Henry James's story "The Beast in the Jungle."

The third-person stories vary more widely in terms of plot and character, although they are consistent in their diminished impact. "Uncle Ernest" recounts a lonely, middle-aged man's befriending of two impoverished young girls and subsequent reprimand by the police; the irony is that the young girls were abusing the man by extorting money and gifts via his emotional dependence on them. "Mr. Raynor the School-Teacher" presents the sexual fantasy life of a ghetto schoolteacher who, while in class, ogles salesclerks in a business near the school as an escape from the ignorance and violence of his students; ironically, he perpetuates that violence and ignorance by teaching poorly during his lustful reveries and then excessively punishing misbehaving students incited by his inattentiveness. "Noah's Ark" traces the desperate attempt by two young boys to enjoy themselves at a traveling fair despite their utter destitution. Reminiscent of James Joyce's "Araby," the story depicts the disillusionment of the younger boy when his stolen ride on the Noah's Ark turns into a nightmare chase on a rapidly moving engine of entertainment (or of death). Finally, "The Match" realistically but cryptically renders the gradual destruction of the life of a middle-aged mechanic, whose worsening eyesight has led him to be ridiculed at work and who is on the verge of being fired because of his violent response to the ridicule. Unable to see clearly the unexpected defeat of the local rugby team but experiencing the anguish of a devoted, even fanatical, fan, he returns home to vent his accumulated frustrations on his family, causing his wife and children to leave for good. Intriguing in their varied plots and characters and embodying significant themes, these third-person narratives nevertheless lack the compelling verisimilitude of the majority of the first-person stories.

Analysis

Although not intended only for young readers, the stories in Sillitoe's collection have great appeal and significance for them, particularly four of the first-person narratives. Those stories present young men coming-of-age in an economically depressed, violent, and even vindictive society, with an emphasis on important realizations by those characters that enable them to survive. The most important thematic similarity of those realizations is existential isolation in an absurdly antagonistic world that the young men must constantly suspect, deceive, and defy in order to maintain psychological integrity.

In "The Loneliness of the Long-Distance Runner," the teenage narrator, in Borstal Reformatory as a result of participation in a store robbery, is allowed to leave the reformatory for running practice in preparation for a nationwide competition among penal institutions. The narrator, however, is not deceived by this "privilege," realizing that the reformatory governor only wants the glory of victory and does not care about the narrator's personal fate. With the runner's loneliness as astute symbol of existential isolation, the narrator realizes that he cannot compromise his personal integrity by allowing himself to be used for others' glorification, but he must deceive the antagonistic powers that be by concealing his intention to lose the race deliberately and then must defy those powers by losing. To do otherwise would be to join a system that killed his father through cancer acquired in horrendous factory conditions and to betray the spirit of his father, who continued his defiance to the point of chasing from his home the doctors who wanted to hospitalize (institutionalize) and sedate (control) him. Doubtless like his father, the narrator realizes the price of his independence, and indeed spends his remaining time at Borstal at the worst possible tasks for the longest possible hours, developing pleurisy as a result. Such stoically endured suffering is necessary in order to maintain his existential freedom from an absurd society with which he (and implicitly all members of the working class) is inevitably at war.

Similarly, in "On Saturday Afternoon," a teenage boy recalls a suicide attempt that he witnessed and in which he briefly assisted. He conveys his defiant determination that "I shan't ever kill myself. Trust me. I'll stay alive half-barmy till I'm a hundred and five, and then go out screaming blue murder because I want to stay where I am." Even at age ten, when he witnessed the attempt, the boy sensed the importance of respecting another's free choice, asking only to observe and obeying when asked to help. The boy's intuition is vindicated, since the man committed suicide after being arrested and institutionalized for his failed attempt. Thus, the man's view (and Sillitoe's) that "It's my life, ain't it?" is endorsed, despite the policeman's (and, by representation, society's) view that "You might think so . . . but it ain't." The man's assertion of existential freedom may be tragically misguided, conveyed by the narrator's contrary determination to struggle for 105 years, but it is nevertheless his individual freedom to assert.

The same kind of crucial lesson learned about independence and survival in existential, antagonistic isolation is conveyed by "The Disgrace of Jim Scarfedale." The young narrator observes and explains the failed attempt by thirty-year-old Jim finally to marry, in defiance of his domineering mother, a symbol of the oppressive society. Jim waits too late, however, and cannot overcome his feelings of guilt or adjust to the eccentricities of his wife, a radical reformer symbolically in opposition to the conservative society represented by Mrs. Scarfedale. Trapped between polarities and lacking the narrator's more developed sense of necessary isolation and independence, Jim returns to his mother, the society that had controlled and molded him for too long. He then defies that society ineffectively by exposing himself to young girls, an action symbolic of his psychologically and existentially arrested development. The young narrator realizes the implicit coming-of-age lesson, that one must consciously establish one's existential independence in order to effectively battle the absurd societal polarities that destroyed Jim Scarfedale.

The same message is conveyed by "The Decline and Fall of Frankie Buller," with the title character, a twenty-five-year-old gang leader of limited intellectual abilities, subjected to shock treatment as a form of societal domination. Like Jim, Frankie lacks the intellectual development and detachment to progress beyond juvenile, misguided defiance (gang turf battles, in Frankie's case) to awareness of existential isolation and necessary deception and defiance of the real enemy, the society as represented by the mental institution and its "therapy." Thus, Jim and Frankie lose, while the younger narrators learn from their failure and truly mature in the war by individuals to survive in an absurdly oppressive, class-based world.

Critical Context

By virtue of its phenomenal success, both critically and commercially—it was even made into an Oscar-winning film in 1962—the title story of *The Loneliness of the Long-Distance Runner* occupies an important position in the history of juvenile and young adult literature. The story was a precursor of and generative force for considerable Angry Young Men fiction to follow, such as that of Stan Barstow in *The*

Desperadoes and Other Stories (1961), which is similarly concerned with the revolt of young men against class hierarchy. Such works have led to the subgenre of working-class fiction, which is often focused on the revolutionary potential inherent in the initial encounters of young adults with a patently unjust society. Although less influential in the more conservative world culture after the demise of Russian communism, Sillitoe's collection nevertheless signifies that stories about the struggles of realistically portrayed young adults with a distinctly dystopian civilization can achieve universal appeal.

John L. Grigsby

THE LOST GARDEN

Author: Laurence Yep (1948-   )
First published: 1991
Type of work: Autobiography
Time of work: The 1940's to 1991
Locale: San Francisco, Brooklyn, West Virginia, Ohio, and Milwaukee
Subjects: Adolescents, race and ethnicity, and writers
Recommended ages: 10-13

Yep describes how he grew up as a Chinese American in San Francisco and how he came to use writing to explore his cultural identity and to celebrate his family and his ethnic heritage.

> *Principal personages:*
> LAURENCE YEP, a Chinese American who searches for his cultural identity through writing
> THOMAS YEP, his hardworking, Chinese-born father, who owns a grocery store
> FRANCHE YEP, his American-born mother
> SPIKE YEP, his athletic older brother
> MARIE LEE, his tough maternal grandmother, whose "Chineseness" greatly affects Laurence's writing
> JOANNE RIDER, his wife, a children's picture book writer who encourages Laurence to write children's books
> FATHER BECKER, the English teacher who inspired Laurence's desire to publish his writing

Form and Content

In *The Lost Garden*, Laurence Yep describes how he searched for his identity while caught between two cultures and seemingly rejected by both. The book has four distinct sections: The first describes his family and family life, the second describes his neighborhood and its people, the third describes the alienation that he encountered, and the fourth describes how straddling two cultures served him well in his career as a writer. In the middle of the book, the author includes photographs of himself, his family, and their grocery store.

Yep's father, Tom, came to the United States from Kwangtung, China, at the age of ten. Yep's mother was born in Ohio and reared in West Virginia, where his maternal grandparents owned a laundry. When his mother was about ten years old, the family relocated to San Francisco. Yep's parents met at high school.

Yep's brother Spike was ten years older and athletic; in fact, everyone in the family was athletic except for the author. Yep often felt like a changeling, wondering how he wound up being born into his family. At the end of World War II, his father bought a small corner grocery store, named La Conquista. Their home, Pearl Apartments, was on the top floor of the grocery store. He and his brother had to help set up the stock, price the inventory, and wait on the customers. As much as Yep hated the endless chores, the habit of establishing a daily routine served him well later when he became a writer. He came into contact with numerous ordinary people while working in the grocery store: Jimmy the Italian truck driver, Saul the junk man, Mr. Vincent the mortician, and Mo-mo the hulking unofficial guardian angel who protected La Conquista from gangsters are brought to life in *The Lost Garden* by Yep's strong characterizations.

When Yep was a child, he did not want to be Chinese: "It took me years to realize that I was Chinese whether I wanted to be or not." He also could not escape Chinese culture because of his grandmother, Marie Lee, who instilled in him a sense of "Chineseness."

Reading was always a part of the family's activities. During Yep's asthma attacks, his mother would always read to him while waiting for the doctor. His favorites were L. Frank Baum's Oz books and Andre Norton's science fiction because children are taken out of their everyday world and travel to new lands where they must learn new customs and adjust to new people.

Yep attended Catholic school, where he had an imaginative chemistry teacher and an excellent English teacher. It was a difficult decision for him to choose between a chemistry major or journalism major, but his teachers suggested that he apply to the college of journalism at Marquette University. There he met Joanne Ryder, his future wife, and she introduced him to the classics of children's literature, including A. A. Milne's *Winnie-the-Pooh* (1926) and C. S. Lewis' Narnia books. After he failed a journalism course, Yep realized that he had more talent for writing fiction than fact.

Analysis

Yep begins *The Lost Garden* by taking readers through his memories of his first home, store, and courtyard garden, which his deceased father so lovingly nurtured. He ends the book with a metaphor of seeds of that garden stirring within his imagination, within his heart, and within his soul.

Yep's skillful use of language can be perceived throughout the book. Metaphors and figurative language create comparisons that make the characters come alive. Even Jezebel, the old family car, is personified: "Being elderly for a car, Jezebel disliked hills and would protest by wheezing constantly up the slope like an old asthmatic." At an early age, Yep realized that "what made people most interesting were their imperfections. Their quirks were what made them unique and set them apart from everyone else."

Yep recounts his childhood as a grocer's son, living in a predominantly African American neighborhood. As a third-generation Chinese American, he found the issue of identity a difficult one. He claims that writing helped him in his search for cultural identity. His books have a wide popularity among young adult readers, probably because his theme of being an outsider—an alien—appeals to them.

In his autobiography, Yep emphasizes how working in La Conquista gave him the discipline for setting a routine in his daily life. As a writer, he tries to write from four to six hours a day, in addition to two hours of notetaking and reading. La Conquista also gave him more tangible help as a writer. For example, Indian-head pennies he found in the grocery store were the inspiration for the book *The Mark Twain Murders* (1982) and *The Tom Sawyer Fires* (1984). Because the people he met at the store were ordinary, his tales are usually about common folk rather than princes and princesses. Taking care of customers also shaped his keen observation of people.

In *The Lost Garden*, Yep also highlights the influence of Marie Lee, his maternal grandmother as the source of his understanding of Chinese culture. Yep gives an honest description of each of his family members. He concentrates on vivid incidents that made moments special. The book is, in a true sense, an autobiography, with no fictional pieces added. Yep pours out his true feelings about being an outsider in two cultures.

His early science fiction often dealt with strange, new lands, which represent his first reactions to white culture, both his fascination and his alienation. Many of Yep's novels are based on his family background. His father, a kite maker, became Windrider in *Dragonwings* (1975), and his grandmother was the source of Paw-Paw in *Child of the Owl* (1977). He used some of his own childhood for the character of Craig Chin in *Sea Glass* (1979). *Star Fisher* (1991) is based on his maternal grandparents' life in West Virginia. His historical novels are painstakingly researched. It took six years of research to find the bits and pieces of Chinese American history for *Dragonwings*.

Yep's writing offers strong characterizations, the sensitive development of relationships, and accurate historical details about China and early California. The author's Asian American perspective has made a significant contribution to children's literature.

Critical Context

The Lost Garden reveals the prolific, award-winning author's source for his books dealing with Chinese American experiences. Readers find a believable portrait of the author as a sensitive, imaginative child, struggling to belong and to find his cultural identity.

Yep has won numerous awards, among them the Children's Book Award, the *Boston Globe*/Horn Book Award, and the Jane Addams Children's Book Award. *Dragonwings* was named a Newbery Honor Book; it is based on a newspaper clipping about a Chinese immigrant who invented a successful flying machine a few years after the Wright Brothers. This book is especially strong in its coverage of Chinese traditions and beliefs. *Child of the Owl* won a *Boston Globe*/Horn Book Honor Award. Yep set the story in a more contemporary Chinatown, where a young Chinese American girl discovers her heritage through Chinese folklore and history. As autobiographical fiction, Yep's *Sea Glass* deals with conflict between generations. *Star Fisher* is about a Chinese family overcoming prejudice in West Virginia during the late 1920's. All of Yep's books cover themes such as poverty, racial discrimination, and loss of identity. In *Dragon's Gate* (1993), which was also named a Newbery Honor Book, a boy in 1867 China accidentally kills a Manchu and is sent to America to join his father, who is helping build a tunnel for the transcontinental railroad through the Sierra Nevada Mountains; some of the same characters also appeared in *The Serpent's Children* (1984) and *Mountain Light* (1985).

Many of Yep's fantasy and science-fiction novels explore the theme of alienation, such as *Sweetwater* (1973) and *Dragon of the Lost Sea* (1982). Other genres in which Yep writes include the folktale, mystery, and horror story.

Winnie Ching

LOST HORIZON

Author: James Hilton (1900-1954)
First published: 1933
Type of work: Novel
Type of plot: Adventure tale, fantasy, and science fiction
Time of work: The early 1930's
Locale: The lamasery of Shangri-La in Tibet
Subjects: Death, religion, social issues, and travel
Recommended ages: 13-18

Four Westerners find themselves transported from a war-torn world to a peaceful but remote sanctuary in the Himalayas.

> *Principal characters:*
> HUGH "GLORY" CONWAY, a British consular official
> CHARLES MALLINSON, Conway's young assistant
> HENRY D. BARNARD, an American businessman and fugitive
> ROBERTA BRINKLOW, a Christian missionary
> CHANG, a lama living in Shangri-La
> FATHER PERRAULT, the High Lama of Shangri-La
> LO-TSEN, a Chinese woman living in Shangri-La
> RUTHERFORD, a novelist fascinated with Conway

Form and Content

Lost Horizon is written in the form of a third-person narrative given to the ostensible author by a novelist named Rutherford and concerns Hugh Conway, a mutual acquaintance. Conway and three other Westerners had been passengers on a plane hijacked from an Indian city during a revolution. The plane was never recovered, but Rutherford found Conway a year later suffering from amnesia in a Chinese hospital. The strange story that Conway related after he regained his memory is the body of *Lost Horizon.*

The four Westerners—Conway, Charles Mallinson, Roberta Brinklow, and Henry Barnard—were powerless to act even when they realized that their plane was being hijacked. Their pilot died after the plane crashed on a ridge high in the Himalayas, and they were saved only because a party of hillmen found them and escorted them to a lamasery named Shangri-La.

The lamasery proved to be comfortable, civilized, but remote. Chang, the leader of the rescue party, assured them that porters who could return them to the outside world would be arriving in a month or two, and that until then they were to be guests of the lamasery. The only other person whom they encountered directly was a young Chinese woman named Lo-Tsen, who entertained them on the piano.

The Westerners reacted differently to their stay. For reasons of their own, Brinklow and Barnard decided to remain. Mallinson himself was anxious to leave, but in the meantime Conway had learned that they were not in Shangri-La by accident. Soon afterward, he was admitted to an audience with the lamasery's High Lama. The aged man told Conway the story of Father Perrault, a friar who had made his way to Shangri-La in the early eighteenth century and who miraculously lived on and on. It was only toward the end of this account that Conway realized that the High Lama himself was Perrault.

In this and subsequent conversations, the High Lama described the lamasery's rediscovery over the centuries by various travelers. Outsiders aged slowly in Shangri-La's air, it seemed, but aged rapidly if they left. Recently, the trickle of travelers had ceased as a result of war and revolution, and so the High Lama had authorized the forced recruitment of new individuals. He shared his vision of a sanctuary that would preserve civilization from the destruction he foresaw for the outside world, and he finally suggested that Conway was destined to be his successor. With this revelation, he died.

At the same time, Mallinson learned that the porters whom Chang had mentioned had reached a point several miles away but would set off again shortly. Mallinson had convinced Lo-Tsen, with whom he had fallen in love, to accompany him. Conway tried to explain that Lo-Tsen was actually an old woman, that her age would reassert itself if she left the valley, but in vain. Torn between remaining in Shangri-La and helping Mallinson, Conway finally decided that his greater loyalty was toward his friend.

In an epilogue, the author described a later meeting with Rutherford, who had tried to track Conway after he had disappeared on another journey. Rutherford did not find Conway—or Shangri-La, where he guessed Conway was headed—but offered several bits of evidence that the story might be true. The most tantalizing came from the doctor who had treated Conway. Rutherford learned that the Englishman had been accompanied by an extraordinarily old Chinese woman who had died shortly after conducting him to safety.

Analysis

James Hilton's short novel is written so carefully that most readers accept the unlikelihood of its setting and story without hesitation. After all, Shangri-La lies high in the Himalayas, one of the coldest and most forbidding regions on Earth, yet the valley's lower reaches are described as almost tropical. Transportation through the high mountain passes would present almost insurmountable difficulties, yet the lamasery boasts modern plumbing, a substantial library, and even such musical instruments as a piano. Readers' doubts are allayed in part because *Lost Horizon* is a story within a story within a story, an adventure related thirdhand, and readers are accustomed to such tales being tall.

Readers also accept the situation because the novel's four Western characters display a perfectly natural range of reactions to the world of Shangri-La. Roberta

Brinklow decides that it is her duty as a Christian missionary to convert the inhabitants of the lamasery and the valley that lies beneath it. Henry Barnard, as Mallinson discovers, is actually Chalmers Bryant, an American financier wanted for fraud. For obvious reasons, Barnard is reluctant to return to the outside world, and he even comes to believe that Shangri-La represents a kind of business opportunity. (In his wisdom, the High Lama suggests that these are shallow interests that Brinklow and Barnard will learn to put aside after a few decades of life in Shangri-La.)

Charles Mallinson himself takes the "official" view—that it is an outrage that he and his compatriots have been kidnapped and that the obvious thing for them to do is to return to "civilization" as soon as possible. He remains oblivious to the life of moderation and contemplation that Shangri-La offers and that most visitors gladly come to accept.

Near the opposite pole is Hugh Conway. Even before he learns the truth about Shangri-La, his interest—if not his passion—is excited. The High Lama at first mistakes Conway's lack of passion for clarity of mind, but Conway explains that his experiences in World War I have simply exhausted him. It is for this reason that the younger and more impetuous Mallinson is able to overcome Conway's better judgment. Mallinson is doomed by his lack of wisdom, and readers are meant to understand that he dies in trying to return to the world that he values so uncritically.

Hilton himself narrowly missed serving in World War I, but he knew the physical damage that it had wreaked on Europe and the spiritual toll that it had taken on those who survived it. He also correctly foresaw the destruction that was to come in World War II a few years after the novel was published. In Conway, he created an example of the very best that the Britain of the 1930's had to offer, and he went on to suggest that the best might not be good enough.

Hilton expresses these concerns in a highly readable novel, but one that makes a forceful moral point. If what the High Lama suggests is true, the world is doomed to destruction and civilization's survival may rest with Shangri-La. Conway accepts the validity of this vision, but he allows himself to be turned aside from what is clearly his duty. He later attempts to rectify his mistake, and readers are left wondering—along with Rutherford and the "author"—whether he finds his way back there.

Critical Context

Lost Horizon is a variation on two important traditions of fantasy literature, that of the lost race and that of the ideal society. H. Rider Haggard's *King Solomon's Mines* (1885) and *She* (1886) are famous early examples of the former, and Hilton, Edgar Rice Burroughs, and Talbot Mundy continued the tradition. For the most part, they were writing for adults, but the color and excitement of their novels have made them popular with young adults as well.

In *Utopia* (1516), Thomas More described an ideal society and in so doing contributed a word to the English language. Subsequent utopias appear in Samuel Butler's *Erewhon* (1872), W. H. Hudson's *A Crystal Age* (1887), and Aldous Huxley's *Island* (1962). *Lost Horizon* may be the best-known example of such a work, and it is perhaps the only one still read for pleasure. It may not be a coincidence that the novel also describes the most moderate and humane utopia of the tradition.

Although James Hilton wrote *Lost Horizon* in 1933 in response to specific world conditions, the book and its message have not become irrelevant over subsequent decades. War on a local or international scale remains an ever-present danger, and other forms of destruction (such as environmental degradation) continue to threaten civilization. Hilton's novel fulfills readers' fantasies of immortality (or near immortality), their yearnings for a better and more colorful world, and their hopes for the world's survival.

Grove Koger

LUCY
The Beginnings of Humankind

Authors: Donald Johanson (1943-   ) and Maitland Edey (1910-1992)
First published: 1981; illustrated
Type of work: Science
Subjects: Nature and science
Recommended ages: 15-18

> *Donald Johanson describes his discovery of Lucy, a 3.5-million-year-old fossil of a human ancestor, and how Lucy fits into the theory of human evolution.*

Form and Content

In 1974, in Ethiopia's Afar Triangle, Donald Johanson discovered the bones of a human ancestor that had lived at least 3.5 million years earlier. The bones were from a small female who walked erect but who had a brain size about one-third that of the average modern human. Forty percent of the skeleton was found, making it the most complete fossil of a human ancestor ever discovered older than seventy-five thousand years. The skeleton was named Lucy, after the Beatles song "Lucy in the Sky with Diamonds." In 1981, with the help of noted science writer Maitland Edey, Johanson wrote *Lucy: The Beginnings of Humankind.* The book describes the finding of Lucy's skeleton and discusses how the discovery forced scientists to rethink their theories about human evolution. For example, it suggested that human ancestors walked erect millions of years before their brain size approached the modern norm.

Particularly controversial, however, was Johanson's decision to create a new species for Lucy, which he named *Australopithecus afarensis.* Two *Australopithecus* species were already known, *africanus* and *robustus*, and it was commonly thought that *africanus* was the direct ancestor of the human line. (Species actually in the human line are designated "*Homo*," as in *Homo erectus*; modern humans are *Homo sapiens.*) Johanson believed that *Australopithecus afarensis* was the ancestor of both modern humans and the other australopithecines. This theory overturned common scientific thinking and caused fierce debate.

Lucy is a first-person account by Johanson of his work and thinking on human evolution. The book contains a prologue and five parts, which are then subdivided into chapters: Part 1 has four chapters, part 2 has eight, part 3 has three, and parts 4 and 5 have one chapter each. Each chapter uses quotes from other scientists as headings. Forty-five photographs and nearly sixty charts and drawings are included, an appendix provides information on the drawings, and an excellent index makes it easy to find topics of interest in the work.

The prologue tells of the actual discovery of Lucy and the excitement that it generated. Part 1 provides background on the earliest fossil finds and on early concepts of human evolution.

Part 2 relates the thinking about human evolution at the time that Lucy was unearthed and describes in detail the scientific process in paleoanthropology, which requires considerable field work. It also introduces many of the personalities involved in Lucy's story, including Johanson's colleagues Maurice Taieb, Tom Gray, and Tim White, as well as the Leakeys—Louis, Mary, and Richard—who were at the time the best-known researchers in human prehistory. Richard Leakey, in particular, was often at odds with Johanson where fossils and theory were concerned.

Part 3 of the book asks the question, "What is Lucy?" It addresses the scientific analysis, the interpretation of the facts, the publication of the results, and the reaction to them. Parts 4 and 5 offer theory and speculation about why Lucy walked erect and discuss the future of anthropology, which Johanson sees as promising. Throughout the book, charts, drawings, and photographs are used to illustrate Johanson's findings and to explore his ideas.

Analysis

Lucy was originally meant not for a young adult audience but for a college-educated reader who lacked formal training in science. Nevertheless, the book's style, its clear explanations, and the numerous illustrations make it suitable for high school students with an interest in science, especially those excited about the process as well as the results of scientific inquiry.

The authors' ability to present complicated material in a way that is accessible to teenagers places them among such science writers as Carl Sagan and Stephen Jay Gould.

The major theme of *Lucy* is one that is of natural interest to young adults. During their teenage years, many people ask questions about where they come from, how they got here, and why they are who they are. This is essentially what *Lucy* is about, although it asks these questions about all humankind rather than about a particular individual.

The strongest connection between writers and readers is made when the reader is given someone with which to identify. Lucy, the *Australopithecus afarensis*, provides that someone. Although she was only three-and-a-half-feet tall and probably weighed no more than sixty pounds, and although she was nothing more than bones when she was found, Lucy becomes a living and breathing creature to the readers of Johanson and Edey's book. They care about Lucy, and the questions that they ask about her are probably the same ones that they ask about themselves. The book even offers some answers, at least partial ones.

Readers are told that humankind originated in Africa but that different groups soon began migrations that carried them all over the world. Young adults are exposed to modern thinking about how humans evolved and the steps that were needed. They learn that they are the product of millions of years of natural selection, that their needs, wants, and even thoughts may be influenced by the environments and dangers that shaped the early human world.

A second important theme in *Lucy* is that science is as much process as it is a collection of facts. The book makes the process exciting, as when Johanson shows how to calculate a fossil's age or how to differentiate between the bones of great apes and human ancestors. Young adults interested in careers in science need to know that results are not the only point, or even the major point, of research. The fun of science often lies in figuring out how to do something. The authors clearly hold this attitude and do an admirable job of conveying it on paper.

A third theme running through *Lucy* is the ambiguity with which scientists must live. The authors point out how few actual fossils exist on which to base a theory of human evolution. Every proposed branch of the human tree is a site of controversy and confusion, and few pieces of uncontested evidence are known. This sense of knowing nothing absolutely is common to all sciences. Scientists live with uncertainty, and every theory can be revised by new discoveries. The book makes this point clear, however, in a way that should not deter interested young readers.

A fourth theme is the importance of the human character in the march of science. Scientific discoveries and theories are produced by people, not by objective machines. Scientists experience fears, doubts, and moments of euphoria. Many are ambitious, wanting to make a name for themselves; others simply want to satisfy their own curiosities.

In *Lucy*, readers are introduced to such personalities as Charles Darwin, whose *On the Origin of Species by Means of Natural Selection* (1859) started the search for human ancestors. Other historically important figures mentioned are Eugène Dubois, who found Java Man, and Raymond Dart, who found the Taung Baby, the first *Australopithecus* fossil. In his research, Johanson meets and exchanges thoughts with the Leakeys, the "first family" of modern anthropology. Sometimes, they agree on the interpretation of a find; often, they are at odds. Throughout, the readers see scientists as people—working together or at cross-purposes, but working steadily to expand human knowledge of the past.

Critical Context

Lucy was Donald Johanson's first book, but it established him as a scientist with the ability to make anthropology attractive to general readers, including young adults with an appreciation for science. *Lucy* became a best-seller, was translated into several languages, and served as a supplemental text in some college courses in anthropology and human evolution. Johanson became one of the few publicly acknowledged experts on human ancestors.

Johanson and Maitland Edey followed the success of *Lucy* with *Blueprints: Solving the Mystery of Evolution* (1989). This book, with Edey as the primary author, focuses on genetic issues in human prehistory. *Blueprints* has not been as popular as *Lucy* and is far more technical. More scientific background is needed to understand the book's arguments, and it is not easy for most young adults to read.

Johanson soon returned to his roots, however, with a series of books written in the mold of *Lucy*: *Lucy's Child* (1989), with James Shreeve; *Journey from the Dawn: Life with the World's First Family* (1990), with Kevin O'Farrell; and *Ancestors: In Search of Human Origins* (1994), with Lenora Johanson and Blake Edgar. These three books are stylistically similar to *Lucy* and deal with the same themes—the origins of humankind, science as a process, and the importance of human personalities in science—but speculate more on human origins. All are suitable for young adults, especially *Ancestors*, which was written to accompany the *NOVA* television series.

Charles A. Gramlich

THE MAGIC FINGER

Author: Roald Dahl (1916-1990)
First published: 1966; illustrated
Type of work: Novel
Type of plot: Fantasy
Time of work: The 1960's
Locale: A small town
Subjects: Animals, social issues, and the supernatural
Recommended ages: 10-13

A young girl, concerned by what she deems senseless cruelty to animals, sets out to teach the offenders a lesson using her unpredictable magical powers.

> *Principal characters:*
> THE NARRATOR, an unnamed eight-year-old girl with magical powers
> THE GREGGS, her neighbors, who like to hunt

Form and Content

Roald Dahl's *The Magic Finger* is a rollicking account of a hunting trip that goes amuck. This grossly imaginative tale is told from the viewpoint of a highly opinionated eight-year-old girl, the story's unnamed narrator. The book is short, containing only forty-one pages in its original edition. The text is interspersed with William Pène du Bois' fanciful black-and-white sketches of the comedic events and whimsical characters described by the author. Some of these illustrations unobtrusively fit into a quarter of a page, or less, leaving the remainder of the page for text; other drawings completely dominate a two-page spread.

The setting for the story is quickly established. Two young boys, whose last name is Gregg, live next door to the eight-year-old narrator. The girl "just can't *stand*" hunting, and the boys next door and their father hunt both animals and birds: "Even Philip, who was only eight years old, had a gun of his own." Adding intrigue to these rather ordinary circumstances is the unusual "gift" that the girl possesses—a magic finger.

The girl does not understand this gift; she only knows that she has always possessed it. It is activated when she becomes angry. A jolt of something akin to electrical power is released from her finger and lands on the person who has angered her, causing all sorts of outrageous things to happen—things over which she has no control. Therefore, when the Greggs begin to hunt and kill deer and wild ducks, the magic finger takes over. It is not until the next day that the girl learns the amazing results of its actions.

The jolt from the girl's magic finger lands on the hunters. At first, nothing out of the ordinary occurs. The hunting expedition is actually quite successful at the outset, and a sizable number of wild ducks are bagged. Then, things suddenly change when a small group of ducks fly into the hunting arena. No matter how persistently the Gregg boys and their father attempt to shoot, how accurately they aim, or how close to the hunters the birds fly, the Greggs cannot even wound their prey. They finally abandon the hunt and return home to retire for the evening, eerily pursued by this band of strangely persistent ducks.

The next morning, to their astonishment and horror, the members of the Gregg family awake to discover that they have been changed into pint-sized people with ducklike wings, while the ducks outside have been transformed into people-sized ducks with human arms. The large ducks quickly proceed to set up residence in the house. In the chaos that follows, the Greggs, locked out of their own home, learn at first hand lessons on survival in the wild. The role reversal presents the Greggs with a very different perspective on hunting and a new sensitivity to animals and birds, especially to wild ducks. Although their problems are resolved by the end of the book, the magic finger continues its relentless pursuit of other purveyors of injustice.

Analysis

In *The Magic Finger*, a number of overlapping concerns are addressed and valid questions are raised about significant social issues: Should hunting be allowed to occur merely for the pleasure of the hunters? Should an eight-year-old child possess, and use, a gun? What happens to animal families when one or more members are slaughtered for sport? Do humans have a greater right to attack animals than animals do to attack humans?

Although narrated in a tongue-in-cheek fashion, Dahl's book presents a provocative look at the issue of hunting from the perspectives of a bold young female activist and the hunters' prey—in this case, the wild ducks themselves. Thoughtful readers will be challenged to reevaluate their own thoughts on the issue because, despite the humor of the story, the question of whether hunting is morally acceptable demands attention. Dahl's viewpoint is clear throughout the lighthearted text, at times thinly disguised in the voice of the female narrator: "It doesn't seem right to me that men and boys should kill animals just for the fun they get out of it." At other times, it is the dialogue between the hunters and the hunted that hints at an underlying bias of the book.

> "No! No! No!" called out Mr. and Mrs. Gregg, both together. "Don't shoot! Please don't shoot!"
> "Why not?" said one of the ducks. . . . "You are always shooting at us. . . . Yesterday you shot *my* children. . . . You shot all six of my children."

Sensitive readers will be drawn into the story and the lives of the wild ducks. Other young readers, however, may be deterred by the concept of humans being hunted, especially when the guns are pointed at the children. Dahl seems to thrive on controversy and goes to daring extremes to get his message across.

A more minor theme of the book seems to be one of survival. The Gregg family's lives are thrown into confusion and initial panic when they are forced to live as birds.

Rather than giving in to despair, however, they work together to adapt to a new way of life and find it not altogether disagreeable. Each of them, at some point, takes on the role of encourager: Mr. Gregg, in directing the building of a nest; William, in commenting on the nest's warmth; Philip, in noting the fun of living in a nest; and Mrs. Gregg, in calming the children with positive words and loving hugs. Each, ungrudgingly, assumes a part of the work load, and each listens and accepts the thoughtful suggestions of others in adjusting to their strange new environment. As a result, the family is able to survive a difficult, stormy night in their new treetop abode. Strangely enough, the ducks appear to adjust more easily to their new surroundings than do their human counterparts and adapt quickly to cooking, eating, and living inside the house. The key to survival, in each case, lies in a combination of acceptance, resourcefulness, and cooperation.

Critical Context

Roald Dahl was a strong supporter of the downtrodden and a courageous crusader against injustice. This common thread runs through a number of his most popular children's books. In *The Magic Finger*, it is deer and wild ducks that are oppressed, and the hero and upholder of justice is an eight-year-old girl with a magic finger. The story ends happily for the antagonists, the Gregg family; this is not the case in all of Dahl's books. In fact, this is not the case for a cruel teacher, the antagonist in a subplot of *The Magic Finger*. When the young girl is unfairly victimized by the teacher, the magic finger's power turns the teacher into a catlike creature, a condition from which she never recovers.

In Dahl's *James and the Giant Peach* (1961), the protagonist, James, is the victim of injustice thrust upon him by wicked and uncaring aunts who make his life miserable. A strange old man gives James magic crystals to add to water. He convinces James that if he drinks this potion, he will no longer be unhappy. The boy falls and spills the crystals at the base of a tree, resulting in the creation of an enormous peach that will provide many magical adventures for James. Things do not end happily, however, for his aunts: The peach rolls down a hill, crushing them—a type of justice seemingly upheld.

Dahl's *Matilda* (1988) features a bright young girl with stupid and self-centered parents who is further victimized by the headmistress at her school. Again, justice is, questionably, served when Matilda gets rid of her parents and goes to live with a favorite teacher. The plot contains cruelty, vulgarity, and violence that will certainly be offensive to some parents and teachers.

Dahl's basic premise for these books is noteworthy: There are many injustices in the world, and there is a need for strong voices raised against them. *The Magic Finger* may be his least-offensive book in addressing this issue. It is a classic work that warrants an open-minded reading.

Katharine D. Herzog

THE MAID OF THE NORTH
Feminist Folk Tales from Around the World

Author: Ethel Johnston Phelps (1914-   )
First published: 1981; illustrated
Type of work: Short fiction
Subjects: Animals, family, gender roles, and love and romance
Recommended ages: 10-15

In folktales representing many different cultures, courageous, quick-witted girls and women overcome difficulties and attain their hearts' desires.

Form and Content

The Maid of the North is a collection of twenty-one folktales from throughout the world. Ethel Johnston Phelps calls them "feminist" stories because they show women as strong not weak, active not passive.

The young peasant girl in the Norwegian story "East of the Sun, West of the Moon" has all the qualities that Phelps values, especially independence. Although her parents have rejected the White Bear's offer of a home for her, she decides to accept it, but only after she has observed him carefully enough to make a judgment about his character. She is not rash or irrational. Like Phelps's other heroines, the peasant girl is brave, insisting, even in the most dramatic circumstances, that she is not afraid.

The same characteristics are evident in the heroine of the English story "The Stars in the Sky." Once she has decided to reach the stars, she sets off, and whatever transpires thereafter, she always keeps her goal foremost in her mind. When the heroine comes across the Little Folk, she asks for their help instead of fearing their magic. Still unafraid, she rides a horse, then a fish, and finally, although extremely tired, climbs to a dizzying height above the earth and manages to touch a star. Although this story is less complex than "East of the Sun, West of the Moon," it follows the same pattern—as, indeed, do all of these folktales.

The reason that the stories in this collection resemble each other so much in form is that, in addition to having such qualities as courage and determination, Phelps's heroines are all analytical by nature. In each story, the heroine identifies a problem and works through to a solution. The problems are varied; many involve a loss. In "Fair Exchange," a child is missing; in "The Twelve Huntsmen," it is a prospective bridegroom. The heroines in "The Old Woman and the Rice Cakes" and "Maria Morevna" have been deprived of their freedom. Other stories feature a threat: a miserable marriage for Bending Willow, the loss of the family livelihood in "The Tiger and the Jackal," and sometimes even death, as in "Elsa and the Evil Wizard" and the story of Scheherazade.

Whether the heroine acts immediately to solve her problem depends on her assessment of the situation. The mother in "Fair Exchange" knows that she will have a better chance at getting her baby back from the fairies if she has something to offer in return; therefore, despite her longing for her own child, she spends months nursing the changeling back to health before confronting the fairy queen. In "Gawain and the Lady Ragnell," the lady must move deliberately by first entrapping King Arthur, then getting Gawain's consent to an unwelcome alliance, and, most difficult of all, making sure that Gawain trusts and respects her enough to let her make the crucial decision. Others must postpone action as well: the forceful Maria Morevna until her lover appears, Bending Willow until the chief dies, and the old woman of the rice cakes until she can think of a plan. The patience shown by these characters should not be mistaken for passivity. Their wills do not waver, and when they can act, they do so.

Clearly, in each tale it is the protagonist who forces events toward a happy ending—or, in the story of Scheherazade, two such endings that differ only in detail, as well as another that the author would prefer. In every case, the heroine's strength of character determines the form that her life, and her story, will take.

Analysis

All the folktales in the collection *The Maid of the North* were invented long before women began demanding their right to compete on equal terms in the workplace or even to vote and hold property. Nevertheless, these stories support the contention of contemporary scholars that there has always been an undercurrent of rebellion against the roles assigned to females in a male-dominated society.

It is interesting that even the heroines who are adept in the areas generally considered to be the province of their gender—cooking, sewing, cleaning, washing, and ironing—use their skills for their own purposes. In "East of the Sun, West of the Moon," the peasant girl removes the spots from a shirt in order to prove that she is the prince's lost bride; in "Elsa and the Evil Wizard," the heroine outwits her antagonist by sewing up a tear in his cloak with her bright hair. One of the most comical stories in the collection is that of Duffy, who, although a good cook, abhors spinning and knitting so much that she makes a pact with the devil to do her work for her. After she has outsmarted the devil himself, admittedly with the help of a female friend, it is child's play for Duffy to persuade her husband that the tasks she so dislikes must be performed by others.

Not only domesticity but also the very idea of marriage is questioned in some of the tales. In the title story, the Maid of the North expresses no interest in exchanging her freedom for the miserable existence of a wife, who she claims is tied to the house like a dog. A similar statement is made by Katrine in "The Twelve Huntsmen." Although both of these young women do eventually marry, Gina the giant's daughter seems unlikely to do so. Having built her own house and attracted plenty of suitors, all of whom bring her gifts, Gina sees nothing wrong with an independent life.

The marriage issue illustrates a broader theme of the folktales in Phelps's collection: a woman's right to power, sometimes over others but always over her own destiny. A number of female figures in these stories do govern others, such as Lady Triamor, the Summer Queen, and the Fairy Queen. Although all these characters are supernatural, and therefore do not represent any challenge to the accepted role for mortal women, *The Maid of the North* also features human leaders such as the warrior princess Maria Morevna and the Indian maiden Bending Willow. After learning about nature from the water spirit, Bending Willow becomes her tribe's expert in preventive medicine, as well as their great healer.

Sometimes, women in these stories merely want influence over their husbands. This theme is found in the familiar Gawain story and, in a sense, in "The Tiger and the Jackal." In the latter tale, however, the husband takes his problem to his wife immediately, evidently having realized long ago that she has the brains in the family.

It is interesting to note that in the one story in which a woman defies society by taking over a man's job, she is motivated by her nurturing instincts. The father of the Zuni girl in "The Hunter Maiden" is old, and her brothers, who always supplied the family with meat, have been killed in battle. Common sense, if not custom, dictates her course of action: The maiden sets out to hunt. With the aid of War Gods, who are impressed by her courage, she comes home with game, thereby winning the gratitude of her parents and the respect of the tribe. In acknowledgement of her new role as hunter maiden, her father presents her with the axes that since her brothers' deaths had hung unused on the wall. In this story, as in all of the others, a woman has asserted herself and, because of her analytical powers, common sense, determination, and courage, has accomplished what she set out to do.

Critical Context

Before the publication of Ethel Johnston Phelps's two collections of folktales *Tatterhood and Other Tales* (1978) and *The Maid of the North*, children and young adults reading works in that genre were exposed almost exclusively to the assumption that males are superior to females. Her works were designed to correct that idea. As the author explains in the introduction to *The Maid of the North*, however, it was not easy to find folktales that would suit her purpose. Most of them focus on heroes, not on heroines, and when women do appear in these stories, they are often beautiful, passive, and docile. Since every society has had its strong, resourceful, and coura geous women, it is clear that the image of women such tales present is a false one.

No sensible person would argue for the suppression of the more traditional stories, such as those in *Die Kinder- und Hausmärchen* (1812, 1815; *Grimm's Fairy Tales*, 1823-1826) and the books of Hans Christian Andersen, or the stories that dominate even the collections from which Phelps drew, such as Kate Wiggins' *Tales of Laughter* (1908) or Andrew Lang's well-known *Lilac Fairy Book* (1910). The books of Ethel Johnston Phelps, however, should appear on the shelves beside them, to remind readers of both genders that there are and have always been strong and decisive women who are courageous enough to make their own choices and to realize their dreams.

Rosemary M. Canfield Reisman

MALCOLM X
By Any Means Necessary

Author: Walter Dean Myers (1937-   )
First published: 1993; illustrated
Type of work: Biography
Time of work: 1925-1965
Locale: Omaha, Nebraska; Lansing and Mason, Michigan; Boston; Harlem; Detroit;
Philadelphia; New York City; and Mecca, Saudi Arabia
Subjects: Activists and race and ethnicity
Recommended ages: 10-18

> *This biography of African American leader Malcolm X traces his life from his childhood through his assassination after breaking with the Nation of Islam.*

> *Principal personages:*
> MALCOLM X (MALCOLM LITTLE, EL HAJJ MALIK EL SHABAZZ), a
> Black Nationalist leader and a member of the Nation of Islam
> BETTY X (BETTY SHABAZZ), the wife of Malcolm X, a former member
> of the Nation of Islam
> ELIJAH MUHAMMAD, the spiritual leader of the Nation of Islam
> EARL LITTLE, Malcolm's father
> LOUISE LITTLE, Malcolm's mother

Form and Content

Walter Dean Myers' *Malcolm X: By Any Means Necessary* follows the brilliant and radical Black Nationalist leader's life from his birth in Omaha, Nebraska, in 1925 to his assassination in Harlem in 1965. The chapter organization divides Malcolm X's life into four stages: his difficult childhood, his troubled adolescence, his ministry within the Nation of Islam, and his life subsequent to leaving the Nation of Islam. Using the third-person point of view and a narrative style, the author has written an excellent biography that recounts major events in the subject's life and analyzes the social forces that influenced him.

The visual materials offered include black-and-white photographs and document reproductions, and the biography also features a table of contents, a superb index, and a chronology. Myers provides an excellent bibliography as evidence of his extensive scholarship in researching the book. Source notes, however, are not referenced in the text.

Malcolm X was the fourth of seven children. Earl Little, his father, was killed when Malcolm was six years old. His mother, Louise, struggled to keep her family together but was committed to a mental institution when Malcolm was fourteen. The family was impoverished. Malcolm had brushes with the law, but was a good student. A turning point in his life came when a teacher discouraged him from becoming a lawyer.

Malcolm later lived in Boston with his half sister Betty. In his teens, he held a variety of jobs but became involved in petty crime. At twenty, he was convicted of burglary and sentenced to eight-to-ten years in a state prison near Boston. His life changed forever when Elijah Muhammad, the spiritual leader of the Nation of Islam, visited him in prison. Muhammad was a Black Nationalist who taught his followers that white people were their enemies and believed in separation of the races. His religion included study from the *Qu'ran* (Koran), the holy book of Islam. Malcolm Little became a minister in the temple in Detroit and changed his name to Malcolm X. This was an important milestone in his life. He ministered to Muslim congregations in several cities and became a public spokesperson. In 1958, he married Betty, a devout Muslim, and their family grew to include four daughters.

Malcolm X's public visibility and growing reputation caused a rift with Elijah Muhammad. Malcolm became disillusioned with the church and in 1964 left to form a new organization. He and his family made a pilgrimage to Mecca, the spiritual home of international Islam. There, he found people of all races and colors working together in spiritual harmony, which changed his perceptions of white people as a group. He took the name "El Hajj Malik el Shabazz" and returned home to begin a new ministry with a new message. He soon received death threats, however, and his home was bombed. On March 11, 1966, Malcolm X was assassinated in Harlem. His murderers were tried and convicted, but who ordered the assassination remains unknown.

Analysis

In his preface to *Malcolm X: By Any Means Necessary*, Myers identifies Malcolm X as the pivotal figure of the Civil Rights movement of the 1960's. His contributions to African American thought and history have survived the test of time as he continues to inspire young people. For many, he remains a symbol of black pride. As a Black Nationalist, he fought the stereotype of "the humble Negro," begging at the table for his rights, and did not disavow violence as a tool for social change. Malcolm X preached revolution "by any means necessary." The author uses the metaphor "the blade of the sword" to describe his subject's role in the Civil Rights movement.

Myers presents an accurate, realistic account of his subject's life and thought. Although the book's scope is limited to the life of one man, the author has also included the relevant information and analysis needed to place Malcolm X's life within a broader historical perspective. Events are presented in chronological order. The author has adroitly interwoven historical facts into the narrative that place the subject's life and thought within the social context of the times. He uses quotations from Alex Haley's *The Autobiography of Malcolm X* (1964) to support his analysis of turning points in his subject's life. Myers' rationale for this approach is expressed in his opening statement in chapter 1 that people "react to ideas that have come before them, and to people who have expressed those ideas."

Using the flexibility of the third-person point of view, Myers not only has produced an accurate, sensitive biography of his subject but also has placed his subject within the broader scope of African American history. Thus, readers with little knowledge of this history are provided with sufficient background information to understand the author's analysis of the subject matter. For example, Malcolm's parents were strong supporters of Marcus Garvey's Black Nationalist movement. Details of Garvey's life are summarized in the text in order to provide readers with an understanding of the controversy that swirled around that figure. Myers sketches a canvas of African American life and thought—from the terrible suffering of families during the Depression to the Civil Rights movement of the 1960's. Interested readers will find many subjects for further exploration.

Myers' writing style is commendable. Although the text is easy-to-read, the author uses phrasing elegantly, with not a word wasted. He paints visual pictures with words, such as his descriptions of zoot suits and conks. Myers' choice of details to elaborate and explore shows unerring judgment, and he writes with clarity and precision. Supplementary information is inserted flawlessly into the narrative and never seems intrusive. Wide margins, chapter heading boxes, and family photographs contribute to the readability of the biography.

The author captures the essence of a complex man whose life and writings continue to generate powerful emotions. Using a neutral voice, he has produced a biography that is not a dry statement of fact, yet effectively avoids an emotional, biased appeal to readers. Reared in poverty, young Malcolm Little craved respect but had no hope for a better life, and he spent much of his young manhood in prison. As a leader, Malcolm X was intelligent and articulate, a man of principles who never stopped learning and growing and whose power was in his ideas. He was loved and hated, vilified and glorified. He was a center of controversy. Myers captures this essence sympathetically, but objectively. He addresses the questions that remain, such as who was responsible for the assassination, and presents controversial issues and relevant facts without taking sides. By avoiding both sensationalism and didacticism, he has created an outstanding biography for young people.

Critical Context

With some fifty books to his credit, Walter Dean Myers is a prolific author whose works are primarily about African American children and youths. In 1994, he was the recipient of the Margaret A. Edwards Award for his writing, "which illustrates the universality of the teenage experience in urban America." *Malcolm X: By Any Means Necessary* has received excellent critical reviews and was a Coretta Scott King Award Honor selection in 1994. He has also written a history of African Americans entitled *Now Is Your Time!* (1991).

Myers' range of works is extremely varied—from picture books to nonfiction to novels. His books frequently reflect social issues as they affect young people. In the novel *Somewhere in the Darkness* (1992), another Coretta Scott King Award Honor selection, a teenage boy leaves home with his father, who recently escaped from prison for a last painful reunion. The death of Myers' brother in the Vietnam War inspired his novel *Fallen Angels* (1988), an account of the day-to-day life of a young soldier in the war; he received the Coretta Scott King Award for that novel. The author's popularity with young people attests the fact that he reaches his goal in his writing to "reach out and touch the lives of my characters and share them with a reader." In doing so, Myers touches the lives of his readers as well.

Inez Ramsey

MANIAC MAGEE

Author: Jerry Spinelli (1941-   )
First published: 1990
Type of work: Novel
Type of plot: Folktale and social realism
Time of work: Contemporary
Locale: Two Mills, Pennsylvania
Subjects: Family, race and ethnicity, and social issues
Recommended ages: 10-13

"Maniac" Magee is an orphan with superhuman skills who runs from place to place trying to acquire a permanent address and who ultimately triumphs over the bitter realities and prejudices of the world.

Principal characters:

JEFFREY LIONEL ("MANIAC") MAGEE, an orphaned twelve-year-old boy who runs away from self-absorbed caretakers to find his place in the world

AMANDA BEALE, an independent young African American girl who lives in the East End of Two Mills and whose family gives the strange new white boy a home

EARL GRAYSON, a grizzled old parkhand at the zoo, who discovers Jeffrey sleeping among the buffaloes and offers him a temporary home until fate intervenes

GIANT JOHN MCNAB, a fastballer and king of the West End Cobra gang, who dislikes Jeffrey until he rescues McNab's little brothers

"MARS BAR" THOMPSON, Jeffrey's candy-bar-eating, African American rival, who eventually becomes his running buddy and friend

Form and Content

Jerry Spinelli's *Maniac Magee* is a fast-paced novel in three parts, each part subdivided into short chapters. The three parts describe three pivotal periods in the life and growth of the main character Jeffrey Lionel "Maniac" Magee, a young orphan with amazing physical abilities who, through a series of adventures, pursues his dream of finding acceptance in a loving home.

The book is written from the omniscient point of view, as if by a narrator looking back on a legendary hero. By using this approach, Jerry Spinelli helps the reader view Maniac not only from the perspective of kids who chant about how fast he could run, how high he could jump, or how he could untie any knot there ever was, but also from the perspective of adults who marvel at how he managed to bring folks from the black East End and the white West End together. The omniscient point of view also enables the reader to see inside Jeffrey Magee, to know his confusion and his solitude, to be a part of his internal struggle and change.

Although Maniac possesses nearly magical athletic prowess, his dealings with racial problems, peer pressures, homelessness, and family situations are all too realistic—and often overpowering. Spinelli has created a novel that is an interesting blend of folktale and contemporary realistic fiction. The superboy dazzles people on the football field but struggles to deal with racial strife. Blending the two genres enables Spinelli to deal with difficult issues in an engaging manner—to create a tall tale out of real-life drama.

The contemporary setting of Two Mills, Pennsylvania, could be any American city that is literally and figuratively segregated into black and white districts. Specific details of time and place are intentionally omitted, in order to suggest that this could happen anywhere or anytime, or perhaps that it already has happened.

The story describes the exploits of Jeffrey Magee, whose parents were killed in a bizarre accident when he was three years old. Sent to live with an aunt and uncle who hated each other, Jeffrey endured eight years of that torture before he could not take any more. He ran away from home and just kept running.

The legend says that Jeffrey ran two hundred miles to Two Mills, where he encountered the friendly Amanda Beale and her suitcase of books. Intrigued by both Amanda and her treasured books, Jeffrey decided to stay awhile with her family. The legend has it that Jeffrey, nicknamed "Maniac" by his peers, amazed the entire town with feats of unbelievable acumen. He caught footballs with one hand, saved a kid from mean old Finsterwald, knocked a frogball for a home run, beat a kid named "Mars Bar" Thompson while running backward in a foot race, and untied the giant Cobbles Knot. Jeffrey became famous. His residence with the kind, African American Beale family was resented by local white racists, however, and soon brought trouble for the Beales. Jeffrey could not bear to see his new family hurt; he felt compelled to run away again.

This time he took up residence living among the buffaloes at the local zoo, running during the day and coming home in time for animal food at night. One day, he was discovered by Earl Grayson, the old parkhand who worked at the zoo. Grayson accepted Jeffrey immediately and provided him with physical and emotional nourishment. Jeffrey and Grayson shared stories, humor, sadness, food, work, and much more, developing a strong mutual respect and affection. Jeffrey taught Grayson to read, and Grayson helped Jeffrey feel a sense of belonging. With Grayson, Jeffrey found contentment. Unfortunately, the contentment was short-lived as Grayson died, once again leaving Jeffrey alone and on his own. At the funeral, Jeffrey began running again, this time in the dead of winter as a dissolute, solitary wanderer, waiting for death.

Just when Jeffrey's life seemed bleakest, two other runaways crossed his path. Because of Hector and Piper, the two young boys whom he coaxed home, Jeffrey wound up living in the twins' house with their brother, Giant John McNab, ace pitcher and leader of the white Cobra gang. Jeffrey tried to bring some order to the lives of the disheveled McNabs; he helped around the house, played with Hector and Piper, and cajoled the twins into attending school. The Cobras, however, were white racists preparing for war against African Americans. Unable to fathom or accept such hatred, Jeffrey felt out of place in the McNab home. Again, he fled to a life among animals at the zoo.

One day during his usual run, Jeffrey encountered a fellow runner, African American rival Mars Bar Thompson. Through their shared interest in running, the two athletes developed a mutual respect and acceptance of each other. Mars Bar determined to help his new friend. He recruited Amanda Beale, and together they sought Jeffrey out at his zoo abode. Amanda called him to come "home," and Jeffrey finally knew where he belonged.

Analysis

Maniac Magee is a moderately complex novel, in form and in content. In form, it offers both social realism and an adventure tale about the life and times of a contemporary legend. In content, it tells an engaging, fast-paced story with a number of subthemes or subjects, including homelessness, the importance of family, the influence of adolescent peer groups, and ever-present racial tensions.

First and foremost, however, *Maniac Magee* is a novel about an adolescent boy in search of his true place in the world, a place that proves quite difficult to find. Jeffrey's search is made more difficult not only because he is orphaned at an early age but also because he is an innocent soul who does not know hatred or prejudice. Jeffrey simply does not see "this color business," and part of his growth as a character is learning what prejudice is, its consequences, and how hard it is to change. Jeffrey's journey symbolizes the journey that all adolescents must make from blind innocence to sighted awareness of the world's evils.

Spinelli wants readers to believe that hatred and prejudice can be overcome, and that people can find where they truly belong if they search hard enough. Jeffrey functions as a catalyst who helps bring together a racially divided town. His eventual home in the black community symbolizes society's potential to heal itself, to be accepting and loving of others, and to live in harmony.

Spinelli realistically captures the rhythms and dialogue of the times, while playfully creating an engaging world of myth and legend. It is notable that the African American characters in the novel have identities and personalities; they do not exist solely as foils for the main character, nor are they stick figures or stereotypes.

Critical Context

Maniac Magee can be considered a landmark in young adult literature by virtue of being one of the earliest and best-written novels to focus on complex societal problems such as homelessness and race relations. It is also unusual in that it blends realism and myth so well; Spinelli commented, in his *Boston Globe*/Horn Book Award acceptance speech, that he found the world children inhabit somewhat indistinguishable from myth and legend. *Maniac Magee* won the Newbery Medal in 1991; since then, it has earned both critical and popular acclaim.

Maniac Magee holds particular appeal for middle school students, for whom family relationships are often volatile and peer (or even gang) pressures are increasingly influential. In this respect, the novel possesses characteristics similar to Paula Fox's *The Moonlight Man* (1986), Walter Dean Myers' *Scorpions* (1988), or Gary Soto's *Baseball in April and Other Stories* (1990).

On one level, *Maniac Magee* makes for engaging reading as simply a fast-paced quest. It would serve well as a read-aloud book for the middle grades. The novel could also be used to precipitate classroom discussions on homelessness, family, peer pressure, or prejudice. On the most serious level, however, *Maniac Magee* may be recommended to encourage private reflection about complex social and personal issues, issues with which each reader must learn to cope.

Cherrie L. Kassem

THE MANY WAYS OF SEEING
An Introduction to the Pleasures of Art

Author: Janet Gaylord Moore (1905-   )
First published: 1968; illustrated
Type of work: Art
Subjects: Arts and nature
Recommended ages: 10-18

Supplemented with numerous illustrations, Moore's book offers a variety of ways to understand and appreciate the visual arts.

Form and Content

The Many Ways of Seeing: An Introduction to the Pleasures of Art presents its contents in several forms and sections. Following an introduction, Janet Gaylord Moore divides the subject matter into ten chapters dealing with various aspects about the visual arts, ranging from a viewer's perceptions to the media that artists use to produce art objects. Between chapter 5 and chapter 6, an "Interlude" is inserted. This section juxtaposes reproductions of artworks with various literary quotations, which are not about the specific pieces of art but rather that serve as textual complements to the visual images. Endnotes document references in the text, and a bibliography of suggestions for further reading enables the reader to pursue topics of interest.

The first two chapters concern general aspects of perception. The author begins by suggesting ways that readers can open their eyes to visual phenomena around them. She shows how to see visual patterns in nature and how to use different perspectives to see new things in ordinary objects. Moore then turns in the second chapter to various artworks to demonstrate how artists and their artworks help one to see the world with a fresh vision. For example, many modern paintings such as the rectangular blocks of color painted by the Dutch artist Piet Mondrian have influenced the modern design of everyday objects.

The third chapter turns to paintings and offers some guidance about how to approach looking at these visual images. Moore uses the example of landscapes by two late nineteenth century artists, Vincent Van Gogh and Paul Cézanne. Van Gogh's paintings are direct and vibrant, while Cézanne's depiction of similar landscapes are more carefully orchestrated and controlled through his use of planes of color to construct the formal elements of the landscape.

The fourth chapter goes into more detail about the visual elements that artists use to create their artworks. Moore concentrates on three key features: line, color, and form. Line is basic because it can be used to define images. Different artists use line almost like a signature, with variations from very clean lines to ones that are filled with energy. She explains the basic elements of color, the primary and secondary colors. In addition, she shows how variations in lightness and darkness of color are called values. Form has two chief meanings: It can be understood as shape, and it can refer to the formal composition of an artwork that places its visual elements in relation to one another.

In the fifth chapter, Moore confronts the important question of why new styles of art challenge the viewer. She reviews briefly the many changes in artistic styles that have succeeded one another, from the mid-nineteenth century to the 1960's. In every case, a new art movement such as Impressionism seemed very daring and different to the public at the time, whereas now such styles are well accepted. Moore implies that part of the function of art is to lead one constantly to see things in new ways.

With this background in the basics of art appreciation, Moore turns in the sixth chapter to some exercises that readers can do in order to experiment for themselves with some of the artistic elements. She begins with some ideas for drawing and then moves on to textures, shapes, and composition. She also suggests that students take sketch books to art museums to work in front of artworks—not to copy them exactly, but to think about some of the visual elements that these works display. The purpose of these activities is to develop one's artistic eye through "hands-on" contact with the practice of art.

After a brief discussion of the possibilities of collecting artworks in chapter 7, Moore presents in chapter 8 an explanation of the various materials and techniques that artists have used over the centuries. She concentrates on drawing, painting, printmaking, and sculpture. In every case, knowing about these materials helps the viewer understand the visual effects that are possible with each medium.

The last two chapters return to the themes relating to the idea of looking at the world with a perceptive eye that were considered at the beginning of the book. The ninth chapter suggests that students keep sketch books or visual journals, particularly when they might be traveling and experiencing new visual sensations. The tenth chapter again juxtaposes patterns in nature with artworks to show how the special way in which artists present their visual ideas may help viewers sharpen their visual senses not only when looking at art objects but also when experiencing the world on an everyday basis.

Analysis

The title of this book, *The Many Ways of Seeing*, succinctly expresses the author's purpose and approach, which is to provide a variety of ways that readers can sharpen their "visual awareness." Thus, the chapters are rather short and offer many different ways to cultivate and heighten visual acuity.

One approach that Moore uses is straightforward textual discussion and explanation. This technique is particularly well suited to conveying basic information about the visual arts. The chapter on the visual elements of line, color, and form and the chapter on the materials and techniques of artists are thorough and clear. Ample illustrations are provided so that each element, material, and technique can be viewed along with the textual discussion.

Similarly, several chapters focus on particular artworks in order to illustrate the special ways that artists present their ideas. The comparison between the landscapes by Van Gogh and Cézanne in chapter 3 shows how different artists approach the same basic subject and composition with strikingly different results. Chapter 5, on ways in which artists change their styles and present challenges to viewers, offers a brief history of the developments in Western art over the previous 150 years.

A second major technique that Moore utilizes is providing actual exercises for readers to follow. In chapter 4, she demonstrates how readers can study the composition of paintings by creating diagrams of their primary compositional lines. Chapter 6, entitled "The Seeing Eye, the Thinking Hand," is devoted to a series of creative exercises that can been done using simple materials such as pencil and paper to get the feel of creating art with the visual elements. These exercises are designed to sharpen the visual senses. In addition, several times, particularly in chapter 9, Moore suggests that students keep notebooks or journals to record visual ideas and impressions.

The Many Ways of Seeing is fully illustrated with reproductions in both color and black and white. The reader is encouraged to study these visual images along with the text. One section, in particular, offers an opportunity use the eyes in a creative way: The "Interlude," by pairing reproductions of artworks with literary quotations, allows the reader/viewer to study and meditate on the interconnections between the visual and literary languages. Throughout the book, Moore presents a variety of creative ways to open her readers' eyes to the appreciation of art and its relationship to other art forms such as literature and to the natural world.

Critical Context

Janet Moore's method of teaching art arises out of her experiences as an artist, art teacher, and education curator in the Cleveland Museum of Art. In addition to *The Many Ways of Seeing*, she has written *The Eastern Gate: An Invitation to the Arts of China and Japan* (1979). Both books provide introductions to aspects of the visual arts for young people.

While *The Many Ways of Seeing* is intended to instill an appreciation of art in a juvenile audience, it is useful for anyone who is interested in learning about how to look at art. The book has been successful, and it was named a Newbery Honor Book by the American Library Association. Critics have praised the book for the clarity with which Moore presents her ideas and material. *The Many Ways of Seeing* has a sensitivity and simplicity, but it never talks down to the reader, whether juvenile or adult. The integration of the text and the illustrated artworks has also been cited as a strength of this book.

A number of books are currently available whose subject is art appreciation. Most, however, are intended as textbooks for courses at the college level or for adult readers who desire an introduction to the visual arts. *The Many Ways of Seeing* remains one of the few books whose primary audience is young people. Its combination of textual discussion and visual exercises is almost unique and well-suited to involve young people directly in the creative process of art.

Karen Gould

THE MARCH ON WASHINGTON

Author: Jim Haskins (1941-   )
First published: 1993; illustrated
Type of work: History
Time of work: 1962-1964
Locale: Washington, D.C.
Subjects: Politics and law, race and ethnicity, and social issues
Recommended ages: 13-18

> *This concise history of the events that led to the March on Washington for Jobs and Freedom includes brief biographies of the African American leaders who were responsible for its organization and successful outcome; the consequences of the march, both positive and negative, are discussed in relation to the Civil Rights movement.*

Principal characters:
>ASA PHILIP RANDOLPH, a civil rights activist who organized the first black union and the March on Washington
>JOHN F. KENNEDY, the president of the United States from 1960 to 1963, a supporter of civil rights for African Americans
>ROY WILKINS, the executive director of the National Association for the Advancement of Colored People (NAACP)
>WHITNEY M. YOUNG, JR., the executive director of the National Urban League
>DR. MARTIN LUTHER KING, JR., the founder of the Southern Christian Leadership Conference (SCLC)
>JOHN LEWIS, one of the founders and the national chairman of the Student Nonviolent Coordinating Committee (SNCC)
>BAYARD RUSTIN, an activist who helped found the Congress of Racial Equality (CORE) and an organizer of the march
>JAMES FARMER, the national director of CORE

Form and Content
   Jim Haskins' *The March on Washington* chronicles the famous march, from the conception of the idea in 1941 to its successful completion on August 28, 1963. Each chapter deals with a specific aspect of the march, and Haskins offers the historical background for each one. He allows the reader to see the vision for the march, how the idea developed, and the effects that the march had on the shaping of civil rights in America.
   The mini-biography that Haskins provides on Asa Philip Randolph sets the tone for the book. Randolph lived through the period of Reconstruction after the Civil War and through the Jim Crow era, and he saw the founding of the Ku Klux Klan and the

NAACP. Randolph organized the first black labor union for Pullman porters in 1934 and in 1941 was responsible for legislation banning discrimination in war industries, opening thousands of jobs for black people. He was also responsible for the 1948 legislation banning segregation in the armed forces.

Randolph was not alone in his struggle to bring equality to African Americans. Lawyers with the NAACP brought cases of discrimination before the U.S. Supreme Court. Dr. Martin Luther King, Jr., organized a successful bus boycott in Montgomery, Alabama, in 1955. National organizations were founded to fight for equal rights, marches were held throughout the country, and some civil rights legislation, although weak, was passed. These and other events brought to the forefront the necessity for laws to provide equal rights for all Americans. President John F. Kennedy made a strong public statement in support of civil rights and proposed a civil rights bill with federal funds allocated to enforce the new laws. Randolph and King believed that the time was right to march on Washington.

Plans for a march to Washington, D.C., for equal rights began. According to Haskins, it would be "the largest organized Negro political event supported by the white power structure." Ten black leaders met to plan the march, but only the six men representing major civil rights organizations were actually involved in the planning: Roy Wilkins, James Farmer, Whitney M. Young, Jr., Randolph, King, and John Lewis. They agreed on the following: The date was set for August 28, 1963; the march would begin at the Washington Monument, with entertainment from the many black stars who were participating; it would end at the Lincoln Memorial, with the leaders giving speeches no longer than seven minutes; the march would be positive, with no violence; and Bayard Rustin, a long-time associate of Randolph and a civil rights worker, would be asked to function as deputy director, organizing the march despite the fact he was homosexual, a former member of the Communist Party, and a conscientious objector during World War II.

Rustin tackled the organization of the march with amazing energy—planning transportation, communication, health and medical services, printing, parking, security, food, and housing for the more than 200,000 people participating in the march. This detailed planning ensured a peaceful, successful march. There were only three arrests, and the world saw "a quarter of a million people, black and white, Jew and Gentile, grandparents and infants, male and female, rich and poor, powerful and powerless walking shoulder to shoulder and hand in hand for a cause in which they believed."

The March on Washington for Jobs and Freedom was the largest peaceful demonstration for racial equality in American history, but it put an end to the nonviolent civil rights movement. After the march, white supremacist groups reacted with violence in cities across the country, and some black leaders began espousing retaliation with violence. Within three years of King's "I Have a Dream" speech, many black people throughout the United States were holding up their fists and screaming "Black Power." Five years after the march, four prominent leaders had been assassinated— John F. Kennedy in 1963, Malcolm X in 1965, Robert F. Kennedy in 1968, and Martin

Luther King, Jr., in 1968—providing further proof that the United States had much to accomplish before the goals of the march could be realized.

Analysis

Haskins wrote *The March on Washington* in the belief that it would be an important work for young adults and children of the 1990's. Books written about events in black history allow young adults of every race to gain an understanding of what African Americans have accomplished in the past two hundred years and of the price that they had to pay to gain what they rightly deserved. Haskins writes about the violent events and loss of life that Americans, both black and white, endured while striving for racial equality. The sacrifices were made by people who believed vehemently in a cause for which they were willing to die, and many of them did.

Haskins' book is written in a narrative style that keeps his readers' attention and helps maintain their focus. The information is accurately conveyed in a clear and concise manner using a tone that models the calm, nonviolent attitude of the march. The author's voice can be heard, but that voice in no way detracts from the content or colors the information conveyed. The black-and-white photographs are clear and appropriately placed throughout the book; they add to the content and illustrate the author's words. The photographs of the black and white leaders show readers the united front presented to America for the success of this event.

The book includes a chronology of important dates in civil rights history, beginning in 1909 with the founding of the NAACP by W. E. B. Du Bois and ending in 1990 when Douglas Wilder of Virginia became the first black governor. Haskins also offers a well-researched bibliography and a comprehensive index. All of these features make the book a valuable resource and a complement to other books on this subject.

The excerpts from the speeches given on the day of the march help the reader develop a sense of the respectful atmosphere that was present at the Lincoln Memorial. The support that President Kennedy gave to the black leaders who planned the march and the positive remarks that he made both before and after the event showed his dedication to achieving racial equality. After the march, Kennedy stated, "The cause of twenty million Negroes has been advanced by the program conducted so appropriately before the nation's shrine to the Great Emancipator, but even more significant is the contribution to all mankind."

On some level, Kennedy shared the dream of Martin Luther King, Jr., whose "I Have a Dream" speech was a universal appeal for racial equality. King and Kennedy both envisioned a world in which, in King's words, "children will one day live in a nation where they will not be judged by the color of their skin but by the content of their character." In the case of the March on Washington, the sword has proved to be mightier than the pen, because racial prejudice continues to exist in the United States.

Critical Context

Jim Haskins is a well-respected educator and author. He has written more than one hundred biographies of African Americans for children and young adults, including

Queen of the Blues: A Biography of Dinah Washington (1987), *Mr. Bojangles: The Biography of Bill Robinson* (1988), and *Rosa Parks: My Story* (1992), which he coauthored with Parks. Haskins has also published books about African American social, cultural, and political history, including *Black Theater in America* (1982), *Black Music in America* (1987), and *Black Dance in America* (1990). His books are written with a style and a voice that touch the soul of his readers. *The March on Washington* is a welcome addition to his corpus of work.

Susan Y. Geye

"MASTER HAROLD" . . . AND THE BOYS

Author: Athol Fugard (1932-   )
First presented: 1982
First published: 1982
Type of work: Drama
Type of plot: Moral tale and social realism
Time of work: A Thursday afternoon in 1950
Locale: St. George's Park Tea Room in Port Elizabeth, South Africa
Subjects: Coming-of-age, family, friendship, race and ethnicity, and social issues
Recommended ages: 15-18

In this play about how a black waiter teaches lessons about manhood to a poor white boy in the early days of apartheid, Fugard critiques the quality of life in South Africa and stresses the importance of recognizing value in other peoples and cultures.

Principal characters:
HALLY, the seventeen-year-old son of the owners of a white tea room
SAM SEMELA, a forty-five-year-old black waiter, Hally's best friend
WILLIE MALOPO, a black waiter who is also in his mid-forties

Form and Content
    "MASTER HAROLD" . . . and the boys is a one-act play using only three characters. All of the action takes place in one hundred consecutive, uninterrupted minutes of real time on a rainy Thursday afternoon at the St. George's Park Tea Room. Influenced by the Irish playwright Samuel Beckett, Athol Fugard uses minimal sets and props. The set design is a simple box with three walls and the fourth side open to the audience. The furnishings are sparse: one table and chair at centerstage, other tables and chairs stacked in the background, a phone, and a jukebox. Fugard uses music and dance to add movement to the play. Throughout, Willie Malopo and Sam Semela practice the waltz and the foxtrot for a ballroom dancing competition. Early in the play, Willie sings Count Basie's "You the Cream in My Coffee, You the Salt in My Stew," and other songs are sung or played on the jukebox throughout the play.
    Less than fully scripted, finite entities, Fugard's plays are existential—happening at the moment of performance as living theater. As the play opens, heavy rain keeps customers away, so the waiters have little to do but practice dancing. Sam has set a place at the centerstage table for Hally to eat his dinner. When the boy comes in from school, he takes for granted that the place is for him. The familiar routine suddenly breaks when Hally learns that his mother is not at the tea room, but at the hospital visiting his sick father. Hally senses that something is wrong because the hospital does not allow visitors on Thursdays. At first he thinks, and subconsciously hopes, that his father may be worse, or even dead. Embarrassed by his father's alcoholism and amputated leg, Hally has enjoyed his absence.

Telephone calls from Hally's mother help move the plot forward. Although the audience hears only Hally's side of these conversations, his responses expose what she is saying to him; he is horrified to learn that his father is being released from the hospital. As Sam tries to stop Hally from talking cruelly about his father, the bond between waiter and boy is quickly established. During a brief phone conversation with his father, Hally lets down his guard and demonstrates his frustration by accusing Sam and Willie of meddling.

The emotional shifts between characters are initially small, but they increase drastically as the play progresses. The audience learns that for years, Hally had relied on Sam as a father-figure. In one remembered scene, Sam built Hally a kite out of scraps and made him fly it in a public park. The boy was initially ashamed of the kite, but its flight made him proud. Sam left Hally alone to fly the kite because the park was for white people only. At the end of the play, the audience learns that some time before the kite episode, Hally had asked Sam to go with him to a local tavern where his father had passed out from drinking too much. Hally had to go in first to ask permission for Sam to enter the whites-only establishment. Humiliated, Hally followed behind as Sam carried the drunk home.

Sam tries to dissuade Hally from hating his real father too much. Tensions turn racial when Hally lashes out and attempts to hurt Sam by saying "You're only a servant here, and don't forget it." For a moment, the boy discards years of friendship and adopts his parents' attitude that white people should not be friendly with black servants. Hally asserts his manhood by telling Sam to call him "Master Harold." Sam, who had always called his friend by the familiar name "Hally," warns that if he calls him "Master Harold" once, he will do so forever, and their friendship will be broken. After Hally jokes about an African's backside not being "fair," Sam drops his pants and shows the boy the truth—that his rear is just as dark as his face. Hally attempts to assert his racial superiority by spitting on Sam. The man is infuriated and initially wants to hit the boy, but as Hally's intellectual superior, he controls his emotions and merely calls him "Master Harold." Signaling the end of their friendship, these words are more condemning than physical violence. Hally tries feebly to get out of the situation, but Sam takes control and guides their relationship to a fresh start. Hally learns that being a man means not always resorting to hatred and violence. The play ends with the jukebox playing Sarah Vaughan singing "Little man you're crying . . . Little man you've had a busy day."

Analysis

Based on an incident in his own adolescence, *"MASTER HAROLD"* . . . *and the boys* is Fugard's most autobiographical work. Harold "Hally" Athol Lannigan Fugard was born on June 11, 1932, near Middelburg, Cape Province, South Africa. Like the character Hally, Fugard is of mixed descent; his Afrikaner mother ran a boarding house, and his British father was a crippled former jazz pianist. In 1935, Fugard's family moved to Port Elizabeth, where the play is set. Like Hally, Fugard completed his secondary education at a local technical college. At the age of thirteen, he spit in a servant's face. From that event, Fugard learned about the pain that people often cause to close friends and family. Thirty-five years after the original incident, he faced his guilt by writing this play.

Fugard's decision to set the play in 1950 instead of 1945 was politically motivated by South Africa's Group Areas Act of 1950, which enforced complete residential segregation between races and "social" or "petty" apartheid segregation in public places such as theaters, parks, and restaurants. Although writing in English, Fugard uses Afrikaner moods and culture. He was the first white South African playwright to blend cultures and the first to violate apartheid artistically by putting black and white actors on stage at the same time. His characters are usually underprivileged white people and black Africans—ordinary people caught in racial and social traps. By dramatizing their interactions, he exposes the quality of life in South Africa, not only for oppressed black Africans but for all races as well.

Fugard creates Sam and Willie as very different characters in order to counter the stereotype that all black South Africans are alike. Willie calls his fellow servant "Boet Sam." "Boet"—brother—is used as a term of affection between friends or with an elder as a sign of respect. Sam and Willie are the same age, but Sam is wiser and more mature. Willie is lazy and abuses his girlfriend; Sam is refined and intelligent, learns Hally's lessons quicker than the boy does, and retains all that he learns.

The central metaphor that Fugard uses for relations between people, races, and countries is ballroom dancing. Willie practices dancing throughout the play, and Hally observes the competition for a school essay. Ballroom dancing also becomes a metaphor for getting through life—communication, maneuvering, people and nations avoiding collisions. Hally suggests that the United Nations is a global dance. Ballroom dancing is not easy; one must practice in order to be good. An accomplished dancer, Sam coaches Willie and shows Hally how to be a man.

The title *"MASTER HAROLD" . . . and the boys* ironically suggests Fugard's concern with the concept of manhood. Although nearly thirty years older, Sam and Willie are considered "boys" by white South Africans, while Hally has been a "master" from birth. As part of his coming-of-age, Hally must learn to recognize the social implications of race and gradually reject institutionalized racism (apartheid). His friendship with Sam transforms from "Master" and "boy" to man and man.

Critical Context

The themes of coming-of-age, racial tensions, and parental conflict in *"MASTER HAROLD" . . . and the boys* have much in common with Mark Twain's *Adventures of Huckleberry Finn* (1884). Its political messages and critique of apartheid fit with Athol Fugard's other works, especially *The Blood Knot* (1961), in which two men—one black and the other white—are half brothers. Fugard's dramatic style is similar to that of Samuel Beckett, Harold Pinter, and other existential playwrights.

"MASTER HAROLD" . . . and the boys was first produced at the Yale Repertory Theater on March 12, 1982, and a television version was produced soon after. Although suitable for mature high school students, this play is taught primarily in

undergraduate college classes. Deeply rooted in South African culture and politics, it can be used in literature or history classes.

Geralyn Strecker

THE MASTER PUPPETEER

Author: Katherine Paterson (1932-   )
First published: 1975; illustrated
Type of work: Novel
Type of plot: Adventure tale, historical fiction, and social realism
Time of work: The late eighteenth century
Locale: Osaka, Japan
Subjects: Arts, family, friendship, and poverty
Recommended ages: 10-15

When young Jiro becomes an apprentice in a Japanese puppet theater, he discovers hidden talents and finds his loyalty to family and friends tested as he uncovers the secret of the bandit Saburo, who is the hero of famine-stricken Osaka.

> *Principal characters:*
> JIRO, a new apprentice at the Hanaza puppet theater
> HANJI, Jiro's father, who makes puppets for a living
> ISAKO, Jiro's mother
> YOSHIDA, the owner and master puppeteer of the Hanaza
> KINSHI, Yoshida's son, who befriends Jiro
> MOCHIDA, one of the "left-hand manipulators" at the Hanaza
> OKADA, the blind and elderly chief chanter at the Hanaza, who was
>   Yoshida's former master and who, in reality, is Saburo the bandit
> WADA, an apprentice at the puppet theater who is initially jealous of Jiro
> MIORU, another apprentice, who likes to eat
> TEJI, a small apprentice who stutters

Form and Content

The Master Puppeteer is at once a fascinating introduction to the complex artistry of the Japanese puppet theater, a gripping historical novel, a mystery, and a study of friendship and loyalty. The novel follows the adventures of thirteen-year-old Jiro, who finds himself caught up in the political events of late eighteenth century Osaka, Japan. When Jiro accompanies his father, Hanji, to deliver a puppet to the Hanaza theater, Yoshida, the owner and master puppeteer, offers to take the boy on as an apprentice. To Jiro's chagrin, his mother, Isako, does not take Yoshida's offer seriously. Determined not to be a burden on his family during the current famine, Jiro runs away to the theater, where he becomes an apprentice; he begins his career by opening curtains and memorizing scripts and eventually graduates to a role as a "foot operator." Along the way, he is helped by an older boy, Yoshida's son, Kinshi, who does not seem able to please his father.

Worried about his father, who is said to be ill, Jiro briefly returns home to discover that Isako has taken his father to recuperate at a relative's farm in Kyoto. When Jiro again returns home on New Year's Day, he discovers that his mother is near starvation. One evening, Saburo, the mysterious bandit who steals from the rich to help the poor, leaves a notice on the door of the theater demanding a special performance of the current play, "The Thief of the Tokaido." The lights go out after the performance, and the police are bound and their uniforms are stolen. One evening soon after, an angry mob dubbed the "night rovers" tries to break into the theater to get food. Jiro and another apprentice, Teji, are forced to guard the door throughout the night, and Jiro is shocked when he hears his mother's voice crying out in the crowd.

When Kinshi begins to sneak out of the theater at night to help the night rovers, Jiro asks him to find his mother and help her. One morning when Kinshi is late returning to the theater, Yoshida orders Jiro to take his place and operate the feet of an important character in their latest play. When Jiro goes to the storehouse to find a puppet to use for practice, he discovers a Samurai sword and concludes that Yoshida is really the bandit Saburo. After Jiro tricks Yoshida into allowing Kinshi to take back his role in the play, the boy makes his friend promise to stop his evening forays into the town if Kinshi can arrange for him to meet Saburo, who might be able to help the night rovers. Jiro then seeks out Yoshida's old master, the blind Okada, asking him to talk to "Saburo." Jiro soon discovers that Okada is really Saburo and that he operates through human "puppets" such as Yoshida.

When Jiro leaves the theater to search for his mother and Kinshi, he is plunged into a riot that leaves much of the town in flames. There, he encounters his father, who is not really ill and who is really one of Saburo's men. Jiro survives by disguising himself as a fireman and helps his mother and Kinshi return to the theater. Because of Jiro's loyalty to Okada, Isako will be allowed to live at the Hanaza. Kinshi, whose right hand has been cut off during the riot, will be apprenticed to Okada, and Jiro, who has proved his talents in the theater and his courage in the outside world, will continue to train as a puppeteer under Yoshida.

Analysis

Katherine Paterson has said that *The Master Puppeteer* grew out of her children's suggestion that she write a mystery story. On the surface, the novel provides a good mystery, one that revolves around the secret identity of the bandit Saburo. Jiro stumbles upon clues to Saburo's identity but learns that, like those who visit the puppet theater, he is focusing on the puppet and not the puppeteer. *The Master Puppeteer* is also a gripping historical novel that introduces young readers to the plagues, famines, and civil disorder of eighteenth century Japan and, at the same time, the beauty, intricacy, and artistry of Bunraku, classical Japanese puppet theater. Various details about creating and manipulating puppets and about the content of the plays are woven into the novel naturally.

Yet, the book is much more than a mystery or history lesson. The novel carefully considers the nature of art, the value of friendship and family, and the fine line between art and reality. Through his adventures, Jiro learns about the patience and practice required to perfect a craft and comes to appreciate the artistry of individuals such as Okada and Yoshida. More important, he learns the value of friendship and loyalty and does not let his desire to excel in the theater affect his friendship with Kinshi.

At the same time, despite his mother's gruff exterior and his father's absence, Jiro comes to appreciate the importance of family and ultimately takes responsibility for his mother's safety. This idea is reinforced by Kinshi's sometimes tempestuous relationship with his own father, Yoshida. Both boys eventually earn the respect of their parents, who have not previously recognized their abilities.

One of the main themes of the book is the way in which Jiro and his people are forced to "play act" in order to survive. At the Hanaza, Jiro learns that everyone is playing a game, whether in the puppet plays or when they are merely preparing to perform them. Stepping out of the bounds of those roles disturbs the drama in which they are involved. Jiro also comes to question some of the roles and ceremony espoused by the adults whom he encounters. Similarly, in a society full of unrest, various characters, including Okada, Yoshida, and Hanji, play roles in order to protect themselves and others. Jiro himself must pretend to be a fireman in order to find Isako and Kinshi. Ultimately, Jiro recognizes the way in which life and art imitate one another. The plays that are performed at the Hanaza, Jiro realizes, suggest various ways in which he might respond to the current political and social unrest. In the end, Jiro learns to create his own story, not to follow blindly those created by others.

On a larger scale, *The Master Puppeteer* introduces the reader to conflicts between social classes and the difficulty of developing one's own moral code or values. Adhering to these values—as when Jiro gives up a coveted role in a play for Kinshi or when Kinshi risks his life and career to help the night rovers—sometimes has serious consequences. Yet, the hope for the future seems to lie in individuals such as Jiro and Kinshi, who value loyalty and friendship over their own needs and ambitions. Paterson has acknowledged that unconsciously woven into her simple adventure story is a plea for justice and compassion.

Critical Context

The Master Puppeteer, Katherine Paterson's third novel, was her first to gain widespread critical acclaim and attention. In 1977, it received the National Book Award for Children's Literature and was a runner-up for the Edgar Allan Poe Award from the Mystery Writers of America. In 1982, the book was also a finalist for an American Book Award. Like Paterson's two earlier novels, *The Sign of the Chrysanthemum* (1973) and *Of Nightingales That Weep* (1974), *The Master Puppeteer* is a historical novel set in Japan, a country where Paterson studied and taught for several years and where she saw Bunraku theater firsthand. In writing the novel, she returned to Japan to do research, including interviewing a modern Japanese puppeteer.

The book also looks forward to Paterson's later novels, such as the Newbery Medal winners *Bridge to Terabithia* (1977) and *Jacob Have I Loved* (1980), whose protagonists, like Jiro, overcome somewhat dysfunctional families and difficult social situations to find true friendship and discover their own special talents. Like a number of other young adult novels, including Elizabeth de Trevino's *I, Juan de Pareja* (1966) and Patricia MacLachlan's *The Facts and Fictions of Mina Pratt* (1988), *The Master Puppeteer* is a *Künstlerroman* in which its protagonist's growth as an artist leads to self-understanding and maturation. Because of its unique combination of adventure, mystery, historical fiction, and psychological realism, the novel continues to be popular and is an important part of Paterson's continued contribution to literature for young people.

Joel D. Chaston

MATHEMATICS FOR THE MILLION

Author: Lancelot Hogben (1895-1975)
First published: 1937, rev. ed., 1967; illustrated
Type of work: Science
Subjects: Education and science
Recommended ages: 15-18

This book introduces the complexities of mathematics to the general reader by relating its concepts to the activities of one's everyday life.

Form and Content

After an introduction indicating the general plan of the book and some specific questions to be discussed, *Mathematics for the Million* is organized as a historical narrative of the development of mathematics and its role as a tool for solving practical problems, particularly those dealing with measurement. Thus, a concept will be discussed as of the time that it was first studied, and only later does the reader see how it was developed by later thinkers, to the level at which it is understood today. In the course of the book, the reader is introduced to many of the main areas of mathematical study, including arithmetic, algebra, geometry, trigonometry, calculus, matrix algebra, and probability. The book is profusely illustrated, with drawings and diagrams of the problems. Each chapter concludes with a substantial series of test problems and a summary list of major concepts and rules to be memorized.

The narrative begins with a discussion of the first number systems and a look at the sort of questions that mathematicians have tried to solve. This information is followed by an analysis of Euclid's geometry, which is seen not as a pure axiomatic system but as a way of applying observations about size and shape in a systematic fashion. Eschewing the rigors of formal proof, Lancelot Hogben demonstrates that Euclid's major results do in fact match the experience of measurement in the real world,

The discussion of Euclid is followed by a treatment of the trigonometric functions, also seen as tools for measurement, leading to a discussion of the concept of pi (the ratio of the circumference of a circle to its diameter) and methods of approximating this number. Hogben then shows how the ancient Greeks used geometrical methods to solve arithmetical problems through the arrangement of numbers in triangular, square, and other regular patterns. This discussion introduces a more general treatment of the idea of number series, which will recur in the book.

Hogben demonstrates that a particularly important change in the Middle Ages was the concept of zero, which enabled the crude early number systems to be replaced by the positional notation used today. This system in turn enabled a general form for linear and quadratic equations. Hogben looks at the solutions of these problems and discusses methods for making sure that one has successfully translated the verbal problem to be solved into the language of equation. The exploration of quadratic equations leads to the concept of the square root of a negative number.

Mention of the great advances in sea travel after the Middle Ages serves as a springboard for a discussion of the use of mathematics in navigation, including a more thorough investigation of trigonometry and the geometry of the sphere. This examination is followed by an analysis of the conic sections—circle, ellipse, parabola, and hyperbola—emphasizing that they can be seen as tracing the movements of a point in accordance with the well-defined rules of quadratic equations. Consideration of the trigonometric and logarithmic functions leads to a treatment of them as the limits of infinite series, which in turn can be generalized and applied to the concept of complex numbers. Calculus is then presented as a way of measuring the rate of change of the sort of functions that have been studied.

Hogben goes on to cover the solution of series of linear equations by the use of determinants—square arrangements of the coefficients of these equations—and methods by which these determinants can be manipulated to make the work easier. As always, the emphasis is on specific practical problems. In the final chapter, the tools derived earlier in the book are applied to the study of probability, first in the sort of gambling problems that inspired the original development of the subject and then with indications of how these tools can be used by governments or insurers.

Analysis

Hogben's declared purpose in *Mathematics for the Million* is to make the mysteries of mathematics accessible to any bright, educated person. He carefully defines the technical terms that he uses and employs vivid language; for example, series "choke off," rather than "converging." Hogben did not create the book for a specific age group, but adolescents might be particularly interested in looking at mathematics in a way other than the standard approach taught in most schools.

In the face of an almost universal treatment of mathematics as a system of pure reason, Hogben presents it as an activity, simply an element in the social life of human beings. This approach has two consequences for the book. One is that rather than construct a system arguing logically from fundamental premises, Hogben tells his story historically. In his view, mathematics is primarily something that people do, and he wishes to inform the reader of the ways in which people have done it, from the simplest forms used by primitive people to the complexities of modern mathematics.

The second consequence is that mathematics is always presented as a practical concern of actual human beings living and working in the world. (Hogben is sharply critical of the ivory tower approach of Plato and his followers.) In keeping with this approach, Hogben describes mathematics as a language of size, shape, and order. In this view, the most fundamental aspect of mathematics is its use for purposes of measurement, with counting seen as only one specific way of measuring.

Despite the limitations of the narrative approach as a way of presenting ideas, Hogben manages to build his view of mathematics in a coherent fashion. Using the concept of mathematics as a language, Hogben begins with the grammar and punctuation of the discipline, clearly explaining the use of its symbols.

Another unusual, and successful, element of the book is its treatment of arithmetic and geometry as related elements that reinforce each other, rather than as theoretically distinct areas. The reader is reminded that the square root of two—which seemed so puzzling to the Greeks because it could not be represented in terms of simple arithmetical operations applied to whole numbers—is in fact a measurement that can be approximated as closely as one wishes by decimal numbers. The perhaps even more puzzling concept of the square root of negative one can be found, without becoming bogged down in theoretical and metaphysical questions, by a geometrical interpretation in which this number is no more and no less than a rotation of the number line by ninety degrees. Conversely, the number series discussed are presented pictorially, so as to give the reader another way to understand them.

Mathematics for the Million presents an extremely thorough treatment of its subject matter, with a profusion of diagrams, drawings, examples, and exercises. Some may find the sheer quantity of material daunting, but the reader is clearly given the chance to study the subject in depth. The book is based on a view of history as primarily a continuing progress in a positive direction, from primitive times to a far more knowledgeable present, and one in which intellectual activities are socially based and largely driven by material forces. Both these assumptions are widely questioned today, and Hogben's repeated animadversions against differing views will be a source of annoyance to some readers.

Critical Context

Mathematics for the Million and its companion volume, *Science for the Citizen* (1938), can be seen as the centerpiece of Lancelot Hogben's career for a number of reasons: They are his best-known works, they were published at around the middle of his life, and they represent a synthesis of his interests. Hogben began as a zoologist, writing technical books on physiology and genetics, and wound up trying his hand at a number of areas—from language, in *Essential World English* (1963), to political reform, in *Interglossa: A Draft of an Auxiliary for a Democratic World Order* (1943). Perhaps his most common theme, however, and the one for which he is best known, is the idea of expressing technical subjects in ways that make them intelligible by, and relevant to the daily concerns of, as many people as possible. *Mathematics for the Million* was followed by more specialized mathematical and scientific books for adults, on probability, statistics, and document design, and by children's books in the same areas, including *The Wonderful World of Mathematics* (1955) and *Beginnings and Blunders: Or, Before Science Began* (1970).

The response to Hogben has been predominantly favorable. Critics praised him for his thoroughness, his expository skills, and his ability to make technical material interesting and understandable, but some have made objections to the polemical nature of his writing. Hogben's attempts to aim *Mathematics for the Million* at a general adult audience—rather than a specifically juvenile or young adult one—have limited the discussion of this text as a school book, but it is one whose ease of exposition makes it accessible to most adolescents.

Arthur D. Hlavaty

MEN, MICROSCOPES, AND LIVING THINGS

Author: Katherine B. Shippen (1892-1980)
First published: 1955; illustrated
Type of work: Science
Subjects: Nature and science
Recommended ages: 13-18

While Shippen focuses on individual scientists and philosophers, her book deals primarily with the evolution and development of scientific thought.

Form and Content

Scientific knowledge is based on information and thought as it developed and evolved over thousands of years. *Men, Microscopes, and Living Things* brings this concept home to the reader. Divided into individual chapters, Katherine B. Shippen's book highlights major figures in science in the context of their own lives and in the world that they knew.

Each chapter is itself a short biography of an individual. Figures are chosen not so much for their prominence but for the impact of their discoveries or thoughts. Each chapter is not merely a compilation of dates; indeed, the inclusion of even specific dates for birth or death is uncommon. Rather, emphasis is placed on the importance of a particular individual to the development of scientific thought.

The philosophy of the author is clear in the opening chapter, which presents a brief discussion of the nature of humankind and its place in the biological order. Humans have always been the dominant species; the question to be addressed, however, is how humans came to understand their relationship to other creatures. By what evolution of scientific thought did human beings come to accept their place in nature and gain a better understanding of the nature of all creatures? Shippen then brings her readers immediately to the story of "the first biologist," Aristotle. Aristotle represents a paradigm of early Greek thought—or philosophy, as science was then called. Shippen's biography contains an overview of Aristotle's life and works. Among the questions addressed are those dealing with what he did, what he wrote, and, more important, why his works had the impact that they did. It was the ancient Greeks who founded the basis for science as it is known today, and it was Aristotle whose ideas had the greatest impact on that thought.

Each subsequent chapter deals with another scientist in a similar fashion. Shippen moves through numerous periods in history, emphasizing the person who had the most significant impact on science during a particular era. From Aristotle, readers move on to the Roman period, with Galen (physician to the gladiators) and Pliny. As readers pass through scientific history, into the Middle Ages and the Renaissance (the twelfth through sixteenth centuries), they can observe the effects of outside influences on science. New trade routes brought Europeans into contact with other cultures, such as Arab and Chinese: Both spices and knowledge were brought to Europe. The scientific establishment remained conservative, while individuals thirsted for new information and answers to questions dealing with nature in general and humans in particular. It was the invention of the microscope by Antoni van Leeuwenhoek, a Dutch lens maker and the owner of a dry-goods shop, that made it possible to address some of these questions.

Pictures and diagrams are rare in the book. It is the written word that brings the subject to the reader. In some cases, a subject's own words are used to convey the importance, and excitement, of the discovery.

Analysis

Men, Microscopes, and Living Things approaches the subject not primarily from the discoveries of the scientists and philosophers themselves but from an analysis of the context in which the work was carried out. It is important for all readers of science, both young and old, to understand that discoveries are not made in a vacuum; rather, they reflect the thoughts and knowledge of the time. This approach is presented well by Shippen; a prime example is her portrait of Charles Darwin.

Darwin is most famous for his theory of evolution. It was an attempt to explain more than simply the existence and reality of evolution; such was well known for decades prior to his work. Rather, Darwin attempted to explain the mechanism of evolution through a process that he called natural selection. The basic facts are well known to most readers of science: Darwin's role as captain's companion and naturalist on the British ship H.M.S. *Beagle* during its voyage in the 1830's and his eventual compilation of his work in both *On the Origin of Species by Means of Natural Selection* (1859) and *The Descent of Man and Selection in Relation to Sex* (1871).

Shippen attempts to place Darwin's discoveries in the context of his times. Darwin was not the first to note the existence of evolution, nor was he the first to attempt an explanation. Shippen begins the story with Baron Georges Cuvier, the inspector of education in France during the late eighteenth century. An extensive building boom was being carried out in France in the years following the French Revolution, and limestone was required for the new structures. During excavation, large numbers of fossils were found in the rock, a discovery of unknown creatures that piqued the interest of Cuvier. Clearly, organisms once existed on Earth that are now extinct. From Cuvier's studies arose modern paleontology. More immediate was the impact of his work on one of his contemporaries: Jean Baptiste Pierre Lamarck.

It was Lamarck who, more than Darwin, could rightly claim a role as the founder of the study of evolution. As Shippen points out, it was Lamarck who suggested that life was not immutable, that it could change from one form to another (although it must be pointed out, his view did not include humans). Lamarck studied a wide variety of life-forms and did so a half century before Darwin published his own work. It was Lamarck who first suggested the existence of evolution.

In such a way, Shippen examines the context of theory and thought in the society known to her subject. Darwin himself is one of the few individuals given extensive coverage in the book, which is only right since an understanding of the relationship between all forms of life is nearly impossible in the absence of an understanding of his work.

Likewise is the work of Gregor Mendel, a Bohemian monk of the 1860's, given prominence. Mendel was not the first to attempt to understand genetics and heredity, but he brought an understanding of mathematics to this new science. Farmers had long known that both animals and food crops could be bred for desired characteristics. What they did not understand was the seemingly random appearance and disappearance of various traits. Using inbred pea plants, Mendel was able to deduce the nature of heredity: that certain characteristics were dominant, and therefore were expressed, while other characteristics were recessive and would sometimes hide. Mendel also came to the conclusion that the forms of such traits were present in pairs. Thus, in a match between dominant and recessive characters, only the dominant one would appear. From such simple forms, Mendel was able to apply this relationship to both animal and human traits.

Throughout *Men, Microscopes, and Living Things*, Shippen moves from a simple example to the wider context of the discovery. Her emphasis on the context of thought and discovery and on the application of the simple to an understanding of the complex creates a fine history of science for the young reader. Further, the emphasis on those individuals whose work had the greatest impact on the evolution of scientific thought ensures that her book itself is never outdated.

Critical Context

Katherine B. Shippen was a noted writer of numerous books for children and young adults for much of her professional career, as well as curator of social studies for the Brooklyn Children's Museum. Her emphasis was on both history, epitomized by *Passage to America* (1952), the winner of the Boys' Clubs of America Junior Book Award, and on science. *Men, Microscopes, and Living Things* was one of several books dealing with scientific history. It was followed by such titles as *Mr. Bell Invents the Telephone* (1955) and *Men of Medicine* (1957). While the specific subjects covered in each of her books varied, Shippen continued to emphasize the role of individual discovery in the larger context of scientific understanding.

In its time, *Men, Microscopes, and Living Things* was an important contribution to the body of science books for the young reader, and it was named a Newbery Honor Book. Rather than a compilation of the famous, the book placed an emphasis on those who laid the foundation of modern science. At an appropriate level, it provided a context for the names, dates, and facts that characterized much of the teaching of science. It addressed the question of the scientist—not so much what he did (and, in this era, it was primarily "he"), but rather why he thought this way. The book avoided controversy; for example, there is only an allusion to Darwin's theory on the origins of humankind. It was, after all, written during the 1950's. Yet, the book remains an excellent source as an overview on the origins of the scientific principles with which students are familiar today.

Richard Adler

A MIDNIGHT CLEAR

Author: William Wharton (1925-   )
First published: 1982
Type of work: Novel
Type of plot: Historical fiction and moral tale
Time of work: December, 1944
Locale: Ardennes Forest, France
Subjects: Coming-of-age, friendship, and war
Recommended ages: 15-18

A group of sensitive young American soldiers, sent on a reconnaissance mission into the Ardennes Forest during World War II, meet a platoon of German soldiers and spend the most memorable Christmas of their lives.

Principal characters:
> WILLIAM KNOTT (aka WON'T), a nineteen-year-old sergeant in charge of six soldiers sent into enemy territory who is responsible for determining German military intentions
> VANCE WILKINS (aka MOTHER), a twenty-six-year-old soldier suffering from battle fatigue, one of Knott's closest friends in the squad
> PAUL MUNDY (aka FATHER), also twenty-six, and a former seminarian who has banned obscenities among his colleagues and who brings a strong sense of moral seriousness to their endeavors
> MEL GORDON, a colonel who is obsessed with his own health and that of his comrades
> STAN SHUTZER, the only Jew in the group and the lone soldier who approaches the war with any zeal
> BUD MILLER, a poet and mechanical genius
> MAJOR LOVE, a mortician and the group's commanding officer, who carelessly sends them off into danger

Form and Content

A *Midnight Clear* is a warm, large-hearted novel about a gruesome subject—warfare—and the ways in which that experience transcends time and indelibly marks its participants. There is no question that the work is a serious attempt at the demystification of heroism and a demonstration of the futility of killing. Nevertheless, the novel also asserts the saving grace of the human spirit and the ways in which true heroism emerges from unselfish, caring concern for others.

The book is divided into six chapters that trace the experiences of a group of soldiers on a reconnaissance mission in the Ardennes Forest in December, 1944. The events are conveyed through the perspective of a subjective narrator, the protagonist

Will Knott, who gives the reader a privileged view into his mind and heart and those of his five compatriots. Knott is a born storyteller, although he is unaware of his abilities and claims that he has "a penchant for telling true stories no one can believe," thus preparing the reader for a sensational tale. Knott punctuates his recounting with brief asides to the audience and glimpses into events that transpire after the central ones of the narrative.

Knott and his colleagues are the survivors of a squad that was attacked in Saarbrücken, Germany. These young men were abruptly dropped at the front although they were originally recruited to be educated at universities because of their superior intelligence. Their division leader, Major Love, is an officious coward who cavalierly sends his men into danger on the pretext that they uncover information about enemy activities in the Ardennes Forest.

The six set up camp in an abandoned château and before long make inadvertent contact with a German platoon that engaged them in a gentle snowball fight and then presents them with a makeshift Christmas tree and gifts. Through awkward translations, the Americans learn that a major offensive is in the offing and that the Germans wish to surrender but only if they can manufacture a false skirmish to disguise their intentions. Five of the Americans decide to hide the plans from their only married comrade, Vance Wilkins, in order to tell their superiors that he was a hero and earn for him a return home to his wife, whom he desperately misses. Unfortunately, however, Wilkins misinterprets the gunfire, kills a couple of Germans, and inaugurates an actual engagement that results in the death of all but one German and the death of Paul Mundy and the grave wounding of Shutzer.

Major Love appears briefly and leaves with Shutzer and the surviving German, and the remaining four Americans flee an advancing column of German soldiers. Both of their Jeeps crash, their communication with headquarters is severed, and they use the blood of their dead friend to create medical insignias that gain for them safe passage back to their unit. Wilkins is decorated and later disappears, Mel Gordon becomes a doctor, and Knott becomes a street painter in Paris, each fulfilling his deepest desire rather than those of parents or other authority figures.

Analysis

Early in the novel, Knott tells readers that an Army briefing is an explanation and that "probably, in a certain way, this whole book . . . is a briefing." His "briefing" is nothing less than a denunciation of the idiocy of war and a vigorous assertion of the value of friendship and love. William Wharton anatomizes the military experience from the point of view of immature soldiers—not, as films so often suggest, battle-hardened, fully grown adults—and the result is anything but an Audie Murphy paean to manhood achieved through combat.

These six soldiers are actually boys who wrestle with their emerging sexuality, desiring yet also fearing sex. Paul Mundy, a devout and aspiring seminarian, leaves his vocation after masturbating and thus breaking his vow of chastity. He is the squad's conscience yet believes that he is a sinner and unworthy of respect. The others scheme to lose their virginity by purchasing the services of a prostitute before they ship out. Instead, they attract a girl no older than they are who is in mourning over a fiancé killed in the war.

Like all young people, these boys have elaborate plans for their futures. Stan Shutzer intends to rid the world of anti-Semitic Nazis and then set off on a career as an advertising executive in his own agency. Wilkins yearns to return home and start a family, Knott plans to satisfy his impulse to doodle by becoming an artist, and Mel Gordon vows to reject his father's dental practice for a career as a doctor.

The theme of innocence confronting experience is foremost in the novel. Each character is an acutely sensitive person, and that sensitivity stands in sharp contrast to their duties as soldiers. They are all aesthetically perceptive: Wilkins is mesmerized by works of art that he finds in the château's attic and insists that the others not destroy the mansion's furniture for firewood, Miller is a poet manqué, and Gordon finds an antique violin and begins to play it. These are also the greenest of warriors, having spent only six months in combat. After the debacle in the forest, the survivors each take a symbolic bath to indicate that they have "definitely turned off the war." Although they contrive to save their own lives and those of their putative enemies, they stumble into a slaughter and the unforgiving compromises of adult life.

Like all young people, these boys experience a series of signal events that define their characters and mark them for the rest of their lives. At every turn in the narrative, the squad members learn crucial truths about human experience, and Knott becomes the filter for those moments of enlightenment. The death of half the squad on the Saar River teaches them the tenuousness and fragility of life, and they approach each day with a sense of hope mixed with a negative expectation. During their sojourn in the château, Knott visits Wilkins in the attic and, while sitting with him before a collection of paintings, realizes that "these intimate presentations of another world, another time, through mind not my own, had an unbelievably profound effect on my deepest psyche. It changed my life. . . . I knew an aesthetic experience. I dimly perceived what it was all about. I'd never be the same again."

Similarly, when he plots with the others to arrange the German surrender, he is struck by the emotional generosity of Shutzer and Gordon and concludes that "they love themselves, and can let that feeling flow over into other people." For Knott, the events in the forest define the course of his adult life and the nature of his emerging sensibility. As Knott resolves, if he survives this experience, "I'm going to do the things I want." In short, he intends to live and love life in all of its grandeur and minutiae.

Critical Context

The critical reception of *A Midnight Clear* was decidedly mixed; some reviewers criticized it as stereotypical and overwritten, while others claimed that it is "destined to become a classic" by "one of the finest writers in English today." Such divergent points of view actually reveal differing notions about adolescent experience. William Wharton's accomplishment, among many others, is his ability to penetrate the thoughts and emotions of the young. In his two preceding novels, *Birdy* (1978) and *Dad* (1981), Wharton also explores the effects of war, family life, and insanity, and each book is characterized by a compelling voice yearning desperately to communicate the intense emotional lives of its characters. Each work demonstrates that compassion, understanding, and love are the most potent palliatives to an individual's sense of isolation and desperation. *A Midnight Clear* is an important addition to such modern antiwar fiction as Erich Maria Remarque's *Im Western nichts Neues* (1929; *All Quiet on the Western Front*, 1929), Ernest Hemingway's *A Farewell to Arms* (1929), Joseph Heller's *Catch-22* (1961), and Kurt Vonnegut's *Slaughterhouse-Five* (1969).

David W. Madden

MIDNIGHT HOUR ENCORES

Author: Bruce Brooks (1950-   )
First published: 1986
Type of work: Novel
Type of plot: Social realism
Time of work: The late 1980's
Locale: A cross-country trip from Washington, D.C., to San Francisco
Subjects: Coming-of-age, family, and social issues
Recommended ages: 13-18

Sibilance T. Spooner, a sixteen-year-old cellist and musical prodigy, learns about the 1960's and sorts out her loyalties during a cross-country trip to find her mother.

Principal characters:
> SIBILANCE "SIB" T. SPOONER, the sixteen-year-old musical prodigy who narrates the novel
> CABOT "TAXI" SPOONER, Sib's father, a product of the 1960's who now edits an environmental newsletter
> CONNIE, Sib's mother, a hippie who turned over responsibility for Sib to Taxi when Sib was only a baby
> DZYGA, a Soviet musical prodigy whose cello music Sibilance knows only from recordings that she has tracked down over the years

Form and Content

Sixteen-year-old Sibilance T. Spooner, the narrator of *Midnight Hour Encores*, considers herself a self-made young woman, even having chosen her own name. A musical prodigy whose talent and hard work has made her one of the world's greatest cellists, she has spent most of her life with Taxi, her unconventional father who publishes an environmental newsletter from their Washington, D.C., home. Although Taxi has always told Sibilance that he will take her to see her mother in San Francisco whenever she wants to go, Sib has never shown much interest in the woman she last saw on January 1, 1970, when she was twenty hours old.

At sixteen, having tested out of her senior year of high school and ready to attend the Juilliard School of Music in the fall, Sib finally tells Taxi that she wants to see her mother. Sib's real reason for wanting to go to San Francisco, however, involves an audition at the Phrygian Institute, a prestigious music school, that she has secretly arranged for herself. If she is successful in the audition, she hopes to study under Professor Dzyga, a brilliant cellist who has defected from the Soviet Union and whose music Sib knows only from a few recordings that she has painstakingly hunted down.

Taxi uses their cross-country trip in an old, green Volkswagen bus to try to teach Sibilance about the 1960's, the hippie lifestyle, and her mother. Sib, however, is sarcastic during the planning phase for the trip, rejects Taxi's "Age of Aquarius" history lessons, and at first devotes most of their travel time to practicing her cello. Even so, the trip provides time for discussion and reflection that gives Sib a greater understanding of her father and why her mother may have given her up.

Prior to arriving in San Francisco, Sibilance expects Connie, her mother, to be wrapped up still in various counterculture beliefs and to be continuing her efforts to become a great macrame artist. Instead, she learns that her mother is now a rich and respected businesswoman who earns her living as an architectural broker. While in San Francisco, Sib and her mother shop together, ride around in her mother's expensive car, and share some intimate conversations during which Sib gains an understanding of her mother. She learns that her mother turned over responsibility for rearing her to Taxi because she recognized that he was better prepared to be a parent than she was. Connie used the freedom that she gained to take control of her life, get off drugs, and study real estate.

Mother and daughter are reconciled, with Connie finally asking Sib to live with her once she is accepted by the Phrygian Institute. By the time that Sib has her audition at the Institute, Taxi is preparing to return to Washington, D.C., and Sib seems prepared to stay with her mother, which makes the ending of the novel somewhat surprising. After a stunning audition, Sib reveals her decision to rejoin Taxi by playing "The Love and Peace Shuffle," the song that she and Taxi wrote during the trip, as her encore. Sib makes her choice "without fear of losing anything," not according to what others feel about her but according to what she herself feels.

Analysis

At first glance, it seems as if young adult readers might have difficulty generating much empathy for Sibilance. She is the type of person whom her peers could easily dislike: self-assured and always wisecracking, extraordinarily gifted, self-sufficient to the point that she does not need close friends, and the only child of a father who dotes on her. Sib seems to have so many strengths that it is a testimonial to Bruce Brooks's talent that most readers will ultimately understand her discontent.

Sibilance is a strong character from the beginning of the novel, but Taxi develops more slowly since he is seen through Sib's eyes and she has always viewed him as a roommate who conveniently stayed out of her way. The cross-country trip provides Sib with time for conversations with Taxi and time for reflection about their relationship, which enables her to understand what Taxi has done because of his unconditional love for her. During one of their conversations, Taxi describes for the first time how demanding parenting has been for him. While Sib was growing up, he had to earn a living editing his newsletter in the odd moments when he did not have to take care of her. When Sib asks if rearing her has been worth it, Taxi replies, "Having you is the best thing that ever happened to me." He goes on to add that "I want you to look back and decide I was a great father." Once he learns that Sib has been accepted by the Phrygian Institute, he tells Connie that he has never been unhappier, but he is prepared to leave Sib behind with her mother because he believes that it is what Sib really wants to do with her life. These scenes make Taxi a full-fledged, complex character whose style of parenting is well worth discussion.

Brooks brings readers into the world of both classical and rock music—composing, practicing, and performing—in a way that is understandable to even the nonmusician. Taxi prepares for the trip by purchasing old records and acquiring a guitar, which enables him to show an aptitude for music that Sib was never aware he had.

Midnight Hour Encores offers an interesting backward glance at the 1960's. During the cross-country trip, Taxi tries to educate Sib about the counterculture in which he and her mother lived at the time she was born, but this hippie lifestyle is only a faded memory. When Taxi and Sib visit a used record shop so that Taxi can purchase some 1960's music, the owner turns out to be a man Taxi knew back then: He once dealt psychedelic drugs, but he now sells nostalgia in the form of old records to former hippies, now members of the establishment, at exorbitant prices. In fact, an old hippie who provides local color for the record store and Taxi, with his environmental newsletter, seem to be among the few people who still hold on to counterculture values. Sib and Taxi compose "The Love and Peace Shuffle," a tone poem based on the Age of Aquarius, during the trip, but the effort seems somewhat forced rather than serving as an integral part of the story. Ultimately, Sib, as well as young adult readers, learn about Bob Dylan and Bo Diddley and are offered a wide array of information about 1960's counterculture. In short, Brooks provided a vivid picture of a time and lifestyle that the parents of many of his young adult readers in the 1980's may have lived through as teenagers themselves.

Critical Context

Bruce Brooks's first novel, *The Moves Make the Man* (1984), was named a Newbery Honor Book for its portrayal of two sensitive young adults coping with racial prejudice and troubled families. Jerome Foxworthy, Brooks's narrator, became the prototype for the protagonists that have become a hallmark of his fiction: teenagers who are wise beyond their years. *Midnight Hour Encores*, an American Library Association (ALA) Best Book for Young Adults, continued Brooks's string of award-winning books that have established him as one of the major figures in young adult literature. Although music rather than sports provides the focus of the book, Sibilance Spooner, like Jerome Foxworthy, is a multifaceted character who offers layers of complexity for class discussion. Since the publication of *Midnight Hour Encores*, Brooks has published the Newbery Honor Book *What Hearts* (1992), which deals with divorce and a child's efforts to fit into a new family, and his other books have appeared numerous times on the ALA Best Books for Young Adults lists. His multidimensional characters, keen ear for the adolescent voice, and use of challenging themes have earned him a large audience of young adult readers. In addition, Brooks has gained a reputation for eloquent and stylish writing that has garnered praise from critics, readers, and other professional writers.

Ronald Barron

A MIDSUMMER NIGHT'S DREAM

Author: William Shakespeare (1564-1616)
First presented: 1595-1596
First published: 1600
Type of work: Drama
Type of plot: Fantasy
Time of work: Unspecified
Locale: Athens and a nearby wood
Subjects: Gender roles, love and romance, and the supernatural
Recommended ages: 15-18

As a result of lovers' inconstancy and the intervention of the fairy Puck, Lysander and Demetrius switch partners before ultimately reverting to their true objects of affection just prior to the wedding of the duke of Athens.

Principal characters:
THESEUS, the duke of Athens, who has subdued Hippolyta in battle and will marry her this night
HIPPOLYTA, the queen of the Amazons, who is betrothed to Theseus
LYSANDER, an Athenian in love with Hermia
DEMETRIUS, an Athenian who seeks the love of Hermia and possesses the approval of her father, Egeus
HERMIA, a woman in love with Lysander, although her father desires for her to wed Demetrius
HELENA, a woman in love with Demetrius, who scorns her in his quest for Hermia
OBERON, the king of the Fairies, who is jealous of his wife's changeling boy
TITANIA, the queen of the Fairies, who engages in a battle of wills with her husband
PUCK, a mischievous fairy who helps Oberon in his struggle with Titania
BOTTOM, a weaver who mistakenly thinks that he knows acting and theater and who thus becomes an object of lighthearted mockery at the wedding of Theseus and Hippolyta

Form and Content

William Shakespeare's comedy *A Midsummer Night's Dream* includes four interwoven plots: the two sets of lovers who flee into the woods, the upcoming nuptials of Theseus and Hippolyta, the battle of the sexes between Oberon and Titania, and the play rehearsals and performance by the "rude mechanicals." The four plots merge in the last two acts as the four lovers pair off (Hermia and Lysander, Helena and Demetrius) and join the newlyweds Theseus and Hippolyta in the viewing of the tragedy *Pyramus and Thisby*. Shakespeare's comedy concludes with the joining of these three couples, as well as with the reconciliation of the fourth, Oberon and Titania.

As the play begins, Egeus, upset that his daughter Hermia desires to marry Lysander rather than Demetrius, demands from Theseus that she be killed or sent to a nunnery. Hermia and Lysander, desperate because of the obstinacy of Egeus, flee to the woods in order to escape him. Helena, Hermia's friend who loves Demetrius, informs him of the plot, hoping that he will forget Egeus' daughter and love her instead. Demetrius, however, scorns her love and follows the couple into the woods—with Helena in pursuit. As the four lovers sleep, Oberon orders Puck to place love juice in the eyes of Demetrius so that he will love Helena, yet Puck mistakenly puts the potion in the eyes of Lysander. Lysander consequently falls in love with Helena; Puck then attempts to rectify the situation by placing the juice in Demetrius' eyes. As a result, both men, who have been pursuing Hermia, scorn her and desire Helena, who previously had no suitors. A significant section of the comedy involves the return of the men to their rightful lovers—Lysander to Hermia and Demetrius to Helena.

Meanwhile, the "rude mechanicals" (poor, honest, and well-meaning working-class men), led by Bottom the weaver, decide to put on a play—a tragedy—to celebrate the marriage of Theseus to Hippolyta. As the men rehearse, Oberon and Titania fight because he is jealous that she possesses a changeling boy. Oberon enlists Puck's help to steal the boy away from her. To humiliate Titania further, Oberon orders Puck to place the love juice in her eyes; she then falls in love with Bottom, whom Puck has transformed into an ass. Satisfied with his triumph, Oberon allows Puck to undo the spell, and the couple reconciles. The rude mechanicals then perform the tragedy in front of Theseus and Hippolyta and the two couples, who have left the woods. Shakespeare's comedy concludes with all four romantic couples being content.

Analysis

Shakespeare's comedies, like those of most Renaissance playwrights, involve love and its obstacles. Much of the comedy in *A Midsummer Night's Dream* derives from the attempt of Lysander and Hermia to remain together while overcoming the "blocking figure" (the adult authority figure who attempts to hinder the love of a young couple). The overcoming of an obstacle (in this case, Egeus) functions as a common motif in Renaissance comedy. The audience must wonder, however, whether Lysander and Hermia, as well as Demetrius and Helena, actually love each other. While it is the love potion that alters the objects of the men's affections, one may interpret the juice as a metaphor for lovers' inconstancy. The juice only contains magic because the male lovers do not possess a fervent and true love. It is significant that Lysander and Demetrius change their minds about whom they love, but Hermia and Helena never waver; perhaps Shakespeare correlates faithfulness with gender.

Audience members generally support the relationship between Lysander and Hermia—partly because her father does not. They are struck by his indifference to his daughter's happiness: He prefers that she die rather than be happy with a man of whom he does not approve. Egeus, furthermore, provides no reason to Theseus as to why he does not support Lysander; it is as if he disapproves for arbitrary reasons—merely to exert his will. His abuse of paternal authority renders him absurd but dangerous nevertheless. His support for Demetrius colors the audience's point of view of the young lover. If one supports Lysander, one cannot approve of Demetrius, who initially enters the woods in the role of obstructionist, not lover.

Male domination also plays an integral role in *A Midsummer Night's Dream*. Shakespeare links the romantic relationships with male authority and aggressiveness. When Demetrius cannot persuade Hermia to love him, he attempts to rape her. Theseus marries Hippolyta after first subduing her physically in battle. Oberon, already coupled with Titania, feels compelled to control her by possessing her changeling, of whom he is jealous.

The rude mechanicals choose poorly by deciding to perform a lover's tragedy at a wedding celebration, yet the choice may not be far-fetched in terms of the plot. Although this comedy ends happily, much of the play demonstrates the potential for tragedy. Demetrius could have raped Hermia. Helena could have ended up with both suitors while Hermia lost both. Oberon could have remained in his bitter struggle with Titania, who, in turn, could have remained in love with an ass (Bottom). These relationships could have terminated forever. Part of the comic charm of the play derives from the fact that the complications work out so that the conclusion, which could be unhappy, results in joy, marriage, and order.

The play is partly about order and disorder. Athens represents the order of a civilized society, while the forest symbolizes disorder and chaos. The woods proves more appealing, however, because it allows for freedom, while the city, with its law that a woman who refuses to marry the man whom her father chooses may die, demonstrates the evils of a restrictive culture. The romantic relationships work themselves out successfully in the disordered, not in the ordered, society.

The play concludes with the play-within-a-play, as the audience watches Hermia and Lysander, Helena and Demetrius, and Theseus and Hippolyta view the play of the rude mechanicals. The lovers gently mock the incompetent actors, with humor but without malice. The play-within-a-play permits Shakespeare to provide commentary and inside jokes regarding stagecraft.

Critical Context

A Midsummer Night's Dream, first performed in 1595 and then published in 1600, is one of William Shakespeare's best-loved plays and remains popular. After such simple comedies as *The Comedy of Errors* (c. 1592-1594), Shakespeare began to write more sophisticated comedies such as *A Midsummer Night's Dream*. In this play, one sees more than a play built merely around mistaken identities (as in *The Comedy of Errors*): One finds more complex, three-dimensional characters and a more sophisticated theme. Although *A Midsummer Night's Dream* does possess the potential for tragedy, the play is much lighter in tone and theme than later Shakespearean dark comedies, also known as problem plays, such as *The Merchant of Venice* (c. 1596-1597) and *Measure for Measure* (1604). These dramas are much darker in tone and much more troublesome in their endings than *A Midsummer Night's Dream*. The problem plays conclude with the success of unlikable and unsavory characters, who unite in marriage with wonderful women; *A Midsummer Night's Dream*, however, ends with perfect order and three marriages that promise to be blissful. The reconciliations are complete and sincere.

Eric Sterling

MIRACLE AT PHILADELPHIA
The Story of the Constitutional Convention, May to September, 1787

Author: Catherine Drinker Bowen (1897-1973)
First published: 1966
Type of work: History
Time of work: 1787
Locale: Philadelphia and its environs and other locales in the original thirteen states
Subjects: Politics and law
Recommended ages: 15-18

Using primary historical sources, Bowen re-creates a narrative history of the birth of the U.S. Constitution, the events surrounding the Philadelphia convention, and the people who composed the document that set up a revolutionary new form of government.

Principal personages:
JAMES MADISON, a delegate from Virginia and the meticulous unofficial note taker during the Constitutional Convention
GEORGE WASHINGTON, a delegate from Virginia, the former commander of the Continental Army, the president of the Constitutional Convention, and the future first president of the United States under the Constitution
ALEXANDER HAMILTON, a delegate from New York, the Continental treasurer under the Articles of Confederation, and an ardent supporter of a strong national government
EDMUND RANDOLPH, a delegate from and governor of Virginia and the author of the original Virginia Resolves, and an eventual opponent of the final Constitution
BENJAMIN FRANKLIN, a delegate from and governor of Pennsylvania, a well-known patriot, inventor, statesman, thinker, and supporter of strong national government
JAMES WILSON, an outspoken Pennsylvania delegate who supported strong government
GOUVERNEUR MORRIS, a Pennsylvania delegate and erstwhile playboy who spoke strongly and eloquently at the convention in favor of the consolidation of national government
ELBRIDGE GERRY, a Massachusetts delegate and the leader of the opposition to strong government and the final Constitution
LUTHER MARTIN, a long-winded delegate from Maryland and an outspoken opponent of the Constitution

Form and Content

Catherine Drinker Bowen provides, in *Miracle at Philadelphia*, an entertaining, exhaustive, and historically accurate record of the events of the Constitutional Convention of 1787. The narrative is drawn from many sources, the most important of which is James Madison's personal record of convention proceedings, which according to Bowen is far more colorful and detailed than the official record of Robert Yates of New York, the convention reporter. She also uses many letters from convention delegates to their friends abroad (such as the letters of George Washington to Thomas Jefferson) and their wives and children at home. In addition, Bowen uses biographical accounts of all important convention delegates to illuminate their character at various points in the narrative. For example, in introducing Alexander Hamilton, she explains his unusual rapport with General Washington: "Alexander Hamilton during the war had acted as Washington's aide-de-camp. It was an extraordinary friendship between the young lawyer, foreign-born, impatient, quick, and his Commander in Chief, infinitely steady, with a slow prescience of his own." Numerous descriptive asides are included about assorted personages, locales, and events when they come up in the course of the story. At various points, Bowen may describe the scene at the State House, the weather on one afternoon in Philadelphia, or the contemporary personal life of a delegate preparing to speak.

Miracle at Philadelphia is divided into two main sections. The first is entitled "The Constitutional Convention" and covers not only the action of the convention itself but also contemporary events in Philadelphia and the other cities of the thirteen States, with some insights into contemporary world events, particularly in England and France. The account begins with a brief description of the circumstances leading up to the Constitutional Convention. The actual coverage of the convention and its delegates is interspersed with personal stories and other background information, but these chapters are also offset with a two-chapter interlude entitled "Journey Through the American States." This section provides a broad cultural, sociological, and historical background of the states from which the delegates came and examines the expectations of common citizens concerning the convention and their attitudes toward the formation of a national government.

The tension at the Constitutional Convention begins to mount with the introduction of the original Virginia Resolves and reaches a fever pitch at the Committee of Style's final presentation of the document now known as the Constitution. At every point, advocates of a strong system of national government are assailed by states-rights advocates. In the beginning, the Virginia Plan is criticized for going against what Congress had expressly requested when it called the convention—merely revision of the Articles of Confederation. Proponents of strong national government push their viewpoint until the convention begins to accept the idea that an entirely new document (if not expressly called a "constitution") and form of government is needed. The "strong-government men" at length persuade the convention to base this document on Edmund Randolph's Virginia Plan. Then, the members of the convention debate for the rest of the summer over what parts of the plan to adopt, what parts to revise, and what parts to throw out altogether.

The convention is afterward constantly in danger of dissolution. The main divisions in American society of that time—North versus South, seaboard versus back country, small states versus large ones—are revealed in the tumultuous debates that ensue over slavery and legislative representation. One by one, the delegates come to a shaky agreement over each of these various contentious issues through vehicles such as the Great Compromise. When the Committee of Style finally presents its final package, the tension comes to a head in the question of whether the delegates will actually approve and sign it. They do, and this section of Bowen's work ends.

Bowen's attention then turns to the arena in which the Constitution once again was in peril of fading into oblivion: its ratification by the various states. The second section of the book is entitled "The Fight for Ratification," and a fight it was indeed. The small states and Pennsylvania immediately approve the document, but the Constitution faces its first real threat in the Massachusetts ratification convention. Elbridge Gerry mounts a formidable opposition to the document's plan for a strong national government, but the Commonwealth of Massachusetts ratifies the Constitution. This sets the stage for the last major battlegrounds: New York and Virginia, whose ratification conventions meet simultaneously. Virginia's meeting proves to be even stormier than that of Massachusetts. The Antifederalists there are led by Patrick Henry, the indomitable and eloquent libertarian firebrand and patriot of the American Revolution. In spite of his fervent arguments against it, however, Virginia narrowly ratifies the Constitution a few days before New York's final vote. Virginia's decision sways its northern sister and the smaller Southern states (with the exception of Georgia, which had ratified the document at the beginning). The tale of the convention ends with descriptions of the grand celebrations across the country in honor of the new Constitution.

Analysis

As the title of the work suggests, Bowen wants her readers to understand the revolutionary change in government that took place as a result of the Constitutional Convention as a "miracle"—that is, a highly unusual and fortuitous experience. She chooses to emphasize the deft way in which many delegates settled problems through clever argument, the magnanimous way in which debaters compromised in order to come up with a government for the common good, and the chivalrous way in which all the debates and disagreements were handled.

Bowen carefully documents her sources. Although relying heavily on Madison's record of the convention, she often notes where his version differs from Yates's or those of other delegates. She also provides multiple perspectives on events and debates by incorporating the journals, personal notes, memoirs, and letters of combatants on every side. Nevertheless, Bowen shaves a bit of the journalistic objectivity for stylistic purposes. She mentions in her "Author's Note" that her original manuscript included "copious footnotes" but that she deleted the vast majority of them from the final text because "It is hard enough for a reader to follow a summer of convention speeches, without wading through exegeses at the foot of the page."

Bowen is somewhat biased toward the supporters of the consolidated, powerful national government, and the narrative is arranged as a story of their progress against, and eventual defeat of, the Antifederalists.

Critical Context

Miracle at Philadelphia has long been a favorite text of high school and college American history and constitutional history instructors. It provides an extremely easy-to-read account of one of the most revolutionary events in history. Perhaps the book's greatest accomplishment is providing an overall context, conceived in unusually intimate human terms, of the often-vaunted characters involved in this historic convention—their lives, their society, and their nation.

Miracle at Philadelphia was Catherine Drinker Bowen's culminating work in a career as writer of numerous critically acclaimed biographies and other historical writings, such as *Beloved Friend* (1937), a story of the intimate relationship between the composer Peter Tchaikovsky and Nadejda von Meck (cowritten with Barbara von Meck), and *Yankee from Olympus: Justice Holmes and His Family* (1944), the story of U.S. Supreme Court Justice Oliver Wendell Holmes and his family. In short, Bowen brought the grandeur of history to the level of the average high school student's knowledge and ability. In *Miracle at Philadelphia*, she does so without diminishing the awe-inspiring significance of the framing of what is today the oldest surviving national constitution.

Rob Marus

THE MIRACLE WORKER

Author: William Gibson (1914-   )
First presented: 1957 (on television); 1959 (on stage)
First published: 1957
Type of work: Drama
Type of plot: Psychological realism and social realism
Time of work: The 1880's
Locale: Tuscumbia, Alabama, and Boston
Subjects: Education and health and illness
Recommended ages: 13-18

> *As a blind, deaf, and mute six-year-old, Helen Keller is uncontrollable until twenty-year-old Annie Sullivan, half-blind and obstinate, finally reaches her with hand-spelled words that open the doors to communication and humanity.*

> *Principal characters:*
> HELEN KELLER, a blind, deaf, mute, and uncontrollable child
> ANNIE SULLIVAN, Helen's teacher
> KATE KELLER, Helen's mother
> CAPTAIN ARTHUR KELLER, Helen's father
> JAMES KELLER, Helen's older half brother
> MILDRED KELLER, Helen's infant sister
> AUNT EV, Helen's aunt
> ANAGOS, Annie's teacher at the Perkins Institution for the Blind

Form and Content

The script for *The Miracle Worker* begins with a general description of the set, which consists of two areas divided by a diagonal line. The area behind the diagonal represents the Keller house and includes two rooms and a porch area. The other area accommodates a variety of sets as needed. According to William Gibson, since the essential qualities of the set "are fluidity and spacial counterpoint," the less set there is, the better.

Act 1 begins with three adults gathered about a crib. Directions are minimal: Kate Keller is described as "a young gentle woman with a sweet and girlish face," the doctor as "elderly" with a "stethoscope at neck, thermometer in fingers," and Captain Keller as a "hearty gentleman in his forties with chin whiskers." The three adults are to appear with "tired bearing and disarranged clothing" to show that they have been through a long vigil. While the dialogue begins with the announcement that the child will survive her ordeal, her mother quickly discovers that the child is blind and deaf.

Although scenes are not noted as such, directions for a scene change are given using lights and distant belfry chimes. Three children and a dog are on stage when the lights rise. Two are described simply as "Negroes," while Helen is described as "six and a half years old, quite unkempt in body, and vivacious little person with a fine head, attractive, but noticeably blind, one eye larger and protruding; her gestures are abrupt, insistent, lacking in human restraint, and her face never smiles."

Since Helen cannot speak, hear, or see, her entire part is described in the parenthetical directions that are interspersed among the pieces of dialogue. The novice reader of plays, especially those who have never seen a live production, may have difficulty in imagining parenthetically described actions. The directions are detailed enough, however, to ensure that all actions required by the plot are included, yet general enough to encourage artistic freedom in acting and directing.

In the next scene, James, "an indolent young man"; Aunt Ev, "a benign visitor in a hat"; Kate, "a woman steeled in grief"; and Captain Keller disagree over help for Helen. This conversation leads to the introduction of Anagos, who reads a letter that he received from Captain Keller to Annie Sullivan, who is to teach Helen. In the remaining scenes of act 1, Annie meets the Keller family, tries to teach Helen to hand-spell, and is locked in her room by Helen.

In act 2, Annie continues to try to teach Helen. A noisy and violent breakfast lesson is presented in several pages of description. Act 2 ends as Annie and Helen begin a two-week stay in the garden house. Act 3 begins in the garden house, where Helen is behaving in an orderly fashion, and continues as Annie and Helen return to the Keller homestead, where Annie and the rest of the family resume their fight over control of Helen. Annie prevails, and Helen finally connects a spelled word "water" to the thing that the word represents and then eagerly seeks the names for other things on stage.

Analysis

The Miracle Worker is not only one work but can be appreciated in three forms: the published script, live performances, and television and film versions. The vast majority of scripts are only read by people involved in preparing a performance. *The Miracle Worker* is one of the scripts written in the twentieth century that has obtained the status of literature. Nevertheless, reading a script as literature is a strange, if not unnatural, activity; it is akin to reading an operation's manual for a product one does not have and cannot obtain. A script is most useful in preparing a play; it can also aid in understanding, analyzing, and evaluating various performances. Yet, even the best script is not an adequate replacement for a performance.

At the time that the play was written, Helen Keller was still alive and was known to most of the educated public. Most theatergoers knew that she graduated from college and, after learning to speak, toured the vaudeville and lecture circuit in the early twentieth century. Her autobiography was widely read, and her name provided an instant image of achievement despite enormous handicaps.

From a historical perspective, Annie Sullivan's description of her own youth in the state almshouse is more indicative of the way in which handicapped children were treated in the late nineteenth and early twentieth centuries than either the indulgent defeatism of the Kellers or the persistent pursuit of the "impossible" by Sullivan. Since no one knew how to reach a child with multiple major handicaps, most people considered the task impossible.

Purchase of the script of *The Miracle Worker* does not include any performance rights. Payment of royalties is required even for amateur performances, and even "lecturing" and "public reading" are specifically prohibited on the copyright page. Nevertheless, drama departments in high schools and colleges, as well as community drama groups, sometimes choose to produce *The Miracle Worker*. One reason is the flexibility and low cost of the set.

The successful production of *The Miracle Worker* requires a child actress capable of playing the strenuous role of Helen and a teenager or young woman who can be a believable Annie; merely adequate or even poor performances by other actors will not jeopardize the play, and considerably less is required of the other roles in both time and talent. The flexible number of roles of children from the Perkins Institute permits a large group where children are readily available or a small group where child actors are limited. Any work that deals with real people with established racial identities can cause problems; the stereotypical and condescending attitude toward the black characters in *The Miracle Worker*, while historically correct, may be offensive to people in some schools and communities.

The 1962 black-and-white film version of *The Miracle Worker* won Oscars for Patty Duke, who played Helen, and Anne Bancroft, who played Annie Sullivan. A copy is available for rent or purchase at various stores, but such rental or purchase does not include the rights to public performance. As with any copyrighted work, rights for educational use must be investigated before the videotape can be played in an educational setting. One advantage of the 1962 film version is that Gibson adapted his play for the screen. While the sets are more elaborate than those prescribed for the play, the black-and-white photography seems appropriate for the time period and the biographical nature of the plot.

The Miracle Worker in any form—script, play, or film—provides an introduction to the lives of Helen Keller and Annie Sullivan. Hopefully, this introduction will encourage readers to turn to more in-depth biographies of the two women, such as Keller's autobiography, *The Story of My Life* (1903), or one of the biographies of Sullivan, such as *The Touch of Magic* (1961).

Critical Context

The Miracle Worker is the story of Annie Sullivan, not of Helen Keller. It is Sullivan who works the miracle, who does the impossible by teaching the blind, deaf, and seemingly unreachable child. Perhaps for that very reason, the play has been a favorite of educators. Sullivan is portrayed as the epitome of the best in all teachers—persistent, long-suffering, confident, yet also human, with a sharp tongue and little tolerance for interference.

Some children are drawn to the character of the young Helen as the epitome of irresponsibility. The real Helen Keller, however, faced much prejudice in her lifetime despite the respect and fame that she eventually earned. People with disabilities, especially disfiguring ones, rarely participated in society in the nineteenth century and were still unwelcome in most social circles of the mid-twentieth century. Although such discrimination had become both socially unacceptable and illegal by the late twentieth century, books, plays, films, and television shows that depict individuals coping with and succeeding despite disabilities are needed as more of these people take their places in society.

Betty-Lou Waters

MISS HICKORY

Author: Carolyn Sherwin Bailey (1875-1961)
First published: 1946; illustrated
Type of work: Novel
Type of plot: Fantasy
Time of work: The 1940's
Locale: The New Hampshire countryside
Subjects: Friendship, gender roles, and nature
Recommended ages: 10-13

Miss Hickory, a country doll abandoned by her owners, survives all winter in an empty bird's nest and is transformed into an apple tree scion in the spring.

Principal characters:
MISS HICKORY, a country doll whose body is an apple twig and whose head is a hickory nut
CROW, a tough but kind-hearted bird
MR. T. WILLARD-BROWN, a barn cat
SQUIRREL, a forgetful and temperamental animal
ANN, a little girl who often visits the farmhouse where Miss Hickory lived before the story begins
TIMOTHY, a young friend of Ann

Form and Content

A doll made of an apple twig and a hickory nut is the protagonist of Carolyn Sherwin Bailey's Newbery Medal-winning fantasy. Miss Hickory's survival in a bird's nest through a cold country winter combines brisk, ironic humor with touches of whimsy and poignancy to form a story with provocative and contradictory implications about motherhood and gender roles. Lively black-and-white drawings by Ruth Gannet illustrate the main event of each chapter, with special emphasis on Miss Hickory's interactions with the various animals whom she encounters.

Miss Hickory opens as the doll's crusty friend Crow informs her that the farm house is being shut up for the winter and that she must plan to move from her corn cob house under a lilac bush to a sturdier and warmer shelter. Initially disbelieving, Miss Hickory soon finds that she has indeed been forgotten by the departing family and must accept Crow's help in finding her a new home in an empty robin's nest.

A series of loosely connected adventures ensues. Her neighbor Squirrel inspires both scorn and fear as Miss Hickory alternately mocks him for forgetting where he has buried his nuts and considers the temptation that her own head might present to the hungry animal. She makes friends with the Hen-Pheasants, whose husbands have deserted them for the winter, and organizes them into a ladies' aid society. At Christmas, Miss Hickory follows a solemn procession of animals to the barn, where her "hardheadedness," a characteristic frequently emphasized in the text, prevents her from seeing a miraculous manifestation of Christ. Along the way, however, she does meet Fawn, who happily tells Miss Hickory that he expects to see his mother, a doe who died trying to protect him from a hunter's bullets. With the approach of spring, Crow returns and takes Miss Hickory on an exhilarating flight high in the sky. Later, a frosty April morning finds her dislodging Bull Frog from the ice. She pulls him free not only from ice but also from his old skin as well.

Fate, however, does not reward her good deeds, for she returns to her nest to find that Robin has resumed occupancy. Remembering suddenly that she has not heard or seen Squirrel for quite some time, she decides to take over his hole. Squirrel, however, is still there and engages her in an acrimonious dispute that ends with Squirrel biting off Miss Hickory's head. Although disengaged from its body, the head continues to think, recriminating itself for its past hardheadedness and selfishness until the Squirrel has eaten it completely. The little twig body, however, surges with life and runs to the apple tree, where it bonds to an upper branch.

The story closes as the little girl, Ann, returns to the farm and climbs the apple tree with her friend Timothy. Timothy explains that the apple twig, formerly Miss Hickory, is a scion, a new graft that has caused the old tree to bloom anew after years of infertility.

Analysis

Although Bailey's story is humorous, the themes that it addresses are serious. Thought-provoking and at times troubling ideas about womanhood, community, and individualism emerge from the small doll's lively adventures. The strong literary qualities of the story give those ideas eloquence and force.

Miss Hickory is an engaging and well-developed character. Sharp-nosed, keen-eyed, and plainspoken at times to the point of rudeness, she is an "intelligent spinster" type, a self-reliant single female with strong opinions and practical abilities. Although the main body of the narrative celebrates Miss Hickory's independence and resource-fulness, the ending translates these qualities into "selfishness" and "hardheadedness," punishing her with death by beheading. There is an unmistakable element of horror in the spectacle of Miss Hickory's severed head recalling the experiences of the past winter in a derogatory light, even characterizing her mentorship of the ladies' aid society as "vanity." Disturbing, too, is the text's portrayal of this mutilation as an act of liberation. No longer "hampered" by her head, Miss Hickory's brainless twig body climbs a tree and happily subsides into somnolent fertility as a scion.

Critic Lois Rostow Kuznets interprets the Squirrel's consumption of Miss Hick-ory's head as a symbolic rape, a masculinist scenario in which a woman finds her ultimate fulfillment in mindless, submissive reproductive activity. The idealization of self-sacrificial fertility is reinforced by the appearance of the doe in the Christmas procession. Both the doe and the Madonna, whose unseen presence is implied in the Nativity scene in the barn, represent an ideal form of womanhood in their total devotion to motherhood.

Although sexist values are thus implied in the story, opposing values also have a strong place. Until her fatal confrontation with Squirrel, Miss Hickory is a forceful and colorful personality. Her independence and determination serve her well in the abrupt transition from her protected life with the farm house family to her new life outdoors, where she must largely fend for herself. Miss Hickory's self-reliance is balanced by a strong social conscience, as evidenced by her friendship with the Hen-Pheasants, her assistance to the ice-bound Bull Frog, and her aspiration to become a schoolteacher. The tough little doll also has a creative side, revealed in the beautiful and stylish outfits that she makes for herself out of forest materials. Her outspoken comments on the foibles of her animal acquaintances are rude but well observed, and in some cases no less blunt than the pithy remarks that they aim at her. In spite of her grotesque fate, Miss Hickory is an attractive heroine whose intelligence and resourcefulness enable her not only to survive in a harsh environment but also to find enjoyment and purpose in an unexpected change of fortune. Indeed, some may even see her transformation into a scion as an ultimate triumph over the harshest turn of events—a continuation of life and productivity after death.

Contrast is also evident in Bailey's portrayal of social relationships among the animals. Tough individualism is the predominant characterization of their interactions, as they compete with one another for homes and food and eschew intimacy and cooperation. The cat, Mr. T. Willard-Brown, epitomizes this harshness when he invites Miss Hickory to view what he expects will be an entertaining sight: the farmer force-feeding medicine to a sick cow. The calf who befriends and shares its food with the bereaved fawn provides a poignant contrast to these anticommunal values, as does Miss Hickory's helpfulness to the Hen-Pheasants and Bull Frog.

The narrative that carries these weighty ideas is related in a clear, straightforward, lighthearted tone. Well-paced, action-filled episodes and brisk, humorous dialogue create an entertaining reading experience. The characters engage the reader's interest not with any charming magical qualities or poetic characteristics but with their arresting similarity both to real animals and to real human beings. Although *Miss Hickory* is a fantasy, it authentically reflects real human virtues and shortcomings and the conflicting moral and social values that shape human destinies.

Critical Context

Miss Hickory lacks the swashbuckling plot lines and magically empowered characters that have become popular in fantasies written in the decades succeeding its publication. Nevertheless, its vivid, authentic voice and appealing illustrations continue to attract readers. It is the only one of the author's seventy-eight fiction and nonfiction publications for children that is still well known.

The book adds a unique element to the body of fiction featuring toys as protagonists. Unlike stories such as Carlo Collodi's *Le Avventure di Pinocchio* (1881-1882; *The Adventures of Pinocchio*, 1892) and Margery Williams' *The Velveteen Rabbit* (1922), it portrays a toy who neither wishes nor attempts to become "real." While some may see her transformation into an insensate scion as a negative contrast to

Pinocchio's and the Velveteen Rabbit's bodily transformations into "real" beings at their stories' conclusions, Miss Hickory's sense of inward completeness and personal sufficiency throughout most of the story is a striking contrast to other toy characters' feelings of anguished inadequacy.

Miss Hickory also contributed to the development of an important character type in children's literature: the "intelligent spinster." P. L. Travers initiated the type with *Mary Poppins* (1934), and the following decades saw the addition of new dimensions to this image of a self-sufficient, mature single woman, including Ellen MacGregor's *Miss Pickerell Goes to Mars* (1951) and its sequels and Betty MacDonald's *Mrs. Piggle-Wiggle* (1947) and its sequels.

Constance Vidor

MISSING MAY

Author: Cynthia Rylant (1954-   )
First published: 1992
Type of work: Novel
Type of plot: Psychological realism
Time of work: The late twentieth century
Locale: A small mountain town in West Virginia
Subjects: Death, family, and friendship
Recommended ages: 10-13

When Aunt May dies suddenly, both Summer and Uncle Ob learn how to ease their deep sorrow and find a new purpose for living through an unexpected journey inspired by Cletus Underwood, a schoolmate Summer had previously scorned.

Principal characters:
SUMMER, an orphan passed from relative to relative until Aunt May and Uncle Ob claim her for their own
UNCLE OB, Summer's devoted uncle, who has been devastated by the sudden loss of his wife
AUNT MAY, Summer's aunt, whose loving presence is still felt
CLETUS UNDERWOOD, Summer's classmate and an inveterate collector
MR. and MRS. UNDERWOOD, Cletus' parents

Form and Content

As *Missing May* opens, twelve-year-old Summer recounts the events leading to her adoption by Aunt May and Uncle Ob: the death of her mother and being passed from house to house among her relatives in Ohio. Summer feels unwanted, "caged and begging," until May and Ob visit from West Virginia when Summer is six years old and recognize her yearning to be loved. They return with her to their rundown trailer deep in the Allegheny Mountains of West Virginia, where Summer realizes that she has come home. Although they are poor, May and Ob give Summer what she needs most: love, comfort, and acceptance.

May dies suddenly in her garden, however, when Summer is twelve, and, although Ob continues to love and care for Summer, both are lost without May. Six months later, Ob suddenly "feels" May's spirit still hovering near them. Desperately wanting to speak once more with May, Ob calls on Cletus Underwood, Summer's classmate. Because Cletus almost drowned when he was seven, Ob believes that he has a special connection to the spirit world and is a conduit through which May can contact them. When they are unable to communicate with May, Ob quickly falls into a deep depression, for the first time not waking on time to get Summer off to school. He confesses to Summer that he doubts he can continue to go on without May.

Cletus provides an unexpected pathway to salvation for all of them through his collection of pictures. He brings Ob a newspaper clipping about the Reverend Young, a spiritualist pastor who communicates with the dead. The coincidence that she is sometimes called the Bat Lady and that May was fond of bats seems strong evidence to Summer, Ob, and Cletus that they should seek her help in contacting May's spirit.

Summer and Ob visit the Underwoods' house to get permission for Cletus to travel with them to visit the Reverend Young. When they arrive, Summer sees Cletus in a new light. Instead of the odd, insecure boy she had known from school, Cletus seems self-assured and comfortable, and Summer realizes it is because of the love and support that his parents give him. She feels ashamed of the disgust that she previously felt for Cletus.

When the three pass through the city of Charleston on their way to visit the spiritualist, Cletus is awed by their proximity to the state capitol, and Ob promises that they will tour the building after they have consulted the medium. Upon discovering, however, that the Reverend Young has died, Ob loses all hope. Summer aches for both of them, knowing that Ob is too depressed to help Cletus realize his dream of visiting the capitol. Ob, however, has a sudden change of heart, turns the car around, and drives back to the capitol building. The three lunch among the legislators in the capitol coffee shop and then tour the capitol, where Cletus is enthralled. They leave Charleston with lighter hearts because of Ob's renewed sense of purpose.

When they reach home that night, an owl flies over Summer's head, bringing back poignantly the loss of May. She finally releases the tears that she has been unable to shed. The next morning, the three of them fill May's empty garden with Ob's "whirligigs," finally setting both her spirit and themselves free.

Analysis

The major subject of *Missing May* is the death of a loved one and its impact on the survivors—their struggle to come to grips with the loss and to deal with their feelings of hopelessness so that they can find new meaning in life. Still torn by the recent loss of her beloved Aunt May, twelve-year-old Summer is desperately afraid that she will now lose her adored Uncle Ob, who continues to pine for May and is slowly losing interest in living. It is only when both Ob and Summer realize that neither can take May's place for the other that they can begin to rebuild their lives without her. Throughout the novel, one sees people handling the deaths of loved ones: the death of Summer's young mother, the death of May's parents when May was only a child, and May's untimely death.

Cynthia Rylant subtly interweaves into the plot reflections on the importance of family and friendship in an individual's development. Although she lives with relatives, Summer has no real family until May and Ob take her in and surround her with their love. She never realizes that they are poor because of the richness of their life together. It is out of May and Ob's deep desire for a child of their own that they recognize Summer's need and decide to share their life with her. After May's death, Ob and Summer keep their family intact by trying to provide for each other as May once did for them.

Even though Summer realizes that the love and support of May and Ob transformed her life, she has not yet learned to step outside her safe cocoon to connect with others. Although Summer rides the school bus with Cletus Underwood, she does not really know him, but she views negatively his obsession with collecting things. While the other kids at school save their potato chip bags and wrapping paper for Cletus, Summer merely watches with disgust. When Ob befriends Cletus and the boy begins visiting the trailer regularly, sharing his latest passion for pictures, Summer reluctantly learns to tolerate him. Even though she is grudgingly grateful to Cletus for helping Ob through the depressing Christmas season after May's death, Summer still refuses to accept him as a friend. It is only after meeting Cletus' elderly parents and feeling his unquestioning reliance on their support and love for him that Summer begins to see Cletus as a unique individual. Summer is finally able to embark on the two-way road to friendship. By doing so, she becomes closer to the spirit of May, who was able to understand people and "let them be whatever way they needed to be."

Through the developing relationship with Cletus, Summer matures and realizes that a "family" consists of those individuals who love, support, and care about a person and that true friendship begins with acceptance and valuing others for the unique gifts that they offer.

Critical Context

Cynthia Rylant has earned a coveted place in juvenile and young adult literature by fearlessly tackling difficult topics and by adding to her readers' knowledge of Appalachia. It is easy to feel Rylant's love of her childhood home in her Caldecott Honor Books *When I Was Young in the Mountains* (1982) and *The Relatives Came* (1985), but it is particularly in her young adult novels such as *Missing May*, *A Fine White Dust* (1986), and *A Blue-Eyed Daisy* (1985) that the Appalachian setting adds dimension to the problems of her central characters. Although the ordinary people featured in Rylant's novels may not perform heroic deeds, readers can relate readily to the everyday heroism that they show in facing life's difficulties tranquilly and accepting as right one's natural place in the world. Her young protagonists encounter problems that keep the adolescent reader riveted: the death of a loved one, a parent's alcoholism, hero-worship and an intense religious experience, the decision of a teenager's mother to have a baby whose father's identity she will not share. Wondering how the problem will be resolved keeps readers enthralled, but learning that each person has a valuable place in the world provides the real satisfaction.

Rylant has written dozens of children's and young adult works, including picture books, poetry, short stories, novels, nonfiction, and works for beginning readers. In the Newbery Medal-winning *Missing May*, she continues the first-person narration, clear, simple writing style, and natural language that made her earlier Newbery Honor Book, *A Fine White Dust*, vivid and compelling.

Phyllis West

MISTY OF CHINCOTEAGUE

Author: Marguerite Henry (1902-   )
First published: 1947; illustrated
Type of work: Novel
Type of plot: Adventure tale, domestic realism, and psychological realism
Time of work: The 1940's
Locale: Chincoteague and Assateague islands, off the coast of Virginia
Subjects: Animals, emotions, family, friendship, and nature
Recommended ages: 10-15

Paul and Maureen Beebe help capture the wild pony Phantom, gentling but eventually freeing the untamable creature, but they win the heart of her precious colt, Misty, who chooses to remain.

Principal characters:
PHANTOM, an almost-mythical Assateague mare
MISTY, her magical foal
PAUL BEEBE, a boy living on Chincoteague Island with his sister and grandparents while his parents are in China
MAUREEN BEEBE, his sister, who is slightly younger but determined to participate equally in all activities that she shares with her brother
GRANDPA BEEBE, the owner of the Chincoteague ranch, where he and his wife reared fourteen children and where they now corral and sell wild ponies from Assateague
GRANDMA BEEBE, the wise and kindly country matriarch

Form and Content
Marguerite Henry's *Misty of Chincoteague* is a thrilling horse story with appeal to readers of all ages. Based on real personalities and true events, the novel occurs in the unusual setting of two little-known islands off Virginia's eastern shore. Here, wild ponies, supposedly the offspring of shipwrecked Moorish ancestors, are rounded up annually. Pervaded by the salty, Atlantic atmosphere, the book discloses much about the unique lifestyle of Chincoteague islanders and of the free-running ponies that inhabit the neighboring isle of Assateague, which is described as "The Island of Wild Things" where no people live.

Part 1, "Before Misty," describes the legendary Spanish galleon *Santo Cristo* swallowed alive by "a wildcat sea"—sparing only one Peru-bound stallion and his fourteen mares, which manage to resurface on the marshes of Assateague Beach. Part 2 recalls two of these survivors' descendants: the ethereal Phantom and her foal, Misty. Paul and Maureen Beebe, two horse-crazy grade-schoolers, decide during an afternoon outing to Assateague that they will catch and financially claim the formerly elusive Phantom during Chincoteague's annual Pony Penning Day.

Four months away from this July celebration, the children resolve to earn auction money by raking clams, gathering oysters, catching crabs, and cleaning chicken houses. They bargain with Grandpa to halter-break his colts for extra dollars. They wash and scrape clean a stall for Phantom, building a manger and scrubbing a rain barrel. When it is time for Paul to assist the volunteer fire department in securing the pony penning grounds, Maureen offers to do his home chores.

Many poignant moments in the novel are exquisitely illustrated by Wesley Dennis' black-and-white pencil drawings. In chapter 6, "Pony Penning Day," Dennis' work highlights the unfolding excitement as, for example, Paul rides off at last to join the roundup team with Grandpa hooting, "Obey yer leader. No matter what!" Amid the thundering chase, Paul is instructed to pursue a straggler. Heeding Grandpa's advice, Paul wheels into the thicket, where he discovers the very prize that he believes himself to have just relinquished: "A silver flash . . . looked like mist with the sun on it . . . just beyond the mist . . . a long tail of mingled copper and silver." The flash is Misty, "brand new, too little" to allow Phantom to keep pace with her flock. Phantom, in response to her mate's summons, leads Misty and Paul straight to the roundup team. Other challenges must be overcome: Paul must swim the channel with the ponies in order to keep Misty afloat, Paul and Maureen almost lose their purchase option on Phantom and Misty, and the ponies are temporarily missing as a result of a storm.

Eventually, ownership of both ponies for the ensuing year teaches the Beebes that, despite the love that they share with Phantom, her chance at happiness is with her mate on the wild island. Paul and Maureen realize that their happiness results from hers and from Misty's joy at remaining in their human world as a loyal, permanent pet.

Analysis

The primary message of *Misty of Chincoteague* concerns the mutual need between people and animals. Paul and Maureen have set their hearts on acquiring ownership of an elusive mare "for our very own." Because Grandpa is one of the few "horsemen" rather than "watermen" on Chincoteague, they have assisted him in the training and sales of all his ponies; parting with their charges has been consistently painful. Their longing for an animal with whom they will never have to sever attachment is a feeling experienced by many people, especially in childhood. In their schemes to obtain Phantom, Paul and Maureen equate ownership with that unbreakable bond.

When Grandpa learns that Paul's plan to ensnare Phantom is the secret that inspired the children's additional employments, he warns him: "The Phantom don't wear that white map on her withers for nothing. It stands for Liberty, and ain't no human being going to take her liberty away from her. . . . She ain't a hoss. She ain't even a lady. She's just a piece of wind and sky." Yet, the children still believe, on the basis of their own instinctive longings, that "Phantom wants to come to us."

Emerging early in the novel is the psychological reality of interdependence among people, as well as that between people and animals. This need is apparent in the islanders cooperative efforts during the pony penning and in the collective spirit displayed when Paul and Phantom win the yearly horse race against a neighboring community. Paul and Maureen, despite normal sibling rivalry, form a viable team working together toward mutual goals. Between them, as between Grandpa and Grandma, exist complementary characteristics. The children share a mutually deep-rooted affection and support, a willingness to sacrifice individual interests for the sake of each other or a cause, just as Grandpa and Grandma form a unit in which they are necessary to each other.

In this same vein, Phantom demonstrates that she, too, possesses a mutual inter-dependence with her mate, Pied Piper. In the final chapter, the stallion swims to Chincoteague calling for his mare, whose captivity he still resents. Although Phantom has returned the love of Paul and Maureen, it is clear to the children and their grandfather that her happiness depends on being able to follow Pied Piper back to Assateague. Paul has learned in his year of hosting Phantom that some spirits be-long more to the world of nature than to that of civilization. He recognizes that this fact does not diminish the bond of love that bridges these two worlds but that if he is to reciprocate the devotion Phantom has demonstrated, he must—like any proper parent or pet-owner—do what is best for her. Throughout *Misty of Chincoteague*, the Beebes show their wonder and respect for the well-being and contentment of animals. When Paul gives Phantom her freedom, Grandpa states, "Ye done the right thing, children."

The competitive desire for personal recognition and worth is another universal quality that the Beebe children exhibit in pursuing and retaining Phantom. Neverthe-less, the value of selflessness and harmony between those who care for one another is undeniable in Paul and Maureen's courageous attempts to raise the purchase money, in Paul's life-risking swim, and, most of all, in their gift of freedom to Phantom.

Critical Context

Marguerite Henry's books are clearly classics that will hold a permanent place of honor in juvenile literature. They are timeless because of their universally important themes regarding relationships between animals and humans and because they appeal so immediately to audiences of all ages. *Misty of Chincoteague* was awarded the Newbery Medal and secured Henry's status as a world-famous author. Motion picture versions of the novel and of several of Henry's other animal stories, such as *Brighty of the Grand Canyon* (1953) and *Justin Morgan Had a Horse* (1945), have been enthusiastically received. Several sequels to *Misty of Chincoteague* have also enjoyed popularity, such as *Sea Star, Orphan of Chincoteague* (1949) and *Stormy, Misty's Foal* (1963).

Henry's style is careful, concise, and purposeful. Her dialogue supports her devel-opments of plot and character, and she delights in the use of appropriate regional vernacular. Her works emerge from meticulous research and extensive travels, and her settings encompass many diverse areas of the United States and Europe. Henry has created charming characters from various horses, dogs, cats, birds, foxes, and mules. Her animal and human characterizations are convincing, the interactions between them utterly believable. Her imaginative works promote wholesome values and positive, optimistic outcomes. Henry's gifts as a storyteller are supreme; her works win and retain the attention of their young readers.

Misty of Chincoteague resulted in the development of a burgeoning tourist industry to Chincoteague Island and its July Pony Penning events, as well as to Assateague Island, which was named a national wildlife refuge. The Chincoteague Pony Association and other organizations have sprung from the ever-escalating public interest that Marguerite Henry's series has done so much to generate.

Michele Perret

MOON-WHALES AND OTHER MOON POEMS

Author: Ted Hughes (1930-   )
First published: 1976; illustrated
Type of work: Poetry
Subject: Animals
Recommended ages: 10-15

Hughes's poems explore an imaginary moon-world, a fantastic dreamscape filled with frightening yet wonderful creatures.

Form and Content

Moon-Whales and Other Moon Poems is a collection of fifty-four short poems that resist easy classification. Individually, the poems describe the bizarre plant and animal life that occupy the poet's fantasy moonscape, creatures ranging from gossiping moon-cabbages to a powerful burrow wolf who hides in "moon holes" and swallows blazing meteorites. Ted Hughes also describes several human (or human-like) inhabitants—for example, a group of people who travel by clinging to one another in a giant ball that rolls across the moon's surface. Despite its strange inhabitants, the geography of Hughes's moon resembles that of the actual moon, complete with deep craters, barren wastes, and vast, eerie silences. Taken together, the poems in the collection evoke a frightening world, part fantasy and part nightmare. Many of the moon-creatures are grotesque and violent, pursuing victims who, in one poem, are "turned inside out/ And sucked dry like an orange" or transformed "instantly into a puff of purple mist." Yet, there is another side to this world. Several poems evoke a sense of wonder, creating a kind of Alice-in-Wonderland distortion of ordinary experience that delights as much as it terrifies.

Among the most striking poems in the book are those describing animals. The title poem, "Moon-Whales," for example, offers a vivid picture of the giant "sea" creatures moving gracefully underground, "lifting the moon's skin/ Like a muscle" and plunging "deep/ Under the moon's plains." The moon-whales' songs includes single notes that last hundreds of years. Other animal poems describe moon-hyenas whose mad laughter comes "to devour the living ones" and silvery white moon-ravens whose "croak" is "not dark/ And ominous,/ But luminous." If such animals have their earthy counterparts, others, such as moon-hops and moon-heads, do not. The latter, which float bodiless among the moon's volcanoes, are menacing "spirit-shapes of unborn prehistoric monsters." The bizarre vegetation of Hughes's moonscape includes jungles of huge nasturtiums swarming with gorillas, marching moon-tulips, and horrible moon-thorns that "make a startling rush/ And stab you to the bone."

Hughes's animal and plant poems constitute about half the pieces in his book. Other poems describe such phenomena as moon-wind, an "utter stillness" in which objects large and small are blown fiercely about. Several poems detail the dreadful symptoms of moon-diseases, one of which—cactus-sickness—causes its victims to sprout a "bunch of ten or fifteen heads," first pea-sized and then melon-sized, all of which are "hungry, arguing or singing." Younger readers may find such descriptions frightening, but they will also sense the comic absurdity that underlies even some of Hughes's most terrifying images. Sometimes, in fact, the mood is predominantly comic, as in "Music on the Moon," in which various instruments make absurd and unearthly "sounds"; the bassoons, for example, produce "huge blue loons" instead of notes. In "The Armies of the Moon," one faction in an unending civil war—the soldiers of the Moon-Dark—fling vampire bats at the soldiers of the Moon-Light, who fight back by shining electric torches into the bats' eyes.

In form, Hughes's poems are mostly irregular, lacking a fixed metrical pattern, with lines ranging from short and clipped ("Moon thirst/ Is the worst") to long and rambling ("Saddest of all things on the moon is the snail without a shell./ You locate him by his wail, a wail heartrending and terrible"). The poems vary in length from four lines to nearly forty, with the bulk falling somewhere in the middle of that range. While some poems follow a pattern of repeated stanzas—four lines or two being the most common arrangement—the majority do not. Most pieces are loosely structured and sound colloquial when read aloud, a feature that should appeal to young readers wary of artificial poetic diction or elevated language. The most notable exception to this informality is the extensive use of rhyme, often in heavy-handed couplets that draw attention to themselves, sometimes for comic effect ("caterpillar" and "gorilla," or "anacondas" and "wonders"). The rhyme gives a degree of control to the otherwise loose syntax of some poems.

Analysis

In his essay "Myth and Education," Hughes argues that children's literature serves an important "therapeutic" function in contemporary society, which tends to over-value rational and utilitarian ways of seeing the world, often at the expense of imagination. The children's writer can offer an alternative vision, invigorating young readers' capacity for wonder, helping them face the irrational forces in themselves and in the world around them. From one point of view, then, the mysterious terrain of *Moon-Whales and Other Moon Poems* is a place where young readers can visit to confront their own fears. Several poems explicitly suggest such a reading. In many pieces, for example, Hughes adopts a technique that makes the reader an active participant, using the second person "you" to place the reader in the middle of the action. In "A Moon-Lily," a mysterious crying flower keeps the protagonist-reader awake: "Then come nights of quiet sobbing, and no sleep for you." In "Moon-Cloud Gripe," the reader is afflicted with a dreadful disease: "Your eyes begin to blur./ Then you go blue." These two poems ask the reader, the "you," to face fearful prospects: death (the sobbing moon-lily is slowly dying) and disease.

"Moon-Shadow Beggars," one of the best and most frightening poems in the book, more fully illustrates the possibilities of Hughes's second-person technique and his capacity to explore hidden fears. The beggars are ghostlike creatures, shadows who pursue "you" across a frontier because "they need your blood"; they want "the body in which you live." If "you pity them, and pause," they will "pour/ Into you through the wide open door/ Of your eye-pupil, and fill you up," making you "nothing but a skinful of shadows." With such vivid, frightening images, Hughes pulls readers into the poem and calls up a host of fears about darkness, injury, death, and loss of self. It should be noted, however, that the violence of this and other poems does not seem gratuitous or designed merely to shock. If Hughes's moon-world is frightening, it frightens in a purposeful way, allowing young readers to act out their fears vicariously and then return safely to the ordinary daylight world of the conscious self. The moon-cloud gripe sickness is curable, and an alert protagonist can avoid the clutches of the moon-shadow beggars.

It is also worth remembering that, taken as a whole, Hughes's moon-world is as much a place of wonder and comic absurdity as of terror. The themes of violence and pursuit in "Moon-Shadow Beggars" exist in a larger context, a world in which fearsome creatures, when faced bravely, dissolve or lose much of their fearsomeness. The moon-hyena, for example, with its "cruel laughter," turns out to be "not dangerous at all"; despite its awesome voice, it is a mouselike creature with a "furry powder-puff tail" who is distressed by its own laughter. Sometimes, Hughes is even more explicit in undercutting the frightfulness of his moon-world. Moon-walkers, dreadful creatures that leave giant footprints on the ceiling, vanish at daylight "as if they came out of your dreams and went back in there (which they probably did)." In other ways, too, Hughes undercuts the terror of his imaginary landscape, such as through the reassuring directness of his language and the sheer beauty of his images: "The big-eyed, up-eared hare I hold/ Is solid flame of living gold."

Critical Context

Moon-Whales and Other Moon Poems is an enduring part of Ted Hughes's contribution to literature for young readers. Like much of his other work—stories and plays as well as poems—this book aims to bring young readers into contact with mysterious, foreboding, often dark aspects of experience that, according to Hughes, are sometimes suppressed or sanitized by contemporary children's writers. His aim is to revitalize, to preserve, and to nurture the child's capacity to imagine, to tap into the inner landscape of the psyche and to face the outer world of raw physical nature. *Moon-Whales and Other Moon Poems* explores a world of dream and nightmare, sometimes fearful but also magical and transforming.

In other books of poetry, Hughes directs attention toward an equally mysterious realm: the outer world of nature, which is powerful, vital, and foreign. *Season Songs* (1975) describes the natural cycles of birth and death that link the human and animal realms, while *Under the North Star* (1981) sees nature as powerful and vast, indifferent to human desires, a source of awe and imaginative regeneration. What all Hughes's collections share is a vision of poetry not as a means of sentimentalizing or prettifying the world but as a vehicle for confronting the powerful, irrational forces that contemporary society, trusting blindly in scientific certitude and the power of technology, often tries to ignore.

Michael Hennessy

THE MOONLIGHT MAN

Author: Paula Fox (1923-   )
First published: 1986
Type of work: Novel
Type of plot: Psychological realism
Time of work: The 1980's
Locale: A boarding school in Montreal, a small town on the coast of Nova Scotia, and New York City
Subjects: Coming-of-age, drugs and addiction, emotions, and family
Recommended ages: 13-18

Catherine Ames spends three vacation weeks with her charming, alcoholic father in a small town on the Nova Scotia coast and finds that, in spite of his selfishness, she can love him for the romance that he brings to her life.

> *Principal characters:*
> CATHERINE AMES, a fifteen-year-old girl who hopes to forgive and love her unreliable father
> MADAME SOULE, the director of the Dalraida Boarding and Day School in Montreal, where Catherine is a boarding student
> MADAME LE SUEUR, Catherine's history teacher, who drinks too much
> HARRY AMES, Catherine's irresponsible, alcoholic father, who has invited her to spend her vacation with him and who calls himself a "Moonlight Man"
> BEATRICE, Catherine's mother, who has recently remarried and is on her honeymoon in Europe
> MRS. LANDY, a local woman hired by Harry Ames to cook and clean the old house that he has rented for Catherine's vacation
> OFFICER MACBETH, an officer of the Royal Canadian Mounted Police who likes Catherine and agrees to take her father on a tour of hidden whiskey stills
> MR. ROSS, a local pastor who is a fine fisherman, a health food addict, and one of the few villagers whom Mr. Ames fails to charm

Form and Content

The Moonlight Man is a short novel about a fifteen-year-old girl who must some-how find a home for herself between two divorced parents who seem never to have loved each other at all. Catherine Ames lives in New York with her mother, Beatrice. At her father's insistence, however, she has been sent to a boarding school in Montreal to "see more of the world"; as a writer, he sees worldly experience as essential. The events of Catherine's summer are seen through her own eyes. She has been invited to spend the entire vacation with her father and his wife, but Harry Ames does not show up on the appointed day to take her home with him. The school director, Madame Soule, agrees to let Catherine remain at the school waiting and, with misgivings, also promises not to call her mother, who is on a honeymoon in England with her new husband.

Three weeks late, Harry calls his daughter and unpersuasively explains his reason for not coming—a disagreement with his wife. She is to meet him in Mackenzie, a small coastal town in Nova Scotia. The next thing that she knows, Catherine is driving three drunk men home over a bad country road and longs to be back in Montreal: "Her mother had not told her how terrible drinking could be." Now she knows why her father had not kept his promise to come and get her: He is an alcoholic.

Catherine manages to live through the next three weeks, and some of that time is wonderful. Her father reads to her; takes her fishing with Mr. Ross, the local pastor who is the best fisherman in town but a hard man to like; teaches her how to shoot windows out of a deserted barn; makes delicious picnics for days in the sun; and applies his romantic charm to everything they do together. He promises not to drink and keeps his promise for a few days.

Soon, Officer Macbeth pays a visit, asking if they know anything about the broken windows, and Harry quiets suspicion with a lie easily told. Sensing that the young officer admires Catherine, he persuades Macbeth to take him on a visit to the local whiskey stills on the pretext that he is writing a book about the area. Harry drinks at each still, and, after seeing him down on the floor pretending to be a dog, Catherine and Macbeth finally take him home, where he collapses. Catherine is afraid that he will die and goes to find Mr. Ross, who turns out to be both useful and sympathetic. He has been there himself: "Forgive it," he tells Catherine, "We're all helpless in one way or the other."

The vacation ends, and Harry knows that it has been a failure. Yet, his daughter knows something else: She can still love her father. When she is at home again with her mother, Catherine defends him, and Beatrice confesses that she once loved Harry. Catherine will be able to admit some of her father's faults, to agree sometimes about his thoughtlessness and unreliability, but she will protect him from her mother's most bitter feelings and will never tell her that Harry dreads seeing his daughter again.

Analysis

Catherine's dilemma is well known to many teenagers. She is caught between two very different parents who are critical of each other. In addition, her father is an unreliable alcoholic whom she must learn to love if she is to be at peace with herself. Catherine must somehow accept both her "daylight" mother—who is dependable, orderly, and unimaginative—and her father—who is a failed novelist and romantic "moonlight man" who uses his considerable charm to get what he wants, which is often alcohol, and who, in the eyes of most people, is a poor father.

Besides learning to love a wayward father, Catherine must come to terms with another important element in getting to know him. She recognizes the value of his romantic view of life, which makes everything so much more intense for her during the time that they spend together. Harry wants his daughter to see the beauty of variety, of faraway places such as Italian hill towns and Paris, and he excites her with poetry and humor. He also teaches her to rebel against the dullness of being obedient and without imagination. Her mother calls the barn shooting "reckless," but for Catherine it is much more.

Paula Fox is especially good at revealing everything about a place through the conversation and behavior of her characters. The small town of Mackenzie becomes real through local people such as Mrs. Landy, the cleaning woman; Mr. Ross, the eccentric pastor; and Officer Macbeth, the awkward young Mountie. The novel also features a vivid emotional topography, with Catherine's feelings changing from anger to delight to fury to fear and back in her continuous search for a "home" between two warring parents who both demand her love and loyalty.

Fox's style employs vivid images that make readers see what the author is describing, but the sentences are not simple, repetitive, or easy to follow. Too many of reality's surprises occur on every page and the reader must be alert in order to recognize them. The story also requires a seriousness on the part of the young reader, which may discourage those who look for predictable characters and happy endings.

Catherine's difficulty in accepting her father is made even worse as she realizes that he is a man who counts on his own charm to get whatever he wants. She herself is cajoled into forgiving him for broken promises. Harry lies cheerfully to Officer Macbeth about shooting out the barn windows and has no qualms about seducing the wife of one of his local drinking partners. With his charm, he has found a rich wife to adore and spoil him. Finally, Catherine realizes that he will sacrifice everything, even his affection for her, to the cold, implacable drive to get drunk. The author has prepared the reader for the final failure of this reunion through three important episodes illustrating the helplessness of Harry Ames to resist alcohol, and the climax comes when Catherine loses patience and tells that him he is not a novelist, as he pretends, but a drunk and a bastard. The break is now inevitable, and no traditional happy ending can come from this story. Nevertheless, Catherine has learned that she can love her father for his magic—there is a truce and an ending after all.

Critical Context

The Moonlight Man is meant for young adult audiences, but it is emotionally sophisticated and could be read with interest by adults. Paula Fox believes that children are able to understand everything adults do and that they lack only judgment, which comes with experience. While she avoids descriptions of extreme violence and sex, she does not shy away from telling young people that life is often confusing and full of questions that have no answers. The author has said that it is her purpose in her books to present young readers with characters who will enlarge their knowledge of other people, and this is true of *The Moonlight Man*. By knowing Harry Ames better, Catherine learns to love what is valuable in him.

Fox has been honored for offering honest stories that often do not have happy endings. Although her books have been tagged "depressing" because of their honesty, they have become an important part of young people's literature. She has received the Newbery Medal for *The Slave Dancer* (1973), the American Book Award for *A Place Apart* (1977), and the Hans Christian Andersen Medal for her collected works for children. *One-Eyed Cat* (1984), a novel for older children, won the Child Study Children's Book Award and a Christopher Award and was cited as a Newbery Honor Book. *The Moonlight Man* was selected by *The New York Times* as one of the notable books for 1986 and also as one of the Child Study Association of America's Children's Books of the Year for 1987.

Lucy Golsan

THE MOUSE AND THE MOTORCYCLE

Author: Beverly Cleary (1916-   )
First published: 1965; illustrated
Type of work: Novel
Type of plot: Adventure tale, fantasy, and moral tale
Time of work: The 1960's
Locale: Mountain View Inn, in the California foothills
Subjects: Animals, coming-of-age, family, and friendship
Recommended ages: 10-13

An adventurous mouse learns about humans, his family, and himself when he strikes up a friendship with a young boy.

> *Principal characters:*
> RALPH, a reckless young mouse hungry for excitement
> KEITH GRIDLEY, a boy fascinated with motorcycles and cars
> MR. and MRS. GRIDLEY, Keith's somewhat overprotective parents
> RALPH'S MOTHER, a worrier with many young children
> MATT, the Mountain View Inn's sixty-year-old bellboy

Form and Content

The Mouse and the Motorcycle follows the parallel stories of two youngsters, one human and one animal, and their adventures when they meet. In some ways, it is a classic "buddy story" of two youngsters learning about and helping each other. The details are fantastic, such as human-animal conversations, and the theme of self-discovery and bonding will appeal to children.

The story is based on a series of adventures culminating in Ralph's "rescue" of Keith from illness. Beverly Cleary introduces readers to the plot and characters by showing the Gridley family's entrance to the Mountain View Inn from Ralph's perspective. Ralph is entranced with Keith's toy motorcycle and is irresistibly drawn to ride it. He falls into an empty wastebasket, where Keith discovers him. They find that they are able to communicate.

Their friendship grows: Keith brings food to the mouse family, and Ralph tells him about life at the inn. The relationship is tested when Ralph borrows the motorcycle without permission and loses it. Keith is hurt and upset, but he realizes that he too has done irresponsible things. Ralph vows to make it up to him.

Keith becomes very ill with a high fever; it is a holiday weekend and drugstores are closed. His parents are frantic. Ralph seizes the opportunity to search the hotel for an aspirin. After a series of near disasters, he delivers the aspirin to Keith.

When Keith recovers, he is overjoyed to see that Matt, the bellboy, has found his motorcycle. Praising Ralph's maturity, he offers to take him back home to Ohio. Ralph is tempted but, on learning that he would be kept in a cage, refuses. Keith, in a gesture of friendship, gives Ralph the motorcycle to keep.

The novel is divided into thirteen chapters and spans several days in the lives of Keith and Ralph. Chapter titles (such as "Trapped!," "The Vacuum Cleaner," and "An Anxious Night") suggest the action to follow; the adventures of mouse and boy are usually followed by conversation and reflection. Louis Darling's black-and-white illustrations often show events from Ralph's vantage point.

The novel is easy to read, even for children younger than the intended age group. The dialogue between Keith and Ralph is often comic, sometimes poignant, and quite believable. Sentences are short and clear, and Cleary relies on vivid description to set the stage for the action. The story is told by a limited omniscient narrator who sees into Ralph's mind and describes his feelings: impatience with his protective mother, curiosity about humans, a longing for freedom and speed, regret at the hurt that he causes Keith. Cleary excels in giving a "mouselike" point of view. Scenes such as Ralph running up a phone cord, trying to escape from a metal wastebasket, and chewing through a pile of laundry rely heavily on sensory impressions; they give a vivid sense of what the world would look like from Ralph's perspective.

Cleary is never condescending to her characters; Ralph never appears as "cute." Instead, he is much like his human friend: adventurous, longing to grow up and go places, irritated at any suggestion that he is too young to be on his own, and reluctant to admit how much he loves and needs his family. Though the story is a fantasy, it is grounded in extremely convincing details that will be familiar to young readers: Ralph's worrying mother and annoying relatives, his fierce desire to do things for himself, and his fear at testing limits are all effectively portrayed.

Although readers feel sympathy for both Ralph and Keith, their dilemmas are both touching and comic, such as Ralph's confrontations with a yappy little dog in the elevator, his boredom and impatience at a "family reunion," and his longing to help Keith when his human friend becomes ill. The fantastic events of the story are treated with matter-of-factness. Never does Cleary suggest that there is anything unusual about the events depicted. Toy cars and the motorcycle run by the driver making realistic engine noises; humans and animals can communicate; and the mouse extended family is modeled on human families.

Analysis

Cleary, in her first attempt at fantasy, includes a number of important themes for young people: responsibility versus recklessness, loyalty to friends and family, courage in the face of pressure to "stay safe," and atonement for mistakes.

Ralph, like Keith, longs to be older and to be able to explore his surroundings freely. He is impatient to see the world and to have adventures. His restlessness causes him to behave irresponsibly early in the novel. Desperate to ride the motorcycle, he tumbles into a wastebasket. Convincing himself that he is doing a scientific study, he pits the motorcycle against a vacuum cleaner and loses. He "borrows" the motorcycle without Keith's permission. It is only when Ralph realizes that freedom brings responsibility—in his dangerous mercy mission—that he is rewarded with true friendship. His newfound ability to consider consequences keeps him from leaving with

Keith and doing the traveling that he has always wanted to do; the price of being kept in a cage is too high. Instead, he decides that he will stay in the hotel and explore the possibilities there.

Ralph's friendship with Keith makes him realize the cost of being a grown-up, a common theme in Cleary's work. Here, a reckless character behaves impulsively and makes mistakes, but, when he sees the consequences of his errors, he atones for his bad judgment by behaving with bravery, kindness, and maturity.

Cleary depicts the courage that ordinary characters can muster under extraordinary circumstances. The story builds to a climax when Ralph is given the responsibility of finding aspirin for Keith's high fever. Cleary creates suspense in showing Ralph's terror at traveling to the dreaded ground floor at 1 A.M. and by having various frightening obstacles—an owl, a capture, a nosy dog, the bellboy—thrown in his path. Added to this fear is the poignant reminder that Ralph's father died from ingesting an aspirin; young Ralph's journey is a terrifying one for both himself and his family. Cleary suggests that concern for a friend can help a young person overcome fear and regret and reap rich rewards. Ralph's concern for Keith and his desire to atone for his carelessness unexpectedly bring him the excitement that he has always wanted, turning him into a hero to his family. Keith, too, praises him as a smart and brave mouse who risked his life to help a friend.

Keith's coming-of-age parallels Ralph's—he longs to grow up and be able to drive a real motorcycle, but he realizes that he has much to do and learn before he becomes an adult. Like Ralph, Keith sees that he must think before he acts and finds out that true friendship can withstand any test.

Critical Context

The Mouse and the Motorcycle was Cleary's first foray into fantasy literature after realistic (and very successful) books such as *Henry and Ribsy* (1954). Her earlier novels also focused on family issues and personal responsibility, but they used an all-human cast. Like the tale of Ralph and the motorcycle, her earlier work treats children and their concerns with affection and respect. Her books look at seemingly small events in a child's life and show what an enormous impact they can have: Henry's paper route, Ramona's first day of kindergarten, and Ellen Tebbits' dance recital are important happenings in the child's world. Similarly, Ralph's small adventures, taken together, change the way in which he looks at life.

The Mouse and the Motorcycle won several state and regional awards; it was one of Cleary's many successes in the field of children's literature and showed that her enormous sympathy and humor extended to the animal kingdom as well. The novel is one of only a handful of children's books to win awards both for literary merit and for popularity. It was critically acclaimed and remains popular with children, being named in national surveys of children's reading choices, placing in the top fifty. It is prominent on recommended lists published by children's librarians, where it is often categorized as "modern fantasy." Critics praised the vividness of Cleary's characterizations and her ability to teach a lesson to children in a humorous and interesting way. She has a solid reputation as a writer who is able to determine what events and emotions are important to children and who has the ability to describe everyday events so that they seem extraordinary. The freshness of her approach—and the fact that she is never patronizing to children—has earned for her lasting popularity.

The Mouse and the Motorcycle was followed a few years later by a sequel, *Runaway Ralph* (1970). In this second installment of Ralph's adventures, Cleary again treats complex topics such as youthful restlessness in a straightforward and humorous manner.

Michelle L. Jones

MY BRILLIANT CAREER

Author: Miles Franklin (1879-1954)
First published: 1901
Type of work: Novel
Type of plot: Psychological realism and social realism
Time of work: 1880-1899
Locale: New South Wales, Australia
Subjects: Coming-of-age, emotions, family, and gender roles
Recommended ages: 13-18

A spirited, rebellious young woman comes of age in the Australian Outback as she struggles with her family's misfortunes.

> *Principal characters:*
> SYBYLLA MELVYN, an intelligent, rebellious adolescent girl who longs
>   for more than life in the Australian Outback can offer
> RICHARD MELVYN, Sybylla's father, whose bad business sense and
>   drinking propels the family from prosperity into poverty
> LUCY MELVYN, Sybylla's refined and well-bred mother, who has been
>   beaten down by poverty
> GERTIE MELVYN, Sybylla's attractive, eager-to-please sister
> HORACE MELVYN, Gertie's twin brother
> MRS. BESSIER, Sybylla's wealthy grandmother, with whom she stays at
>   Caddagat
> HELEN BELL, Sybylla's kind and beautiful aunt
> HAROLD BEECHAM, a handsome young land owner who falls in love
>   with Sybylla
> PETER M'SWAT, an old school chum of Richard Melvyn who employs
>   Sybylla as governess to his children
> MRS. M'SWAT, Peter's fat, lazy, but good-natured wife

Form and Content

Miles Franklin's *My Brilliant Career*, the story of Sybylla Melvyn, an intense, passionate young woman growing up in the nineteenth century Australian Outback, is a phenomenal achievement for such a young author. Narrated by Sybylla in an autobiographical style, this novel consists of thirty-eight chapters, beginning with her earliest recollections of life in the Outback but focusing on her sixteenth through nineteenth years. An early landmark in feminist literature, *My Brilliant Career* is more relevant to contemporary audiences than it was to early twentieth century readers.

Sybylla Melvyn, born on a large estate in the Australian Outback, is the high-spirited, rebellious daughter of a wealthy landowner and a woman of aristocratic background. When Sybylla is nine years old, her adored father sells the family's estate to try his hand at dealing cattle. Dick Melvyn's poor business sense, coupled with heavy drinking, propels the family into poverty within a year and transforms him from "a kind and indulgent parent, a chivalrous husband, a capital host, a man full of ambition and gentlemanliness" into a "despicable, selfish, weak creature." Sybylla's heroic image of her father is destroyed, and her idyllic life disappears. Their existence at the new family home, Possum Gully, is harsh, and Sybylla, who longs for a "brilliant career" as a writer, foresees nothing in her future but mind-numbing, back-breaking labor.

When Sybylla accepts an invitation from her wealthy grandmother to stay on her estate at Caddagat, she is thrust back into the world of culture, beauty, and refinement that she has so sorely missed. She blossoms among the music, books, and good conversation for which her soul had been thirsting, and even her appearance, usually judged "plain" at best, improves tremendously. Although she still does not believe herself a beauty, her exuberant nature captivates several marriageable men in the district.

Sybylla, however, admires only Harold Beecham, the young, handsome owner of a neighboring estate. She finds his seeming indifference to her intriguing, but when he finally declares his love, her attraction to Beecham is at odds with her fierce need for independence. When her suitor's fortunes suffer a reversal, he departs to seek his fortune anew, extracting Sybylla's promise that she will marry him in three years if he still wants and needs her.

With Beecham's departure, Sybylla's idyll at Caddagat also comes to an abrupt end when she must take a job as governess to the unruly M'Swat children to help repay a debt that her father has incurred. The utter ignorance and filth of the M'Swats and the dramatic contrast between their home at Barney's Gap and her previous life at Caddagat plunges Sybylla into a deep depression, and a nervous breakdown eventually forces her return to the family at Possum Gulch.

Back at the less odious, but nevertheless harsh surroundings of her family home, Sybylla receives another proposal from Harold Beecham, restored once again to his fortune. Sybylla, realizing that she does not love him enough to settle for a safe marriage over a "brilliant career," refuses him and remains at Possum Gulch, with little hope of a brighter future but with dreams of a brilliant career intact.

Analysis

The passionate intensity of *My Brilliant Career* is both its principal weakness and its greatest strength. Although the novel descends into melodrama, the authenticity of its young author's voice eloquently expresses juvenile anguish and gives articulate utterance to the universal adolescent concerns of self-doubt, isolation, and gender identity.

Franklin convincingly conveys the self-obsession and insecurities typical to many young adults. For example, Sybylla becomes fixated on her appearance, convinced that she is unbearably ugly, and no amount of evidence to the contrary will persuade her otherwise. Also sure to resonate with young readers is Sybylla's conviction that her torrential emotions are utterly unique, as she agonizes, "What was the hot wild spirit which surged within me? . . . Why was I not like other girls?" These adolescent uncertainties regarding appearance and emotion have fueled popular literature, including teen magazines, for years.

Also like many adolescents, Sybylla feels misunderstood and estranged from both family and society. Her father has become an embarrassing disappointment to her, barely able to keep his family from starvation as he drinks away what little he is able to make. Her mother has lost her refinement in the family's hard-scrabble existence and has become bitter, unhappy, and completely unsympathetic to her rebellious teenage daughter. Sybylla finds little solace or understanding from her siblings, who, although they love their sister, have no sympathy with her woes. Even society has no role other than housekeeper, governess, or wife for an independent young woman such as Sybylla.

My Brilliant Career addresses not only youthful alienation but issues of gender as well. Sybylla lashes out repeatedly against the strictures of her sex:

> As a tiny child I was filled with dreams of the great things I was to do when grown up. My ambition was as boundless as the mighty bush in which I have always lived. As I grew it dawned upon me that I was a girl—the makings of a woman! Only a girl—merely this and nothing more. It came home to me as a great blow that it was only men who could take the world by its ears and conquer their fate. . . .

Sybylla struggles with the mutually exclusive choice between marriage and independence. She is offered the choice of marriage to a wealthy, intelligent, kind man who can offer her a life full of the books, music, and culture that she desires. Yet, she must weigh the option of a comfortable and happy life against the chance of a "brilliant career." Despite the fact that Beecham is a sympathetic character, and that a career is only the remotest of possibilities, Sybylla opts for a miserable but self-reliant existence over a life lived as merely an extension of another person.

An enriching experience for young adult readers, particularly young women, *My Brilliant Career* addresses themes of universal interest to adolescents. Although lacking the perspective of an older, more experienced author, Miles Franklin compensates for a deficiency in maturity and with a heartfelt expression of emotion that addresses the universal nature of youthful agonies. Young readers will come away from this book with the comforting knowledge that even their most troubling thoughts and emotions are not unique and that others have experienced, and survived, the agonies of adolescence.

Critical Context

My Brilliant Career, essentially a nineteenth century novel embracing a twentieth century sensibility, had an unusual publication history. Perceived by its readers to be autobiography rather than fiction, the book brought such an unwelcome notoriety to its young author that she withdrew it from publication. In fact, the public's reaction to her book so disturbed Miles Franklin that she left her native Australia for nearly thirty years, and *My Brilliant Career* did not appear in print again until well after her death, in 1966. Clearly, the novel was ahead of its time—too disturbing for an early twentieth century audience uncomfortable with the feminist sentiments expressed by its rebellious narrator.

As a notable early example of feminist literature, *My Brilliant Career* parallels another novel, *The Awakening* (1899), by Kate Chopin, whose heroine chooses to end her life rather than live within the strictures of society. These novels both reveal an understanding of the repercussions of being female in a "man's world," which did not begin to be widely understood and written about until nearly sixty years later, in works such as Betty Friedan's *The Feminine Mystique* (1963) and Kate Millett's *Sexual Politics* (1970).

My Brilliant Career is more closely akin to twentieth century coming-of-age novels than to any contemporaneous works. Sybylla Melvyn, like Holden Caulfield in J. D. Salinger's *The Catcher in the Rye* (1951) and Esther Greenwood in Sylvia Plath's *The Bell Jar* (1963), questions the most basic assumptions of her society and her elders, and she suffers a nervous breakdown when the realities of life in the adult world prove more than she can bear. The novel's authentic adolescent voice and autobiographical tone also recall Anne Frank's *The Diary of a Young Girl* (1947), which expressed the depth of adolescent passions.

Mary Virginia Davis

MY LIFE AS A DOG

Author: Reidar Jönsson (1944-   )
First published: Mitt Liv som Hund, 1983 (English translation, 1989)
Type of work: Novel
Type of plot: Domestic realism and social realism
Time of work: 1958-1959
Locale: Småland, a rural village in Sweden, and Happy Heights, a housing development in urban Sweden
Subjects: Coming-of-age, death, emotions, family, and friendship
Recommended ages: 13-18

Ingemar Johansson works through feelings of guilt and grief over his mother's death while being forced to become an adult before he is emotionally ready.

Principal characters:
INGEMAR JOHANSSON, a thirteen-year-old struggling to be accepted and loved
INGEMAR'S MOTHER, a woman who suffers from tuberculosis and openly admits to her son that he was not wanted
INGEMAR'S FATHER, a banana boat sailor who is often remembered by Ingemar as the man who brings fruit
MANNE, Ingemar's best friend in Småland, the son of the village inventor
SAGA, a player on the local soccer team and the girl to whom Ingemar loses his virginity
INGEMAR'S UNCLE, a kindhearted man who shelters Ingemar in Småland after the death of his mother
THE MANUFACTURER, a rich man who once loved Ingemar's mother

Form and Content

My Life as a Dog is a touching story of a lonely boy's struggle to survive in a world that is forcing him to become an adult before he is ready. Although it takes place in Sweden, this autobiographical novel raises social issues found throughout the world. Neglected in his childhood and, as a result, confused as a teenager, the protagonist, Ingemar, faces life with a blind resignation—he continually tricks himself into believing that soon he will be loved. The protagonist at times seems to be mentally ill, but anyone who has felt totally alone in the world will be able to relate to his precarious grip on sanity.

Narrated by Ingemar, the story mixes the present tense and flashbacks. In this manner, Ingemar Johansson tells how he spent the last two years of his childhood, being passed from one guardian to another and living with the constant fear as well as the certainty that he will manage always to do the wrong thing. He compares himself to the dog that was sent into space by the Soviet Union, and he comforts himself by deciding that the dog's life must have been even more uncomfortable and lonelier than his. Ingemar's one wish is to believe that his mother loved him, but he is forced to face the fact that neither she nor anyone else ever really wanted him.

Ingemar's childhood is spent in fear of angering his mother, who suffers from tuberculosis. Whenever her attacks become too bad, he and his sister and brother are sent away to the children's home or to their grandparents' house. Ingemar, however, is described by the adults as being "too much trouble," so he is often separated from his siblings. When he is at home, he is forbidden to disturb his mother, and he must cook and care for himself without any help.

One summer, he is shipped off to his uncle's house in a small village, where he manages to make a few friends and to play on the football (soccer) team. After his mother's death and a short stay with a man known as the Manufacturer, he returns to live with his uncle, but this time his stay is not as successful. Although he finds friends in Manne, the son of an inventor, and Saga, a tomboy who is distressed by her growing breasts, Ingemar disrupts the village through a series of blunders and is finally retrieved by his long-absent father.

Unfortunately, as soon as Ingemar shows signs of being able to take care of himself, his father leaves to work once again on a banana boat, and Ingemar is left alone. He realizes how angry he is and begins to avenge himself by smashing windows at night and stealing from the pharmacy where he works. His anger is totally unleashed when his brother returns and produces a hidden airgun. Ingemar is finally arrested, and he breaks down at the police station. Although he claims that he will go and work with his father, it is clear that he will continue to be alone, since he ends his story the same way that it began—forming a circle of loneliness.

Analysis

Reidar Jönsson's *My Life as a Dog* is a novel that deals with loneliness and rejection. Although it does not offer much hope of comfort to young readers, the story of Ingemar Johansson helps to identify some of the questions that teenagers ask. It also presents a variety of emotional responses in a manner that does not judge what is "normal," but instead simply acknowledges that growing up is a confusing and frustrating task that is often accomplished in spite of—rather than because of—the efforts of the young adult.

The novel illustrates the challenges that all teenagers must face, such as trying to fit in with and be accepted by one's peers, dealing with sexual urges and temptations, recognizing and controlling anger, and developing relationships. For Ingemar, however, these challenges are even more difficult because of his mother's untimely death and his father's notable absence. In addition to the usual struggles of a thirteen-year-old, Ingemar must deal with grief and guilt, as well as a growing despair because nobody wants him.

In an effort to develop an identity for himself, Ingemar lives on the edge of reality, sometimes even unsure himself how he has come to be in the situations in which he finds himself. His attempts to comfort himself by reading about accidents and disasters and telling himself that he is better off than the people in the news raise the question of why children such as Ingemar are not considered newsworthy as "disasters." His belief that all of his misfortunes are somehow his own fault causes readers to ask not only who is really at fault for his circumstances but also who should be responsible for rectifying his situation.

It is not surprising that Ingemar rebels by stealing from his employer and by smashing windows and shooting streetlamps. What is surprising is that none of the adults in Ingemar's life realizes that his violent behavior could have been avoided if someone had simply allowed him to believe that he was loved.

A related issue is that of Ingemar's first sexual experience. His search for love leads him to "marry" a girl whom he refers to as "Tree Frog" because they take American Indian names and pretend to live in a tent. When he is with Tree Frog, he alternates between the roles of husband and infant, and he admits that he sometimes enjoys being held as an infant more than as a husband.

When he is sent to live with his uncle, Ingemar is teased by an older woman named Berit, who pretends to accept his marriage proposal and then takes him along on a date with another boy. He is also teased by a girl named Louise, who is his own age and very attractive but who is willing only to flirt. He is finally satisfied sexually by Saga, a tomboy who first teaches him to box and then seduces him. He spends a whole night in her arms, happy and content, but, when morning comes, they are separated forever without being given the chance to explain why.

Although Jönsson's message may be intended for an adult audience, through Ingemar, he allows young readers to realize and admit that everyone needs help, and his novel suggests that all children have a right to demand that help. It also shows what happens when they do not do so.

Critical Context

Written in the 1980's, *My Life as a Dog* deals with social issues that were in the spotlight at that time. The book appeared in the United States in the late 1980's, around the same time that the acquired immunodeficiency syndrome (AIDS) epidemic was gaining momentum. Even though sexual and health issues are not the main themes of the novel, his mother's slow death and the theme of loneliness and separation touched a nerve with readers. Furthermore, Reidar Jönsson portrays a young adult who is forced to live without guidance from a caring adult. This seemed to be a recurring theme by the 1990's, as more and more attention became focused on welfare reform and the cycle of poverty.

A critically acclaimed film version of *My Life as a Dog* was made by Lasse Hallström in 1985.

Amy Shollenberger

THE MYSTERIOUS ISLAND

Author: Jules Verne (1828-1905)
First published: L'Île mystérieuse, 1874-1875 (English translation, 1875)
Type of work: Novel
Type of plot: Adventure tale and science fiction
Time of work: 1865
Locale: An uncharted Pacific island
Subjects: Science and social issues
Recommended ages: 13-18

Prisoners of war escape in a hot-air balloon only to find themselves tossed onto a remote island where they need ingenuity and courage to survive.

> *Principal characters:*
> CAPTAIN CYRUS HARDING, a first-class engineer whose courage, dexterity, and tenacity command the respect of the other men
> GIDEON SPILETT, a brave and persistent reporter for the *New York Herald* who follows the Northern army and chronicles its battles
> NEB (NEBUCHADNEZZAR), a former slave who is a devoted servant to Captain Harding because Harding granted him his freedom
> JACK PENCROFT, a bold, adventurous sailor who devises the dangerous plan for escape from the city of Richmond
> HERBERT BROWN, a fifteen-year-old orphan of a former captain whom Pencroft loves as his own son
> AYRTON, an exiled sailor who attempted mutiny on his ship and was dropped off on a neighboring uninhabited island
> CAPTAIN NEMO, the commander of the submarine *Nautilus* and the mysterious benefactor for the colonists

Form and Content

Finding themselves detained in Richmond, Virginia, during the Civil War, five Union soldiers and a dog dare to escape in a hot-air balloon during the worst hurricane of the decade. The balloon sails haphazardly through the storm, tosses Captain Cyrus Harding and his dog, Top, into the ocean, and crashes with the rest of its passengers onto the shore of an uninhabited island in the Pacific Ocean. Fearing that the captain is dead, his servant, Neb, searches the island until he finds Top, who leads him to Harding. This is to be the first of many mysterious occurrences involving the group of men.

They build up a settlement as best they can. The men call themselves "colonists" and name their island Lincoln Island after their great president. They establish a permanent camp in a cave on the side of a cliff and call it Granite House. They plant crops from seedlings that they find and establish a farm with the animals that they capture. They build a boat in order to visit nearby islands and find Ayrton, an exiled sailor who comes to live with the colonists and becomes one of them.

Throughout these adventures, a mysterious force seems to be at work on the island that helps the men in dire times of need. Although Harding is clever and is able to make tools and weapons for the colonists, things they cannot manufacture from the natural resources of the island mysteriously appear as they need them. For example, an intact, waterproof chest of books, clothes, and other items washes onto shore one day, although no ship has been sighted. Another time, the colonists find that wild orangutans had invaded their cave but were scared off by some force before they could do much damage. When fifteen-year-old Herbert is wounded by pirates during an attack, a box of quinine, the only thing that could save him, appears by his bedside one night.

All these mysterious happenings are discovered to be the work of Captain Nemo, the commander of the submarine *Nautilus*, who has been hiding in seclusion beneath a reef of the island. He has abandoned civilization and has lived near the island for many years. Nemo decided to help the colonists because he recognized the goodness and humanity of these men.

Even with Nemo's anonymous help, the colonists must deal with many dangers. Marauding pirate ships, wild animals, and the weather are constant threats, but the most fearsome threat is the volcano that created the island. The volcano becomes active, and the colonists know that they have little time to build a seaworthy vessel before the volcano erupts. It does so before they have a chance to sail away, and they survive for nine more days on the small rock formation that remains before being rescued by a passing ship.

Analysis

The Mysterious Island is a science-fiction adventure that glorifies the adaptability and survival instincts of the human body and spirit. Frenchman Jules Verne has made all the characters in the novel Americans, partly to present a social commentary of the United States and of the historical period surrounding the American Civil War. Thus, Verne not only spins a tale of intrigue and adventure but also portrays the traditional American qualities of individualism, courage, and resourcefulness. The colonists are not easily defeated when confronted with adversity. From the beginning, they are willing to escape imprisonment in a balloon during a hurricane. They face certain death but manage to survive against terrible odds. While on the island, which they name after Abraham Lincoln in a patriotic gesture, the colonists come across every conceivable danger and setback, but they prove to be masters of their own destinies and persevere. Although they are helped by a mysterious benefactor, they personify the rugged American spirit.

The figure of Captain Nemo serves as a counterpoint to the other characters. As his past is revealed to the colonists, they realize that he is an anarchist who has abandoned society and its flaws. He considers the human race to be in decline and sees the source of its demise in the technological wonders of the time. Nemo is a genius who has built an extraordinary vessel that travels underwater, but, instead of using his invention for the good of society, he frightens away and destroys ships that pass in the surrounding ocean as revenge for his exile.

Captain Nemo's submarine is a magnificent vessel created in Verne's mind. In his time, underwater travel was considered, at best, a topic of research and debate and, at worst, a figment of the imagination. As Verne described the vessel, however, it appeared to be quite feasible. Introduced in Verne's earlier work *Vingt milles lieues sous les mers* (1870; *Twenty Thousand Leagues Under the Sea*, 1873), Captain Nemo's *Nautilus* became a symbol of how rapidly science and technology advanced during the Industrial Revolution. Although *The Mysterious Island* is not truly a sequel to *Twenty Thousand Leagues Under the Sea*, Captain Nemo's character is revealed and explained more fully in *The Mysterious Island*, and the reader comes away with a more satisfactory explanation of Nemo's motivations and inspirations in this book than in the earlier novel.

Critical Context

This classic novel offers an example of Jules Verne's extraordinary ability to make science fiction seem real. Truly the father of this genre, he mastered the art of describing in minute detail the design and workings of machines and technologies unknown to most people of his time. As a child, Verne was able to witness experiments of an underwater vehicle tested by Brutus de Villeroi. By 1800, Robert Fulton had designed and built a practical submarine that he named the *Nautilus*. Influenced by these innovations, Verne wove miraculous tales that anticipated the development of such a machine. Like Leonardo da Vinci and H. G. Wells, Verne was able to foresee many technological advances that humans would achieve. This limitless hunger to learn about and build new technologies epitomized all of Verne's works.

In his novel *De la terre à la lune* (1865; *From the Earth to the Moon*, 1873), Verne's design specifications for his rocket ship are similar to those from which the Apollo spacecraft were made a hundred years later. Verne's spacecraft was made from aluminum and had approximately the same dimensions as the Apollo spacecraft, was launched from Florida, and was made to splash down into the ocean upon return. Along with such detailed foresight, however, Verne also includes a social commentary of how technology can erode the fabric of society: Technology makes the life easier for the human race, but it also introduces new weaponry that destroys lives. In *Twenty Thousand Leagues Under the Sea*, Captain Nemo is dehumanized and exiled by his own country and then uses technology to seek revenge. Afterward, he finds a home in *The Mysterious Island* where he can continue to experiment and build his machinery. Mired in a time when humanity was seen as pitted against the inevitable progress of technology, Verne uses Nemo's character to warn society of both the good and the evil of technological advances. Nemo's motto for *Nautilus*—*mobilis in mobili* (everything circulates)—is truly a lesson to keep in mind in an ever-changing world. Technology has far-reaching effects and does not occur in a vacuum. The wonders that technology presents are exciting and compelling to investigate, but society must weigh the costs involved against improvements to the quality of life and the aspirations of the human spirit. New technology may be readily available and may help humankind, but it may also tear irreparably at the fabric of society in the interest of progress.

Verne's works are classic, easy-to-read stories that will always be popular with readers of all ages. They are especially suited for the young adult audience because they speak to the uninhibited imagination and adventurous spirit of young people who can still believe that anything is possible.

Denise Marchionda

THE MYSTERY OF THE ANCIENT MAYA

Authors: Carolyn Mae Meyer (1935-   ) and Charles Gallenkamp (1930-   )
First published: 1985; illustrated
Type of work: History
Time of work: Prehistory to the mid-twentieth century
Locale: Guatemala, Yucatan, and Belize
Subjects: Race and ethnicity, religion, and travel
Recommended ages: 15-18

This compelling book tells the story of the headstrong explorers who faced personal peril to study and publicize the glory of the sophisticated Mayan civilization.

> *Principal personages:*
> THE MAYA, a highly civilized Central American populace
> JOHN LLOYD STEPHENS, the nineteenth century explorer-author whose writings publicized the magnificence of Mayan ruins
> FREDERICK CATHERWOOD, an artist who teamed with Stephens and whose pen-and-ink drawings gave the world its first detailed images of Mayan ruins
> DIEGO DELANDA, a bishop of the Yucatan, a self-professed savior of the Maya and the author of *Relación de las Cosas de Yucatán*, a complex, complete detail of Mayan daily life
> EDWARD HERBERT THOMPSON, an American scholar who lived in the Yucatan and studied the Maya for more than forty years
> ALFRED P. MAUDSLAY, an Englishmen archaeologist who quantified Maya research as a science
> ALBERTO RUZ LLUILLIER, an archaeologist from the Center for Maya Studies in Mexico whose research and digs provided substantial information about the Maya

Form and Content

The Mystery of the Ancient Maya suggests answers to the enigmatic demise of the Mayan civilization. Carolyn Mae Meyer and her coauthor Charles Gallenkamp follow the wanderlust and exploits of mid-nineteenth century explorers, adventurers, and thrill seekers. One such explorer, John Lloyd Stephens, journeyed to Guatemala to uncover significant ruins belonging to one of the most fascinating cultures of the Americas, the Maya. The book describes the unrelenting pursuit for a lost civilization that followed.

Meyer is a studious writer who actively becomes involved in her subject matter. Gallenkamp is an archaeologist, student of the Maya, and the author of several books about the subject and is highly respected by his peers. His solid archaeological expertise complements Meyer's writing style.

The book follows a chronological format when reviewing the explorations but reverts to past centuries in order to discuss the Mayan civilization, its rituals, lifestyle, sacrifices, and wars. The book's four parts describe the mid-nineteenth century exploration of Mayan ruins, the Mayan royalty, the day-to-day routine of a Mayan city, and theories about the disappearance of the Maya. Each section is well organized, although the omnipresent anecdotal lead-in becomes tiresome, if not confusing. Some beautifully detailed artistic renderings dot the verbal landscape and are accompanied by archival photographs and illustrations—of particular note are the representations of tomb paintings. Pen-and-ink drawings accurately illustrate the emblem glyphs, numerical graphics, and hieroglyphs of Mayan cities. Maps appropriately orient the reader. The index is strong enough to withstand detailed research within the book, and a three-page glossary clearly marks the pronunciation of Mayan terminology.

Although the book's language is technical at times, the authors carefully define their terms and the processes, items, or tools under discussion. Scientific, technical, archaeological, and Mayan terms are used accurately throughout the text, and most young readers will understand.

Analysis

The mystery of the Maya is their disappearance. Researchers, archaeologists, and historians have not satisfied their piqued curiosity about the lost culture. The Maya are not extinct: An estimated two million Indians of Mayan descent live in roughly the same geographical boundaries as their ancestors. These Maya are the second largest surviving indigenous American culture, after the Quechua of Peru and Bolivia. Long since divided into small, isolated groups, few Maya speak a tongue familiar to those of other Mayan populations.

John Lloyd Stephens, a lawyer in New York City who had the spirit of wanderlust, was one of the first nineteenth century explorers of the Mayan ruins. After working and traveling in the United States for a decade, he went on an extended vacation, on doctor's orders, to recover from an illness. Stephens spent two extravagant years roaming Europe and North Africa. Upon his return, his peers convinced him that a financial boon was his in the writing of travel books. He had met Frederick Catherwood, an architect and artist whose penchant for travel matched his own, and they began travel plans for the lands of the Maya. Despite travail and severe discomfort, they chopped their way to Copan in Guatemala and spent the next six months in discovery and drawing. The Copan chieftain was under pressure to rid the village of these interlopers, and Stephens miraculously arranged a deal that matches the heralded purchase of Manhattan: He bought Copan for fifty dollars.

Stephens and Catherwood continued their journeys—visiting, writing, drawing, and being astonished by ruins of a magnificent civilization. They suffered dismal weather and deplorable conditions, and they fought health problems that few could survive. The ruins of Palenque followed those of Copan, and the rainforests of Uxmal finally drove them from the land. They were exhausted, ill, and sick of each other's company. Stephens did write his book, which is still read, but he and Catherwood never traveled together again.

The Spanish *conquistadors* invaded the New World during the mid-sixteenth century, suppressing the descendants of the Maya and ignoring their historical significance. At the same time, Franciscan monks arrived from the Old World to convert the uneducated natives. Diego DeLanda became bishop of the Yucatan, and he brutally tortured the subdued descendants of the Mayan culture. He not only imprisoned, mutilated, and killed the natives but also systematically destroyed their cultural icons, including all written history, or codices. Eventually, DeLanda's superiors, furious at his actions, removed him from his post. Ironically, DeLanda provided the most accurate treatise on Mayan life and traditions as part of his punishment. He was ordered to write everything that he knew, resulting in *Relación de las Cosas de Yucatán*, a classic text still studied by modern-day researchers.

Edward Herbert Thompson felt the fire of enthusiasm for the Maya—called *Mayismo*—from reading Stephens' books. This gentle man knew at an early age his route in life and prepared himself by studying medicine (in order to care for himself), psychology (in order to develop positive relations with the natives), photography (for documentation), Spanish, and archaeology. Thompson's research at Chichen Itza in the upper Yucatan Peninsula revealed human sacrifice rituals in which the Maya threw victims into a well. Thompson verified the ritual by diving, in decrepit gear, to the bottom of the deep pool, where he gathered pottery, carved jades, copper bells, golden bowls, spears, and knives. In 1883, Alfred P. Maudslay established a research camp at Chichen Itza and confirmed Thompson's findings. In 1949, Alberto Ruz Lluillier made several important discoveries in the ruins at Palenque. He unearthed a stairway to a burial vault system used to hide the tombs of priests. His workers spent arduous months uncovering stairway passages that led to spectacular artifacts and, more important, increased knowledge about this civilization.

The concentration of material in the middle of *The Mystery of the Ancient Maya* offers detailed, documented facts about Mayan life, rituals, and traditions. The Mayan civilization featured beautiful art, intelligent hieroglyphs, superb time-marking systems, playfulness in the form of games, and religious fervor. The Mayans also practiced bloodletting, human sacrifice, games to the death, and brutal warfare. The descriptive text carries the reader through the average day of a Mayan child, relates the perspective of the average farmer, examines the Mayan royalty, and details the rituals that led many to their death.

The ultimate question of why the Mayan culture vanished requires careful response. Scientists are not in agreement concerning the fate of this sophisticated, advanced society. Meyer and Gallenkamp visit the theories and offer several accepted conclusions, but they leave the debate unfinished.

Critical Context

Carolyn Meyer has published dozens of fiction and nonfiction books for young adults, as well as several books for a middle-school audience. She is a hands-on author who relishes the learning experience that is involved in the writing process. In order to enhance her skills at character development, she may study kung fu, go camping and kayaking, and research quicksand, wildflowers, plastic surgery, and opera—all for one novel. One of her series, *Hotline,* demanded knowledge of suicide hotline operators, and so she became a volunteer for a year. Meyer enjoys doing her homework.

Although Meyer has written many crafts and how-to books, she is no stranger to descriptive writing about cultures and peoples. In the United States, she studied crafts and craftspeople for *People Who Make Things: How American Craftsmen Live and Work* (1975); immersed herself in the Amish community for *Amish People: Plain Living in a Complex World* (1976); and presented a viable point of view in *Eskimos: Growing Up in a Changing Culture* (1977). Meyer has also analyzed other cultures and other times; she traveled to Africa to explore the southern part of the continent and wrote *Voices of South Africa: Growing Up in a Troubled Land* (1986). She repeated this successful formula for books about the Irish and Japanese cultures.

Consequently, it was not a huge step for Meyer to team with Charles Gallenkamp for their corroborative study of the Maya. Gallenkamp, a scholar, archaeologist, and compiler, organized a traveling exhibit of Mayan artifacts called "Maya: Treasures of an Ancient Civilization."

Craig Gilbert

THE NATURAL

Author: Bernard Malamud (1914-1986)
First published: 1952
Type of work: Novel
Type of plot: Allegory
Time of work: The early 1920's and fifteen years later
Locale: Primarily New York and Chicago
Subjects: Sexual issues and sports
Recommended ages: 15-18

This novel teaches about heroism and how difficult it is to achieve success if one is unwilling to grow up and take responsibility for one's actions.

> *Principal characters:*
> ROY HOBBS, a man trying to achieve greatness in major league baseball
> IRIS LEMON, a young single mother who gives Roy emotional support
> MEMO, a glamorous young woman whom Roy loves
> HARRIET BIRD, a crazed young woman who shoots Roy
> JUDGE BANNER, the principal owner of the New York Knights baseball team
> POP FISHER, the manager and part-owner of the Knights
> MAX MERCY, a newspaper sports reporter
> GUS SANDS, a shadowy underworld figure working for gambling concerns

Form and Content

The Natural is the account of a talented athlete who wants to play major league baseball more than anything in the world. The story opens when Roy Hobbs is about nineteen and traveling from somewhere out west to Chicago for a tryout with the Cubs. After winning a pitching contest against a major leaguer named Whammer Whambold, he attracts the attention of a crazed young woman, Harriet Bird. She follows him to a hotel in the city and, after inviting him to her room, shoots him as he enters. The material in this section is entitled "Pre-game."

The second and much longer part of the novel is entitled "Batter-Up!" Roy reappears at the age of thirty-four after signing to play for the New York Knights. The intervening years are a mystery. Well past his prime to start major league baseball, he surprises the manager, Pop Fisher, and the rest of the team with his skill. He is so good that he begins to give them hope of winning a pennant. Roy's big chance for a starting position as well as for love begins when a player named Bump Bailey dies from an injury in the outfield, thereby vacating that position and leaving behind his beautiful girlfriend, Memo Paris, who is also Pop Fisher's niece.

Roy's relationship with Memo begins to interfere with his ability to play ball, so much so that Roy sees everything that he has a dreamed about for so long threaten to disappear. He falls into a midseason slump and becomes the object of fans' derision. At a game in Chicago, however, Iris Lemon, a young woman who has followed his career, literally and symbolically stands up in the bleachers for Roy. As if by magic, he hits one into the stands. At this point in the story, Bernard Malamud's direction becomes clear. How Roy Hobbs deals with these two women is symbolic of the choices all people make. Iris and Memo are opposite forces: To choose the first, who is good, is to risk suffering, but to choose the second, who is beautiful but dangerous, is to court disaster.

Roy's life becomes more complicated when newspaper reporter Max Mercy thinks that he recognizes Roy from the unsavory shooting incident fifteen years before. It is also revealed that Memo is primarily interested in men with money and is not interested in how they earn it. She is involved with an underworld figure, Gus Sands, and he is involved with Judge Banner, who is trying to wrest total control of the team from Pop Fisher.

Ultimately, they concoct a way to bribe the Knights players, including Roy Hobbs, to throw the World Series. They bet heavily on the Knights to lose because then the Judge can force Pop to relinquish ownership of the team: Pop has agreed to sell his shares to Judge Banner if the team does not win the World Series that year. The team does indeed lose, and Roy is the player who makes the final out in a pitcher-batter duel that is riveting to read. Roy returns the thirty-five dollars in bribe money to the evil trio of Judge Banner, Max, and Memo. He understands that he has not learned from his mistakes of the past and that the cycle of suffering must begin all over again.

Analysis

The meaning of *The Natural* can be readily understood but readily denied, which is what makes the novel interesting. Malamud makes the case that life involves suffering and, hopefully, learning from that suffering. When one does not learn, the cycle starts again. In Roy Hobbs's case, his youthful, nearly fatal attraction to the young Harriet Bird could be understood and forgiven. His infantile attachment to Memo Paris cannot, however, especially given the alternative of Iris Lemon. Iris explains to Roy the suffering and learning in her own life, which has included single motherhood and the fact that she is a grandmother at the age of thirty-three. Roy cannot cope with a mature woman or relationship. To his ultimate regret, he single-mindedly pursues the glamorous, gold-digging Memo.

Iris Lemon is Malamud's idea of a realistic, good person. Through her, the most eloquent ideas of heroism in the modern world are voiced. She pleads with Roy to be a hero because the world has so few of them and because children especially need them so desperately. Her name is also symbolic of the real world: It consists of both a flower and a sour fruit, just as life is a mixture of the beautiful and the bitter.

The novel is particularly interesting for its brilliant incorporation of both Arthurian legend and factual information related to American baseball history.

Roy's first name is derived from the French word *roi*, meaning "king." He comes to save a baseball team called the Knights with the bat Wonderboy, a weapon reminiscent of Arthur's sword, Excaliber. Memo can be seen as a kind of Guinevere or Morgan le Fay. The forces of evil are embodied in Judge Banner, Gus Sands, and Max Mercy. Magic works in the story much like it does in Arthurian legend. The elements of lightning and rain punctuate events. There is even a collection of weird characters, usually in the stands at games, similar to the dwarves and jesters found in Arthur's court.

The entire novel is also loosely based on the World Series scandal of 1919, when the Chicago White Sox (which came to be known as the Black Sox) was accused of throwing the World Series. The White Sox owner was the infamous Charlie Comiskey, and Judge Banner's nastiness is not coincidental. The team included such famous players as Shoeless Joe Jackson, Eddie Cicotte, and Happy Felsch. The last spoken line of the novel is based on the perhaps apocryphal plea that a newspaper boy shouted to Shoeless Joe after his trial: "Say it ain't so, Joe."

The character of Roy Hobbs also has some basis in the legendary Babe Ruth. Ruth was an orphan, and, although Hobbs mentions his parents, the reader is led to believe that he was deserted by them. Both Ruth and Hobbs started their careers as pitchers and ended them in the outfield. Both were womanizers. In real life, Babe Ruth hit a home run for a sick little boy in the hospital, as Roy Hobbs does in the novel. Finally, Ruth died of stomach cancer, and Hobbs is hospitalized during the World Series for excruciating stomach pains that are apparently life-threatening.

Critical Context

In all the works that Bernard Malamud wrote, the theme of suffering and the necessity of learning from it is a major concern. He does not romanticize this theme, however, and restricts his characters' advancements only to learning from their suffering. Rarely do his characters triumph, at least not in the usual American sense of that word. For Malamud, life is a perpetual struggle. Perhaps the best illustration of the difficulty that American readers experience in dealing with this concept can be seen in the happily-ever-after ending given to the story in the film version of *The Natural* (1984), which starred Robert Redford.

The Natural is the Malamud novel most likely to appeal to young adult readers, because most of his protagonists are much older and still going through the cycle in which Roy is found in his thirties. This novel was not written specifically for teenagers, but that may indeed be part of its attraction. Young people are given insights into the adult world to which they look for leaders and heroes, and they learn how confusing and difficult that world is even for adults.

Judith L. Steininger

NEVER TO FORGET
The Jews of the Holocaust

Author: Milton Meltzer (1915-   )
First published: 1976
Type of work: History
Time of work: 1933-1945
Locale: Northern Europe, primarily Germany, Poland, Ukraine, France, Belgium, Holland, Austria, and the Soviet Union
Subjects: Death, race and ethnicity, religion, and war
Recommended ages: 15-18

Meltzer chronicles German dictator Adolf Hitler's movement to exterminate the European Jewish population in the 1930's and 1940's by examining the history of hatred against the Jews, the systematic murder of Jewish people in Hitler's Germany, and the Jewish resistance movement.

Principal personages:
ADOLF HITLER, the German dictator and Nazi Party leader in the 1930's and 1940's
CHAIM KAPLAN, a Holocaust victim whose diary of his years in the Warsaw Ghetto has survived
M. I. LIBAU, a fourteen-year-old Berlin resident who survived *Kristallnacht* (the night of broken glass)
RIVKA YOSSELEVSCHA, a Ukrainian Jewish woman who survived attempted execution by the German army
REUBEN ROSENBERG, a survivor of four Nazi death camps, including Monowitz, the slave labor camp attached to Auschwitz
PRIMO LEVI, an Italian chemist and Auschwitz survivor
ABRAHAM LISPER, a Polish youth who survived by jumping off the train transporting his family to Auschwitz and hiding for two years underground
SIMA, a twelve-year-old resistance fighter from Minsk

Form and Content

Never to Forget: The Jews of the Holocaust is Milton Meltzer's highly personalized look at the attempted extermination of an entire ethnic group during the 1930's and 1940's. Meltzer looks specifically at the years between 1933, when the Nazi Party came to power in Germany, through 1945, the year that it lost power. During those twelve years, two out of every three Jews in Europe were murdered. These events are known collectively as the Holocaust.

The work is divided into three sections, labeled books. Book 1 deals with the history of hatred, persecution, and discrimination directed against Jews. The background of how and why the Holocaust occurred in Germany and the events leading to Adolf Hitler's rise to power are explored in five chapters. Although Germany is the country in which modern anti-Semitism reached its zenith, the roots of discrimination against Jews goes back much further in history. The accusation that the Jews were to blame for the crucifixion of Jesus was used to make them outcasts in society as early as the fourth century. This popular and enduring hatred of Jews was systematically exploited by Hitler. Through a well-orchestrated propaganda campaign, Hitler used anti-Semitism brilliantly to unite the German people. Jews were portrayed as parasites on society and blamed for the ills of post-World War I Germany. While persecution of Jews was not new, the Nazi anti-Semitism was preached with a boundless fury, beyond the portrayal of Jews as scapegoats or inferiors to charges that they were the cause of every major problem—and thus, the solution to all problems existed in the elimination of the Jews. As the persecution and violence escalated against the Jewish population, no one intervened. Hitler continued until the plan called the Final Solution was in place: the death of all Jews.

This Final Solution, the systematic destruction of the Jewish population as carried out by Hitler's government, is the subject of book 2. The historic tragedy unfolds as told through first-person narratives, eyewitness accounts, and surviving diaries of Holocaust victims. Starting with November 9, 1938, the *Kristallnacht* (the night of broken glass), a nationwide German program in which the Nazis destroyed Jewish shops, synagogues, businesses, and homes, Meltzer takes the readers through the Holocaust years. Stories from the Warsaw Ghetto, mass murders in Germany and Russia, and life in the concentration camps are chronicled.

Book 3 tells the story of Jewish resistance to the Holocaust. One question asked in the third part of *Never to Forget* is "How could the Jewish people fight back?" Another question examined is "What degree of resistance existed among non-Jews?" Hitler's army swept over Europe with incredible speed. How could Jews who had nothing retaliate? Nevertheless, many Jews did. Resistance fighters, those who worked underground and those who organized violent rebellion, are profiled. Included in the story of the resistance is the rebuilding process that the Jews faced at the end of World War II. Those who survived had no family, no home, and a difficult future. Although the Jewish homeland of Israel was created, it was not a peaceful land. For Jews, the Holocaust had nearly been their destruction. It happened once; it could happen again.

The book is supported with maps, a comprehensive index, and a chronology. Chapter notes and source documentation are provided. An extensive bibliography is included, as well as statistical data and charts concerning the death toll of the Holocaust.

Analysis

Meltzer begins with the question "Why remember?" It is his belief the Holocaust did not occur in a vacuum. It was the logical outcome of certain conditions; given the nature of Nazi beliefs, the crime of the Holocaust could be expected. Because the world of Hitler is not totally alien to the world today, according to Meltzer, the

Holocaust must be examined in order to understand why it happened and to prevent it from happening again.

This examination is at a very personal level. The author recalls how he felt as a teenage Jewish boy in the United States reading newspaper accounts about Hitler and the Nazis. Young Meltzer found the knowledge terrifying that Jewish people lived under a threat. He asked what most people would ask, "Could that happen to me?" In order to create this personal perspective of history, Meltzer relies on the eyewitness accounts of those who experienced the Holocaust. The truth does not consist of merely the facts and figures of the Holocaust but is found through the stories of those who experienced the terror and grief. Meltzer articulates the meaning of being set apart by something over which one has no control not only through his own experiences but through those of others as well. What sets Meltzer apart from other nonfiction writers for young adults is his use of a definite point of view in his work. He usually does not attempt to present more than one side of his story, and *Never to Forget* is told totally from the Jewish perspective.

Never to Forget also deals with the basic conflict of good against evil. The Holocaust demonstrated that all people have the capacity to be both good and evil. It is the story of those who treated other human beings as less than human and the story of those who tried to resist or held out a helping hand. Forces exist that can cut off human response and make it possible to be evil without feeling responsibility; this is how the massacre of a whole people can be organized by a government. The individual conscience vanishes when given orders from superiors or perceived superiors. Not enough people in Nazi Germany said "no" to the Holocaust. Meltzer wonders what would have happened if more people, not only in Germany, but in the rest of the world had said "no." Would the Holocaust have happened? Readers are confronted with the dilemma of what would they have done in this situation.

Critical Context

Never to Forget makes an important contribution to the understanding of one of the most tragic events in history by making it a personal story. The tragedy that befell one group of people is presented by sharing the experiences of a few who lived it; this approach is responsible for the powerful impact of many of Milton Meltzer's works. This personal face on history offers a different perspective to those readers who may know of the Holocaust only from a few paragraphs in a history text or a list of facts.

Meltzer demonstrates an awareness of his audience, the young adult reader. His books seek to help adolescents become aware of themselves and their role in society by leading readers to ask "Would I have done that?" or "How could people have allowed this to happen?" Many of the voices heard in *Never to Forget* are those of young adults. This book can serve as validation that young people can make their voices be heard and make a difference in their world.

Twelve years after he wrote *Never to Forget*, Meltzer addressed the Holocaust again in *Rescue: The Story of How Gentiles Saved Jews in the Holocaust* (1988). This book tells the stories of some of those courageous people who aided the Jews. Once again, Meltzer puts a personal face on history by using first-person accounts to tell the story, and he leads the reader to ask "Would I be able to do that?" These two works are recommended reading for young adults studying World War II, the Holocaust, and Jewish history.

Meltzer has been quoted as saying "the writer's voice must be heard on the pages of the book." Whatever he writes comes out of his own personality and experiences. In *Never to Forget*, Meltzer's voice provides insights to the experiences of those caught in the nightmare of the Holocaust.

Jane Claes

THE NEVERENDING STORY

Author: Michael Ende (1929-1995)
First published: Die Unendliche Geschichte, 1979 (English translation, 1983)
Type of work: Novel
Type of plot: Fantasy
Time of work: The 1970's
Locale: The attic of a school and the imaginary world of Fantastica
Subjects: Animals and the supernatural
Recommended ages: 10-15

A misfit boy steals a magical book and is absorbed into its text, where he learns about the marvelous opportunities and problematic seductions of fantasy.

>   *Principal characters:*
>   BASTIAN BALTHASAR BUX, an ineffectual schoolboy
>   CARL CONRAD COREANDER, a mysterious bookseller
>   THE CHILDLIKE EMPRESS, the ruler of Fantastica
>   ATREYU, a young hero
>   CAIRON, an old centaur
>   MORLA THE AGED ONE, a giant turtle
>   FALKOR, a luckdragon
>   DAME EYOLA, the matriarch of the House of Change

Form and Content

The Neverending Story is an extended fable detailing the rewards and hazards of escapism. The text is typeset in two colors, with sequences occurring in the world of Bastian Balthasar Bux being set in red and the story that he is reading reproduced in green. In the early phases of the novel, Bastian's world and the world of the book-within-the-book are distinct, but they gradually intersect until Bastian is incorporated into the story that he is reading.

The miserable and overweight Bastian, whose widower father is a remote figure and who lives in fear of the ridicule of his schoolfellows, takes refuge in an attic so that he may read a book called *The Neverending Story,* which he has stolen from a strange shop and its mysterious bookseller. He discovers that the story is set in Fantastica, an imaginary world whose outlying regions are being consumed by Nothing—an affliction whose onset corresponded with the illness of the Childlike Empress, who lives in the Ivory Tower.

The empress divines that the hero who can save the world is one Atreyu, and she commissions the centaur Cairon to give him the talisman AURYN. Cairon is alarmed to find that Atreyu is a mere boy but sends him forth nevertheless on the Great Quest.

In the Swamps of Sadness, Atreyu learns from Morla the Aged One that the empress can only be healed if someone from outside Fantastica gives her a new name. After encountering the monster Ygramul the Many, Atreyu and the luckdragon Falkor brave the baleful sphinxes that guard the Great Riddle Gate, the first of three through which he must pass in order to reach Uyulala, the Southern Oracle. Uyulala tells Atreyu that only a human can give the Childlike Empress a new name but that humans have forgotten how to enter Fantastica. Subsequently, Atreyu discovers that humans are, in fact, bent on Fantastica's destruction, not realizing that the health of the human world and the health of Fantastica are dependent on each other.

Atreyu returns to the Ivory Tower to confess his failure to the Childlike Empress, but she is able to look out from the text at Bastian, who realizes that her new name is Moon Child. The Childlike Empress also has a book called *The Neverending Story*; at her command, the Old Man of the Wandering Mountains begins to write in its pages the story of Bastian Balthasar Bux, which has already been set in red, thus drawing him into the green-set text to give the Childlike Empress her new name. This event occurs at the half-way point of the novel.

The remainder of the green-set text tells how Bastian is rewarded by becoming the possessor of AURYN and having all of his wishes granted. He uses this gift to save Fantastica all over again from various new enemies, but ultimately he becomes ambitious to establish himself as the Childlike Emperor. Atreyu is forced to raise a rebel army against him, and, although he cannot be defeated, Bastian is brought to recognize the extent to which unlimited power has corrupted him.

The humbled Bastian sets forth on a Great Quest of his own to figure out how best to use his wishes—and how to get back to his own world. In the House of Change, he encounters the maternal Dame Eyola, who sets him on the right path. In the end, he must willingly surrender everything that the Childlike Empress gave him and drink the Water of Life in order to return to reality.

When he does so, Bastian finds that although many years have passed in Fantastica, he has only been away one night in the real world. Fortunately, even that brief absence has persuaded his neglectful father to take notice of him, and the mysterious bookseller reappears to prophesy that he will one day become a writer who will show many others the way to Fantastica, from which they will bring back abundant supplies of the Water of Life.

Analysis

The Neverending Story is an allegory that provides a neat analysis of the psychological functions of fantasy and eloquent propaganda for its use. The imaginary world of Fantastica provides a refuge for the unhappy child who is as alienated from his father as he is from his peers. At first a mere fellow traveler with Atreyu, Bastian eventually discovers that in Fantastica he can become anything he wants to be—all that he has to do is make up the story for himself. One of the first things that he does after receiving the gift of the Childlike Empress is to conjure up an imposing library filled with his own works, which presages the bookseller's judgment that Bastian's encounter with *The Neverending Story* will make a writer of him.

In providing this conclusion, Michael Ende accepts the common suspicion that the kind of creativity that remains secret and self-centered may be unhealthy but insists that the power of creativity is nevertheless uniquely precious. The healthy use of fantasy, in this way of thinking, is to derive some benefit from it that can be carried back to the real world, and Ende takes this view seriously enough to suggest that the prize that can be carried back is the "Water of Life" itself: something not merely useful but actually vital to enrichment of everyday existence.

The moral of *The Neverending Story*, therefore, is that fantasy—far from being a threat to the ability to live in the real world—is the natural and invaluable partner of reason and common sense, provided that one can move easily back and forth across the boundary separating fantasy and reality and provided that the world of fantasy can be constantly renewed by the efforts of new fantasists. (This moral is travestied in the film version of the novel, released in 1984, which only reproduces the first half of the plot and thus ignores Bastian's education in responsibility.)

As with all honest fantasies, *The Neverending Story* is in some respects a victim of its own frankness. It is utterly and unashamedly a boys' book. Its careful development of Bastian's fantasies is relentlessly masculine, not so much by virtue of its heavy concentration on masculine endeavors as by virtue of its curious idolization of feminine archetypes such as the Childlike Empress and Dame Eyola. Few female readers would be inconvenienced by the task of identifying with Atreyu's adventures in derring-do, or even Bastian's imitations thereof, but many might be hard-pressed to empathize with the reverence afforded to one character whose main narrative function is to be pathetically ill and another whose sole function is to provide an implausibly saintly mother-figure for a boy who has lost his real mother. Presumably, the author could not have done otherwise without resorting to a measure of artifice that would have robbed the book of some of its intensity; it is when writing fantasies that authors are most likely to reveal themselves most fully and most intimately.

The Neverending Story is rather vague in detailing exactly what Bastian does bring back from his experience, apart from the ability to become a writer. It is the fact of his temporary absence rather than anything he has learned that improves his relationship with his father, and it is not clear that he will be any better equipped to face the school bullies. Ende is, however, wise not to overstate the value of fantasy (as the film ludicrously does by importing the luckdragon into the real world). The Water of Life has provided Bastian with psychological refreshment by raising his spirits, offering him an arena in which he can be free of his physical limitations, and confirming the potential of his own creativity. As the story admits, this is not power in any vulgar sense, but it is a kind of mental strength that everyone requires.

Critical Context

Many fantasy novels make a case for the necessity of fantasy, but few have ever done so as elaborately and as steadfastly as *The Neverending Story*. The book sold more than a million hardcover copies in its native country of Germany—a success which emphasizes that although the story is designed for children, the message it contains is relevant to everyone. Its allegorical apparatus aims to be universal, occasionally echoing devices from mythology and folklore (as with the centaur Cairon) but refusing any single anchorage. The novel appeared when fantasy role-playing games were becoming widely popular, and it has many parallels to them.

Brian Stableford

THE NIGHT JOURNEY

Author: Kathryn Lasky (1944-   )
First published: 1981; illustrated
Type of work: Novel
Type of plot: Historical fiction and psychological realism
Time of work: 1900 and the early 1980's
Locale: Russia and Minnesota
Subjects: Family and social issues
Recommended ages: 10-15

> *Thirteen-year-old Rachel learns about the importance of family and connections in time from her great-grandmother's story of escape from the persecution and pogroms of czarist Russia.*

Principal characters:
> RACHEL LEWIS, a thirteen-year-old girl who helps her great-grandmother relive childhood memories
> SASHIE, Rachel's great-grandmother, who tells the story of her escape from czarist Russia when she was nine years old
> JOE, Sashie's father, a machinist
> GISHA, Sashie's young unmarried aunt, an excellent seamstress
> IDA, Sashie's mother
> ED, Rachel's father
> LEAH, Rachel's mother and Sashie's granddaughter
> WOLF, a man haunted by his past who helps the family escape
> REUVEN BLOOM, a second man who assists the family, who later becomes Sashie's husband

Form and Content

The Night Journey connects Sashie's childhood experiences in czarist Russia with her great-granddaughter Rachel's experiences at home and at school in the United States. The story within a story shifts back and forth from the dangerous plotting and journey out of Russia to Rachel's secure life. Rachel is expected to spend time visiting with her "old old" great-grandmother about topics of conversation that are approved by her family. Both she and Nana Sashie are displeased with this arrangement: Rachel wants to hear the story that Sashie wants to tell about her family's life in and escape from Russia. Sashie tells Rachel the tale in small segments in their private time together, often in the middle of the night when Rachel sneaks into her great-grandmother's room. In the contemporary story, Rachel is involved in coaching her friend in the lead part for the school musical, an interesting counterpoint to the guise of Purim players that Sashie's family uses for their escape. The stories also intertwine when Rachel finds the top piece of the family's samovar (an urn with a spigot used for making tea) when rummaging though the scrap box for costume material. In honor of Leah's birthday, Ed manages to reconstruct an authentic samovar, which Nana Sashie insists on keeping in her room.

The larger portion of the escape story is devoted to the planning and preparation rather than to the actual events of the escape. Sashie has overheard the adults talk of escape and of their frustration with their inability to devise a plan. One night, she conceives a plan of traveling as Purim players. Sashie's family members lend their strengths to solve each of the problems to be encountered on the journey: Her mother, Ida, bakes the gold to be used as a bribe into *hamantaschen* (hat-shaped cookies); her aunt, Gisha, sews Purim costumes that can be reversed to resemble peasant dress; and her father, Joe, wins the trust of Wolf, who devises a plan to carry them out of town in a wagon under a load of chickens. Each person is allowed to take one special item. Gisha brings a photograph of herself and a friend with Sashie, Sashie chooses a cloth book that Gisha had made of scenes of Nikolayev, and Joe brings his box of tools. Ida chooses the samovar even though it seems an unwise choice because of its size. She wears its top as a crown for her costume, and the cookies are packed in the other part. Narrowly escaping detection by the czar's soldiers, Wolf with his quick thinking is able to get them to the countryside, where Reuven Bloom provides a wagon, a hot meal, and an open-air violin concert. Sashie is moved by the passion of the man and his music and knows that their paths will meet again.

The incidents that occur as the family drives to the border are sometimes light-hearted, sometimes sad, and sometimes frightening. Sashie feels all things—from the wide night sky, to the colors and sights of the forest, to her aunt's sadness at leaving behind a life that she loved. The tension builds as they twice encounter a band of soldiers. They pass the first time in the Purim costumes and the second time as a mourning Christian family in peasant clothing. Although tense, the actual border crossing is also humorous as Sashie, in her anger that the bribed guard is taking the samovar, switches the gold-filled cookies for ordinary ones. As the family members celebrate the escape, they discover, even to Sashie's surprise, that most of their remaining cookies contain gold.

The book is written using third-person narration, but in the epilogue the reader learns that the writer is a nineteen-year-old Rachel, who has matured and gained perspective, as well as more details about the story, in the intervening years.

The black-and-white drawings by Trina Schart Hyman help convey the strengths of the characters and, with their romantic quality, the mood and passion of the story. The illustrations provide a sense of time and place for both the contemporary story and the tale from the past.

Analysis

The two stories within the novel are deftly woven together. The contemporary scenes are often humorous, and the characters' relationships are conveyed convincingly. Kathryn Lasky maintains the tension of Nana Sashie's story even though it is revealed bit by bit with intervening events in the contemporary story. The balance between the two stories is such that the reader is kept focused on Nana Sashie's story, which is illuminated by the contemporary events. For example, readers find out about Joe's toolbox and Sashie's mechanical abilities early in the story as she fixes a valve for the dishwasher. Since there is not a strict pattern of alternate chapter presentation of the two stories, readers must be alert at the beginning of each chapter to place themselves in the appropriate time frame. The transitions between the stories are smooth, however, and the timing of the events in the dual plots is well-conceived. For example, the newly acquired samovar is revealed just in time so that the recounting of the escape can be told in the glow of its light.

The portrayal of warm supportive families in both stories links the past and the present. The contrast between life in the two time periods poignantly reveals the real meaning of freedom. The inclusion of the Purim story also illuminates the theme of freedom that permeates the novel, illustrating the centuries-long struggle for freedom of the Jewish people. This theme is directly stated at the end of the book with Joe's toast, "To all of us, not just here at this table but all over the world, who love freedom, for we are the best lovers!"

A second idea explored in the book is the interweaving of lives across time. Rachel tells readers that "'time marching on' is a bore and it is the circles and deviations of time that makes time curiously alive." Nana Sashie's story involves young Rachel by using the past to understand the present and give insight into the future. Yet, it is not only time that is alive; the people and the stories are alive as well. Even though readers may be saddened by Sashie's death, they realize that she will continue through her story and through Rachel. The complexity of Nana Sashie's character is reflected in Rachel, who exhibits her spunk and her passion for life. The samovar, the tool box, and the photograph of the young Sashie are symbolic reminders of the continuity of life.

Readers are reminded that all people need to listen to the stories of others in order to have a wider perspective on life, both the storytellers' and their own. Rachel and Sashie's relationship demonstrates that people of very different ages can be brought close together through the continuity of a shared story. Although the author offers an intricate and well-developed plot, she leaves one story waiting to be told. Sashie and Reuven were reunited ten years after the escape, but readers do not know how he came to the United States to become a famous musician; they are left wondering if Lasky will write this story in the future.

Critical Context

Comparatively little fiction about this phase of Jewish history has been written for young adults. Readers often learn more about the significance of events in a historical period by identifying with individuals who have experienced those events rather than from reading numbers, dates, and generalizations of facts. Kathryn Lasky has made a strong contribution to this understanding with her compelling story of one family's ordeal. The traditions, stories, and customs included in *The Night Journey* not only add to the richness of the story but also foster understanding of the Jewish heritage. For her contribution in this area, Lasky received the National Jewish Book Award for *The Night Journey* in 1982.

Carol Lauritzen

NIGHT KITES

Author: M. E. Kerr (Marijane Meaker, 1927-   )
First published: 1986
Type of work: Novel
Type of plot: Social realism
Time of work: The early 1980's
Locale: Seaville and New York City, New York
Subjects: Coming-of-age, family, friendship, health and illness, and sexual issues
Recommended ages: 13-18

Erick Rudd struggles with his physical attraction to off-beat Nicki Marr, his best friend's girlfriend, while trying to deal with his own, and his family's, reaction to learning that his older brother, Pete, is gay and has contracted AIDS.

Principal characters:
　　ERICK RUDD, a seventeen-year-old high school senior who has always been part of the popular crowd at Seaville High
　　JACK, a star athlete at Seaville High and Erick's best friend since grade school
　　"DILL" DILBERTO, a cheerleader at Seaville High and Erick's long-time girlfriend
　　NICKI MARR, a seventeen-year-old girl with a reputation for being "fast"
　　PETE RUDD, Erick's older brother, a French teacher and an aspiring writer who lives in an apartment in New York City
　　ARTHUR RUDD, Erick and Pete's father, a straight-laced corporate executive who usually spends his weekdays at an apartment in New York City
　　MRS. RUDD, Erick and Pete's mother, a housewife who occupies her time with local theater and charitable works

Form and Content
Night Kites was one of the first novels for young adults to deal with the issue of acquired immunodeficiency syndrome (AIDS). M. E. Kerr has woven the problems confronting a family that must cope with this devastating illness into a coming-of-age story of a young man struggling with his emerging sexual attraction for his best friend's seductive girlfriend. Much of the action of the novel is set against the small town of Seaville, New York, which was "practically founded" by Mrs. Rudd's family. The upper-middle-class setting of the Rudd home provides a striking contrast to Kingdom by the Sea, the motel owned by Nicki Marr's father. Once a tourist attraction with rooms, a restaurant, and a pool named after the writings of Edgar Allan Poe, it now resembles a run-down amusement park.

Kerr weaves complex ideas and emotions into a simple, first-person narrative told from the viewpoint of seventeen-year-old Erick Rudd. In the second chapter, she provides readers with a foreshadowing of the contrasts that dominate this novel. Erick remembers a time when he was five years old and Pete was fifteen. Pete had made a special kite, a "night kite," for Erick with battery lights strung around its edges. Night kites are different, Pete told Erick, and, like night kites, some people are different too.

Until his senior year in high school, Erick's life had been uncomplicated: dates with his girlfriend, Dill; spending time with his best friend, Jack; working in the bookstore where Pete had worked. Then Jack began dating blond, green-eyed Nicki Marr, who is "seventeen going on twenty-five" and openly attracted to Erick. Nicki persuades Erick to arrange a weekend in New York City for the four of them, staying in Pete's apartment. When Dill and Erick return from a visit to Dill's aunt, they are surprised to find Arthur Rudd, Erick's father, waiting for them. Pete is very ill and, as their father explains privately to Erick, has been diagnosed with AIDS.

In the weeks that follow, the family tries to cope with Pete's homosexuality and his devastating illness. Mr. Rudd, who had always been critical of Pete, seems unable to refrain from the patronizing comments that place him in conflict with Pete and the rest of the family. Angry exchanges become commonplace, and, as Erick observes, the family is "coming apart at the seams." Meanwhile, Erick gives in to his physical desire for Nicki, thereby losing both Dill and Jack from his life. Soon, he is isolated from his friends, spending more and more time at Kingdom by the Sea. When Nicki and her father learn that Pete has AIDS, however, Nicki turns on Erick, refusing to see him and finally taking a new boyfriend. Erick becomes a loner and spends more time with Pete, who observes that his father's "old chestnuts," such as "family first," suddenly sound good to him.

Analysis

Although the story is told simply through first-person narration by its seventeen-year-old protagonist, *Night Kites* is a complex novel with many subthemes: AIDS, sexuality, family issues, friendship, and maturity. These themes are explored through contrasts: adolescent heterosexuality versus homosexuality; upper-middle-class support and conflict among the Rudds versus the permissiveness of Captain Marr; belonging among the popular crowd versus the rejection of the loner; physical desire versus friendship; loving relationships that, under stress, either falter or grow stronger. Kerr has chosen to display unconventional behavior against a background of conformity, providing glimpses of the positive and negative aspects of both. She makes no overt value judgments; however, despite anxiety, anger, and conflict, family loyalty remains a clear theme throughout the book. The contrast between the conventional and the unconventional in this novel is symbolized by the "night kite" that Pete made for his younger brother. Most kites fly in the daytime, Pete says, but some go up in the dark. They go up alone, and they are not afraid to be different. Pete is a night kite, but Erick sees himself as cautious and conservative—definitely "the regular day kind" of kite.

As Erick interacts with the two significant "night kites" in the novel, Pete and

Nicki, he learns much about himself and the important people in his life. Fleeing his father's anger and confusion over Pete's illness, Erick turns to the solace of a physical relationship with Nicki. By doing so, he loses his comfortable ties to Dill and Jack. Suddenly, he, too, is living like a night kite. His feelings toward this new role are ambivalent—sometimes incredible loneliness, and sometimes soaring too high to care: "And always, there was Pete on my mind." When Erick finally accepts Nicki's rejection of him, he comes to realize that he, just like Pete, is completely on his own. Yet, by the end of the story, he and Pete have grown closer. They recognize that, although change is inevitable, there are sweet parts of life still to be enjoyed.

Kerr has treated the issue of homosexuality and AIDS subtly. Pete's desire to keep his sexual orientation a secret while still at home, and his promiscuity when he finally moves to an accepting environment, is presented as an understandable reaction to these different circumstances. Through various characters, Kerr presents the spectrum of the responses to Pete's homosexuality and illness that might be anticipated in real life: Erick's ready acceptance and support; Mr. Marr's anger and embarrassment despite his love for his son; Mrs. Marr's attempt to understand; Nicki's fear of contracting AIDS through her relationship with Erick; and the homophobic reaction of Toledo and Captain Marr.

Nicki, like Pete, is a "night kite," unable or unwilling to become part of the popular crowd at Seaville High, and through her character Kerr shows both the weaknesses and vulnerabilities of the loner. As Jack's girlfriend, she is offered the opportunity to "fit in," but she chooses instead to antagonize Dill by ignoring her and overtly attempting to attract Dill's boyfriend. When she succeeds in luring Erick away from Dill, she pulls Erick into her world but is comfortable only when they are alone together in her familiar environment at Kingdom by the Sea. After Nicki rejects Erick when she discovers that his brother has AIDS, her character is further revealed. Nicki, who once wanted Erick because she thought that he did not like her, attracts a new boyfriend, Roman Knight, about whom Nicki had once said, "See, that sleazeball doesn't like me." Throughout the story, Kerr shows Nicki struggling for acceptance in the only way in which she knows, through her sexuality, and losing interest once she has captivated those who once rejected her.

Critical Context

Night Kites introduced AIDS as a subject to be explored in fiction for young adults. In 1986, when this book was published, information about AIDS was not very accessible. The presentation of AIDS within the context of homosexuality and promiscuity is consistent with the time period in which this novel was written; because Pete contracted AIDS, it was assumed that he was gay and had been promiscuous. While this assumption can no longer be made in the light of the universality of the AIDS epidemic, it does not deter from the overall effectiveness of the novel. By focusing on the events in Erick's life that were caused by, or affected by, his brother's illness, M. E. Kerr has created a coming-of-age story that continues to be relevant for young adults.

Night Kites, like many of Kerr's other novels, depicts events that influence the movement of the protagonist from adolescence to adulthood. Her novels do this by presenting both adult and adolescent characters who are realistic and well-rounded. Since many novels for young adults focus on the earlier stages of adolescence, with adult characters who are untrustworthy or stereotypical, Kerr's novels, regardless of topic, continue to have an important place in young adult literature.

Constance A. Mellon

NIGHTS WITH UNCLE REMUS

Author: Joel Chandler Harris (1848-1908)
First published: 1883; illustrated
Type of work: Novel
Type of plot: Folktale and moral tale
Time of work: Before the American Civil War
Locale: A plantation in Putnam County, Georgia
Subjects: Animals, family, friendship, race and ethnicity, and social issues
Recommended ages: 15-18

From late fall until Christmas, Uncle Remus tells black folktales in dialect for the entertainment and instruction of the young son of the white owner of the plantation, frequently in competition with three other narrators.

Principal characters:
UNCLE REMUS, an eighty-year-old black slave, originally from
  Virginia, who is an authority figure on the Home Place plantation
MASTER JOHN, the white owner of the Home Place and Georgia coastal
  plantations
MISS SALLY, Master John's wife
THE LITTLE BOY, Master John and Miss Sally's young son
'TILDY, a young black slave, the ladies' maid to Miss Sally and the
  sometime attendant of the little boy
DADDY JACK, also called African Jack, the eighty-year-old black
  Gullah-speaking overseer of the coastal plantation
AUNT TEMPY, a black female slave who is an authority figure for the
  other female slaves
BRER RABBIT, the usually successful trickster figure and hero of the
  animal tales told by the various narrators
BRER TERRAPIN, another successful trickster figure in the tales
BRER FOX, BRER WOLF, and BRER BEAR, the usually unsuccessful
  adversaries of Brer Rabbit and Brer Terrapin

Form and Content

Nights with Uncle Remus is a thematic novel of seventy-one chapters, sixty-one of which contain animal stories and one of which contains a witch tale. The final chapter provides a climactic celebration of Christmas Eve festivities led by Uncle Remus, including the marriage of Daddy Jack and 'Tildy, a dance, and a communal song session. The white plantation owners and their guests are appreciative onlookers.

In most of these chapters, Uncle Remus tells stories in a rural black dialect to the young son of the plantation owner. The device of stories within a frame was introduced in Joel Chandler Harris' first book, *Uncle Remus: His Songs and His Sayings*

(1880). In *Nights with Uncle Remus*, however, the time has shifted to before the Civil War to allow for more variety in black narrators and black dialects and for differences in storytelling techniques. A lively competition between narrators ensues in the sessions.

Reconciliation, a major theme of the book, is established in the frame of the novel when these narrators come to appreciate their differences as individuals and as storytellers. At first, they argue over the authenticity and details of tales, but eventually they become a mutually appreciative and cooperative group. Their tales provide contrast to this harmony by focusing on the negative and destructive aspects of the animal community. Brer Rabbit, along with Benjamin Ram and Brer Terrapin, must constantly be on guard to avoid being captured and eaten by Brer Fox, Brer Wolf, and Brer Bear. When the animals do undertake a communal project—such as building a house, digging a well, or planting a garden—Brer Rabbit manages through trickery to take it away from the others. Several of the stories show Brer Rabbit tricking his enemies into selling their kin for food. Other conflicts over courtship and property arise in this self-destructive animal community.

Nights with Uncle Remus begins on a dull rainy night in late fall when the little boy and 'Tildy bring an evening meal to Uncle Remus, who is unable to get about. As a reward, Remus tries to amuse and interest the little boy in his stories of Brer Rabbit tales, but he has to tell five stories before the boy shows much enthusiasm. This nightly pattern of exchanging meals for stories continues until chapter twenty-four, when Daddy Jack, an overseer on the coastal plantation, visits the Home Place plantation.

Soon, Jack objects to Uncle Remus' storytelling and offers more authentic African versions. Smitten with affection for 'Tildy, he also begins a serious flirtation, which she rejects. When Jack's physical advances become known, Aunt Tempy is sent as a chaperon to the young boy at the nightly storytelling sessions. Aunt Tempy and 'Tildy become regular and occasionally quarrelsome members of the group. The competitive storytelling continues along with the aged but vigorous Daddy Jack's courtship of the young, pert 'Tildy.

All in all, Daddy Jack tells ten tales; Aunt Tempy, five; and 'Tildy, three. Uncle Remus tells the remainder. The storytelling sessions contribute to the development of characters and plot. For example, 'Tildy's ghost story (chapter 29), based on "The Golden Arm" story suggested to Harris by Mark Twain, allows her to make physical contact with Daddy Jack when she shouts, " 'You got my money!' " and grabs him. In turn, Daddy Jack shows respect by complimenting her telling of a second story (chapter 61). Criticized by Uncle Remus for her telling of a third tale (chapter 65), 'Tildy shows modesty, courtesy, and respect for his authority and age by listening to his corrected version of the story. Similar interactions between Uncle Remus and both Daddy Jack and Aunt Tempy show the characters overcoming their argumentative natures and jealousy of one another's place and authority. These developments lead to the joyous, harmonious final chapter of the book, with its Christmas Eve festivities.

Analysis

Nights with Uncle Remus is a difficult book for readers, especially those who do not have any experience with black dialects. Seventy stories are written in both nineteenth century rural black dialect of Middle Georgia and the Gullah of the coast, a language even more foreign and difficult to many, despite Harris' simplified introduction to Gullah and his glosses.

The thematic development of the novel can be obscured by the numerous tales, the arguments by the various narrators, and the repetition of themes and story elements. Harris had used many of his most distinctive stories in *Uncle Remus: His Songs and His Sayings*. In this book, he had to rely more heavily on stories from informants.

Harris' thirty-one page, scholarly introduction to the book addresses "ethnologists and students of folk-lore," unlike the general audience in his first book. His extensive comparison of some of his individual stories to those in academic collections by folklorists may put off young adult readers expecting a work of fiction. Harris intended to give the reader "a volume embodying everything or nearly everything, of importance in the oral literature of the negroes of the Southern States." With this and his first book, he nearly succeeded but at the danger of exhausting a reader who must struggle through more than four hundred pages mainly in black dialect. The competition among the narrators is most intense in chapters 31 and 32; 39, 40, and 41; 47 and 50; and 55 and 56. These chapters offer variants of the same tale.

The pastoralism and benevolence of the frame, with its four narrators, is at odds with the realism and violence of the animal tales. Since the novel is set in the late fall, a more leisurely time in the country, these black slaves can spend long nights telling stories. Less is revealed about the real work on a farm or plantation than in Harris' first book.

While the frame of this book does not give a realistic depiction of farm life—it is far too pastoral in the classic sense—the realistic violence of the animal community in the stories is often relentlessly harsh and naturalistic. Occasionally, this realism intrudes into the frame: For example, in one story Brer Rabbit steals a wagonload of money from Mr. Man, but what is a rabbit doing with money? The extensive competition for food results occasionally in cannibalism, as when Brer Rabbit tricks the wolf into eating his grandmother. Three stories in a row have plots that involve selling one's relatives for food (chapters 39, 40, and 41).

The focus on food gathering, sharing, and stealing is thematically significant for family preservation in addition to being suitable for the fall season of the frame. As such, it is also a familiar and recurring subject in children's literature. The stories also stress loyalty to and protection of family and kin, as opposed to interests of the larger community, natural enemies, or unrelated neighbors. This is clearly a book about maturation and the necessity of belonging to a community.

Critical Context

Collections of Negro folklore were just beginning in the late nineteenth century. Some folklorists praised the stories in Joel Chandler Harris' Uncle Remus miscellany as a contribution to this new science. *Nights with Uncle Remus* resulted from Harris' ambition to combine a work of fiction, a thematic novel, with an academic collection and anthology. After this book, many more collections of black folklore appeared, either for the amusement and entertainment of a general audience, such as those of Charles C. Jones, Jr., and Mrs. A. M. H. Christensen, or for folklorists, by such scholars as Elsie Parsons, Alan Dundes, and Richard Dorson.

Harris soon realized that *Nights with Uncle Remus* was a failure both as an academic contribution and as a commercial venture even though the reviews were good. Sales were not as large as those for his first book, and academics took no notice of it. In one inscribed copy of *Nights with Uncle Remus*, he wrote humorously and deprecatingly concerning the subject of "comparative folklore" that the author "knows no more on the subject than a blind horse knows about Sunday." In *Uncle Remus and His Friends* (1892), his third Uncle Remus book, which follows the much simpler miscellany structure of his successful 1880 *Uncle Remus*, Harris announced the end to his Uncle Remus books, apologizing for the stories as authentic folktales. Later, he satirized folklore as a science in the essay "The Late Mr. Watkins of Georgia: His Relation to Oriental Folk-Lore" (1898) and through the academic narrator of a children's book in *Wally Wanderoon* (1903). His last three Uncle Remus books (1904, 1905, 1907), which were mainly lavishly illustrated picture books, made no pretense to being authentic folktale collections.

Nights with Uncle Remus regularly appeared on lists for children from 1912 to 1941 and occasionally afterward. The book deserves rediscovery, however, because it gives a thorough, detailed description of oral storytelling techniques. The stories have an authentically oral structure in interspersing prose with verse. Florence Baer's *Sources and Analogues of the Uncle Remus Tales* (1980) has proved that most of the sixty-nine animal stories in *Nights with Uncle Remus* have African or African American sources. Only five stories have European sources, five are American, four are American Indian, and one is unknown. Both storytellers and academics have come to a greater respect for Harris's amateur collection. Stripped of Harris' frame, the stories have been restored to a general audience of children's literature through retellings such as Julius Lester's four volumes of Uncle Remus tales (1987, 1988, 1990, and 1990) and by Van Dyke Parks's three *Jump* books (1986, 1987, and 1989). *Nights with Uncle Remus* deserves more consideration as a complex but unified novel.

Hugh T. Keenan

NINETEEN EIGHTY-FOUR

Author: George Orwell (Eric Arthur Blair, 1903-1950)
First published: 1949
Type of work: Novel
Type of plot: Science fiction
Time of work: 1984
Locale: London and environs, in the province of Airstrip One (Britain), in the state of Oceania
Subjects: Politics and law, social issues, and war
Recommended ages: 13-18

Winston Smith and Julia attempt to join a revolutionary group to overthrow the ruling government in Oceania and keep their individuality, but their efforts are doomed to failure.

Principal characters:
 WINSTON SMITH, a writer in the Ministry of Truth who is unsure of the rightness of the revolution that has established Ingsoc, the government under which he lives
 JULIA, the young woman with whom he falls in love
 O'BRIEN, an Inner Party member whom Winston and Julia believe to be a leader in the revolutionary society called the Brotherhood
 BIG BROTHER, the enigmatic leader of Oceania

Form and Content

Nineteen Eighty-four is George Orwell's unswervingly grim vision of a dystopian future. The author always intended it as more warning than prophecy, so that even though its title date has passed, its lessons about the dangers of conformity, mental coercion, and verbal deception retain their validity and relevance. Orwell's careful use of clear, understandable language makes the unfamiliar world of *Nineteen Eighty-four* comprehensible to every level of reader, and his theme of personal individuality and human emotion, particularly love, trying to establish themselves in spite of the relentless pressure of the modern industrial state has perennial appeal to young adult audiences.

The novel depicts a world divided into three totalitarian superpowers that are constantly at war with one another: Oceania, dominated by the former United States; Eurasia, dominated by Western Europe; and Eastasia, dominated by China and Japan. Since the novel belongs to the genre of the dystopia, a negative Utopia, much of its content is necessarily involved in describing Oceanian society—not only in the features of its everyday life, much of which reflects British life in 1948 (a year whose inverted numbers may have suggested the novel's title), but also in detailed explanations of the historical origins of Ingsoc and Oceania, as well as its official language,

Newspeak. Orwell, rather clumsily in the view of some critics, gives much of this information in the form of a book-within-a-book, the supposed handbook of the revolutionaries, and an appendix to the novel itself about Newspeak.

Not until the second main part of the novel does the story really begin. Winston Smith is a writer for the ironically named Ministry of Truth, whose chief job is to assist in the constant rewriting of history so that it conforms with the predictions and pronouncements of Big Brother, the possibly mythical ruler of Oceania, whose minions in the Inner Party are nevertheless omnipotent and omniscient. Winston, who was born in 1945 and thus was named after Britain's wartime leader Winston Churchill, vaguely remembers life before the revolution and the establishment of Ingsoc, and he gradually comes to believe that life was not always as dreary, mechanical, and deadening as it now is in Oceania, although he has no means of proving it. Another worker in the Ministry of Truth, Julia, a young woman whom Winston suspects of spying on him, turns out to be attracted to him, and they enter into a complicated, dangerous love affair that they both internally believe can only end in disaster.

O'Brien, an Inner Party member to whom Winston has been vaguely drawn, provides a ray of hope when the lovers become convinced that he is a secret member of the Brotherhood, the revolutionary group committed to the overthrow of Ingsoc and Big Brother. O'Brien—naturally, one is almost tempted to say—turns out to be a double agent, and the last part of the novel depicts in graphic detail Winston's torture and conversion by O'Brien into an unconditional acceptance of the power of the party and Big Brother. To accomplish this acceptance, Winston must master the mental skill of "doublethink," a form of reality control involving "the power of holding two contradictory beliefs in one's mind simultaneously, and accepting both of them." To some critics, the descriptions and explanations in this section of the novel are the book's weakest parts. This ordeal culminates in Winston's betrayal of his love for Julia. A broken man, Winston is set "free" to spend his last days in a semi-alcoholic stupor, mindlessly cheering on huge mythical victories by the forces of Oceania as he awaits the inevitable bullet in the back of the head. *Nineteen Eighty-four* ends with the chilling—and inescapable—sentence "He loved Big Brother."

Analysis

Critics of every aspect along the political spectrum, no matter what their views about the validity of Orwell's social analysis in *Nineteen Eighty-four*, agree on one thing: Considered politically and historically, *Nineteen Eighty-four* is one of the most important books of the twentieth century. The bleakness of its vision of a totalitarian society became a profound warning, and Orwell's accuracy was attested by dissidents in Eastern Europe and Russia both before and after the dissolution of the Soviet empire; Orwell, said a Russian philosopher, "understood the soul, or soullessness" of Soviet life. Not only did the words "Newspeak" and "doublethink" enter the English language but Russians refer to the *Novoyaz* of Communist Party language. Orwell's examination of the political uses and abuses of language became the basis for a more critical perception of governmental pronouncements and declarations everywhere. For these reasons alone, *Nineteen Eighty-four* deserves to be studied, and the clarity and transparency of Orwell's language make it particularly appropriate for young adult audiences.

Some critics have pointed out that another layer of meaning exists within the novel. They connect Orwell's dissection of Oceanian society to his portrayal of his depressing and unhappy preparatory school days, which he discussed in his essay "Such, Such Were the Joys" (1952). Young English boys were removed from the warmth and security of their families, mini-societies governed by love and respect, and hurled into a world dominated by fear, repression, and an all-pervading sense of guilt. There, Orwell was imprisoned "not only in a hostile world but in a world of good and evil where the rules were such that it was actually not possible for me to keep them." In such a society, rebellion or even dissent becomes almost impossible, and even personal relationships are viewed with hostility and suspicion by the ruling "class," that is, the masters and proprietors of the school. That Orwell's school was run by a husband and wife made the situation even more ironic and perhaps gave Orwell the unconscious inspiration to have his totalitarian society ruled by Big Brother, a pseudo-member of a much larger "family."

Thus, as far as a young adult audience is concerned, Orwell's theme of establishing one's individuality in the face of an all-powerful and inimical society might be the most important, and it is intensified by the way in which he reproduces the psychic atmosphere of childhood and adolescence in his portrayal of Winston's rebellion. Winston knows that life is not meant to be lived as it is in Oceania, and he tries to construct his ideal society out of fragments of dreams, nursery rhymes, and his love for Julia. Their affair is an attempt to set up briefly and furtively an independent life of their own. This freedom of personal relationships echoes Winston's struggles to establish the freedom of his own mind, if only to assess the existence of external reality, symbolized by the equation "$2 + 2 = 4$." That Winston's and Julia's rebellion is doomed to failure—O'Brien demonstrates to Winston that "$2 + 2$" can equal "5" if the Party declares it so—will trouble some readers. Yet, since Orwell's vision is that of a satirist, prophetic only in the sense that it is a warning, such a conclusion is inevitable both within and outside the framework of the novel, as are the endings of Jonathan Swift's *Gulliver's Travels* (1726) and Orwell's own *Animal Farm* (1945).

Critical Context

Textbooks are uncertain whether to classify *Nineteen Eighty-four* as a young adult novel or as a "classic." Whatever its designation, the novel has been often assigned in the classroom, sometimes for political reasons, but not as widely as *Animal Farm*, largely on the basis of length. *Nineteen Eighty-four* also often turns up on lists of censored works, often for its theme of sexual relations as a legitimate form of political rebellion.

The novel continues to be read even though the year that it so remorselessly depicts is long over. *Nineteen Eighty-four* brought the rich tradition of the dystopian novel into the heart of the twentieth century. It acknowledges and builds upon the heritage of *Gulliver's Travels*, H. G. Wells's *When the Sleeper Wakes* (1899), Jack London's *The Iron Heel* (1907), Yevgeny Zamyatin's *We* (1924), Aldous Huxley's *Brave New World* (1932), and *Animal Farm*. The gloominess of its tone persuaded some critics that it was the bitter, twisted outcry of a dying man (Orwell died of tuberculosis seven months after it was published). Yet, the humor of its satire, the overwhelming seriousness of its message, and the clarity of its exposition ensure its continuing place in the ranks of both young adult literature and the classics.

William Laskowski

NORTH AMERICAN INDIAN CEREMONIES

Author: Karen Liptak
First published: 1992; illustrated
Type of work: Social science
Subjects: Gender roles, nature, race and ethnicity, and social issues
Recommended ages: 13-15

Liptak describes a wide variety of North American Indian ceremonies and rituals.

Form and Content

Karen Liptak's *North American Indian Ceremonies* depicts a wide spectrum of ceremonies practiced in both the past and the present by a variety of American Indian tribes. The book's introductory section gives an overview of the purpose of these ceremonies, stressing how they help children to grow closer to other tribal members and to learn about themselves, the world around them, and, most important, their own particular American Indian culture. Subsequent sections focus on specific kinds of ceremonial events, including those for birth and death, coming-of-age, courtship and marriage, hunting and gathering, war and peace, initiation into secret societies, abundant food, and healing. The book's final section discusses the ceremonies still performed today, usually on reservations and sometimes at American Indian cultural centers, pageants, fairs, and museums. These contemporary ceremonies, Liptak suggests, serve two purposes: to instill pride in the American Indians watching and performing in the ceremonial rituals and to educate non-Indians about American Indian life.

Illustrated with numerous photographs and works of art depicting the ceremonies, costumes, and sacred objects, this thin work seems to be almost as much picture book as a reference text. A short list of other works about American Indian ceremonies and a glossary of terms, including the names and geographical locations of many of the tribes that Liptak's discusses, concludes the book.

Except for the introduction and conclusion, Liptak organizes each section similarly, beginning with a general description and definition of the ceremonial event under discussion before moving to specific examples of how different tribes conduct a particular ceremony. When Liptak writes about girls' coming-of-age ceremonies, for example, she defines puberty and discusses several tribes' practices of isolating a girl when she first begins to menstruate before describing how one tribe, the Sioux, stage this type of celebration. During the Sioux ceremony, which honors the strong role that women play in the family, a feast is held. The girl being honored receives gifts from other tribal members, as well as instructions about her adult duties from the tribal medicine person. Liptak follows this example of the Sioux, a Great Plains tribe, with a second example of a more elaborate coming-of-age ceremony practiced by the Apaches, a Southwestern tribe. According to Liptak, in the Apache ceremony several girls are simultaneously honored through singing, dancing, eating, tepee-building, entertaining, and gift-giving in a four-day event called the Sunrise Ceremony. After these public ceremonies, the girls spend four days in isolated huts with older women from the tribe, who conduct private rituals. When the girls return home, they are ready for marriage.

By contrast, the introduction of the book depicts the costumes, music, dancing, sacred objects, and cleansing rituals of these ceremonies in general terms, without offering specific examples from individual tribes. The book's conclusion is also general in nature.

Analysis

By organizing the book in this way and by including certain information, it is clear that Liptak wants to dispel the stereotype of American Indians as belonging to a monolithic cultural group. Although she occasionally speaks generally about all American Indians, for the most part Liptak distinguishes not only among various tribes but also among the various regions in North America that these tribes inhabit. Thus, she makes reference to the kachinas and prayer sticks of the tribes from the Southwest as well as the buffalo robes and sun dances of the Great Plains tribes and the wood carvings and potlash ceremonies of the tribes from the Pacific Northwest. Her inclusion of regional differences—she also mentions the Southeast, Northeast, Great Lakes, Eastern Woodlands, and Plateau regions—stresses that American Indians were and still are living and practicing ceremonies in many areas of America. (Despite the book's title, *North American Indian Ceremonies*, Liptak makes no reference to Central American, Mexican, or Canadian Indians or their ceremonies.) Besides her focus on these regional identities, the author also mentions a dozen and a half individual tribes, making reference not only to larger, well-known tribes such as the Navaho and Cherokee but also to smaller tribes such as the Tlingit, Kwakiutl, Quinault, Tsimshian, Nootka, and Tohono O'odham that are, most likely, less familiar to young readers.

The differences among these tribes' ceremonies resonate because of the thematic organization of the book. When Liptak writes about fertility ceremonies, held to give thanks for American Indians' current blessings as well as to ask for abundant food and other good fortune in the future, her readers learn that while tribes in the Southeast and Northeast hold the Green Corn Ceremony, the Great Plains tribes participate in the Sun Dance Ceremony and the Southwestern Pueblo villages hold many annual fertility ceremonies to honor the kachina that represents one of the rain-bringing ancestral spirits. By juxtaposing these ceremonies, Liptak allows readers to compare and contrast different tribal rituals and to make connections between a tribe's ceremony and its location. Landscape, animal and plant life, and weather all help determine the makeup of American Indian ceremonies.

Liptak also seems interested in dispelling any stereotype of the American Indian as warrior, as a hard-hearted enemy of nineteenth century wagon trains and the settling of America. In her discussion of the war and peace ceremonies, she focuses on the many rituals that take place behind the scenes of battles—the singing and fasting, the cleansing and dancing. This presentation of how American Indians deal with war gives a more in-depth portrayal of what it means for them to engage in battle than most Hollywood films or other forms of media, which often focus on incidences of violence such as the scalping of homesteaders or the kidnapping of women and children. Moreover, Liptak mentions the four days of war ceremonies that took place in 1991 before eight Apaches living at Arizona's San Carlos Reservation left, as members of the United States armed forces, to fight in the Persian Gulf War. This brief anecdote portrays American Indians as Americans, as friends to non-Indian Americans rather than as foes.

Despite the book's in-depth look at so many ceremonies, Liptak acknowledges that she cannot show or tell all about them. In the section of the book describing initiations into secret societies, many details are absent, since only the initiates would know them. When describing children's initiation into the Kachina Society, for example, Liptak talks generally, without elaboration, about the "unexpected, yet traditional events" that take place during the ceremony. She honors the ceremonies by honoring American Indians' right to privacy.

Critical Context

Interest in enlightened works about and by American Indians (and other minority groups) began in the 1970's when intellectuals began challenging the traditional literary canon, which was primarily made up of white, male, American and British writers. A substantial body of literature within this canon, including the novels of James Fenimore Cooper, celebrated the American frontier and in doing so depicted the decline of the "red man" and the triumph of the "white man." Reenvisioning the literary canon has had two results: the publication of anonymous American Indian writings and stories (handed down orally), which have survived from the eighteenth and nineteenth centuries, and the publication of contemporary American Indian writers, such as N. Scott Momaday, Leslie Marmon Silko, Louise Erdrich, Joy Harjo, and James Welch.

This reformation of the canon eventually affected the juvenile and young adult literature. *North American Indian Ceremonies*, with its enlightened, nonstereotypical portrait of American Indians, is a product of the literary academy's embracing of multiculturalism. This book and other works by Karen Liptak in this field—such as *North American Indian Medicine People* (1990), *North American Indian Sign Language* (1990), *North American Indian Survival Skills* (1990), and *North American Indian Tribal Chiefs* (1992)—mark the author as an important spokesperson for American Indians.

Cassandra Kircher

NOTHING BUT THE TRUTH
A Documentary Novel

Author: Avi (Avi Wortis, 1937-   )
First published: 1991
Type of work: Novel
Type of plot: Social realism
Time of work: The early 1990's
Locale: Harrison Township, New Hampshire
Subjects: Coming-of-age, education, politics and law, and social issues
Recommended ages: 10-15

Ninth-grader Philip Malloy's attempt to manipulate his teachers escalates into a national news story that foils his plans, threatens a teacher's career, and challenges notions of ethics, truth, and the American way.

> *Principal characters:*
> PHILIP MALLOY, a ninth-grade student
> BEN MALLOY, Philip's father
> MRS. MALLOY, Philip's mother
> MARGARET NARWIN, an English teacher at Harrison High School
> COACH EARL JAMISON, the track coach
> DR. ALBERT SEYMOUR, the school superintendent
> DR. GERTRUDE DOANE, the principal of Harrison High School
> DR. JOSEPH PALLENI, the assistant principal
> TED GRIFFEN, a neighbor of the Malloys who is running for election to the school board
> JENNIFER STEWART, the education reporter for the *Manchester Record*

Form and Content

Philip Malloy's dream is to join Coach Jamison's track team. Unfortunately, he is ineligible for the team because of his low grade in Miss Narwin's English class. Philip is further upset when he learns that Miss Narwin is to be his new homeroom teacher. Rather than sit down and talk with Miss Narwin as Coach Jamison suggests, Philip hatches a plan that he thinks will get him transferred out of both Miss Narwin's homeroom and her English class. During homeroom, when school policy dictates that students are to "stand at respectful silent attention" during the playing of the national anthem, Philip loudly hums along. When Miss Narwin reprimands Philip, he insists that his previous homeroom teacher allowed him to hum along because of his patriotic feelings. When her attempts to talk to Philip lead nowhere, Miss Narwin sends him to the principal's office. Philip asserts to Dr. Joseph Pelleni, the assistant principal, that he has a patriotic desire to sing the national anthem during homeroom. The next day, Philip again hums along and is sent to the principal's office; he is given a two-day suspension from school for his failure to follow stated rules. Philip maintains to his mother that Miss Narwin dislikes him and that the whole situation is her fault.

Philip's parents are easily led to believe that Miss Narwin is to blame. Philip's father is under pressure at work to be more productive. He is frustrated by needing his job and being unable to protest his supervisor's demeaning attitude. Philip's treatment at school provides an arena in which Mr. Malloy can find vindication. Philip's assertions that his teacher is against patriotism motivate his father to take the story to his next-door neighbor, Ted Griffen, a candidate for a seat on the local school board.

Mr. Griffen is quite responsive to Mr. Malloy's tale of woe about the schools. When he learns that Miss Narwin refused to allow Philip to sing the national anthem in class, he is easily convinced that this is another example of eroding community morals and the folly of allowing the free-thinking intellectual elite to run the schools. Mr. Griffen cites the incident in speeches to several community groups.

Through Ted Griffen, Jennifer Stewart, the education reporter from the *Manchester Record*, the newspaper of the state capital, learns about Philip's case and contacts him for an interview. Mr. Griffen and Mr. Malloy dominate the interview to make sure that Philip's story comes out in full detail. Unfortunately, their version contains many errors. Jennifer Stewart does cross check her story with the school superintendent, Dr. Albert Seymour, and Dr. Gertrude Doane, the principal of Harrison High School, who refers her to Dr. Pelleni, the assistant principal. The story becomes more confused as the reporter checks her facts with Dr. Pelleni and Miss Narwin, as both are inexperienced at dealing with reporters.

When the newspaper article appears, it precipitates conversations among the school administrators and others. As one group tries to iron out a uniform story, others interpolate even wilder conclusions. Ted Griffen cites the newspaper article in more speeches, and finally a news media wire service picks up an abbreviated version of the newspaper story. A national talk show picks up the case from the wire service and begins to discuss it with telephone callers. National newspapers hear of the story and begin telephoning Harrison, New Hampshire, as they prepare their versions. A patriotic group in another state sends a telegram of condemnation to Miss Narwin, while another sends congratulations and a pledge of support to Philip. Letters from around the country are sent to the major players of the story. Some call for banning Miss Narwin from teaching.

Under pressure from the school board, school administrators meet and try to effect a cooling off of the situation. Philip is transferred to another homeroom and then another English class. When he tries to raise his English grade by doing extra work, he discovers that this is impossible because he is no longer in Miss Narwin's class. Coach Jamison tells Philip that sports is all about being a team player and that it is his fault he is not on the team. Miss Narwin is asked about retirement and then is offered a leave of absence until the next year. Ted Griffen is elected to the school board. Philip's parents decide to enroll him in a private school. Unfortunately, the private school has no track team.

Analysis

Avi's *Nothing but the Truth* is told through a series of documents, including school policy statements, conversations, diary entries, telephone conversations, newspaper articles, transcripts of a talk show, letters, and memoranda. When Philip Malloy's low English grade prevents him from joining the track team, he creates a disturbance during homeroom in order to be transferred to a more sympathetic teacher. Philip's juvenile stunt of loudly humming along as the national anthem is played on the loudspeaker during school opening exercises is blown out of all proportion. The author shows how through a series of misrepresentations, misperceptions, and hasty conclusions, the alleged facts of the incident are used by a political candidate as evidence in a crusade for increased morality in the schools. The national news media make matters even worse as they join the parade of misunderstanding that obscures the real truth. There are ramifications to Philip's actions: The career of a popular and highly respected teacher is jeopardized through innuendo, and Philip is forced to transfer to a school without a track team.

Nothing but the Truth presents a stark picture of the self-centered thinking of the young, the preoccupations and poor listening skills of parents and teachers, the prejudice and posturing of politicians, the timidity of school administrators, and the hasty and shortsighted assumptions of journalists. While all these people pay lip service to high ideals and patriotism, their actions raise important questions about the believability of what is said, reported, and written. This story challenges the reader to think carefully about human communication and value systems.

Critical Context

Nothing but the Truth was designated one of two Newbery Honor Books by the American Library Association in 1992, as a runner-up for the best book for young people published in the previous year. If notable fiction for young adults is supposed to challenge them to think about important issues, this book could well have warranted the medal itself. The plot is a masterpiece of clever construction, without extraneous elements. The author weaves a complex set of story threads into a powerful tale that is accessible, intriguing, and fast-paced. The significant theme of half truths leading to perdition marks this book as a modern classic.

Avi's work is quite varied, including historical adventures such as *The True Confessions of Charlotte Doyle* (1990), which was also a Newbery Honor Book; historical mysteries; contemporary comedies; and fantasies. Unlike many of his other works, which have a strong sense of period and a sweeping narrative style, *Nothing but the Truth* operates in a dramatic mode, presenting documents for the reader to interpret. The author never steps in and tells the reader what to think of the characters or theme. The book is quite easy to read, but it demands attention to the facts and sharp inferential reasoning if the subtle ironies strewn through it are to be appreciated.

John D. Beach

NUMBER THE STARS

Author: Lois Lowry (1937-   )
First published: 1989
Type of work: Novel
Type of plot: Historical fiction
Time of work: 1943
Locale: Copenhagen and Gilleleje, Denmark
Subjects: Friendship, race and ethnicity, social issues, and war
Recommended ages: 10-15

Annemarie Johansen gradually discovers the reason for a hurried trip from Copenhagen to the port city of Gilleleje, the Danish resistance to the cruel actions of the Nazis in their attempt to "relocate" the Danish Jews, the value of true friendship, and the nature of bravery.

Principal characters:
ANNEMARIE JOHANSEN, a ten-year-old girl who helps her friend Ellen and other Jews escape to Sweden
ELLEN ROSEN, a Jewish friend of Annemarie
INGE JOHANSEN, Annemarie's mother, who knowingly assists the endangered Jews
MR. JOHANSEN, Annemarie's father
UNCLE HENRIK, Mrs. Johansen's fisherman brother
KIRSTI JOHANSEN, the youngest daughter in the Johansen family
LISE JOHANSEN, the oldest Johansen daughter, who is killed by the Germans
PETER NEILSEN, the former fiancé of Lise Johansen
MR. and MRS. ROSEN, Ellen's Jewish parents

Form and Content

This historical novel, set in German-occupied Denmark in 1943, includes in its account of two fictional Danish families—one Christian and one Jewish—many factual incidents that occurred as the Danish people successfully helped many of their Jewish fellow citizens escape to Sweden and thus avoid death and deprivation at the hands of their Nazi captors. In seventeen brief chapters, author Lois Lowry recounts the fear, secrecy, uncertainty, and subterfuge experienced by the Johansens as, in the spirit of all Danes during World War II, they protected and assisted the Rosens and other Jewish friends, demonstrating their individual courage, their innate humaneness, and their unrelenting empathy for a persecuted people. Annemarie Johansen learns from her father the various stories about the bravery of their good King Christian X and the Danish Resistance, and she wonders whether she could be as courageous. The events over the next few days will tell.

For three years, German troops have occupied Denmark, but everyone becomes worried when two soldiers question Annemarie and her friend Ellen Rosen on the way home from school and when on the following day the Hirsches' shop is found locked by the Germans and the Hirsches are mysteriously gone. The Jewish community knows that it must act when the rabbi tells them he has word the Nazis plan to "relocate" the Jews. The Rosens make hasty arrangements for Ellen to stay with the Johansens under the guise of being Annemarie's sister Lise, who had been killed, according to her parents, in an automobile accident. Annemarie learns the wisdom of such a ploy when German soldiers break into their house that night.

Annemarie has already learned firsthand to fear the abuse of the rude Germans, and she understands somewhat the dangers facing the Jews in Denmark. What is she to make, however, of the cryptic telephone call by her father and the sudden trip by Mrs. Johansen and the children, including Ellen, to the seaport village of Gilleleje to visit Uncle Henrik? She perceives that her parents and Uncle Henrik are lying to her. Piece by piece, the puzzle comes together. First, the wake for Great-Aunt Birte—who, Annemarie knows, never existed—is actually a gathering of Jews, the Rosens included, whom Uncle Henrik will take in his boat across the short distance to freedom in Sweden. Annemarie unwittingly plays a crucial role in the success of the escape when she delivers to Uncle Henrik an important packet containing a handkerchief. She experiences a fearsome night and rough treatment by German soldiers who roughly search the contents of her decoy lunch basket.

Only after the success of the rescue of Jews that night does Annemarie discover fully the truth about coded messages, secret compartments on boats to hide escaping Jews, a special drug to block temporarily the sense of smell by German police dogs, and the valiant efforts of the Danish Resistance, which cost the life of her sister Lise and her fiancé, Peter Neilsen. To her surprise, she learns that she, too, is courageous, for as Uncle Henrik explains, bravery is "not thinking about the dangers." Perhaps more important, she learns about the terrible injustice of racial prejudice.

Analysis

Through one family's efforts to aid Jewish friends in their escape to free soil in Sweden, *Number the Stars* captures the heroic spirit of many compassionate Danes during World War II who risked their lives and property by defying Nazi persecution of their Jewish citizens. It is a story that young people need to know; it is a story that promotes a tolerance that all people need to possess. Beyond the particulars of historical fact, the novel addresses universal issues that maturing youths must resolve: the natures of social justice, racial prejudice, personal responsibility, and courage.

The story of King Christian X fearlessly riding alone through the streets of Copenhagen because, as her father said, all Denmark is his bodyguard greatly impresses Annemarie and introduces the central theme of the true definition of bravery, which she doubts that she has. Yet, without consciously deciding to be brave but instead employing unrecognized inner resources, she acts courageously when she snatches Ellen's necklace with the Star of David pendant and hides it in her hand while

German soldiers search their bedroom and when later she races to Uncle Henrik's boat to deliver the handkerchief. The Jewish families also exhibit courage as they face the dangers and deprivations of the escape route. Bravery is thus defined dramatically as doing what is necessary without considering the possible costs. Its genesis is in a concern for people, a conviction of rightness, and a determination to do what is right.

The juxtaposition of the Nazis' hatred and persecution of blameless Jews with the Danes' caring protection of them is telling. Moreover, the interrelated themes of social justice, racial acceptance, and personal responsibility permeate the novel from the beginning and invade the story from several sources. The Johansen family is a microcosm of the Danish people, for they are unwilling to sit idly by when the Danish Jews are threatened. The Johansens risk disastrous reprisals by passing Ellen off as their gentile daughter, by smuggling the Jews out of the country, and, in the case of Lise and her fiancé, Peter, by participating in the Danish Resistance. They understand that one must go beyond mere intellectual agreement with justice and equality to the level of personal involvement, regardless of the cost. Annemarie demonstrates this spirit of identification with others in the closing line of the book: She says of Ellen's Star of David that until the return of the Rosens, "I'll wear it myself."

The final, symbolic action of Annemarie's decision to wear Ellen's necklace, undeniably striking in itself, is overshadowed by a similar symbol early in the novel when, to prevent Ellen's being detected as a Jew by three Nazi officers who burst into their bedroom, Annemarie jerks Ellen's necklace off and clasps it tightly in her hand. After the officers leave, she relaxes the clenched fingers and sees the Star of David imprinted in the palm of her hand. The implication is clear; she, a Gentile, bears the mark of a Jew. Lowry's point is just as clear: The answer to racial prejudice lies not in mere tolerance of other races but in active identification of oneself with them.

In some sense, *Number the Stars* is a suspense story. Annemarie is not always told the truth about what has happened and why certain actions and precautions are being taken. Thus, she (and the reader) is puzzled and must either figure out what is going on—and what is likely to happen—or be told later in the concluding chapter. She is told that the closed lips are for her safety; nevertheless, the lack of information makes for suspenseful reading.

Critical Context

Although she had already established herself as a noted author of children's books through many previous novels, especially those about Anastasia Krupnik, Lois Lowry reaches new heights of achievement with this historical novel, which won the coveted Newbery Medal in 1990. Her other well-loved books deal mostly with the perils of puberty, but the depth of content exhibited in *Number the Stars* and later in *The Giver* (1993), for which she won her second Newbery Medal, show her to be a writer of the first order.

For much of the historical information in the book, Lowry is indebted to her friend Annelise Plat, who was a child in Copenhagen during the German occupation. The story of the Danes' love for King Christian X, the blowing up of the small Danish navy to prevent the ships from falling into the hands of the Germans, the warning to the Jews by a high German official that allowed the smuggling of almost all of the seven thousand Danish Jews to Sweden, the hiding places on boats, the use of a special drug on handkerchiefs to deaden police dogs' sense of smell, the execution of young freedom fighters—all make their way into the fabric of this much-needed novel for youths.

Maverick Marvin Harris

OF MICE AND MEN

Author: John Steinbeck (1902-1968)
First published: 1937
Type of work: Novel
Type of plot: Allegory, psychological realism, and social realism
Time of work: The 1930's
Locale: Salinas Valley, California
Subjects: Death, friendship, jobs and work, poverty, and social issues
Recommended ages: 13-18

> *Lennie and George's dream of putting together a stake and buying a farm ends abruptly when Lennie inadvertently kills the wife of the boss' son; George, out of loyalty and friendship, is forced to shoot Lennie in order to save him from an angry mob.*

Principal characters:
LENNIE SMALL, an inarticulate itinerant worker who is unable to
   control his brawn and passions
GEORGE MILTON, Lennie's friend, protector, and traveling partner
CURLEY, a scrappy former fighter who is the son of the ranch owner
CURLEY'S WIFE, a recently married woman who uses flirtation to dispel
   her loneliness
SLIM, the ranch foreman
CANDY, an old, broken swamper
CROOKS, a crippled, black stable hand

Form and Content

Of Mice and Men recounts the story of two itinerant ranch hands who, despite their apparent differences, are dependent on each other. Lennie Small, by far the better worker of the two, suffers not only from limited intelligence but also from an overwhelming desire to caress soft objects. These traits, combined with his uncontrollable strength, set the stage for disaster.

The fact that a disaster has not already occurred is largely the result of the vigilance of Lennie's traveling companion, George Milton. Being aware of Lennie's limitations, George does his best to keep Lennie focused on their mutual dream of owning their own spread, raising rabbits, and being in charge of their own lives. He also ushers Lennie out of town whenever the locals misinterpret his friend's actions.

When the reader first encounters Lennie and George, they are setting up camp in an idyllic grove near the Gabilan mountains. It is lush and green and inhabited by all varieties of wild creatures. It represents, as the ensuing dialogue makes clear, a safe haven—a place where both humans and beasts can retreat should danger threaten. This setting provides author John Steinbeck with a context against which to portray the ranch to which George and Lennie travel the next day. The ranch, as he describes it, is a world without love and in which friendship is viewed as remarkable.

Steinbeck frames the desolation of ranch life by having George and Lennie comment on how different their lives are and having the other ranch hands comment on how unusual it is for two men to travel together. The hired hands have no personal stake in the ranch's operation and, for the most part, no stake in one another's well-being. Although they bunk together and play an occasional game of cards or horseshoes, each is wary of his peers. It is for this reason that Lennie and George's friendship is questioned by everyone and why their dream of owning their own place is so infectious, especially to men such as Crooks and Candy, both of whom long to escape this loveless, isolated existence. Complementing this theme are the description of Candy and his dog and Crooks's analysis of what it means to have a friend. Even Curley's wife is used to reinforce the message. She is a woman who, despite her own dreams of grandeur, finds herself living on a ranch where she is perceived as a threat and an enemy by all the hired hands.

To underscore the situation, Steinbeck adopts restricted third-person narration and employs a tone that can best be described as uninvolved. His technique is an outgrowth of his desire to fuse dramatic and novelistic techniques into a new literary format, which he called the "play-novelette." Accordingly, he relies on setting and dialogue to convey his message. For this reason, he begins each chapter with a compendium of details that allows readers to envision the scenes much as they might were they watching a staged presentation. Once he has outlined the surroundings, however, he steps away and relies on dialogue to carry the main thread of the story.

Significantly, Steinbeck begins and ends the novel at the campsite. This circular development reinforces the sense of inevitability that informs the entire novel. Just as Lennie is destined to get into trouble and be forced to return to the campsite so, too, will George be forced to abandon the dream of owning his own farm. Instead, he will be reduced to the status of a lonely drifter, seeking earthly pleasures to alleviate the moral isolation and helplessness that Steinbeck suggests is part of the human condition.

Analysis

When Steinbeck began *Of Mice and Men*, he was planning to write a children's book called *Something That Happened*. His intent was to demonstrate that events often have a momentum of their own and need not reflect the existence of a higher power that is exacting punishment. Perhaps it was for this reason that he decided to retitle the book, drawing from Robert Burns's oft-quoted poem "To a Mouse," which contains the line "The best-laid schemes o' mice an' men gang aft a-gley."

Casting Lennie as he does, Steinbeck forces the reader to deal with the fact that well-intentioned people commit acts that are beyond their control or understanding. Lennie, although slow, has no malice. Even when he is under physical attack from Curley, he restrains himself until George orders him to take action. Lennie, however, stricken by fear, loses control and cannot let go of his attacker.

At this point, Steinbeck is clearly asking the reader to understand Lennie's dilemma and to empathize with him. He depicts him as a terrified giant who, when threatened, loses all control of his faculties and unleashes his enormous strength. He injures Curley because Curley has attacked him, not because of any willful animosity. If there is blame to be cast, therefore, it resides with Curley.

Throughout the novel, Steinbeck depicts Curley as a vain and shallow little man. Being the boss' son and a former Golden Glove finalist, he picks fights with impunity, generally targeting larger men so that he will get praise if he bests his opponent and be seen as a martyr if he does not. His attack of Lennie, however, is so unprovoked and one-sided that everyone witnessing it sides with Lennie, leaving Curley no alternative but to invent an accident to explain his crushed hand.

When Curley's wife, suspecting the truth about her husband's injury, begins toying with Lennie, she replicates Curley's error of judgment by failing to understand how uncontrollable Lennie's fear and anger can be. When the taunts begin, Candy and Crooks attempt to intervene, but both are quickly emasculated and rendered powerless by Curley's wife, who gains what, in retrospect, is clearly a Pyrrhic victory. While she can lord her position over Candy and threaten Crooks with a lynch mob, her haughtiness and contempt for the workers are ultimately her undoing. Because she views Lennie as easy prey, she ups the ante and encourages him to stroke her hair. When she has had enough, however, she demands that he stop. Her protest leaves Lennie in a panic, and the inevitable outcome occurs.

Hers is not a tragic death. Instead, it is a vehicle that Steinbeck uses to contrast the reactions of the various men. While George, Candy, and Slim know that Lennie is the personification of innocence and never meant to harm anyone, Curley, Carlson, and Whit are bent on vengeance. They give no thought to the man or the sequence of events. George and Slim, however, do assess the full situation and are able to elude the posse long enough for George to usher Lennie out of the world without destroying his hope of attaining a better, more hospitable future. By allowing Lennie to die humanely, Steinbeck concludes what would otherwise be an overpoweringly depressing novel with the faint hope that loyalty and friendship are a necessary antidote to the cruelest aspects of reality.

Critical Context

Of Mice and Men is one of the most widely assigned modern novels in high schools because of both its form and the issues that it raises. John Steinbeck's reliance on dialogue, as opposed to contextual description, makes the work accessible to young readers, as does his use of foreshadowing and recurrent images. Equally important is the way in which he intertwines the themes of loneliness and friendship and gives dignity to those characters, especially Lennie and Crooks, who are clearly different from their peers. By focusing on a group of lonely drifters, Steinbeck highlights the perceived isolation and sense of "otherness" that can seem so overwhelming when one is growing up.

Of Mice and Men is also important because it explores the way in which events can conspire against the realization of one's dreams. It pits a group of flawed individuals against a set of circumstances that they are unable to master or, in the case of Lennie, even to comprehend. This is a theme that Steinbeck also explores in his classic novel *The Grapes of Wrath* (1939).

C. Lynn Munro

THE OLD MAN AND THE SEA

Author: Ernest Hemingway (1899-1961)
First published: 1952
Type of work: Novel
Type of plot: Moral tale
Time of work: A September in the 1930's
Locale: The Caribbean Sea off Havana, Cuba
Subjects: Emotions, friendship, jobs and work, and nature
Recommended ages: 13-18

Santiago fishes alone and catches an enormous marlin, but, when sharks destroy it
and hence his profit, he concludes that he went out too far without help.

Principal characters:
    SANTIAGO, an old, professional fisherman who seeks to reverse his bad
       luck by catching a big fish
    MANOLIN, a young boy who used to fish with Santiago as his
       apprentice and still helps him whenever he can
    A MARLIN, an 18-foot, 1,500-pound fish that Santiago hooks, comes to
       respect and even love, but must kill

Form and Content

The Old Man and the Sea, although usually called a novel, is not divided into
chapters; yet, at 27,500 words it is too long to be called a short story. Efforts to split
it into recognizably separate parts are haphazard at best, because its simple action
moves along a time line of morning, noon, sunset, midnight, and dawn, which is then
repeated, and with little reminiscing by the protagonist and no interpolations by the
author.

The action may be arbitrarily, but perhaps helpfully, divided into introduction, three
dramatic sections, denouement, and coda. In this introduction, the reader learns that
for forty days Santiago fished off Havana in the Gulf Stream, aided by his friend and
admirer Manolin, and then for forty-four more days alone, all without success. In
part 1, the action begins. On the eighty-fifth day, Santiago rows his skiff "far out" and
at noon hooks an enormous male marlin. In part 2, the fish is so strong that it tows
Santiago's skiff northwest into the night and beyond. The following afternoon, the old
man first sees his quarry when it suddenly surfaces. All through the second night, it
tows the old man, whose hands are cut and whose back is strained. It circles at dawn,
and Santiago harpoons it at noon and lashes it alongside the skiff. In part 3, a mako
shark attacks and devours part of the marlin. Santiago kills the shark, but his fear that
more sharks will follow the bloody wake is soon confirmed by their awesome
appearance. In the denouement, the scavengers complete the ruin of his prize, leaving
only the marlin's skeleton, which he brings to shore. Bone-tired, he sleeps again in his

shack. In the coda, Manolin brings Santiago coffee next morning, and the two determine to fish again.

Most of the time, Santiago is the only person whose words and thoughts are recorded. When he talks aloud to himself, as he often does, Ernest Hemingway puts his exact words within quotation marks. At other times, his unspoken thoughts are recorded but without the use of quotation marks and with the pronouns "he" and "I" used without evident distinction.

The Old Man and the Sea displays the classical unity of time, place, and action—with a distinct beginning, long middle, and end. It comprises three days and nights, occurs mostly on the vast sea, and presents one sequence of events. It is knit together by skillful foreshadowing, largely through Santiago's repeated refrain of going out too far, his frequently calling his quarry his "brother," his thoughts about baseball (especially his hero Joe DiMaggio), and his dreaming about playful lions that he saw long ago on African beaches. Manolin is involved in the action only in the first several pages and in the last few pages of the story. Thus, the novella has a sonata form, with Manolin constituting the short first and third motifs and a man pitted against the sea and its creatures as the more elaborate second motif.

Analysis

This short work is deceptively simple on the surface but very puzzling deeper down. It narrates basic events in generally short sentences and with a minimum of figurative language; simultaneously, however, it raises many questions without providing enough evidence for conclusive answers.

Santiago combines pride and humility. He performs heroically, conquers the marlin, but then loses it. Therefore, he is not a triumphant hero returning to his admiring people. Tourists even mistake the marlin's skeleton for that of a shark; furthermore, it is not preserved but instead waits to be washed back out to sea as "garbage." Nor does the hero have a heroine to comfort him, his beloved wife being long dead. He has no son to carry on, although he treats Manolin lovingly and often wishes that the boy were with him on this mission. The old fisherman is partially a Christ figure: His wounded hands pain him as though they were nailed to a piece of wood; toward the end, he carries his mast like a cross and stumbles under its weight; and, once home again, he sleeps in a cruciform position with arms out and palms up. Yet, Hemingway disavowed any consciously developed symbolic or allegorical import in this work. Furthermore, Santiago often tries to pray but puts off such attempts and regards himself as an unsatisfactory Catholic.

The marlin is another source of puzzlement. Why is its maleness emphasized? Hemingway, notoriously macho, may be suggesting that a female quarry would not be sufficiently challenging to his hero. On the other hand, Santiago calls the sea *la mar* (the feminine form in Spanish), which Hemingway depicts as a creative, loving, but often cruel mother. He makes much, here and elsewhere, of his heroes' being "destroyed but not defeated." Also, his heroes, when they win, must take nothing. Santiago killed the marlin, but he can never sell its meat for the $300 that he hoped to gain. He reveres his prize but despises the sharks and attacks them with commendable if unavailing ferocity. Yet, after all, both marlin and sharks are explicitly said to function precisely as designed.

The subject of free will thus enters. Winds, clouds, water, birds, and fish, all colorfully depicted by Hemingway, are linked parts of the great chain of marine life. What Santiago calls the marlin's choosing to dive deep is obviously instinctive, as is its subsequent surfacing. Surfacing causes its air sacks to fill and thus prevents its diving soon again, in turn predictably causing it to circle and hence be harpooned and killed. Santiago says both that he was born to fish and that he chooses to fish. To the degree that he has free will, his flaw—determining to go out too far—is a tragic one. Yet, perhaps he was fated to do so. Hence, being a partly naturalistic figure, he is an incomplete hero; the sentimental aura cast about him further diminishes him in the eyes of some critics.

The Old Man and the Sea has autobiographical overtones. Hemingway was an accomplished deep-sea fisherman and provides the reader with many details concerning the art of capturing marlins. (His big-game hunting and attending bullfights are obviously related activities.) It is not farfetched to equate Santiago's marlin with Hemingway's decades-long effort to write, to pull from the depths of his being, a vast book about the sea. Santiago's story was planned as a segment of a four-part novel, of which only it and *Islands in the Stream*, appearing posthumously in 1970, were completed. In this ambitious aesthetic adventure, the author tried to go too far. It may be added that the sharks ravaging the marlin can be likened to Hemingway's critics— ever eager, in his almost psychotic view, to pick his writing apart. Just as Santiago calls his enemy his brother, so Hemingway, in capturing on the printed page an artwork of his creation, may be presenting his readers with aspects of his hidden self. This possibility has teased psychoanalytically inclined critics.

Critical Context

Ernest Hemingway published "On the Blue Water: A Gulf Stream Letter" in *Esquire* magazine in April, 1936. It is an essay about marlin fishing and mentions an old sailor who hooked a marlin that towed him for days, was too big to get aboard, and was gnawed by sharks. In 1950, Hemingway published *Across the River and into the Trees*, which was so poor that many reviewers wrote him off as finished. Two years later, however, he rebounded with *The Old Man and the Sea*, a brilliant expansion of "On the Blue Water." It was first published in *Life* magazine on September 1, 1952, which sold more than 5,300,000 copies in two days. When the story was published in book form, it became a runaway best-seller in the United States and England. It made its author a fortune, augmented by rights paid for the rather poor 1958 film based on it and starring Spencer Tracy. It is more significant that the book earned for its author the Pulitzer Prize in fiction in 1952 and contributed to his being awarded the Nobel Prize in Literature in 1954.

Although *The Old Man and the Sea* may tease would-be explicators, it is a perennial favorite of young readers. It is a rousing quest narrative. It has a hero whose virtues are worth remembering and emulating. It teaches readers to guard against pride, to set workable limits to laudable goals, and—above all else—to love and respect God's beautiful creatures even as one must struggle daily to survive in a world red in tooth and claw.

Robert L. Gale

OLD POSSUM'S BOOK OF PRACTICAL CATS

Author: T[homas] S[tearns] Eliot (1888-1965)
First published: 1939
Type of work: Poetry
Subjects: Animals and social issues
Recommended ages: 13-18

An ostensibly whimsical survey of the secret lives of cats provides uneasy glimpses into a civilized jungle where madcap mayhem is the order of the day.

Form and Content

On the surface, *Old Possum's Book of Practical Cats* is a surprising change of pace, coming as it does from one of the most serious and, as some regard him, gloomy poets of the twentieth century: T. S. Eliot, the author of such somber works as "The Love Song of J. Alfred Prufrock" (1915), *The Waste Land* (1922), and "The Hollow Men" (1925). In sharp contrast, *Old Possum's Book of Practical Cats* seems refreshingly lighthearted and devil-may-care in the sheer energy of its play of both language and imagination. Yet, lurking beneath its surface is the potential of a darker intent, just as the potential of a lighter or at least ironic intent peaks continuously out of the corners and from behind the lines of Eliot's more sober and serious literary endeavors.

The volume is composed of fourteen poems, none longer than two full pages, composed in a variety of rudimentary stanzaic patterns, ranging from quatrains to stanzas whose varying lengths, like those of prose paragraphs, are determined more by content than any preconceived structural principle. One outstanding prosodic feature is the nearly complete use of couplets, although several of the poems—"The Naming of Cats," "The Song of the Jellicles," and "Old Deuteronomy"—employ true quatrains, utilizing an *abab* rhyme scheme throughout, and "Of the Aweful Battle of the Pekes and the Pollicles" uses three-line rhymes.

The poetry saves its true inventiveness for the clever use of language, which at times approaches the sprightliness of nursery rhymes and nonsense verse largely because of the obvious pleasure that Eliot finds in naming his various feline characters. Jennyanydots, Mungojerrie, Rumpelteazer, Bustopher Jones, and Skimbleshanks represent as good a sampling as any. That a cat's name is significant is stressed in the opening poem of the sequence, "The Naming of Cats," which includes such delicious sounds as Coricopat and Jellylorum, and which, with the concluding poem, "The Ad-dressing of Cats," provides a generalizing frame around the twelve poems comprising the main body of the text. These each deal with a very particular, very individualistic sort of cat.

They range from the Old Gumbie Cat, whose ironically nurturing treatment of mice and roaches makes for "well-ordered households," to Growltiger, a criminal cat whose "last stand" echoes a bit of the burlesqued violence to be found in the Lost Boys, pirates, and Indians of Sir James M. Barrie's *Peter Pan* (1904) and in Bertolt Brecht's *The Threepenny Opera* (1928), with its host of underworld characters. Meanwhile, more typical cats such as Rum Tum Tugger either are the model of domestic contrariety or, like Mungojerrie and Rumpelteazer, make a shambles of their adoptive household, while other cat characters portrayed in human guises, such as the title roles in "Bustopher Jones: The Cat About Town" and "Gus the Theatre Cat," are presented as out-and-out cads and general ne'er-do-wells. Added to these bounders are the further criminal exploits of the Great Rumpuscat, who puts the battling Pekes and Pollicles on their ears, and Macavity, a Holmesian "master criminal" "called the Hidden Paw," suggesting that there is no more intractable creature in all the animal kingdom than the cat.

The hero of "Skimbleshanks: The Railway Cat" is a rather winning sort, seeing to it that things go smoothly on all the various mail runs, but the general tone and tenor of the volume impresses primarily two feline features upon readers: that cats do as they please and that their self-possessed swagger is no laughing matter. Thus, the volume's final poem, "The Ad-dressing of Cats," which recommends calling a cat by his name, expresses the frustration of trying to come to mutual terms with cats by bringing readers back full circle to the first poem in the volume, "The Naming of Cats," which had insisted that each cat has a name only "the cat himself knows, and will never confess." In sum, there is no getting the better of cats, even when one is attempting to be deferential, politic, and cautious.

Analysis

A clue to Eliot's intention is found in his choice of title: *Old Possum's Book of Practical Cats.* "Old Possum" was the contemporary American poet Ezra Pound's nickname for Eliot. The sobriquet refers to what Pound perceived to be Eliot's ability to play at being what he was not, as the possum plays dead to thwart the plans of potential predators. Eliot's forte in much of his so-called serious poetry is the allusional hint that is as likely to lead readers into a blind alley as into some revelatory meaning. Thus, that he would choose to allude to Pound's identification of him as a trickster in the title of a volume of poetry that appears to be children's verse bordering somewhere among the whimsical, the satirical, and the nonsensical is encouragement enough to warrant reading the poetry with a mildly jaundiced eye.

To start with what the poetry of *Old Possum's Book of Practical Cats* is very likely not, the poems are not animal fables in the same way as Aesop's stories or George Orwell's *Animal Farm* (1949); that is to say, Eliot maintains the authentic tone of someone who is mainly having fun with the words, images, and characterizations. This essential quality of a poetic *divertimento* is found both in the sonority and wit of the language and in the sing-song rhythms of the verses themselves, and so cannot easily be dismissed.

It would be as wrongheaded, however, to assume that there is no serious intention to the poetry. For all the heady erudition of his major works, Eliot was always a fancier of popular forms and appeals to the popular mind as audience. Hanging on the wall of his office was a photograph of the popular film comedian Groucho Marx, with whom the poet developed a personal friendship, and Eliot wrote an essay on the passing of Marie Lloyd, an equally popular comedian on the English music hall circuit. He was also a lover of popular mystery novels, often personally reviewing them for his otherwise lofty journal, the *Criterion*. Eliot himself proved to be quite successful on the London stage as a playwright. Indeed, his first successful play, *Murder in the Cathedral* (1935), about the murder of Thomas Becket, the archbishop of Canterbury, was originally more appealingly titled *The Archbishop Murder Case*.

Even in his major poetry, Eliot was as likely to allude to popular song lyrics as to the Greek and Roman classics; it is perhaps fitting that *Old Possum's Book of Practical Cats* has been successfully translated to the Broadway stage by Andrew Lloyd Weber as *Cats* (1983), although the musical's most notable song, "Memories," is actually a loose adaptation of a much earlier, far more serious Eliot poem, "Rhapsody on a Windy Night" (1917). Eliot also constantly eschewed the incredibly complex interpretations applied to his work, arguing that poetry can communicate before it is understood, and he once observed that the best audience for poetry was one made up of people who could neither read nor write. Whether he meant that an illiterate or a preliterate culture was more conducive to poetic production and appreciation, it is clear that Eliot did not regard poetry as the exclusive preserve of highbrow scholars and critics. He spoke for the auditory imagination—the one that is most stimulated by intriguing sound patterns—and for what he called the music of poetry—its ability to transmit degrees of meaning through tonal variations in rhythms rather than through processes of pure intellectual thought.

Critical Context

Taken together, the foregoing suggests that Eliot was as serious about the poetry comprising *Old Possum's Book of Practical Cats* as he was about any of his other poetry. The fact that hints of the volume's mood and tone appear in earlier work identified as minor poetry in *The Complete Poems and Plays* (1969), specifically "Lines to a Persian Cat" and "Lines to a Yorkshire Terrier," further suggests that the work went through a gestational period during which Eliot was also composing some of his most serious and philosophical poetry that would later comprise *Four Quartets* (1943), which explores the complex interrelatedness among God, person, and nature in Christian terms.

It cannot be mere happenstance that one of the twentieth century's most notably Christian poets also focused on an animal as self-absorbed and likely to do as it pleases as the domesticated cat, or that the poet who virtually first gave voice, in *The Waste Land*, to what critic Hugh Kenner termed the "urban apocalypse" created a cast of primarily city cats. Like all good literature, *Old Possum's Book of Practical Cats* first should delight readers by giving them the pleasure of enjoying words beautifully used. Nevertheless, the amorality and the outright violence and criminal chicanery of these "practical cats" can be viewed as a way of also delightfully instructing readers in the deleterious moral consequences of action centered only and wholly on self and self-aggrandizement.

Russell Elliott Murphy

OLYMPIC GAMES IN ANCIENT GREECE

Authors: Shirley Glubok (1933-   ) and Alfred Tamarin (1913-1980)
First published: 1976; illustrated
Type of work: History
Time of work: 776 B.C.-A.D. 393
Locale: Greece
Subjects: Arts and sports
Recommended ages: 13-18

> *Glubok and Tamarin re-create the experience of an ancient Greek Olympiad through descriptions of the various sporting events and colorful anecdotes from throughout its history.*

Form and Content

Olympic Games in Ancient Greece presents a colorful account of how the ancient Greeks played the Olympic Games. Each chapter describes one day in this five-day festival, beginning with the day-long opening ceremonies, proceeding through three days devoted to various sporting events, and concluding with the Victory Banquet on the last day. Shirley Glubok and Alfred Tamarin give an almost hour-by-hour account of the festivities and sporting events, giving the reader the feeling of having personally witnessed an ancient Olympiad. Brief but evocative details of the typical sights, sounds, and smells of the festival add to the impression of immediacy. Although the emphasis is on a "typical, ideal" Greek Olympiad of the fifth century B.C., information about the history of the games and anecdotes about famous athletes from different time periods are incorporated into the narrative so that the reader has a sense of how the festival evolved over time. Black-and-white photographs of ancient pottery and statuary depicting Olympic athletes provide a visual extension to the authors' description of most of the sports. A note on the modern Olympics, a list of important dates, and an index conclude the book.

A procession of judges, games officials, trumpeters, athletes, and their trainers initiated the Olympiad on its first day. The marchers would start in Elis and proceed thirty-four miles to Olympia. Travelers from throughout the Greek-speaking world representing all classes and professions also converged on Olympia, the sacred site of the Olympiads, which first took place in 776 B.C. and every four years thereafter for more than a thousand years.

Religious rites were an important part of the games. A sacred truce was declared throughout the Greek empire in order to enable Greek citizens to travel to and from the games; contestants took sacred oaths in front of a huge statue of Zeus; an official sacrifice to Zeus marked the high point of the five-day festival; and the victors of the games would dedicate their olive crowns of victory to their peoples' gods and goddesses. Winning was considered pleasing to the gods; cheating was an insult.

Chariot races, horse races, and a pentathlon took place on the second day of the

Olympiad. The pentathlon consisted of the discus throw, long jump, javelin throw, stade race (a sprint down the length of a stadium), and upright wrestling. With his tall, slim figure and strong torso and legs, the pentathlete was considered the ideal of Greek youth and beauty. Lampis of Sparta, a victorious pentathlete of the eighteenth Olympiad in 708 B.C., timed his discus and javelin throws to the rhythm of flute music.

After the great sacrifice to Zeus on the morning of the third day, the boys' events took place. These consisted of some of the same events staged for older athletes: the stade race, wrestling, boxing, and the *pankration*, a mixture of boxing and wrestling. The fourth day of the Olympiad saw a return to adult competition, with three different types of foot races, upright wrestling, boxing, a *pankration*, and the *hoplite* race (a race in armor).

On the fifth day, the victorious athletes processed to the great Temple of Zeus and exchanged their palm branches for olive crowns. The enormous gold statue of the god was also crowned with olive leaves to salute his victory over the old gods at Olympia. A banquet for all the victors ended the festival, with the main course consisting of the hundred animals that had been sacrificed to Zeus on the third day of the Olympiad.

Analysis

The subject matter of *Olympic Games in Ancient Greece* presents a formidable challenge to the writer of nonfiction for young readers. The history of the games spans a thousand years and enfolds the politics, art, and religion of a large empire. Although many of the sports of ancient Greece have modern-day analogues, the cultural context surrounding those sports is vastly different from the experiences of a modern reader. In order to participate imaginatively in an ancient Olympiad, the reader must be made to understand the significance of the Olympic Games in ancient Greek culture. Glubok and Tamarin have addressed this challenge in part through the device of structure: The book is divided into five main parts, each describing one day of an ideal Greek Olympiad. The focus of each section is on the sports played on that day. This way of organizing the text provides a concrete and easy-to-understand overview of the information. It also allows the authors to create a sense of immediacy, as they note the bright colors of the chariots, the bitter smell of burning sacrifices, and the glistening sun reflected on hundreds of eager faces. Readers feel that they are witnessing the events of the festival as they happen.

The authors convey the historical and cultural context of the ancient world with ingenuity. Information about religious beliefs and historical events that affected the development and execution of the games is imparted through lively anecdotes and vivid details interwoven throughout the narrative that dramatizes each day's sports. For example, the authors show the influence of political rivalry on the Olympic Games by recounting a dramatic encounter between King Iphitus of Elis and a victorious runner from Pisa. Other anecdotes emphasize more brutal elements of the ancient world, such as the story of Callipatria, who was nearly thrown off a mountain as punishment for having broken the ban on women attending the games.

The authors also include the stories of several legendary Olympic athletes, such as

Polydamas, winner of the *pankration*, who was so strong that he held up the falling ceiling of a cave long enough for his friends to escape. Through these stories, interspersed frequently throughout the text, the reader becomes aware of the importance of storytelling in ancient Greece. In addition, the reader gains a sense of the heightened drama that these legendary personalities added to the ambience of the ancient Olympiads.

Visual presentation is critical in nonfiction works for young readers. With the exception of a map and a few photographs of Olympia's present-day ruins, the authors have focused illustrative material exclusively on ancient pottery and carvings. The large black-and-white photographs of athletes jumping, twisting, fighting, running, and dancing on the smooth, curved sides of vases and plates add a consistent and strong visual dimension to the book. Images are well-integrated with the contiguous text. In spite of these strengths, the visual design and content are clearly dated. The decades since the publication of *Olympic Games in Ancient Greece* have seen dramatic advances in the sophistication of visual media, and nonfiction books have reflected these developments in the amount, variety, and finesse of their visual elements. Consequently, Glubok and Tamarin's book is likely to strike young readers as visually unexciting, with its predictable approach to page layout, media, and color.

Critical Context

Shirley Glubok, both individually and in her joint works with husband Alfred Tamarin, is noted for her consistent ability to distill intellectual rigor and scholarly authority into an appealing and easily understood text for young people. Always readable, clear, and lively, her books do not oversimplify their subject matter or employ faddish gimmicks in their presentation of information. These qualities have earned for her books numerous awards and citations as well as inclusion on prestigious professional bibliographies such as the American Library Association's *Best Books for Young Adults*.

Like Glubok's many other works of nonfiction, *Olympic Games in Ancient Greece* shows how art reflects the history and values of its culture. Unlike her books about art history, such as the series beginning with *The Art of Ancient Egypt* (1962), it emphasizes a particular ritual of a society and uses art exclusively as illustrative material rather than as a focus of the text itself. Unique to this work, too, is the device of presenting information in a dramatized form.

Olympic Games in Ancient Greece is an extensive account of the ancient games for young readers. Before its publication, no other treatment of this topic had attempted its comprehensive approach to the artistic, historical, and cultural context of the ancient sports. In years when the Olympics are held, demand for this title typically increases, according to the publishers. With the timeless appeal of sports as its focus and the added impetus of the interest created by modern-day Olympiads, *Olympic Games in Ancient Greece* is likely to remain a widely read classic of nonfiction for children and young adults.

Constance Vidor

ON THE BEACH

Author: Nevil Shute (Nevil Shute Norway, 1899-1960)
First published: 1957
Type of work: Novel
Type of plot: Science fiction
Time of work: One year after a nuclear war
Locale: Australia and Seattle
Subjects: Death, suicide, and war
Recommended ages: 15-18

People in Australia try to cope with the end of the world resulting from a nuclear holocaust.

Principal characters:
PETER HOLMES, a lieutenant commander in the Royal Australian Navy
MARY HOLMES, his wife
DWIGHT TOWERS, a commander in the U.S. Navy and the captain of the American submarine *Scorpion*
JOHN OSBORNE, a scientist
MOIRA DAVIDSON, a young woman
RALPH SWAIN, a radar operator on the *Scorpion*
LIEUTENANT SUNDERSON, a radio officer

Form and Content

On the Beach is an account of how the world might end. About a year before the book begins, everyone in the Northern Hemisphere died in a nuclear war that lasted thirty-seven days. It started when Albania managed to drop a nuclear bomb on Naples, Italy. Then Egypt bombed Israel. Eventually, the United States, the Soviet Union, and China unleashed their nuclear arsenals.

Australian scientists estimate that 4,700 warheads were detonated, but little else is known. Lethal levels of radiation are spreading into the Southern Hemisphere, all the principal characters know that they have less than a year to live. They plan to use drugs to commit suicide when they develop the symptoms of radiation disease, which are vomiting, diarrhea, and fever.

Surviving vessels of the U.S. Navy in the Pacific journeyed to Australia after the fighting stopped. A shortage of oil curtailed their operations after they reached Brisbane. Only the nuclear submarine *Scorpion* is still operational until Commander Dwight Towers scuttles it at the end of the novel.

There is little plot to *On the Beach*, although the *Scorpion* makes two journeys. Towers is in command, with Peter Holmes as his Australian liaison and John Osborne as his scientific adviser. The first journey is to other cities in Australia to confirm the deaths of their populations. The second is to North America to investigate mysterious radio signals originating in the Seattle area. While the submarine is in the harbor, Ralph Swain jumps ship. Seattle was his home town, and he finds the corpses of his parents in their house. When the crew of the *Scorpion* last see him, he is fishing, but already running a fever. When Lieutenant Sunderson goes ashore in a radiation suit, the only items that he brings back are the last three issues of *The Saturday Evening Post*. Another purpose of the trip was to test a theory that radiation would decrease the farther away they traveled from the equator. Unfortunately, they prove the theory false.

Most of the action consists of people finding ways to cope with their own impending deaths and those of everyone else. Towers pretends that his family in Connecticut is still alive and that the United States still exists: His relationship with Moira Davidson remains platonic because he still considers himself married, he sinks the *Scorpion* because it contains much classified technology, and, when he takes the boat out on its last voyage, he brings presents for his wife and children with him. Peter and Mary Holmes take care of their child and work on a garden; Peter clears some trees a few weeks before he expects to die. Osborne buys a Ferrari, takes part in automobile races, and wins the last Grand Prix race; he dies in the car, sitting in the driver's seat after he has put it on blocks. In the first chapters, Davidson drinks and attends parties to forget her imminent doom; later, she learns shorthand. Her parents take care of their farm until the very end. A minor character sets for himself the goal of drinking all the wine in his club's collection; ironically, he outlives all the others, because alcohol in the bloodstream slows the advance of radiation sickness.

Analysis

On the Beach is a prime example of a science-fiction story based on the premise of "if this goes on." In such a story, the author warns the reader that if a particular trend or practice is allowed to continue, the results will be disastrous. Accordingly, Nevil Shute is warning the reader that if nuclear weapons continue to be developed and if small countries obtain them, the extinction of the human species is inevitable. For example, Shute assumes for the story that the hydrogen bomb will be superseded by the cobalt bomb, which generates more radiation than previous nuclear devices. His other premises are that countries such as Albania and Egypt will be able to buy Hiroshima-like bombs from arms dealers and that some of them will have leaders irrational enough to use them.

Shute shows the danger of relying too heavily on systems. During the war, Washington, D.C., and London were bombed by Russian-made Egyptian planes disguised as Russian planes. The people left in command reacted as they had been trained to do and ordered a retaliation on Russia. By the time that the mistake was realized, it was too late: North Atlantic Treaty Organization (NATO) forces had bombed Moscow, Leningrad, and other targets in the Soviet Union.

What makes the novel so effective is that Shute does not preach. He lets the reader get to know and like the main characters, and then he kills them off. Shute is also restrained. He does not sensationalize them or resort to gory descriptions of corpses.

No one in the book ever sees a city in ruins. If anything, the main characters are below average in imagination.

In one sense, they are fortunate in knowing the approximate date of their deaths. They can put their lives in order and spend their remaining days doing what they want to do. Osborne indulges in his secret ambition of car racing. Towers and Davidson go fishing in the mountains, where they meet other fisherman spending their final days. All the major characters die on their own terms: Towers is in his submarine, Osborne in his Ferrari, Peter and Mary Holmes in their house, and finally Davidson watching the *Scorpion* sail from Melbourne on its last voyage.

In an unrealistic move, Shute chooses not to portray characters who have crackpot schemes to save themselves; no one moves into a cave or builds a bunker. While such actions may be irrational, so are the actions of many of the book's characters.

The male characters reflect Shute's interest in ships and technology. His 1954 autobiography was even entitled *Slide Rule*. Shute was an officer in the Royal Navy during World War II and worked in the Department of Miscellaneous Weapon Development on the development of rockets, torpedoes, flame throwers, and other weapons. A large part of his earlier life was devoted to the construction of an experimental airship, and he founded an aircraft manufacturing company.

The technology that Shute describes dates the book. For example, the challenge of transmitting a long document from Rio De Janeiro to Australia would be easily handled today with a fax machine. No one has developed a cobalt bomb; the story requires this premise, because hydrogen bombs would not poison the atmosphere in the way that Shute describes. Furthermore, Shute's description of the ecological changes resulting from the detonation of so many warheads is not consistent with contemporary theory. No nuclear winter occurs in the novel; the submarine crew even marvels at what a beautiful day it is when they visit Seattle. Second, no effects of electromagnetic pulse are found; the radio station in Seattle survives almost two years after the deaths of the operators. None of these flaws, however, lessens the book's power.

Critical Context

On the Beach dramatized the potential effects of nuclear warfare better than any book before it. Because Nevil Shute was already one of Great Britain's most popular authors, it had a wide audience. The novel was his biggest best-seller and never went out of print. It reached a larger audience when it was made in a major motion picture starring Gregory Peck, Ava Gardner, and Fred Astaire in 1959, although Shute considered it the worst film made from one of his books.

Later works by other artists explored aspects of nuclear war not dealt with directly by Shute. The film *Dr. Strangelove* (1964) is a satirical examination of the irrationality necessary to initiate a nuclear exchange. It points out that such irrationality is not confined to small countries: An insane U.S. Air Force general orders sixty B-52 bombers to attack the Soviet Union. Eugene Burdick and Harvey Wheeler's book *Fail-Safe* (1962), which was made into a film in 1964, is a serious look at how people can become prisoners of the systems that they build: A computer malfunction sends the attack order to a squadron of American B-58 bombers, and the system works so well that the bombers cannot be recalled or stopped.

Antinuclear political activists are normally associated with the political Left. Shute, however, was a conservative who was strongly procapitalist and antisocialist, as shown in his books *A Town Like Alice* (1950), *In the Wet* (1953), and *Slide Rule*. Shute's political position adds to the credibility of his message in *On the Beach* because critics cannot dismiss the book as left-wing propaganda.

Tom Feller

ONE DAY IN THE LIFE OF IVAN DENISOVICH

Author: Aleksandr Solzhenitsyn (1918-   )
First published: Odin den Ivana Denisovicha, 1962 (English translation, 1963)
Type of work: Novel
Type of plot: Historical fiction and social realism
Time of work: The early 1950's
Locale: A Soviet labor camp in Siberia
Subjects: Crime, politics and law, and social issues
Recommended ages: 15-18

Ivan Denisovich Shukhov, an ordinary Russian serving time in a Stalinist labor camp on trumped-up charges, does his best to live through the indignities and brutalities of one more day in captivity.

Principal characters:
  IVAN DENISOVICH SHUKHOV, an ordinary honest Russian of peasant origin who is caught up in the injustices of the Soviet camp system
  TIURIN, a fellow prisoner, the leader of Ivan's work squad
  GOPCHIK, a fellow prisoner, a boy from Ukraine
  TSEZAR, a fellow prisoner, an intellectual
  ALYOSHA, a fellow prisoner, a pious Baptist
  BUINOVSKY, a fellow prisoner, a former naval captain

Form and Content

The clang of the wake-up call at five A.M. starts the day for Ivan Denisovich and hundreds of other prisoners at a bleak Siberian labor camp. In this short novel, Aleksandr Solzhenitsyn offers the reader a view of the realities of life behind the barbed wire. Men struggle to get enough food in the mess hall. They try to keep themselves from freezing in below-zero temperatures. They obey the arbitrary rules of the armed guards and the orders of a few prisoners who have ingratiated themselves with the powers that be and have become camp leaders. They avoid being sent to the punishment cells, where men can weaken and die in a few days. They swear obscenely at one another and at the system. They work when they can and rest when they can, saving their strength to live another day.

The camp is presented through the eyes of a middle-aged man from a peasant village, Ivan Denisovich Shukhov. He was sentenced to ten years of hard labor after he had been falsely accused of spying for the Germans during World War II. With no chance for appeal, Ivan was sent off to the camp system, the Gulag. Every day, he tries simply to get by as best he can. He generally obeys the rules, takes small pleasures in small things, and stoically awaits the end of his sentence.

The plot of the story is simply the events of an ordinary day. It is a relatively good day for Ivan. He avoids the punishment cells. He must work outside, building a wall, but there are places to find shelter from the snow and biting wind and even a stove to warm himself during the lunch time break. He swipes an extra bowl of oatmeal at breakfast and "earns" an extra soup at dinner by doing a favor for another inmate. He helps build the wall and enjoys his accomplishment. He smuggles a piece of a hacksaw blade into his bunk that he can later make into a little knife for repairing shoes. He buys a bit of tobacco from an inmate who has gotten a package from home. He has not fallen ill. In short, he has survived.

The lives of other prisoners who are close to Ivan are vividly drawn as well. Tiurin, his squad leader, is a shrewd and basically honest man, who knows how to get work out of his men but also how to protect them from the worst excesses of the Gulag. Gopchik is a teenager, anxious to please the men in the squad, smart and willing to learn. Alyosha is a dedicated Baptist, a man of humble Christian virtues who believes that he has been called to suffer for the sake of Jesus Christ. Tsezar is something of an intellectual who has wangled himself an inside job as a bookkeeper. Buinovsky is a former naval captain who cannot get used to taking orders from men like those who once obeyed his every command. His pride gets him in trouble with the authorities, and he is sent to a punishment cell, an ordeal that he might not survive. There are glimpses of the camp guards who realize that, although they are carrying the guns, in a sense they are also victims of the Gulag.

After the last count of prisoners for the night, Ivan climbs wearily into his bunk, nibbles a bit of sausage that he has saved, covers himself with his thin blanket and his overcoat, and awaits another day.

Analysis

Throughout this deceptively simple story, Solzhenitsyn reflects on the nature of the Soviet Union and its Communist system. The protagonist, Ivan, is not a troublemaker, but he is a firm opponent of the regime. He does his best to maintain bits of private property, even though they are only personal items. He once was issued a pair of leather boots, which he cared for lovingly, cleaning them and softening them with grease. The authorities, however, demanded that all leather boots be returned to the warehouse when winter felt boots were issued, and Ivan did not have a prayer of getting his own leather ones back in the spring. At the job site, Ivan carefully kept his own personal trowel for laying cement blocks, rather than taking the shoddy one from the common tool shed. The message is clear: Private property and private enterprise is superior to communism.

Religion is another major theme in the novel. Ivan believes in God, but he has little use for institutional religion. The Russian Orthodox priest in his village, he recalls, was in league with the government authorities to keep his own privileges. Alyosha is a genuine Christian, a dedicated member of a baptist sect. He secretly reads from the Bible whenever he can, and his behavior is full of Christian charity, even in the harsh camp environment.

The dignity of work is important. Ivan dreads the punishment cells not only because they are cold and unhealthy but also because prisoners there are forced to be idle. He gets satisfaction from accomplishing real tasks, such as installing a stovepipe, so that his work squad can have a bit of heat at the construction site, or building a cement block wall straight and true.

The one young adult in the story is Gopchik, a Ukrainian teenager. He is naïve but resilient. Ivan, who remembers that he once had a son, likes the young man and teaches him the realities of the camp so that he will have a good chance to survive.

Although the book is clearly based on Solzhenitsyn's own experience in the camps, it is not really autobiographical. Ivan is a peasant, without formal education. Solzhenitsyn had a formal education in mathematics and the sciences, and he had been an artillery officer in World War II. He, like all the men he described, had been sentenced on false charges. Perhaps at one time he was like the naval captain, Buinovsky, learned and proud of his former status, but Solzhenitsyn must have acquired the peasant shrewdness of Ivan in order to survive.

Solzhenitsyn is contemptuous of the Soviet system, labeling the worst possible place for the squad to be assigned work as "The Socialist Way of Life" settlement. Yet, he is uncertain about the nature of real freedom. In the camp, prisoners are free to complain about dictator Joseph Stalin in ways that civilians on the outside cannot. Even the camp guards, presumably free men, are under iron discipline and face the same cold winds as the prisoners.

One Day in the Life of Ivan Denisovich is a short book that carefully understates the brutalities of the Soviet camps. A decade later, Solzhenitsyn brought out three massive volumes detailing the deadly viciousness of the camps under the title *Arkhipelag GULag* (1973-1975; *The Gulag Archipelago*, 1974-1978). The brevity and restraint of *One Day in the Life of Ivan Denisovich* makes it comparable to Elie Wiesel's *Un di Velt hot geshvign* (1956; *Night*, 1960), a short memoir about death and survival in the Nazi concentration camp system.

Critical Context

When *One Day in the Life of Ivan Denisovich* was published in 1962, it created a sensation. Aleksandr Solzhenitsyn was an unknown high school mathematics teacher who wrote in his spare time. *Novy Mir*, the Moscow literary magazine, published it only after getting permission from Soviet leader Nikita Khrushchev himself. The little book was quickly translated and published abroad, and foreign publishers sought more material from the eloquent dissident. After Khrushchev fell from power and the anti-Stalinist "thaw" proved temporary, Solzhenitsyn was pressured by Soviet authorities to be silent, but he continued to write. When he was awarded the 1970 Nobel Prize in Literature, the Soviet Union refused to allow him to go to Sweden to receive the prize. Like Ivan, Solzhenitsyn submitted outwardly, but he continued to write in private.

In 1974, just after the publication of *The Gulag Archipelago* abroad, the Soviet government exiled him. He settled in Vermont but remained largely in seclusion. Although an eloquent anti-Communist, he did not like the freewheeling materialism of the West either. After the dissolution of the Soviet Union in 1991, Solzhenitsyn returned to Russia and continued to write and speak as a prophet of conservative and Slavophile virtues.

Gordon R. Mork

ONE FLEW OVER THE CUCKOO'S NEST

Author: Ken Kesey (1935-   )
First published: 1962
Type of work: Novel
Type of plot: Psychological realism
Time of work: The late 1950's
Locale: A state mental hospital in Oregon
Subjects: Emotions, health and illness, and social issues
Recommended ages: 15-18

Committed to a state mental hospital, a rambunctious drifter inspires his fellow patients to resist an oppressive system and to achieve self-reliance and self-respect.

Principal characters:
RANDLE P. MCMURPHY, a hustler, roustabout, and former prison farm
     inmate committed to the mental hospital for observation
CHIEF BROMDEN, a 6-foot 8-inch Columbia Indian suffering from
     paranoid schizophrenia
NURSE RATCHED, the head nurse on the ward, who is devious,
     determined, and authoritarian
DALE HARDING, an intellectual and somewhat effeminate patient
BILLY BIBBIT, an extremely insecure and sometimes self-destructive
     patient who admires McMurphy

Form and Content

One Flew over the Cuckoo's Nest is a tragic yet inspirational account of one man's self-sacrifice in a struggle against hypocrisy and oppression. Set on a ward of a mental hospital in Oregon, the novel depicts characters who could be found in many settings and a conflict between authoritarianism and individualism that is truly universal.

Ken Kesey tells the story through the eyes of Chief Bromden, a longtime patient who is uniquely knowledgeable about hospital routines and procedures and privy to staff secrets. As important as what Chief knows is what he does not know; he can only infer Randle McMurphy's motives, a process of discovery that gives the novel its focus. A paranoid schizophrenic, Bromden reports his hallucinations faithfully; while they cannot be taken literally, they do make sense. As Chief says, his story is "the truth, even if it didn't happen."

The action begins when McMurphy is admitted to Nurse Ratched's ward for observation. Authorities at the prison farm where he had been a convict are not sure whether he is a psychopath or merely a malingerer. On the ward, McMurphy proves himself to be a master manipulator, hustling his fellow patients in card games and persistently challenging the authority of Nurse Ratched. The patients quickly accept him as a leader and begin to see him as their champion. Nurse Ratched is infuriated by this challenge to her authority, but she bides her time. McMurphy finds out that because he has been officially committed, Nurse Ratched and the hospital staff control his release, and he becomes more prudent and conformist. Nurse Ratched appears to have won, and McMurphy's fellow patients understand and regretfully accept the change in his behavior.

McMurphy then learns that Dale Harding, Billy Bibbit, and many of the other patients on the ward have not been committed and are there voluntarily, and his behavior changes again. Once more, he is loud and irreverent, challenging Nurse Ratched at every opportunity. He charters a fishing boat, persuading ten of his fellow patients to sign up for a salmon-fishing trip despite Nurse Ratched's opposition; he even persuades the staff doctor to go along. The trip is a great success: McMurphy spends time with a teenaged girl, one of the patients manages the boat masterfully, the men catch fish, and they are all able by the end of the day to hold their heads up in society. Nevertheless, this outing sows the seeds of disaster.

Nurse Ratched demands that those who went on the trip undergo a particularly disagreeable hygienic procedure. One of the patients resists, and a fight breaks out between the staff orderlies on the one hand and McMurphy and Bromden on the other. In response, Nurse Ratched orders electroshock therapy for McMurphy and Bromden. When McMurphy refuses to apologize for his role in the fight, he is subjected to repeated treatments.

After McMurphy returns to the ward, Harding and the other inmates convince him to escape from the hospital to save himself from further retaliation by Nurse Ratched. McMurphy is determined not to leave, however, until Billy Bibbit has had a "date" with Candy, the teenager who went on the fishing trip with McMurphy and the other patients. McMurphy persuades the night orderly to let Candy and another young woman onto the ward with bottles of wine and vodka for a midnight party. Billy and Candy eventually disappear into the ward's seclusion room, and everyone falls asleep. In the morning, Nurse Ratched discovers Billy sleeping with Candy and threatens to tell his mother. Billy pleads with her not to do so. He blames Candy, McMurphy, and the others for what has happened and then, when left alone, commits suicide. McMurphy attacks Nurse Ratched and is dragged away by hospital staff members.

In the denouement, many patients leave the hospital or transfer to other wards. McMurphy is lobotomized; his mindless body is smothered by Chief Bromden, who then makes good his escape.

Analysis

Intended for a general audience, *One Flew over the Cuckoo's Nest* has been popular with high school and college students because of its vivid prose, its sharply drawn and readily comprehensible characters, and its theme of self-reliance and self-respect.

This theme can be clearly seen in Kesey's presentation of McMurphy as a Christ figure. McMurphy is crucified on a cross-shaped table when he undergoes electroshock therapy. The party that he and the others have on the ward is a kind of Last Supper, with pills and codeine-laced punch taking the place of bread and wine. Candy is a Magdalene, Billy Bibbit is a Judas, Nurse Ratched and her staff are Pharisees, and the twelve people whom McMurphy takes on the fishing trip are Disciples. Yet, there is a significant difference between McMurphy's story and the Christian Gospels. According to the Gospels, when a storm blew up on the᷾ sea of Galilee, the Disciples awakened Jesus, who miraculously calmed the waters. In *One Flew over the Cuckoo's Nest*, when McMurphy's followers on the fishing trip ask for help, he stands in the doorway and laughs. In the Christian worldview, salvation comes by the grace of God; in McMurphy's worldview, salvation can only come from within each individual.

A gambler, brawler, ladies' man, and drifter, McMurphy also resembles figures from folklore such as the Roving Gambler and the Wagoner's Lad, about whom he sings his first morning on the ward. He reminds Harding of the Lone Ranger. In an era when even the West has been settled and civilized, McMurphy makes Nurse Ratched's ward a last frontier. The great American Dream that he pursues is the existential authenticity of nonconformity, or even of madness. (True madness, unlike neurosis, has its own authenticity, at least in this novel.) The worldview that presents nonconformity as such an unquestioned ideal divides the world and the people in it absolutely. Individualists are "good guys," and representatives of restraining or civilizing forces are oppressive "bad guys." Readers must decide whether such an antithetical worldview is a simplification that clarifies important truths or an oversimplification that distorts reality.

Paradoxically, this novel, which so clearly challenges oppression, uses sexist and racist language. Even more significant is that the novel generally characterizes women and African Americans unsympathetically. While the little Japanese nurse on the Disturbed Ward might provide an attractive role model for young female readers, the novel's most vivid characterizations of women are all negative: McMurphy's nymphomaniac, underage lover; the stereotypical prostitutes with hearts of gold and minds of plastic; and overwhelming, mechanistic, hypocritical, and emasculating figures such as Billy Bibbit's mother, Chief Bromden's mother, and, above all, Nurse Ratched. Similarly, although the African American night orderly, Mr. Turkle, is presented as relatively benign, he is also shown to be an incompetent substance abuser; and although Nurse Ratched's day orderlies—Washington, Williams, and Geever—are presented as victims of oppression themselves, they are also characterized much more emphatically as hate-filled, perverted, sadistic instruments of oppression in their turn. While the novel's language referring to minorities and women surely may be taken as representative of the American society in the late 1950's, the pattern of these characterizations is unfortunate and not in keeping with the novel's sensitive and sympathetic treatment of Chief Bromden's problems with cultural assimilation and its championship of oppressed persons in general.

Critical Context

The protagonists of *One Flew over the Cuckoo's Nest* and of Ken Kesey's second novel, *Sometimes a Great Notion* (1964), belong to the American tradition of the romantic hero, which extends from James Fenimore Cooper's Natty Bumppo through all the heroes of popular Westerns to the superheroes of contemporary comic books. Kesey's novels also find a place in the American tradition of iconoclastic individualism extending from Henry David Thoreau through Herman Melville and Mark Twain to the Beat authors of the 1950's, such as Jack Kerouac and Allen Ginsberg.

One Flew over the Cuckoo's Nest has been more successful than many other works popular during the counterculture movement of the 1960's and 1970's—a success that stems more from its artistic excellence than from its social philosophy. Kesey's effective use of emblematic scenes (reminiscent of some scenes in the works of Melville), his telling use of allusions, his vividness, his economy, and his thorough integration of detail all combine to make the novel a classic of modern American literature.

David W. Cole

ORIGINS
What New Discoveries Reveal About the Emergence
of Our Species and Its Possible Future

Authors: Richard E. Leakey (1944-   ) and Roger Lewin (1946-   )
First published: 1977; illustrated
Type of work: History
Time of work: Human prehistory
Locale: Mainly Africa
Subjects: Nature, race and ethnicity, and science
Recommended ages: 15-18

This well-informed but highly speculative account of the evolution of the human species includes the authors' theories about human nature and its development.

Form and Content

Several terms are useful to master before reading *Origins*. The small, apelike creatures who appeared twelve million years or so ago are known as *Ramapithecus* and were the first hominids, or primates of the family Hominidae. *Ramapithecus* were the ancestors of two long-extinct species termed australopithecines, *Australopithecus africanus* and *Australopithecus boisei*. *Ramapithecus* were also the begetters of *Homo erectus*, who around half a million years ago evolved into *Homo sapiens* and later, perhaps fifty thousand years ago, into the modern humans that Richard E. Leakey and Roger Lewin name *Homo sapiens sapiens*.

After a chapter that puts "Humanity in Perspective," the authors explain "The Greatest Revolution," or the series of events in the nineteenth century that led to understanding the great age of the earth and the rudiments of evolutionary theory. Five chapters on the development of humankind follow: "The Roots of Humanity," "Hominid Beginnings," "The Cradle of Mankind," "From Africa to Agriculture," and "The First Mixed Economy." The chapters "Intelligence, Language, and the Human Mind" and "Aggression, Sex, and Human Nature" argue very strongly the authors' views on these topics; the final essay is entitled "Mankind in Prospective."

Leakey and Lewin state the goal of *Origins* clearly:

> Through an exploration of the forces that nurtured the birth of the hunting and gathering way of life perhaps three million years ago, and through studying the question of why such a long-established mode of existence was superseded, beginning some 10,000 years ago, by a sedentary agricultural society, we can hope for some insight into modern society, and with it some guide to our future. That is the aim of the book.

As they proceed with this aim, the authors dispute the thesis that humans are innately aggressive, a position held notably by Konrad Lorenz, Raymond Dart, and Robert Ardrey. The vigor with which Leakey and Lewin rebut their opponents gives *Origins* a sharply tendentious tone.

If possible, readers should obtain the original hardbound edition, with its many illustrations that parallel the text throughout and bring alive much of the discussion. The only advantage of the unillustrated paperback edition published in 1991, aside from its compactness, is its greatly enlarged bibliography. Slight changes occur in the text as well, reflecting changes in scholarly thinking. For example, the hardbound edition begins with the words "Close to three million years ago . . . ," whereas the paperback shortens the period to two million years.

Special attention should be given to the several hundred illustrations, half of them in vivid color, in the hardbound edition. The photographs are sometimes grouped by theme, depicting the varying responses to similar challenges of widely different cultures. The chapter "Mankind in Prospective," for example, juxtaposes five photographs on facing pages to compare a variety of habitats: a Moroccan nomad's tent, an Inuit's igloo, a Mali dweller's grass hut, a French farmer's home, and a Solomon Islander's house built over the water on stilts. Similarly, the self-adornment practices in dress and cosmetics of six different cultures are compared in colorful photographs printed side-by-side.

Analysis

The dramatic account of how the earth's great age was discovered is one of Leakey and Lewin's most interesting stories. They explain how the Western world accepted for two millennia the Judeo-Christian story and how James Ussher (1581-1656), the archbishop of Armagh, calculated that the Creation had occurred in 4004 B.C. Dr. John Lightfoot of Cambridge University even narrowed down the event to nine o'clock on the morning of October 23. The evidence from geology, however, made this dating difficult to maintain, and true believers resorted to various explanations to ward off assaults from science. The diluvial theory, for example, explained fossils as the remains of animals drowned in the biblical Flood. When this hypothesis collapsed, French geologist Baron Georges Cuvier (1769-1832) proposed that the sequences of fossils found in sedimentary rock indicated a succession of catastrophes—hence, the term "catastrophe theory."

In 1830, Charles Lyell (1797-1875) published the first volume of *The Principles of Geology*, thereby founding the modern science of geology. This great work was the beginning of the end for the faithful Creationists who followed Archbishop Ussher. Other scholars, such as Charles Darwin's grandfather, Erasmus Darwin (1731-1802), had already done important research in embryology and comparative anatomy that suggested one single source for all life. Yet, even the most devoted of Erasmus Darwin's followers could not explain exactly how life had evolved.

Jean Baptiste de Lamarck (1744-1829) theorized that evolution occurred through the inheritance of acquired characteristics. For example, he claimed that giraffes acquired long necks because they would stretch for food high up, thereby lengthening their necks, and that each generation of offspring would be born with longer necks than those of their ancestors.

The dramatic conclusion to this chapter in history was to be written by Charles

Darwin (1809-1882), whose five-year voyage around the world on HMS *Beagle*, concluding in 1836, led to the publication on November 24, 1859, of *On the Origin of Species by Means of Natural Selection*. This 502-page opus sold out its entire first printing of 1,250 copies on the first day. A long intellectual debate ensued, with late skirmishes still breaking out, but evolution now has a firm foundation in scientific theory.

From the mix of fact, hypothesis, and speculation that Leakey and Lewin generate, a central thesis emerges: that *Homo sapiens* is not the instinctively aggressive creature for which some scholars have argued. Hunting, for example, is not to be confused with aggression and with some vague need to release the impulse to violence; instead, it is commonly a group endeavor that offers many practical advantages, and it is not even the hunters' major food source. Hunting and gathering dominated life during the period of transition from *Homo erectus* to *Homo sapiens*, roughly half a million years ago, and continued down to the invention of agriculture, which occurred about ten thousand years ago.

It is from this transition to an agricultural life that the authors derive their main argument rebutting the claims for humans as innately aggressive and asserting the primacy of culture over heredity in establishing patterns of behavior. For example, cannibalism is a culturally influenced form of aggression of which there are two types: exocannibalism (eating members of another tribe) and endocannibalism (eating members of one's own tribe). Leakey and Lewin minimize the aggression in exocannibalism by declaring that it is "much more often an accompaniment of hostilities than the cause of them," and they declare that "endocannibalism at its simplest may be the customary way of laying the dead to rest."

Why, then, if humans are not by nature aggressive, does war remain a threat everywhere on the globe? The authors' answer again relies on their thesis that *Homo sapiens* is conditioned by cultural factors. Whereas the hunting and gathering economies succeeded because of their need for cooperation, the transition to an agricultural economy encouraged people to live in larger groups and in permanent communities, where they accumulated material possessions in quantities sufficient to encourage raids on affluent neighbors. This thesis is clearly a controversial one and is virtually impossible to prove.

Critical Context

The cautious reader will approach *Origins* with considerable respect for the erudition of its authors and the fluency of its arguments. Yet, not only are many of its claims controversial—such as the one that follows the linguist Noam Chomsky in assuming that humans have an innate capacity for language structures—but the knowledge of the human past changes rapidly and not much can be taken for granted.

Indeed, in 1992 Leakey and Lewin published *Origins Reconsidered: In Search of What Makes Us Human*. Most of this volume is devoted to updating discoveries in the field, but the last chapter, "Origins Reconsidered," apologizes for their suggestion in *Origins* that the species has had a telos, or end, toward which it has been marching to the tune of some cosmic principle. The chapter also introduces some compelling philosophical issues that will be of great interest to readers of the original book.

Frank Day

OUR GOLDA
The Story of Golda Meir

Author: David A. Adler (1947-   )
First published: 1984; illustrated
Type of work: Biography
Time of work: 1898-1978
Locale: Kiev and Pinsk, Russia; Milwaukee, Wisconsin; and Palestine (later Israel)
Subjects: Activists, military leaders, and politicians
Recommended ages: 10-13

Meir hears the message of Zionism from early childhood and grows up to become a political activist and eventually the prime minister of Israel.

Principal personages:
GOLDA MEIR, whose life is traced from birth to retirement from the
    position of prime minister of Israel
MOSHE YITZHAK MABOVITCH, her father, a carpenter and cabinetmaker
BLUME MABOVITCH, her mother
SHEYNA, Golda's older sister, a Zionist
MORRIS MEYERSON, a cultured sign painter and eventually Golda's
    husband
DAVID BEN-GURION, the first prime minister of Israel

Form and Content
David A. Adler's *Our Golda: The Story of Golda Meir* is a biography of Israel's famous prime minister. Adler did not know Meir or her times personally, but he obviously admires her. His admiration adds a warmth to the text that is often missing from biographies of important but distant personages. The reader is drawn in closer yet by the soft black-and-white pencil illustrations by Donna Ruff. The twelve drawings of Meir and her family and compatriots help put a human face on the legend.

Meir's story is told chronologically, with little dialogue or description. The emphasis is always on describing events and giving information, not on putting the reader at the scene. Each of the book's five chapters is named for a different part of the world where Meir lived out an important stage in her development. The first chapter, "Kiev," shows the strength of Meir's parents and grandparents, who lived in poverty and oppression because they were Jews. This chapter provides an excellent overview of the hardships faced by Russian Jews in the nineteenth and early twentieth centuries; Adler understands the power of the truth simply told, without dramatics. Golda Mabovitch is only the second of her mother's first six children to survive. Her father leaves Russia for the Golden Land—the United States—to establish a better life for his family.

In the second chapter, the remaining family members are forced to move to Pinsk, within the Pale of Settlement for Jews. Life is even harder here, and the threat of pogroms is always present. As Golda grows up, she overhears and is fascinated by the planning of groups of Zionists. The third chapter, "Milwaukee," covers the harrowing journey to the United States to join her father and follows Golda's formal and informal education as a schoolgirl and as a Zionist. She struggles under her parents' old-fashioned demands and their inability to understand her desire for education. They believe that education is wasted on a woman and that at fourteen Golda ought to be thinking of marriage. At fifteen, she runs away to Denver, where her older sister Sheyna lives, and becomes involved in Zionist activism. She meets Morris Meyerson, whom she will later marry.

The fourth chapter, "Palestine," shows Golda and Morris settling on a kibbutz in Palestine, their name Hebracized to "Meir." Golda becomes more and more involved politically, especially with labor issues, and less involved with her husband and children. She travels throughout Europe and North America seeking support for a Jewish state and refuge for Jews fleeing Nazi persecution. In 1947, the United Nations votes to partition Palestine into an Arab and a Jewish state. Thus, the fifth chapter is entitled "Israel," and it begins with war against the Arab nations. Golda Meir again travels to North America, returning with millions of dollars for weapons, which help Israel prevail. She signs the Israeli Declaration of Independence, becomes minister of labor and then foreign minister, and retires in 1965. In 1969, Meir is elected prime minister, and she serves in that position through the Six Days' War, until her second retirement in 1974.

Analysis

In *Our Golda*, Adler brings together several skills and interests demonstrated throughout his career, which has produced more than one hundred books for children and young adults: The book is nonfiction, features a strong female central character, and presents an important part of Jewish history and culture. These elements come up repeatedly in Adler's work and help account for the continuing popularity of this biography.

For Adler, the line between fiction and nonfiction is a clear one. He stands at a respectful distance from his subject, presenting only information that he can somehow verify. He was not able (or did not seek) to interview family members or to examine private family documents. He is not himself a contemporary, able to recount his own sensations of the terror of the pogroms or the Holocaust. Most important, he does not attempt to fictionalize Meir's life, to present words that she must have spoken under the circumstances or to describe how their family's apartment probably looked. The tone and the stance throughout is somewhat distant, with a focus on actions and events rather than on motivations and feelings.

One happy result of this distance, of keeping the focus on events, is that the book avoids taking on a strident political voice of its own. Clearly, the central character is Golda Meir, and clearly she is working and fighting against great odds to create and maintain a Jewish homeland. Yet, Adler does not put in his characters' mouths the arguments, the rhetoric, or the biblical quotations. He could easily supply adjectives for Meir, calling her "brilliant" or "righteous" or "wise," and he could refer to Arabs as "misguided" or "evil," but he does not. He presents events in clear factual language, with few adverbs or adjectives. He trusts the power of simple language to guide the reader gently: "During the next few months in Israel there were shootings, roadblocks, attacks, and bombings. The Arabs were fighting to keep Israel from being born, and the Jews were fighting back."

Adler, however, is not totally removed from his subject. He obviously sees Meir as a hero, as a fighter for justice and freedom. He explains in a brief "About the Book" section that he grew up during Meir's rising career in the Israeli government. Although she held important offices, he and his family always "referred to her affectionately as 'Golda,' as if she were a close personal friend."

It is interesting to note that although *Our Golda* is part of Viking's Women of Our Time series, Adler does not make much of the fact that Meir was a woman in what is usually thought of as a man's world. Just as he does not argue for the rightness of the Zionist cause, but simply assumes it, neither does he devote much ink to pointing out that it is unusual for a woman to be the elected leader of a modern nation engaged in war.

There are a few places where gender becomes an issue. Golda's parents had clear assumptions about a daughter's role. She could attend school, but working in the family store was more important than homework. By her mid-teens, she should be settled into marriage—and her parents went so far as to select a successful (and much older) husband for her. Although she married a Zionist and a scholar of her own choosing, Golda soon found that her physical and mental powers were greater than his. She also was more interested in political life than in family life. Her ambition and ability led her to positions of greater responsibility and prominence, while her husband faded into the background. The marriage ended, and Meir spent far less time with her children than she would have liked. In a biography of a successful man, these separations would hardly draw a comment, and Adler does not make issue of it here. His concern is with presenting a straightforward story of a strong leader, and he lets that story speak for itself.

Critical Context

David Adler has written several books about Jewish history and culture for children at all levels, including *A Picture Book of Passover* (1982) and *A Picture Book of Hanukkah* (1982), *The Number on My Grandfather's Arm* (1987) for middle schoolers, and a well-known book of essays and photographs, *We Remember the Holocaust* (1987), for older students. He is also the author of the Cam Jensen series of young adult mystery novels, featuring another strong and intelligent female character.

As public education becomes more concerned with celebrating the rich diversity of the world's people, *Our Golda* is an important book, both for its portrayal of a strong female leader and for its presentation of an essential piece of Jewish history. When the book was new, it received an Outstanding Social Studies Book for Children citation from the Children's Book Council and was named a Carter G. Woodson Award Honor Book by the National Council for Social Studies. Teachers and school librarians still select *Our Golda*, as well as other titles in the Women of Our Time series, for its soundness, its even-handed treatment of difficult political issues, and its lively writing.

Cynthia A. Bily

OUR TOWN

Author: Thornton Wilder (1897-1975)
First presented: 1938
First published: 1938
Type of work: Drama
Type of plot: Domestic realism, fantasy, and social realism
Time of work: 1901-1913
Locale: Grover's Corners, New Hampshire
Subjects: Coming-of-age, death, family, and love and romance
Recommended ages: 13-18

Wilder portrays ordinary events in the life of a turn-of-the century town, with a special emphasis on the coming-of-age of Emily Webb and George Gibbs, their marriage, and Emily's untimely death.

> *Principal characters:*
> THE STAGE MANAGER, the presenter of the play and the manipulator of
>   the action
> FRANK GIBBS, the town doctor
> JULIA GIBBS, his wife
> GEORGE and REBECCA GIBBS, their children
> CHARLES WEBB, the editor of *The Grover's Corners Sentinel*
> MYRTLE WEBB, his wife
> EMILY and WALLY WEBB, their children
> JOE CROWELL, JR., the paper boy, who is killed in World War I
> HOWIE NEWSOME, the milkman
> SIMON STIMSON, the alcoholic choir director
> LOUELLA SOAMES, the town gossip

Form and Content

This three-act play chronicles typical episodes in the life of Grover's Corners, New Hampshire, beginning in 1901 and ending in 1913. In the first act, called by the Stage Manager "The Daily Life," Grover's Corners is set forth in minute detail, including the locales, history, geography, and demographics of the area, to create a backdrop of small-town America against which the lives of its citizens are played out. Thornton Wilder's focus is on a single day, May 7, 1901, as two prominent neighboring families, the Gibbses and the Webbs, go about their daily lives. George Gibbs is more interested in baseball than in helping his mother chop wood, to the chagrin of his father. Emily Webb, a star student in high school, agrees to give George hints about his algebra problems. Toward day's end, Simon Stimson's drinking is the talk after choir practice.

The Stage Manager calls the second act "Love and Marriage." The tender and awkward courtship of George and Emily at Mr. Morgan's soda fountain concludes with George deciding not to go off to State Agriculture College but to stay in Grover's

Corners in order to be with Emily. The Stage Manager as minister performs their marriage, which town gossip Louella Soames thinks is the nicest wedding she has ever seen. Wilder prepares the audience for the grim final act with the Stage Manager's commentary on the course of life: "The cottage, the gocart, the Sunday afternoon drives in the Ford, the first rheumatism, the grandchildren, the second rheumatism, the deathbed, the reading of the will,—."

In the third act, several years have passed, and Mrs. Gibbs, Simon Stimson, and Mrs. Soames have died. The scene is the Grover's Corners churchyard, and the occasion is the funeral of Emily Webb Gibbs, who died in childbirth at the age of twenty-six. The Stage Manager philosophizes about the state of the dead, and, in an immensely imaginative scene, the dead speak about how troubled the living are. Against the advice of Mrs. Gibbs and others, Emily returns to the land of the living to relive her twelfth birthday. As an invisible presence, she observes her family and exclaims, "Why did they ever have to get old?" She realizes that she truly cannot go home again and, regretting that life passes by so quickly without true appreciation and understanding, returns to the world of the dead. The Stage Manager bids the audience a good night.

Analysis

From the very beginning of the play, the illusion of the invisible wall is abolished and the audience sees an empty stage in half light. After some time, the Stage Manager appears and begins placing a table and chairs on stage. Not until the lights dim and the audience is left in total darkness does the Stage Manager—director, puppeteer, and illusionist—speak. He functions as an all-knowing citizen of Grover's Corners: He manipulates time by re-creating the past and revealing the future, interrupts the dialogue of the characters, invites questions from the audience, provides information, at times fills the roles of other characters, and philosophizes about the meaning of life. He is the central figure of the play, full of simple wisdom and unself-conscious humor. He is a spellbinder, appealing to audiences and readers of all ages.

An element of *Our Town* that must be attractive especially to young people is the simplicity and directness of the language. Wilder was a master of colloquial speech who did not resort to too many rhetorical devices. His diction and syntax are easily understandable without being in the least monotonous. In fact, much variety of tone is evident in *Our Town*. One can consider, for example, Dr. Gibbs's statement to his wife about a father-son relationship that "there's nothing so terrifying in the world as a son. The relation of father to a son is the damnedest, awkwardest—. I always come away feeling like a soggy sponge of hypocrisy." One may also note George's earnest outcry before the wedding—"Ma, I don't want to grow old. Why's everybody pushing me so?"—and Emily's beautiful farewell to the world—"Good-by, Grover's Corners . . . Mamma and Papa. Good-by to clocks ticking . . . and Mama's sunflowers. And food and coffee. And new-ironed dresses and hot baths . . . and sleeping and waking up." Finally, there are the Stage Manager's poetic remarks on the cemetery and the profound peacefulness of the dead: "Yes, an awful lot of sorrow has sort of quieted down up here. People just wild with grief have brought their relatives up to this hill. We all know how it is . . . and then time . . . and sunny days . . . and rainy days . . . 'n snow . . . tz-tz-tz. We're all glad they're in a beautiful place and we're coming up here ourselves when our fit's over."

Perhaps the clearest clue to the meaning of *Our Town* is the address that a young girl receives on a letter from her minister: "Jane Crofut; The Crofut Farm; Grover's Corners; Sutton County; New Hampshire; United States of America; Continent of North America; Western Hemisphere; the Earth; the Solar System; the Universe; the Mind of God." Grover's Corners, the little town where nothing extraordinary ever happens, is a microcosm of all towns and its people are prototypes of all people. The universal appeal of this play, for young and old alike, rests largely in the recognizable nature of its characters. With few exceptions, they are static. Wilder had a profound knowledge of human cognition, knowing that people come to understand others not through sequential actions over extended periods of time but rather in isolated episodes when any change in appearance and behavior is subtle if noticeable at all.

Because Emily dies and people age, *Our Town* could have been a darkly pessimistic play, but it is not. In this play, people generally need other people, and the daily business of life is carried out not alone but with others. As Mrs. Gibbs says, "People are meant to live two by two in this world."

Our Town presents life's archetypes—school, first love, marriage, child rearing, aging, death—without being maudlin. Rather, the play affirms a kind of Emersonian self-reliance that is ultimately optimistic. "Everybody has a right to his own troubles," Dr. Gibbs says. The Stage Manager in his role of minister talks about the underlying goodness and oneness of nature. *Our Town*, in title and substance, affirms that people are not alone. Perhaps that is the ultimate source of its universal appeal.

Critical Context

When Wilder wrote *Our Town*, he had virtually no American models of dramatic expressionism. This play predates Tennessee Williams' *The Glass Menagerie* (1944) and Arthur Miller's *Death of a Salesman* (1949) and is contemporaneous with Bertolt Brecht's alienation drama. Wilder relied on a bare stage with only the most rudimentary props; his technique of creating a sense of illusion through language alone is reminiscent of William Shakespeare. It is the antithesis of the representational realism of Henrik Ibsen or Anton Chekhov.

The final act of *Our Town* is one of the most original and powerfully imagined scenes in all of theater. The awful peace of the dead as they have been weaned from the earth, Emily's sad farewell visit to her family on her twelfth birthday, and the Stage Manager's final speech sounding so much like Ecclesiastes provide an unforgettable theatrical experience. It is no wonder that *Our Town* is a perennial favorite with high school and college drama groups. For decades, it has been one of the most studied texts in the public schools and one of the most performed plays in the American theater.

Robert G. Blake

PALE HORSE, PALE RIDER
Three Short Novels

Author: Katherine Anne Porter (1890-1980)
First published: 1939
Type of work: Novels
Subjects: Coming-of-age, death, and love and romance
Recommended ages: 15-18

Although not written specifically for a young adult audience, these novellas center on important concerns for youth: love, death, coming-of-age, and the relationship among past, present, and future.

Form and Content

Taken together, the three short novels in Katherine Anne Porter's *Pale Horse, Pale Rider* provide a rather bleak account of life in the late nineteenth and early twentieth century Western United States. In "Old Mortality," as Miranda matures she rejects her family's romantic view of the past and determines to create her own version of truth. In "Noon Wine," Thompson purportedly kills in self-defense, but, when he fails to convince others and ultimately even himself of his lack of guilt, he commits suicide. In "Pale Horse, Pale Rider," Miranda confronts death and manages to escape, only to learn that her sweetheart has died and that she is left to face a bleak future alone.

"Old Mortality" begins in late nineteenth century Texas and is divided into three parts. In part 1, Miranda and Maria continually hear stories of their family's romantic history, especially the tragic tale of their beautiful late Aunt Amy and her dashing beau and husband, Uncle Gabriel. In part 2, the sisters are sent to a convent school in New Orleans, where they feel "immured" in their cloistered existence. On a weekend escape, their father takes them to a horse show and introduces them to Uncle Gabriel, whose drunken state and slovenly appearance evoke skepticism about the romantic legends and force the girls to modify their view of the past. In part 3, the story is seen through Miranda's consciousness as she boards a train on her way home and bumps into Cousin Eva, who is coming back for Gabriel's funeral. The antithesis of Amy, Cousin Eva has devoted her life to the woman suffrage movement. She maintains that she was fond of Amy but that Amy "was simply sex-ridden, like the rest." Miranda listens quietly but rejects Eva's view of the past as equally romantic and false as the view the family has tried to force on her. She realizes that continual re-creation of the past through memory produces a lie, and she determines to detach herself from that past and to create her own version of truth and define her own future.

"Noon Wine" takes place in southern Texas from 1896 to 1905. Olaf Eric Helton appears on the farm of Royal Earle Thompson to ask for a job. Because Thompson's wife is in poor health and he is more concerned about his dignity and reputation than in doing the necessary farm work, he has allowed his farm to fall into miserable condition. Helton begins work immediately, and his industriousness eventually makes the farm prosper. His only negative qualities, in the Thompsons' view, are that he does not eat or talk enough and that he reacts violently when the young Thompson boys damage the harmonicas on which he daily plays the same haunting tune. Nine years after Helton's arrival, Homer T. Hatch arrives, completely unexpectedly, to arrest Helton for a murder committed in North Dakota. Hatch, a bounty hunter, maintains that Helton killed his own brother in a quarrel over a lost harmonica. As Thompson orders Hatch to leave, he sees Helton approaching. When Helton charges in between the quarreling parties, Thompson, thinking that Helton is being stabbed, hits Hatch on the head with an ax and kills him. Thompson claims self-defense and a jury finds him not guilty, but he realizes that no one truly believes him despite his continual attempts to tell his story and to convince them and himself of his innocence. Finally, when he realizes that even his wife and children do not believe him, he commits suicide.

"Pale Horse, Pale Rider" returns to the character Miranda, now a twenty-four-year-old struggling drama critic for a newspaper in a small Western town near the Rocky Mountains. An opening dream summarizes the novel. Miranda envisions a stranger who has come to ride with her. Thinking that she must "outrun Death and the Devil," Miranda selects the horse Graylie because he does not fear bridges, and she rides along with the stranger until she suddenly recognizes him, stops her horse, and declares that she will not ride with him this time. The stranger rides on, and Miranda awakens.

In a novel filled with realistically grim details of a life controlled by war and disease, the growing relationship between Miranda and Adam, a soldier of her age from a nearby camp, provides a positive contrast. Miranda becomes seriously ill with influenza, however, and Adam attempts to nurse her before she is finally provided a bed in an overcrowded hospital. Adam must return to camp, leaving Miranda with her feverish dreams. She lies seriously ill for several weeks, finally awakening to the sounds of bells celebrating the Armistice and to the news that Adam has died of influenza in the camp hospital.

Analysis

Each of the three novels is short and has a simple plot, but the meanings are quite complex and, for many readers, disturbing. An effective coming-of-age novel, "Old Mortality" centers on the conflict between romance and reality, between past and present. While the first two parts of the novel incorporate the viewpoint of both Miranda and her sister Maria, the third shifts entirely to Miranda's consciousness. The action of the novel is designed to reveal Miranda's growing awareness of how the past is shaped by persons in the present. Despite her growth toward maturity, however, Miranda's journey is not complete, as the narrator subtly reveals in the final sentence of the novel: "At least I can know the truth about what happens to me, she assured herself silently, making a promise to herself, in her hopelessness, her ignorance."

"Noon Wine" also focuses on the relationship between the past and the present, but the conclusion is more pessimistic. A greedy bounty hunter who has no concern for Helton as an individual, Hatch determines to turn Helton in and collect his money.

This determination sets in motion the chain of events that destroys him, Helton, and Thompson. The other characters are not without weaknesses, however, and they too contribute to the tragic conclusion. Helton's weakness is a passion for harmonicas so strong that he values them above life. Thompson is so overly concerned with appearances that he would allow his farm to deteriorate rather than do work that he considers unmanly or inappropriate for a landowner. Because Helton's industriousness has enabled Thompson to prosper, Hatch poses a threat. Thus, Thompson's motivation to protect Helton becomes questionable. Is it actually self-interest? Even Thompson does not know for certain, and without any support from community or family, he cannot bear his condition and commits suicide.

The characters are well developed and the scenes of the novel carefully built to lead to the ultimate tragedy. The use of foreshadowing is especially effective. For example, Helton's overreaction to the boys' playing with his harmonicas foreshadows the revelation that Helton earlier murdered his brother for a similar action.

In "Pale Horse, Pale Rider," the major subjects are death and isolation. Although Miranda herself escapes death, she loses Adam. She reacts by determining to return to a world that is greatly changed—a world without plague, without war, without Adam. She faces a world of "noiseless houses with the shades drawn, empty streets, the dead cold light of tomorrow," a world in which "there would be time for everything."

The novel uses stream-of-consciousness techniques, carrying the reader directly into Miranda's feverish dreams and at times leaving both Miranda and, consequently, the reader confused about the sequence of events. The use of war and death as metaphors emphasizes the helplessness of the individual. Allusions pervade the novel and contribute to its theme of mutability. The phrase "pale horse, pale rider" recalls both an old folk song and a biblical passage (Revelation 6:2). Adam's name recalls the biblical first man, while Miranda's evokes William Shakespeare's heroine in *The Tempest* (1611).

Critical Context

Written long before young adult fiction was viewed as a distinct genre, the three novels in *Pale Horse, Pale Rider* have nevertheless become accepted classics for young adults as well as for a broader audience. The novels, along with her collection of stories in *Flowering Judas and Other Stories* (1930) and *The Leaning Tower and Other Stories* (1944), established Katherine Anne Porter as one of the best American writers of short fiction in the twentieth century. *Pale Horse, Pale Rider* reflects the careful craftsmanship, the rich symbolism, and the recurrent themes of all of her best works. Although each novel reveals the isolation, mutability, and spiritual poverty that characterize most of Porter's works and although each ends tragically, each also produces the final effect of great tragedy—a cathartic renewal.

Verbie Lovorn Prevost

PAPER MOON

Author: Joe David Brown (1915-1976)
First published: Addie Pray, 1971 (as *Paper Moon,* 1973)
Type of work: Novel
Type of plot: Social realism
Time of work: The 1930's
Locale: The rural South and New Orleans
Subjects: Coming-of-age, crime, family, friendship
Recommended ages: 13-18

Addie Pray learns about life, friendship, and responsibility during her travels with Long Boy, in which she participates in con games that are eventually turned to the benefit of a would-be victim.

> *Principal characters:*
> ADDIE PRAY, an eleven-year-old orphan
> MOSES "LONG BOY" PRAY, a confidence man, possibly Addie's natural father
> TRIXIE DELIGHT, a former carnival dancer
> IMOGENE, Trixie's maid
> MAJOR CARTER E. LEE, an experienced confidence man
> AMELIA SASS, a New Orleans heiress
> MAYFLOWER, Amelia's maid and companion

Form and Content

Paper Moon is the comic and ultimately touching tale of Addie Pray's coming-of-age adventures as assistant to a master confidence man during the Great Depression and her eventual decision to use her skills in a compassionate way. The story, related by an adult Addie, begins shortly after the death of Addie's mother when she is taken in by Moses "Long Boy" Pray, who may be Addie's biological father. He is initially more concerned with her potential as an accomplice as he uses her in his schemes to sell personalized Bibles or photographs. Addie soon proves that she is intelligent beyond her years and that she has a natural affinity for their chosen line of work, since her youth and innocent façade disarm victims.

The novel's structure is episodic, with each section focusing on a different confidence game, but each event illustrates a portion of Addie's education and reveals aspects of her character. Addie and Long Boy make a brief foray into legitimate business after an appearance by President Franklin Delano Roosevelt. Long Boy acquires a stack of Roosevelt photographs from a printer, and he and Addie set out to sell the pictures to shopkeepers. Since Roosevelt's programs to assist the poor are so popular, the pictures sell readily for one dollar to a dollar and a half. The work does not turn as quick a profit as selling a five- to ten-dollar Bible, however, and going store to store soon exhausts the Prays. The incident illustrates Long Boy's need for the excitement of the con game and his lack of interest in legitimate business. It also explores Roosevelt and Depression era programs; these will trouble Long Boy later. Long Boy next moves to a scheme involving dropped wallets, which relies on the dishonesty and greed of his victims, a theme that will remain important throughout the novel as well.

The first hint of Addie's sense of compassion, as well as her ability to utilize what she has learned from Long Boy, arrives when they come upon a carnival. It is there that Addie sees a hermaphrodite in the freak show. She observes that the townspeople expect the promise of a half-man, half-woman to be fake. They are uncomfortable when they encounter a true biological curiosity, and Addie notes they would rather have been cheated in this case than to find something that makes them uncomfortable. Later, she is polite to the man from the freak show, and that kindness delights him.

Also at the carnival, Addie and Long Boy pick up dancer Trixie Delight and her maid, Imogene. Trixie is not only a dancer but also a sometime prostitute, but Long Boy's vision is clouded. Addie vows to reveal Trixie for what she is, partly out of necessity and partly out of jealousy. In exchange for freedom from Trixie, Imogene helps set up a tryst between Trixie and a clerk. Addie then arranges for Long Boy to catch the two together.

Addie and Long Boy move on to con a moonshiner by selling him his own stock. The incident gets them in trouble, since the moonshiner attempts to squash competition, but, in their escape, they wind up with a bale of cotton. In selling the single bale, Long Boy realizes that warehouse practices are exploitable in much the way that he planned to cheat the moonshiner. Cotton sales are handled by samples only, and the actual bales are warehoused. The system relies on the honesty of the poor farmers, who are frequently cheated by buyers paying less than what their cotton is worth.

Addie and Long Boy make a small fortune in cotton using samples and false warehouse receipts. This scam works well until a buyer realizes that Long Boy has no knowledge of a Roosevelt program to reduce the cotton supply. They escape the police only with the help of Major Carter E. Lee, who becomes a mentor to Addie and Long Boy. Lee deals in worthless silver mines and the sale of stock in dummy corporations. Long Boy and Addie work with him on several schemes before heading off on their own again for a time.

They encounter Lee again in New Orleans, where he is developing a plan to con the aging heiress Amelia Sass, who once disowned a daughter. The daughter died in a hurricane, but she is believed to have had a child who survived. The idea is to have Addie pose as the granddaughter so that Lee and Amelia's nephew, Beau Goldsborough, can obtain her fortune.

Addie successfully infiltrates the Sass household but comes to care for Amelia and Mayflower, her maid. When she learns that most of the fortune was lost to a swindler, she convinces Long Boy that they must help. With Major Lee's assistance, they convince Beau that he must become Amelia's guardian. He does this because of his own greed, assuming responsibility for her bills and expecting eventually to inherit her vast fortune. Amelia is well cared for until her death. Addie mourns for her but is soon off with Long Boy on a new excursion.

Analysis

Paper Moon is an entertaining work with focal characters who are petty criminals. The novel is both cynical and optimistic in its humorous examination of human nature. Themes of loyalty and integrity are developed. Addie and Long Boy travel a Depression era landscape of corruption where few people are honest. The people whom they cheat are often trying to cheat others.

Yet, while Addie is quite willing to scheme with Long Boy, she ultimately displays a capacity for compassion and a sense of justice. The compassion is developed in part during their dealing with widows who are thrilled that their deceased husbands remembered them with the cheap Bibles that Addie and Long Boy broker.

A degree of Addie's compassion, however, seems to be inherent. Although Major Lee suggests that Addie has no concept of right and wrong, actually she has a well-developed sense of the two concepts. She is pure not because she is devoid of conscience but because she is capable of exercising her intelligence and her kindness for others. Although she acts partially out of jealousy, Addie reveals Trixie Delight's true nature to the lovestruck Long Boy. In breaking Trixie's spell over Long Boy, she also makes it possible for Imogene to escape Trixie's employment. Addie grows angry when she realizes that cotton buyers are offering Long Boy cheaper rates on the same samples for which they earlier paid more. It is amusing to Long Boy that she is mad about the shoddy practices of people whom they have swindled, but to the reader it is apparent that Addie has a basic goodness.

Never is that goodness more evident than in her dealings with Amelia and May-flower. Addie is willing to participate in the swindle of Amelia when she believes that she is a greedy penny-pincher, but, when she learns how victimized Amelia has been, she is quick to change her mind. Addie is also able to persuade Major Lee and Long Boy to go along because of the wisdom that she has displayed in other dealings.

Major Lee, in fact, decides that Beau, whom he has known for many years, needs to be taught a lesson. Using the already-wealthy Beau's lust for what he believes are Amelia's millions, he is persuaded to do what conventional social responsibility would suggest that he do anyway—take care of his aunt.

Ironically, Addie becomes what she pretended to be: a granddaughter for the aging Amelia, who has paid dearly for mistakes with her daughter. This relationship both connects and sets Addie apart from many other characters who have an outward, misleading façade. Often, the appearance of outward honesty and uprightness is revealed to cover corruption and dishonesty.

Although Addie is a con artist, beneath her exterior she holds values of loyalty and integrity. She is loyal to Long Boy. She loves the unlovely, turns evil back on evil, and reaches out to those who need her. She is one of the most endearing young heroines of modern fiction.

Paper Moon is ultimately an upbeat, comic novel that is relevant for young people as a reflection on a particular historic era and in its presentation of coming-of-age lessons.

Critical Context

Paper Moon, originally titled *Addie Pray*, was Joe David Brown's final novel. It returns to the reflections about the rural South that began in Brown's short stories and in his first novel *Stars in My Crown* (1946). *Paper Moon* was heralded upon its publication for the novel's rousing style and humor. Addie Pray has been compared to the similar narrator-heroines of such works as Charles Portis' *True Grit* (1968) and Harper Lee's *To Kill a Mockingbird* (1960) because of her precocious development.

Sidney Glover Williams

THE PEACOCK SPRING

Author: Rumer Godden (1907-   )
First published: 1975
Type of work: Novel
Type of plot: Psychological realism
Time of work: The early 1970's
Locale: Delhi, India
Subjects: Coming-of-age, family, love and romance, race and ethnicity, and sexual issues
Recommended ages: 13-18

Una Gwithiam learns how difficult it is for romantic love to survive when one is burdened by ethnic differences, economic dependency, and extreme youth.

Principal characters:
UNA GWITHIAM, a bright, sensitive fifteen-year-old schoolgirl whose goal is to study mathematics at an English university
HALCYON "HAL" GWITHIAM, Una's pretty, carefree, twelve-year-old half sister
SIR EDWARD GWITHIAM, their father, a United Nations official in India
ALIX LAMONT, his beautiful, manipulative Eurasian mistress and future wife
RAVI BHATTACHARYA, a handsome young Indian student and poet, who is temporarily working as a gardener on Sir Edward's estate

Form and Content

The Peacock Spring is a poignant story of love and loss set in postcolonial India, where a rigid social system has not been markedly altered by political independence. In selecting their associates, both Indians and British residents are still very much aware of class and, when it comes to marriage, of ethnicity as well. If even so powerful a person as Sir Edward Gwithiam meets with resistance when he crosses the established lines, it is obvious that two young lovers, still financially dependent, cannot hope to marry, no matter how sincere their feelings for each other. Rumer Godden's novel is of special interest to young Western readers because it shows them what life can be like in an exotic world very different from their own and at the same time emphasizes the fact that, wherever they live, young adults have the same problems with teachers, parents, and their own emotions.

The story begins with a mystery. Two days into the term at their expensive school in England, Una Gwithiam and her younger half sister, Halcyon (or "Hal"), are told that their father, Sir Edward, has sent for them and that they must return to India immediately. While Hal accepts the news with equanimity, Una is appalled, since she is preparing for the examinations that will ensure her admission to an English university. She is even more disturbed when, on arriving in Delhi, she finds that the girls will be taught by a beautiful Eurasian woman, Alix Lamont, who Una soon discovers is only half-educated, incapable of teaching her mathematics or much else. Soon, Una and Hal realize that Edward has brought them home not because he was lonely for them, as he claimed, but because if the girls are in the house, Alix can live with him, under the pretext of being their governess.

Hal is soon enjoying the lavish social life in which, as Edward's daughters, the girls are automatically involved, but Una resents Alix both because of her influence over Edward and because of her ineptness as a teacher. Edward is too infatuated to listen to Una. The estate's young gardener, Ravi Bhattacharya, sympathizes with her, however, because he too has had his education interrupted. A college student from a good family, Ravi had to drop out of school and is working a menial job until the authorities forget about his rash involvement in a political movement. At first, Ravi and Una are only friends. Ravi arranges for Una to be tutored in mathematics, Una listens to the poems Ravi has written, and they talk about life. The two are more attracted to each other, however, than they realize. After Alix whips her for disobedience, Una turns to Ravi for comfort, and, almost inevitably, they make love.

During the next few weeks, Una is too happy to worry about her future, but then she becomes pregnant. Ravi and Una decide to run away and hide at the home of Ravi's grandmother until they can be married. Edward tracks them down, however, and informs Ravi's father as to what has happened. Both parents agree that the young lovers must be separated. Alix forces Una to drink something that causes her to miscarry, and Una is sent back to school in England, while Hal is dispatched to America, to live with her mother. Later, Una learns that Ravi has won India's most prestigious award for poetry. Sir Edward makes Alix his wife, thereby assuring her of wealth, prestige, and social acceptance.

Analysis

Like most other stories of initiation, *The Peacock Spring* shows how painful it is to lose one's illusions. With her mother dead, Una has persuaded herself that her father loves her as much as she does him. Ignoring the fact that he had previously sent her away when his second wife, Hal's mother, took a dislike to her, Una has continued to think of herself as her father's favorite companion. Only her anticipation of once again being close to him tempers her unhappiness about leaving her school and giving up her hopes for a university education. Almost as soon as she arrives in Delhi, however, she realizes that she is not particularly important to her father. This is her first disillusionment.

Ironically, in her relationship with Ravi, Una repeats the pattern and thus makes a second disillusionment inevitable. Abandoning her interest in mathematics, Una focuses on Ravi, his poetry, and his future. She appears to be to Ravi what Alix has become to her father. She forgets how careful Edward has been to safeguard himself, however, so that he will not have to sacrifice his career for his romance. Ravi, too, is prudent when he sees that marriage to Una would cost him his position in his family and his future as a poet. Because she has given up her mathematics to become his muse, Una cannot believe that Ravi will not sacrifice everything for her and for their child. Again, she is disappointed.

Una's perception is of personal betrayal, in both cases by a man whom she had made the center of her life. She is too young and too inexperienced to comprehend Godden's primary theme: that only the most ruthless can force society to bend its rules. On the face of it, Una and Ravi would seem better candidates for marriage than Edward and Alix. Although the younger pair are of different ethnic stocks, they are of the same social class. Alix, on the other hand, is not only Eurasian but also has a vulgar background, reflected only too clearly in her mother's behavior, and an unsavory past, including some notorious liaisons in addition to a marriage as yet not dissolved. Alix's inferior social status is evidenced by the fact that she is not invited to the parties that Hal and Una attend.

At the end of the novel, however, Alix has penetrated upper-class society in the only way that she could, by marrying Edward. She has been ruthless and clever enough to catch him, and, although Godden shows him as a man obsessed by his desire for a beautiful woman, in fact he too has been clever and ruthless—clever enough to conceal their relationship until it could be made legitimate and ruthless enough to use his daughters as pawns in his game. Ironically, though Una and Ravi are destined to be separated, the fact that their relationship was never sordid or selfish offers hope for a time when such lovers, a bit older and wiser, can be united, despite their ethnic differences.

Critical Context

An award-winning author of books for children, Rumer Godden has also seen many of the novels that she wrote with adults in mind find a place on the shelves in school libraries and even on textbook lists. In addition to *The Peacock Spring*, especially popular with young adults are *An Episode of Sparrows* (1955), a story of war-ravaged London, and *Greengage Summer* (1958), a semiautobiographical account of adventures in France's wine country. Like her novels *The River* (1946) and *The Battle of the Villa Fiorita* (1963), these are coming-of-age stories, with appealing young protagonists, told with Godden's characteristic sensitivity and understanding.

Increasingly, however, Godden is recognized as a writer about multicultural issues. Her love of India, where she spent the first twelve years of her life, and of the people who live there is evident in all of her works with an Indian setting. These works include books for children, such as *The Valiant Chatti-Maker* (1983); novels whose protagonists are young adults, such as *The River*, *The Peacock Spring*, and *Breakfast with the Nikolides* (1942); and works focusing more specifically on adults, such as *Black Narcissus* (1939), which concerns a group of nuns in the Himalayas, and *Kingfishers Catch Fire* (1953), whose central character is a widow living in Kashmir. In her autobiography *A Time to Dance, No Time to Weep* (1987), Godden describes her Indian childhood as a wonderful period in her life, when she and her sisters lived happily within a close and loving family, stimulated by the beauty and the richness of the alien culture that flourished just outside their door. Although Godden recognizes that Indian society had rules as rigid as those of the British subjects, it is significant that she herself did not feel repressed until, at twelve, she found herself immured in a boarding school in England, nor did she feel alienated until she was, in expatriate terms, "at home." It is appropriate that, as young adults learn to appreciate cultures other than their own, they turn to Godden who, while recognizing the problems that are inevitable when one lives in a multicultural society, believes that they are far outweighed by the rewards.

Rosemary M. Canfield Reisman

THE PEOPLE COULD FLY
American Black Folktales

Author: Virginia Hamilton (1936-   )
First published: 1985; illustrated
Type of work: Short fiction
Subjects: Animals, race and ethnicity, and the supernatural
Recommended ages: 10-13

This collection of American black folklore includes tales of tricksters and ghosts as well as tales of freedom.

Form and Content

In *The People Could Fly: American Black Folktales*, Virginia Hamilton, a descendent of early African Americans, recounts twenty-four stories from the rich oral history of the black culture in the United States. Written in a readable, mild dialect, the tales capture the spirit of the slave culture that spawned them and are effectively illustrated by Leo and Diane Dillon, Caldecott Medal winners for two of their earlier works involving African tales. The reader is led through four genera of black folktales: animal tales; tales of the real, extravagant, and fanciful; tales of the supernatural; and slave tales of freedom.

The folktales retold by Hamilton originated not only in Africa and North America but in Europe and South America as well. Many of the tales involve the theme of the weak and oppressed triumphing over the strong and powerful. In such a way did the slaves often weave allegories of their own existence with their hope of victory over the powerful and rich landowners who were their masters. This approach is especially evidenced in the animal tales wherein the hero is often the rabbit, a trickster by trade.

In the "Animal Tales" section, the reader is reintroduced to a number of stories commonly associated with the Uncle Remus tales of Joel Chandler Harris. In her retelling, Hamilton avoids much of the thick dialect found in some other stories about "Bruh Bear and Bruh Rabbit," the Tar Baby, and other well-known characters that many readers first met in the stories collected by Harris. Following each tale, Hamilton provides a brief discussion of the origin and variations of the tale. For example, the Tar Baby tale is said to exist in about three hundred versions from such diverse locations as Africa, India, the Bahamas, Brazil, and the southeastern United States.

In the section entitled ". . . And Other Tales of the Real, Extravagant, and Fanciful," the reader is led through a number of tales of the impossible varying from "The Beautiful Girl of the Moon Tower," wherein the hero Anton receives the ability to change himself into a number of different animals, to "Wiley, His Mama, and the Hairy Man," a story about an ogre who must be overcome by the quick-wittedness of a small boy.

". . . And Other Tales of the Supernatural" takes the reader through the frightening world of ghosts and devils, with many stories offering a moral. These tales are often calculated to scare youngsters and thereby promote behaviors that adults consider proper. A number of these stories have long since transcended ethnic barriers and are found in various permutations in cultures throughout the world.

The final section of the collection is ". . . And Other Slave Tales of Freedom." In this section, Hamilton provides six selections, including "The People Could Fly." The selections are unified in their origin, all being American slave tales, although the title story and several other tales reveal elements of African folklore in their themes. All these tales involve the escape of enslaved people from their masters. One of the stories is a true account, while the others are more fanciful, but each of the tales carries a message of hope from the people who told it.

Analysis

Folklore is said to provide insights into the collective experiences, aspirations, and values of a cultural group. Hamilton provides readers with a looking glass through which to view some of the common experiences from the early heritage of the people who are now known as African Americans. One such experience is demonstrated in the manner in which black folklore uses animal heros to portray both the oppressed slaves and their masters. The ubiquitous "Bruh Rabbit," small and weak but clever, plots, schemes, plays tricks, and uses humor to outdo his larger and stronger rivals, often "Bruh Bear" and "Bruh Fox." The rabbit almost always eventually overcomes adversity and escapes his predicament. It is said that the black slaves told stories of this type because they dared not to portray themselves and their masters in stories directly but rather had to rely on subtlety and personification. "Doc Rabbit, Bruh Fox, and Tar Baby" is one tale in which the trickster resorts to cunningness and subtlety in order to achieve happiness and freedom from persecution. Doc Rabbit uses his cleverness to get himself out of a predicament: He tricks Bruh Fox into throwing him into the briar patch, which looks dangerous but is his natural home, and thereby avoids a more grisly fate.

The aspirations of the slaves, as portrayed in this collection, were centered on freedom and a better life. Using one's wits to outsmart the powerful and thereby win riches and a beautiful woman are common themes in a number of the tales. Often, the prize won is freedom from slavery, whether by escape across the Ohio River in a rowboat or by rising up into the sky and flying away from the Mas' and the Overseer. In a number of the tales, the hero gains gold, silver, or property. Since slaves had little hope of possessing these things in actuality, they sought and achieved them in their tales. "John and the Devil's Daughter" portrays the success of a poor man in capturing the affection and hand of a beautiful woman, the daughter of the Devil. "Manuel Had a Riddle" shows the reader how cleverness and riddling (a prime pastime of the slaves) enables Manuel to gain great treasure from the king and his scheming family.

The values of the African American community are shown in the significance of the familial relationships and friendships portrayed in the tales. Often the hero of the tales is a rescuer of his family or loved ones. In "The People Could Fly," the hero rescues a plantation's slave population and flies away into the sky with them. The esteem awarded to cleverness and an interesting story are clearly shown; most of the stories in this collection have little to do with things as they are (or ever will be) but rather deal with life in an exaggerated way.

Each story has at least one, and usually more, illustrations. The drawings are done in black, white, and gray tones in a simplified, almost primitive style. They effectively extend the stories and offer additional insights about the characters in the tales. Hamilton also provides footnotes for terms that are used colloquially or that may be unfamiliar to most readers. In "Bruh Alligator Meets Trouble," which is partially presented in the Gullah dialect, the author includes a glossary of Gullah terms to promote understanding of the story.

Critical Context

Virginia Hamilton has gained renown for a number of her works, notably for *M. C. Higgins, the Great* (1974), which won the Newbery Medal, the *Boston Globe*/Horn Book Award, and the National Book Award. Her books *The Planet of Junior Brown* (1971) and *Sweet Whispers, Brother Rush* (1982) were also awarded Newbery Medals. In addition, she was given the Edgar Allan Poe Award for the best juvenile mystery for *The House of Dies Drear* (1968).

In *The People Could Fly*, Hamilton drew on her considerable talent and her African American heritage in order to pull together these tales of black American folklore and to create a coherent glimpse into the culture that generated them. *The People Could Fly* could be used to give young readers a portrait of the early years of the evolving black culture in the United States. It can provide insight into the minds of an oppressed population and how the members of that population cope with adversity. Hamilton has chosen tales that highlight humor and cleverness. The tales should enchant and entertain readers and listeners of many ages. Some of the stories will be familiar to most readers, while others will not. All can be taken at two levels: as entertainment and as a way to look into the hearts and souls of slaves.

Duane Inman

PERRAULT'S FAIRY TALES

Author: Charles Perrault (1628-1703)
First published: Histoires: Ou, Contes du temps passé, avec des moralités, 1697;
   commonly known in French as *Contes des fées* or *Contes de ma mère l'oye*
   (translated as *Histories: Or, Tales of Past Times,* 1729; also known as *Tales of
   Mother Goose* or *Perrault's Fairy Tales*)
Type of work: Short fiction
Subjects: Animals, family, gender roles, and love and romance
Recommended ages: 10-13

   *The original "Mother Goose" tales, this collection draws upon folk motifs in an
imaginative and sometimes satiric look at human nature.*

Form and Content
   Perrault's Fairy Tales consists of eight short stories, modeled on French folktales,
with morals appended to each. Five of the tales are almost universally familiar to
English readers: "Sleeping Beauty" ("La Belle au bois dormant"), "Little Red Riding
Hood" ("Le Petit chaperon rouge"), "Puss in Boots" ("Le Maître Chat: Ou, Le Chat
botté"), "Cinderella" ("Cendrillon: Ou, La petite pantoufle de verre"), and "Tom
Thumb," sometimes called "Hop o' My Thumb" ("Le Petit Poucet"). The others,
"Blue Beard" ("La Barbe bleue"), "The Fairies" ("Les Fées"), and "Riquet with the
Tuft" ("Riquet à la houppe"), are not as widely known in English.
   Although scholars debate the actual portion of folk material in Charles Perrault's
collection, the stories generally resemble folktales in their brevity and matter-of-fact
reporting of events. The action begins immediately, following the formulaic "once
upon a time" ("il était un fois") in all the tales except "Puss in Boots." As with
folktales, the stories emphasize action and dialogue, making them well suited for oral
presentation. Although often called "fairy tales," only four of the eight—"Sleeping
Beauty," "Cinderella," "The Fairies," and "Riquet with the Tuft"—feature fairies as
characters.
   While all the tales are widely read, not all have achieved equal popularity. In
particular, readers have often found "Blue Beard" disturbing. A young woman is
married by her family to a grotesque but wealthy man with a blue beard. When his
bride disobeys his command not to enter a certain storeroom in his castle, she
discovers several bodies—those of his previous wives, whom he has murdered for
similarly disobeying him. She survives only because her brothers arrive at the moment
that Blue Beard is about to kill her.
   As the inclusion of morals suggests, the tales deal with ethical issues. Good is
always rewarded, and evil is always punished. Modern readers, however, often miss
the satire that is often present. For example, the good daughter in "The Fairies" shows
kindness to a fairy and is rewarded with magically produced precious stones; a prince
soon falls in love with her, but only after he notices her jewels. The morals themselves

are more obviously sardonic. One of the morals to "Blue Beard" remarks that such cruelty as Blue Beard shows could no longer occur, since modern men know better than to expect the impossible of women; whether the impossibility is for women not to be curious or for them to obey men slavishly is unclear.

Analysis

Perceived as "fairy tales," Perrault's tales seem disarmingly simple and innocuous, and perhaps too familiar, to interest any but the youngest readers. Nevertheless, they bear considerable historical significance. Although neither the first book written for children nor one written solely for them, *Perrault's Fairy Tales* is a landmark, a collection of stories that offer their lessons by employing satire and imaginative appeal rather than the overwhelming didacticism found in most early children's literature. They entertain more than they preach.

Students of French culture may be interested in knowing that these tales were once the subject of heated debate. By 1697, Perrault and Nicolas Boileau-Despréaux had been arguing for ten years concerning the moral value of contemporary literature (espoused by Perrault and many female writers) and classical learning (supported by Boileau-Despréaux and most male intellectuals). *Perrault's Fairy Tales*, drawn from folklore and popular short stories, embodied the "modern" ideas and added new fuel to the quarrel. Unlike classical mythology, Perrault's stories allow no evildoer to go unpunished. While classical myths chasten irreverence for the gods and the fates, other evils, especially cruelty, often incur no punishment. Blue Beard is executed and the fairies offer justice, while Hera, for example, is savage toward her often unwitting rivals for Zeus' affection.

One of Perrault's claims, and the one that most enraged his critics, was that contemporary society was more humane than ancient civilization had been, particularly in the attitudes expressed toward women. Among other things, Perrault's tales feature many female protagonists. Of the eight, only three—"Puss in Boots," "Tom Thumb," and "Riquet with the Tuft"—have male protagonists, and a female character in "Riquet with the Tuft" is given equal importance in the plot, as she makes a decision upon which Riquet's happiness depends. Although some of the stories, especially "Sleeping Beauty" and "Cinderella," have come under criticism for depicting women as stereotypically passive, Perrault and much of his audience believed that women were being treated much more favorably because of the interest taken in their decisions and feelings. For example, although Aurora in "The Sleeping Beauty" is awakened by the prince's kiss, she is not simply a trophy awarded to a gallant knight; she is the principal character in the story, and the one with whom the audience has sympathized. Perrault's opponents, on the other hand, claimed that such tales only encouraged useless fantasizing, especially in women, and made readers unlikely to be content with their necessary social roles. They further maintained that such tales were childish and unworthy to be compared to the writings of Homer, Vergil, and other great figures of classical literature.

Along with encouraging a humane morality, Perrault also thought that he was depicting a universe in harmony with Christian belief. Not only pagan moral values but pagan gods as well were replaced. Cinderella's "fairy godmother" is an adaptation of a Christian image from French folklore. In many French folktales, young virgins are aided by *"la Marraine,"* or "the Godmother," who is understood to be a manifestation of the Virgin Mary. Perrault made the character a fairy so as not to offend Christian readers for whom Mary would have been too important to treat as a fictitious character, but the essential nature of the godmother would have been familiar to any of his contemporaries. Similarly, Riquet's fairy recalls saints or guardian angels in folklore, and Sleeping Beauty's battling fairies echo confrontations between the forces of good and evil familiar from religious narratives.

Perrault claimed to have discovered the tales in his son Darmancour's copybook, presumably adapted from stories that Darmancour had heard in childhood, although scholars generally agree that Perrault himself was largely responsible for their composition. Since Darmancour was nineteen in 1695 when the first five tales appeared in manuscript, however, some believe that he may have had a hand in their creation. Either way, fables and stories based on folk motifs were fashionable in France at the time, and the tales were in accord with contemporary tastes in literature for adults as well as for children. Perrault especially recommended that his stories be read to children in a contemporary periodical, *Le Mercure galant*, claiming that the morality of the tales made them ideal to educate and stimulate young minds.

Critical Context

Although some men composed the popular fairy novellas, they were mostly the work of women. Originally, just like *Perrault's Fairy Tales*, the works of the fairy writers were meant to be read aloud or told from memory like folktales. Stock situations, such as that of a beautiful maiden being forced to marry against her will, were elaborated upon and interwoven with other elements to produce stories that took an hour or more in the telling. Many of these narratives were eventually published, either individually or in collections. Judging from those that were published, storytellers would often compliment their friends or comment on recent events through oblique references within the story; in addition to such commentary, the authors primarily strove for wit, satire, playfulness, and graceful language. The most famous and successful of these adult fairy writers was Marie-Catherine d'Aulnoy. Her *Contes de Fées* (1690) and *Les Fées à la mode* (1695), translated together as *Fairy Tales by the Countess d'Aulnoy* (1856), are still widely read in French and are occasionally retold for children in English. The best known of these tales in English are "The White Cat" ("La Chatte blanche") and "The Yellow Dwarf" ("Le Nain jaune"), both of which were popular in the nineteenth century.

Charles Perrault, as a moralist, drew upon such works as Aulnoy's vehicles for philosophical examinations of human behavior and thought. Another influence on him was an older contemporary, Jean de La Fontaine, whose fables, written between 1668 and 1695, were similarly intended both to appeal to young readers and to offer insight to older ones. Perrault adapted La Fontaine's simplicity of language and brevity of plot for his new genre, the fairy (or nursery) tale. Later writers took up Perrault's ethical fairy stories, including moralist and educator Jeanne-Marie Leprince de Beaumont, now most remembered for her children's version of Suzanne-Gabrielle de Villeneuve's 1737 adult fairy romance "Beauty and the Beast," ("La Belle et la Bête").

Paul James Buczkowski

THE PETERKIN PAPERS

Author: Lucretia P. Hale (1820-1900)
First published: 1880; illustrated
Type of work: Novel
Type of plot: Fantasy
Time of work: The 1870's
Locale: Boston
Subjects: Emotions, family, and social issues
Recommended ages: 13-18

The members of the Peterkin family become perplexed while trying to solve everyday situations and often turn to their friend, known as the lady from Philadelphia, to save them from themselves.

> *Principal characters:*
> MR. PETERKIN, the father of the household
> MRS. PETERKIN, the mother
> AGAMEMNON, the eldest son and the only one who has been to college, who tries to invent useful devices
> ELIZABETH ELIZA, the daughter who often suggests asking the lady from Philadelphia for advice
> SOLOMON JOHN, another son
> THE LITTLE BOYS, the youngest of the Peterkins' children
> THE LADY FROM PHILADELPHIA, the Peterkins' wise friend

Form and Content

The Peterkin Papers is a hilarious account of life in the mid-nineteenth century. From the opening story of Mrs. Peterkin accidentally putting salt in her coffee to the last page when she explains that it was not their luggage that was lost, "But we, as a family," the reader laughs at the adventures of the Peterkins. The novel is an important example of humor in young adult fiction. Set in Boston in the 1870's, the novel gives readers a satirical view of genteel family life. Lucretia Hale portrays the Peterkins as extremely unwise, but few young adults would argue that they or their families have never behaved as foolishly as the Peterkins.

Each chapter in the book is a complete story in itself. The plots are neither difficult nor complex. The members of the Peterkin family find the most mundane daily decisions to be incomprehensible. In the first episode, and one of the most famous, Mrs. Peterkin accidentally puts salt in her morning coffee, which is considered a tragedy. The entire family gives advice, and they seek a solution from a chemist and an herbalist, but neither can rectify the situation. Finally, the lady from Philadelphia is consulted. She suggests that Mrs. Peterkin simply be given a fresh cup of coffee, to which Elizabeth Eliza exclaims, "Why didn't we think of that?"

Throughout the novel, readers are reminded of Elizabeth Eliza's question. In another episode, Mrs. Peterkin decides to go for a ride in the carriage, but nothing that she or her children attempt will make the horse move. They try reducing the load on the carriage, whipping the horse, and even giving the horse sweets to induce it to move. Finally, the children ask the lady from Philadelphia, who peers out her bedroom window and calmly suggests that they untie the horse from the hitching post.

Eventually, the Peterkin family resolves to become wise and independent from the lady from Philadelphia. They decide that what they need is a library, and material is gathered to build a bookcase. The question of books, however, remains. Solomon John declares that he will write a book. After several obstacles are overcome, including finding paper, gathering nuts and ingredients to make ink, and a deciding on a pen, Solomon John announces that he is ready to begin—only to discover that he has nothing to say.

In the last episode of the novel, the Peterkins take their long-awaited vacation. Instead of the resort where they had planned to stay, however, the Peterkins find themselves at the poor farm without their luggage or their friends.

Each of the episodes demonstrates the Peterkins' inability to cope with simple, everyday situations. Whether deciding to raise the ceiling instead of chopping the bottom off the Christmas tree, delaying a vacation because the trunk is too heavy to lift, or playing the piano outside because the movers placed the keyboard in front of the window, the Peterkins provide a humorous look at family life.

Analysis

The Peterkin Papers, like most satires, may be enjoyed on two levels: a straight story of a family who has the uncanny ability to complicate everyday situations and a pointed social parody of contemporary times. On the first level, readers laugh at the Peterkins' misadventures, delight in the illogical solutions to problems, and discover that they themselves, like the lady from Philadelphia, were able to find the simple answers that the Peterkins overlooked. Several themes for the reader can be found on this level: for example, that respect should be given to others within and outside the family, that foolish behavior can be forgiven and overlooked, and that such behavior is not confined to young people.

In each episode, the Peterkins demonstrate, through their words and actions, the respect and concern that they have for one another and for the people they meet. For example, when Mrs. Peterkin puts salt in her coffee, the whole family rushes to find someone to solve the problem so that mama can have her morning cup of coffee. The Peterkins listen and follow the advice of the chemist, who adds a multitude of chemicals to the coffee without the desired effect, pay him for his trouble, and politely send him on his way. The same is true for the woman who attempts to undo the results of the salt and other chemicals with herbs. Mama is not criticized for her mistake or for the trouble that it causes; instead, the family shows only concern for her plight.

In another story, Solomon John decides to write a book for the Peterkin library, and the family tries to help him collect the necessary supplies and waits expectantly for him to begin writing. They have provided Solomon John with their help, time, and efforts. When Solomon John at long last sits down to write, they do not laugh as he exclaims that he has nothing to say. Examples such as these are found in every chapter in the book. The young adult reader cannot fail to understand the importance of demonstrating respect for others.

In much the same way, young adults begin to understand that foolish behavior is not confined to any particular age group. All the Peterkins make mistakes or behave in foolish ways. The other family members forgive the foolishness and act in supportive ways toward one another. For example, when Mr. Peterkin decides to raise the ceiling instead of chopping the bottom off the Christmas tree, the family stands behind his decision. When Agamemnon decides to patent a master key, so that all locks can be opened with the same key, his family supports his efforts. When Solomon John decides that he may become a doctor if he does not have to see sick people, his family offers helpful advice about ways that he could prescribe treatments without having to be close to those who are ill or come at inconvenient times.

While the novel is enjoyable as a chronicle of the Peterkins' life, more sophisticated readers will view it as a social satire of genteel life in Boston in the mid-nineteenth century. Attitudes toward education, foreign travel, and social obligations are all comically satirized. For example, in one story, the Peterkins decide to learn foreign languages. Elizabeth Eliza stops her French lesson after a few weeks because, as she says, she has learned the five or six useful phrases. Another story satirizes the social teas of the era. The Peterkins count their plates and cups and decide to invite that number of friends and neighbors to afternoon tea. They then decide to invite several more people in order to fulfill their social obligations, reasoning that not everyone will come. Naturally, not only do all those invited come but several uninvited visitors arrive also. A satirical look at education is offered in several episodes. In one story, the Peterkins decide to educate the little boys at home, beginning with an alphabet breakfast. They start with applesauce but are stuck on items for x and z until the lady from Philadelphia offers some advice. The Peterkins decide that educating the little boys is too difficult and send them back to school.

The Peterkins illustrate lessons in family and social relationships that are sometimes difficult for young adults to comprehend. Through the use of humor, the novel helps readers to understand better their own complex relationships.

Critical Context

The Peterkin Papers is one of the earliest examples of nonsense prose written for young adults. Prior to its publication in 1880, most stories that explored family relationships were heavily didactic, such as Mary Sherwood's *The History of the Fairchild Family* (1812). Strict obedience to parents, especially to one's father, was stressed and accompanied by moralizing on the nature of sin and repentance. Parents were portrayed as wise, with a strong sense of what was right, as in Martha Finley's Elsie Dinsmore books, beginning in 1867. These parents did not condone foolishness, nor did they demonstrate foolishness in their own behavior. The humorous treatment of the Peterkins is the more remarkable and memorable for this reason. Despite Lucretia Hale's example, most authors writing for young adults continued in their didactic approaches. One exception was E. Nesbit's Bastable family in *The Story of the Treasure Seekers* (1899). These stories, narrated by the oldest son, Oswald, offer the same sense that children have the ability to initiate actions and to think of grand schemes on their own. Nesbit's humorous touch to the situations is similar to Hale's. Other notable humorous books of this era include Lewis Carroll's *Alice's Adventures in Wonderland* (1865), Rudyard Kipling's *Just So Stories* (1902), and Kenneth Grahame's *The Wind in the Willows* (1908).

Linda Runyon

THE PHANTOM OF THE OPERA

Author: Gaston Leroux (1868-1927)
First published: Le fantôme de l'Opéra, 1910 (English translation, 1911)
Type of work: Novel
Type of plot: Thriller
Time of work: The 1880's
Locale: The Paris Opera
Subjects: Crime, death, and love and romance
Recommended ages: 15-18

This novel offers a reconstruction, thirty years after the event, of the career of the "Opera Ghost" that briefly terrorized the Paris Opera, killing several people and causing the disappearance of a young singer.

> *Principal characters:*
> RAOUL, Vicomte de Chagny, a young nobleman
> CHRISTINE DAAÉ, a singer at the Opera with whom Raoul falls in love
> PHILIPPE, Comte de Chagny, Raoul's older brother
> FIRMIN RICHARD and ARMAND MONCHARMIN, the new managers of the Opera
> MADAME GIRY, a box attendant at the Opera
> THE PERSIAN, a regular visitor to the Opera
> THE OPERA GHOST, a skull-faced blackmailer with the seemingly supernatural power to appear and disappear at will anywhere in the Opera house

Form and Content

The Phantom of the Opera was written for publication as a feuilleton (a newspaper serial) in *Le Gaulois,* one of three such daily serials that Gaston Leroux wrote in 1910. Works of this kind inevitably tend to be episodic, crammed with incident and full of such narrative hooks as mysterious apparitions and seemingly inexplicable disappearances; in these terms, *The Phantom of the Opera* is a bravura performance. Like many feuilletons, it is presented as a quasi-journalistic endeavor: a story carefully pieced together from interviews with the parties involved, which can only be displayed in its entirety by virtue of the investigative flair of the reporter.

Having credited his "sources," the reporter lays down the background history of the Opera Ghost, a mysterious figure with a face like a death's head. The main story concerns a period when the Ghost's appearances suddenly become more frequent and the demands that he makes upon the theater's managers more forceful, after which he was never seen again.

The Ghost's increased activity begins with the insistence that a particular box always be left empty for his use and that regular payments of money be deposited there. He also issues instructions to the effect that a singer named Christine Daaé be promoted to leading roles. The intimidated managers of the theater immediately hand the problem over to a new team, Firmin Richard and Armand Moncharmin. Believing that it is all a practical joke, these resolute skeptics refuse to give in to these demands and set out to trap the supposed joker.

In the meantime, Raoul, Vicomte de Chagny, who knew Christine Daaé when they were both children, falls in love with her after hearing her sing. Unfortunately, Philippe, Comte de Chagny, disapproves strongly of the possibility that his younger brother should marry so far beneath him, and Raoul encounters further difficulties in pressing his suit because he has a rival. Christine has a mysterious singing tutor whom she never sees and who claims to be the Angel of Music about which her father used to tell her stories when she was a child. The "Angel" demands that she renounce Raoul, and Christine initially does so, but Raoul will not accept defeat. His attempts to confront the "Angel" are frustrated, but it quickly becomes clear that this enigmatic individual and the Opera Ghost are one and the same.

The stubbornness of the managers leads the Ghost to spoil a performance by a diva who refuses to make way for Christine. The great chandelier that lights the auditorium crashes down on the audience and kills the concierge, whom the managers intended to appoint in place of Madame Giry, the box attendant who seems to them to be the Ghost's accomplice. The Ghost cultivates a closer acquaintance with Christine, taking her down to his "house" on the shore of an underground lake in the catacombs beneath the Opera house, where he composes music of his own. There, she snatches away his mask and sees his horrible face, but she persuades him that she loves him in spite of his appearance in order to prevent him from murdering Raoul. During a masked ball where he appears as the Red Death (from Edgar Allan Poe's story "The Masque of the Red Death"), however, the Ghost eavesdrops on a rooftop meeting between Christine and Raoul. When he learns that they plan to elope, he kidnaps her from the stage in mid-performance.

Raoul is befriended by a regular operagoer known as the Persian, who tells him that the Opera Ghost is a stonemason named Erik whose career was blighted by his horrific deformities. Erik helped to build the cellars of the Opera house and incorporated many trapdoors into the edifice. The Persian guides Raoul to the Ghost's lair, but they are trapped in a curious mirrored "torture chamber." Philippe, who approaches the house by a different route, is drowned in the lake.

Erik has filled the cellars with barrels of gunpowder. He demands that Christine choose between marrying him and the total destruction of the Opera house, but he knows full well that she will promise him anything and then betray him. There is no way forward for him, and the only question at stake is how much damage the climax of his madness will do. Raoul and Christine escape, leaving him to die alone and unmourned.

Analysis

The Phantom of the Opera is a melodrama in the great French tradition, full of theatrical flourishes; it seems to have been written with the cinema in mind, although it was not until 1913 that any of Leroux's works reached the screen. Oddly enough, although a dozen of Leroux's novels were filmed in France during his lifetime, it was left to Hollywood to produce a version of *The Phantom of the Opera* in 1925, with Lon Chaney in the lead.

Making the most of the scenes where the phantom appears as the Red Death and the scene where Christine first snatches away the mask, the silent film became a classic. It was remade several times, most effectively in 1943, with Claude Rains in the lead. These film versions gave the phantom a more powerful motive than Leroux had, transforming him into an ambiguously tragic figure. Andrew Lloyd Webber's Broadway musical, first staged in 1987, followed suit and provided quasi-operatic music to match.

The film and stage versions deemphasize the subplot in which Firmin and Moncharmin try to thwart the Ghost, although they do exploit its comic aspects for the sake of light relief. In the book, the Ghost's ability to make things disappear (including himself) is so frequently invoked as to become tedious, and few readers can be surprised by the eventual revelation that it was all done with mirrors and trapdoors. Leroux had built his career on the presentation of seemingly impossible events that he then explained rationally; his greatest success was the pioneering "locked room" murder mystery *Le Mystère de la chambre jaune* (1904; *The Mystery of the Yellow Room*, 1908). He seems to have regarded narrative moves of this kind as his chief stock-in-trade and never bothered overmuch if they became frankly preposterous, as the "torture chamber" scenes of *The Phantom of the Opera* unfortunately do. The book makes no pretense, however, to be anything other than pure entertainment. The fact that the implausibilities strain the credulity of the reader far more than any frankly supernatural tale could have done may well be attributable to the fact that Leroux was making up the serial version as he went along, under the pressure of a daily deadline, but it is by no means inappropriate to the kind of story that resulted.

Beneath its flamboyant surface, *The Phantom of the Opera* does have one serious element. The plot turns on the observation that a man might have great talent in his chosen profession and sing like an angel and yet be an abhorred outcast from society simply by virtue of his looks. It observes, too, that a man regarded as a monster has little alternative but to become one—but that no extreme of monstrousness can contrive to redeem his situation. Unlike those who rewrote the story, Leroux does not compromise in the matter of Erik's monstrousness, but that approach makes the tragedy all the more brutal. It is not only the happy ending vouchsafed to Raoul and Christine that is withheld from Erik; he cannot even make his fatal exit with dignity.

Critical Context

Were it not for the text's provision of the key scenes that have kept the story alive in the public imagination and for the films and the stage musical that followed, Gaston Leroux's novel would have been forgotten. It must also be remembered, however, that the actual Paris Opera provided the inspiration for *The Phantom of the Opera*. Paris is set above a network of catacombs so extensive as not to be fully known, and Leroux was not the only Parisian writer to be fascinated with them. The fact that the focal point of French high culture was situated above a dark labyrinth provided a golden opportunity for symbolism. The symbolism embodied in this kind of sensationalist text is inevitably crude and overblown, but it is there nevertheless, and it cries out for recognition and recapitulation. Such caricaturish cinematic homages as *The Phantom of the Paradise* and *The Phantom of Hollywood* (both 1974) are as appropriate, in their own way, as the famous stage musical.

Brian Stableford

PHILIP HALL LIKES ME. I RECKON MAYBE.

Author: Bette Greene (1934-   )
First published: 1974; illustrated
Type of work: Novel
Type of plot: Domestic realism
Time of work: The early 1950's
Locale: Pocahontas, Arkansas
Subjects: Animals, education, friendship, and gender roles
Recommended ages: 10-13

Beth Lambert competes with Philip Hall through one year of rural activities, including a church picnic and a calf-raising contest, until they realize that winning is a partnership when they enter the square-dancing contest.

> *Principal characters:*
> ELIZABETH (BETH) LORRAINE LAMBERT, an eleven-year-old African American girl with a spunky personality who is possessed by affection for her class rival, Philip Hall
> PHILIP HALL, the cutest boy in the sixth-grade class at J. T. Williams School
> MA and PA LAMBERT, Beth's parents, who live on a farm, where they sell pigs and turkeys and grow fruits and vegetables
> ANNIE, Beth's sister, who thinks that Beth should be a farmer's wife or a teacher, rather than becoming a veterinarian
> THE COOKS, a family that steals livestock and the Lamberts' turkeys
> CYRUS J. PUTTERMAN, Pocahontas' leading merchant, who is willing to sacrifice his morals for money
> MISS JOHNSON, the schoolteacher

Form and Content

From September to September, the seven chapters of *Philip Hall Likes Me. I Reckon Maybe.*, divide the seasons and the year into a story of the growing relationship between two sixth-graders. Beth Lambert and the most handsome boy in school, Philip Hall, vie for leadership and academic excellence. Beth realizes early in the year that Philip wins because she lets him. It is her Pa who reminds her that she need not be the second-best arithmetic solver, the second-best speller, and the second-best reader at the J. T. Williams School. Beth's crush on Philip gets her into trouble with her family, her friends, and herself.

Beth persuades her friends and herself that Philip will invite her and the other girls to his birthday party because she is Philip's best friend. After completing her own chores at the farm, she helps Philip brush down the cows at his farm. Philip does not send her an invitation to his birthday party, however, because he is afraid of being called a sissy. Beth accuses Phil of being a "fraidy cat" because he avoids her. This nickname takes on a humorous twist because Philip, his friend Gordon, and other boys belong to the club known as the Tiger Hunters, who are not afraid of tigers; in rural Arkansas, not a single soul has ever seen a tiger. In like manner, Beth has her own club, known as the Pretty Pennies, who attempt to outrace the Tiger Hunters, while their most noble efforts are used to picket the Busy Bee store and its owner, Mr. Putterman, for selling bad merchandise. Both clubs compete during the Old Rugged Cross Church Picnic, with the losers becoming slaves to the other group for an entire week.

Lighthearted fun, preadolescent banter, and nonserious conflicts keep the novel moving toward an obvious conclusion whereby the protagonists do become friends, warm to the idea of accepting the opposite sex, and continue to achieve together as partners. One episode that is not so lighthearted, however, occurs in December, when Pa's turkeys begin to disappear mysteriously. The adults are seemingly helpless, while Beth and Philip catch two thieves as they arrive by automobile in the dark of night, the youngsters waiting with Philip's pop gun in the branches of a tree.

Bette Greene uses the character of Beth to narrate this story of life in the African American community in Pocahontas, Arkansas, during a time when life was simpler. People went into town for shopping and socializing, young girls did embroidery, and church suppers, the county fair, square dancing, and letters to the Answer Man were a way of life. This first-person narrative appears to contain a hybrid mixture of Southern dialect and black English. Greene's effort to appeal to all children, however, may mean that something is lost in authenticity.

Analysis

The strong, lively, and resourceful character of Beth Lambert provides energy and spirit to this story of life in rural Arkansas during the 1950's. Her drive and spunk ring true for young readers, just as noble qualities are also manifested in her rival, Philip Hall. Both characters win readers' affection as they experience adventures, which include stopping a turkey theft, operating a vegetable stand, getting lost on a mountain, running a foot race, raising calves, and competing with each other.

The eleven-year-old within a peer group is shown with the two clubs, the Pretty Pennies and the Tiger Hunters. Both groups are populated with likeable young friends who support one another, fuel the controversies with good humor, and show acceptance of one another. That these characters are part of a group while at the same time maintaining individuality and independence shows a healthy balance for readers to emulate. The author conveys the importance of intellectual prowess, physical stamina, and common sense for an interesting and active life; these are the same components that are necessary for solving problems. No great difficulties are encountered by the protagonists, and their many minor triumphs allow readers to experience the warm glow of success and achievement.

Greene's description of small-town life evokes the smells and sounds of the countryside. Life in the community and its inhabitants, who depict human nature with all of its foibles, are shown. Greene presents the kindly Doc Brenner, who makes house calls, as well as the merchant Cyrus J. Putterman, whose concern for financial gain outweighs his better judgment. Readers are made to feel participants in the neighborly community of Pocahontas, Arkansas, where attending a picnic and square dancing are popular forms of entertainment.

When Beth discovers that she is allergic to first a collie, next a chihuahua, and then a poodle, Ma states, "Life don't always be the way we want it to be. Life be the way it is. Ain't nothing we can do." Beth desires something little, soft, and cuddly that is all her own, and her allergy to dogs keeps her from this dream. Her disappointment turns to joy, however, when a new baby brother, Benjamin, is born into the family. Parental support and caring helps to convey a warmth of understanding, enabling Beth to feel secure to reach out and challenge the boundaries intellectually, athletically, and emotionally.

Greene's writing style in *Philip Hall Likes Me. I Reckon Maybe.*, resulted in the novel being named a Newbery Honor Book; she demonstrated the same proficiency of writing in her earlier book, *Summer of My German Soldier* (1973). The short chapters, copious dialogue, fast pacing, and month-by-month chronological organization make the novel easy to follow. Each chapter's story is complete within itself, with each conflict resolved, making this work a good read-aloud book. The thread that runs throughout the story is the ongoing relationship of the protagonists, who participate in a battle of the sexes in an honest and wholesome adventure that is realistic in its portrayal of schoolgirl crushes on boys. Philip learns to respond and to respect Beth, while she gains understanding of Philip and of herself.

Charles Lilly's black-and-white illustrations, strategically placed throughout the text, create a sense of place, intimacy, and warmth. Beth's no-nonsense, bright-eyed approach to the world is conveyed through her eyes, her smile, and the tilt of her head. Full-page and double-page spreads show the farm land, the Lamberts' kitchen, Pa's worried face, and Mr. Putterman's dismay. The characters' expressions upon winning or losing at the calf contest demonstrate a major theme of the story. One of the most telling portrayals of the story is the illustration of a huge tractor being driven by Philip while Beth sits beside him with her arm casually placed on his shoulder. These are authentic characters realistically drawn, and the drawings are a wonderful addition to the book.

Critical Context

Understanding the life of an African American sixth-grade girl growing up in Arkansas in the 1950's provides a complement to a social studies unit on communities, the South, or black history. Racial understanding should not be confined to one month in February, Black History Month, and *Philip Hall Likes Me. I Reckon Maybe.*, is appropriate for reading and study anytime. Its themes go beyond the color line to universal truths about friendship, affection, and achievements. A special aspect of the book is the humor, fun, and relaxed life in a small town. For some, this is a remembered experience of the past, but for others who reside in similar communities today, the story will be timely. *Words by Heart* (1979), by Ouida Sebestyen, also offers a female student bent on success; this book takes place during the early twentieth century and includes violence toward black people.

Bette Greene's sequel, *Get on out of Here, Philip Hall* (1981), continues the story of this duo in a cheerful and adventurous style. For a more serious example of Greene's work, *Summer of My German Soldier* explores history, tolerance, and acceptance. In *Philip Hall Likes Me. I Reckon Maybe.*, and in all of Greene's writing, the protagonist becomes a person of value, which is a worthy message for all readers. When Philip finally says, "Sometimes I reckon I likes you, Beth Lambert," a sense of closure has been reached for the main character and for the novel.

Helene W. Lang

PICNIC

Author: William Inge (1913-1973)
First presented: 1953
First published: 1953
Type of work: Drama
Type of plot: Social realism
Time of work: The early 1950's
Locale: A small Kansas town
Subjects: Emotions, sexual issues, and social issues
Recommended ages: 15-18

Madge Owens abandons the prospect of a secure but dull life with affluent Alan Seymour and yields to her sensual yearning for a materially unsuccessful but physically charismatic vagabond.

Principal characters:
MADGE OWENS, a beautiful eighteen-year-old whose vague
    discontentment is resolved by the animal magnetism of her local
    suitor's friend
HAL CARTER, a handsome, athletic college dropout
MILLIE OWENS, Madge's tomboyish sixteen-year-old sister
ROSEMARY SYDNEY, a schoolteacher living in dread of "spinsterhood"
HOWARD BEVANS, a storekeeper who regularly dates Rosemary
ALAN SEYMOUR, a local suitor of Madge and a former college friend of
    Hal
FLO OWENS, Madge's protective mother
HELEN POTTS, an unwed middle-aged neighbor of the Owenses

Form and Content

During the Labor Day holiday in a small Kansas town, seven lives are disrupted by the arrival of a sensually attractive, indigent young man who performs some cleanup work for a meal. The young man, Hal Carter, carries out the work for "Mrs." Potts (who is unmarried); the experience of a male presence in her house increases her sense of vitality and gives her a new perspective on the life that she has led as her mother's aide and, currently, nursemaid. "Mrs." Potts's neighbor, Flo Owens, is unsettled by the young man, in whom she sees, first, a threat to the plans that she has for her daughter Madge and, second, the embodiment of her own desire for a man, following a decade of adjustment to her husband's desertion. Madge is captivated by Hal and finds in him the direction in life that she chooses to take. Her younger sister, Millie, finds her own sense of female maturity awakened by Hal and becomes ready, as a result, to pass from tomboyhood to intellectualism.

The person most dramatically influenced by Hal's arrival is the town's schoolteacher, Rosemary Sydney: She resents Hal for reminding her of her lost youth and unsatisfied desires, and she is stimulated by her resentment to pressure Howard Bevans, her only marital prospect, into a guarantee of wedlock. Therefore, Howard's life of easy and unchallenging bachelorhood is ended as a result of Hal's appearance. One other man, Alan Seymour, is also affected: He loses Madge, who he had assumed would marry him, to Hal. Alan engineers Hal's flight from town by falsely accusing him of car theft, but Madge subsequently leaves town to follow Hal.

The disruptions of the seven lives are highlighted by various social differentials: middle-class affluence versus moderateness of means, the married state versus forms of the single state, high intelligence versus mediocre intellectual ability, physical attractiveness versus plainness, and differences of age.

Madge Owens, a dime-store clerk, is unhappy despite her beauty, which ensures her ability to catch the most desirable bachelor in town, the Cadillac-driving Alan Seymour. Her romantic dreaming is punctuated by the distant train whistle at evening and comes to center on Hal, who can offer her no material security and with whom she falls in love. Hal and Alan, once roommates in college, present the contrast of an exciting failure and a successful dullard, respectively. Madge's younger sister, Millie, resents Madge's beauty because it brings people, including their mother, to prefer Madge. Yet, Millie is as superior in intelligence to Madge, as Alan is shown to be to Hal. The play ends with the intimation that Millie and Alan, both destined to respectable citizenship, are ideally suited as marriage partners and with the departure of Madge in pursuit of the unlucky Hal.

The three middle-aged women are left in the wake of the young. Helen Potts, whose marriage was annulled by her domineering mother but who has kept the name, Potts, of the boy whom she married, cherishes her memory of Hal as she continues to nurse her aged and now-invalid mother. Flo Owens, whose husband abandoned her and their two young daughters ten years earlier, looks sadly upon her daughter's flight from the nest. Rosemary Sydney leaves for a honeymoon with a reluctantly compliant Howard Bevans after having emotionally coerced him into a promise of marriage. Each of the three women has had her frustrations intensified and redefined by the sensual presence of Hal.

The Labor Day holiday is the scene of two annual events: a town picnic and the eve of the reopening of schools at summer's end. The picnic is not seen on stage. In the 1956 film adaptation of the play, the picnic was shown as a lavish extravaganza hardly tenable by the modest appointments of a small Kansas town. The stage's unseen picnic, however, adequately underscores the unreality of life-as-fun, particularly in view of the fact that the audience's only acquaintance with the picnic are the problems of those going to it and returning from it.

Analysis

William Inge's artistic preoccupation is with the quiet desperation of middle-class midwestern American lives, in which the burdens and frustrations of convention and responsibility are shown to defeat the romance of ambition and dreams in direct proportion to the physical or intellectual limitations of the dreamers.

Of the characters in *Picnic*, only Rosemary gets what she wants—the certainty of marriage. Yet, it is the form and convention of marriage that she wins, exactly what Madge has feared being led into. Neither Rosemary nor Howard displays the vaguest symptoms of love. Theirs will be a material partnership, as opposed to the exclusively subjective relationship of Madge and Hal, with their deep and overriding passion. It is clear that actual happiness is to find neither couple: Rosemary and Howard will have conflicting and unreconcilable notions of what their marriage must be; Madge and Hal will live in uncertainty, financial insecurity, and, as it is intimated, an eventual separation not unlike that of Madge's parents.

The essential unhappiness of human life, which is the theme of Greek tragedy wrought through larger-than-life characters, is brought by Inge into the ambience of realistic middle-class Americans. In *Picnic*, he spans the generations from teenage to octogenarian to illustrate the persistence of frustration: Millie and Madge are in their teens; Hal and Alan are in their twenties; Rosemary and Flo are in their late thirties; Howard, "rapidly approaching middle age," is forty-two; "Mrs." Potts is "close to sixty" and her demanding, vocal mother (heard but not seen on stage) is eighty years old or close to it. For all the characters in all these age groups, the aura of despair is, patently or inferentially, unrelieved.

Inge's disclosure of the conventional pursuit of materially informed happiness as tragic misdirection is inherently suggestive of the appropriate alternative—namely, the commitment to one's individual dignity. Each of the principal female characters finds an inner reserve of self to which happiness is not requisite and in which the meaning of one's life is to be determined; the exception is Rosemary, who sacrifices dignity to conventional security. Helen Potts, having become aware of the absurdity of her situation, accepts it and achieves equanimity. Flo, left to her own resources by the departure of Madge, with Millie soon to leave as well, stands in the last scene as an individual, her stance and steady gaze evidence of her newfound ability to cope with the necessity that she had hoped to elude. Millie has found her self in her commitment to follow her intellectual impulsion and, eventually, to "write novels that'll shock people right out of their senses" and become "great and famous"; significantly, she does not say "rich."

The male characters are left in transitional gaps—Hal not knowing that Madge is on her way to him, Alan not knowing that Madge will not be his, and Howard about to be tested as a married man after his habitual lack of spousal responsibility.

Critical Context

The 1950's, those "happy days" before the Vietnam War, were marred by a subsurface of disillusionment that had earlier found expression in *film noir* and was coming to the surface in the Beat movement, rock music, and the government's explicit fear of communist infiltration. In tune with this changing of the times, William Inge wrote five plays examining the interior reality of the middle-class ethos. He diagnosed a midcentury, midwestern, middle-class fear of facing life on its own terms and a sublimative quest for security in convention and status, a quest that led to frustration in success as well as in failure. *Picnic* is the second of these plays. Like its predecessor, *Come Back, Little Sheba* (1950), and its first two successors, *Bus Stop* (1955) and *The Dark at the Top of the Stairs* (1957), it had a successful Broadway run. Inge appeared then to reweave his already perfected texture of quietly desperate lives. *A Loss of Roses* (1959) and his subsequent work fell noticeably short of his consistent tetrad, the one exception being his Academy Award-winning screenplay for *Splendor in the Grass* (1961). The countercultural revolt of the young, anticipated in the character of Madge Owens and implicitly invoked in *Splendor in the Grass*, was a reality by 1961, and Inge, who may rightly be called the first playwright to examine the Midwest and its people, is more accurately recognized as a playwright who exposed a profound malaise of the 1950's.

Roy Arthur Swanson

PILGRIM AT TINKER CREEK

Author: Annie Dillard (1945-   )
First published: 1974
Type of work: Science
Subjects: Education, nature, religion, and science
Recommended ages: 15-18

> *By close observation of the natural world near Tinker Creek, Dillard shows how to see into the life of things.*

Form and Content

Pilgrim at Tinker Creek is a series of meditations on Annie Dillard's illuminating observations of the natural world. In her engaging conversations with herself, Dillard invites readers along as she wanders out, like the bear that went over the mountain, to she what she can see. She sees in the details of nature amazing and enlightening things, things that one would miss without her clear-eyed perspective: sharks outlined in waves of the Atlantic, caterpillar droppings, the green ray at sunset. Her close observation discovers that beauty is all around if people are able to notice it. "The least we can do is try to be there" for the loveliness with which nature surrounds people and the insight to which the details of natural life can lead.

The way to gain that inspiration is to look closely. This author shows how to find what one has been missing of life. Dillard observes things most people do not know enough to look for. People see what they expect to see. She shows readers how to expect more in seeing, to become expert observers, like the herpetologist who finds snakes where the natives never noticed any. Dillard shows how to look curiously as children, cherishingly as lovers, carefully as scientists.

The author sees things that most of people think they see but which they mostly miss, things as close as the bloody ferocity of pet cats, the neighborliness of spiders in the bathtub, and the glory of light through the trees. No detail is too minute for her notice, and no notice is insignificant. She is not only an onlooker but an "inlooker" as well, discovering how much there is in details where most people do not even perceive the details. She looks at things honestly and shows unhesitatingly how fierce the natural world can be. She describes unflinchingly the death throes of the mating praying mantis, the horrors of parasites such as the giant water bug sucking the juices out of a frog, and wolves so hungry that they cannot resist licking the blubber from an exposed knife and slicing their tongues until they bleed to death.

Yet, Dillard relates with equal clarity the grace and beauty of the natural world, and how that beauty can help people live more abundantly, more intensely and with awareness of the present moment. Where most people notice only a cedar tree with sunlight shining through its branches, she recognizes life transfigured. She urges the reader to make the most of the light, to "catch the solar wind" and "spread your spirit." "Seeing," the pivotal second chapter of *Pilgrim at Tinker Creek*, encourages readers in its every deeply envisioned line: See better and live better. See well enough and see God.

Analysis

Dillard's poetic prose paints vividly her inside view of nature, making tangible what most not only do not observe but do not even think about—the soul of the living world. *Pilgrim at Tinker Creek* is a challenging book for young adult readers, but it is an invaluable one. The challenge is not a matter of difficult writing. Dillard's prose, although it can be intimidating in its allusiveness, is as naturally lyrical as the reader's heartbeat. The challenge of the book lies in the complexity of the life-and-death issues that it invites the reader to ponder: "'If I did not know about God and sin, would I go to hell?' 'No,' said the priest, 'not if you did not know.' 'Then why,' asked the Eskimo earnestly, 'did you tell me?'" The book is not only an exploration of Tinker Creek, but of the human soul, "a meteorological journal of the mind" that provokes readers to reexamine their experience. *Pilgrim at Tinker Creek* explores lovingly human beings' relationship to the natural world, to one another, and to God. Its openness to new possibilities may be the book's greatest appeal for young adult readers.

This volume stands in a long tradition of pilgrimage books that recount expeditions undertaken in search of faith. It also stands in a tradition of American writers who meditate upon nature, who find in the physical world stimulus for metaphysical contemplation. Dillard taps directly into the thoughts of Henry David Thoreau, the most influential of those transcendental observers whose book *Walden* (1854) explores the Walden Pond area near Concord, Massachusetts, as thoughtfully as Dillard explores the Blue Ridge Valley near Roanoke, Virginia. Dillard's version of Thoreau's close analysis of nature, however, is updated by the perspective of a modern woman. Where Thoreau sees incursions of society into nature, Dillard looks at nature breaking through into society. Where Thoreau yearns toward simplicity and unity, Dillard finds variety. Where Thoreau fights toward resolution of the great questions of life, Dillard insists on asking questions. *Pilgrim at Tinker Creek* replaces the secular heroism of *Walden*—the kind of ennobling of nature that can be seen in Thoreau's battle of the ants—with a spiritual perspective. Behind both the beauty and the terror of nature looms God.

The only source more influential on Dillard's book than *Walden* is the King James version of the Bible. It is not merely that Dillard often quotes from it; passage after passage of *Pilgrim at Tinker Creek* sounds as impassioned, as morally intense, as sonorously visionary as Isaiah or Amos or Malachi—and as beautiful. Her words taste good in the mouth, roll out so rhythmically, that it is hard to keep from reading the entire book aloud, hard not to speak such sentences as "New shows roll in from over the mountains and the magician reappears unannounced from a fold in the curtain you never dreamed was an opening."

The book is a fertile merger of art and science. Scientifically meticulous as Dillard is in her observations, the book goes well beyond science. It does not so much explain the world as ponder its wonders. *Pilgrim at Tinker Creek* is less a scientific disquisition than a conversation, a poem, a prayer. In form, it is a walk together with Dillard's wide-open eyes and wider-open heart beside Tinker Creek. The book's natural rhythms, from winter to winter, are irresistible—the "Winter" chapter, for example, focuses on the kind of storytelling anecdotes that bloom in front of fireplaces on January evenings. "Intricacy," where Dillard argues for the complexity of nature, is a longer chapter than most and features shorter, more detailed, paragraphs.

Dillard's prose voice is unusually inviting, so honest and open that it seems as if she is thinking aloud and allowing readers to overhear. That invitational quality is heightened by the concentration of the writing, as if the reader were being invited to share honey. The most satisfying aspect of the book is the way in which the author can encapsulate in words what readers have only known as feelings, can squeeze bare essences of emotional experience into concrete metaphors, as in "you catch grace as a man fills his cup under a waterfall."

Its basic technique, meditation, reflects its essential genius. Dillard translates sight into insight. She returns repeatedly to an image, each repetition of that image making it richer. This leitmotif technique—reiterating as it does the bloody tracks of the cat, the sucked-dry frog, and the tree full of lights—works almost musically, like a refrain in a symphony, so that by the time one reaches the full-chorus climax, one is overwhelmed by its cumulative power.

Ultimately, Dillard not only sees what is really there and how much it matters but also helps the reader see it. She opens her readers' eyes to fuller life, urges them not to miss the life before their very eyes. The world is more than people see "in all directions, more dangerous and bitter, more extravagant and bright. We are making hay when we should be making whoopee; we are raising tomatoes when we should be raising Cain, or Lazarus."

Critical Context

Pilgrim at Tinker Creek, Annie Dillard's first volume of prose, was a national best-seller when it was first published in 1974 and won the Pulitzer Prize the following year. Although Dillard has published several popular volumes since—especially *Holy the Firm* (1977), *Teaching a Stone to Talk* (1982), *Living by Fiction* (1982), *An American Childhood* (1987), and *The Writing Life* (1989)—*Pilgrim at Tinker Creek* remains recognized by most readers as her masterpiece.

There is much in the book, as can be seen by what different readers get from it. Orthodox religionists find in the book a reaffirmation of faith. Feminists discover it to be a declaration of female independence, a celebration of the differences that separate women from men. Perhaps the most impressive thing about *Pilgrim at Tinker Creek* is the range of its appeal: Although readers like it for very different reasons, all readers seem to like it.

Steven C. Walker

PIPING DOWN THE VALLEYS WILD
Poetry for the Young of All Ages

Editor: Nancy Larrick (1910-   )
First published: 1968; illustrated
Type of work: Poetry
Subjects: Animals, emotions, nature, and the supernatural
Recommended ages: 10-13

This anthology of verse on themes enjoyed by young readers contains selections intended to promote a lifelong appreciation of poetry.

Form and Content

Piping Down the Valleys Wild derives its title from the introductory poem to *Songs of Innocence* (1789), by William Blake, the eighteenth century English Romantic poet and engraver. Editor Nancy Larrick could not have chosen a better poem to set the tone and to serve as prelude for her collection for young readers. Just as Blake's poem emphasizes the musical quality of poetry with his piper, or poet, "Piping songs of pleasant glee" that "Every child may joy to hear," so Larrick's selections are generally those that will appeal to the ear. As she states in her introduction, "poetry itself is music," and perhaps it is for this reason that young readers respond enthusiastically to it, asking to hear a favorite verse again and again. She based this belief on years of working with students and claims that it guided her in choosing the 245 poems in this volume. This enthusiasm for aural elements is evident in examples such as Karla Kuskin's "Full of the Moon," with its dogs that "howl and growl" as they "amble, ramble, scramble"; or in Eve Merriam's "Bam, Bam, Bam," in which workers "Slam, slam, slam" as they demolish neighborhood houses with pickaxes and wrecking balls.

Piping Down the Valleys Wild is divided into sixteen chapters grouped by subject matter. Each chapter takes its title from a portion of a poem contained within that section: for example, the title of chapter 5, "I saw a spooky witch out riding on her broom," comes from the poem "October Magic," by Myra Cohn Livingston; and the title of chapter 13, "I must go down to the seas again . . . ," is the opening line expressing the adventurous longing that suffuses John Masefield's poem "Sea-Fever." Thus, each section offers a satchelful of poems on a particular topic, although the subjects are not always apparent from a quick perusal. While chapter 2, "Sing a song of laughter . . . ," is obviously about humor, readers will have to look more closely at the poems themselves in chapter 8, "I'll take the hound with drooping ears . . . ," and chapter 10, "I found new-born foxes . . . ," to determine their distinguishing feature. Both seem to be about animals, but closer scrutiny reveals that the first concerns pets or domesticated animals, whereas the second focuses on wild animals and insects.

Other organizational characteristics of the collection include drawings by Ellen Raskin, an author, illustrator, and recipient of the prestigious Newbery Medal for *The Westing Game* (1978), a young adult mystery novel. Each illustration suggests the theme that follows. On the title page, the bird singing in the branches parallels the idea of the piping music of poetry, and the juggling clown introducing chapter 7, "I chanced to meet . . . ," suggests verse on characters such as Kaye Starbird's intrepid summer camper Eat-It-All Elaine, who devours tissues, buttercups, birch bark, prune pits, stinkbugs, and anything else in the poem of the same name.

Study aids within the book consist of a table of contents, two indexes (one of authors and titles and another of first lines), and acknowledgements. This last feature, which cites sources for the selections, should be especially useful to anyone who discovers a favorite poet and wants to read more of his or her work. For example, those who enjoy T. S. Eliot's "The Rum Tum Tugger" and desire further feline capers can find his book *Old Possum's Book of Practical Cats* (1939) referenced here. One caveat is that the acknowledgements are alphabetized by author but place each poet's name within the bibliographic citation, following the title of that particular poem. Nevertheless, this format should prove only a slight, initial inconvenience.

Analysis

Piping Down the Valleys Wild possesses virtually everything that younger audiences cite as their poetry preferences. In addition to the musical qualities of rhyme, rhythm, alliteration, assonance, and other sound effects, many of the poems in the anthology are about familiar experiences. David McCord's "Kite" speaks of the thrill of flying a kite in different kinds of weather—from sunny to cloudy to dark, windy, and gray. Patricia Hubbell's "Concrete Mixers" compares the machinery of her poem to ponderous pachyderms that move, bellow, and spray with their trunks as they raise a city. Although it offers unique insights into the ordinary, the language is everyday, never obscure, and easily comprehensible to the urban and suburban audiences for whom Larrick intended her book.

Three sections are devoted to animals, also a favorite topic among children. The verses range from the lighthearted descriptions of a puppy's antics in Marchette Chute's "My Dog" to the gentle, poignant, and sometimes humorous characterizations that Carmen Bernos de Gasztold gives her animals as they offer special prayers to God and simultaneously hold up a mirror to human thoughts and wishes. None except those with hearts of stone could fail to be touched by the request of the Old Horse who, with threadbare coat and stiffened legs, asks God for a gentle death after long years of labor.

Another preference to which this collection caters is the strange and fantastic. The poems on people feature characters such as Beatrice Curtis Brown's poor old Jonathan Bing, who cannot remember the appropriate attire for his visit to the king. Karla Kuskin's Catherine serves up a special blend of mud, water, weeds, nuts, gravel, bark, thistle, and sand as a "most delicious chocolate cake," while the beneficiary of her concoction insists on having it with ice cream. Indeed, an entire chapter on the supernatural is included, encompassing ghosts and ghouls along with elves, wee folk, and other creatures from fairy lands.

Throughout the book are dozens of humorous poems, a further favored category.

Some of these will be found amusing because of their wordplay. In "The Squirrel," an unknown author describes the "whisky, frisky," "whirly, twirly," and "furly, curly" features of a squirrel. Other poems will inspire humor because of their content. In a manner reminiscent of Mother Goose, Dylan Thomas creates nonsense when Johnnie Crack and Flossie Snail put their baby in a milking pail and serve it "stout and ale." In the "Adventures of Isabel," Ogden Nash describes an unflappable girl who, when confronted with a ravenous bear, calmly washes her hands, straightens her hair, and turns the tables by eating up the bear. In addition to Nash, readers will find such other stalwarts of light verse as Lewis Carroll, John Ciardi, and Shel Silverstein. No collection for young readers would be complete without a smattering of limericks. Edward Lear makes one perfunctory appearance, but the best are those penned by "Anonymous."

A final appealing component of this anthology is its widespread incorporation of narrative. Audiences will enjoy story poems such as James Reeves's "The Old Wife and the Ghost," a humorous tale of a woman living alone who is so deaf that she thinks a poltergeist to be such "tidy big mice" that she fetches a "tidy big cat" to rid herself of the pests.

For readers whose taste is not with the majority, Larrick has other offerings, including occasional bits of free verse and stray haiku. Pieces from the Bible, Walt Whitman, William Carlos Williams, and Asian authors can be found among these selections. Yet, not one poem is marred by the indecipherable images that frequently turn poetry into a riddling sphinx—something that, as the choices herein make evident, it need not be.

Critical Context

Because this collection is intended to appeal to a wide array of interests, almost by necessity it will not satisfy everyone. Critics not having a penchant for end rhymes and regular rhythms may find the volume too full of poems that jingle to the ear. Others inclined to favor poetry about contemporary topics or with a social conscience may also be disappointed. For example, African American poets are scarce, and the few represented such as Gwendolyn Brooks barely emit an audible whisper about the experiences of black people in the United States.

These objections, however, are more cavils than criticisms. Nancy Larrick has provided for more specialized interests elsewhere among her numerous collections. Because of its incorporation of photographs and its inclusion of poems selected by more than one hundred youngsters from inner cities and small towns, Larrick's *On City Streets* (1968) is a good choice for audiences who want poems about a more contemporary scene. For those who prefer controversial fare, *Male and Female Under Eighteen* (1973), which Larrick edited with Eve Merriam, contains language and ideas that some people might consider inappropriate for juveniles and young adults. Even so, such collections may become easily dated for readers whose environments and problems are ever-changing. *Piping Down the Valleys Wild*, however, will continue to have broad appeal. It not only attempts to make poetry as necessary a part of living as speaking or breathing but also is a treasure trove of favorite verses that vary in form, style, and content—all hallmarks of a good anthology.

Terry L. Norton

A PLACE APART

Author: Paula Fox (1923-   )
First published: 1977
Type of work: Novel
Type of plot: Psychological realism
Time of work: The 1970's
Locale: New Oxford, Massachusetts
Subjects: Coming-of-age, family, and friendship
Recommended ages: 10-15

After the death of her father, Victoria Finch seeks security in the friendship of Hugh Todd, an older boy from a wealthy family, whose influence in Victoria's life becomes overpowering.

Principal characters:
VICTORIA FINCH, a thirteen-year-old who is left in a state of confusion after her father's death
HUGH TODD, an enigmatic high school junior with whom Victoria becomes infatuated
LOIS FINCH, Victoria's mother
ELIZABETH MARX, Victoria's best friend
TOM KYLE, a new student during Victoria's sophomore year
UNCLE PHILIP, Victoria's uncle

Form and Content

The first-person narration of *A Place Apart* is provided by Victoria Finch, a sensitive and somewhat vulnerable thirteen-year-old. After her father's sudden death, Victoria and her mother must move to New Oxford. The dreariness of the new house, the need to adjust socially, and the death of her father make Victoria's outlook bleak and confused. As a freshman, she becomes best friends with Elizabeth Marx. Soon after, she meets Hugh Todd, a junior from a rich family whose mysterious aura fascinates Victoria: "I never thought as much about another human being as I thought about him." Hugh takes an interest in some scenes that Victoria has written about her father's death and decides that she should expand them into a full-length work, which he will direct as next year's senior play—the first senior play to be a student's work. Victoria is fascinated and frightened by this prospect, but she realizes that she cannot say no to Hugh. One day, Hugh draws Victoria into a game of throwing stones and shouting; although Victoria realizes how easily she can be controlled by Hugh, her infatuation with him continues.

During the summer, Hugh goes away and Victoria becomes closer to Elizabeth, although she thinks of Hugh constantly. Victoria knows that she cannot speak of Hugh to her friend because Elizabeth does not like or trust him. Victoria's mother begins a relationship with a new man, which makes Victoria think of her father more than ever. With a week and a half left until school begins, Victoria turns her attention to her play again and feels intense excitement at Hugh's return.

In school, Hugh conducts a meeting of the Drama Club, complete with a new student, Tom Kyle. Victoria feels betrayed as Hugh, Tom, and another student suggest major changes to her play. After another of Hugh's games, Victoria finds herself alone in a cemetery. Among the gravestones, she is able to put her problems into perspective, and she realizes that she will have to stand up to Hugh. Victoria's determination, however, is not as strong as she would like. She is unable to complete her play but equally unable to forget about it. Deep down, she still hopes that she and Hugh can be close again, but she sees that Tom Kyle is Hugh's new friend. In addition, Elizabeth now has a boyfriend, Frank Wilson, and Victoria is further isolated. Victoria finally tells Hugh that he cannot use her play. She then tells Mr. Tate, the faculty producer of the senior play, and is shocked to learn that Hugh had never cleared her play for production as he had told her.

The novel moves toward its conclusion with a car ride that Elizabeth, Frank, Tom, and Victoria take on Mt. Crystal. On the way down the icy roads, Tom becomes so frightened that he wets himself. In town, Hugh sees Tom, witnesses his humiliation, and abandons him. Victoria now realizes why Hugh had an interest in Tom and herself: Both have timid natures easily manipulated by Hugh. A few days later, word spreads that Tom has been in a severe accident on Mt. Crystal, and Victoria understands that Tom tried to conquer his humiliation by driving up the mountain. Although Victoria is skeptical, Frank claims that Hugh drove Tom to such desperate behavior, and the entire school views Hugh with suspicion and contempt. In Boston, Victoria visits Tom in the hospital, but she tells no one. Shortly after, Hugh leaves school. As the novel ends, Victoria walks past the hill where she first met Hugh, contemplating what has happened in the past year, hoping for some new experience, and looking back "just once."

Analysis

The title of the novel comes from Robert Frost's poem "Revelation," in which "a place apart" represents some hidden part in each person. As she matures, Victoria comes to realize that there is less that can be said, more that must be kept hidden. This realization leads to the eventual acceptance of her mother's new and private love life; moreover, it allows Victoria to develop her own private existence when, for example, she keeps her meeting with Tom in the hospital a secret. Along with privacy, *A Place Apart* deals with several common themes: loss, teenage anxiety, and, most prominently, relationships.

Structurally and thematically, the novel is designed to reflect Victoria's search for security and certainty. The first sentence is one of her reminiscences: When she was ten, she thought that all of her confusion would be cleared up if someone told her the meaning of life. At thirteen and after the sudden and unexpected death of her father, Victoria comes to suspect that the world is random and incomprehensible. After the move to New Oxford, her sense of displacement and insecurity becomes greater. Thus, when she meets Hugh Todd, Victoria is especially vulnerable to his manipulation. Instead of a confused, indefinite perception of the world, Hugh offers a simplistic, judgmental point-of-view to which Victoria readily clings. While his ability to categorize others underscores his belief in his own superiority, it represents to Victoria the certainty that she cannot find elsewhere. Hugh, however, is a master manipulator and understands how to attract and control Victoria and how to coerce her into writing a play for him. This relationship between dominance and submissiveness, which is the center of *A Place Apart*, is wish-fulfillment for Victoria—someone is telling her what life means—and a new chance for control for Hugh. As this relationship begins to break down, Victoria finally understands that she has been misled by her desire for certainty and the security that follows.

At the beginning of the novel, Uncle Philip tells Victoria that she must search for her place in the world, her "own country." As Victoria begins to break away from Hugh and assert herself, she is coming to realize the full importance of Uncle Philip's advice: The meaning of life cannot be dictated; it must be experienced and learned on one's own terms. Along the way, Victoria obtains the most essential pieces of knowledge from her mother, who helps her understand that Hugh is manipulating her, that writing a play is not her "own country," and that life continues after loss. Other lessons are provided by Elizabeth, Uncle Philip, and Victoria's own insights. At the novel's end, Victoria has not yet found her place, but she has taken a huge step forward by moving past Hugh's self-serving influence.

In *A Place Apart*, Paula Fox provides several crucial lessons for the young adult reader. The book demonstrates the need for independence and privacy, the value of family, and the importance of getting on with life after loss. The most important lesson, however, seems to be that the world is not a simple place with easy answers. Only after Victoria discovers that the certainty Hugh provides is false certainty, that the world and human relationships are complex and often puzzling, is she free to discover who she is. This is the discovery that awaits Victoria as the novel ends.

Critical Context

In the works of Paula Fox, the lines between adult and young adult literature are indistinct. Like Victoria Finch, many of Fox's young adult protagonists must face a harsh, confusing, or unjust world. Fox does not pamper her readers with nonabrasive themes or happy endings and instead, as in much serious adult literature, depicts the world in realistic and complex terms.

In *How Many Miles to Babylon?* (1967) Fox tells the story of James, an African American child who experiences the severity of life in the ghetto. *Blowfish Live in the Sea* (1970) is about the difficulty that nineteen-year-old Ben encounters in trying to reestablish a relationship with his father. In *The Slave Dancer* (1973), a thirteen-year-old boy is kidnapped and forced to play the fife on a slave ship, where he witnesses the cruelty of slavery. A teenage girl spends a tense summer with her alcoholic father in *The Moonlight Man* (1986). These works, along with several others in both adult and young adult fiction, have established Paula Fox as a master in the exploration of interpersonal relationships and as a writer who is never afraid to confront reality head-on.

Matthew J. Perini